THE LAST OUTLAW

Also from Crowbar Press

Inside Out
by Ole Anderson with Scott Teal
0-9745545-0-2

Wrestlers Are Like Seagulls
by James J. Dillon with Scott Teal and Philip Varriale
0-9745545-2-9

Assassin: The Man Behind the Mask
by Joe Hamilton with Scott Teal
0-9745545-3-7

"Is That Wrestling Fake?"
by Ivan Koloff with Scott Teal
978-0-9745545-4-9

Bruiser Brody
by Emerson Murray
978-0-9745545-5-6

Wrestling with the Truth
by Bruno Lauer
0-9745545-7-0

The Solie Chronicles
by Bob Allyn with Pamela S Allyn and Scott Teal
978-0-9745545-8-7

Wrestling in the Canadian West
by Vance Nevada
978-0-9745545-9-4

Long Days and Short Pays
by Hal West
978-0-9844090-0-6

Drawing Heat
by Jim Freedman
978-0-9844090-1-3

ATLAS: Too Much, Too Soon
by Tony Atlas with Scott Teal
978-0-9844090-2-0

The Last Laugh
by Bill De Mott with Scott Teal
978-0-9844090-3-7

HOOKER
by Lou Thesz with Kit Bauman
978-0-9844090-4-4

NIKITA
by Nikita Koloff with Bill Murdock
978-0-9844090-6-8

The Last Outlaw

By

Stan Hansen

with

Scott Teal

CROWBAR PRESS
Gallatin, Tennessee

THE LAST OUTLAW

Published by Crowbar Press
106 Tattnal Court
Gallatin, Tennessee 37066.

http://www.crowbarpress.com

Book layout and cover design by Scott Teal

Library of Congress Cataloging-in-Publication Data

Hansen, Stan
The Last Outlaw / by Stan Hansen with Scott Teal

1. Hansen, Stan. 2. Sports—United States—Biography. 3. Wrestling—United States—Biography. I. Teal, Scott. II. Title.

Printed in the United States of America
ISBN 978-0-9844090-5-1

First Edition / August 2011

Table of Contents

Acknowledgements

by Stan Hansen

I began writing this book because I wanted people to enjoy stories and remember some of the great characters from the professional wrestling business. When people look back and remember professional wrestling of the past, the individual wrestlers weren't carbon copies of each other. They all had different styles, physiques, personalities, and talent. I think most of the modern day wrestling fans have no idea of the amount of talent the wrestlers from the '60s through the '90s had. Not only were they independent, but they were innovative, both in and out of the ring. They brought wrestling to the cities on a weekly basis and only had their charisma to draw fans to the arenas. Their success was solely dependent on how well they sold their character to the people. They didn't have nationwide television programs to sell their shows. They had nothing more than their own talent and ring psychology. And with the new era of "sports entertainment," that psychology and empathy with the audience has faded into history.

For those reasons, it is to those great professionals that I dedicate this book.

Most of all, I want to thank my wife Yumi, the love of my life. She saved me by changing the direction I was headed years ago. She righted the ship (Hansen in Japanese) and made my life.

I want to thank my family for putting up with all my faults and all the long periods of time that I was away from them. They were the backbone for my purpose of wrestling all these years.

Two special people in my life who deserve special mention are —

— Terry Funk, who broke me into the wrestling business. Without him, I never would have had the opportunity to write this book.

— Pete Roberts, the true brother that I never had. His friendship is one of the best things that came out of my years of wrestling.

I also would like to acknowledge:

— Bruiser Brody, my partner, and friend. Together, we achieved a position that few others have achieved. He was definitely a major part of that success.

— Giant Baba, who gave me the opportunity to be promoted in Japan and to be an integral part of All Japan's business.

— Andre the Giant, for helping "make" Stan Hansen in Japan.

— Antonio Inoki, for giving me my first opportunity to get over in Japan.

— Ole Anderson, for being a friend during some hard personal times and for being up front with me from the promotional side of the business in the States.

Stan gives the "Longhorns" sign to the fans

Last, but not least, I want to thank all the great talent I fought over the years: Bruno Sammartino, Terry Funk, Andre the Giant, Steve Williams, and Terry Gordy, just to name a few. And most of all, I want to acknowledge the Japanese wrestlers: Giant Baba, Antonio Inoki, Jumbo Tsuruta, Genichiro Tenryu, Mitsuharu Misawa, Toshiaki Kawada, and Kenta Kobashi. Without those great Japanese opponents, there could not have been the great matches I was involved in over the 27 years.

A big thank you to my friend in Japan, Koji Miyamoto, who answered questions about wrestling in Japan when my editor couldn't find what he needed elsewhere. J Michael Kenyon's expertise in both my football and wrestling background also proved invaluable to us and Bill Burnett is to be commended for doing a fine job of proofreading.

I also want to thank Scott Teal for all the time he has invested in this book. We have been working on it for a little more than four years and his patience is surely appreciated. Although the words are mine, his proofreading and editing have made it so much better and it could never have been published without his expertise. I also thank him for adding historical data to the many, many years and matches that are referenced to. After years of working together, we have developed a friendship through both our common Christian faith and our love for the wrestling business.

Foreword

by Pete Roberts

Stan and I first met in January 1977 when we were both booked on a tour with New Japan Pro Wrestling. At the time, the promotion would bring in a variety of nationalities — a few Americans, a couple of Canadians, and a couple of Englishmen. I went over with Dave Taylor, another Englishman, but he contracted peritonitis and went to the hospital. Stan and I went to the hospital to visit him. We hit it off and our friendship grew from there.

The thing I remember the most about that first tour was that we had to sleep on the floor of one of the hotels. Another story I like to tell took place in a club to which we were invited by the Japanese. They had a small band playing on a stage. After we downed several drinks, they invited Stan to get on stage and sing something. With two guitars and a drummer trying to follow along, Stan proceeded to belt out his rendition of *"Deep in the Heart of Texas."* The funny thing was, none of the Japanese there could understand English, so they didn't know what he was saying. When he finished, Stan said, *"You guys take it easy. After the band takes a fifteen-minute break, we'll be back."* As soon as he finished the last sentence, he tossed the microphone over his shoulder and jumped down off the stage. What Stan didn't realize was that the mike hit the drummer in the forehead. Stan just walked on as if nothing had happened.

When Stan left New Japan and went to the other side (All Japan), we stayed in touch. I had been booked into New Japan by Karl Gotch, who was the booker for Antonio Inoki. After Stan established himself with All Japan, he got me booked with them. From then on, I worked for Baba in Japan.

Stan is one of the nicest guys I ever met. In fact, his whole family is fantastic. He visited me here in England and I go to the States about once a year. We both like the history of the Old West, so we make trips to places of interest. He always takes me someplace interesting. One year, we drove through Lincoln County, where Billy the Kid was imprisoned while awaiting his execution. We saw the place where the Kid escaped after killing the two deputies who were escorting him. This year, we visited Death Valley and the Alamo.

Stan and I both enjoyed Japan. It was a great place and we were there at a great time. When we would go out on the streets, everyone recognized him. We were in a restaurant in Tokyo one night when a group of students came in and sat down. All of a sudden, one after the other, they stood up and began chanting, *"Stan-san! Stan-san!"* On another night, we left a bar and were trying to find our hotel. Stan said, *"Let's go this way. We'll cut across."* He knew Japan better than I did, so I just followed. As we walked past one house, some people opened their front door and said, *"Stan Hansen!"* They invited us in and served us a delicious Japanese dinner of cooked shrimp and other delicacies.

Other wrestlers came and went, but Stan lasted longer in Japan than any other gaijin. He was the main guy. In fact, many of the Japanese people considered him to be a god. He changed the style of wrestling in Japan. He weighed 280 pounds, but moved and ran like somebody who weighed 120.

I'm proud to have been asked to write this, but I'm more proud to call Stan Hansen "my friend."

Stan and Pete Roberts

Foreword

by Terry Funk

The first time I heard the name "Stan Hansen," he was coming to West Texas State to play football. During the years he was there, our paths only crossed occasionally. I was wrestling during that time, but I heard a lot about Stan because I still followed football closely. I even went down to watch him play. He was a big boy. I remember him being a very good linebacker and he played extremely physical on the field. The one thing I will never forget about those days was that he wore the same tennis shoes all the way through college, into the wrestling business, and on the day he first arrived in Japan. Like Cactus Jack, Stan was so tight with his money that he squeaked when he walked. Actually, he was smart. Being frugal paid off for him in later life.

It wasn't easy to get into the wrestling business in those days. It was very protected and we were selective about who we brought in. At the time, my dad and I were looking for a tough guy, not someone who could do flips or cartwheels. I can remember it like it was yesterday. Stan came to my house to talk about getting into the wrestling business. When he left, my father and I talked about it. We both thought he would be good.

When I called Stan, he asked me, *"How much can I make?"*

I said, *"Well, we'll start you off at about three hundred dollars."*

He said, *"Well, I'm makin' $550 now."*

I asked him, *"Is that a week?"*

He said, *"No. That's a month."* All of a sudden, it dawned on him: *Holy crap! I can make $300 a week?"*

In 1976, Stan was the biggest thing they had in New York. At that time, New Japan pulled Abdullah right out from underneath us. My brother and I were booking for All Japan, so we called Stan and made him an offer he couldn't refuse. When he came to work for us, Vince McMahon Sr. called and asked me, *"Why did you steal my boy?"* We got a tremendous amount of heat over it. When Stan came over, he came to the ring during a match between Bruiser Brody and Jimmy Snuka and my brother and me. His appearance popped the building, and later, the territory.

We were competing against New Japan during a new age and Stan was a very important part of the company. He wasn't the wheel. He wasn't just a cog in the wheel. He was the most *important* cog in the wheel. He was as important as anyone could possibly be. Things looked bad for All Japan when they took Abdullah, but Stan brought the numbers back up for the company.

Wrestling at that time wasn't like it was in the old days, but it was still very combative. New Japan had moved to a format that featured a lot of wrestling, particularly with light-heavyweights. They gave people things they hadn't seen before. We were in a wrestling phase, but we gave the fans matches that were very physical. We wanted to be known as tough guys, and as we got more and more physical on TV, our matches became very believable. Everything we did was as solid as we could make it. When Stan caught me with a clothesline, I felt it, and I believe the fans could, as well. The bottom line was we wanted to give the fans realistic entertainment.

Scott Teal asked me to share a funny story or two about Stan. Let me tell you this. I can't remember anything funny because he rattled my brain so many times, I can't remember most of what took place during the time I was around him. I do remember he had very selective hearing in the ring. When I'd talk to him, he'd say, *"What? I can't hear you."* Everything he did hear was in his favor. If I said something about me wanting to look a little bit better, he couldn't hear me. My brother will tell you the same thing. Shoots were easy. Working with Stan Hansen was hard. Having said that, Stan might have been the stiffest SOB in wrestling, but he knew what it took to draw money. He knew being physical was necessary.

We hated New Japan. If Baba asked us to go to one of Inoki's show and kick the shit out of their guys, we would have done just that. Inoki would have done the same to us if he had been given the opportunity. I hated the opposition ... and so did Stan Hansen. He didn't want to just draw a bigger crowd than Inoki. He wanted to bury them, and I did, too. That's the only way you can have a war. Did I talk to their guys? No! Did Stan? No! We were pissed if we didn't outperform their guys. It was a matter of pride, and Stan had that pride.

Stan was wrestling as I was brought up to know it. He was wrestling as my father knew it. The Funk family is very proud to say we were the ones who put him in the business. He could have been a star anywhere, but I thank God he came to All Japan for us. I'm not saying Stan was the only one — there was Brody and Butcher, as well — but he was an intricate part of our success. He enabled us to dominate and do as well as we did over there.

I have all the respect in world for Stan and I truly mean that. I started very, very few people in the business. I helped many people after they were already in, but I started very few from the very beginning. Stan was one of those I did, and that was because I always knew he would be a star. He didn't prove me wrong.

Stan vs Terry Funk

Prologue

The Phone Call

January 31, 1999

The phone broke the silence of the night, jarring my wife and myself awake. In Colorado, where we lived, it was only four in the morning. I picked up the phone and groggily mumbled, *"Hello?"*

A distraught voice yelled, *"Baba-san is dead."*

It was Koichi Yoshizawa, a long-time friend who was a wrestling reporter in Japan. As I waited for a second, trying to compose my thoughts, he repeated, *"Baba-san is dead. I just saw it on the TV."*

I was finally wide awake. *"Are you sure?"*

Crying as he spoke, he said, *"I just saw and heard it announced on TV. It is true."*

We talked for a few minutes and I told him I would make some calls to see what was going on. I asked him to keep in touch and told him I appreciated him calling me. I turned to my wife, who knew something bad had happened. I told her, *"Baba died!"* She sat up in bed and we stared at each other. We were both in shock. We knew Baba had been sick. He had undergone surgery to remove a blockage from his intestine, but his death came as a shock. We wondered how and what Mrs. Baba was doing, and how she was handling this huge loss.

Shohei "Giant" Baba's death signaled the end of an era. A defining point in my life, and in professional wrestling, had just taken place. The passing of a legend had just taken place. People use the term "legend" loosely, but if there was a true legend in Japan, Baba most certainly was one.

As I sat in bed, I came to the realization that both wrestling and Japan would never be the same for me. I had lost more than a man for whom I worked for almost twenty years. I had lost a friend, and perhaps one of the most stable relationships of my whole life.

A few minutes later, the phone rang again. It was Mrs. Baba. Naturally, she was very emotional, but she managed to give me some of the details of Baba-san's passing. I told her how sorry I was and that I wished I could do something to help her. As with Koichi, I thanked her for calling me and told her I would be in touch.

As I hung up the phone, it finally sank in. Baba really was dead. It had really happened.

Chapter 1

Tomatoes and Pasta

My great-grandfather on my mother's side of the family was Rufus King Shaver. In 1915, Rufus, along with his four sons and two daughters, loaded all of their possessions onto three rail cars and moved from the country east of Austin, Texas, to Knox County. In the rail cars were wagons, furniture, household goods, and all their worldly possessions, including the all-important farming equipment which would be used on the sandy loam farmland of Knox County. Edward Shaver, my grandfather, was one of Rufus' sons. When he was twenty years old, he married Molly Anderson, his childhood sweetheart. She was only 15 years old at the time. Molly gave birth to my mother at their home in 1925. She was the fourth of five kids.

On my father's side, my grandfather, George Hansenanis Hansen, was 12 years old when he left his home on the island of Borhome in Denmark. That was in the 1880s. He set sail on a "Hansen," which in Japanese means a four-mast sailing ship, hiring on as an apprentice cabin boy. He sailed around the world four times and wouldn't return home for years at a time.

I can't even imagine how it must have felt to leave home, sail out onto the high seas, and be separated from family. He set out on a journey without knowing the destination or the type of life he would lead. I'm sure it's hard for the youngsters of today to even comprehend this, but there was no technology that would even allow him to communicate with his family. Telephones and e-mail would not be invented for many years.

During his journeys, he learned to speak seven languages, including two dialects of Chinese. When he got older, he was promoted from cabin boy to chief cook.

When he was 31, he jumped ship in New York Harbor. While there, he met my grandmother, who had immigrated from Alsace Loraine a few years earlier. Alsace Loraine is located on the northeast border of France and Germany. They fell deeply in love, but she refused to marry him until he returned to Denmark and came back legally through Ellis Island.

After he returned to the United States, they got married and he took up an occupation as a baker, using many of the skills he had learned while he was on the sailing ship. Over the next decade and a half, they had 12 children. My father, John Stanley Hansen, Sr., the second youngest of the children, was born in 1921.

The family lived in a three-story house in Brooklyn, New York, with the children sleeping three to a bed until my father was a young man. He had to quit school to help support the family and worked at different jobs, one of them being a stock boy for the Pfizer company. When World War II broke out, he tried to enlist in the Navy, but was turned down when the doctors discovered he had a heart murmur. He also was turned away when he tried to enlist in the Merchant Marines. He was eventually accepted by the Army. After completing his basic training at Fort Dix, New Jersey, he was sent to Camp Barkley in Abilene, Texas, to undergo training to become a medic. Abilene was a town with a population of about 16,000, but with the huge influx of soldiers preparing for the war, it had swelled to more than 80,000.

My mother, Nella Shaver, grew up in Knox City, a small town just south of the Salt Fork of the Brazos River, but she was working in a hospital and taking classes at a nursing school in Abilene when my father arrived in town.

My parents were two opposites from two completely different cultures. One lived in the big city, the other in the rural country, but it was a love-at-first-sight connection that resulted in a lifelong relationship. They were married in Knox City, just a few months before he was shipped out to the war in Europe.

Attached to the U.S. Third Army under the command of General George S. Patton, my father participated in four invasions: the North African Campaign [1942], the Allied Invasion of Sicily [July 1943], the Allied Invasion of Italy [September 1943], and the Allied invasion of southern France [summer 1944]. He hit the beaches under fire, and as a medic, he had to deal with the deaths of many soldiers as he tended to their injuries. He fought all the way into Germany and was with Patton's Third Army Division forces when they liberated Mauthausen concentration camp on May 5, 1945. He once told me that after witnessing the killing and carnage that took place in Europe during the war, he had begun to question exactly why he was there. It was the liberation of the concentration camp that made him realize he was fighting in Europe for a reason.

My father returned home with a unique perspective on life. He saw many of his buddies killed on the beaches of Europe, and he lived every day of his life like the gift it was. He felt lucky to be alive and able to return home to a loving wife. He never complained about the many disappointments he experienced. He knew when he put his problems into perspective with what others had suffered both during and after the war, his problems seemed insignificant. I'm grateful to have been raised by that kind of a man, one who taught me to always forge ahead and not stop to feel sorry for myself.

I'm jumping way ahead in my story, but in 1993, my father lay dying of congestive heart failure and emphysema in a hospital in Mississippi. I was finishing up a tour of Japan on June 4. I called the hospital several times each day, never sure whether or not I would be talking to him for the final time. He refused to give in until I got home. My family told me that he kept asking, *"Is Stan here yet?"* I walked into his hospital room the following day, June 5. I spent the night with him there and he died in my arms early the next morning. I miss him so much and I am so proud to be his son.

My mother, in turn, was dedicated to my father. She also was a very strong influence in my life. After marrying my father, she quit nursing school and went to work at a hospital in Knox City. Years later, at age 48, she re-enrolled in a nursing program. She made straight A's and was named to the Who's Who. Four years later, at age 52, she graduated with a B.S. in Nursing. I learned a lot by watching her as she endured many physical hardships during her lifetime. Through example, she taught me to be tough. She never complained or felt sorry for herself. I owe my spirit to her. God bless them both.

In 1946, shortly after he returned home from Europe, my parents had their first child — my sister, Jan. Three years later, on August 29, 1949, I was born. I was named John Stanley Hansen, Jr. after my father. My son John Stanley Hansen III carries on the family name.

The year my sister was born, 1946, was the first year of the era which would become known as the Baby Boom years. With World War II ended, along with the economic prosperity that followed the war, people once again felt comfortable having large families. As a result, there was a large increase in the number of children born, and those born between 1946 and 1964 created what we know as a "baby boom."

After the war, my father made a living by dryland farming on 350 acres in Knox City with my grandfather Shaver. A large portion of the surface of our world is considered arid, and too dry for conventional rain-fed agriculture. Dryland farming is farming without irrigation. Farmers had to depend on the unpredictable rainfall and it was either boom or bust, all according to the amount of rain that fell and the price they received for the crops.

I learned at a very early age how tough it was to make a living. In the '50s, we lived through a seven-year drought. To make ends meet during those lean years, my father worked two other jobs. One job was in the oil fields that were being developed west of Knox City. He often worked the morning tower shift from seven at night until seven in the morning. In the daytime on the weekends, when he wasn't busy on the farm, he worked helping the butcher at the local grocery store.

We were not poor, but we were definitely in the lower, middle class. We never went hungry, either, but our meals were planned and we had to follow a strict budget. We had homemade fried chicken almost every Sunday afternoon. Once a month or so, we would have round steak when Dad could get a good deal on it from the grocery store. My mom would stretch it out by being innovative. She could do so many things with a can of tomatoes and different types of pasta. We loved it. And even though things were tight, we never realized we were living during hard times. To us, it was just the way life was. I always thought life was good to us. Even living through the hard economic times, my parents had a great, loving relationship, so I had no complaints.

As was the custom in those days, my mother stayed at home to raise us. She also kept busy by planting a garden, being involved with our school, sewing her own clothes, and making dresses for my sister.

My clothes always came from the Sears Roebuck catalog. The only way my parents could buy clothes was to order them on credit and pay for them over time. I can remember going barefoot all spring and summer, but I'm not sure if it was because we couldn't afford shoes, or if I just didn't want to wear them. I do remember always having patches on my jeans.

During the months leading up to Christmas, I would spend hours looking through the Sears catalog. I would put pencil marks beside the items I wanted. The next day, I would erase them and mark other items. That went on for months, until the pages were worn through from the constant marking and erasing. My final choice was always a Fort Apache play set. I loved to play with the miniature cowboys, soldiers, and Indians. I would sit in the back yard and play with them for hours on end.

I played sports from the time I entered elementary school. Texas schools offered tackle football in the fourth grade, and even at that early age, I loved the physical part of it. My grandfather Shaver, who played semi-pro baseball in the central Texas area, had been a very good baseball player. My dad also was a good baseball player, having grown up playing stickball on the streets of Brooklyn. He also played baseball on local teams that competed against other small towns in that part of Texas. He was the fastest player in the area and set several stolen base records. By the time I was born, however, Dad no longer played baseball. He was working almost around the clock and didn't have time for leisure activities.

In 1960, my father had a successful crop, which allowed him to pay off his farming debt. Since he was out of debt, he decided to take a job as a salesman with Murray Company, one of the largest manufacturers of cotton gin machinery in the world. The company, founded in 1900 when it took over a small gin manufacturing plant in East Dallas, was the first company to perfect a machine for cleaning cotton at the gin, and the first to build a gin to run at 700 revolutions a minute with a loose roll.

We moved into an upstairs, two-bedroom apartment in east Dallas that was located directly across the street from Woodrow Wilson High School. I was in the sixth grade at the time and I walked about ten blocks to Lipscomb Elementary School. My sister went to J.L. Long Junior High School, which stood right beside Woodrow Wilson High.

My father finally had a job that paid a steady income. My mom also landed a job, working at nights as proof reader for the Taylor Publishing Company. They were still young and they were excited about having an opportunity to make a new start in a new place. The budget was still tight, though, and they struggled to make ends meet, but again, we never went hungry

I was excited about the move. I wanted to see new places and know more about the areas, so I rode my bike all over east Dallas. I had a great time getting to know the kids in the area.

As an avid football fan who had collected at least two trading cards of every pro football player, I went to several of the first-year pro games of the brand new Dallas Cowboys, which joined the NFL in 1960 as an expansion team. They played their first game in the Cotton Bowl and finished the season winless with a record of 0-11-1 (with a tie vs. the New York Giants). That same year, I also went to see the Dallas Texans, who were also in their first year of play as charter members of the newly formed American Football League.

One day about a year later, I heard the San Diego Chargers were coming to Randall Park to practice. Since they were a start-up league, I don't think the Texans had a practice facility for visiting teams, so they picked a nearby park for practice on the day before the game. There weren't any fences or yard lines. They just practiced in a wide, open area of the park.

By the time I heard about it, the practice had already begun, so I hopped on my bike and raced down to the park. I got off my bike and got as close to the action as I dared. As time passed, I shyly inched closer and closer, until I was about 30 yards from the players. I was so excited. I couldn't believe I was so close to the players, and being so close, I couldn't get over how big they were. They were huge!

I was squatted down on my knees, watching the players go through their repertoire of plays. They would often run straight towards me. There was one play that stands out vividly in my memory. The players began a play which came in my direction, with most of them breaking off and running around me, but one huge player was running towards me at full speed. Before I had time to even think about getting out of the way, he was on top of me. Without breaking stride, he hurdled over me and kept running for a few yards before returning to the huddle.

I was a big-time football fanatic, so I knew who the player was.

Number 77 — Ernie "Big Cat" Ladd.

I was so excited. The biggest man in professional football had just hurdled over me. I had his football card at home. For the next several weeks, I talked about that with everybody who would listen.

That was my first meeting with Ernie Ladd. I don't know if he had been nicknamed "The Big Cat" at that time, but he is in the record books as the largest pro football player of his time. He stood 6-foot-9, weighed 315 pounds, had a 52-inch chest, a 39-inch waist, twenty-inch biceps, a 19-inch neck, and wore 18D shoes. He is a member of the American Football League Hall of Fame. Our paths would cross many times in later years, but at the time, I just couldn't believe I had been that close to Ernie. I will never forget the excitement of him barreling down on me, and then going up and over as I ducked down a little.

Years later, when Ernie and I were booked in the same place, I would tell him that story and we would laugh. He would grin and say me telling him I met him when I was a kid made him feel old. But as an 11-year-old kid, I never would have dreamed I would be in the same car, in a dressing room, or in the ring, interacting and joking around with my childhood football idol. I think that's pretty cool. Ernie didn't know it until I told him years later, but he was a big influence in developing my ring character. I'll explain that later.

My family stayed in Dallas during my 6th and 7th grade years. During that time, my dad made frequent trips to South America to sell machinery for Murray. To prepare, he spent many hours in our living room, listening to and studying Spanish on a record player. One time, he traveled around the continent for three months, visiting every country except Brazil. It was the first time we had been apart, and it was hard on me and my family.

I struggled in school. I did not have good study habits and I did just enough to get by. One of the classes I did enjoy was history. I was in the 6th grade in 1960, which was an election year. Richard Nixon was running against John F. Kennedy for the office of president of the United States. My parents were yellow-dog democrats, a term which came from the idea that a Southerner would vote for a yellow dog before they voted for a Republican. I was for JFK, of course, because my parents were.

In one of our class sessions, every student had to stand up and give an election speech for the candidate they preferred. Out of 25 students, there were only three of us who wanted JFK to be our next president. When it was my turn to speak, I stood up and repeated what my parents had said about JFK being "pro-farmer" and for "the little guy."

At the end of the debate, my teacher stood up and said, "*John F. Kennedy was born rich and is not a good American. Anybody who votes for him is not an American, either.*"

As soon as I got home, I told my mother what my teacher had said. It was the first time (but not the last) I saw my mom take on the establishment. She went to the school and raised all sorts of Cain, demanding a meeting with the school principal and my teacher. I had to stay out in the hall, but I heard every word she said as she lit into my teacher with both barrels. "*Don't EVER tell my boy that he is un-American because he votes for a Democrat or John F. Kennedy!*" She really let them have it. If I lay quietly at night, I can still hear her unloading on them. After a long silence, there were voices of apology from both the teacher and the principal. That was the last I heard of it, but the teacher seemed to give me a little more leeway from that time on.

I played football and basketball in the 7th grade, but I didn't get to play baseball because I missed the deadline for signups. That summer, my dad was transferred and we moved to Tempe, Arizona. I was glad we were making the move, and looking back on that time in my life, it was for the best because we were living in a section of Dallas where there was a lot of juvenile crime. My friends and I would do mischievous things that could be considered illegal, like sneaking into the movie theater. I suppose the worst thing I did was shoplift. We stole water balloons because we didn't have the money to buy them. We went through a stage that a lot of kids go through, but I was fortunate to not get caught before I grew out of it.

I believe the reason I never went beyond that was due to the morals instilled in me by my parents. Many times in the future, I found myself making decisions based on those values of right and wrong. Dad once told me a story about a time when he was growing up in Brooklyn. His mother answered the door one day to find a policeman holding onto Dad and two of his brothers. They had "borrowed" a trolley car while the driver was on his coffee break and drove it a few blocks down the street before they were stopped. Dad's mother gave Dad and his brothers a withering look, and then said, "*Those are not my boys! My sons aren't thieves.*" She then slammed the door shut.

The policeman took my Dad and his brothers to the local police station. The next morning, one of Dad's older brothers came and got them out of jail. It made a lasting impression on Dad, and it made one on me, too. I always assumed Dad would treat me the same way if I were to get myself into a similar situation. Having said that, I'm definitely not a saint, and I've done a lot of things which might be considered to be wrong, but having parents who set a boundary for me seemed to keep me from stepping out too far.

Moving to Tempe the summer before the eighth grade was a great step forward for Dad and our family. We lived in a hotel for the first three months while our house was being built on the edge of Tempe and Scottsdale. Dad paid $13,000 for a new 1,100 square-feet, four-bedroom, two-bath house on Normal Avenue. Mom was so excited and everything seemed to be going well for us. My sister was going into the 10th grade and I was going to be in my last year of junior high school. The move was much harder on my sister because it's harder for girls to make new friends. I was into sports, so I made new friends almost instantly. I played Pop Warner Football and basketball on the junior high team, and then played baseball during the summer.

I always loved baseball. In my opinion, it's the true American sport. I used to play with my father when he would come home from work. He worked long hours as a farmer, but he always seemed to find time to play catch with me. He was a left-hander and taught me to write with my left hand. Early in my childhood years, I threw with my right hand, but batted left-handed. As I got older, I could do things with either hand, like handball or racquetball. I swung a golf club right-handed, but was a natural left-hand hitter with the baseball bat.

As a Little League player, I played the outfield, first base, and pitched occasionally. I pitched one perfect game over a six-inning series. I struck out everyone except two players, and they both popped up fly balls which I caught at the pitcher's mound. My grandfather shook hands with me after the game. Hidden in his palm was a silver dollar. I took it gratefully. A dollar was a lot of money in 1959. I later joked about it, telling people that I was a professional baseball player since I had been given money during that game.

But as much as I loved baseball, I gravitated towards football because I loved the contact and getting down on the ground and getting dirty. My mom was a big influence on me when it came to sports. She taught me to be tough. If I got hit in the nose, she would tell me to wipe off the blood and get back on the field. One day, I came close to being knocked out by a big, defensive lineman. I was staggering around the field. She came out onto the field and stopped the game until I could regain my senses.

Soon after we moved into the new house, my dad's career took a bad turn. The executives at Murray Company had promised him the district manager position, but when he arrived, there was a conflict with the local manager in Phoenix and miscommunication between the home office in Dallas and Phoenix. In the end, my father found himself out of a job. That was the beginning one of the most trying times in my family's life.

My father was out of work for six months. He tried to find another job in the ginning business, but there were only a few big ginning companies. He tried to find anything to make a living, but in 1962, Phoenix was not a thriving metropolis. We had moved twice in the previous two years, and Dad wanted to avoid moving us again. We had to borrow a few thousand dollars from my grandfather to cover the house payment and living expenses, and in those days, that was a lot of money. We had a lean Christmas for the first time in my life. I was old enough to understand what was going on, but as a kid, I was somewhat insulated from the horrors of being unemployed.

Dad traveled back to Texas and eventually found work with an irrigation pump company in Friona, Texas, a small town of about 1,200 people. He took the job in the spring of 1963, but we stayed in Tempe until school was out in May.

Friona is located in the Texas panhandle between Clovis, New Mexico, and Amarillo, Texas. At the time, it was a small, conservative, farming town. Friona High School was comprised of two tiers of students: the locals who were born and raised in Friona, whose parents were either farmers or had important jobs in town, and the laborers like my father, who worked for the farmers. There wasn't any real trouble between the "haves" and the "have-nots," but there were kids in the 9th grade who had brand-new cars to drive. We had one used car, while Dad drove the company pickup truck.

One of my first friends was a kid my age named Alvin Ruffin. Alvin was the first black person in my life that I befriended. I was fortunate to have known my grandmother's house helper in Knox City, a black lady named Pearl Coward. She helped raise my mom and her siblings. Though she was an old woman when I knew her, she was one of the sweetest women I can remember. She was like family to us, and we respected and loved her just as if she were an aunt. Our relationship with Pearl taught me that I shouldn't judge people by the color of their skin, but accept them for how they treat others.

I also befriended Bill Weatherly, who was from a well-to-do farming family. We got along well and became good friends. During this time, my family was very short on money, so I would often bum off of others — a quarter here, a quarter there. Bill would loan me money to buy a snack, or a candy bar. I would always tell him that I would pay him back, but I never did. I hated to do that, but I wanted to have a snack like the rest of the kids. The fact that I had to bum off of others, especially Bill, really bothered me for many years. Years later, when I began to make money as a wrestler, I always saved a percentage of my earnings, even if I was only able to save five dollars.

Years later, Bill and I both visited West Texas State University as football recruits. We both were accepted into the school and became roommates during our freshman year.

When we moved to Friona, my sister once again had to endure a move to a smaller town, where it is even harder to become accepted and fit in. And once again, she suffered the anguish of being the new girl in town who had no friends. Even though she had a hard time of it, she did manage to adjust and make friends.

I spent the first summer running around town and playing with the kids who lived across the street from us. We rented a two-bedroom house and we were glad to have it. I made a bedroom on the screened-in porch and slept there until the weather got too cold. I can remember it being so cold that I would pile on the blankets and sleep wearing a sock hat, while a howling, cold wind blew through the porch. It really wasn't that bad, though. It was just something I had to do.

One of the things I remember most about Friona was a local celebration called Maize Days. The celebration had been held every September since 1957 and came when the maize was being harvested. During that time, they held a talent contest which anybody in the community could enter. The high school auditorium was packed with people and there were all sorts of acts, from singing to comedy to skits. Dad, who had sung on the radio in New York City during his youth, entered and sang two songs, "They Call the Wind Maria" and "Old Man River." When Dad walked out on stage and began to sing, there was a sudden silence as everybody hushed to listen. To say the least, he really did mesmerize the audience. He received a standing ovation after each of the songs. It was one of the proudest moments of my life.

On November 22, 1963, the students at Friona High were called to an assembly in the auditorium. There were more students than could fit into the auditorium, so the room was packed. As soon as we were all settled, the principal walked out onto the stage and said, "*President John F. Kennedy was shot and assassinated in Dallas earlier this morning.*" I was shocked. There were a few seconds of silence, and then suddenly, a loud cheer went up. The majority of the kids were clapping! I could not believe it. The principle restored order and reprimanded them, but I was more in shock about the applause than I was about the assassination.

The next day, most of the students came to school in a somber mood. After they went home, the gravity of the situation sank in and the realization of what had happened hit home. For the most part, most of the students who had cheered were sorry for their reaction and felt badly. It was just a childish reaction to news to which they thought their parents would have applauded. I remember talking to my parents about the teacher in Dallas who had shown so much hatred for JFK a few years earlier, and we all agreed that we weren't shocked that the assassination took place in Dallas.

Chapter 2

The Invisible Line

The 9th grade holds a special place in my life when it comes to sports. At that time, the Friona varsity football team had the longest losing streak in the state of Texas: 27 straight games. That year, a new coach, Don Light, and his assistant, Bob Owen, came in and turned the whole football program around. The varsity won eight straight games, and the whole town was ecstatic.

I played defensive end and tight end on the freshman team. Bill Weatherly, our biggest lineman, got hurt and was out the whole year. Without him, we struggled, and we had a fullback who was susceptible to fumbling. He had fumbled the ball a number of times during the year and the freshman team was looking for its first win. Coach Owen made him carry the football around with him all day — in class, at lunch, and, of course, to and from football practice. I really felt bad for him because he tried hard, but he just couldn't hold onto the ball.

We went into the last game of the year without a win. Not only were we winless, but we hadn't scored a single point during the whole season. We were playing Dimmitt, a rival school, and late in the game, we were down by six points. When we took the ball to the two yard line, the Friona supporters were on the edge of their seats, optimistic that we were going to win the final game of the season. With four downs available to make the score, our quarterback gave the ball to the fullback. When he was hit, he fumbled the ball and Dimmit recovered on the one yard line. We were so upset. We all piled on top of the fullback.

When the school yearbook photographer took the team photo, Coach Owen wouldn't stand with us. Months later, when we got our yearbooks, we found a full-page photo of the team, along with a list of our opponents and the scores of each game. There was a big, fat, "0" in every column under "Friona." That had to be one of the most embarrassing things that happened to me in my whole life.

Years later, the fullback who had fumbled also was going to school at West Texas. Every time I would see him, I would remind him about fumbling the football. There weren't any hard feelings over what happened in the 9th grade, but I kept kidding him about it. He didn't think it was funny, though. He had heard about it so often over the years that he was sick and tired of it.

We moved again when I finished the 9th grade. Dad got a opportunity to buy into an irrigation pump company in Las Cruces, New Mexico. We all hoped this would be our last move, especially Jan, who found herself back to square one. She had attended four different high schools in four years. Fortunately, we stayed in Las Cruces for my final three years of high school.

When we moved to Las Cruces in May 1964, I worked full time for my father. I was 14 years old and it was not your typical "boss's son" job. I worked all summer with one of the two three-man crews that my father had working for him. The only previous job experience I had was working on our farm in Knox City, and everybody was looking at me as the typical 14-year-old boss's son, but I was all ears and eager to learn.

During my first week on the job, I got a lesson in being careful and staying alert about what was going on around me. I was helping one my crew members unload six-inch, concrete water pipes from a trailer. We were on top of a ten-foot high stack of pipe. We used a rope to lower one pipe at a time over the edge and down to the ground. All of a sudden, the pipe we were standing on began to shift. The other guy leapt down to the ground, leaving me holding onto the rope. I did my best to keep the pipe from rolling over the edge, but the rope slid through my hands. I managed to slow it down, but it still raced through my hands, and I wasn't wearing gloves. When the pipe finally hit the ground, I dropped the rope and looked down at the palms of my hands. The top layer of skin had been burned off and my hands were bleeding. They looked bad.

I didn't want to go to the hospital, so I went straight home, where Mom put on some Vaseline and white, cotton gloves. I suffered the whole night. I don't remember if my mom said I could stay at home or not, but the next morning, I got up and went to work. My hands were really sore and I wore the white gloves, but I reported to work. That really impressed the other workers. They never thought the son of the owner would come to work with hands that looked like hamburger, let alone a kid who was just 14 years old.

That was one of my first lessons in "taking care of yourself" and not depending on anybody else. When the pipe shifted, my co-worker jumped off, leaving me to hold the rope by myself. I didn't resent him for doing that, but it was a lesson I would experience many times throughout my career. That job also taught me about getting along with people. In life, we are often pushed into positions where we have to spend time with people we might not like, or have anything in common with, but we have to accept that and learn to get along.

In 1964, the minimum wage was $1.25 an hour, but because of my age, I worked for just $1.00. I worked long hours, often putting in 50 to 55 hours a week, and was paid twice a month. I kept $25 to $30 and turned the rest over to my mom. With this additional income, she was able to buy my sister some clothes for her senior year, and later, for college. I didn't mind. I didn't have a car at the time and I was working so much that I really didn't have time to spend the money. I also was happy to contribute to the family. Those hard times taught me the value of saving. Years later, when I was wrestling, saving my money for the future became my number one goal.

I tried to instill a work ethic in my kids. Each generation of Americans has had it easier than their parents. My parents gave me more than they had when they were growing up during the Depression, and I wanted to do the same for my children. I'm not so sure my kids' generation really understands the importance of work and family. They didn't experience hard times like my parents' generation did in the years immediately following the Depression, and thank God, neither did I. However, I am proud of my children, who are now adults. They are working hard to raise families and continue to work towards getting a degree from college.

As a 14-year-old, working alongside those grown men, doing the same work they were doing, and for less money, prepared me for hard work in the future. I learned early that if I didn't work, then I didn't get anything. There was no free lunch. Somewhere along the way, I feel our country has lost a lot of that work ethic.

Okay, that's the end of the sermon. Let's get back to the story.

As with our last move, I missed out on playing baseball because I worked all summer. When school began, however, I dove right into sports, beginning with football in my sophomore year at Las Cruces High School. I would play for the Bulldogs during the 1964-1966 seasons. I was the new kid again, but I had been playing tackle football since the fourth grade. In those days, the earliest we could play organized football in New Mexico was the seventh grade, so I had a three-year advantage over most of the kids. I weighed 165 pounds and played both linebacker and center on the junior varsity team. I enjoyed both positions. I also was on the junior varsity basketball and baseball teams. I hadn't played baseball since my 8th grade year and my skills were lacking, but I did improve quickly and was getting the skills back by the end of my sophomore year.

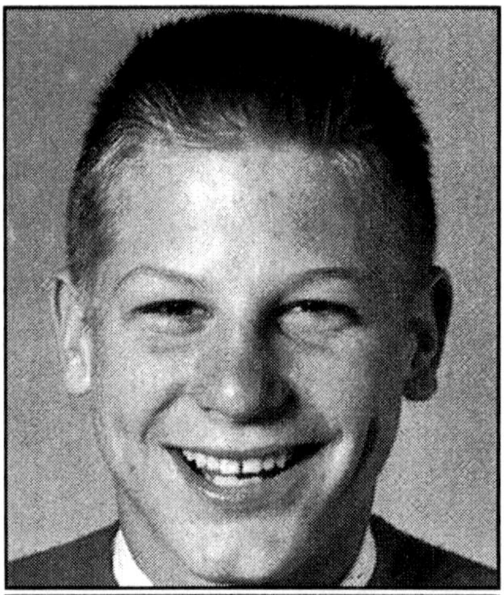

Sophomore year, Las Cruces, Mexico

I worked for my dad again the following summer. I didn't get to play summer baseball because I was working long hours and couldn't work it into my schedule. It really hurt me because baseball is a sport that requires constant repetition to improve and develop skills.

In my junior year on the varsity football team, I started as both center and middle linebacker. I loved playing defense the most. We had a 4-6 win-loss record that year, but I still managed to earn post-season honors, including All-State. My coach was Ed Boykin, who also taught my youth class at church. After football, I was the seventh man on our basketball team, which means I was the enforcer on the team. I had a couple of good games. My best scoring in a single game was 17 points and hitting 100 percent from the floor, but most of the time I was a substitute.

One of the toughest decisions I had to make that year was to give up baseball. I had missed so much during the off-season I really didn't have the skills necessary to reach the next level. Coach Dave Graham was really disappointed with my decision, but he understood my reasons and we've remained friends ever since. We still stay in touch and talk a few times each year. I don't have many regrets in life, but one of them is that I wish I had continued to play baseball in high school. Coach Graham was a great coach and I would have liked to play for him.

Even though football, basketball, and wrestling were a big part of my adult life, I think baseball is still the greatest of all sports.

After school during the off-season, I worked at the local Baskin-Robbins ice cream shop to earn spending money. I really enjoyed the daily treats the owner gave to us, and I always took some back to Mom and Dad at the end of my shift.

I still didn't apply myself to my academics. If I had just dedicated myself to the classroom one-third as much as I did to sports, I would have done well. I always did just enough to get by, however, and I squeaked through with C's and a few B's. I wasn't aware of just how much grades meant when it came to getting admitted to a good college. My dad had not gone to college, and my mom had to quit after one year, so none of us knew anything about the process of getting into college on a football scholarship. Winning a scholarship had always been my dream, but I was really unaware of the importance of good grades, and that would prove to cost me in the future.

During the summer following my junior year, I began to receive letters from schools all over the country: Oklahoma, Michigan State, University of Texas, Texas Tech, Southern California, and a host of smaller schools and junior colleges. Sure enough, my grades disqualified me from qualifying for a scholarship to several of the big and powerful football schools. I was disappointed at the time, but as I would eventually discover, the Lord has ways of working things out.

I made trips to a number of colleges as a potential football recruit, including the University of New Mexico and Texas Tech. The University of New Mexico was very interested in recruiting me and offered me a scholarship. They were having a hard time competing at that time, but they had high hopes of rebuilding their football program.

The next stop on our campus visits was West Texas State University [WT], which was located in Canyon, Texas, a small city south of Amarillo. While there, not only did we visit the school, but we paid a visit to my aunt and uncle, who lived in Canyon. My family made occasional visits to Canyon when I was a kid, and one of my cousins was my age, so we knew the town. To be completely honest, our main reason for making the trip was to visit our family, and when we were presented with the opportunity to go using expense money provided to us by the WT athletic department, we jumped at the chance.

I hadn't given much, if any, thought to attending WT. However, head coach Joe Kerbel was one of the great characters I've had the pleasure of meeting during my lifetime. He won over my mom by telling her, *"I'll take care of your son, and I'll provide tutors, or whatever else he needs, to get an education."* He had honey flowing out of his mouth. It worked on my mom, and again, to be honest, it worked on me, too. He sold me on the WT football program. Also, as I mentioned earlier, by chance, Bill Weatherly was visiting WT on the same weekend, so we both committed to WT.

During the visit, I was shown around campus by Phil Hampton, a senior center on the team. I had already visited several other colleges, so I was expecting to be shown the dorms where I would be living when I came to the university. Phil walked me from one side of the campus to the other, but he never volunteered to show me his dorm room. I wanted to see where he was staying, so I finally summoned up the courage to ask. He seemed to hesitate before answering, but he finally agreed.

When we reached the door of his room, he hesitated again and told me that all football players have roommates. He also said he had a roommate, and that we don't normally have a choice as to who our roommate will be.

When he opened the door, the first thing I noticed was there were two beds — one on each side of the room. It was as if an invisible line was painted down the center of the room. On Phil's side were a neatly-made bed and a desk on which his books were neatly stacked. His closet was open and the clothes were all hung neatly inside. His side of the room would have passed an Army inspection.

The other side of the room was a different story. It was messy beyond belief. Newspapers, trash, food, and food containers were everywhere. Just like Phil's closet, the hangers were hung neatly in a row ... but there wasn't a stitch of clothing on a single one of them. Dirty clothes were piled up on the floor and draped over the back of the desk chair. There were no sheets on the bed, and a big guy was sleeping on the bare mattress. As we walked in, he woke up. This was two in the afternoon. He rolled his eyes, said, "*Hi,*" turned over, and went back to sleep.

That was my first meeting with Frank Goodish, who would later become a big name in professional wrestling as Bruiser Brody. Years later, when Frank and I were both wrestling, we would laugh when we talked about our first meeting.

Several things happened during my first visit to West Texas State. Coach Kerbel had a minor heart attack a few months before my visit. I was concerned because I wanted to play football at a school where the coaching position was stable, and not likely to change.

Several of the recruits, including Bill Weatherly and myself, were invited to Coach Kerbel's house for dinner. It was close to dinner time and this would be our first meeting with the coach. When we got to his house, he was sitting in the kitchen at a dining bar which overlooked the kitchen stove. He was excited to see us and was very jovial and outgoing. As we were all standing around talking, he dipped a folded piece of white bread into a big bowl of what looked like tomato sauce, and then almost ate it whole. He ate one piece of bread after another, while his wife was busy frying steaks and cooking other items on the stove. He didn't offer any of us a piece of bread. He just sat there and ate in front of us. After visiting for awhile, we all went to a basketball game at WT. While there, we all discussed his strong personality, but wondered about the scene we had witnessed.

The next day, when my mom and I were visiting with Coach Kerbel in his office, I asked about his heart attack. He said he was on a strict diet and that his heart was fine. I was somewhat reassured by his explanation, but I couldn't get the vision of him dipping one piece of bread after another into the sauce out of my mind.

After my trip to West Texas State University, I was scheduled to visit University of Arizona, but I opted out. I had decided to accept the offer from West Texas State University. During my senior year in high school, there were fifteen guys from WT who were signed to the pros. WT ran an offense that was almost a carbon-copy of the Dallas Cowboys offense. The potential for being drafted into the pros, along with the fact that WT had a winning football program, was instrumental in my decision to accept a scholarship from WT.

While I was busy planning out my future, my dad was working hard to keep his business running. He had laid off half of his employees and was barely able to keep a three-man crew active. At the end of my junior year, I went to work for him again. Since I was 16 years old, he could now pay me the full minimum wage. I was happy to get it and turned most of it over to my mom, who used it to help pay for my sister's college bills. They had to borrow, of course, to send her to college, so my contribution was greatly appreciated. Nothing was more important than family, and loyalty to family roots ran deep in the Shaver clan. I always tried to put my family first, a principle which cost me a good amount of money when I was in the wrestling business, but I don't regret it for one moment.

My senior football year in Las Cruces, New Mexico, was a mixed bag. I gave up basketball that year in order to concentrate on football and train for my first year of college. The football team once again struggled to a 4-6 win-loss record. Personally, I had a pretty good year playing both offensive tackle and middle linebacker. I was selected All-State again (defensive first-team) and won Honorable Mention All American.

In March 1967, I became the first kid from "the New Mexico-West Texas area" to merit inclusion among the 100 top athletes recognized, nationally, by *Coach & Athlete* magazine. From the article: "Hansen has been an outstanding leader and aggressive competitor for the three years he has played football at Las Cruces High School," said his coach, Ed Boykin, present at the award ceremony along with an El Paso-based RC Cola bottler (RC Cola was the national sponsor of the "Prep America Football Awards"). The award program was four years old at the time.

I was so excited and happy to be recognized. Years later, it doesn't mean much, but when you're a high school student with the world at your fingertips, you think the whole world is standing in awe of that achievement.

1967 • 17 year old high-school senior

Chapter 3

A Gallon Jug of Blood

The head coach at WT, Joe Kerbel, was a legend among Texas high school football coaches. At West Texas State, his teams won the most games of any other coach before or since at that level. He also was one of the most dynamic individuals I have ever met. We always treated him with respect because he deserved it. Then again, perhaps it was because he demanded respect.

Coach Kerbel wasn't more than 5-foot-9, but he weighed more than 350 pounds, and his personality was as big and impressive as his size. He spoke loudly, too. He had a booming voice that could be heard clear across campus. He would cuss and swear at us one second and compliment us the next.

On and off the football field, his word was the law, and everybody within eyesight of him walked on their tiptoes. Everybody, even the first-string players, was afraid of him. We did whatever we could to avoid attracting his attention because he was a master of psychology. If we were unlucky enough to be stopped by him on campus, he would begin to question us about our classes or something.. Vince Lombardi was a choir boy compared to Kerbel. He had complete rule over the West Texas football program and made all of the major decisions. He put West Texas on the map, so he was given leeway to do just about whatever he wanted to do.

Coach Kerbel trained us really well to react to his whistle. At least one time at every practice, he would blow his whistle, lift his hand above his head, and move it around in a circle. It didn't matter what we were doing. Everybody — coaches, players, managers, and support staff — would run in his direction and form a circle around him. When we were on the field, he usually blew his football whistle, but if he saw us walking across campus, and we made eye contact with him, he would physically whistle, lift his hand, and circle it over his head. It didn't matter whether we were trying to get to class on time or headed to the cafeteria. If we heard that whistle and saw him, it usually meant he saw us, and we knew we "were under the eye."

One day, we were waiting to board a plane at Chicago O'Hare International Airport. We had 30 to 40 minutes to kill, so we were all scattered around in the various shops. Each of us was wearing a maroon school blazer. All of a sudden, we heard "the whistle." As we looked down the aisle, we saw Coach Kerbel, standing on a small table in the boarding area, circling his hand above his head. Instantly, more than 50 players broke into a fast trot to circle Coach Kerbel. The average traveler must have got a good laugh to see powerfully built, muscular football players running towards one central point. I laugh when I think about it now, but at the time, it was pretty embarrassing, but we did what we were expected. If we didn't, we knew we would have to endure his wrath.

Joe Kerbel

One weekend, the WT football team traveled to Detroit for a game against Western Michigan University. Before we got to the school, we stopped at a restaurant for a pre-arranged meal. As the horde of players filed into the restaurant, Coach Kerbel asked everybody if they wanted some "Buff Dessert." Buff Dessert was the official Kerbel term for vanilla ice cream and Hershey chocolate syrup, a dessert we had with almost all of our pre-game meals.

After our meal, Kerbel yelled, "*Give everybody some Buff Desert.*" He repeated that fast and loud at least four times. The waitresses and restaurant manager were tripping over themselves as they ran around, trying to figure out what "Buff Desert" was. One of the assistant coaches finally told them what it was. A few minutes later, every player was served Buff Desert.

Coach Kerbel also was one of the first coaches to recruit black football players. The first was "Pistol" Pete Pedro in 1960. He was so fast and quick. He set quite a few rushing records during his time at WT. Another black player was Hank Washington, who was the quarterback at WT in 1965 and 1966. During that time, he completed 282 of 524 passes for 3,510 yards and 26 touchdowns. In October 1966, Washington was touted as someone who could possibly become the NFL's first black quarterback. He was drafted by the New York Giants and spent two years with the team before being traded to another team. Sadly, Washington died from cancer when he was just 23 years old.

While I was playing, Duane Thomas and Mercury Morris were in the backfield — at a time when Southwest Conference schools were reluctant to start one black, let alone two. Having two incredible players like Thomas and Morris in the same backfield is something that doesn't often happen. Ralph Anderson and Ray Brown were in the secondary at the same time. All four went on to have great careers in the NFL.

Not only was Kerbel a great coach, but he was an incredible motivator. He could get every last ounce of energy and ability out of every one of his players. Of course, in the process, he also ran off a number of players who wouldn't accept his style of coaching. In the long run, however, he turned out many great football players who left college and went into the pros: Jerry Don Logan, Bobby Richardson, Mercury Morris, Duane Thomas, Rocky Thompson, Ted Wheeler, Ralph Anderson, Ray Brown, Bobby Duncum Sr., Frank Goodish, Mark Allen, and myself, to name a few. He treated everyone fairly, but at times, he could be harsh and unforgiving. As the saying goes, it was his way or the highway. He didn't take anything from any of his players. If we didn't listen or did something wrong, he would physically hit us. He would even grab our face mask and sling us off the field. He would never get away with that in the politically correct world we live in today, but in the wild and wooly days of Texas football in the 1960s, he pretty much had license to do whatever he wanted to do.

To this day, football players in Texas tell stories about "The Fat Man," which was our nickname for Kerbel. Of course, we only used that name behind his back and when he wasn't within earshot. Many of them sound bizarre and unbelievable, but I have no doubt the biggest percentage of them are true.

Bobby Duncum, a pro wrestler during the '60s, '70s, and '80s, played for Kerbel before I arrived at West Texas. During one game near St. Louis, he was sent to the hospital for heat exhaustion. In the meantime, the team lost the game. Several players who were there told me that after the game, Kerbel had the bus driver make a detour to the hospital. He got out of the bus and found Bobby sitting in the emergency room, hooked up to IV lines. Kerbel walked up to him and told him, "*The bus is leaving. Get your ass on it right now.*" When Bobby didn't move, Kerbel pulled out his IVs and proceeded to drag him off the stretcher and out to the bus.

Over the years, many of us, who played for Kerbel and ended up wrestling, would talk about how we were all treated pretty harshly by Kerbel at one time or another. We would all laugh about our shared experiences and considered them to be a rite of passage that we had to endure. Bobby was the only one who never laughed. He still harbors ill feelings towards the Fat Man.

Frank Goodish transferred to WT from Iowa State University as a redshirt sophomore. He was a very talented high school athlete from Warren, Michigan. He was All-State in both football and basketball.

Frank once told me a story about a time when he was in Amarillo, which was 17 miles north of Canyon. Canyon was located in Randall County, a dry county, which means the local government forbids the sale of alcohol. Amarillo was wet, so we went there to drink beer. I never drank alcohol in high school. I drank my first beer during my freshman year in college. That came about as a result of me getting involved in a fraternity, the Kappa Alpha Order. We saw ourselves as southern gentlemen, and the inspiration for the fraternity was based on the chivalry and manners of Robert E. Lee. To be honest, our primary goal was to drink, to party, and to have as good a time as possible. Being in a fraternity gave me the opportunity to get to know people outside of football, and that was a real benefit. I still have a bond with several of those people today. However, in other ways, getting involved in that scene was a big mistake for me. I was really underfunded and I drank much more than I should have, and in the process, learned that my body couldn't assimilate alcohol well.

Late one night during the time when he was going to school at WT, Frank was in a small, after-hours Pit Grill restaurant. He didn't have much money on him, so he ordered breakfast, ate, and then went to the restroom. A few seconds later, the cook rushed into the restroom with a meat cleaver in his hand, only to find Frank crawling out the window. He escaped in the nick of time and took off running.

A few weeks later, Frank was told the Fat Man wanted to see him. You can rest assured that when the Fat Man asked to see you personally, it wasn't to congratulate you for something good you might have done. When Frank walked into Kerbel's office, Bobby Hudson, the WT head of security, was there. Kerbel said there had been a report that one of his football players had skipped out on a meal in Amarillo, and they had identified Frank as the culprit. "*What've you got to say about this, Frank?*" Kerbel asked.

Of course, Frank denied it. "*That's fine,*" said Kerbel. "*Just go down and take a lie detector test and this whole thing will be over with.*"

Frank denied it again.

Kerbel stood up and walked around his desk, got close to Frank, put his arm around his shoulder, and leaned in real close. "*Now you go on down with the officer and take that test.*" Kerbel paused for about ten seconds, and then said, "*But, if you fail the test, I am going to personally kick your ass out of town.*"

Frank walked out of Kerbel's office and down the steps to the first floor. A minute later, he climbed back up the steps, knocked on the open door, and stepped in. Kerbel was still talking to the school's head security officer. Frank said hesitantly, "*Coach, I can't pass the lie detector test.*"

Kerbel did not even hesitate. "*That okay, Frank. I just wanted you to come clean with me. I will take care of it.*"

That was the type of coach that Kerbel was. He would do anything for his players, but in return, he demanded loyalty and honesty from them. Of course, if you were 6-foot-5 and could run the 40-yard-dash in 4.5, he really did like you.

In spring 1968, when I was a freshman, Frank left West Texas State and took a job as the doorman/bouncer at a couple of honkytonks in Amarillo. Once we learned that, we went there because Frank would let us in, even though we were all under the drinking age.

Frank was a Yankee. He was born in the coal mining area of western Pennsylvania, and his family moved to Warren, Michigan, a suburb or Detroit, when he was young. When he arrived at WT, he made friends with a large group of guys from back east that Kerbel had recruited. By the middle of my freshman year, Frank had gotten into some trouble off campus. It seems that while a number of his Yankee buddies had been drinking beer, one of the other football players got a chain saw. They cut down three or four big trees in Canyon, where WT was located. A witness to the incident recognized Frank as one of the players. The Fat Man called them all into his office and said there were witnesses to them doing it. They all denied participation, and Frank was the only one who was identified.

Kerbel had a lot of influence with both the university and the townspeople. He used his power on many occasions to get players out of trouble. He wasn't able to save Frank this time, however, and Frank, true to his character, took the rap and never told who was with him. As a result, he was kicked out of school.

My freshman coaches were John Fritch, Jim Young, and Ronnie Mankin. Young and Mankin had both played football at WT with Terry Funk and were good friends with him. When I arrived on campus, they were graduate assistants. They were just a few years older than us freshmen and they were still crazy guys. Before practice, they would act like professional wrestlers and beat up each other.

Before I went to WT, my only memory of professional wrestling was from a time when I was five or six years old. I remember watching a snowy picture on a TV station from Wichita Falls, Texas. One wrestler, holding his opponent in an arm bar, rubbed the inside of his opponent's arm with a shoe until he gave up.

The very first time I met Mankin and Young, they made the comment that I looked just like Terry Funk. I had heard of Terry, but I had never met him. He was wrestling in the Amarillo territory, but he also was traveling around the country. At that time, Terry and I both parted our hair on the right side, and there really was a striking familiarity between the two of us. I was often mistaken for him. In fact, one time when I was out on a date in Amarillo, a young kid ran up to me as I was walking out of a movie theater. He said, "*Terry, you are my favorite wrestler. Can I have your autograph?*"

That had happened before, but I always told them they were mistaken, and that I wasn't Terry Funk. That time, however, I took the paper and signed it, *Terry Funk*. The kid said, "*Thank you, Terry, and good luck with the match this Thursday.*" My date was embarrassed, but impressed, and we laughed about it.

1971 • West Texas football, sophomore year

Mankin and Young must have mentioned to Terry that somebody on the freshmen team looked a lot like him. As time went by, my friends and I began to watch wrestling on TV, and Terry was heavily involved in the wrestling programs that were going on in the territory at the time. One of the feuds was between Terry and "Mad Dog" Harley Race. We first heard about their matches on TV. I don't remember watching the match on TV, but everybody knew who Terry was, so when the feud began, word spread around campus. They had a hot angle going and their series of matches built in intensity until they met in Amarillo in what was known as a Russian Chain Match. They were very deliberate in their working style and the people believed in what they were doing. Harley was deliberate and solid with everything he did and really looked the part of the nasty heel. He really impressed me during the match when he press slammed Terry, even though they were chained together. That was the first time I had ever seen anybody press slam their opponent, and Terry probably weighed 265 pounds at the time. He was much bigger than he was later in his career. The match ended when Terry "damaged" Harley's eye to a point where Harley had to wear a patch over his eye for the remainder of the time Harley was in Amarillo.

Terry Funk

During that time, we would make the rounds of the bars in Amarillo, and on occasion, Terry would be at one of them. Terry knew who we were and we became casual acquaintances. One night, we were in Luigi's, a popular nightclub on Amarillo Boulevard. When we walked in, we saw Harley sitting at a table with some of his friends. He was wearing the patch over his eye. A few minutes later, Terry came in with a few of his friends. We were really excited to see both Terry and Harley in the same place, and we wondered if anything would happen. After just a few seconds, Harley stood up and left. He had seen Terry come in, so he did what was expected of him. Whenever possible, the heels and babyfaces would almost never occupy the same place. It was just good business. The wrestlers really protected the business back then, and it paid dividends because the people were really into their matches and many of the shows were sold out.

Terry played football at WT from 1963 until 1966, so the football players were big fans of Terry and they were really into his matches. Even though he had only been out of college for a few years, Terry was already a great worker and he was really over. He had a wild and exciting style of wrestling that really hadn't been seen before. His brother, Dory Funk Jr., was the wrestler of the family. Terry was more of a brawler, like his father, Dory Funk Sr. All three of them would be featured on the card at the Fairground Sports Arena in Amarillo on Thursdays nights, although Dory was the National Wrestling Alliance [NWA] world heavyweight champion at the time and was in and out of the territory. Terry, Dory, and Ricky Romero were the top babyface wrestlers. Harley, the Beast, Gorgeous George Jr., and Pak Song were the top heels. The program between Terry and Harley, however, was the one that got all the football players into wrestling. Harley would beat up Terry. Terry would come back and get his revenge. That scenario was repeated over and over, and there was no end to their feud.

We were told that during the football off-season, we could get a student rate, which was 50 percent off the regular price of tickets to the wrestling matches. Ringside tickets were $3.00, so we could get them for $1.50. That was a real bargain. Around four on Thursday afternoons, before the matches, a large group of us would go to the Jockey Club, a local beer dive in downtown Amarillo, for happy hour. By the time we got to the matches, we weren't feeling any pain and we were ready to have a great time. We were big, so we all stood out. We would yell and holler, and just make a spectacle out of ourselves. The local fans would get annoyed because we were so loud and boisterous, but we were just having a good time. When Terry would come to the ring, we would all yell in unison, over and over again, "*Funk! Funk! Funk! Funk!*" He occasionally acknowledged us, but most of the time, he was all-business and concentrating on his match.

While watching those matches, I wasn't so hooked on the wrestling as I was on Terry and his wrestling personality, especially his matches with Harley, which we really enjoyed because they were action-packed and violent. There was a lot of blood in every one of their matches, and I knew the blood was real. I can remember someone once saying that it was "chicken blood," but I didn't buy that because Terry bled so much that he would have had to have a gallon jug in his hair.

We always left the Amarillo Sports Arena with a feeling of excitement, and Thursday nights just didn't come around soon enough. We just couldn't wait to see what was going to happen the following week. Terry and Harley were the masters of psychology. They kept the fans coming back, week after week, to see what they were going to do next. That's an art that has been lost in wrestling today.

One day, somebody came into the dorm and said they had been watching the TV wrestling program, and in a interview, Terry had said, "*I saw Stan Hansen and some of the West Texas football players down at the matches last week.*"

"Wow!" I thought. "My name was mentioned on TV!"

From that day on, we went to the shows in Amarillo as often as we could. One night, someone said Terry would like us to all come back by the dressing room. Terry came out, talked to us for a few minutes, and thanked us for being there.

I can still remember the match Terry had that night. In the middle of his match with Ciclon Negro, Terry chased him back to the heel dressing room. When Negro went inside, the referee tried to keep him from following. We were with the crowd that had moved with them down the aisle. The police were holding the crowd back, but we were really up close. Terry broke free of the referee and ran into the dressing room after Negro, slamming the door shut behind him as he went. All of a sudden, we heard a loud pounding and raised voices as a fight took place behind the door. All of a sudden, there was silence. After a few seconds of suspense, the door swung open. Negro and a couple of his cohorts threw Terry through the doorway and out onto the arena floor. Terry lay on the ground, bleeding and twitching. When the referee finally pulled him to his feet, Terry, in a state of semi-consciousness, began swinging at the air (as only Terry could do), fighting invisible opponents.

That was great wrestling. At the time, I had no idea those matches would have a great influence on me in my later years.

Coach Kerbel was our head offense coach. At the time, sports analysts considered him to have one of the top offensive minds in college football. Few coaches were able to run the complicated Dallas Cowboy offense that I mentioned earlier. Coach Kerbel knew the strengths and weaknesses of every player on his offense, and he really trained them hard. As a freshman, I also was on the card defense team. The freshmen players always ran what was called the card offense and defense, or the plays of our next opponent, so our team could practice defending against what the other team could possibly do. That was very important since our next opponents' plays were drawn on cards and our coach would hold up a card so the "card team" could see it. Each player had a position on the card and we would run the play as it was drawn.

The card defense team helped the varsity offense learn our opponent's defensive alignments. The offense had two different teams that alternated running plays against the card defense. The offensive team that wasn't involved in a play would huddle about ten yards back from the ball, and either to the left or the right side. As soon as the first offensive team ran a play, Coach Kerbel immediately sent out the other offensive team. That only gave the defensive team a few seconds for a huddle, so we had to do it over the ball. He ran one play on the heels of another, so we had to be on our toes in order to keep up with the offensive teams. We looked forward to the games so much because they were always easier than the practices by a large margin.

Coach Kerbel had a very stout, wooden, straight-back chair that he would sit on when he coached from the field. When he wanted to make a point, or give instruction, he would stand up, and then return to the chair and sit down as the play was run. He did that hundreds of times every day. Up, down, up, down, up, down. There were about 50 players who made up the offense part of the practice: two offensive teams, several subs, and the card defense team.

One day, practice was moving along at a rapid pace, and Coach was getting up and down, up and down. After one scathing critique, he backed up and dropped himself into a sitting position onto the chair. Or, at least, where he thought the chair should have been. He dropped hard onto his rear end and rolled backwards onto his back. There was dead silence. Nobody made a sound. I swear that even the birds quit their singing for fear of being noticed.

Coach Kerbel rolled around as he tried to get up off the ground, but being as big as he was, he just couldn't manage to get to his feet. As the seconds ticked by, the field remained silent. Finally, a couple of the trainers ran over and helped him get up. The silence continued as he slowly glared at each and every person on the field. He looked from player to player, one at a time, and stared directly into their eyes. Still no sound. Nobody said anything. I don't know what was going through his mind, but he stood there staring at each of us, for at least three minutes. He finally said, "*Huddle up!*"

When we (card defense team) got into the huddle, we all broke into silent laughter. We were only ten to fifteen yards from where Coach Kerbel sat, so we made sure we didn't laugh out loud, but it was hard to keep from doing just that. We were literally crying, with big tears running down our cheeks. When Coach Ostrander, one of the offensive coaches, walked towards us, we thought we were in big trouble. If Coach Kerbel had heard our laughter, there would be hell to pay. However, when the coach bent down and leaned into the huddle, as if to tell us something, all he did was break into his own silent laughter. He had found himself unable to hold it back, and the only way he could hide it from Coach Kerbel was to join us.

I weighed in at about 205 pounds and stood 6-foot-3. Frank Goodish was 6-foot-4 and weighed about 215 pounds. He was on the thin side, but he was wiry. He was a defensive end and was quick and agile, but he got frustrated by having to play on what was known as the "sh— squad," our name for the card team. He ended up butting heads with the head defense coach.

To a guy like Frank, being red-shirted was mentally tough and depressing. The red shirts were required to practice and do everything the other players did. They had to take the hits and wrath of the starters. But as red shirts, they had no chance to play. Frank was a good athlete and football player, and he just hated having to just run plays on the card team. Kerbel's head defensive coach, Clarence "Dirk" Dierking didn't like Frank's attitude, so they often butted heads. Frank later told me that he often messed up on a card play, just to make Dierking mad. Coach Dierking could really get mad, and he wasn't shy about venting his anger on a player. He was second only to the Fat Man as far as the players being scared of his wrath. He would get into Frank's face and yell at him. Frank, in turn, would give him a cold stare and not show any emotion. That made Dierking even angrier. Most of the time, Dierking would end the standoff by making Frank run laps. Needless to say, they didn't like each other at all.

In mid-winter of my freshman year, I found myself on the other end of high school recruiting when I was asked to show a high school prospect around campus. The recruits arrived on campus during the short off-season between the fall football season and the spring drills that began in March. That was an important job because it can influence the recruit in lots of ways. Most of us didn't really like doing it because it interfered with our other important activities (beer drinking, partying, dating, driving around town, etc). It also meant we had to report to the Fat Man and the other coaches.

As I got to know one of the kids that I was showing around, he told me that he wanted to know where he could go to have a good time. We always took them to the basketball game, but he was interested in meeting some "college girls." The kid told me that he had visited some other schools, and at one, he had been taken to a fraternity party. I wasn't in a fraternity at the time, but I had some friends in one of them, so I took the kid. When he got sloppy drunk, I took him back to his dorm room and then returned to my own room where I hoped to sleep until at least noon. However, around ten in the morning, somebody began to pound on my door. "*Stan! Stan! Coach Kerbel wants to see you. He's mad as hell.*"

Oh, no. I didn't know what Coach wanted, but whenever he sent somebody to get one of us, we could assume that we were in real trouble. I dressed as quickly as I could and sprinted across campus to the Buffalo Courts, the ancient building which housed the football office. After running up the steps to Kerbel's office, I hesitated for just a second before I walked around the corner and into his office. As I did, the Fat Man stormed around his desk, grabbed me by my shirt collar, and pushed me backwards into the wall. "*What did you do to that kid?*" he yelled at me. I swear I could see flames blazing in his eyes as he held me against the wall. He "bumped" me into the wall a couple of times and then hissed, "*I said, what did you do to him?*"

I remember focusing in on his mouth. The corners of his lips were white with froth. "*He's sick and hung over so bad that he left campus and went home without telling anybody but one of his buddies.*" Then he paused for second and said, "*I'm gonna kick your ass, Hansen, you son of a bitch*"

Before he could finish his sentence, one of the booster ladies (we'll call her Mrs. Johnson) walked into the office. In the millisecond between *"son of a"* and what would have been *"bitch,"* he let go of me, smiled, turned, and held out his hand to Mrs. Johnson. "*Oh, Mrs. Johnson. How nice it is to see you.*" He then proceeded to pull her hand to his mouth and kiss the top of it.

He began to make small talk and walked her deeper into his office, leaving me still leaning against the wall. As he helped her into a seat, he turned towards me, and the sweet, cherub angel expression on his face changed to that of Satan personified. "*I'll see you later,*" he said, with his lips curled up in anger. I was out of there in a flash. I spent the next couple of days making myself scarce. We didn't have cell phones in those days, so as long as I stayed out of sight, I thought my chances of living to age twenty were good. Coach Kerbel never brought up the subject again, even though we were together for the next three years.

In the fall of 1968, as a sophomore, I was the starting middle linebacker. We finished the season with a record of 8-2 and had an opportunity to play in California in what was called the Junior Rose Bowl. The previous year, while I was a freshman, West Texas won the Junior Rose Bowl when they beat San Fernando Valley State College. For the second year in a row, we would be playing in that bowl, but during a team meeting at the end of the season, Kerbel said he wanted us to practice every day until the game, which was sometime around Christmas. When some of the seniors complained that they wanted some time off, Kerbel exploded. He went into his office and turned down the bowl. I was disappointed, but I have to admit that after a long season, I was tired, too. We never had another opportunity to play in a bowl game. If the seniors hadn't played in the Junior Rose Bowl the year before, they would have jumped at the opportunity. That experience taught me to never look a gift horse in the mouth. Never expect to come down the same road again. When I was wrestling, I kept that memory foremost in my thoughts. I returned time after time to Japan, and never took for granted that there would be another tour. I accepted every tour offered to me, all the while knowing that one day, I would not be going. I never dreamed, however, that it would last for 25 years.

After my sophomore season, I was playing intramural basketball as a tool to help develop my quickness. I went up for a rebound and landed on one foot. The impact caused my knee to cave to the inside and tore the interior cruciate ligament. I had surgery and was in a cast for seven weeks. In 1969, the medical technology in orthopedics was way behind where we are today. It took me the whole spring and summer to rehabilitate my knee into a condition where I could play football. The recuperation cost me all of spring practice that year. By the time I was able to get back onto the field, I had lost a step or two in running, so in my junior year, I was moved down to a defensive end position. To play on the line, I had to put on weight, so I bulked up to 250 pounds, the heaviest I had ever been in my life.

Before I injured my knee, several pro scouts had been looking at me as a prospect for the NFL. However, I disappeared from their sight when I was moved to defensive end.

Early in August 1969, while I was recovering from the knee injury, West Texas sports information director Tommy Bryant issued the pre-season football brochure, which featured a picture of Duane Thomas and me mounted on a huge white statue of a buffalo. Some press writers wondered if the team would be know as the "White Buffaloes," or "White Buffs," in the future.

By the time I was a senior, my knee had completely healed, and I was moved back to middle linebacker. I started all the games and did pretty well, but I never quite recovered the quickness I had before the surgery, even after dropping my weight to 240. During that time, the middle linebackers were in the Dick Butkus mold — big, strong, and mean — and I fit into that mold. Pro scouts were always hovering around our practices, primarily because we had Duane Thomas, who ended up being drafted during my junior year in the first round of the 1970 NFL Draft by the Dallas Cowboys. The following year, two other defensive backs were drafted that year — Ralph Anderson went to the Pittsburgh Steelers, Ray Brown went to the Falcons — and Rocky Thompson, a kick returner, was a first-round pick for the New York Giants.

I wore a brace on my knee and my time in the 40-yard dash was 4.9. In 1970, it wasn't a bad time for somebody who weighed 240 pounds, but it wasn't blazing speed. It was enough to get me noticed by the scouts, but even though a number of scouts told me they were going to draft me, they all passed me over.

When the pros didn't call, I was devastated. Ever since I was seven years old, I had dreamed of playing professional football. I was so depressed. In 1971, shortly after the draft, WT chose not to renew Coach Kerbel's contract and he was forced to resign on February 8. Our record for the 1970 season was 7-3, but the politics of college coaching had probably clashed with his unique style. He was the last of the real dynamic, "do things my way or it's the highway" coaches of college football. During the years when I was playing for him, he had grabbed me and hit me, as he had with just about every other member of the team, but in time, and with the advent of political correctness, that kind of action had to come to an end. I don't hold a grudge against him. In fact, I remember those days of hard work fondly. Coach Kerbel was instrumental in helping me develop into the man I am today.

Coach Kerbel died of a heart attack on March 20, 1973, just two years after leaving West Texas State. He was 51 years old.

In 1971, I was signed as a free agent to the Baltimore Colts camp at Western Maryland University. I was given a minimum contract for $12,000 a year. There were 12 games in the season and I would be paid $1,000 per game. If I made the team, I would be given a $2,000 bonus. In 1971, the contract for a top lineman was only $30,000 to $35,000 a year. The $12,000 contract they offered me was an incentive, money wise, but I was excited to just have an opportunity to make a club. I worked out hard, ran, and lifted weights every day that spring and summer, and walked into camp in great shape at a lean 230 pounds.

In 1970, the year before I arrived at the training camp, the Colts won Super Bowl V against the Dallas Cowboys. They had some great players on the team: Earl Morrall, Bubba Smith, Ted Hendricks, John Williams, Mike Curtis, Bill Curry, John Mackey, Jerry Don Logan (a West Texas alumni), and, of course, the legendary Johnny Unitas.

For me, going to the Baltimore training camp was a dream come true. In the late 1950s, when I was growing up, football was my love. My favorite teams were the Baltimore Colts and the Chicago Bears. Johnny Unitas, who played for Baltimore, was my favorite player in the National Football League. In Knox City, my friends and I played football in the yard almost every day. My best friend, Greg Knight, and I would alternate being Unitas or Raymond Berry, the wide receiver for Baltimore. We worked on the patterns of Unitas and Berry until we had them down pat and beat everyone in two-on-two games.

When I arrived at the training camp, I walked through the Colts locker room, gawking somewhat like some of the younger wrestlers walked around the dressing room at some of the independent shows later in my wrestling career. It was neat to be in the same locker room as Johnny Unitas. I never went up to him and told him, but I was in awe of him. He looked just like his football card pictures. Of course, I kept my being in awe to myself, but it was really neat to see those players on their level. The difference between college and the pros back then was interesting. Talent wise, most of the players in pro football were within reach of really good college players. However, the All-Pro players were, and are, a step above everyone.

In my eyes, Mike Curtis, Ted Hendricks, and "Big John" John Williams stood out because I was signed as a center, even though I played middle linebacker in college. I had been the backup long-snapper at West Texas and the Colts needed a backup center for Bill Curry. Curry was an All-Pro center with the Colts in 1971 and 1972. He wasn't too big, but he knew his position and was able to position himself to block. Curry had been the center for the Green Bay Packers when they won Super Bowl I and for the Colts in Super Bowl V. In addition to his playing skills, he was a real nice guy. He tried to teach me a lot of technique, but it takes time to learn to pass block. I hadn't pass blocked since my freshman year at WT when I played offensive guard. He later went on to coach at Georgia Tech and the University of Alabama and is now a football analyst for ESPN. He probably doesn't even remember me.

I had a lot to learn as a center because I hadn't played center since high school and I had played middle linebacker in college. The center in pro football is a skilled position. He calls all the blocking schemes for the offensive linemen. He has to read the defense, make the blocking calls, remember the play, and remember the snap count. A number of times, I got over the ball, called out the blocking assignments, made a decision as to whom I was going to block ... and then snapped the ball too early. Of course, that was a big no-no. Unitas or Morrall weren't ready for the ball, so it would hit their fingers. The head coach got mad at me. Unitas and Morrall weren't too mad the first few times, but they became hesitant to put their hands down for fear I would snap the ball at the wrong time. I can laugh about it now, but at the time, it wasn't funny.

During training, we had to run from workout position to workout position. I was always the lead guy and ran as hard I could. Compared to the Fat Man's drills, the Colts practices were a piece of cake. Another player, Bobby Wuensch, an offensive guard drafted from the University of Texas, also ran hard with me. We were always way ahead of everyone when we changed areas on the practice field. The veterans complained because we ran so fast and it made them look bad, but I knew that if I was going to make the club, I would have to stand out.

For the first two weeks of camp, I was the only center because the veterans didn't have to report. I did both offense team huddles that they were doing during the rookie part of camp. I was in good shape, so it didn't bother me. As the vets came in, it became apparent that my lack of pass blocking skills, and the time it took to learn them at this level, was going to hurt me. That proved to be true when coach Don McCafferty picked up Ken Mendenhall, a center who had been cut late from the Atlanta Falcons. Mendenhall started 118 consecutive games for the Colts over the next ten years, so McCafferty made a good decision when he brought Mendenhall onto the team. I was bigger than him, and I may even have been a little bit faster, but he knew how to pass block and had experience playing center. I think if I had had past experience with pass blocking, I might have made the team. In the end, that was the difference between me making the team or not.

Most of the other rookies had already been cut. I was the only person left on the whole floor of the college dorm and had been by myself for a week or so. I was there by myself every night. It was depressing, especially knowing that it was just a matter of time before I would be cut. One night, somebody came into the dorm and yelled, "*Hansen, get your playbook. Coach McCafferty wants to see you.*" I had heard that many times before with other rookies, and most of them had been draft choices. I felt almost relieved, because in my heart, I had known that it was coming, but I was satisfied knowing that I had given it my best and had outlasted most of the other rookies. In my opinion, if I had played offensive line in college, I think I would have made the team. However, that's not an excuse. I just wasn't good enough.

When I went to see Coach McCafferty, he asked if I would be interested in going to Roanoke, Virginia, to play a season in the Continental Football League. I could get some experience at pass blocking and come back to camp the following year. It was enticing, but I had one full year, or two semesters, of college left before I would graduate. I told him that if I didn't finish then, I might not ever graduate, and I wanted to complete my degree. He understood and shook my hand. He was a nice guy.

I'm so grateful for the opportunity to attend that camp. If nothing else, I had the opportunity to snap the ball to my all-time favorite football player, Johnny U. I also met other great players and got to hang around with legitimate All-Pros. I witnessed one of the best (and longest) fights I had ever seen on the football field between John Williams, the offensive tackle, and Mike Curtis, the middle linebacker. That was really something to see. Most altercations on a football field would results in tempers flaring, followed by cursing and yelling. When Curtis and Williams locked horns, there wasn't a sound for at least a couple of minutes. All we heard was their labored breathing and grunting. That's a long time to be bulling around in football pads in 95 degree heat and 95 percent humidity. They were facemask to facemask, glaring at each other. It was really intense. That was 38 years ago and I can still see it like it was yesterday.

I played in both pre-season exhibition games, the first at Soldier Field in Chicago, Illinois, against the college All-Stars. In my last game, that time in Baltimore, I got to go onto the field with about a minute on the clock. I wanted to be able to show my stuff, so I went all out during those final plays, and in the process, I got cussed out by a bunch of the veterans. They just wanted to lay back and wait for the clock to play out.

That attitude stayed with me during my wrestling days. I remember wrestling in the small towns, where just a small number of fans attended. Mitsuharu Misawa, Toshiaki Kawada, and even Jumbo Tsuruta, wanted to "take it easy." Instead, I would go out and work hard. I think that's one of the reasons why I got over with the Japanese fans. The press recognized that fact and wrote about it several times over the years. I never, ever let up.

When I left camp, I went home and re-enrolled in West Texas State. I needed two semesters to graduate with a degree in education. West Texas had a new football coach: Gene Mayfield. Ronnie Mankin, who had been the freshman assistant coach when I was playing, had been hired to be the freshman coach, so I asked Coach Mayfield if he needed anybody to fill the freshman assistant coach position. Coach Mayfield took me on, and in return, paid my college fees and expenses. It sure helped because I was really short on money.

Coach Mayfield, who played quarterback at West Texas in the early '50s, had been very successful as a high school coach, especially at Permian High School in Odessa, where he coached his team to the 1965 state championships and took that same team to the state finals in 1968 and 1970. (The 1988 Permian football team was featured in the movie *Friday Night Lights*) Coach Mayfield brought a whole different philosophy of coaching to WT, one which was 180 degrees different from that espoused by the Fat Man. It was natural that he wanted to implement his own style, and he was successful in leading the team to the Missouri Valley Conference championship soon after he took over.

During my last year at WT, I was an assistant coach for the freshmen. One of the better freshman players was Merced Solis, a rugged tight end from Mission, Texas, which is located in the lower Rio Grande valley. After graduating WT, he tried out with the Kansas City Chiefs, but was cut during training camp. He played for the BC Lions of the Canadian Football League for one season [1976] and then broke into the wrestling business under his real name. When he went to the Atlanta territory in April 1977, Jim Barnett changed his name to Richard Blood, which is the real name of Ricky "The Dragon" Steamboat. Steamboat was wrestling in the Charlotte territory at the time. Jim Barnett, the promoter in Atlanta, always liked the name "Richard Blood," so he asked Ricky for permission to use the name. Ricky agreed and Barnett gave it to Solis. Solis had only been in the business for two months at the time, so he wasn't given much of a push in Atlanta, but he stayed there for nine months. He later changed his ring name to Tito Santana and became a top star with the WWF.

During that time, Terry Funk brought a young man named Teddy DiBiase to the football office. Teddy played football for a local high school in Arizona and came to the campus as a prospect for WT. After introducing me to Teddy, the subject turned to pro wrestling, and Terry asked me if I would be interested in getting into the business. I told him that I had just contacted the San Diego Chargers, and had been invited to attend their camp as a middle linebacker. I wanted to give football, my first love, one more chance.

In my position as a freshman assistant, I tried to fit into Coach Mayfield's style. However, I was a Kerbel man. I just didn't fit into his style of coaching. He tolerated my attitude and allowed me continue working in the program until I graduated in the spring of 1972 with a degree in education. I am indebted to Coach Mayfield for helping me get through that fifth year.

When I graduated, I was 22 years old, and I wanted one more chance to see if I could make it in pro football. I missed playing and I wanted to see if I would fare better as a linebacker, the position I had played in college. My wife and I moved to California and rented an apartment close to the University of Irvine, where the San Diego Chargers held their training camp. My wife took a job as a secretary.

Once again, I went into camp in good shape. At 245, I was a little bit heaver than I was at the Colts camp, but I was in good shape. Since it was my second pro camp, I knew a little about how I might be able to make the team. I asked linebacker player/coach Rick Redman to put me on all of the special teams: kickoff, kick receiving, punt, and punt return teams. I also was a backup deep snapper to the punter and field goal kicker. I made all of the special teams and was making the deep snaps. In the preseason games, I made a good showing and even intercepted a pass against the Falcons. I was doing pretty good for a free agent and thought I was well on my way to establishing myself as a potential backup to Tim Rossovich, the starting middle linebacker.

San Diego originally hoped their starting linebacker trio would be Bob Babich, in the middle, flanked by Redman and Ed Philpott, who had been acquired from the New England Patriots. Philpott didn't look good, so they aquired Rossovich from the Philadelphia Eagles before the first exhibition, which was a 30-7 win over Atlanta in San Diego. Babich was moved to Philpott's projected strongside linebacker slot and Rossovich took over at middle linebacker, with Redman on the weak side.

The second of six preseason games was at Minnesota against the Vikings. On the opening kickoff team, I was running down the field, tracking the ball, and staying in my lane. Out of nowhere, someone hit me from the side with a blindside block. Walter Gillett, the Vikings kickoff return man, ran the ball back for a 90-yard touchdown, right through the hole I left when I got blocked. Later in the game, we kicked off again, and once again, someone hit me, and Gillett again went 60 yards before getting tackled. After the game, I was pretty despondent.

Before leaving West Texas State, I had applied for a job as junior high football coach and elementary physical education teacher at Las Cruces, New Mexico, my high school alma mater. The athletic director had agreed to hold the position for me, but as time passed by and I wasn't cut from the Chargers camp, a phone call from the athletic director in Las Cruces forced me to make a decision about my future. School was starting in a matter of weeks, and if I wasn't going to take the position, he needed to make alternate plans to fill the position. I quickly thought about my chances to secure a position on the San Diego team. I knew I wasn't an All-Pro level player, but I knew I could hold my own on the pro level. However, knowing that I was on the borderline of being cut from the camp, I made a tough decision and told the director I would like to accept the job.

The next day, I went to see the Chargers head coach, Harlan Savare, and asked about my chances of making the team. I was the second team middle linebacker and the final cut would take place in seven days, after the final preseason game. Four players were scheduled to be cut and I felt pretty good about my chances to make the team. I had outlasted three high college draft picks and three veterans who were picked up from other teams during the off-season.

Coach Savare, however, couldn't give me a clear-cut answer. If someone got hurt, there was a chance that I might make the taxi squad, the extra players on the team roster who substitute for injured players. I told him about my job opportunity and that it would probably be best if I got into coaching and teaching. He said he understood and paid me a high compliment when he said I was one of the best tacklers he had ever seen.

He also said that I lacked the speed needed to play at the top levels of the game, and that was the one thing which might keep me from having a long career in football. I had to agree with him. It was the honest truth. I wasn't slow, but there are some real quick and speedy linebackers in pro football. Speed and endurance are two different things, and football is all about speed. I could stay with anybody when it came to endurance. I could run long distances without getting winded, but speed is the key, especially in today's pro football ranks.

That ability to keep going, however, would serve me well in my future career as a wrestler. Having the "gas" [energy] to keep going in the ring was one of the things which kept me in a top spot in wrestling for years. There weren't many people who could keep up with me, and a lot of that came from my years of training for football.

As I was leaving camp, John Hadl, the quarterback for the Chargers, came to me and said, "*Why are you leaving? I think you're going to make it.*" He'll never know how much those words meant to me. Coming from the quarterback, especially one who was a four-time AFL All-Star, that was a high compliment.

I packed everything I owned in a rented trailer (the smallest the company rented) and moved to Las Cruces. I was ready to begin my career in coaching, and even with the letdown of giving up on my dreams of a pro career, I was excited about what the future had in store for me. I wasn't going to look back and think "what if?" I had given it my best shot and had just missed reaching my goal. There were players, the All-Pros, who were quite a bit better than most of us, but the majority of the players were so close in ability that, on any given day, any of us could have beaten out the other. I was satisfied knowing that I had been able to play on that level and compete with some of the best.

Looking back, I have no regrets. Accepting the teaching position was the first of many deals which I would make in my lifetime, and I made most of them with just my word or handshake as the bond. I learned that from my father. He once told me, "*Once you give your word and shake hands on a deal, you must honor that deal. Two of the most important things in life are your health and your word, and you will be judged by how you honor your word."*

My father's words stuck with me throughout my entire life, and I always tried to live up to them. Most of his life, he worked hard and had to struggle to support his family, but he never deviated from his own standards. He might not have given me monetary things, but he taught me something which was much more valuable: respect others and honor your word. I'll always be grateful to him for teaching me that. Many times in my life, when I found myself wondering what to do when conducting business, I would always end up asking myself, "*What would Dad do?*" That might sound trite, but it's true. His example served me well over the years. I always used his example to make my choices. It cost me money several times during my career because I chose to honor my word which I gave to people, rather of jumping to the next and better deal.

As I reflect back over my life and my career in wrestling, my Dad has been my hero. I wish I had more of his personality traits. I thank him for being the type of man he was.

Amarillo Sports Arena

Chapter 4

Forearm Class

Having made my decision, I went into coaching with every bit of enthusiasm and energy I had. I coached the 8th grade football team at Court Junior High School and Physical Education at Alameda Elementary School. The school's football program had already developed a reputation. Unfortunately, that reputation was for being the worst in sports in all the county schools. I didn't let that discourage me, however, and I brought my enthusiasm and experience of playing college and pro football to the team. Somehow, we turned things around and went 6-2 for the season, and for the first time in more than ten years, we beat the rival team with a score of 30-7.

After one month of teaching, I brought home my first paycheck. I had worked and studied in college for five years to get myself into a position where I could make a good living for my family as a teacher and a coach. As I ripped open my pay envelope, I looked at a check for a whopping $477 ... which was for an entire month of work. That was when I came to the realization that we would just be making a living. Needless to say, I was both discouraged and depressed. How would we be able to live on so little?

My father, who was living in Amarillo, was selling crop irrigation systems to farmers. In mid-October, one of his prospective clients was Dory Funk Sr. During the course of their conversation, Dory asked my dad if he had a son who had played football for West Texas State University. When my dad told him I had, and that my name was Stan Hansen, Dory asked him what I was doing. When he was told I was teaching in Las Cruces, Dory asked him if I was happy with teaching. My dad didn't know the answer to that question, so Dory asked, "*Why don't you ask Stan to give me a call sometime. I'd like to talk to him about getting into wrestling.*"

My father called that night and told me about his talk with Dory Funk Sr. I didn't waste any time. I called Funk Sr. back right after I hung up. "*Stan, if you're interested in getting into professional wrestling, come by sometime and we'll talk about it.*"

"I'll drive up this weekend if that's okay."

The trip from Las Cruces to Amarillo was about 350 miles. I drove to Terry's house in Canyon and we talked about wrestling. I told him I was only 23 years old and still in my prime, and with my football playing days behind me, I had little to occupy my time. I didn't like sitting around, and if possible, I wanted to do something with my life that was athletic. Terry was very receptive to what

I had to say. He finally told me to get into his car and he drove me over to his dad's house.

They put me over and made me feel good when they said they had been watching me when I had played football at WT. They told me they were always interested in breaking in new talent, but they were very selective about who they let into the business. They wanted to be sure I would be good for the wrestling business and not someone who would be an embarrassment. I told them I would try my best and I thought I would be a good learner. After going to pro football camp, and seeing the respect the veterans demanded and got, I felt it would be easy for me to do the same thing with the veterans in pro wrestling.

As our conversation came to an end, I found myself excited about getting into wrestling. I realized that wrestling would be a good opportunity to make money. In fact, I was so excited I almost forgot to ask about how much money I could expect to make. "*We can't give you an exact figure, but we'll do our best to take care of you,*" said Funk Sr. "*If you work out, you can probably count on three-hundred to three-hundred-and-fifty dollars.*"

The feeling of excitement I had experienced a few minutes before vanished. When I heard Funk say, "*three-hundred to three-hundred-and-fifty dollars,*" all the air went out of me. With my mouth hanging slack-jawed, I sat back down on the couch, and I slowly shook my head. "*I'm bringing home $477 a month now and I can barely make it through the month. I'd love to give pro wrestling a try, but I can't afford to quit my job for less money.*"

In unison, Dory and Terry slowly turned their heads, looked at each other, laughed, and said, "*That's $300 to $350 a WEEK!*"

I couldn't believe it. That was more than $1,200 a month; more than twice what I was bringing home as a teacher. It was even more than I could have expected to get if I had landed a contract with the San Diego Chargers. I jumped to my feet, shook their hands, and said, "*I'll turn in my resignation tomorrow morning!*" I was so excited I could barely control myself, and I was willing to do whatever it took to make that kind of money.

Funk Sr. cautioned me and told me to wait awhile before resigning. He suggested I go back and resign at the end of the semester, right before the Christmas break. He was absolutely correct in making that suggestion. Giving the school notice was the right thing to do. I shook both of their hands, thanked them, and told them they would not regret it. I floated out of the house on cloud nine.

Terry encouraged me during the ride back to his house, telling me I was going to do well and that he would do his best to help me make it in the business. He also told me something I always remembered and lived by: "*If you respect the business, it will respect you.*"

As I made the long drive back to Las Cruces, I set my goals. I made them right then. My primary goal was that within three years, I would be in the main event. That was where Funk Sr. had said the real money was. During our conversation, he had said the goal was $1,000 a week, and everything over that was gravy.

I had never dreamed of making $1,000 a week. That was big money to me. I mean huge money. In pro football in the early '70s, only the top quarterbacks and certain key players were making that kind of money. I was going to have the potential to make that kind of money. I was elated and determined that I was going to take the opportunity handed to me and give it my very best.

When I was in football camp, I knew I would have to prove myself. I knew that nobody would just lie down and let me have their job. My football experience taught me to fight for my position, and I was ready to take on that challenge in a new industry. From what little I had seen, most of the wrestlers were big, strong, and tough. I never thought any of them weren't able to take care of themselves. I had seen too many hard fought matches between Terry Funk and Harley Race, as well as others, who convinced me that most of the guys were good athletes and as tough as nails. I knew that in the process of my training, I was going to be beaten up, but it didn't matter. If you can take getting hit on the football field by Bubba Smith, an All-Pro with the Baltimore Colts, you can take anything a pro wrestler can dish out.

Or so I thought at the time. I didn't have a clue as to what wrestlers could do to the joints and tendons in a person's body.

I finished out the semester at Las Cruces, and then turned in my resignation and left on good terms. It was one of those pivotal points in my life. I had put teaching behind me and I was about to set out on a new journey. It was a time of opportunity, and I was willing to do whatever it took to make it.

After the initial shock of seeing my first paycheck, I bought a motorcycle in order to save money on gas. I didn't have it too long before I had an accident. As I was making a turn, the tires slipped on some sand. The bike slid to the pavement and over in front of an oncoming car. Fortunately, my momentum carried me past the car and over to the curb. I sold the bike shortly after my visit with the Funks because I didn't want to do anything which might jeopardize my chances to get into wrestling.

During my final weeks in Las Cruces, I trained hard by running and lifting weights at the elementary school. I also began to watch wrestling on an El Paso, Texas, TV station, which was about 45 miles from Las Cruces.

I made my first official appearance at a wrestling event was on Thanksgiving night, November 23, 1972, at the Amarillo Sports Arena. Funk Sr. had told me that he wanted to introduce me to the audience. At the end of the intermission, I made my way to the ring (for the first time). I was dressed up in a nice sweater (bless my heart) and excited beyond belief.

On the floor surrounding the ring, there were several small posts with a small chain connecting one to another. As I stepped over a section of the chain, a cameraman took my picture. His flash blinded me for a second and I almost tripped. As I walked up the steps which led to the apron of the ring, the announcer was saying, "*I'd like to introduce Stan Hansen, a former football star at West Texas State University. You'll be seeing him wrestle in the near future. Let's give him a hand.*"

When I had attended the matches, I had seen hundreds of wrestlers get into the ring, but as I stood on the ring apron, I suddenly realized that I didn't know how they did it. I squatted down and went under the middle rope. By the time I was about halfway into the ring, I realized I should have been going over the middle rope, and not under it. By that time, however, it was too late, so I continued going under. I had to squat really low to make it. Two wrestlers were waiting in the ring for me, and I could feel their eyes on me as I struggled.

When I finally stood up and looked across the ring, I detected a grin on the face of Lord Alfred Hayes. The other wrestler in the ring was Alfred's opponent, former NWA world heavyweight champion, Pat O'Connor.

I went to Hayes first and shook hands with him. He smiled and said good luck. I then turned and walked over to where Pat O'Connor stood, and shook hands with him. I smiled, nodded my head to him, and tried to turn to leave. O'Connor, however, held onto my hand and refused to let go. I wasn't sure about what was going to happen next. We were standing in the ring, smiling and shaking hands, with a few thousand people watching. When I tried to pull my hand away, he gripped it tightly. He waited several seconds before releasing my hand. I was so relieved. I turned and waved to the crowd before leaving the ring … "over" the middle rope. Years later, I met O'Connor in the Louisiana territory and we laughed about it. It was my first experience, but not the last, at being on the receiving end of a wrestler's rib.

In addition to O'Connor and Hayes, the wrestlers on the card that night included Jerry and Nick Kozak, Mack Quarry, Ricki Starr, El Gran Tapia, the Viking, Terry Funk, and Hank James.

The first two wrestlers I met were Jerry and Nick Kozak. They were smaller than most of the wrestlers, but they were in great physical condition. They trained hard and were very conscious of how their bodies looked. In addition to being a wrestler, Jerry was the figurehead promoter for Amarillo. After being introduced to Jerry and shaking his hand, I was introduced to his brother, Nick.

Jerry was an avid hunter and fisherman. When he first moved to Texas, he had never done much hunting, so he was anxious to hunt deer. Before hunting season began, he bought a brand-new hunting outfit and a powerful rifle. He went all out and had everything a hunter could want.

Don Slatton was the the promoter in Abilene and surrounding towns. Known to everyone as "The Lawman," Slatton had been a deputy sheriff of Taylor County, of which Abilene is the county seat. I was told Slatton had been in on the arrest of Billie Sol Estes, a west Texas businessman who was convicted (a decision which was later overturned) of swindling investors, banks, and the federal government of at least $24 million dollars. The Lawman was a colorful guy. He always had a smile on his face and he never acted seriously, even when we talked to him about the wrestling business ... and especially when the discussion concerned our payoff.

Slatton owned a large ranch on the outskirts of Abilene, so when he heard about Jerry Kozak's desire to hunt deer, he set things up for Jerry to hunt on his property. A few days before Jerry was due to arrive, Slatton found a good-sized buck with a large rack of antlers that had been killed or had died of natural causes. He put the deer into the back of his pickup truck and took it back to an area of land near his home, where he used bailing wire to tie it to a tree in a standing position. The deer was as stiff as a board from rigor mortis, and from a distance, it looked like a live deer.

When Jerry arrived with his hunting gear, Slatton told him to take a few shots to see if the rifle was properly sighted in. He then took him farther out into the woods. Slatton kept looking in the direction of the deer, hoping Jerry would notice it, but to no avail. They continued to walk. Slatton circled around so they once again came within sight of the deer, but Kozak still didn't see it.

Slatton finally stopped and whispered, "*Jerry! This one is too big. I've got to take him.*"

Jerry said, "*What are you talking about?*" As he followed the Lawman's gaze, he finally saw the deer. With his eyes glazed over with excitement, Jerry said, "*Please, Don. Let me have him. I've got to have him.*"

Slatton said, "*Well, okay I guess, but if you miss, I'm gonna have to take a shot at him.*"

Slatton told Jerry he needed to sneak up on the buck and to get within 100 yards before he took a shot. Jerry began crawling through the brush, making all kinds of noise as the thorns ripped his new clothes and scratched him. About fifteen minutes later, Jerry figured he was close enough. He took careful aim and pulled the trigger. When the buck didn't move, Jerry shot again. He reloaded and shot one more time. When the buck still didn't budge, Jerry raced back to Slatton (who had tears in his eyes from laughing so hard), grabbed Slatton's rifle out of his hands, and said something about the sight of his rifle being out of adjustment. He ran towards the deer at full speed and began firing as he ran. As he came to a halt about 40 yards from the deer, Slatton drew out his hunting knife and ran towards Jerry and the deer. "*Let me gut him, Jerry. Let me gut that $(*#& @.*"

Slatton stopped running as he came up alongside Jerry. The deer had been torn to pieces from the rifle shots and Jerry was looking down at the ground, ,shaking his head. He finally said, "*Now who ... what ... who would do something like that?*" Slatton acted as if he didn't know anything about it. Jerry finally said, "*Please don't tell any of the boys* (wrestlers) *about this, Don.*"

Don said, "*I won't tell anyone, Jerry. Somebody has a sick sense of humor. Hey, I got a deer hanging in my shed. Why don't we go and I'll show you how to butcher it?*"

After giving Jerry a few pointers on how to butcher a deer, Slatton made an excuse to go into his house ... where he called as many of the boys as he could to let them know about the rib.

I didn't have much interaction with Jerry because he didn't go out on the road too often. I made a few trips with his brother, Nick. Nick had a van in which he would sleep at night in order to save money by not having to rent a motel room. I later followed suit when I bought a van and converted the back into a full bed. Nick was one of the first people who really inspired me to save money. He once told me, "*It's not how much money you make, but how much you save that's important.*"

Ricki Starr was quite a character. He had been a big star in England for many years before coming to the United States. He had an unusual style of wrestling that wouldn't seem out the ordinary today, but in the '70s, it was quite unique. His gimmick was wrestling as a ballet dancer. Ricki even wore ballet slippers. He had a unique finish for his matches. After whipping his opponents into the ropes, he would catch them when they rebounded and lift them up onto his shoulders. He would then spin around and around before he finally threw them to the mat and pinned them.

Ricki was only in the Amarillo territory for a few months. One night, I was driving to El Paso, Texas, from Clovis, New Mexico. Clovis ran every Sunday night, but it was the smaller of the two towns that ran on Sundays. The big show was in Albuquerque. After the show in Clovis, we had to drive about 275 miles to El Paso for the next show, which was held on Monday night. It took all night to drive through the winding New Mexico Mountains. On this particular week, Ricki had asked if he could ride with me to both Clovis and El Paso. It was a cold winter that December and there was black ice on the road. As we were driving on the truck route which took us around Roswell, I downshifted my Chevy Rally Nova just as I hit a patch of black ice. We spun out of control and slid into a ditch. Other than my pride, nothing was hurt.

Ricki had a reputation for being tight with his money. I remember somebody telling me that he was so frugal that he never spent more money on anything than was absolutely necessary. That night, when we left Clovis, Ricki pulled out a bottle of whiskey. He was going to mix himself a drink before starting on our long ride. I noticed the bottle was almost empty and watched as he poured the very last drop of whiskey into his cup of coke. As I pulled onto the road, he continued to hold the inverted bottle over the cup. He held it in that position for at least five minutes, making sure he got every last drop of the whiskey from the bottle. I remember thinking of how that was going to the extreme to get the very last bit of value out of something.

The Viking was quite a character, too. His real name was Bob Morse and he came to Amarillo from the Kansas City territory when the Funks were rotating their middle-of-the-card talent. I had first seen him on TV when I was in college. He had snow-white, bleached-blond hair, and he wore a Viking helmet with horns jutting out from the sides. One Saturday afternoon, I saw him at a mall in Amarillo. He stood out from the crowd, not only because of his white hair, but because he was such a big guy. I stood and watched as he walked along, before sitting down on a bench. I don't know why that memory stuck with me. I suppose it was because I was a complete mark at the time, and that was the first time I had seen a wrestler in public and during his private time.

Later, when I was broken into the business, I had an opportunity to meet him. I didn't get to talk to him too much because, as a heel, he was always in the other dressing room. He was a good, cheap-heat heel, as I called them. Wrestlers got cheap heat by pulling hair, gouging eyes, and sparring verbally with the fans. I'm not knocking that style. There is a place for it, just as there is for serious heat heels. In fact, some of the cheap heat heels actually get more heat than other heels because they get into it personally with the fans.

El Gran Tapia, another cheap-heat heel, was a carpenter wrestler who came from Mexico. A "carpenter" was a word we used for someone who worked the bottom matches on a wrestling card and got beat by guys who were being pushed. He was a good addition to the territory and drew from the large Hispanic population.

Mac Quarry, who would later wrestle as George McCreary, was a smaller guy with a dry sense of humor. At Southern Illinois University at Carbondale, he was a very good amateur wrestler, and he wrestled on the team with Bob Roop. He wasn't too big and he worked the opening matches. I worked with him in Clovis one night, just a few days before he was supposed to leave the territory. I was green [inexperienced] and I hurt his back when I didn't body slam him correctly. When we finished our match, we went to our separate dressing rooms. He sent over word to "*Go fu— yourself.*" I thought he was kidding, but somebody later told me he was serious. He was going to the Charlotte, North Carolina, territory, and he was afraid the back injury would hurt his chances of getting any kind of a push there. I don't think the injury, if you can even call it that, was too serious, but you always wanted to go into a new territory in the best of shape. I never got a chance to see him again. I heard he later retired from wrestling and opened a business in the mountains of North Carolina. I learned a valuable lesson that night. Not only do you have to protect yourself in the ring, but you have to protect your opponent. If somebody gets hurt and is unable to work, they don't make any money.

Hank James was supposed to be the brother of Bobo Brazil, one of the greatest black wrestlers to ever step into the ring. James was tall and greased his hair straight back, and being from the big city of Detroit brought him a lot of natural heat in Texas. When he first came into the territory, he didn't wear wrestling tights. He just went into the ring in street clothes and jumped on the babyfaces. I later heard that the Funks kept him in street clothes because he couldn't work. Regardless, he got over and drew big money for quite awhile. He also had a black valet named Little Joe, who wore a black, afro wig. His presence at ringside added to James' heat. When I started, they were both in the territory.

The Beast, [real name Yvon Cormier of the famous Cormier wrestling family] who was billed from New Brunswick, Canada, was a short, but strong, heel. When I wrestled him, he body slammed me and I laid motionless on the mat. He climbed to the top turnbuckle, jumped off, and landed with one foot on my head. The Beast was really good at making that move. It looked devastating and very few people could do it as well as he could. Later in my career, I wouldn't allow too many people to come off the top rope onto my head. There was too much room for error. That says a lot for my opinion of the Beast.

Ciclon [pronounced and sometime spelled Cyclone, or Cyclon, in promotional material] Negro was awesome. In real life, he was so different from his ring character. He was such a nice guy. He was tough, though. During a TV interview, he smacked a real, 10-pound sledge hammer into his forehead. He didn't hit his forehead softly. He hit himself with real force. The hammer made a loud thud as it made contact. He never missed a beat as he continued to talk about his devastating head butt. At another TV taping, I was in the ring. He was standing on the floor with his hands locked behind him. He bent over and head butted the ring post, over and over, until the whole ring was shaking from the force of it. I was really impressed. Years later, I was with him when Shohei "Giant" Baba booked him in Japan. It was great to see him because I hadn't seen him since I had broken into the business. It seemed, however, that he was having problems. Having seen what he did first-hand, I have no doubt that the blows to his head had taken their toll on him.

I met "Big Cat" Ernie Ladd for the second time when he came to the Amarillo territory for a couple of weeks. After a show in Odessa, he asked me to give him a ride to Lubbock. I was happy to have him along, but there also was the incentive of picking up the "two-cents-a-mile" trans [transportation money] the boys paid to whoever drove. I was always interested in talking to the top guys. I asked endless questions about the territories in which they had worked and about wrestlers I hadn't met. I was all ears that night. Some of the stories sounded a bit farfetched to be true, and perhaps that was the case, but I didn't care. I enjoyed hearing the stories about different places and situations inside the business. When I told him I had met him in Dallas when I was in the sixth grade, he told me he didn't remember it.

Ricky Romero was the top Hispanic wrestler in the territory. I didn't see him until he was in his later years, but he was extremely over with the fans. He used to throw out miniature sombreros to the fans at every show, long before the wrestlers or promotions sold souvenirs. Ricky was hard to work with because he wouldn't allow himself to stay on the defensive too long. He was very protective of himself and his image with the fans. He was protected by the office, and rightfully so because he had a lot of value as a babyface. Over the years, he made a lot of money for and with the Funks and he was close to Dory Funk Sr.

Bull Ramos was a big Mexican wrestler who billed himself as a Native American. He was about six-foot tall and weighed close to 300 pounds. He had the look of a mean Indian and worked as a heel when I was with him in both the Amarillo and Dallas territories. Bull was always on a diet. Like most of us, he was a little over weight. He was always talking about how much weight he was losing, but for the life of me, I never was able to see any difference in his size. One night at the matches in Houston, he was talking about how he wasn't eating any fattening food. Later that night, when I drove past a Pizza Hut, I saw Bull's black pickup truck parked outside. The next night, I ribbed him about it. When I was around him, Bull was a carpenter. At other stages of his career, however, Bull was a main event wrestler in Los Angeles, Oregon, and New York.

One of the great characters in the Amarillo territory wasn't even a wrestler. He was the promoter in Albuquerque, New Mexico — Mike London.

If you wonder what Mike London looked like, just think of how the Devil was pictured in old books, and you'll have an image in your mind of London. He had platinum-colored hair, pointed eyebrows, a wicked-looking moustache, and a pointed goatee. London was born Harold Russ Anshutz to a family of South Dakota farmers. London wrestled for a long time, throughout the 1930s and '40s, and then settled in Albuquerque, where he ran restaurants and saloons. In the '40s, he began promoting wrestling at the Ice Arena, and then moved to the Civic Center, where he promoted wrestling through the early '80s.

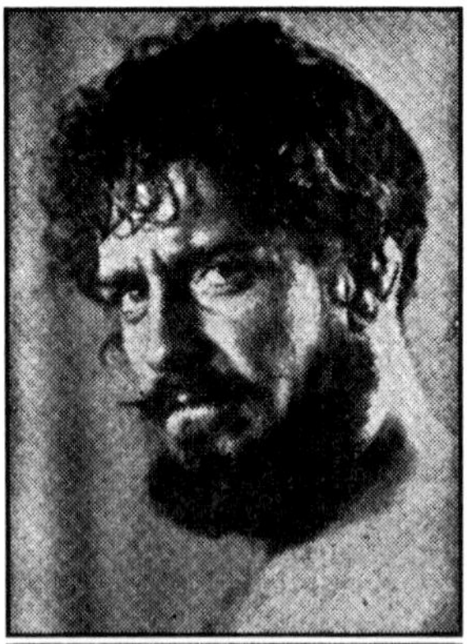

Mike London

London, who held his house shows at six o'clock on Sunday evenings, did the interviews for his shows live at eleven that same morning. The actual wrestling program which aired on the Albuquerque TV station was the tape from Amarillo, while the interviews were live and to be inserted between the matches. London injected himself into the program by conducting the interviews with the talent, which helped make his promotion more personal for the Albuquerque area. He also was the ring announcer at the house shows. Occasionally, he would introduce the underneath referee, who worked the first few matches, as "Kay Faben," which always got a laugh from the boys in the know. "Kay

Faben," of course, was a takeoff on the carny word "kayfabe," which was a word most often used by the wrestlers to let other wrestlers know that a "mark," or someone who was not a part of the business, was within earshot.

London might have had some input as to who and what matches he promoted, primarily because Albuquerque was the best town in the Amarillo territory. We could make $100 dollars in the opening match, which was a great payday. Knowing that, everybody wanted to be booked in Albuquerque on Sunday night, and not in Clovis, New Mexico, where we would be lucky to make $75 in the main event.

Often, in the middle of an interview with a wrestler, London would break into double talk, sometimes referred to as doublespeak. Double talk is speech consisting of nonsense syllables mixed with intelligible words, which is meant to confuse a listener. Double talk is a lost art. When I broke into the business, there were only a few guys who could do it, or for that matter, who even knew what it was. I never could figure it out, but it was a real art to those in the know. When London spoke it, we really had to be listening to him to catch it. He could say something to us that sounded legitimate, but a second after he finished his sentence, we would shake your head and think, "*What did he say?*" Before we had time to think about it, he would be continuing with the original conversation.

Pat O'Dowdy was another old-time wrestler who had moved to Texas and stayed to promote in Odessa. He was short, and during his prime, he was a junior heavyweight. For most of his wrestling career, he was billed as Pat Dowdy, but I suspect his real name was O'Dowdy. I heard he had been a very good amateur wrestler before he turned pro. He wrestled for Southwestern State Teachers College in Weatherford, Oklahoma, where he was a member of an incredible wrestling team which won five individual AAU titles in 1934 ... Jack Gott (126 lbs), Ernie Stout (135), Foy Stout (145), Orville England (165), and the legendary Ralph Teague (heavyweight). O'Dowdy, though, only got as far as the 155-pound quarterfinals before bowing out. O'Dowdy always walked around the Ector County Coliseum with a dip of snuff in his gums. He didn't command as big of a presence to the audience as some of the other promoters. He was always quiet and non-assuming, while the other promoters were more out in front as they promoted their towns.

Ken Farber was the main referee in the Amarillo territory. He was short, but strong and stout. He protected the business and made sure I respected it. He was an assistant to Herman Gust, Dory Senior's real brother, in the front office, and was a key player in the territory behind the scenes. A retired Hammond, Indiana, policeman, Herman Funk took the name of his mother's father, Herman Gust, when he transplanted to Amarillo and became part of brother Dory's promotion.

The following weekend, the Funks took me to the Sports Arena to show me some basic holds. Dory Funk Jr., who was usually on the road defending his NWA world heavyweight title, was in town that weekend, so he joined us. We spent a grand total of about 60 minutes in the ring. When I asked, "*Is that it?*", I was told I would learn everything else in the ring in front of people. "*What?*"

That was it. There was no camp where I would spend a week learning all the various moves and holds. I was going to learn day by day through experience. I was disappointed, but if that was what they wanted, I would do the best I could with what I had. I would listen and soak up everything I could in order to learn what I had to know to survive and thrive in the wrestling business.

As we were standing outside the dressing room after the one-hour session ended, they decided to show me how to give a forearm blow to the chest. Funk Sr. said, "*This is the way you do it.*" He bent me over backwards and hit me hard in the chest. I have to admit, it was a pretty hard blow.

Dory Jr. stepped in and said, "*No, Dad. Not that way. Do it this way.*" Junior proceeded to bend me backwards and hit me with a blow which was much harder (and louder) than what I had received from his dad.

Then Terry said, "*No, no! Not that way. This is how you should do it.*" He pounded me with a forearm blow which sent a resounding "smack" throughout the arena.

Dory Sr. said, "*Well, you could do it this way,*" and proceeded to hit me again, only harder. Dory Jr. decided he knew a better way, and then Terry followed suit. They continued to "teach me" for about five minutes. I stood there and took everything they had to give. When Senior finally said, "*Okay, forearm class is over,*" my chest was red, and even bleeding in a few places. I didn't mind. I was going to take anything they were going to dish out. I don't know what this says about me, but I was excited about getting hit and feeling the pain. I liked it. I was having fun learning and taking the pounding.

In later years, Terry, Dory, and I have laughed about that so many times. They describe to the boys, in great detail, how my eyes were wild and glazed over as they each took a turn, time and time again, smacking me in the chest. They had done it as a rib and in good fun. That incident showed them I could take a pounding without complaint, which meant I was a good prospect for the business.

The Funks didn't break many people into the business. They were very selective. I believe Bobby Duncum was the last one to be broken in before me, but he had been in the business for at least four years by the time I arrived.

I had one other training session. The Funks asked a wrestler named Gordon Nelson to show me the basics. Gordon was the territory shooter, or what we called an enforcer. When I was in college, I watched him wrestle challengers from the crowd. At the time, Gordon was wrestling under a mask as Mr. Wrestling. If a challenger could stay in the ring with Gordon for ten minutes, they would win $1,000. A lot of the marks took him up on his offer, and 100 percent of them regretted it. I saw Gordon put the sugar hold on one guy and make him scream, "*Okay, I quit! I quit!*" They brought the mark onto the television set and had the announcer ask him if wrestling was fake. The guy, who had snot spread all over his face, swore it wasn't. That was more than 35 years ago, and I can still remember the guy's face.

While I was waiting in the ring, I noticed Funk Sr. pull Gordon to the side and quietly talk to him. I figured he was talking to him about working out with me, and from what little I had heard about the business, I thought he was telling Gordon to make me scream. I knew the veterans did their best to weed out new talent by punishing them. They wanted only the best in professional wrestling, and if a guy couldn't take a little pain, he wasn't going to make it in the business. I was willing to take whatever they put me through, primarily because I wanted to make $300 a week. What Funk was saying, however, was just the opposite. He didn't want Gordon to hurt me and he was explaining that to him. That fact was revealed to me later by Ken Farber.

When we got into the ring, Gordon showed me how to get a headlock, and what to do if somebody got one on me. I learned the basics of the body slam, and the proper way to apply an arm bar to an opponent.

A month or so later, when I was working a match with Gordon in Colorado Springs, we were scheduled to go fifteen minutes broadway. I was still green and stiff. During the match, Gordon told me to get him in a headlock. After I had held him for a few seconds, he said, "*Squeeze harder.*" I did what he said, but each time, he would repeat what he had said. "*Come on. Squeeze harder!*" After a few minutes, I discovered I couldn't squeeze at all. My muscles had tired out and were limp. I held his head in my arms so loosely that I could barely feel his head. Gordon then whispered to me, "*This is how you're supposed to hold your opponent. It's called working.*" That was one of the first, great lessons I learned.

When Gordon was with WCW, one of the wrestlers made a negative comment about Gordon's girlfriend. The guy was a top talent, and, like Gordon, he had a reputation for being tough. Gordon confronted him about the remark and they wound up in a scuffle. In a matter of seconds, the guy was hollering, "*Okay, I give up! I give up!*" When Gordon released him, the guy went after him again. In less time than it took the first time, he was hollering again. That was a great lesson. You might not always like what other people do, but if you're smart, you'll keep your opinion to yourself when it comes to making personal remarks to people. You never know when you'll run into someone like Gordon Nelson.

Gordon Nelson

Gordon was typical of the great talent that wrestled in the Amarillo territory during that time. Years later, he worked for World Championship Wrestling [WCW], carrying one of their rings from town to town. Most of the talent working for WCW had no idea about what a great wrestler he actually was. In both 1952 and 1956, as the Canadian amateur middleweight champion, he was chosen as the Olympic representative in Freestyle Wrestling, but a lack of funds prevented the Canadian Olympic team from taking freestyle wrestlers to the games in Helsinki and Melbourne. He had his first pro match in 1956 and was active in rings in both Europe and the United States until 1983. I will never forget how much he helped me.

For a long time, the Funks didn't tell me much of anything in regards to the workings of the business. A week or so after that training session, I went to the TV station to watch the show. The word had spread around that a "green kid" was getting broke into the business by the Funks. Dory Sr. pulled me aside and said something like, "*You know, wrestling is a business, and we're trying to make money. We do it by working together to make a good and exciting match. The better you learn to wrestle with your opponent, and how to excite the crowd, the more money you'll make. We're going to show you a few things and let you take your time learning to work so we can all make money."*

At least, that's my best recollection of what he said.

Dory then took me into the dressing room to introduce me to the boys. At the time, the TV station control room was only divided from the back room (which we used as a dressing room) by a door. It was small and crowded, and by necessity, the heels and babyfaces were all together, but everybody did their best to maintain kayfabe.

When I broke in, two of the top heels in the territory were Moose Morowski and Ciclon Negro. I had seen both of them on TV and they both seemed to be nasty characters that I wouldn't want to mess with. In fact, after I made my decision to get into the business, I remember watching them on TV and being scared at the thought of getting into the ring with them.

When we walked into the back, Senior introduced me to Moose. I was totally shocked when he stood up and gave me a big smile. He shook my hand, called me Staush [Polish for Stan], and said, "*It's nice to meet you."* I stared at him for a longest time because he seemed to be the total opposite of what I had seen on interviews and in the ring. I almost was unable to believe it. It really had a lasting impression on me. To this day, we talk on the phone a few times each year. He is truly one of the nicest guys in the business. I did, however, get to see his "rough" side. When I accidentally hurt him in the ring a few times, he took me down and "kindly" taught me a lesson in "Taking care of your opponent."

Senior then introduced me to Ciclon Negro, the other top heel in the territory. If looks could kill, Ciclon had that look. He was definitely not the average pretty boy. I say that as a high compliment because I loved the look of the heels. Even at that early stage of my career, I knew I was destined to be a heel, and I wanted to look like them. Ciclon wasn't quite as friendly as Moose, but he was friendly and looked at me with a sly smile on his face. He mentioned that he had heard of me and was glad to meet me because the Funks had said I was a nice guy. As with Moose, I had seen Ciclon beat people over the head with chairs, and knock them senseless with his deadly head butt, so I was totally unprepared to find him to be such a nice person.

Of all the wrestlers, I really expected Moose and Ciclon to be the mean, tough heels they were on TV. And yet, they were both the nicest, most laid back guys I had ever met. I could not believe how different their personalities were from their ring characters. It was one of the biggest surprises I can remember happening to me in wrestling. I'm not saying they weren't tough. I grew to respect them fast as I saw how their personal character was so different than the way they presented themselves in the business. I saw both of them take on "marks" [wrestling fans] so many times when the fans' emotions were hot and out of control.

As time went by, I came to realize that the heels of the wrestling business were usually the good guys, and the good guys, or babyfaces, were the bad guys. That's a true statement. I discovered that many of the babyfaces had ego problems, and thought they were something special. They often treated the fans badly and took advantage of them. On the other hand, the heels just wanted to do their job and make a living. Inside the ring, they were loud and boisterous, but outside of the ring, they just wanted to be left alone.

For the rest of that morning, I thought a lot about what Funk Sr. had told me ... that wrestling was a business. Some of my friends had often said wrestling was "fake," but if you had seen the matches between Terry and Harley, you would most certainly have your doubts about that. Regardless, I made up my mind that I wasn't going to dwell on it. I would give the veterans the respect they deserved by not asking questions which might be insulting. I wasn't going to be cocky, either. I was going to take whatever they gave me and do what they asked of me because the money was so good.

As far as people claiming that wrestling is "fake," I have to weigh in on the subject. To this day, when everybody thinks they know about the business, I strongly object to that term. If wrestling was "fake," I wouldn't have artificial knees and shoulders, and I would still be able to scratch the back of my neck. If it was "fake," then very few of us would have the injuries we have to live with every day, and there are hundreds of stories about wrestlers getting hurt, maimed, and dying in the ring. Most people don't have a clue about just how much stress and strain the body takes in professional wrestling. Most of us are heavyweights. When we get body slammed, or hit the mat, the stress the organs and joints take is tremendous. There's nothing "fake" about that. Each time we made a move, we tried to make it look more impressive than the last time we did it. We pushed our bodies hard in order to get noticed by the promoters and earn a spot on a card. There were times when I was running a fever, or feeling nauseous, and I was pressured to *"at least show up at the building because the people are coming to see you."* I've worked with fluid on my knees from the night before. We just had to go out and do our job, especially since the promoter wouldn't give us time off because they didn't care about our health. Their only concern was their show. In Japan, that attitude was even worse. Due to their culture and work ethic, there is almost *no* sympathy for pain or injury. No. "Fake" is what actors do when they use camera angles to throw a punch and miss their target completely. And no, wrestling wasn't full-blown competition, but the blows were solid and damage was often inflicted. However you look at it, we all took a beating.

I moved to Amarillo in December 1972, and on Monday, January 1, 1973, I traveled to El Paso to have my first match. For my debut, I was booked to wrestle in a tag-team match with Alex Perez as my partner against Jerry and Nick Kozak.

I borrowed my mom's car and drove to El Paso with Alex. Alex was a native of Amarillo who began his professional sports career as a catcher in semi-pro baseball. Prior to that, as a youth, he had won the light-heavyweight and middleweight Golden Gloves titles. He wrestled in the pros in the early '50s. He was short, stocky, and strong. I was later told that Alex had a reputation for giving a hard time to guys like me, who were new to the business. I also was told that most of the guys didn't like to drive with him because he was moody. Fortunately, he was going to be my partner, so I didn't have to worry about him taking advantage of me in the ring. Outside the ring, we also got along well, and he never gave me any trouble. He did break the doorknob on one of the back doors of my mom's car during the trip, but it was by accident.

At that time, I didn't own wrestling trunks or shoes, so Terry Funk gave me an old pair of each. I didn't have a ring jacket, either, so I went to the ring wearing only my borrowed trunks and shoes.

I didn't know what I was supposed to do, so I just sat and listened to everything being said in the dressing room. Before the match, Ken Farber came in and discussed the match. Alex would be disqualified for using a chair on one of the Kozaks. I was told to go in when Alex tagged me, get a few holds, and then tag out.

Gory Guerrero, the promoter in El Paso, had a lot to say about what went on in El Paso. He didn't get involved with the discussion about my match, but he had a lot of input when it came to the main event and the Funks. I didn't really understand much of what he was saying, but in later weeks, I realized he had a lot to say about who would be featured in El Paso, and what angles he thought would be good for business, which was his main town in the States. He also ran pure Mexican wrestling in Juarez and the surrounding area.

A few of my high school friends from Las Cruces had driven up to watch my debut at the El Paso County Coliseum, a building large enough for the locals to hold indoor rodeos. For the wrestling matches, the ring was set up in the center of the arena floor. The only one I can remember was John Gutierrez. As I walked to the ring, I felt absolutely naked, and the aisle leading to the ring from the dressing room seemed to be a mile long. I don't know why I thought this, but the first thing that went through my mind as I walked down the aisle was, "*There are people standing on both sides of the aisle,*" and then it was, "*... and they're all looking at me!*" Or so I thought. Alex was walking behind me, but I felt like everybody was staring at me alone.

I was so nervous, but I also was excited beyond belief. When I reached the ring, I climbed up onto the ring apron and got into the ring. This time, I did it the right way ... going *over* the middle rope.

Nick and Jerry, who were the babyfaces, were already in the ring. I was with Alex, and he was a heel, so by association, that made me a heel. In reality, nobody knew what, much less who, I was. I felt like the people didn't care about me at all. They were there to see the Kozaks and Alex. I got a very small reaction from the crowd when they announced me as being from Las Cruces.

Alex began the match against Nick, while I stood on the ring apron at the corner of the ring, holding onto the tag rope. Alex did a few things, and then came over and tagged me in. I only knew the few moves the Funks had taught me a few weeks earlier. When Nick and I came together in the center of the ring, I grabbed him in a headlock and held on as tightly as I could. Nick let out a scream and scrambled to the ropes, where the referee ordered me to break the hold. When I broke, Nick backed away with fire in his eyes, and then rushed at me and grabbed my arm. When I tried to do something (I couldn't tell you what it was because I didn't know, myself), he countered and took me down to the mat. After a few seconds, he let me up and all but pushed me back to my corner so Alex could tag me. He looked relieved when I got out.

I had been in the ring for less than 30 seconds, but as I stood on the apron, holding onto the top rope with both hands, my head began to spin. I felt dizzy and light-headed. I suddenly realized I wasn't breathing. I tried to take a breath, but I couldn't. I tried to breathe in, and then out, but I couldn't do it. I began to panic. I was out of breath, and I couldn't breathe. The noise of the crowd around me seemed to disappear and I felt my legs begin to weaken.

The thought passed through my mind that I was going to faint and fall to the arena floor.

Just when I thought things couldn't get worse, Alex made his way over to where I stood, pulling Nick along under his arm in a headlock. He stuck out his hand to tag me. I looked at him in horror. I can still see Alex's face as he urged me to tag him. I just stood there and shook my head. I'm sure I had a wild look on my face because Alex abruptly turned around and did something else to Nick.

All of a sudden, somehow, I began to breathe. The fresh air that rushed into my lungs felt so good. As I breathed in and out, my strength began to return.

It was just nerves. That was all it was — just nerves. I learned a valuable lesson that night. Most of the time, if I forced myself to relax when I was really winded, I would begin to breathe deeper and better. I have relied on that technique so many times during my career, such as when I had been wrestling for 40 minutes, and I was trying to make it to the 60-minute time limit. It saved me so many times.

After Alex was disqualified, Jerry and Nick left the ring and went back to their dressing room, Alex, Ken Farber, and I stood on the arena floor next to the ring apron. Alex had taken a beating and was bleeding heavily. My nerves had taken over again and my knees were weak and shaking. Farber told me to throw Alex over my shoulder and carry him back to the dressing room. It was a good 35 yards to the dressing room, and my legs barely had enough strength left in them to carry me back to the dressing room, much less a wrestler who weighed almost 300 pounds. I told Farber, "*I don't think I can make it myself. There's no way I can carry Alex back.*"

Farber laughed and laughed about that. He couldn't wait to tell everybody about the "college boy, football player" who couldn't carry someone back to the dressing room. I didn't care. I had survived my first match. I didn't do too well, I suppose, but it was a start, and I felt hopeful about my future. I knew I had a lot to learn, but I couldn't wait to get more experience.

I didn't work on the Amarillo show that week [January 4], but on January 3, I wrestled to a draw with Mack Quarry in the opening match in Lubbock. The main event that evening featured NWA world heavyweight champion Dory Funk Jr. defending his title against none other than Ernie Ladd.

Two nights later, on January 5, I was booked in Abilene, Texas. This time, my partner was Karl von Steiger. Karl was a new heel in the territory and he was really getting over. He was new to the territory, so he wasn't taking many bumps, but he got a lot of heat with wrestling holds. He also had a great mind for the psychology of wrestling and his timing in the ring was near perfect. Once again, we were booked against Jerry and Nick Kozak. This time, however, it was a two-out-of-three fall match.

For the first fall of the match, Jerry beat me with a small package. After getting to my feet, I walked over to our corner to talk to Steiger, but he wasn't there. I looked around the ring, both inside and out, and he wasn't anywhere to be found. Like the dumb rookie I was, I got out of the ring and walked back to the dressing room, hoping to find him and get some advice on what I was supposed to do next. He wasn't there, either. Where I stood in the back of the building was a long way from the ring. I suddenly realized the referee was counting, "*Three, four, five ...*" He was counting me out! I didn't know much about the rules, but I did know that if I didn't get back into the ring by the count of ten, I would be disqualified. I took off with my best football sprint, moving as fast as I could.

Jerry was still in the middle of the ring. He saw me coming and could read the panic and intensity on my face. As I got close to the ring, he began walking backwards and put out both of his hands, as if telling me to stop. I vaulted over the top rope just as the referee opened his mouth to count ten. I sprinted over to where Jerry stood, scooped him up, and body slammed him to the mat. It all happened in the space of about five seconds.

It was funny that Jerry would back up like he did, because typically, the babyface doesn't do that. However, the heel will. At times during a match, when the babyface gets angry at the heel and begins to threaten him, the heel will begin to backpedal, with his hands held palms outward, as if begging for mercy. Jerry was backing up because he was genuinely scared of me. I was wild-eyed and out of control, and he wasn't quite sure what I might do. Both his reaction and my own were genuine.

Jerry got to his feet, rolled out of the ring, and stared at me. He had fire shooting from his eyes. Nick, who was on the other side of the ring, was laughing so hard that he fell off the ring apron. When I turned around, Steiger was standing on the apron with a big grin on his face. I was so glad to see him because I didn't want to be out there alone.

I never did find out where Steiger went, but it was all a big rib on his part. When I went to the back after the match, the wrestlers were all laughing about it. They had all been standing in the back, figuring they would be entertained by the antics of "the green guy." Watching new guys stumble through their first matches is big entertainment to the boys. They had no idea that I would provide the best "entertainment" they had seen in many years. They kidded me about that for a long time. Karl and I talk occasionally, and even though it's been 38 years since that happened, he still talks about it.

I also was told that Jerry Kozak hadn't taken a slam for more than ten years. He had a bad back and that was the one move he did not want to take. He would do everything he could to keep somebody from slamming him. However, in my youthful excitement and enthusiasm, I slammed him before he knew what I planned to do, and I slammed him hard.

Once again, I didn't do very well, but I was learning more in every match. Even though I had been thrust into the ring without having the benefit of a structured wrestling training program, I learned to work from some of the best talent in the business. Most of the guys were main event talent, from the top of the cards to the bottom. They might wrestle on the under-card matches in Amarillo, but just about any of them could carry the main event in one of the other towns, like Abilene or Odessa. They could keep people interested in their programs and bring them back to the arenas week after week. They were good at what they did, and fortunately, they were willing to help me, even though I quickly developed the reputation of being "the stiffest guy around." They didn't hold that against me, but they were wary when they were in the ring with me. Fortunately, I never hurt anybody seriously.

Whenever a new wrestler came into a territory, he was booked as either a heel or a babyface. I was so green that I wasn't considered to be either. I was just booked into matches where I could get experience. If I wrestled a heel, then the people automatically considered me to be a babyface, and vice versa if I wrestled a babyface. In regards to working, I really didn't know what to do in either category. I just went out and did the limited things I could do.

I didn't have a character, either. I was simply billed as an ex-football player from West Texas State. Over time, I adopted the "cowboy" and "Texas" character used by both Terry Funk and Dick Murdoch, the two guys who probably had the most influence on my character of anybody in the business.

When I first broke in, a lot of people compared me to Bobby Duncum, who I mentioned earlier. He was big and blond, as I was later in my career. He spent his entire career as a "cowboy." And finally, our most striking similarity was that he could hurt you accidentally, even when he was just working with you. Bruno Sammartino, the greatest WWWF heavyweight champion of all time, said Bobby and I were the only two guys who really hurt him. Bobby broke Bruno's arm. I broke Bruno's neck. (That story will come in a later chapter)

I got beat up several times, but I learned from those experiences. One night, Karl von Steiger chopped me in the chest so hard (as he had a number of times in previous matches) that it really hurt. The next time he drew his hand back, I gritted my teeth and prepared myself for the pain, only this time, he hit me with a working chop. It made a loud, popping noise, but it didn't hurt at all. That was another great lesson. Karl had me psyched out, ready for a blistering chop to my chest, and I barely felt his hand when it landed. I learned that I didn't have to feel it to make it believable.

Another night, this time in El Paso, I hit Moose Morowski with a potato [blow that lands with force]. He hooked me and laid a few hard slaps into my chest with his open hand. He was just trying to teach me a lesson. (Most of the boys say I never learned that lesson) I was extremely lucky to be brought into the business by the Funks, and taught by good, talented guys who were willing to put up with a crowbar like me.

I believe "on the job training" works better, in most cases, than anything a person could learn at a wrestling school. There were times during my first few weeks in the business when I wished I had been trained more on the basics, but "baptism under fire" gives you a real feel about how to do things. You listen to the crowd reaction to determine what works and what doesn't work. Unfortunately, wrestling schools are now the best (and only) available option because potential wrestlers don't have the opportunity to travel and work in more than 30 different territories, as we did during my formative years.

Those early months were a great time for me. I was as happy as I had ever been and I could hardly wait for another night to come around so I could wrestle again.

During the first couple of weeks, somebody would prepare me for what could happen during the introduction of my match, and talk to me about situations which might come up during the match itself. After that, however, I was given very little, if any, direction regarding my matches. Ken Farber usually came to the dressing room with instructions and he kept mine pretty simple. We weren't handed a script of the match beforehand. We didn't say, "*I'll do this, this, and this. You do that, that, and that.*" The opening and guts of the match were worked out by the wrestlers involved when they were in the ring.

Killer Karl Kox was a master at wrestling psychology. There are a lot of wrestlers today who can do amazing physical moves in the ring, but few of them had the knowledge and ring ability that talent had in the '70s and '80s. Karl Kox was one of the masters. He could do so little and get so much heat. He could make the wrestling fans stand up from their seats and push them to a point where they were ready to come to the ring, but just before they did, he would do something which would make them sit back down. He played with their emotions like a yo-yo. When the fans saw him use his finishing move, the brainbuster, they knew the match was over. I watched Karl protect his finish, and through his example, I learned to protect my finisher, the Lariat, in the same way. It's hard to get a finish over, but it's even harder to protect it.

Killer Karl Kox

I worked with Karl one time in Amarillo. After we got into the ring and the introductions had been made, I advanced towards him. He backed up and put his head and upper body through the ropes, as if he was afraid of me. After milking that for a few minutes, we began to circle each other. As we did, he "spotted" a heckler in the crowd and exchanged words with him, and then stepped out onto the ring apron and made gestures as if he was going to do something to him. When he got back into the ring, we prepared to lock up, but just before we made contact, he "heard" the fan again and went back to the ropes to restart the whole scenario over again.

I wasn't too happy with the way things were going. I wanted to get it on and try a few things I had learned the night before. I looked at every match as an opportunity to learn new moves and holds. Kox delayed the start of the match so long that I really became angry, especially because it made me look somewhat foolish. He worked the whole match without locking up ... until he finally made a few moves and beat me

Kox did the right thing for business that night. He was the heel, and as the heel, he led the match. He was supposed to dictate what we would do and when we would do it, and the in-ring antics were a part of his character. In the pecking order of talent, he was so far above me that the only other thing he could have done was to beat me in the strongest way. By doing things the way he did, he kept me from getting squashed and let me save face, and in the process, he kept himself over so he could draw money down the road.

Unfortunately, that mindset (concern for others) isn't seen much in wrestling today. Everybody acts and talks like their only concern is to get themselves over, never stopping to think that everybody has to sacrifice something for their opponents in order to do business in the future. I ran into that a lot in Japan when American wrestlers came to work for Giant Baba and Antonio Inoki. They thought they were bigger than the business and didn't want to do what was right for the long-term success of the All Japan or New Japan Pro Wrestling promotions. It's not a disgrace to put somebody over if it's for the advancement of the business. The whole purpose of wrestling is to draw money weeks and months down the road. When Baba and Antonio Inoki were personally running their companies, the Japanese wrestlers had the best attitude. They would do whatever was asked of them if it meant the business would succeed and thrive. Egos weren't allowed to interfere with business. Perhaps that had something to do with the fact that those guys knew how to put somebody else over, and still keep themselves looking strong. Many of the guys don't know how to do that, so they just refuse to do business when they're asked. Over time, however, even in Japan, attitudes changed. As a result, business went down the toilet, just as it did in the States.

The Amarillo territory was not what you would call a "big money territory," like New York, the Carolinas, or Georgia. The Funks owned and booked the territory, but most of the towns were run by local promoters: Gory Guerrero (El Paso), Pat O'Dowdy (Odessa), Nick Roberts (Lubbock), Mike London (Albuquerque), Don "The Lawman" Slatton (Abilene), and, of course, Jerry Kozak in Amarillo. The local promoters paid the Funks a booking fee for providing the talent, as well as a regular payoff when the Funks wrestled in their towns. At the time, I didn't know too much about that part of the business. I was only interested in learning as much as I could about wrestling, and working my way to the top so I could get the big payoff in the main event.

Our main loop began in Amarillo on Saturday morning, where we filmed our TV show. We would leave Amarillo and drive to Pueblo or Colorado Springs, Colorado, which were 325 and 360 miles away. After the show on Saturday night, we drove anywhere from 345 to 380 miles to Albuquerque, New Mexico, where we did live interviews on Sunday morning at eleven o'clock, and wrestled on the house show on Sunday night. When we arrived in Albuquerque around four in the morning, we tried to find a good deal at a motel which would give us an early check-in for the following night. That way, we didn't have to pay for a room which we would only use for a few hours. We called it a 2-for-1 deal. That was important to us because it saved us the expense of a motel room for one whole night. In Albuquerque, we usually stayed at the Alamo Plaza, which was the cheapest hotel chain at the time. I stayed at Alamo Plaza motels all over the southern and western states.

After the Sunday night show, we left Albuquerque and drove 265 miles to El Paso, Texas. We got a good deal at the Holiday Inn east of downtown, and if we arrived after four o'clock, they would give us an early check-in. If we arrived earlier, we would kill time by eating breakfast.

On Monday night, most of the guys would drive 240 miles to Odessa, Texas, especially if they didn't get the 2-for-1 motel deal. If we left El Paso immediately after the show, we could get a 2-for-1 deal at the Antlers Motel when we arrived in Odessa. Others would stay in El Paso and get a good night's sleep after the show, and then drive to Odessa the next day. Most of the guys with families chose that option. After a good night's sleep, they would drive to Odessa, and return to Amarillo as soon as they finished wrestling. That trip was 235 miles. The trip from Odessa to Amarillo took us right through Lubbock, Texas, which was our Wednesday night town. At only 115 miles from Amarillo, Lubbock was the shortest trip to a weekly-run town.

We loved Thursday because that was the night we wrestled in Amarillo. Of course, we were right back on the road the next day, driving 285 miles to Abilene, Texas. That trip was a killer because we drove to Abilene on Friday afternoon, wrestled that night, and drove straight back to Amarillo after the show.

The Amarillo circuit was a hard loop. Every week, we traveled over 2,000 miles of highways and spent three to four nights away from home. It was a hard life and one which wasn't conducive to our family life.

The Amarillo territory was spread out over a lot of miles, but most of the roads were smooth and well-maintained. I don't remember too many bad roads in the territory. In Texas, the small roads were better than many parts of the interstate highway system in other states. The interstate ran most of the way from Amarillo to Albuquerque. There was road construction in the mountains east of Albuquerque. It was all interstate highway from Colorado to Albuquerque, from El Paso to Odessa, and from Lubbock to Amarillo. South of Albuquerque, there were small sections of construction on I-25 south towards El Paso. Odessa to Lubbock was four-lane, but not interstate. We traveled on two-lane highways all the way Raton on I-25 in New Mexico and freeway to both Colorado towns. Amarillo to Abilene was two-lane most of the way.

Due to the size of the territory, everybody in the Amarillo territory thought the travel was tough. However, I drove more miles each week in Florida because we drove home to Tampa every night.

When it came to payoffs, Dory Funk Sr. lived up to his word. I averaged about $300 a week during my first two months in the business. A few times during the first couple of weeks, when they didn't have a spot for me on the card, the Funks used me as a referee in order to give me an extra payday.

As a referee, I thought I might get a different perspective on the business, but I didn't learn very much from the experience. Don Fargo and Johnny Fargo [later known as Greg Valentine] were in one match I refereed in El Paso. They were working as the Chain Gang. At the finish of the match, when I was distracted and looking the other way, they used a chain on one of their opponents, which led to a pin. Unfortunately, they used the chain right in front of me. Of course, since I witnessed the blatant infraction of the rules, I should have disqualified them. That put me in a bad situation because the heat from the wrestling fans went on me, rather than the two heels. The crowd went nuts. "*Hey, dumb ass ref. Are you blind? Didn't you see them use the chain? You were lookin' right at 'em!*" After the match, I told Don and Johnny what I thought about it, and then I told the Funks that I didn't want to referee again. That experience taught me one thing. When you get heat, it should be on the heels, and not the referee. The smart heels did their best to hide their nefarious tactics from the referee. That way, the heat came to them, rather than making the fans mad at the referee. You can't always get into a position where the referee won't see the infraction, but you can at least make an effort to hide it from him.

Don was way out there. He was a pervert who did things which shocked even seasoned wrestlers. I was as green as a gourd and had never been exposed to the things the things the Fargos did to each other. I hate to leave it that way, but I can't even write about the things they did. They were sick almost to the point of being unbelievable. I gave them a ride to Abilene one night, but when we got there, I told Dory Jr. that I wasn't going to take them back. I ran into Don and Greg later and they were a lot mellower. Don is infamous for doing things which most people would never think of doing. He told me quite a few stories about the days he spent hanging around with bikers and local gangs. The last time I saw him, he was at the Gulf Coast

Wrestlers Reunion. He seemed to be a changed person ... at least, morally. He didn't look much different from what I remembered other than being older. He said he had found God and his life had changed. Don is a good example to everyone that it's never too late to change. Good for him.

At times, when they couldn't work me enough times to pay me the full $300, the Funks would work me more the following week to make up for it. It was hard to find work every day for such a green kid, but they did their best and took good care of me. After all, I was making much more money than I was teaching and I was getting paid while I learned my craft.

Out of my payoffs, I had to pay for my food, motel, and transportation. When I was told I would make $300 to $350 a week, I never thought about the road expenses I would incur. Transportation, or what we called "trans" at the time, was three cents a mile, and was paid to the person we rode with. If a trip was 300 miles (600 round trip), our trans was $18. If I stayed in a motel by myself, it cost me at least $25 to $30. Food expenses were entirely up to the individual. When you add up all of those expenses, you can see how easy it was to spend $45 to $60 a night. The minimum pay was $40 a night, so we really prayed that we would be booked in one of the bigger towns, where our payoff could be as much as $60.

To offset some of those expenses, and make it possible to have money left on a $40 town, there were many things we could do. The first was to "heel a room." In those days, most of the motels charged per person, so we would have one guy check into a motel as a single, and two or three others would sleep on the floor. Sharing a room would cut our motel expense by 50 percent or more. When it came to food, we looked for restaurants that offered "all you can eat," or ate bologna sandwiches.

Most of the guys knew where to go for the best deal on food. We looked for the places where we could get "the mostest for the leastest." The old-timers will agree that the "king" of the eaters was Johnny Heidemann. I was with Johnny for a few weeks when he was in the Dallas territory. His home base was Charlotte, North Carolina, but he was temporarily "on loan" to the Dallas office. He traveled with me during the few weeks he was there. He loved (or lived) to eat. As soon as we got into the car, he would start talking about the buffet. "*I don't want any vegetables. I want meat, chicken, beef, and pork. I don't have time for vegetables.*" He would almost work himself into a lather talking about it. You wouldn't believe how much he could eat. He was stout, but he wasn't huge.

One time in particular, we went to a Holiday Inn in Houston, where we had eaten the week before. He was so excited about going there again because they had three meats on their Sunday buffet. He was just about beside himself by the time we pulled into the parking lot. I jumped out of the car first and purposely blocked his path to the front door by moving in front of him and slowing down. When he tried to pass by and get to the door before me, I would speed up and move over in front of him. When he tried again, I broke into a run. He was right on my tail. When I reached the door, I acted like it wouldn't open. He was almost in a panic as he tried to push me aside and open the door, but I kept a firm grip on the door handle and acted like it was locked. Finally, when he began making animal-like sounds, I opened the door. He raced around me and ran into the hotel. I was laughing so hard.

When I reached the buffet a few seconds later, Johnny already had a plate of chicken in one hand, and in the other ... he held a single piece of chicken which he was wolfing down with gusto. By the time I filled a plate and was starting to sit down, he had been through the line a second time. As I sat down, he was making growling sounds, like a hungry wolf. It was really humorous. He told me that owners of some buffets make him pay double because he eats so much.

Just off of I-40 on the east side of Amarillo, there is a famous steak house called The Big Texan Steak Ranch. For hundreds of miles, on roads leading into Amarillo from every direction, there were billboards which advertised Big Texan's "Home of the FREE 72 oz. Steak." Of course, there was a catch to the offer. You had to eat it all in one hour. The price at the time was $35. Today, the steak will set you back $72. Of course, your money will be happily refunded if you manage to eat it in 60 minutes or less. Out of the more than 42,000 people who have tried, only 8,000 have managed to accomplish the feat. Winners have included an 11-year-old boy and a 69-year-old grandmother, and advertising for The Big Texan says professional wrestler Klondike Bill ate two of them at one sitting.

Big Texan Steak Ranch

Of course, we also had to spend a few dollars for beer after the matches. Wrestlers liked to drink beer after the show, at the motels, on the road in the cars, or whenever we had the opportunity. Most of the time, the guy driving would have a cooler full of beer and cokes in the back seat. Not only that, but everybody drank and drove. I'm not saying that was the right thing to do, but those were the days before the police got serious about drinking and driving offenses. If they stopped us for speeding and saw an open container of beer in the car, they would just let us go. We were more worried about the speeding ticket than a drunk-driving ticket. Considering how much we drank, and how often we drank, it's a wonder we weren't involved in more serious accidents than we were. We (at least, most of us) weren't drinking to get drunk. Drinking was just the social part of traveling together. That changed later when the police began treating drinking and driving as a serious infraction of the law. By that time, though, I was traveling on the company bus in Japan.

Lord Alfred Hayes had great psychology. If I was the stiffest guy in the world (and there are those who will say I was), he was the loosest. When he held my arm in the ring, I had to look down at my arm to see if he was holding it. One time in Odessa, when I was still really green, we had a battle royal. For a wrestler to be eliminated, he had to be thrown over the top rope. When someone tried to put me out, I fought hard to keep them from eliminating me because I was having so much fun. Most of the wrestlers think battle royals are a pain and they didn't enjoy them, but I was having a ball. When someone finally threw me over the ropes, I landed on the apron, but held on to the ropes so I wouldn't be eliminated. I grabbed Hayes' foot and brought him down to the mat inside the ring. He commenced to kick me in the face ... with a very light kick. I held on and tried to pull myself back up towards him, but he read my intention and kicked a little harder. I sold it, but I held on for dear life. He kicked me several more times, each time, with more force. He later told me that he was legitimately scared that if I made it back into the ring, I would be hard to handle. I finally had to let go and I fell to the arena floor.

Hayes, who really spoke the "King's English," was a babyface in Amarillo. Later, in other territories, he turned heel and really hit his stride. When I first met him, I couldn't imagine that he could have been a heel, but by turning the King's English around and talking down to the fans, he got serious heat.

The story going around was that when he first came to Amarillo, he didn't know any of the Funks. In fact, when he showed up early at the TV studio on his first day in the territory, he didn't know anyone. Funk Sr. was the only person there. When Senior realized Hayes didn't know who he was, he took a mop and broom from a closet and began to clean up the studio. While Hayes continued to wait for someone from the wrestling office to show up, Senior began mopping the floor. He looked at Hayes and asked, "*Are you one of those fake wrestlers?*" Hayes was put off by the question and really got uptight. They got into a verbal fight and Senior egged it on by saying all kinds of bad things about wrestling and the wrestlers. When Hayes reached a point where he was ready to fight, Senior began to laugh. Meanwhile, while they were arguing, several other wrestlers had walked in and were enjoying the show.

En route to El Paso one night after wrestling in Albuquerque, Hayes, Moose Morowski, and I stopped at a small restaurant/bar about fifteen miles outside of town to meet two of Moose's friends. It was late at night and there was just the five of us in the place. Al and I decided to play a game of 8-ball pool while Moose visited with his friends. Neither of us were too good at shooting pool, but we had played a couple of games when a guy came into the bar. He ordered something at the bar, and then staggered over to the pool table and slammed a quarter down onto the table. That meant he got to play the winner of our game. Without saying a word, he stood there and stared at us for a few seconds, while Hayes and I both looked at each other. If you've been to places like that, you can feel the bad vibes that guys like that put out. Hayes beat me, so he had to play the guy.

Since he was the challenger, the guy began the game by breaking the rack of balls. When he did, the cue ball went into a pocket, which is an automatic loss. In his most arrogant English accent, Alfred said, "*You scratched. You lose.*" The guy's back stiffened and he stepped in front of Hayes, glaring at him with a hard, challenging stare. After a couple of seconds, he turned around and fast-walked out the front entrance. I knew exactly what he was doing. I had been around those kinds of places a lot and things turn bad real quick. I yelled at Hayes, who was laughing at the guy. "*He's going out to get a gun. We need to get out of here.*"

I began to look for the back door. All of a sudden, the front door slammed open and the guy walked in. He wasn't in any hurry. He walked slowly to the pool table, close to where Moose was standing. Hanging out of the waistband of his pants was the butt of a huge pistol. He stopped and slowly turned his head, looking each of us in the eye. After a few seconds of dead silence, Hayes, once again, in his best King's English, said, "*Your shot.*"

Lord Alfred Hayes

The game resumed where they had left off, and as before, the advantage went back and forth. I moseyed over to the bar and ordered a beer. The bartender whispered, "*That guy is a bad hombre. He was in prison for murder and just got out.*" Now I was really on edge. As the game continued, Moose had moved closer to the pool table and was watching the game intently. Only the eight ball remained on the table and it lay directly between the cue ball and a corner pocket. It was an easy shot, and it was Hayes' turn. Still holding my cue stick, I nonchalantly walked over until I was standing just a couple of feet from the guy. In my mind, I was thinking, "*If Hayes sinks this shot, the guy is gonna bring out the gun.*" I was ready to drill the guy with the cue stick if he tried it. Moose and I both held our breath as Alfred lined up on the eight ball, judged the distance to the hole, took careful aim, and ... he missed!

I didn't realize at the time that I had been holding my breath, but when Alfred missed, it rushed out of me. The guy then took his turn and pocketed the eight ball for the win. Hayes threw a few dollar bills onto the table for the bet. The bartender immediately yelled out, "*Bar closed. Everybody out.*"

As we all walked out, the guy said, "*I know a place that's open all night where we can play.*"

Hayes said, "*Where is it?*"

I whispered, "*Are you nuts, Al? I'm going to El Paso, either with you or without you.*"

The three of us got into the car and drove in silence for a few miles. As if on cue, we all broke out into laughter at the same time.

On the days when I was on the road and couldn't get back to Amarillo, I would go to the matches and watch, even though I wasn't being paid. The Funks had suggested that I watch every match I could, so I took them up on their advice. If I saw somebody do something I wanted to learn, I would ask an opponent if he would let me try it. Most of the time, they were willing to let me do it.

When I was in the dressing room, I listened to everything being said, partly because I wasn't told anything other than what I needed to know for a particular match or situation. We hear the phrase "need to know" used a lot today, particularly in our government. Sensitive information is only given to those who have a specific reason for needing that information. The wrestling business operated much the same way. For instance, I was taught basic holds, counters to those holds, and the psychology of a match. I wasn't, however, taught about other, more secretive things. Scott Casey let one of those things slip out one day and he found himself in hot water with the Funks.

Scott, who was one of the younger wrestlers in the territory, worked out with me a few times at the Sports Arena. One day, he told me a few things about the business that nobody else had shared with me. Ken Farber overheard him tell me and chewed out Scott in private later that day. Farber felt that if the Funks had wanted me to know about that subject, they would have told me. For one reason, the less a newcomer knows, the less they'll be able to share with their friends if they don't make it in the business. A lot of people who tried to make it in wrestling didn't last longer than a week or two, and when they were booted out, they spilled their guts about the business to anybody who would listen. Until you proved you had what it took to be in the business, you were told only what you had to know.

It took a long time before I became comfortable doing interviews, or what we called promos, on television. I was very nervous the first time I was asked to do one. I was booked in a battle royal and the winner was supposed to win $1,000. The announcer asked me, "*How do you feel about your chances of coming out as the winner?*"

I didn't say much. "*I'm going to come and do my best to win. I need the money.*"

How clever.

Interviews never came naturally for me. I am, and always have been, pretty shy. However, once I established my character, I loosened up and felt more comfortable in front of the cameras. One of the reasons it got easier was because my eyesight was so bad that I couldn't see anything more than a few feet away. That kept me from being intimidated by the camera and the people in the audience. It wasn't until I went to Louisiana in 1974 that I really began to feel comfortable about getting a point across. There were times when I really messed up, but unless I left out something important, I learned to go along with the flow. Most of the time, I was the only person who knew I had screwed up.

For the first several months, it felt strange to get up in front of thousands of people, dressed only in wrestling trunks and boots. There again, my eyesight (or lack of it) helped because I couldn't make out faces of people in the audience. Once I took off my eyeglasses, I was "safe" behind a haze which knocked out anything more than fifteen feet away.

I met a lot of great guys during my first run in Amarillo. One of them was an old-timer named "Gorilla" Frank Marconi. Frank was a fairly short, but stocky, guy who had a carpet of solid, black hair which covered most of his body. He wore a small beret hat and loved to smoke his pipe. He smoked it constantly in the dressing room.

I was supposed to work with Marconi on the opening match in Albuquerque. He was passing through the Amarillo territory and only wanted to work a shot or two. He also was late in his career and didn't want to take any chances of getting hurt.

He told me a story of how he had one of Bobby Duncum's first matches at the same building in Albuquerque. Before their match, and before the fans arrived, some of the boys had Bobby trying out a new finish in the ring. Bobby was supposed to slam somebody, and then climb to the top rope and jump off, stomping on his opponent's head as he landed. To assist with learning the move, Bobby practiced using a tin can as a substitute for his opponent's head.

Marconi watched as Bobby began to practice. He climbed to the top turnbuckle and leaped off, landing with his right foot on the can. Of course, the practice was to help him learn and judge distance, so that when his foot hit the can, it would make contact, but not with enough force to flatten it. The first time Bobby landed, he smashed the can flat. He tried it again, with the same results. He tried it again and again, and every time, the can was smashed. After he destroyed a number of cans, Bobby figured it out and began to hit the can with just the right amount of force.

Frank "Gorilla" Marconi

Marconi went to the dressing room and got ready for the show. He was scheduled to wrestle Bobby in the opening match. Bobby, of course, was pretty green at that time. After a few minutes of wrestling, Bobby was blown up. It was much the same situation that had happened to me in my first match. His nerves took over and he didn't breathe properly. After five minutes, he body slammed Marconi in the middle of the ring. Bobby cinched up his tights and climbed up the ropes to the turnbuckle. Halfway up, he slipped and fell back to the mat. On his second attempt, he climbed more slowly and reached his goal. As he stood up, he realized he was facing the crowd, and not Marconi, who was in the ring behind him. Not knowing how to turn around on the small turnbuckle, he climbed back down, got out onto the ring apron, and climbed up the ropes on the outside of the ring. When he finally stood on the turnbuckle, he balanced himself and got ready to jump off with his new finishing move ... the stomp to the head.

As he looked out over the ring, he saw Marconi standing up in the opposite corner of the ring. Marconi lifted his hand, with his index finger pointing upwards, and shook it slowly at Bobby. *"Not today, Bobby."*

Terry Funk was in the room when Marconi told me that story. We were all laughing so hard. I can't remember how the match ended, but I do remember that our match was slow and methodical. Marconi, who had probably been told about my reputation, wasn't going to take any chance of getting hurt.

While we were wrestling, one of the guys put ground-up rubber bands in Marconi's pouch of tobacco. The first thing Marconi did when he got back to the dressing room was fill his pipe and light it. After a few seconds, the most putrid odor filled the dressing room. It really smelled bad. Marconi, however, must have realized that somebody was playing a rib on him. To his credit, he never put the guy over. He sat on the bench and smoked it for the rest of the night. So, who ribbed who?

After I had been wrestling for a few weeks, Moose Morowski told me, "*The people in the cheap seats, who sit the farthest away from the ring, way up at the top of the stands, have the right to as good a show as the people in the front row.*" Another rule that stuck with me is one I really tried to follow: "*You should work just as hard at a show where there are only fifty people in the arena as you would if there were thousands.*" There was a tendency for the top guys to take it easy at spot shows, but the people who bought tickets paid just as much money as the people at sold-out shows in big arenas. Regardless of the size of the crowd, the people deserve a good show. That was a lesson I learned and followed, and it became one of my biggest assets. Never laid down or took it easy. I always put out hard when I wrestled, even when I had an opponent who wanted to "take the night off" in the ring. In those cases, I often had to drag my opponent along and force him to work hard.

My mom wasn't too crazy about my choice of profession, but she always supported me. She had seen how Ciclon Negro, Moose Morowski, and other heels acted, so she always made a face whenever she thought of me as one of them. Dad didn't care one way or the other. He was happy for me and willing to support me in whatever decision I made about my future. I never discussed the business with them, and never mentioned the possibility of getting hurt. In 1976, however, they came to see me wrestle in Madison Square Garden. It would be their first opportunity to see me wrestle in person. At that time, I thought it best to have a talk with them and explain that, "*I want you to remember that no matter what happens to me tonight, I'm going to be okay.*" It was the same thing I had always told them before football games, so it was natural to say it to them now. By that time, I'm pretty sure they knew there was more about the wrestling business than met the eye, but they did express their worry about the possibility of me getting hurt. I did my best to put them at ease.

Perhaps the biggest highlight of my first few months in the business came when I wrestled in Knox City, Texas, the town where I was born and raised. When we drove into town, we saw the town billboard, which read, "Big Stan's Coming Home!" That was really neat. At the matches, my Uncle Eddie and Aunt Faye were at ringside, as was my fourth grade teacher, Mrs. Hazel Long, who had also taught my mom. Mrs. Long gave me my first whipping in school.

Chapter 5

Dressing Room Promo

One thing all new wrestlers need is "ring time." The Funks had done just about everything they could with me. Honestly, I don't think anybody was as green as I was when I started. Dory Funk Sr. felt that going to a new territory would give me an opportunity to wrestle new talent. I was excited about going, and I hoped that by going out and working in other places, I would come back knowing enough to draw money. From what I understand, they did the same thing with Bobby Duncum.

Funk had a good relationship with Eddie Graham, the promoter in Florida, so he contacted him and got me a starting date. My last shot in the Amarillo territory was on April 3 in Gorman, Texas. The problem was that Tampa was almost 1,300 miles from Gorman, and I only had two days to get there. I had to be at the Tampa Sportatorium, where the wrestling office and TV studio was located, on the morning of April 5. The TV show for the Florida territory was filmed there every Tuesday morning, and the Tampa house show was held later that night.

At the time, Louie Tillet was the booker. The top heels were Johnny Valentine, Buddy Colt, Paul Jones, and Dick Slater, while Blackjack Slade and Gorgeous George Jr. were middle of the card heels. The top babyfaces were Jack Brisco, Mike Graham, Kevin Sullivan, Ron Fuller, and Tim Woods. Eddie Graham and Buddy Fuller, who owned the Florida territory, would also wrestle occasionally in the main events. There were several other wrestlers I had heard of, or had seen when I was in college, so it was exciting to get to know them personally.

In those days, Florida was a haven. Most of the wrestlers would take less money than they would get in other territories just to live there. Florida had good weather, sunny beaches, and beautiful girls on those beaches. It was a dream territory. For those reasons, wrestling fans in Florida had an opportunity to see a wide variety of talent. Wrestlers would come to vacation there, and wrestle a few times to help pay for the expenses. As a young, green guy, I was happy to be in Florida, but I was more excited about working against new talent in new arenas.

For a month or so, I shared a room in a suburb of Tampa with Bob Bruggers. Bob had played football with the Miami Dolphins and the San Diego Chargers, and then retired after the 1971 season to become a pro wrestler. He left San Diego the year before I went to their camp. I remember seeing his picture in one of the Charger's publications, which I was studying in order to get familiar with the linebackers I had to compete against.

Bob had been sharing an apartment with Greg Gagne, the son of AWA wrestling legend Verne Gagne. Greg had returned to Minneapolis just before I arrived, so the office told me Bruggers was looking for somebody to share expenses. We talked about football and the Chargers for a short time, but the subject quickly turned to wrestling. Football was a thing of our past and we were both more excited about our new careers.

When Bob left Florida, I was forced to move into a different apartment. Bob's apartment was really nice, but it was way over my head in regards to being affordable. In fact, when Bob was there, he picked up the majority of the rent. I'm grateful to Bob for helping me during a time when I was really struggling, both professionally, as I learned the business, and financially. Bob left Florida and eventually wound up in the Charlotte territory. After working there for almost two years, his career ended when he was injured in a plane crash which also ended the career of Johnny Valentine. Bob broke his back, but he had no nerve damage. However, he never worked in the wrestling business again. The last I heard, he was working as a janitor for a lounge and package store in Fort Lauderdale. It was a sad way for the career of a fine athlete to end. Tim Woods and Ric Flair were also in the plane and suffered injuries, but none were serious enough to curtail their careers.

Bob Bruggers

My new apartment was very small, cheaply furnished, and dirty, but it was all I could afford. The rent was $47.50 a month, which included all utilities. That was unbelievably cheap. I was the third or fourth wrestler to live in that apartment. Ed Wiskowski, who had been working under a mask with Bill White as the Mighty Yankees, had lived there before I did. It really was dirty, but I cleaned it up the best I could. The cockroaches were so bad I finally gave up trying to kill them all and just tried to keep them on the other side of the room. The bed had bed bugs and fleas in it, so I had to spray the sheets with Raid flea killer before getting into bed at night. There was a small TV in the apartment which only picked up one channel. There was no air conditioner, but I did have a window fan which circulated the air at night. It didn't do too much to dispel the June heat, though, and the humidity was so bad that the temperature was still hot in the room at night. By nine in the morning, it was so hot that I was unable to sleep or remain in the apartment.

Many times, at ten or eleven in the morning, I would drive to a local motel and walk into the air-conditioned lobby. I would ask, "*Has Joe Johnson checked in yet?*" Of course, Joe Johnson was a name I had pulled out of the air, so they would say, "*No, we don't have anybody registered under that name.*"

I would say, "*Well, I'm supposed to meet him here,*" and sit down on the couch. I would wait there for two or three hours and watch TV. I couldn't do that too often because it would look suspicious, so I visited every motel in the area.

When the heat was too much to bear, and I didn't want to leave my apartment, I would stand in the shower with the cold water running over me. At times, I would do that three or four times a day, just to beat the heat. At night, arguments broke out from the neighboring apartment, and with the windows opened all the time, I could hear every noise outside. I would even hear gunshots in the distance.

The first two months I was there, I ate lunch at McDonald's every single day. I could buy a meal for three dollars. I got so sick of the food. After two months, I switched to Burger King. I did that for the next two months. To this day, I can't stand to eat in either McDonald's or Burger King.

Eddie Graham would pay us $25 for every job we did on the TV show. I just wanted to work, and $25 was $25, so I didn't mind putting somebody over. Eddie also subscribed to the idea that if you won your match on TV, then you didn't get paid. Your compensation was the free promotion of your character and an opportunity to get yourself over on TV.

During the four months I was there, I had an opportunity to work with Johnny Valentine, Paul Jones, and Buddy Colt. They each had different styles and were three of the top heels in the business.

I had heard stories about Valentine. He was a legend in the business who had worked on top in every major territory in the country. He was famous for his facial expressions in the ring, and for his ring psychology. Johnny liked to work solid and stiff [wrestling terms which meant how you physically felt to another wrestler in the ring], and he would knock you to the mat with his wicked forearm punch. He would chop people in the chest harder than just about anybody else in the business, and he was willing to take just as much in return. In fact, he preferred to have his opponents work stiff with him. I had heard the stories about Johnny, and how he seemed to "get off" on the pain. He would say, "*Lay it in,*" which meant, "*Hit me hard.*" He was famous for saying that to his opponent, over and over and over.

Johnny Valentine

I worked with him on Tampa TV. I was fired up because I knew that by working on TV, I would earn an extra $25, and in the process, have a chance to work with one of the top heels in the world. It really was a thrilling opportunity for me. In the dressing room before our match, he pulled me aside to give me some advice. He talked in a very slow, deep voice. "*Now, when I say, "Lay it in, I mean LAY IT IN!*" He really emphasized "lay it in." I told him, "*Okay,*" and began to leave. As I turned away, he grabbed me by the arm and repeated, "*I mean, lay it in.*"

Johnny also was famous for getting a wrestling hold on his opponent and holding it for a long period of time. There were times when he would have a hold on his opponent for three or four minutes and never move a muscle. The fans of today would be yelling "boring" after less than a minute of that. Back then, however, wrestling was actually based on holds, and Johnny was a master of getting a big reaction from the crowd with that style. The wrestlers who had that ability are all gone now.

Our match was going to end up with me hitting him several times in the face with a hard punch. He would do his routine of not registering the punch, and staring coldly at me as he slowly walked towards me in his "death walk."

When he whispered "*Lay it in*" while he had an arm bar hold on me, I knew it meant to start the finish. I was green (have I mentioned that already?) and really didn't know how to throw a punch, so I reared back and hit him with a pretty stiff punch to his forehead. He held onto my arm and didn't react whatsoever. "*Harder,*" he breathed, as he hunched his shoulders and glared at me.

I hit him harder, just like he said. He shook his head and glared at me again. "*Harder!*"

My hand had hurt when I hit him the last time, but I thought, "*All right. If that's what you really want.*" I reached back and hit him as hard as I could, right between his eyes. His famous glare actually slipped for a moment. He broke the hold he had on me and stepped back. That was something he rarely did during a TV match, especially for a job guy like me, but step back he did. There was quite a reaction from the crowd, who knew he was going to kill me in the end. As he stepped backwards, the corners of his mouth turned upwards slightly and he whispered, "*Beautiful, baby.*" When I heard that, I knew I had hit him hard enough. After a few seconds more of working the crowd, he went on to beat me in quick fashion.

When we got to the back, Johnny came up to me and thanked me for what I did. He was happy with the match, and that made me feel good. It felt good to know I had stayed in there with Johnny and that I had given him everything he had asked for. It wasn't often that a top guy like Johnny gave a green boy a compliment.

Buddy Colt

Another experience from the Tampa territory that had a lasting effect on me took place when I was working on TV with Buddy Colt. In those days, most of the TV matches were squash jobs, matches in which a "job guy" would be there only to make his opponent look good. I mean no disrespect to the underneath talent when I call them job guys. That was just a term used in the business at the time. The "job" of the job guys was to go out and have a match with someone the office was promoting as a top talent in a way that made the talent look good. They were very, very important to our business. Without them, none of the main eventers would have a chance to get over and draw people to the house shows. In those early days, a job guy was treated pretty well. He could make a living by traveling from territory to territory and have matches with the wrestlers who were being promoted. They all had the hopes of being given an opportunity by a booker to be figured in on an angle. As time passed, the quality of the talent went down, a consequence of the fact that the promoters quit supporting the job guys with decent payoffs.

On this occasion, I was the job guy, and my only purpose for wrestling that day was to make Buddy look like a world-beater. To many of the fans who remember Buddy in his heyday, he was the personification of the brutal heel. However, Buddy did more wrestling in his matches than Valentine did. Our match didn't last more than a couple of minutes, and when Buddy covered me for the finish, as the referee was making the three-count, Colt whispered to me, "*Thank you.*"

Wow! That was the first time I had experienced that. My opponent thanked me for doing the job and putting him over. It was a small gesture, but it had a huge effect on me. It showed respect to "me" as a man and as a wrestler. In later years, as I moved up the ranks in wrestling, I found myself on the other end of the TV squash jobs. If at all possible, I would whisper down to my opponent, "*Thank you.*" It's been more than 30 years since I've seen Buddy, but I hope he knows he played an important role in teaching me how to conduct business with class.

Paul Jones was really over in the Florida and Charlotte territories. He was one of the top heels in Florida and was really over. He didn't stand out physically, but he knew how to get heat and he understood the psychology of the wrestling business. It wasn't until later that I realized it wasn't what a person looks like, but how they project themselves.

I settled in with the hopes of working every day of the week, but as a rule, I was only booked three to four days a week. During my first week in the territory, I made $250. I was so excited the second week when they asked me to do a job on television because I could make an extra $25. A few times, they asked me to wrestle twice on television, so I made an extra $50 those weeks. If I was booked on five or six house shows in a week's time, my payoffs were better, and I would be happy. The following week, however, I would only have three bookings, so my pay would drop below $250. I finally realized that no matter how many times a week I worked in a set period of time, at the end of the month, my pay always averaged out to $250. Financially, I was having a tough time. Money was so tight that I often volunteered to drive because the trans money helped me make it through the week. I suppose that was Eddie Graham's version of a guarantee. I didn't know that when I went there, but from what I heard later, that was fairly standard for the territory. The underneath guys were making about the same. Today, the Florida office is remembered for low payoffs. They knew a lot of guys would come to Florida to wrestle because of the beach and weather, so they felt they could pay whatever they wanted.

One night, I heard Gorgeous George Jr. say he made $600 that week in the semi-finals, and he was pretty mad about it. I remember thinking that if I made $600, I would never complain again. I never thought I was on salary, but when my pay averaged to the same amount every week, that's pretty much what it was. I didn't get into the business to draw a salary. I wanted the opportunity to do well and advance in the ranks, and if I drew bigger houses, I wanted to get compensated for it. The pay in Amarillo was a little more than what I made in Florida, but I think it was because the Funks took care of me.

Each week, I sent $200 to my wife, which left me $50 a week to pay for car, gasoline, food, and rent expenses. That was why I was content to live in such a run-down apartment. I'm definitely not perfect, and I've made my share of mistakes in my life, but I'm very proud to say I always tried to take care of my responsibilities first. To me, it was family first, Stan second. That was something I learned by watching my parents, who struggled financially when they were raising us. Having so little was very beneficial to making me who I am today. I learned that I could endure hardship and loneliness, and living in those conditions made me a stronger man. I admit that in the beginning, I didn't have any choice but to accept those conditions, because I didn't have the money to buy a better way of life. By the time I was making better money, however, saving money and living frugally was ingrained into my personality.

Those days in Florida were formative times for me. I worked with a few of the top guys during my run in Florida, but for the most part, I was booked against other green guys, or older guys who were on their last legs. Many of them were living paycheck to paycheck and trying to stay in the business as long as they could. Age had caught up with them and they didn't want to do much in the ring. I tried to have a good match with them, but they were only there to enjoy the weather and make a little money on the side. I was young and gung-ho about learning. I wanted to have good matches and "get" the wrestling fans with every match. However, I lacked experience and didn't know how to make a match when my opponent didn't put forth any effort.

A few times, I got frustrated and forced my opponent to work. I was in good cardiovascular shape and I could move, so I would stay on them until they blew up. Usually, when that happened, they were willing to go in whatever direction I wanted to go. There wasn't much discussion about it later because my opponent rarely knew I had been doing it on purpose in order to get "a match" out of them. Later, when I was working for Giant Baba in Japan, it became a part of my style. However, I want everybody to understand that my purpose for being aggressive wasn't to "eat up my opponent." It was to do what Baba expected me to do: take care of his business and keep myself strong. At one point, the gaijins [pronounced *gay-gins*, means foreigners] who made several tours for All Japan Pro Wrestling got frustrated and talked late into the night about my style. They didn't want to get eaten up or made to look weak. I can understand that frustration. However, professional wrestling is "business," and I did what I had to do to give the fans the match they had paid for.

While in Florida, I also learned a lot about the business itself, both inside and outside the ring. I realized that wrestling was no different than any other business, and politics were being played in the background behind the office doors. I began to understand what "stooges" were. They were the guys who went to the office and snitched on their fellow wrestlers, telling the powers-that-be about their actions both inside and away from the business. Stooges thought burying others would help them get ahead, and went so far as to make up stories which would cast a negative light on other talent.

Seven weeks after I began my tour of Florida, I arrived at the wrestling office to ride to a town with Paul Jones. The first thing Paul said when I walked up was, "*It's too bad about Funk Sr.*" I didn't know what he was talking about. When I asked, Paul told me Senior had died of a heart attack on May 26. He was only 53 years old. I was shocked. I didn't have a close relationship with Senior, but he was a nice man who gave me an opportunity to do something with my life. One of my regrets in life, and one we all face at one time or another, is that I didn't get to know him on a more personal basis. After hearing the news, I called Terry right away, but I couldn't get through to him. I wish I had been able to attend Senior's funeral, but being so far away from Amarillo and with obligations to the Florida office, I couldn't get away.

One guy in Florida who made quite an impression on me was Dick Slater. Slater got started in the business about six months before me. Like me, he was big and he could move, but he was a natural to the business. For someone so green in the business, he was one of the best workers I had ever seen. He had a sixth sense about how to generate real heat with the fans. At that time in Florida, he was already working on top in the smaller, weekly towns, like Fort Myers, West Palm Beach, Tallahassee, and Lakeland. Fort Myers and Tampa both ran on Tuesday nights. Of course, everybody wanted to work on the Tampa show because that was the town where we lived, while Fort Myers was 100 miles away. On the other hand, a wrestler could make more money in the main event in Fort Myers than they could on the undercard in Tampa. Slater, who had serious heel heat there, regularly headlined the shows.

1973 • Stan in Florida

One night at the National Guard Armory in Fort Myers, Slater was on top. At the time, I was a babyface teaming with Steve Keirn. The dressing room was a big room which was divided into smaller rooms by pulling out dividers, allowing the heels and babyfaces to dress in separate rooms. One night, after a hot finish in which Slater used illegal tactics to beat Tony Charles, we were helping Tony back to the dressing room. Suddenly, we heard a loud boom and the sound of breaking glass come from the heel dressing room where Slater had gone after his match. Everybody dropped to the floor and shouts began to ring out from the heel area. A disgruntled wrestling fan had fired a shotgun at Slater through one of the wire mesh windows in the heel dressing room. Luckily, the buckshot went into the ceiling and nobody was hurt. That night, I got a lesson about real heat. The people really believed in what we were doing.

Slater became good friends with Terry Funk when they were making a tour of Japan. In fact, Slater liked Terry so much that he almost became a clone of Terry. I also became good friends with Slater in Japan. He lost his job there when he thought Riki Chôshû wasn't taking him seriously during a match. As a friend of the Funk "family," Slater had been coming to Japan quite often. Slater had a few signature moves that he liked to do, just like everybody else. Chôshû blocked a number of Slater's moves, and then tried to do his own things. Slater decided he wasn't going to put up with it and punched him in the face. Chôshû backed up and tagged out. Afterwards, in the back, Slater was yelling, "*Who does he think he is? I'm no piece of shit!*"

It was obvious that Chôshû was really mad about the incident, and he carried a lot of weight with Baba. Slater wasn't fired because it was highly unusual for that to happen in Japan, but he wasn't booked again after that.

I do remember one incident where a couple of wrestlers were fired. At one time, Johnny Powers, who was in a good position with New Japan and Antonio Inoki, and Ox Baker were booked on a four-week tour. Powers' problems began when he wasn't able to keep up with the fast Japanese style. Ox, who wasn't a bump taker in the first place, blocked Inoki when Inoki tried to slam him. After the match, I told Ox (who had given me some good advice on my first tour for Baba) that the match didn't look too good. Later on the bus, I continued ribbing Ox by telling him, "*Man, if you refuse to do something the boss wants you to do, they might fire you.*" I really laid it on thick. Both Powers and Ox were quiet and didn't say too much. When we got back to the hotel, they went in, packed their personal belongings, and took a bus to the airport. What I didn't realize at the time was that they had both been fired at the show. I felt really badly about the situation because I had no idea they were being sent home, and my ribbing must have cut them like a knife. As they got onto the bus, I stammered out an apology to them. I haven't seen Powers since then, but I've seen Ox a number of times and there are no hard feelings.

The week I came in, I worked the Tampa house show. Four months later, I worked in Tampa again. From what I remember, for the remainder of the time I was there, I worked in Fort Myers, their secondary show, on Tuesday nights. I didn't mind, though. I traveled with Steve Keirn and Mike Graham. Mike was being used on top in some of the secondary towns. I remember Mike ribbing people, but he didn't like being ribbed in return. He had a lot of heat with the other talent. In my opinion, it was unjustified heat because he did nothing to deserve it. Mike worked hard in the ring and his ego wasn't beyond that of anybody else in the territory. The heat was based solely on the fact that he was the owner's son. Second-generation guys always took a lot of heat from the other boys. During my career, I always kidded second-generation guys about having it made, but most of them were hard workers who would have made it without help from their fathers.

My old acquaintance, Alex Perez, came through the territory while I was there. During the time when I was staying at a motel which they gave the boys a rate, Alex was staying there, as well. We got along well. I think the link which kept us together was the common bond of the Amarillo territory. I also treated Alex with respect, as the veterans deserved to be treated, and he appreciated that. He was older, but he had been a top guy in his glory days.

I would also like to mention a great character named Charlie Laye. Charlie was an old-timer who "ran" the front desk in the wrestling office and set up rides for everybody. He had been doing that for the Florida office for almost two decades. Charlie didn't waste words. When I called the office in Florida, Charlie would answer the phone. I would say something like, "*This is Stan Hansen. I need a ride to Miami tonight.*" In his slow, monotone voice, he would say, "*Four o'clock ... with Paul and Bob,*" and he would hang up. That was it. Nothing more, nothing less. He was often imitated by the boys. No matter how much of a hurry somebody was in, or how urgent their need was to talk to somebody, he was so slow in both actions: tone and voice. It irritated some people because he never got in a hurry. Twenty years later, I really got to know him well when we were both living in Mississippi, where he had grown up years before.

One of the guys I drove around in the Florida territory was the Great Malenko. Malenko was one of the all-time greatest heels in the business and his matches in Florida against Eddie Graham were the stuff of legend. I first met him in Amarillo when I was breaking into the business. He was past his prime by then, but he was nice to me and I respected him. Years later, when I was with All Japan, I met his sons, Dean and Joe [Jody].

Tony Nero was a great guy. He was funny and he had a lengthy career in New York and other places. At that time, however, his career was winding down and he seemed to be just getting by. He worked even less than me, if that's possible. For four weeks in a row, I worked with him in the opening match at the National Guard Armory in Lakeland. He would get into the ring and say, "*I am the captain and you are the soldier. You just follow the orders.*" He would then lead the exact same match. Week after week, it was the same match. I was 23 years old and he was in his 50s, and we had the same match. I didn't mind putting him over, and I really didn't mind having the same match, but to use the same finish every week was ludicrous. Each week, I would try to change it up, and he would say, "*Who is the captain?*" It was ridiculous, but I followed his lead.

Man Mountain Mike made a swing through the territory. I first met Mike when he spent a few weeks in the Amarillo territory. Mike must have weighed about 500 pounds at the time. One night, we were wrestling in the Lakeland Armory. The dressing room was upstairs and it was pretty crowded. That in itself wasn't too bad, but there was only one restroom in the building and it was downstairs, so the fans used it, as well.

Whoever designed the Armory didn't design it with any thought of privacy. The toilet was set in a corner of the restroom. There were no doors and no stalls — just a naked toilet sitting out in the open.

One night after my match, I walked into the restroom and saw about ten kids standing in a semi-circle around Man Mountain Mike. He was sitting down, signing autographs. To start with, it struck me odd that he would be signing autographs in the restroom. Then it hit me. Mike was sitting on the toilet, as pretty as you please, and going to the bathroom, with his overalls down around his ankles. I cracked up.

I kidded Mike about that in 1976 when we were both wrestling in the WWWF. Mike later moved to New Hampshire and opened a laundry business. In 1981, when I went through New York again, I was told that Mike had come to one of the shows in New Hampshire. He had lost over 300 pounds and nobody in the dressing room recognized him.

I also had the pleasure of working with Tosh Togo in Tampa and Miami. I was excited to work with him because I had seen him in the James Bond movie, *Goldfinger*. He played a villain named "Oddjob." I have a large picture of him chopping me during that match. The camera angle made it look as if he was as tall as me, but he was only 5-foot-9 inches tall. The photo also shows off his powerful legs.

There were a number of the guys in the territory who flew private planes. Eddie Graham was one of them. One night, two of the planes took the boys from Tampa to Jacksonville. Terry Funk was a passenger on one of them. During the flight, while Eddie was listening to the two-way radio on the U.S. Navy frequency which originated from the Jacksonville Navy Air Station, a mayday call was broadcast. A Navy airplane had crashed.

Later that night in the dressing room, the wrestlers who were pilots themselves were having a serious discussion about how horrible that was, and what must have been going through the pilot's mind at the time of the accident. About the time that Terry Funk walked into the dressing room, somebody asked the question, "*What was the last thing the pilot said before he crashed?*" Everybody was looking around, waiting to hear the answer from somebody who had been listening to the broadcast. Terry piped up, "*I heard what he said.*"

Knowing Terry had been on the other private plane, everybody turned to look at Terry. Terry didn't say anything. Finally, someone asked, "*Well, what did he say?*"

Terry paused, and after a few seconds of shaking his head, he said, "*He said, 'Oh shi-iiiiiit.'*"

Everybody got so mad at Terry for telling such a bad joke that they refused to let him return to Tampa on either plane. He had to get a ride with one of the boys who drove.

I met Hiro Matsuda, the trainer for Florida Championship Wrestling, a couple of times. I never worked out at the Sportatorium. In fact, I never trained in the ring the whole time I was there, even though I had heard Matsuda trained a lot of guys who were just getting into the business. I did train with weights at a local gym. I later met Matsuda again when I was wrestling for New Japan Pro Wrestling. He was highly respected and had a reputation for being a good wrestler.

I also met Karl Gotch at the Sportatorium on one of my days off. A couple of small guys wanted to break into the business as a tag team. Eddie Graham liked to get those kinds of guys into the ring at the Sportatorium. He had somewhat of a masochistic attitude and loved to see wrestlers punish young guys until they literally screamed for mercy. I only witnessed that happen one time, and when I did, Dick Slater and Bob Roop were both selected to dole out the punishment.

When the two kids got into the ring, they tried some working moves on Slater. He played along with them, like a cat playing with two mice, until they were blown up, and then he stretched them. When the two kids were worn out and begging for their lives, Eddie got into the ring and punched both of them in the face. From what I understand, that was typical of Eddie. After Eddie took his shot at them, Slater chased them out the front door. I remember thinking, "*Wow! I'm sure glad that I got broke in by the Funks, and not these guys.*"

I didn't know who Gotch was at the time, but I remember thinking he could take care of himself. He had age lines in his face, but his body was big and solid. He was wearing shorts, and his legs looked muscular and powerful. Gotch had the reputation of being one of the toughest men ever in the wrestling business. To his credit, Gotch didn't get involved in this incident, and just stood and watched with several of the other guys. Tony Charles, who was a tough wrestler in his own right, was there, as well. He made a comment to me that he didn't like what they were doing. I had to agree with him. The two kids weren't knocking the wrestling business. They didn't come up with an attitude, or disrespect anybody. They just wanted to get into wrestling.

Tony was solid and a real rounder who could throw a great dropkick. He hit Bob Roop with a dropkick one day that looked like it took off Roop's head. For a long time, that video clip was featured in the opening of the *Championship Wrestling from Florida* television show.

Off and on, I teamed up with Steve Keirn. Steve also was green, but he was somewhat ahead of me in the ring. We got along well together and hit it off from the start. We both had high hopes of being pushed as a top babyface team, but at the time, there wasn't a need for a team which was probably too green to work a money program. Steve was a local Florida boy who was good friends with Eddie Graham's son, Mike. As a friend of the promoter's son, he was given more opportunities to work because he was "taken care of" by the Florida office. I don't mean that in a disparaging manner when I say that, but that was another lesson I learned. Many times in the wrestling business (and I have to admit that the rest of the world often operates in much the same way), when it came to getting bookings, it wasn't "what" you knew, but "who" you knew. Steve had the talent and he deserved to be booked as often as he was, but his "in" with the office was definitely a boost for his career.

Steve Keirn

I had an opportunity to meet Steve's father, Col. Richard P. Keirn, who was one of only two Americans held captive in both World War II and Vietnam. He spent more than seven years as a prisoner of the North Vietnamese and was released on February 12, 1973. Steve hadn't seen his father since he was 14 years old, so the elder Keirn's return was a happy reunion for the Keirn family. Steve's dad impressed me so much and I really felt for him for the hardships he had suffered through in Vietnam. He had sharp and intense eyes. When he smiled, I could see something dark and enduring in his mind, no doubt stemming from the torture he had endured. I respect and honor the sacrifice he made for our country.

The four months I spent in Florida was a great experience for me. I learned a lot and met some top talent. I endured some hard times, but they were instrumental in forming my character. When I left, I was ready to travel to more places in my quest to get to the top of my profession.

I was ready to head back to Amarillo at the end of July. On my next to the last night in the territory, I was booked against Don Carson at the Jacksonville Coliseum. Carson was a middle-of-the-car heel who had just come in from Tennessee. He wore a black welding glove on one hand and used it to get heat during his matches. He would work over his opponent with the glove, leading the people to think he had something in it that gave him an illegal advantage, and then refuse to let the referee inspect it.

During our match that night, when he threw me into the ropes, I pushed myself up and onto the top rope, catching myself just before I went completely over. My intent was to pull myself back in, but being hot and sweaty, I lost my grip and slipped over onto the ring apron. In most wrestling territories, one of the things we weren't allowed to do was throw our opponent over the top rope. If we did, we were automatically disqualified. In this case, the referee had no choice but to disqualify Carson, even though the match was set up to promote Carson, who was the new heel in the territory. When I went over the ropes, I was declared the winner of the match.

As Carson exited the ring, he went out where I was laying. As he jumped to the arena floor, he gave me one last parting shot with his glove. I went down and sold it. It was the least I could do to help him get over. It was his first match in Jacksonville, so he wanted to impress the fans with a strong match, but my getting him disqualified had deprived him of that opportunity.

When I got back to the dressing room, Carson was shouting at Eddie Graham, ranting and raving about having lost the match. He knew I was green and that I was leaving the territory. Jack Brisco, Paul Jones, Buddy Colt, and all the other top guys were there, as well. When I walked into the room, Carson vented his rage towards me. I was shocked by the anger he showed towards me, but I realized he was doing it in order to look important to the other guys. What he didn't realize was that I wasn't going to sit back and take it. I jumped right back at him. *"For the past four months, I've done everything that's been asked of me. I haven't complained ... not about money, not about putting over guys who are in their late 50s, and not even about how I've been living in a dump. I've done nothing but jobs for everybody the whole time I've been here. I've done exactly what I've been asked, but if you think you can treat me like a piece of sh—, then you'd better think again because I'm not gonna sit here and take it ... from you or anybody else."*

Nobody in the dressing room, and I mean nobody, made a sound. As I finished my rant and looked around the dressing room, nobody would look me in the eyes. Everybody simply looked down at the floor, as if they wanted to be anywhere but there. I thought I was through, but as I was undressing for my shower, I began again. *"Don't EVER yell at me again, especially when you're just doing it to impress somebody."* Carson began to backtrack and said I misunderstood him. That didn't calm me down, whatsoever. I told him to stay away from me or I would knock him out. He must have known I meant what I said because he sat down and shut his mouth. I looked around at the others, curious to see if anybody would chastise me for my threats. Nobody did. I realized later that there are very few guys in the business who would stand up for themselves, especially green guys who were at the mercy of the bookers and promoters.

The incident was forgotten as quickly as it had erupted, but I learned a great lesson that night. It made me realize that there are all kinds of people who try to look big in front of the boss and their peers. Some of the boys would tell lies about other wrestlers, make fun of them, or belittle them. They saw it as an easy way to make themselves look big in the eyes of the booker or the owner. They were known as the stooges, and many of them treated green guys with disdain. A big part of their reasoning was to prevent somebody else from stepping up and taking their spot. In my opinion, the promoters encouraged the guys to become stooges by rewarding them for those actions.

They wanted to know about everything that was going on, even when that information was personal and didn't pertain to wrestling. There were certain bookers and territories which didn't operate that way, but for the most part, the majority of them did. It was always a pleasure for me to work for someone who would judge me on my ability in the ring. In the long run, I found that by doing my job well, and then I would get over in wrestling and reap the benefits. It was a matter of just doing my job and staying out of the business of others.

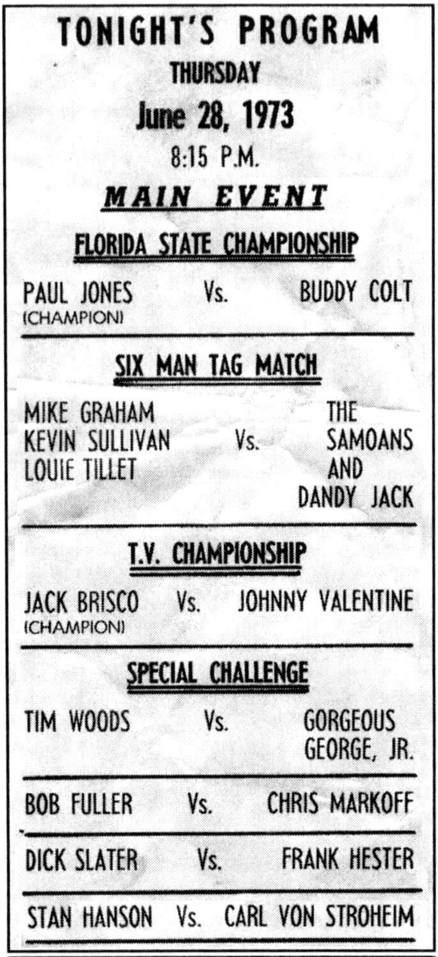

TONIGHT'S PROGRAM

THURSDAY

June 28, 1973

8:15 P.M.

MAIN EVENT

FLORIDA STATE CHAMPIONSHIP

PAUL JONES (CHAMPION) Vs. BUDDY COLT

SIX MAN TAG MATCH

MIKE GRAHAM, KEVIN SULLIVAN, LOUIE TILLET Vs. THE SAMOANS AND DANDY JACK

T.V. CHAMPIONSHIP

JACK BRISCO (CHAMPION) Vs. JOHNNY VALENTINE

SPECIAL CHALLENGE

TIM WOODS Vs. GORGEOUS GEORGE, JR.

BOB FULLER Vs. CHRIS MARKOFF

DICK SLATER Vs. FRANK HESTER

STAN HANSON Vs. CARL VON STROHEIM

Jacksonville program lineup

I'm sure there were stooges in Amarillo, but the Amarillo crew I broke in with was working up and down the card. I wrestled in preliminary matches, but I occasionally found myself booked in a semi-final or main event in the small towns. Basically, that scenario allowed everybody to feel like they were a part of the overall business of the territory. In Florida, I wasn't privy to anything but the opening two or three matches.

That night in Jacksonville, I made my first real stand in the business. And my decision to not take crap from anybody else would form the foundation for the future career of Stan "The Lariat" Hansen.

I drove to Tallahassee, Florida, for my final match. Most of the crew there had been in Jacksonville, but Carson was booked in another town. I didn't see Carson again until years later, at the Omni in Atlanta. Time heals all wounds. We talked for a few minutes, just as if we were old friends, and that's the way it should be. That night in Tallahassee, however, I felt a distance between myself and the other wrestlers. One of the veterans walked up and told me, "*You shouldn't have done what you did. Complain to the office or somebody, but don't do it like that.*" That was good advice, but I hadn't been the one who began the verbal confrontation. I was more than willing to "give" and "take" in the business. I had given my share, but I also was learning to stand up for myself when I felt it was necessary. I worked the opening match that night and put somebody over, just like I had almost every night during the previous four months. It was no big deal. That night, I was on my way out of Florida and headed back to Texas before the matches were over.

Chapter 6

Decision Time

I returned to Amarillo in August 1973. For the next six months, I continued to sharpen my skills in the ring and wrestled new talent. After my experience during the last couple of nights in Florida, I was glad to know I could concentrate on wrestling and not worry about stooges trying to waylay my career. Amarillo was a small-money territory and they rotated the talent base fairly often, but even so, one could count on staying there for eight months to a year. Some of the talent was asked to stay longer. Guys in the middle of the card made about $500 a week, while the top guys often brought home $800 to $1,000. It wasn't big money by today's standards, but in those days, that was considered to be a good living. That was very evident to me, a former teacher who made one-fourth of what the guys on the bottom made.

Amarillo gave everyone a chance to show their stuff. The top talent would be on top most of the time, but after they had a run, they would be put on the back burner and would work the second or third match from the top. There were also top guys who would work the main event in one town, but in another, they would be the second or third match from the bottom.

I was fortunate enough to be given the opportunity to work with the top guys who were being kept warm on the back burner. They not only taught me some great lessons about the business, but the most important thing they taught me was the psychology of "working," and working is what it's all about.

The word "work" means being able to go out and have a match which will entertain the fans, and also get them excited enough to buy a ticket for the show the following week. Unlike today, when wrestling is held in a city only a few times a year, the territories held weekly shows in a number of towns. We really had to work to get the people to come back week after week. It took a concerted effort between the promoters, bookers, and talent to make it interesting enough to entice the fans back to the arenas each and every week. It's easy to put together a lineup for a show that's held in a town one time a year, but it's an altogether more difficult task to book five to ten matches in a town every week and keep it interesting for the fans. Today, the emphasis is on the television shows, and the networks pay millions of dollars to the WWE for their TV show. In our day, the house show was the most important thing because that was the promoters' and wrestlers' only source of revenue.

One of the guys I wrestled when I returned to Amarillo was Jumbo Tsuruta [Tomomi Tsuruta]. Jumbo had been a top amateur wrestler at Chuo University in Tokyo, winning the 1971 and 1972 All Japan amateur wrestling championships in both freestyle and Greco-Roman in the super heavyweight class. He also competed in the 1972 summer Olympics in Munich, West Germany. Scouted by All Japan Pro Wrestling promoter Giant Baba, he was sent to Amarillo to train under Dory Funk Jr.

Jumbo was tall and thin at the time, but he weighed about 240 pounds. On the day we met, we struck up a friendship. He was learning pro wrestling moves and getting experience in the ring. His amateur wrestling background was a great foundation to build upon, and he quickly learned the basics of the professional style.

The first time we went to the gym together, I was amazed by Jumbo's strength. I was bigger than he was, and I had occasionally worked out with weights, but I wasn't that strong in respect to my size. Jumbo, however, outdid me on reps with the same weight. I was really surprised. That experience taught me that I should never judge somebody by how they looked. He was smaller than I was, and yet, his Greco-Roman training had taught him how to use his strength for maximum effectiveness.

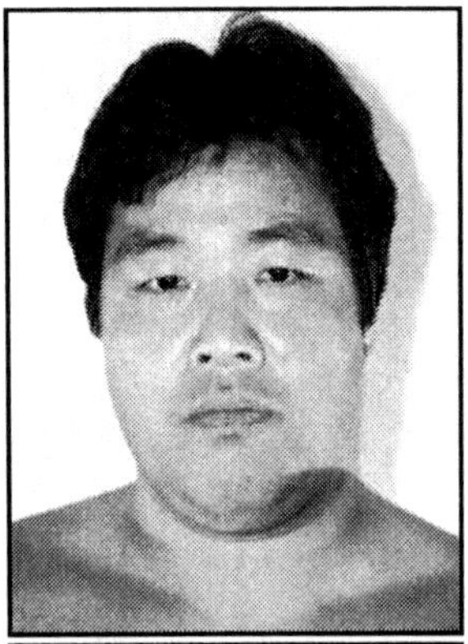
Jumbo Tsuruta

He understood a little English. We spent hours together on the road, talking to each other in broken English and Japanese. We discussed the fundamentals of working and holds. It was always tough for Japanese wrestlers to come to the States. I don't believe the American promoters looked at Japan companies as equals, but simply as a place where they could send talent to get exposure and experience. I know how well the American talent was taken care of in Japan, but there wasn't a fair exchange in the way the Japanese were treated when they worked in the States. Most of the Japanese boys were relegated to spots in the middle of the card. Akihisa Mera, who wrestled as the Great Kabuki, probably had the best run in the States and drew a lot of money as a heel, but he was the exception to the rule. In most cases, the boys themselves tried to help them. In return, when we wrestled in Japan, we were treated well by the Japanese.

Jumbo and I had something in common throughout our career. While we were wrestling each other in Colorado Springs, he rebounded off the ropes and came towards me like a runaway freight train. He ducked down and I did the standard leapfrog over him, with him continuing to move towards the ropes on the other side of the ring. When he came back towards me, I was going to do another leapfrog, but he had the same idea and tried to leap over me, as well. We hit each other face to face and chipped off pieces of our front teeth. We both sported a small chip in our teeth for the rest of our career.

Two other Japanese wrestlers, Motoshi Okuma and Shinya Kojika, were in Amarillo before I got into the business. Okuma was a nice man who always worked hard in the ring. I wrestled him many times in Japan in the mid '80s. As far as the promoter knew, Okuma couldn't speak a word of English, but he sent Okuma out onto the interview set to "*say something ... anything.*" Okuma spoke the only English words he knew: a long list of filthy curse words.

Everybody laughed, but they had to re-shoot the interview. It's a shame that the first words we taught the Japanese were curse words, although they got their revenge when we traveled to Japan. Unbeknownst to us, they taught us the same words … in Japanese.

Kojika wrestled as Kung Fu Lee, playing off the popularity of the "Kung Fu" TV series. He was another good worker. The people hated him and he knew how to get heat. He did good business in the Amarillo, Dallas, and Kansas City territories.

I would often ride with Terry Funk if we were in the same town. He always left as late as possible. He had a 1970 Buick Riviera which was really fast, and Terry drove it fast all the time. It was as if he was obsessed with speed. When the police clocked him speeding, he would run from them.

On one particular night, I was riding home from Abilene with Terry and Dick Murdoch. Veterans always had their choice of seats, so naturally, I rode in the back. The Riviera is a two-door car with a fairly small back seat, but it was big enough for me and, of course, a cooler of beer. My job was to keep Terry and Dickie supplied with beer. They could really put it away, and it seemed as if I was constantly opening a new can and passing it to the front.

As I mentioned earlier, Terry played football at West Texas State. Dickie was a good athlete who had played football at Caprock High School in Amarillo. He loved watching football and supported both the University of Texas and West Texas State. Both Terry and Dickie began talking about WT and their football program, and launched into rants about how the Fat Man was "one mean son-of-a-bitch." After a few beers, they had me reminiscing right along with them. Regardless of what they said, both Terry and Dickie had a lot of respect for Coach Kerbel.

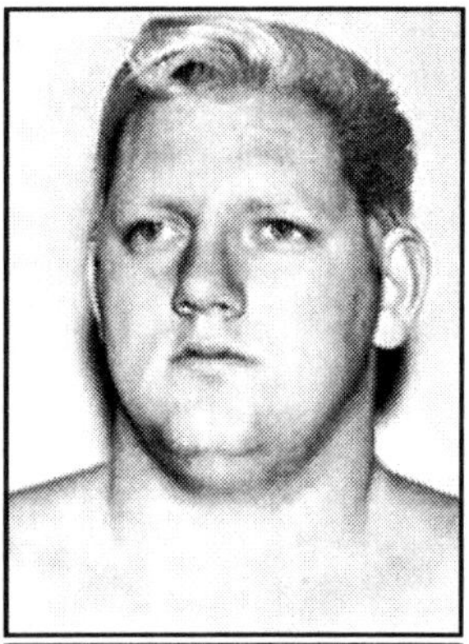

Dick Murdoch

Early in our careers, the young guys all wanted to be accepted by the veterans, so we went out of our way to impress them, even if it meant we had to do something stupid. Perhaps it was just my personality to do some things which were dangerous, but now that I'm older and wiser (maybe), I realize we did a lot of stupid things while we were under the influence of alcohol. As I grew older, I learned where the boundaries were and stopped before I became a danger to myself and others.

Since we wrestled in the same towns on the same nights, week after week, we would always take the same route. The police would then know that late on a particular night, the wrestlers would be coming through town. Most of the time, we were driving fast, and often, we had beer in the car.

There was a small town in Texas named Happy, located about 17 miles from Canyon, where Terry lived. Terry, Dick Murdoch, Larry Lane, and I were all coming back from Abilene, the Friday night town, and it was late at night. Larry later became one of the top babyfaces in the West Texas territory, but at the time, he was just breaking in and was green like me. I first met him during this time. As I've stated before, I was considered to be a stiff worker [very aggressive], but Larry was even more so. He had an amateur wrestling background and was in good shape.

We had several cases of beer in the car. Yes, cases! Terry was driving his Buick, Murdoch was in the front passenger seat, and Lane and I were in the back. Since Larry and I were the green guys, we had to take some ribbing and joking. Some of it bordered on abuse, but most of it was just good-natured fun. That night, instead of putting the beer cans into the trash bag, Terry and Dickie would throw them over their shoulders and into the back seat where we were sitting. The trip was a long 3½ hour trip, and by the time we were driving through the town of Happy, the beer cans filled the floorboard of the car all the way up to the seat on which Larry Lane and I were sitting.

Happy, Texas, couldn't have been more than ¼ mile long from top to bottom. Terry and a local policeman had a mutual hatred for each other. On Friday nights, the cop knew it was highly likely that Terry would be driving through town around two in the morning. The cop had given Terry quite a few speeding tickets over the years, and he was always waiting for Terry to drive by.

We drove through a lot of small towns where the speed limit dropped from 55 mph to 25 mph. It really was an inconvenience, not to mention waste of fuel, to slow down at every town, especially at two in the morning. When we reached Happy, we were all looking for the cop. All of a sudden, we saw the police car on the side of the road, facing outwards. Terry didn't slow down until he was almost directly alongside the cop, at which time he slammed on the brakes. Terry slid down the highway and came to a complete stop in a huge cloud of dust. He then pushed the accelerator pedal to the floor and sped off down the road and into the night.

The cop turned on his lights and sped off after us. As Terry drove at speeds of more than 100 miles an hour, we slowly pulled away from the police cruiser. When his lights had faded to a dull glow, Terry turned off his headlights. We were outside the city limits and it was pitch black. We could barely see the road. I hunkered down in the back seat and began to pray.

After two or three minutes, the headlights of the police car had disappeared into the distance. Less than ten minutes later, we drove into the outskirts of Canyon, Terry's hometown. Looking ahead, we saw two police cars, evidently waiting for us. As we approached them, they turned on their flashing lights and motioned for Terry to pull into the parking lot of a store. While Terry talked with one of the cops, the cop from Happy pulled up. Steam was billowing from the hood of his car and the engine was making a loud knocking sound. He got out of the car with his gun drawn and pointed it at Terry, cursing and yelling at him. "*I would've shot you, you son-of-a-bitch, if it hadn't been for the other guys in the car.*" The other cops, who were from Canyon and knew Terry personally, stepped in-between them and tried to calm down the cop from Happy.

Larry Lane and I were in the back seat of the car, watching all of this happen. Neither one of us was feeling any pain, but we were sober enough to realize that Terry might be in a lot of trouble. When the cop from Happy finally calmed down, he said, "*I'm gonna give everyone in the car a ticket for doing ninety miles an hour.* "

A citation for speeds that high would cost more than $100, and while I can't speak for the others, to me, that was a *lot* of money. As I stepped out of the car to protest, my feet pulled at least 50 beer cans out onto the ground, which made a lot of noise and got everybody's attention. "*You can't give me a ticket,*" I protested. "*I wasn't even driving!*" Everybody, except the policeman from Happy, of course, laughed out loud, not for what I said, but for how it looked when the beer cans clattered to the ground around my feet.

The four of us had to follow the Happy policeman to the Canyon police department. I thought we might be placed under arrest once we got into the building, but we weren't. The Happy officer didn't have his ticket book, so he wrote Terry a ticket on a plain sheet of notebook paper for driving 90 miles an hour. Terry went to court and challenged the citation, since the ticket wasn't written on a legal document, and the charges were dismissed.

For the next two decades, Dick Murdoch took every available opportunity to remind me (and everybody else) about how I looked as I dragged the beer cans out onto the parking lot. Every time we ran into one another, he told the story. It was a night to remember, for sure.

Kojika had a similar experience while riding with Terry. The incident took place in the exact same place and with the same cop. With the cop in hot pursuit, Terry took a short cut through some country roads which led to his house, bypassing the town of Canyon. However, three or four police cars were waiting for him, this time at an intersection near his house. Evidently, the cop had radioed Terry's identity to the Canyon police, and they knew the routes he would take to get home. As Terry came to a stop, he got out and began jumping up and down on his car hood, yelling, "*Okay! You cops win! I give up.*" One of the policemen stepped out of the darkness, with a loaded rifle in his hand. If Terry hadn't stopped, he was going to use it. They were that serious. Kojika, meanwhile, got out of Terry's car. With a big grin on his face, and in broken English, he said, "*Just like Kojak!*" Kojak, a popular TV series at the time, was about a detective with New York City's 13th Precinct.

Bob Backlund came in and impressed everybody with his athletic ability. To this day, he is probably one of the best athletes to enter the ranks of professional wrestling. He was in great shape. Bob had been a star linebacker and wrestler at North Dakota State in Fargo. After college, he played semi-pro football and trained for pro wrestling in Minnesota with Eddie Sharkey. Bob broke into wrestling in Oklahoma, but after being paid $10 for his first match, sleeping in the trunk of his car, and getting involved in a bar fight with a local, tough guy, he decided to learn more about pro wrestling from Dory Funk Jr., so he came to Amarillo.

Because of his amateur background, the promoters in Oklahoma and Louisiana had forced Bob to wrestle challengers from the crowd. That was a dangerous thing to do. It's one thing to wrestle or fight somebody with an organization which has sanctioned rules, but it's entirely another thing to get into the ring with somebody you don't know. Most of the wrestlers could take care of themselves in a fair fight, but you never knew what some of the street fighters might do. They were too unpredictable.

Tim Woods, who wrestled under a mask as Mr. Wrestling #1, found that out the hard way when he accepted a challenge from a guy named Arnold Spurlin in Columbus, Georgia. Woods, who was no slouch when it came to legitimately taking care of himself in the ring, was caught by surprise when Spurlin sucker punched him, ripped off his mask, and threw it to the crowd. Woods took

Spurlin down with a wrestling hold, but when Spurlin saw Woods' hand exposed, he bit off one of Woods' fingers at the knuckle.

Backlund took on challengers in Oklahoma because the promoter paid him an extra $10 to $15 a night to wrestle them, and he was desperate for money. The marks, in turn, would be paid a money prize if they were able to stay in the ring with Bob for a specific length of time. When Bob got into the ring against his first challenger, he pulled his opponent into a side headlock. There are shooting holds which can be put on people to make them quickly give up. Some of those holds are very painful and put tremendous pressure on the joints. The side headlock, however, isn't one of those holds. It's used to control somebody, not to force them to concede. Bob, however, was very strong. Once he had his opponent in the headlock, he would rotate his arm and place the bone of his forearm across their cheekbone. He then squeezed so hard that the pain forced the challenger to give up. The promoters, who were shocked (and a little bit worried) that Bob would use a hold which wasn't normally considered to be a concession hold, asked why he did it. He said it made sense because the side headlock was one of the most-often-used holds in professional wrestling, and by using it in a shoot [real] situation, the hold would be accepted as a legitimate wrestling hold. Bob was 100 percent correct in his assumption and his efforts gave credibility to the wrestling business.

Bob Backlund

Bob has a young, boyish face, even today. In the 1950s, there was a puppet character on TV named Howdy Doody. With his red hair and freckles, Bob was the spitting image of Howdy. However, he didn't like being called Howdy Doody. He even hated for people to tell him that he looked like Howdy Doody. Of course, that just encouraged the boys to call him that as often as they could. Wrestlers were merciless when it came to ribbing.

One day, we were driving home from a show. Bob had won the Western States title a few days before that. When we stopped at a roadside café in Dickens, Texas, Karl von Steiger told him he would help promote the business by wearing the title belt into the café. Bob agreed with him and walked into the café, wearing the title belt around his waist on top of his street clothes. Karl wanted everybody to notice him, so he walked around to all of the tables and introduced Bob. The people were polite and didn't say much. Bob turned ten shades of red. I think he knew it was a rib, but being the good person he is, he went along with it. The funny thing about it was that I wasn't involved, but I was probably more embarrassed by the attention we were getting than Bob was.

In the fall of 1973, Larry Lane and I shared a motel room, One night during a trip to El Paso, being young and wild, we went to a liquor store and each of us bought a half gallon of wine. Later that night, a number of the guys wanted to go across the border to Juarez, Mexico, to get something to eat. I drank a good portion of the wine before they decided to do that, so I wasn't in the best of shape. Dick Murdoch said I shouldn't go because I could get into trouble and end up in jail. I was mad at him, but he was so right and probably saved me a lot of grief. I ended up wrestling with Terry Funk outside the motel and we both fell into the pool. Of course, because of the drug wars, Juarez is now considered to be the most dangerous city in the world, but back then, it was pretty safe and a good place to go and have fun.

A freak accident later that night almost put an end to my career. While walking down a motel corridor, I came to a wooden door which had vertical strips of glass embedded in the frame, which allowed people to see through to the other side. Since I had my suitcases in my hands, I kicked the door open with my foot. I must have kicked too hard because the glass broke and my foot went through. To make matters worse, my foot got stuck between the jagged edges of glass. Off balance, I fell backwards to the floor, and when I did, the glass cut my Achilles tendon three-fourths of the way through. I knew I was seriously injured because blood was pouring out of my shoe, and I was bleeding badly as I limped to my room. When I sat down on the bed and took off my shoe and sock, blood spurted out in a three-foot-long stream every time my heart beat. I knew I was in trouble. I put my finger on the wound to slow the bleeding. Larry immediately rushed me to the hospital emergency room.

The doctor told me that unless I was a coward, I would get up and walk out. To this day, I don't know why the doctor had that attitude towards me. He told me my tendon was almost cut through, and that I would need an operation to fix it. I was driven back to Amarillo, where I saw the orthopedic surgeon who had operated on my knee in college. He said the wound was serious and that I needed to go right to surgery. I wouldn't be able to wrestle for three months or more.

I was devastated. I was just beginning to really make headway in the business. To make matters worse, I was scheduled to go to Japan for Giant Baba in a few weeks. Baba had recently left the Japanese Pro Wrestling Association [JWA] and had formed his own company, All Japan Pro Wrestling [AJPW]. In the process of getting the company off the ground, he reached a deal with Dory Funk Sr., who would provide talent for Baba's promotion.

For the next three months, I was in a walking cast. That presented a whole set of problems. Wrestlers were considered to be independent contractors. The promoters were not their employers in the strict sense of the word, so wrestlers weren't given health or disability insurance to help them get through circumstances like the ones I found myself in. We were left to fend for ourselves.

When I began wrestling, I took out my own health insurance policy. At the time, the premium was $50 per month. I'm thankful I had the foresight to do that because it paid for the surgery to repair my Achilles tendon, a knee operation, and other injuries. It also covered everything through my youngest son's birth in 1991. The premium skyrocketed twenty-fold over the years, but I kept that policy until 1988, when I qualified for insurance through the Screen Actors Guild, which I had joined while working on the *No Holds Barred* movie with Hulk Hogan. I had to let that policy lapse in 1993 when I couldn't qualify for membership in the Guild due to not working in the performing industry. I regretted having to let it go because the company I went with had premiums which were off the charts and the policy had a huge deductible. Those expenses are tough on people who are self-employed. Regardless of the cost, I knew I couldn't do without it. The premiums continued to rise each year until I retired and let it lapse in 2005.

Of course, the best "insurance" was to avoid getting injured, but with the amount of bumping we did, it was inevitable that we would get hurt sooner or later. I can remember many instances of guys being hurt when they didn't land correctly, or do what they were supposed to do to protect themselves from injury. One example that comes to mind took place during a match between Tony Russo and John Black at a TV taping in Shreveport, Louisiana. I saw the whole thing. Black held on when Russo tried to back drop him and brought Russo down on top of him. Black's face was buried in Russo's back as their bodies crashed to the mat and he broke his neck on impact. Russo didn't know what to do because Black was holding his head and telling him to not touch him. When Russo came to the dressing room and told us what had happened, I went out to the ring because I was in the next match. I got into the ring and bent over him. Black was scared, of course, and he was holding his head and neck, trying to keep them in a straight line. I honestly thought he was just selling the back drop, until he said, "*Don't touch me. I broke my neck. Don't touch me. I really did. Don't touch me.*" When I realized he really was hurt, I returned to the dressing room to let everyone know that he really was hurt badly.

Not knowing what to do with the injured Black, the referee had left the ring shortly after stopping the match and went to the back for help. Someone from the promotion made the decision to leave him in the ring for a few minutes ... so they could get the cameras in position to show him being loaded into the ambulance. That was one of the times when I realized how cold and impersonal the wrestling business could be.

That incident also taught me another lesson. Whenever you are coming down and someone is falling on top of your face, always turn your head a little to the side because the neck has more give in that position.

Russo felt badly about what had happened, although it wasn't really his fault. Sadly, we [the wrestlers] were somewhat cold in our reaction to Russo's feelings as we ribbed him about hurting Black. There just isn't much sympathy for injury in professional wrestling. The old feeling of "better you than me" was the norm.

That was the last time I saw John Black. I never heard a word about him after that day.

I had come full circle. Up to that point, I wasn't getting ahead or saving any money, but I was able to make a living. Now, however, I found myself suffering through another round of hard times. Fortunately, the Amarillo territory had a small fund which the promoters doled out to wrestlers if they got hurt in the ring. That was the only territory I ever knew to do that. I wasn't injured in the ring, but the Funks still gave me a little money to help me get by. And "get by" is all I did. I received about $75 a week. The Funks also were kind enough to give me some small office jobs, as well, and let me promote the town of Elk City, Oklahoma, but the money I made wasn't enough to live on. Of course, I wasn't hurt in the ring, so they couldn't be held responsible. I appreciate what they did because they did it from the kindness of their hearts. I also went to work for a company which made plastic fishing lures, making minimum wage, which at the time was $1.60.

During the next two months, I was very depressed. My attitude and feeling of self-worth dropped to one of the lowest points in my life. I pushed myself to come back early, keeping my upper body in shape by lifting weights. In the first week in November, just two months after the injury occurred, I sat on the back porch of our rental house and cut off the cast. It was a month early, but I wasn't going to wait around any longer. I called the office and told them the doctor had released me and I was ready. They booked me in Lubbock, Texas, against Dick Murdoch.

During our match, Dickie and I began to run the ropes. As I hit the ropes, I heard a loud popping noise in my Achilles tendon. It was so loud that even Dickie heard it because he stopped in mid-ring and stared at me. Of course, when the tendon snapped, I lost the strength in my ankle and immediately fell to the mat. As I sat on the canvas, I wiggled my toes, trying to assess the damage. Dickie walked over, pushed me down, and pinned me.

The doctor put another cast on my ankle and I was out for another month. I wasn't too discouraged about the time I missed because I should have let my tendon heal for at least another month. Sure enough, a month later, the doctor removed the cast and it felt as good as new. When I began wrestling again, I wore wrestling boots for a short time, rather than my standard cowboy boots. I took good care of my ankle and to this day, it has not been re-injured.

The little bit of money I had saved went quickly and I had plenty of time to think about what I had done, and how I would handle my business and life more wisely if I was given the opportunity to wrestle again. In the long run, the injury changed my life for the better. I realized a day would come when I would either be injured, or I would get old and not be able to wrestle. Before then, I had made it a habit to save something from every paycheck, even if it was only a dollar a week, but the injury wiped out everything I had saved. That incident made me that much more aware of how important it was to save as much money as possible.

The experience taught me three huge lessons about life. One, I wasn't indestructible. Two, I had to make better choices and control my actions. It was pretty much the last time I ever got that drunk. I drank a lot of beer during my life, but I learned to drink in moderation. Being out of work for more than three months with no income taught me a life-long lesson. And finally, nobody was going to help me if I got injured and couldn't work.

While I was still on the sidelines, I began to question whether or not wrestling was going to be my life's work. I looked at where I had been and the direction in which I was headed. After one year in the business, I was dead broke. I had to make a decision. I could get back into teaching and coaching, but that really wasn't what I wanted to do, so I decided to give wrestling another chance. I would give it one more year. If things didn't turn around by then, I would quit and find another line of work.

Chapter 7

The Little Blue Pill

In April 1974, the Funks asked me if I would like to work in the Dallas, Texas, territory for a couple of weeks. Relishing the idea of working with new talent, I jumped at the opportunity. My first match there took place at the Stockyards Arena in Fort Worth, where the promotion taped their TV show. Bronco Lubich, a retired wrestler who worked in the office during the day and refereed at night, was the first person to introduce himself to me. He had heard that I had played football for West Texas State, and that made him curious, because they were breaking in another guy who played for West Texas State. "*He's a real nice, quiet guy.*" Those were his exact words. I remember them as if they were etched into my brain. He then said, "*His name is Frank Goodish.*"

"*That wild and crazy guy?*" I asked.

Bronco said, "*No, this guy is real quiet, and nice. He's a huge guy, but he's easy to get along with.*"

I couldn't contain my astonishment. "*Are you sure? I know Frank Goodish, and he's a wild and crazy guy.*"

Bronco again said, "*No, this guy isn't wild. He's soft-spoken and keeps to himself.*"

I couldn't believe what Bronco had said. I had to see the guy for myself. There must be two guys from West Texas with the same name. I walked over to the other dressing room … and there was Frank. And just as Bronco said, he was sitting down and being quiet. I couldn't believe it.

Frank had a reputation in college. When I went to WT as a freshman, he was already playing football on a scholarship. He was a very good football player and the coaches had great hopes for him. But even then, there was one thing about Frank which set his personality and course in life. He wasn't coachable. In every sense of the word, he was an outlaw. He frequently got into trouble off campus, and as I explained earlier, he was kicked out of school when he pulled one prank too many.

I was excited to see Frank sitting there, and I was amazed at how big he was. He was huge. He weighed almost 300 pounds at the time. The last time I had seen him, he weighed about 230 pounds. I didn't know what kind of a reception I would get because it had been seven years since I had last seen him. When I walked up to him, he smiled, stood up, shook my hand, and sat back down. I talked to him for a few minutes, while Bronco stood beside me, listening to every word. When Bronco finally walked away, Frank immediately became animated, as if he had been woken up from a trance. As I told him about telling Bronco that he was a wild guy, Frank put his finger to his lips. "*Keep quiet about all that stuff. I'm trying to break into the business. Fritz is really watching me and my attitude, so I have to keep it low key.*" Fritz, of course, was Fritz von Erich, the owner and promoter of the Dallas wrestling office. Apparently, nobody knew about his past life. For the two weeks I was there, we traveled together and laughed about old times.

Frank wasn't working yet, but he being trained by some of the younger guys in the territory, like Doug Somers, a young wrestler from Minnesota. Doug was training Frank in the ring at the Dallas Sportatorium, the building where they held their weekly Tuesday night matches. I watched one morning as Doug had Frank run and do forward flips, as if someone was hip-tossing him. He had Frank do them over and over and over. Doug thought it was funny to make Frank go through the drills. Frank, however, wasn't very good at taking bumps like that. When the session was over, I told Frank, "*You know he's messing with you.*"

"*I know,*" said Frank, "*but I'm gonna take whatever they put me through.*"

Later that week, Doug bought a used Pontiac from a local dealership for $800. It was the first car he had bought himself. He was so excited about it and was showing it off to everybody. When I asked him if he got any kind of a warranty with it, he said, "*No, that's why I got such a good deal.*"

Frank Goodish

That night, as Frank and I were driving through the toll booth on the Dallas-Fort Worth Turnpike (now a part of I-30), we saw Doug standing in front of his car on the side of the road. The hood was up and smoke was pouring out of the engine. He was looking around with a dumbfounded look on his face. He looked so pitiful, as if he just couldn't believe that his new car had already broken down. I pulled over onto the emergency lane and we got out. I was laughing so hard. I mean, I could not stop. Frank even poked me in the ribs to get me to stop, but I couldn't. It just struck me as being so funny. We took Doug with us to the Fort Worth show and left the car on the side of the road. He later had it towed to a repair shop, where it cost him $1,000 to get it fixed. I saw Doug later that year in Louisiana, and I never stopped kidding him about it.

Frank was living in San Antonio with his best friend, Pete Ortega, and for the two weeks I was in Dallas, when I was working on the south end of the territory, Frank let me stay with them. Pete, who Frank always referred to as "The Mexican," was a huge weightlifter. He was a big influence on Frank, who was taking a lot of protein and working out hard, with the objective of getting bigger than he already was. Frank had adopted the idea that bigger is better, and he was right, because a few years later, the business moved towards the bigger guys. That was when I first decided to bulk up. I thought there might be a niche in the business for a huge guy, so I increased my food intake and began hitting the weights with Frank. At Frank's urging, I also began to take protein supplements.

Later, a couple of weeks after I left Dallas, when I was back in Amarillo, I woke up one morning with an acute case of the gout. My body had overloaded on protein, which raised the uric acid levels in my body. The result was gout. After that, I was careful about taking excessive levels of protein. It didn't seem to bother Frank, though. He used to swallow handfuls of concentrated liver pills. Two years later, when Frank and I were in New York, we were working out with "Superstar" Billy Graham at the YMCA in New Haven, Connecticut. After the workout, Billy saw Frank swallow a handful of liver pills. He told Frank, "*It's a lot easier to just take this little blue pill,*" and held it out in the palm of his hand. I guess it was easier, but in the end, I think it hurt a lot of the guys. Superstar learned first-hand about the damage the "little blue pill" could do to a man's body.

Blackjack Mulligan and Black Jack Lanza were the top team in Dallas at the time, and the first top heel team I got to know outside of the Amarillo territory. I'll never forget their kindness. I was just a young, green, inexperienced kid, who didn't own a car, while Mulligan and Lanza were top guys. Even so, they took the time to talk to me and let me travel with them around the Dallas loop. The funny thing about it was that the three of us were crammed into the front seat of Mulligan's pickup truck. Of the three of us, I was probably the smallest, but none of us were small guys. Both Mulligan and Lanza stood over 6-foot-4, so they were really tall and stout. In my eyes, next to Andre the Giant, and possibly Big John Studd, physically, Mulligan was the biggest and most impressive wrestler I knew. I loved to watch the big, nasty heels, and Mulligan sure fit the bill.

Blackjack Mulligan

Black Jack Lanza

One story which stands out in my mind illustrates the true character of Mulligan and Lanza. One night after we wrestled in Laredo, which was a spot show taking the place of Corpus Christi, Lanza had plans to meet friends in Houston. The trip from Laredo to Houston was 350 miles, so we had a long drive ahead of us. As we left Laredo, I began experiencing stomach cramps. The cramps were so severe that we had to stop several times so I could go to the bathroom. Before we had reached the first small town outside Laredo, we had stopped three times, so we decided to stay over at a motel. I was sick all night long, and by morning, the sickness had run its course.

Mulligan and Lanza didn't give me a hard time about forcing them to change their plans, or making things inconvenient for them. They were just glad my problem wasn't anything serious, or contagious, for that matter. They treated me like I was a good friend and an equal.

It also was customary in those days to pay trans of three to four cents a mile to the driver to help pay for gas. When I offered trans to Mulligan he refused it. "*Someday, Stan, you'll be on top and making good money. You don't need money from the underneath guys who are barely making it."* I never forgot that, and years later, when I was working on top, I never charged trans. It was all because of a lesson I had been taught by Mulligan.

I also met Ken Patera during my time in Dallas. I heard Verne Gagne had bought a piece of the Dallas territory, so he was trading talent with Fritz. Ken, a former Olympic Weightlifter, won the Pan American Games in 1971. He also was the first American to press 500 pounds over his head. In late 1972, Verne Gagne broke him into the wrestling business. Gagne later sent him to Dallas to get experience. Ken was still a little green (but not as green as Frank and me), but he had achieved a lot of notoriety stemming from his weightlifting feats in the Olympics, so he was already getting a big push.

Frank and I were staying at the Alamo Plaza on the west side of Dallas near Oak Cliff. Ken also was staying there. The boys were all guided there as it was the cheapest motel in town. One night, we were standing outside our rooms at the motel, which was an old-style, single-story motel, with grass growing between the rows of rooms. Somehow, we got on the subject of agility. As we talked, Patera laid down on the ground, on his back, and did a nip-up to his feet. That was very impressive considering the fact he weighed 320 at the time. That impressed Frank and I so much. We couldn't believe a guy that big could be that agile. He was a real horse. While I was there, I had the pleasure of working with Ken in Dallas.

My scheduled two weeks in Dallas passed by quickly. When I think back on those 14 days, I think about how "chance" plays such a big part in our futures. My chance meeting in Dallas with Frank Goodish resulted in a long and enduring business relationship between the two of us ... and a close friendship which would last until the day of his death.

Alamo Plaza Hotel, Dallas

Chapter 8

Gadget Man

In September 1974, I told Dory Funk Jr. it was time for me to get out and find work in other places, and that I would appreciate it if he could help me get booked. Karl von Steiger had told me that Portland, Oregon was a good territory. It covered a small area of the Northwest, the trips were fairly short, and a wrestler could make $500 each week working underneath. I also told Dory that the two places I didn't want to work were Kansas City and Louisiana/Oklahoma. Both territories were well-known for long trips for little money, much like Amarillo, and I was tired of traveling long distances. I made my preferences real clear to Dory.

A week later, he told me he had me booked in Louisiana ... one of the places I had specifically told him I did *not* want to go. I had no choice other than to take the booking. In those days, when a promoter went to bat for someone and got them booked in another territory, they were expected to fulfill the obligation. Looking back on things, though, I can't fault Dory for what happened. There's a very good chance that Louisiana was the only place that would take me. However, other than the time when Vince McMahon Sr. booked me to New Japan in January 1977, that was the last time I depended on somebody else to book me into another territory. I promised myself then and there that from that day on, I would take care of my own bookings.

Today, when I'm asked which territories were the worst when it came to the travel, the Amarillo and Louisiana/Oklahoma immediately come to mind. The Louisiana territory, which covered six states, was worse than Amarillo. The drive from Houma, in southern Louisiana, to Tulsa, Oklahoma, was 700 miles ... one way! Tulsa was one of the Monday shows, so we made that trip on Sunday night. It was a brutal drive which Frank and I had to make quite often. We would often stop in Shreveport and check in for a few hours at the Alamo Plaza (three to a room), and then leave early in the morning for Tulsa, which was a good 350 miles from there. The other Monday show was in Monroe, Louisiana. However, everybody wanted to be in Shreveport because TV was taped there on Tuesday morning. Shreveport was halfway between Houma and Tulsa, so if we were in Tulsa, we had to drive back to Shreveport after the show on Monday night.

At one time, when LeRoy McGuirk was still running the territory, we also cut promos in Tulsa. McGuirk and Bill Watts [wrestler and part owner of the territory], both lived in Tulsa,

The Louisiana/Oklahoma territory was divided into two sections: the north and the south. The north, which we referred to as the Oklahoma territory, consisted of Tulsa (Oklahoma), Springfield and Joplin (Missouri), Little Rock and Fort Smith (Arkansas), Wichita Falls (Texas), and TV in Shreveport, Louisiana.

The south, or Louisiana territory, was the money territory, and all of the main towns — Shreveport, Alexandria, New Orleans, Monroe, Baton Rouge, Lafayette, and Houma — were in Louisiana. The other big town, and the best money town of them all, was Jackson, Mississippi.

The south loop began in Shreveport on Tuesday where we taped our TV interviews in the morning and had a house show at night. On Wednesday, we would drive 245 miles to Baton Rouge, or 225 miles to Jackson. On Thursday night, we wrestled in New Orleans or Greenville, Mississippi, which were 225 or 130 miles from Jackson, and 100 or 290 miles from Baton Rouge. Friday nights were usually relegated to spot shows in places like Lafayette, Louisiana, or one of the towns in Missouri, such as Joplin or Springfield.

On Saturday, we wrestled in either Greenwood, Mississippi, or Loranger, Louisiana. Houma was the Sunday night town. Houma was a weekly town, but it had a smaller population, so even though the arena was usually packed, the payoffs weren't very good. The small payoffs were also due to the town being promoted by the "one-armed bandit," the name we gave to the local promoter who had just one arm. We would often have to do a TV taping on Saturday morning in Shreveport, and then drive 320 miles to Loranger for the show that night.

If we wrestled in the north end, we began in Shreveport for TV, and then drove to Fort Smith or Little Rock. From there, we made the circuit through Oklahoma City, Tulsa, and either Joplin or Springfield Missouri. Wichita Falls, Texas, was the last stop on the tour before we made our way back to Shreveport for TV. When I first went into the territory, they also taped television in Tulsa, but they eventually consolidated the two territories into one TV show. In my opinion, that was a good idea, but the downside was that the trip was longer. Wichita Falls was 325 miles from Shreveport, but only 240 miles from Tulsa.

The office ran a lot of other towns, as well. It wasn't unusual for them to have three shows running every night of the week. The south would have two shows running on any given night, while the north would have one. Regardless of where we were wrestling on Monday night, we always had to be back in Shreveport on Tuesday mornings for TV interviews, as well as Saturday mornings for the taping of the television show. Very few territories demanded that much travel, but the Louisiana territory covered six states, so there wasn't any way to avoid it. To make matters worse, the territory was notorious for making small payoffs to guys who worked below the main and semi-main events. I often drove 3,000 to 3,500 miles a week for an average of $350 a week.

When Watts was the booker of the territory, Bill Watts could fly his own plane and write off his expenses. The talent who worked for him didn't have that option. Many nights, we drove three to four hours a night to get just *part of the way* to the next town. We were jealous of Bill. We would gripe and complain about having to drive long hours, while Bill flew in the comfort of his airplane in a fraction of the time it took us. I have to admit that if I had been in his shoes, I would have done the same thing. However, at the time, I was like all the rest of the guys and was pissed at him for it. Years later, when I went back to work for Watts, he gave me a ride from Lake Charles to New Orleans in his plane. It was a nice treat, and even though I knew nothing about airplanes, I could tell that Bill was a very conscientious pilot.

Getting home was a real problem because we wrestled seven nights a week. The bookers would often have bookings planned out a month in advance, so we had to really fight to get time off, especially if we were involved in a program. The young, green boys (like me) were really in a bad spot because we needed the experience (not to mention the money) and we wanted to work as much as possible. In some ways, we were in a Catch-22 situation. When we first began wrestling in Louisiana, Frank and I complained because we weren't working every night. Even though we had a night off, we had the same hotel, food, and car expense we would have if we had worked. Little did we know that once we began working every night, we would be begging for a night off.

One of the ways we saved money was by car pooling, but it was hard to plan rides. For instance, I could ride with someone to a couple of towns, but if we were booked in different towns on the third night, I would have to find a ride with somebody going to the town where I was booked. Most of the time, the bookings were so haphazard that we all had to drive our own cars. I solved that problem when I bought a Ford van and built a bed into the rear. I lived in that van as much as I could, but the weather in the south was so hot in the spring and summer that I couldn't sleep. I would just lay there and sweat. Occasionally, when the weather became just too hot to bear, I would stay with Luke Brown and Frank at their apartment in Baton Rouge. As a rule, however, we were all going in different directions, so I was usually on the road by myself. Luke had a wrestling ring he took to the towns. He wasn't wrestling very often, which was typical of the older wrestlers. Very few of them saved their money, so they had to take any job they could get. Frank and I both took notice of that. It helped us see the end results of not saving, and it influenced us to save as much money as we could.

Luke was a great guy who was really smart to the business. He knew everything there was to know about most of the boys and the workings of the territories. He spent a lot of time educating Frank and me.

Most of the guys didn't have apartments because there was no ideal, central place to live. We were in town only a few days a week. The guys who did have an apartment lived in either Baton Rouge or Shreveport because they were in a central area, but neither city was ideal because we had to zigzag through Louisiana, Mississippi, Arkansas, Missouri, Oklahoma, and Texas to get to the towns. There was a good chance we would only be in our apartment for five days out of a month. As always, there were certain motels the boys would stay in when they were in town. When a newcomer arrived in the territory, they would ask the other boys which motels were good. Our definition of "good" was "cheap."

At that time, the Alamo Plaza was in decline, but they still had good rooms for what they charged. I stayed in Alamo Plaza motels in Dallas, Shreveport, Jackson Mississippi, Albuquerque and Baton Rouge. The Ten Flags Inn Motel in Baton Rouge was even cheaper than the Alamo Plaza, but it was, beyond any doubt, the worst motel I ever stayed in. They were located right around the corner from Luke Brown's apartment. When Luke gave up the apartment and left the territory, the Ten Flags became the place where most of the boys stayed. One time, I checked in and went into the bathroom, but there was no toilet. I had been given one of the "two nights for one" deal, but that was ridiculous. When I went to the check-in desk to complain, they gave me a room with a toilet, but not the special deal.

One problem with the wrestling business is that wrestlers aren't employees of the wrestling company. Wrestlers are self-employed. There were a lot of territories to choose from, but we never knew when the booker or promoter would decide we were no longer needed and give us our notice. That notice was usually two weeks before we were through, which didn't allow us much time to find a new job.

Most wrestlers lived week to week, meaning the money they made was just enough to cover their expenses. In addition to renting an apartment in the territory where they worked, most of the boys also had the expense of a family in whatever town they permanently lived. Most of the underneath guys moved their families with them, and with that came a lot of expense, so they looked for a territory which would book them for at least a year. That gave bookers and promoters power and control over the boys, who were always worried about being cut from the roster. It was common knowledge that when we moved our family to a new territory, registered our kids in school, and set down roots, then we were locked in and had to take just about whatever the bookers chose to give us.

There were exceptions to that rule because at least a third of the wrestlers did just that. Louisiana wasn't a good territory to do that because we were always on the road, and might not get home for three weeks. Most of the guys would leave their families at a home base. I remember Silento Rodriguez bringing his family into the territory. Silento was deaf and couldn't talk much, but in spite of those handicaps, he was smart, in good shape, and was a good babyface talent. He had been in and out of Louisiana over the years and was considered to be one of LeRoy's boys.

Leroy McGuirk

The owner of the entire territory was LeRoy McGuirk, an old-time wrestler who had been a huge star in the '40s and '50s. He had to quit wrestling when he lost his eyesight in a car accident. He lived in Tulsa, Oklahoma, which is where the official office of the territory was located. Of course, the boys didn't live there because, as I said earlier, Shreveport and Baton Rouge were more centrally located.

I met LeRoy in Tulsa, but the only other time I saw him was when we went to Tulsa TV. He didn't come to the Louisiana part of the territory very often. While I was there, I saw a picture of LeRoy which had been taken before he lost his eyesight. When he was young, LeRoy looked like a movie star, and in the picture, LeRoy was standing next to Roy Rogers, one of the most famous singing cowboys of radio and television.

Skandor Akbar told me a great story about LeRoy. Several years after LeRoy had lost his eyesight, Akbar was driving him to one of the towns. LeRoy called Akbar, "*Skakak,*" drawing out the "aakkkkk." After they had been on the road for several hours, LeRoy said, "*Skakak, if you get tired, let me know and I'll drive for ya.*"

I don't remember seeing LeRoy very much after Bill Watts came back into the territory [he had been booking in Florida] and took over the book. That was around the time when Watts took over the territory.

George Culkin, who had wrestled years before with his brother as George and Jack Curtis, was the promoter in Jackson, Mississippi. He was a good promoter and the top guys all loved working there because it was a great wrestling town. When I first got there, George personally made the payoffs, and his payoffs were along the lines of those made by Paul Boesch. I was told that when the Great Mephisto [Frankie Cain], Dr. X [Jim Osborne], the Spoiler [Don Jardine], and Bill Watts had the town on fire in 1972 and 1973, the guys would make $1,000 on top. I was never on top, but even in the opening match, I was paid $300. George also ran two weekly towns — Greenville, Mississippi, on Thursday, and Greenwood, Mississippi, on Saturday. They were good towns, although the crowds were small, and the payoffs were average. Later, when Watts came in and took over, the money went back to the office in Tulsa to be paid out later, and the payoffs dropped way down. There were a lot of complaints made about it. George was very unhappy with the change, but he was beholden to the office and his hands were tied. Even when he wasn't making the payoffs, everybody still wanted to work for George because he was a gentleman and he treated the boys with respect. In my opinion, along with Paul Boesch, George Culkin was one of the last, great payoff men in the business.

George Culkin

I met and worked with a lot of great characters during my time in Louisiana. Bobby Jaggers, who had a lot of talent, was one of them. His strongest personality trait, however, was that he tended to exaggerate. Well, maybe "tended to" isn't the right way to describe Bobby. He liked to exaggerate a lot. No matter how exciting or fantastic a story was, Bobby could always top it. One time, Killer Karl Kox and Bobby were traveling together after a show in Arkansas. Kox decided to lead Bobby down the primrose path, just to see what Bobby would say. As they were driving down a long stretch of road, Kox pretended like he saw a deer run across the road. "*Wow,*" he said. "*Did you see that deer? We almost hit him.*"

Bobby never missed a beat. "*Yeah. He was a big one, wasn't he?*"

Jerry "Duke" Miller was a great character. I learned a lot about being a heel by watching Jerry in the ring. He wasn't a particularly big man, but with long, black hair, a moustache, and goatee, he had a southern look about him. He never went anywhere without a little black bag of "marital aids" that he said he liked to use. Back when CB radios were used by most of us, his handle was "gadget man." He died in a car accident in 1976. The story circulated that three Mrs. Millers showed up at his funeral. We thought that was funny, but knowing Duke, there was a good chance the story was true.

I also liked Treach Phillips, who was at the end of his career when we met him. He was built like a bulldog — stocky, but short. Frank and I would rib him about his height. Sometimes, when we got into the ring, we would drop down to our knees and lock up with him. He gave us a lot of grief for doing that. Regardless of his height, I thought he really looked like what a pro wrestler should look like. Like me, he had bad eyesight and wore thick glasses, but without glasses, he really looked the part.

There are many stories of wrestlers who were injured or killed on Louisiana highways. Bob Sweetan, Duke Myers, and Ken Mantell were involved in a serious accident in which they were hurt pretty badly, but they were able to return to work when their injuries healed. Terry Gordy and Buddy Landel had a bad accident between Lafayette and Baton Rouge. Terry told me Landel sued both him and the car dealer who leased the car to Gordy. Ronnie Paul, a journeyman wrestler, was killed on the road between Alexandria and Monroe, Louisiana. I was lucky because I was never involved in an accident. That's pretty amazing considering the number of miles we drove.

One of the biggest stars ever to wrestle in the Oklahoma-Louisiana territory was Danny Hodge. As an amateur wrestler on the University of Oklahoma wrestling team, he had a record of 46 wins and no losses, and won 36 of those matches by pin fall. He won the NCAA title three times and was the first amateur wrestler to appear on the cover of *Sports Illustrated*. He wrestled on the U.S. Olympic team twice, placing 5th in 1952, and winning a Silver Medal in 1956.

Danny Hodge

As a professional wrestler, Danny had the reputation of being the real deal. He wasn't a great worker, as most shooters aren't, but he had a lot of charisma and was good enough to get the job done. As the top man in the territory, he held the NWA world junior heavyweight title for the better part of fifteen years [1960-1976].

Frank and I worked with Danny and his partner, Jay Clayton, a number of times. Clayton was a personal friend of Watts, who broke him into the business. Danny had unbelievable tendon strength, and the strength in his hands was legendary. He would walk into hardware stores and squeeze a pair of pliers, breaking them into pieces, and then tell the salesman that the pliers were defective. During interviews, he would crush an apple with one hand. One day, Frank and I went to a store and bought the hardest apple we could find. That night, while Danny and Jay waited for us in the ring, we walked out and tossed it to him. We thought he would be unable to crush the apple and he would be embarrassed in front of the crowd of wrestling. He caught it in mid-air and squashed it with no hesitation at all.

I never had a problem with him in the ring. One night, I used an amateur move (which I knew very little about) to pick him up and take him down to all fours. I knew he would reverse and get behind me, but as he did, I quickly released him and slid out under the bottom rope to the arena floor. I wasn't going to take any chances. I had heard about what Danny would do to guys who got cute with him. Danny just laughed about it, though.

When I first went in, the bookers of the Louisiana end were Grizzly Smith and Rip Tyler. Griz, as he was known to his friends in the business, had been a big card [someone who drew a lot of fans to the shows] in the Charlotte, North Carolina, territory for promoter Jim Crockett Sr. Crockett Sr., of course, was the father of Jim Crockett Jr., who expanded the Charlotte territory to a national level under the name World Championship Wrestling [WCW]. Grizzly was a huge man, standing 6-foot-10 and weighing almost 400 pounds. He and his partner, Luke Brown, who was almost as tall, were known as the Kentuckians. They worked in almost every territory in the United States and portrayed the poverty which was prevalent in the states located near the Appalachian Mountains. They were huge men for that day and time and were one of the first "big man" tag teams in wrestling. They wore overalls, had long hair, and grew full beards which hung down onto their chests.

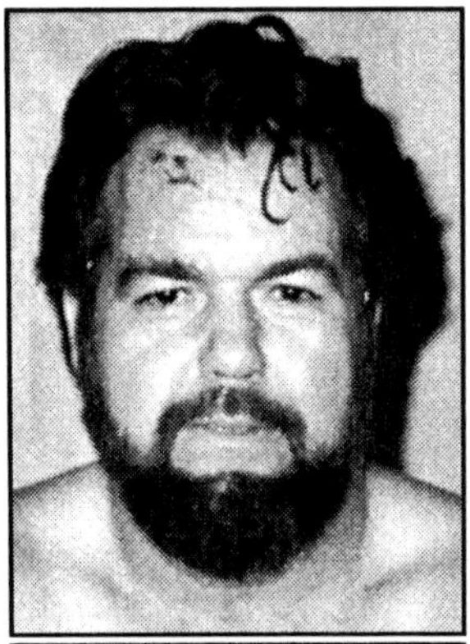
Grizzly Smith

I was told that the first time they went to Japan, in the '60s, the people were awestruck by their size. By any standards, they were huge, but to the Japanese, they seemed to be real giants. Other than Giant Baba, they had never seen wrestlers that tall. Baba-san was tall, but Griz and Luke probably weighed almost two times as much as he did. The promoters in Japan put them into the back of a cattle truck with side rails, and advertised the shows by driving them through the streets. Luke told me that one time, he climbed out of the cage, dropped to the ground, and chased the crowd through the streets. One middle-age lady ran so hard and finally collapsed in front of him. She was so scared that she urinated on herself. Luke felt badly about that, but that was how different and unique the gaijin were to the Japanese.

By the time I met them, however, Grizzly and Luke had all but retired from the ring, but they would work occasionally. Grizzly chose to concentrate on booking, and gave his old friend, Luke, the job of setting up and hauling the ring from town to town.

Grizzly ended up booking me every night of the week and put me against some of the top heels in the territory. It was hot and humid in Louisiana, and many of the arenas weren't air conditioned. The fans were a real mixture: blue collar workers, the poor, rednecks, coon-asses (Cajuns), and blacks. They really got into the toughness portrayed by the wrestlers and the violence in the ring. When those ingredients were mixed together, the setting was just right for violence. It was the perfect culture for wrestling.

The bookers were well aware of that underlying psychology and tried to relate programs to the people in each area. What worked in New York might not mean anything to the sugar cane workers in Alexandria, Louisiana. If they booked black wrestlers like Tom Jones or Porkchop Cash, and later,

Junkyard Dog, they subtly referred to race in order to make it a personal issue. It worked well and the people really got into toughness and violence. In most of the towns in that part of the country, everybody carried a knife. I'm not talking about a small penknife, either. They carried switchblades, gravity knives, and straight razors, and they wouldn't hesitate to use them when they got worked up enough. A lot of people carried guns, as well. That was just the way it was in the south. It made for a very dangerous environment.

Thanks to Grizzly for giving me the opportunity to work some small programs, I began to get comfortable with my ability.

Frank Goodish was already in the territory when I got there. Fritz von Erich had sent him there from Texas to get some experience. Frank was 28 years old when he broke into the business, which was pretty old. When I arrived, Frank was only working three or four days a week, but even when he was off, he would go to the towns and watch the matches. Griz liked him a lot and used him as often as he could, but when they had somebody as big as Frank, they almost had to book him as a heel. Frank, of course, was too green to work heel. On the other hand, he didn't look anything like a babyface, either. Griz booked him in both roles when he could, but Frank had so much going against him that Griz could only give him a limited number of bookings.

As usual, everybody ribbed and played jokes on the new guys. One of the wrestlers played one on Frank when he and Buck Robley were booked in the north end of the territory, as I was, but we traveled separately because Frank was involved with a girl in Tulsa. She was a mixture of a couple of races and treated Frank really well. One day, when Buck and Frank were staying over at her apartment, Frank noticed she had an 8x10 picture of him in a glass case on the TV table. Frank and Buck decided to act like they were going to take out the picture. When they did, they found a picture of another wrestler behind Frank's picture. They really laughed about that and assumed that Frank's girl was playing a rib on him. The wrestler had been in the territory, but was out working in another one at the time. When he came back, there was a bit of unspoken heat between Frank and the other guy, but nothing ever came of it.

Before I met Frank in Dallas, he was training hard in an effort to get bigger. He had a strict schedule for everything: training, eating, and resting. That caused a problem in his marriage, and when he was faced with either divorce or readjusting his training habits, he chose to keep his regimen.

I believe a lot of Frank's "Bruiser Brody" character came from his time spent bouncing at one of the biggest and most popular bars in San Antonio, Texas. Fights broke out there all the time. Just like in the movie, *Road House*, with Patrick Swayze, things could get out of hand quickly. When Frank was hired to do the bouncing, he took his job seriously. His answer to the problem was to meet violence with more violence. He did his job so well that the owner gave him a substantial raise and let him name his own hours. When he walked into the bar, the people knew "the law" was there. Of course, everybody wanted to be his friend, but he never talked, smiled, or introduced himself to anybody. It was as if he was always "in character" as the bad-ass bouncer. Frank felt that by doing so, nobody would try to get into his good graces and take advantage of him or a situation. On a number of occasions, after closing, people would wait for him to leave, and he had to wait in the darkened bar for the police to arrive. He was tough, but he wasn't a fool. In my opinion, his experience as a bouncer played a big part in the development of the Bruiser Brody character he later adopted.

Frank really put an emphasis on saving money. In fact, he was even tighter with a dollar than me, if that's even possible. When Frank wasn't around, I would tell other people that he was a miser when it came to money. Of course, he was telling people the same thing about me. Frank once went four weeks without cashing his wrestling checks. Griz finally had to call to tell him that, at the very least, he had to deposit them in the bank.

We liked each other because we were on the same foundation. The wrestling business was a fun business. A lot of the boys were attracted to it for the good times. They were enticed by the travel, the money, being in the public eye, and the other perks which came with that type of life.

The main reason Frank and I got into the business was to make money. We had both been football players who dreamed of playing in the professional leagues, and we had both failed to achieve those dreams. In those days, wrestling paid as well as pro football. I'm not talking about the wrestling superstars, either. I'm talking about the average guy. On the other hand, most of the boys lived high and gave no thought to the fact that it might all come to an end. That's what separated Frank and I from the rest of the guys. We were in the business to get ahead.

After a few months, Grizzly Smith put us together as a tag team. He knew we were friends, and that we were young, green, and willing to work hard. It was almost a natural for him to put us together. Griz saw something in us. He noticed that even though we were green, and didn't know too much about the business, the people believed we were real. When two big wrestlers were willing to go out and do anything, and I mean anything, to get over and get noticed, then Grizzly knew he had the potential for success. We were willing to take a lot of bumps for our opponents. I took more bumps than Frank, but we developed similar styles and played well off of each other in the ring. We were unpredictable, too. Every night, we tried to come up with something new and different, and many times, we did something just a few seconds after it came into our heads. Not knowing where or what we were going to do, our opponents had to stay alert in order to react properly. The people in the audience reacted in a positive way, too.

The toughest thing about the business is getting over. Once you're over, it's fairly easy to stay over. For Frank and I to get over, we had to go out and get real heat. "Heat" is the key word in wrestling. It's almost non-existent in the U.S. today, and it's almost gone in Japan. Basically, heat is the end product of making the people mad at you, and keeping them mad at you. Frank and I had a goal of always wanting the people to leave the building hating us. That would entice them to return the following week in the hopes of seeing our butts kicked by one of the popular wrestlers.

Compared to many of the boys in the business, our appearance was intimidating. I was, and always will be, a cowboy. I had long, bleached-blond hair and wore a cowboy hat and boots, which I copied from Terry Funk and Dick Murdoch. Frank and I decided to dress alike, so I gave him one of my extra hats and we bought boots that matched. In later years, Frank and I would always laugh when we saw the picture of him dressed like a cowboy.

It was during this time that I first believed that my goal of becoming a top wrestler might actually become a reality. As I mentioned earlier, Louisiana was a wild and violent part of the country. One of the reasons we got over and had heat was that we were wild and did things the other wrestlers didn't. We ran into the crowd and went after people who gave us a hard time. I believe that innovation was unique to Frank and me. Looking back, that was a dangerous and stupid thing to do, but Frank and I were willing to do whatever we had to do to get over. We were driven by a desire to make money and climb the ladder. Nobody told us to do the things we did. We did them on our own. To tell the truth, it was fun and exciting to walk into the arena and act reckless. I have to admit, there were times when Frank and I took stock of what we had done when we got back to the dressing room, and questioned whether or not we had done the right thing. It almost became a game to see what kind of trouble we could get into with the fans, the police, and last, but not least, the promoters.

The boys were somewhat in awe of us, too. Some of them told us we were crazy, and warned us that we were risking injury or getting into trouble. Others didn't like what we were doing because they realized we could be a threat to their job or positions. Most of the guys, however, liked what we were doing

Since we were being given more opportunities to work, and pushed higher on the cards, Frank and I were able to sharpen our skills both in and out of the ring. We were together 24 hours a day, seven days a week. During that time, we developed a great relationship. When you're in a car with another person for days at a time, with nothing to do but talk about your past, your opinions on what was going on in the world, and your philosophy of life, you either build close ties, or you grow to hate each other. Frank and I grew close. We both came from lower-middle-class families and we had to work for whatever we wanted. We had both gone to college on scholarships, but even then, we were on tight budgets. We just didn't have the money to do things most of the other college students did.

When we were teaming up, Frank and I were making about the same money: $300 to $350 a week. We both lived frugally and saved as much money as we could. Frank was a master of living cheaply. He set aside much more money than I did during that time. Frank was single (divorced), and that worked to his advantage in the early years. However, I was married, so I had the additional burden of supporting a household in Amarillo. At the time, I sent home $200 every week and tried to live on what was left. I believe our dedication to saving money was one of the closest bonds we had together.

Grizzly had given Frank and me an opportunity to wrestle near the top as a team. However, when Watts came back from Florida and took over the book, he booked us into the "second tier" towns like Tulsa, Wichita Falls, Springfield, Joplin, and Fort Smith, where we didn't have an opportunity to make good money. In the good towns like Jackson and New Orleans, where the real money was made, he booked wrestlers he had done business with before into the top programs. In retrospect, they were seasoned veterans and better talent than Frank and I were, but at the time, we didn't like the fact that we were moved out of a better position.

1973 and 1974 were the years of the oil embargo in the Middle East. The price of oil quadrupled in 1974 and the price of a gallon of gas went from 38 cents to 55 cents. That doesn't sound like a bad deal now, but in addition to the increase in gasoline prices, we were worried about just getting gas. Gas was being rationed and long lines of cars formed at the pumps. In order to be sure they had fuel when they needed it, a lot of the boys installed spare gas tanks in the trunks of their cars. I didn't do it myself because they were too expensive to install. Bob Griffin had a huge tank mounted underneath his car. I never felt comfortable sitting on top of 100 gallons of gasoline, so I was leery about riding with him.

During our time together in Louisiana, Frank and I befriended a wrestler named Mr. Chin. He worked as a Chinese, but he was actually Japanese. His real name was Ideguchi Hajime. When we met him, he was an old-timer. He wore long, loose tights, a pointed hat, and Japanese-style sandals to the ring. He wasn't a big man. If anything, he was small in stature, and he was a typical "cheap-heat heel" that was very important to any territory.

One night, Mr. Chin was paid after a spot show. He was really mad about the payoff because he didn't get what he thought he deserved. He drove back to Baton Rouge, and at three in the morning, he walked up to Grizzly's house and began pounding on the door. He kept it up until Grizzly came to the door. Grizzly refused to open the door and asked who it was. In his broken English, Mr. Chin told him about being mad about the payoff. When Grizzly still refused to open the door, Mr. Chin began kicking it. When the door finally opened, Grizzly stood in the doorway, holding a pistol aimed at Chin's chest. He told him he was fired, and if he didn't leave immediately, he would call the police. Mr. Chin left the territory, but not before he talked to Frank and me. We were impressed by his bravado and respected him for doing what he did. We thought it took a lot of nerve to show up at Grizzly's house and demand his money. Mr. Chin held a special place in our minds as someone who stood up for himself when he thought he had been screwed, even knowing it might cost him his job.

Years later, when I was working for All Japan, Mr. Chin, who had by then retired from wrestling, came into the dressing room in Tokyo. We talked and reminisced about Louisiana and that incident. He also told me he was involved in a company named Capital Ace which made sports sweat suits. He sold Frank and me several of those, and years later, I became a sponsor for the company. Today, I still own several Capital Ace sweat suits which I wear to the gym. Mr. Chin died of kidney failure at age 62 on June 26, 1995.

Frank and I found ourselves in a good position when we were given the U.S. tag-team belts. We were figured into a number of main events, but most of our matches were billed as a semi-final in support of the main event matches which featured single wrestlers.

There were some really good personal issues going on in the territory at the time. In the southern states, personal issues were always hot. In fact, I witnessed my first riot in Alexandria, Louisiana.

When the heat gets turned up enough and wrestling fans break out into a riot, there is very little that security or police can do. They will do whatever they can to break or destroy the object of their wrath. In wrestling, that object is usually the heel of a match, and to that heel, a riot is a scary thing to witness.

Alexandria was a hot bed for wrestling, and the audience was made up of Cajun and wild, country people. At the time, Buck Robley was working in a

1974 • Bruiser Brody and Stan Hansen, Louisiana

personal issue match against Ken Mantell, a babyface who had a large following of fans. At one time, Ken had been a heel himself, but the people in Louisiana liked the rough and tough characters, and as so often happens, they began to develop a liking for Ken's character. Heels who are brought over from the "dark side" by the fans themselves, often make the best babyfaces and develop the largest following. It is really hard to get to that point because you have to be a really hot and believable heel. Dusty Rhodes is one of the best examples of that happening. Dusty was passionately hated by wrestling fans in Florida, but as the people began to take an interest in his character, he was all but forced to turn babyface. When he did turn, Dusty became one of the hottest babyface properties ever to appear in the Florida territory.

When Frank came into the Louisiana territory, Buck and Ken had been embroiled in an ongoing battle for more than a year. On that particular night in Alexandria, the people rioted after a particularly hot finish. Frank and I were in different dressing rooms, but we were both standing outside, watching the matches. Frank had the night off, but he came to the show with Luke Brown to watch the matches. We watched every match we could, hoping to learn more about how different wrestlers did things.

The match was stopped when Buck was disqualified for doing something dastardly to Mantell. Even after the bell rang, Buck kept pounding on Mantell. As always, there was a contingent of policemen on hand to keep people from the ring, and to escort the heel to and from the dressing room. When the riot began, Buck was on the ring apron, waiting for the police to come escort him to the dressing room. When they reached Buck, they surrounded him and slowly walked up the aisle. It was difficult to get through the crowd because the show was a sell-out and standing room only tickets had been sold. To get to the dressing room, Buck and the police had to walk down a fenced aisle. There was a balcony walkway above which stretched around the top of the bleachers, with a barrier to keep the people from moving all the way around the top of the walkway. The people up there were rioting, too. Somebody picked up a heavy piece of the barrier, a large piece of wood, and threw it down at Buck. It glanced off the side of Buck's head and sliced him open like a knife in a watermelon. With the crowd in full-blown riot mode, the police weren't about to stop and administer first aid. They just dragged him bodily into the dressing room.

Frank and the wrestlers who were standing near the dressing room where Buck was being taken decided to get involved. When a riot is likely to happen, we often forgot about being a babyface or a heel. We felt like we had to help the guy in trouble in some way or another. There have been many instances of wrestlers being the only factor in preventing one of their own from being injured or killed. In this case, everybody came out, if for nothing else than to make a presence to try and control the crowd. I was on the other side of the building, but I could see the odds weren't in the boys' favor, so I ran over to help. Frank began to throw chairs at the people. Well, that just added fuel to the fire because the people just threw the chairs right back at him. I saw kids and old people hit and knocked down by flying chairs which had been thrown by the people. Somebody threw a four-by-four-inch board at Frank, but it missed and crashed into the wall beside him. He picked it up and threw it at knee-high level into the crowd, spinning it like a Frisbee as he released it.

The people looked like dominoes as they fell down, one after the other. He cut a huge gap into the crowd of people. We stood our ground and held back what was a veritable "wall" of angry wrestling fans, until an additional detachment of police arrived to restore order, but not before several people were injured. Buck Robley was taken to the hospital where a doctor used 60 stitches to close his head wound.

When a heel would do something hot, which he almost always did, he was expected to deal with the fans who were out to do bodily harm to him. The best way to do that was to act as if the people don't matter. Focus on your opponent and avoid making eye contact with the fans. More importantly, a heel must act as if he was in control of every situation, and not show fear to the people.

I had trouble in other territories, too. When I was in Corpus Christi, Texas, Terry Funk was working as a masked wrestler called "The Big T." He had been banned from the building, so he came back under the mask to wrestle Jose Lothario. Of course, the fans all knew it was Terry. During the hot finish, a number of people got into the ring and attacked Terry. I was watching from the back, so I ran to the ring to help. Terry had a guy pinned against the ropes and was really giving it to him. By the time I got there, another guy had come up behind Terry and was about to hit him in the back. I tackled the guy from his side and sent him out through the ropes. Terry was still hitting the guy when I walked up behind him and grabbed him with both of my arms. I was wearing a coat and he didn't recognize me. He tried to turn around, but as he did, he recognized me. As the two of us combined efforts to throw the guy out of the ring, somebody threw a long piece of angle iron at us like a spear. It skimmed off the top rope and shot across the ring into the crowd on the other side. Terry and I looked at each other with wide eyes, and then proceeded to exit the ring in a slow, controlled manner. It was a scary moment, but we knew enough to never show fear, even when it might be called for, because to show fear would just embolden the marks.

Another time, when I was wrestling Andre in Japan, we were battling on the floor area outside the ring. When I climbed back into the ring, Andre reached through the ropes and tried to grab me. I began kicking at him, keeping him from getting back into the ring. Earlier in the match, I had thrown the ring announcer's table into the ring. I picked it up, held it high over my head, and charged to the side of the ring where Andre stood. Andre saw me coming and barely had time to duck out of the way when I threw it down at him.

At the time, the ring was surrounded on four sides by a three-foot high iron fence, and the ringside seats were right outside the fence. The first foot or so of the table went over the top of the fence, followed by the longer and heavier end of the table. When the table hit the top rail, the weight of the longer end pushed the front end of the table up. The table glided over the railing and shot out into the air, traveling about twenty to 25 feet into the ringside crowd. My feet were glued to the mat where I stood, and I looked on in horror as the people in the first two rows all dove out of the way. They were lucky they did because the front edge of the table would have smashed into their faces with a lot of power. By that time, Andre also was standing motionless, watching the event unfold. It was one of those surreal moments in which the table seemed to fly in slow motion. The people in its path all moved as it landed flatly on the backs of several rows of empty seats. When it finally came to rest, Andre and I looked at each other in shock. We both knew what could have happened. We were so relieved that no one had been hurt.

On another night, when I was working at the Sportatorium in Dallas, I was working in the semi-final event with Paul "Butcher" Vachon as my partner. The ring there was really high off the ground. The distance from the ring apron to the floor was probably four to five feet. I had just met Paul and didn't really know him. It was the first time we had been partners, so I didn't know anything about his style of wrestling. While we were waiting for our opponents to come to the ring, someone jumped up onto the apron of the ring near to where I stood. When I realized he was a mark, I turned and gave him a pretty good push. He swayed out, holding onto the ropes with just one hand. As he slowly swung back to the ropes, I realized that he was drunk, so I just walked away from him. As I did, Paul walked over and smacked him really hard with an open hand to the face. The guy fell backwards off the apron, as if he was taking a long, back dive to the floor. The first thing that hit the floor was the back of his head. It made a sickeningly loud thud. I was really worried that it had killed him. My first thought was that the guy might sue, so I moved away from Paul. I didn't want anyone to think I had been the one who had knocked him off the apron. The oddest thing about the whole incident took place when the guy hit the ground. Three security guards grabbed him and dragged him to the front of the building, beating him with billy clubs the entire way. Later that night, when I asked the guards about his condition, they said he was an illegal alien, so they had him arrested. Wow! That's Texas justice.

In 1976, when I was working the WWWF territory, we were in Harrisburg, Pennsylvania. Four or five of us were standing on the stage in the building during a match between the teams of Chief Jay Strongbow and Chief Billy White Wolf and Chuck O'Connor [aka Big John Studd] and Walter "Killer" Kowalski. Chuck and Walter were working under the hood as the Executioners. Chuck, whom I had befriended, was on the floor of the arena, and had done something to one of the Indians. All of a sudden, a guy built like a football linebacker grabbed Chuck's mask and began twisting it around. John couldn't see and was trying to keep the guy from pulling it off. Killer was doing something with the other Indian, so he didn't even know it was going on. When I turned to look at the other guys, they all disappeared behind the curtain. I could see the crowd was "smelling blood." When a mark gets out of control, it emboldens others to get involved. I jumped off the stage and ran down to the ring. As I got close to the ring, the mark saw me and let go of Chuck. I went ahead and gave him a big push. After landing on his rear end, he stood up quickly and moved back into the crowd. By then, Chuck had turned the mask back around so he could see. He didn't know who had attacked him, but he was so mad that he hit and kicked a couple of fans who were sitting nearby. He was embarrassed and pissed off that somebody had gotten to him. I was able to calm him down enough for the match could continue. Later that night, Chuck thanked me because he realized the guy had him at a distinct disadvantage.

I was surprised the other guys on the stage had taken off, rather than go to the aid of a fellow wrestler who was in trouble. In the south in the NWA, the heels always protected the other heels, regardless of the circumstance and even if it got us into trouble. On most nights, there were some pretty salty guys in the crowd, so the possibility of being attacked was an ever-present danger. If a heel wasn't able to count on their fellow heels for protection, then he could really find himself in trouble. That was my first indication that protection for heels in the WWWF was different than it was in the south. The hired security was good there, but the attitude of the heels was quite different from that which I had been familiar. Not only were the guys indifferent to the situation, but they criticized me for going to the ring because it could have caused "*trouble between the fans and the office.*"

There also was the danger from people who threw things. I've been in matches where people threw paper cups (some filled with ice), rocks, spark plugs, and metal chairs. One night, I was getting out of the ring in the old Atlanta City Auditorium. It was a long walk back to the stage, where we had to climb a set of stairs that led up onto the stage. There was an upper deck which jutted out close to the edge of the stage. As I was walking up the steps, an empty whiskey bottle sailed down from high above my head. Not having good eyesight, I didn't see it. Luckily, it came down at an angle and just grazed my sweaty chest, shattering into the wall on the other side of me. If it had been a few inches to one side, I could have been hurt badly.

In Puerto Rico, kids stood outside the stadiums and sold rocks to the fans, and when we walked to and from the ring, we held metal chairs over our heads to protect ourselves from spark plugs thrown at us by the marks. The last time I was in Puerto Rico, I was hit by a rock wrapped in a paper cup. It hit the fat part of my cheek and sent me to my knees. I was very lucky that night. I hate to think of what might have happened if it had hit my jaw bone, my teeth, or my eye socket. Some of the guys told me stories about people saying they were going to throw acid on them. That was scary to think about, but we had to put threats like that out of our minds.

Carlos Colón and I were working one night when someone threw a 10-inch knife into the ring. The point buried itself into the mat beside where we stood. We charged at each other and went down to the mat, each of us trying to get the bottom position underneath the other. We were giggling under our breath as we fought to use each other's body as a shield. The reality is that at times, "they" were trying to kill us. It was a sobering thought on which we tried to avoid focusing.

We saw guns and knives in the States, especially in Louisiana, but never in Japan. Luckily, nobody ever tried to cut me. I was shot at only one time, and that was in Lubbock, Texas.

On that occasion, I was supposed to meet Terry at his home in Canyon and ride with him to the Wednesday night matches in Lubbock. Terry had called earlier that day, telling me that the Odessa promoter, Pat O'Dowdy, had called the office. Apparently, a fan, who had been at the show the night before in Odessa, was mad about something I had done, and he was coming to Lubbock to shoot me. Terry thought it might be a good idea for me to ride with him.

As usual, Terry was running really late. That wasn't normally a problem for Terry because he was on the last match of the card, but I was in the opening match, so I had to be there on time. The standard rule was that we were expected to be at the venue at least an hour before the show began. Being the promoter's son, Terry could get away with being late, and he usually showed up when the first match was getting into the ring.

I wasn't very excited about going to Lubbock. I was still in my first year in the business and I had never been in a position where I had to deal with serious heat, and as I thought about my match the night before, I couldn't figure out what I had done to generate that kind of heat. I put the threat out of my mind, but Terry brought it up a few times during the trip. When I showed Terry a pistol I had brought along, his eyebrows raised and his eyes got a little bigger than normal, but he didn't comment.

As expected, we arrived late to the Lubbock County Fairgrounds Arena, but we were there in time for me to wrestle. As I ran into the dressing room, a couple of the guys who had stayed over in Odessa told me somebody had been looking for me at the Antlers Hotel, where some of the boys stayed. As I rushed to the ring, I turned my head from side to side, scanning the crowd. I was so relieved when nothing happened that I put it completely out of my mind.

Since Terry was on last, I had to wait around until the end of the show. In typical Terry Funk style, which he did really well, his match developed into a wild brawl which went on for what seemed like forever. Nick Roberts, the Lubbock promoter and father of Baby Doll [Nickla Roberts], liked to end the show by ten o'clock. On this night, however, Terry took a long time to shower after his match, and it was eleven before we were walking out to his car.

The parking lot for the Lubbock Fairgrounds Arena was huge. At that time of night, the nearest car in the lot was more than a hundred yards away. We got into Terry's Buick Riviera and drove towards the parking lot exit. About that time, a car about two hundred yards away started their engine and turned on their lights. As the car moved towards us, Terry and I both looked at each other. With a smile on my face, I said, "*Terry, I know this has got to be a rib, but I'm going to cock my gun and fire it.*" As I pulled it out, Terry muttered, "*I think someone's comin' to get you.*" I was almost laughing as I rolled down the window and pulled the gun out of my pocket. As we watched the car get closer, we saw a hand holding a gun stretch out one of the windows. Still smiling, I cocked my gun and aimed it at the car. Before I could fire, Terry grabbed my hand and moved it. While I was trying to react, I heard a shot, and a bullet smacked into the panel of Terry's car behind the rear wheel. The car sped off into the distance and disappeared.

Terry brought his car to a stop and we got out to inspect the car. Sure enough, there was a big dent where the bullet hit the car. I was laughing, but Terry tried to keep up the pretense. "*That guy was trying to kill you.*" By the time we got back into the car, he was smiling and laughing, but he continued to keep up the pretense of it being a real incident. As it turned out, the guy who shot at us was none other than Nick Roberts, the promoter. Those guys would go to any extreme to pull a rib.

I had heard of fans flattening the tires on the heels' cars, or using their keys to make deep scratches in the paintwork. I was concerned that it might happen to me, but I was lucky they never did. More than likely, they thought it wasn't worth the effort because I always drove an older car, like my Toyota Corolla or Ford van.

One of the worst arenas for fans getting out of control was the arena in downtown New Orleans. I also remember Holyoke, Massachusetts, as being pretty bad on a few occasions. Going to and from the ring, most of the

Louisiana territory was pretty dangerous, as were Greenwood and Greenville, Mississippi. I had a few scary moments at the old White House Hotel in downtown Baton Rouge, where we wrestled at the Convention Center.

For the most part, we accepted the risk. If the promoter was promoting us the way he should, then it *should* be somewhat dangerous. That's the one reason why I always thought the heels should get a few extra dollars, but that was the risk we took for being a bad guy.

The security details at the arenas were usually comprised of cops moonlighting for extra pay. They were just doing a job. Security in Puerto Rico was good. They were dressed in Army uniforms and were well-organized. The absolute best security forces were in New Orleans at the St. Bernard Parish building. I was so thankful to have them watching my back. There were some fanatical wrestling fans there whose idea of a fun evening on the town was to beat up somebody. I always treated the security people with respect. I went out of my way to be friendly with them and get to know them since they were so important to my well-being. Most of the time, their presence along kept trouble from happening, but that wasn't always the case.

Promoters would give us strict orders to keep our match in the ring. They didn't want us fighting outside the ring or using chairs because they were worried about lawsuits. Not every promoter held us to those guidelines. In the '70s and early '80s, people weren't sue-happy, so we could get away with carrying the action outside the ring, but by the late '80s, just about every promoter tried to enforce that rule. When I first got into wrestling, there wasn't a barrier of any kind around the ring, but as time went by, some kind of a barrier was found in most arenas. Most of the time, however, only a small chain or velvet rope separated the ringside seats from the ring.

Japan was a dream territory for heels. I could go out into the crowd and do just about anything I wanted to do. I threw chairs into the crowd, giving them enough elevation so the people could see them and move out of the way. Years later, Baba told me to stop throwing chairs either into or near the crowd. I made the mistake of doing it a few more times. One night, after I threw a chair in Kochi, a town on Shikoku Island, Baba loudly yelled down a corridor at me. I got the message. That was the only time he ever raised his voice or acted upset with me.

I made people panic by chasing them, causing them to run over each other in their effort to escape, but I did whatever I could do to avoid hurting anybody. When I saw people begin to pile up, I would change direction, allowing them to get up without worrying about me coming after them. However, if somebody made a stand and acted like they weren't going to move, then I would run right over them. The excitement my actions created was really unique. Most of the fans enjoyed getting close to the action, and it made them feel as if they were a part of the overall experience. Several of the guys tried to do what I did, but most of them found it too hard to run after the people. Frank (as Bruiser Brody), Tiger Jeet Singh, and Abdullah the Butcher also had success using that style. What separated me from them was that I could chase people for five minutes without stopping. That might not sound like a long time, but try moving through a crowd and changing directions, grabbing fans and whirling them around, and slinging chairs. That took a lot of gas [wind] and lung power. A few people tried to imitate me, but few of them could keep up with me. When I was young, I could go and go and go. It might sound like I'm bragging, but it's the truth. Singh, Butcher, and Brody all had a wild style of their own, and they were successful with it, but my constant movement inside and outside the ring was what separated me from them.

Frank and I were working a hot series of matches against Tom Jones and different partners in Baton Rouge. Tom was a black guy who was very popular with wrestling fans in the south. When I walked into the dressing room one night, I found three uniformed police officers and one plainclothes detective talking to Frank and Jimmy Killshaw. Killshaw, the promoter in Baton Rouge, was a retired deputy sheriff. It seemed an informant for the police had overheard a conversation by someone who said "he was going to shoot Stan Hansen to death in the ring that night." We heard threats like that quite often, but when a threat like that was made away from the arena, that was unusual. The police were taking it seriously and advised me not to wrestle, but told me it was my choice. I have to admit I was scared. There was real heat in my program with Tom, but I felt compelled to go on. I was working on top that night against Tom Jones in a single match and the house was sold out.

Tom Jones

After getting dressed, I said a prayer and went to the ring. There were about ten uniformed policemen in the building and ten undercover cops mingling with the crowd. The people yelled and jeered at me as I walked to the ring, and threw objects like soft drink cups and ice at me. None of that was unusual or out of the ordinary.

As soon as I got into the ring, I began to criss-cross, running from rope to rope. I kept in constant motion. I did that often just to loosen up, but on that night, I did it to give any possible assailant a target that would be hard to hit. When they announced Tom Jones, he ran to the ring and the people cheered. As soon as he entered the ring, I charged him and we began to wrestle. Tom was probably as scared as I was. Many times in the past, when wrestling fans took shots at the heels, they usually missed the heel, the object of their hatred. When that happened, the bullet either hit wrestling fans on the other side of the ring, or the babyface. Tom had heard those stories. As we grappled, he mumbled under his breath that if somebody took a shot, he hoped they were a good aim and hit me, not him. We both chuckled at his attempt to lighten the tension. The match ended in a hot finish with me being disqualified. While we were wrestling, the police had stood facing the crowd, never once turning to look at the ring. The house lights weren't turned off during our match, either. Normally, the only light left on was the light above the ring, but the police wanted the house lights to remain on so they could see the crowd more clearly.

I was so relieved when I got back to the dressing room. For all of my stress and fear, I was paid $110, which was a whopping $10 more than I made for the show the previous week. That was one of the few times in my career when I honestly questioned whether or not the money was worth it. That was the complaint most of the heels had about the business. We literally put our lives on the line, all so the promoters could make most of the money. Don't get me wrong. I'm not against the promoters making money. No, not at all, but wrestling was one of the few professional sports where the talent was paid little more than a living wage. That was one of the reasons why I chose Japan as my mainstay. Japan would guarantee us a specific amount of money. In the States, we were never quite sure what we were going to get. It was up to the sole discretion of the promoter to decide how much he would pay.

One night, Frank and I were leaving Jackson, Mississippi, after a show. We were crammed into Frank's 240Z. Frank was too big for the 240Z and he developed back problems, so that might have been the last time in his career that Frank drove. He learned it was cheaper and less hassle to just ride with somebody else and pay trans, so he sold the Z and never had a car on the road again. Can you imagine two 300-pound guys in a small, two-seat sports car? It was so tight in the front that our shoulders overlapped. Shortly after we left, a car full of rednecks pulled up behind us, honking their car horn and shouting obscenities. We were on a two-lane road, so when they pulled up beside us, we assumed they were going to pass us. Instead, they held steady alongside us while someone rolled down their window and pointed a gun at us. Frank braked hard and they shot out in front of us. As we slowed, we both pulled out our pistols, rolled down our windows, and Frank hit the gas. When we were alongside them, we stuck our guns out the window and fired two or three shots apiece over the roof of their car and into the air. The driver slammed on his brakes and skidded to a stop. He turned around and sped off in the other direction. Frank and I put our guns away and continued with our journey, as if nothing untoward had happened.

Another incident occurred when I was wrestling in Monroe, Louisiana. When Grizzly Smith and I took our match out onto the arena floor, a fan tried to kick me in the groin. He missed, and in the process, he slipped and fell to the ground. By instinct (and the desire to protect myself), I turned and football punted him in the face. While Grizzly and I continued our match, somebody called for an ambulance, which arrived before we finished. After the match, I had to walk close to the ambulance to get to the dressing room. The guy was on a stretcher and being carried out the back door, while the police were holding the people back. While that was going on, a woman ran out of the crowd. Just as I spotted her, a policeman caught her arm and raised it up into the air. She was holding a gun, and her objective had been to use it on me. I continued into the dressing room, packed my stuff, and left.

A few weeks later, I was back in Monroe. I figured the promotion knew I had been involved in an altercation with a fan. In a case of bad judgment, the promoter put me on last, rather than putting me on early so I could leave with no problem. By the time I got to the dressing room, everybody was gone. After showering, I left the almost empty building. Nobody was in the parking lot and all the other wrestlers had gone. As I was walking towards my car, I heard the engine of another car fire into life. It was all the way on the other side of the large parking lot and it began to roll towards me. I was wearing a long, western duster, a type of trench coat, and held my wrestling bag in my left hand. As the car slowly drove up, I reached into my right coat pocket and cocked my gun. I didn't say anything, but I kept a close eye on the car as it drove by. Somebody yelled, "*I'm going to kill you!*" I just held my ground and kept the gun, still hidden in my pocket, pointed at them. I was thinking that if they shot at me, I would at least get one return shot off at them. However, they continued driving and it ended there. That was pretty scary, especially when I realize I could have panicked and pulled the trigger. That action could have changed my life. I might have found myself in serious trouble, and possibly have served time in prison. I later made the decision to not carry a gun. It was just too dangerous. A few years later, in 1976, I carried a gun while I was working in New York. When a state policeman stopped Frank and I in my van, I had a gun in the back under the mattress. At the time, carrying a firearm in New York and New Jersey was an automatic one-year sentence. That scared me, so shortly after that, I quit carrying one.

The promoter in Monroe was Larry Tillman. One night, Larry ran a spot show in an old, high-school gym in Arkadelphia, Arkansas. The show was a disaster. There were probably less than one hundred people there. There was so few people that only two or three people sat in the front row of ringside. Earlier that evening, Buck Robley saw a big baboon on a leash, running up and down a handrail which ran along the front of the bleachers. It was one of those that had a huge, red rear-end. Buck and I were working against Argentina Zuma [Manuel Chaij] and someone else. At one time, Zuma had been a big card. At this stage of his career, he was completely bald and wore a huge afro wig to the ring. Buck and I went to the ring first, and then Zuma and his partner came out. Zuma went over to the baboon and acted like a wild man, mimicking the sounds of a monkey. Buck and I jumped out of the ring and went after him. We fought throughout the entire building, knocking over every chair that had been set up. Of course, most of them were empty. By the time we finished, the place looked like a tornado had torn through it.

After the show, we asked Larry Tillman about the baboon. He told us the guy who owned it had wanted to bring it in. Larry said, "*I told the guy that if he wanted to bring in the baboon, he would have to buy a ticket for it. He didn't hesitate and handed me the money.*" Larry Tillman is probably the only wrestling promoter to sell a ticket to a baboon. We thought that was funny. Larry also told us that Arkadelphia had never been the same since Ox Baker had killed it five years earlier. When I asked him what Ox did, he said, "*Nothing. It was just his work in the ring.*" To this day, whenever I see Ox, I always remind him of that.

The purpose of a heel was to make the people mad enough that they would buy a ticket to see him get beat. However, a good heel could work the people into a frenzy, and get them so angry that they would come to the ring to take on the heel. It's also the heel's job to keep the heat as long as possible. At times, it was hard to do that, because the heel had to deal with the babyface's ego, and the direction in which the promoter wanted to go.

That was the crux of what Frank and I learned in Louisiana. We had both been in the business for almost two full years, but we still had a lot to learn. We were willing to go out and do what we could to get over and learn. Most of the other wrestlers were supportive and willing to help teach us, but others weren't. Pro wrestling is an "every man for himself" business. There is a lot of competition for just a few top spots. Most of the new, young talent doesn't have a real chance of making it to the top, but given an opportunity, they could do it. The problem is, and was, getting that opportunity. The boys who were already on top were often reluctant to help newcomers because they were afraid of losing their own spot. That's why Frank and I had such a soft spot in our hearts for Grizzly Smith. He gave us our first opportunity to work our way to the top. Note that I didn't say he "put us on top." He started us on the bottom, and gave us the "opportunity" to work our way to the top, which is what we did. In the process, we proved we could draw money in that position. I believe Grizzly liked us because we were big. Grizzly was big, too. In fact, he was much bigger than either Frank or me.

I always tried to be serious during my matches, but there were a few occasions when I had to laugh over something my opponent did, or even something I did. When that happened, I would stretch out my face in a horrid grimace to cover up. That didn't happen often, but it did occasionally. One time, I was working against Grizzly in Loranger, Louisiana. We fought outside the ring and into the concession stand. I pushed his head under the beer tap and turned it on. He lost all pretense of being in a serious contest and laughed out loud. I'm sure I was laughing on the inside, but I didn't want the fans to think we weren't serious about what we were doing, so I maintained a staid front. I remember how mad I was when he got to the back for not grabbing me and returning the favor.

Things changed when Bill Watts returned as the booker. As Cowboy Bill Watts, he had been a big drawing card in New York and in the south, including his own territory. When Frank and I began our run in Louisiana, Watts was in Florida, learning the booking end of the business from Eddie Graham. From our point of view, he also learned how to treat the boys in a way in which he wouldn't want to be treated, and in my opinion, he paid them in a way that was highly in favor of the office. He had one of the better wrestling minds, but he treated most of the boys as inferior to himself. When he came back to Oklahoma, he bought the territory from LeRoy McGuirk, and brought in his own crew of talent. It wasn't unusual for a new owner or booker to do that, and Watts did bring in good talent like Dickie Murdoch, Killer Karl Kox, and the Spoiler. However, with Watts booking himself as the new top babyface, and Kox, Murdoch, and Spoiler getting the push as the heels, Frank and I were slowly edged out of the main programs. Grizzly was demoted to assistant booker and left with little power and no real influence as to what was going on.

The one thing that should have been a positive about the new direction was that Watts did a good job promoting his ideas and talent. Business began to increase and the towns began to draw. Frank and I were still used on top during this time, but only in the secondary towns up north where the payoffs were smaller. The hot angles were all done with the new group of talent and in the big (money) towns. Because of that, we were only making $300 to $350 a week, driving 3,500 miles, and starving. We should have been making more money just due to the fact that the gates were up. That wasn't the case, however. We made no more money in the spots we were in than we did when we were in those same positions months before, and the towns were drawing much more money now than they had been then. It was a tough pill to swallow and hard work, but Frank and I looked at it as a learning experience that, hopefully, would pay off in the future.

That ended when Watts decided to split up Frank and me. He said it was the best for us. We disagreed, but we continued to work for him as singles. It's been more than 30 years since that happened, and looking back on it, perhaps Watts did the right thing. Frank and I enjoyed working as a tag team, but we had a lot of growing to do. We had reached a point where we had become complacent in our matches. We were no longer trying new things. We also needed to work on character development, and that was something we each had to do alone. Not only that, but Frank was riding and running with Buck Robley. Most of the time, we were still booked in the same towns, but in an effort to save money, I was traveling on my own and sleeping in my van. Frank and Buck were both single at the time, so they saved money by staying with different girls around the territory, or by heeling a room in a cheap motel. Frank and Buck became good friends and did business together in the States for a long time. Frank even got Buck booked in Japan for Baba. Robley influenced Frank a lot, and in my opinion, not in the best way. He was a good talent, but he had some bad habits, as I must say applied to all of us.

The fun of wrestling slowly diminished as the travel became the job. The trips were long and brutal, and the road expenses ate deeply into our payoffs, even though I got good gas mileage in my Toyota Corolla. Most of the time, I was on the main event, so I would be one of the last to leave the arenas. I would get home at three or four in the morning, and then have to leave at noon the next day. However, unless I was working on top and got the bigger payoffs, it was hard to see much of a profit at the end of the day. In retrospect, the small payoffs were an expected part of the Oklahoma-Louisiana territory. I did make a little money when I returned to Mississippi in 1977, and Watts treated me as well as could be expected, but the two trips to New Japan before, and after, my six-month run was what allowed me to make a profit. The guarantee I got in Japan was the main reason I went in that direction. I knew exactly how much money I was going to make. That allowed me to set a budget. I knew how much I was going to pay in taxes, and how much I would bring home. That was so much better than driving thousands of miles and not knowing what I was going to make. Not only that, but whenever we worked a show, we had to wait two weeks to get paid.

After several months of working hard for little money, word filtered back to Frank and I that Watts and his clique had been overheard making negative comments about us. One that really hit hard came from Watts, who said, "*I got those big, dumb, goofs running around up there in the small towns.*" Everybody laughed out loud when he said it. Of course, even though he was an insufferable a—hole, Watts was the boss, and everybody laughed because they all wanted to keep their jobs. Looking back on the incident, I think they were just ribbing, but since we weren't there when Bill made the statement, we took it seriously and were hurt. For him to make light of the fact that we were driving thousands of miles and sleeping in my van for very little money, and he was making a lot of money, that was a pretty low-class thing to say. That really hurt us and made us even more determined to break away and make it on our own. It had more of an effect on Frank than it did on me. For everybody who wonders where Frank got his attitude, that specific incident was "the" cornerstone of his personality development. From that day forward, Frank looked at the promoters as "the enemy." He held fast to that point of view every time he conducted business. If he had the opportunity, he would even try to double-cross them. I can't begin to count the number of times he said; "*They're all lying to us, so I'll lie back to them,*" "*I don't trust them,*" and "*I'm out for myself.*" Regardless of what the promoters paid him, Frank always felt like they were trying to screw him.

Frank followed that philosophy for the rest of his life, and he was very successful in doing so, but he burned a number of bridges along the way. Whenever I would mention that, he would tell me, *"If you've got talent, they'll build another bridge for you."* As he was such a good and unique talent, promoters were forced to do business with him whether they liked him or not. The fact that Watts thought it was so funny that he was sending us to the little towns had a major effect on Frank, and he was never able to put it to rest.

I had bad feelings towards Watts for a long time, too, and I developed somewhat of the same reputation for being an outlaw that Frank did, but I didn't do it for personal reasons. I did it because it was something I had to do to move ahead. At the very least, if I wasn't going to be paid what I considered to be a decent wage, I should be treated with respect as a talent who was working hard to draw money. On the other hand, I didn't hate, or spend time trying to outthink, outmaneuver, or throw curves at the promoters. They had every right to make a good return on their investments, but I should get my fair share, too.

Years later, after I had established myself as a top talent in other territories, I returned to work for Watts and he treated me well. The experience made me realize that a person can do business with somebody they might not have had a good experience with in the past.

The one positive thing to come from that incident was that I developed an attitude of my own. I promised myself I would never treat young talent as if they were beneath me. That attitude stemmed not only from the incident with Watts, but by the way Murdoch treated me in Amarillo. I vowed to treat young talent as I had wanted to be treated when I was green. Most of the guys went the other way. Frank often made the comment, *"I'm not helpin' no one. You never know when someone'll take your job."* I was always ready to help a new guy, and I never worried about losing out to somebody new. I replaced a number of veterans who had time on me, and I knew it could and would happen to me, but I didn't take that personally. Frank did. That was *the* major difference between the two of us.

Shortly after Watts split us up, I jumped off the top rope and tore some cartilage in my left knee. I could barely walk, so I gave my notice and went home to Texas for knee surgery. I hated to leave the territory like that, but I needed the operation and the time was right to leave. A confrontation with Watts and the other top boys was building, and I wanted to avoid that. I had learned a lot during the time I was there, but it was time to move on. Unfortunately, I had to use my meager savings for living expenses while I recovered from my operation. That was proof, however, that I had been correct when I made the decision to save as much money as I could.

After a two-month recovery, Dory Funk Jr. booked me in Japan for All Japan Pro Wrestling in the fall of 1975. As before, I was glad to be going somewhere new, and Japan was an opportunity to recover some of the money I had lost while I had been on the sidelines.

Chapter 9

Land of the Rising Sun

In October 1975, I was booked on a five-week tour of Japan. My knee was feeling fine and I was excited to be going to a foreign country. I was even more excited to be getting $1,000 a week. When you're used to making $300 a week, $1,000 a week was big money. I would finally have an opportunity to save some money and get ahead.

I arrived at Haneda Airport (also known as Tokyo International Airport) in Tokyo with Bobby Jaggers, Ox Baker, Prince Pullins, and Larry Zbyszko. Abdullah the Butcher had arrived a day or two earlier. I hung out with Jaggers and Zbyszko. We were the three green guys, each on our first tour of Japan. The Butcher spent time with Prince Pullins, but for the most part, he kept to himself. He had lots of sponsors, so he went out and did his own thing. Nobody, bar none, worked Japan outside the wrestling business better than the Butcher.

"Sponsors" were one of the great things about Japan. Sponsors were people who would take us out once in awhile and treat us to dinner at the small Japanese-style restaurants and nightclubs. They were always eager to show us a good time. Others were promoters of the shows, who enjoyed taking us out and showing us off to the public. Most, however, were just common salary men (Japanese term for a typical office worker) who enjoyed having us share their table. They might also have been on an expense account. Often, the upper bosses would take out co-workers who worked under him in the hierarchy of the company.

There were numerous times when we suspected that certain people were members of the Japanese underworld, also known as the Yakuza. They never came across in any way but respectful and honestly seemed to enjoy taking us to their favorite establishments. The places ranged from elaborate discos to small clubs that only held five to seven people. We weren't quite sure as to the amount of the tab the sponsors paid, but everything in the clubs had a price, and those prices weren't cheap. Everything in Japan is expensive. A beer cost six to ten dollars and the price went up with other drinks. Food prices could be off the charts. So, often, sponsors offered to take us out and show us a good time. They would pick up the tab for our food and drinks, and on occasion, give us a contribution of cash for pictures and autographs. We were there to make and take home as much money as we could, so any help with our expenses was really appreciated. However, I never went looking for sponsors like some of the guys did, or set out to milk them out of money. If a sponsor offered money to me, I would accept. When I was with Brody, I learned that if I was friendly and gave the sponsor a small gift, or showed them some kindness, then it would be returned one-hundred fold. I never sent a gift to a sponsor, although on occasion, I would do the custom of pouring the first beer, or sending a few beers to a table. No matter what I did, I always got it back ten-fold. That was the Japanese custom.

I can remember my first taxi ride from the airport to the Ginza; the main shopping and commercial district in Tokyo. As a kid, I used to watch a lot of the Japanese movies which featured monsters like Godzilla and Mothra. In those movies, the monsters always demolished the buildings in downtown Tokyo. The square buildings located along the freeway near Haneda Airport looked exactly like the fake buildings I had seen in the Godzilla movies. It left quite an impression on me. To this day, whenever I land in Tokyo, I think about that first tour and how everything looked. Of course, things have changed so much since then. Japan is now one of the most modern countries in the world and they boast some of the most unique and advanced-style skyscrapers in the world.

If there was ever a great ambassador for Japan, it is Joe Higuchi [Kanji Higuchi]. When I say that, I don't just mean as an ambassador for All Japan Pro Wrestling. I mean for the whole country. Known to everyone as Joe-san, he has been a great influence on so many gaijins over the years. There is no wrestler in Japan who did not respect and appreciate him. I never knew or heard a wrestler make one negative comment about him. Of all the people in the business I have met over the years, Joe-san and Baba-san are the only two who can make that claim. Even the wrestlers at New Japan knew Joe-san, and to the American boys, he was a legend.

Joe Higuchi

Joe-san trained in Judo when he was just a child and learned the English language after World War II while training American service men in judo. He has been around pro wrestling since 1954 and was trained by Paul Romero and Tojo Yamamoto [Harold Watanabe]. In 1963, he joined Nippon (Japan) Pro Wrestling as an interpreter for gaijin wrestlers, and in 1965, he began refereeing. When Baba formed All Japan Pro Wrestling in 1972, Joe-san went to work for him. Joe-san is the only Japanese referee to referee an NWA world heavyweight title match in the United States, which was a match between Jack Brisco and Dory Funk Jr. at the St. Louis Kiel Auditorium in 1975.

The only time I heard Joe-san complain about anything was when he talked about being tired of taking the heat for heels who didn't know how to get heat on themselves. The wrestling office frowned on heels who tried to get cheap heat by pulling hair or trunks, or switching the heat to the referees by hiding illegal moves from them. The referee will always take a certain amount of heat, but when too much of it is directed at them, the heel doesn't get over as strongly as he should.

Joe-san once told me a story about a time in November 1982 when Victor Rivera was on tour with Brody and Jimmy Snuka. Like most of the wrestlers, Victor was a nice guy, but when he drank too much, he turned mean. They were staying at a hotel in Tokyo and some bad feelings developed between Snuka and Rivera. Their hostilities built up over time and came to a head one night as Brody and Snuka came into the hotel. Rivera had been drinking and he was in the hallway of the hotel. They exchanged words and a fight broke out with Snuka getting the best of Rivera. Rivera would give up, but when Snuka let him go, he would come back at him. Each time, Snuka would beat Rivera into submission. However, the alcohol clouded Rivera's common sense and he continued to return for more punishment. Snuka finally took Rivera down and began pounding his head against the floor.

When Joe-san heard the commotion, he came out into the hallway. Snuka was letting Rivera get to his feet and was trying to convince him to stop fighting. Rivera refused to listen and once again attacked Snuka. Before he could reach him, however, Joe-san stepped in and slapped Rivera across the face three or four times with his open hand, and then dragged him down the hallway and threw him into his room. He said, "*Don't you ever come to my country and act like a fool again.*" Joe's words must have penetrated Rivera's drunken haze because he never came back again.

Another time (Brody told me this story), there was trouble between Brody and Snuka on the street outside Ribera's Steakhouse. They had been drinking in separate establishments. Jimmy was walking by and saw Brody. I don't know what set Jimmy off, but it was around the time when All Japan brought me in as Frank's partner. We thought Jimmy might have been upset over the fact that he had been left out in the cold. Whatever it was, Jimmy wasn't happy. There were a few blows exchanged and the police were called. Frank took the heat because Jimmy was pretty much out of it and could have had a bad run-in with the police. Joe-san was called and Brody was saved by Joe-san, who helped smooth things over.

Joe-san stepped in so many times to help gaijins who had gotten themselves into trouble. I phrase it that way because most of the time, the gaijins were at fault. There were times when trouble just seemed to find us, but most of the time, it was our fault. I can't think of one gaijin who didn't get some kind of help from Joe-san in situations like the ones described above, including me.

Joe-san also was a strong, tough guy. Everyone respected him. However, you would have to grab hold of him to realize just how strong he was. He was notorious for being almost unmovable in the ring. Often, during our matches, we try to move the referee out of the way. Well, you couldn't move Joe-san. He had spent many years studying judo and trained daily, keeping himself in shape for years longer than almost anyone else. He was a man to respect. All of us, even the younger Japanese wrestlers, thought he was amazing.

Joe-san also acted as a liaison between the office and the wrestlers. He was trusted and carried information between the gaijins and the office all the time. We knew that if we had a complaint, or needed to know something, then Joe-san was the man to deliver a message or get the information we needed. He also smoothed over many hard feelings which naturally develop between talent and the office. I'm sure he also smoothed things over with the office on our account when we messed up or did something wrong. And yet, even though he worked closely with the office, there was one thing he wasn't. He never was a stooge. Year after year, he did his job silently and properly. He was one of the most stable things about the All Japan company.

More importantly, he was a gentleman, and a one-of-a-kind person who I grew to love and respect so much. During the many tours I made of Japan, it was my pleasure to be around such a nice, straight man. I am sad to know that he has retired. He loved the wrestling business so much, but I know he is going to enjoy being off the road.

Joe Higuchi retired as a referee after refereeing the Triple Crown heavyweight title match between Steve Williams and Mitsuharu Misawa at the Budokan on March 1, 1997. During his 32 years as a referee, it is estimated that he officiated more than 20,000 matches. After his retirement, he continued to ride on the bus and help make things easy for the gaijin talent who came to All Japan. He is still active in the business today as the acting president of Pro Wrestling NOAH.

I miss being with him on the bus. I used to kid Joe-san that as long as he and the Butcher were on the tours, I would never be the oldest guy on the bus. When Abdullah left All Japan in 1981, it left Joe-san and me. When Joe-san retired in 1997, I was finally the oldest guy on the bus.

When we traveled, we had no idea where we were going, and at times, we weren't even sure how to navigate to or through an airport or train station. What we *all* knew, however, was the saying, "*Follow the bald head and you'll never get lost.*" Of course, the "bald head" was Joe-san. During my last months with the company, I really missed seeing the "bald head" on the bus, and the bus seemed empty.

Personally, throughout my career, Joe-san was a great influence on me. I love and respect him so much. He was like a father to me, and he is still a trusted, close friend. I know he will be embarrassed to hear me say these things about him, but we are all so proud of knowing him. To the public, he is not as well known as the talent who appeared in the ring and on television, but he is truly a Japanese living legend.

Baba passing away and Joe Higuchi retiring are the two things which changed the face of wrestling in Japan, and it hasn't been a change for the good.

Joe-san passed away on November 8, 2010 at the age of 81. I always remember his age because he was 20 years older than me. I talked to his wife and son after his passing and we all felt a real loss. To me, Joe-san represented all the best of Japan. He was a gentleman and he had a lot of class as a person. It was just a pleasure to know him.

I can't imagine Japan without Joe-san. For decades, he was one of the most stable things in the country for all the gaijins who came to Japan, and he was never anything but a gentleman to all of us. He was always seeking to make life easier for wrestlers in a foreign land where food, accommodations, and other things were very strange to us. Many times, he was forced to smooth over problems caused by gaijins who got into trouble. At other times, he had to get up in the middle of the night to sort out their problems. He did that time and time again and was always on the front line. I think All Japan was very fortunate to have had him as their representative for so many years. He kept us all in line and gave us great advice and discipline.

When we arrived in Japan for my first tour, Joe-san took us directly to our hotel. I never went to the wrestling office until years later. At the time, the boys weren't really welcome at the office. If there was business to be done, it was done at the hotels. While at the hotel, we met Yoshi [Yoshihiro Momota], the eldest son of Rikidôzan [Mitsuhiro Momota], who established Japan's first professional wrestling promotion, Japan Pro Wrestling Association [JWA], in 1953. He is remembered by Japanese wrestling fans as "The Father of Puroresu." Puroresu means Japanese pro wrestling.

Yoshi was just starting to work himself. On October 21, 1972, he got his start in the wrestling business as the ring announcer for Baba. He trained with wrestlers every day and made his debut in the States in 1978, wrestling in the Amarillo and Kansas City territories as Yoshi Momota. He returned to Japan in the summer of 1979 and wrestled until 1984, at which time he took a position in the office. Yoshi and his younger brother, Mitsuo, inherited a percentage of the business from their dad, so they were involved in a lot of the business of All Japan.

In 1975, Giant Baba and Jumbo Tsuruta were the top single wrestlers, while Motoshi Okuma and Shinya Kojika were the top tag team. Abdullah was the top gaijin. Nobody else came close to him in popularity. He had his own style, which was wild violence, but he could move quickly. The wrestling fans respected him and his fellow wrestlers supported him.

I wound up in a tag-team combination with Bobby Jaggers, who I had known in Amarillo and Louisiana. He was a good worker and we had been in the business about the same amount of time. Bobby had a knack for talking on interviews, producing in the ring, and he became one of the great psychologists in the wrestling business. He had his own style and has been overlooked as being one of wrestling's better workers. Danny Kroffat [Philip Lafond], who wrestled with Doug Furnas in Japan as the tag team known as the "Can-Am Express," speaks highly of Jaggers. He said when he tagged up with Jaggers in the States, Bobby taught him a great deal of ring savvy. I agreed with him because it showed in Dan's ability in the ring.

Bobby Jaggers

On this tour, we spent a great deal of time trying to figure out the Japanese style of wrestling and determine what we should be doing. One of the first things we were told was "there is no noise," which meant the audience didn't make noise. In America, the audience was never quiet. They were always cheering, booing, yelling, or screaming. If it was anything close to quiet in an American arena, then you can bet you weren't doing your job. We were told not to worry if the Japanese people didn't react to things we did.

For the first week or so, it was really strange, because when Jaggers or I would grunt, we could hear it echo through the arena. In an attempt to rile up the audience and get some feedback, Jaggers yelled at the people at ringside. He didn't get a response, whatsoever. He just got blank, seemingly uncomprehending, stares. "*That's out,*" he muttered to me. It was so very different from the States, and it took a long time before we got used to it. Of course, by the early '80s, that began to change and the crowds became a little more vocal. Today, there is a lot of noise, and the audience reacts much like they do here in the States.

Another thing I learned on that tour is that there are differences in position. It was obvious that Abdullah was the top gaijin, but I wasn't aware that some people got better deals than others. The office took good care of him. He had a bigger hotel room than the rest of us, and, of course, more money. Other than that, things were fairly equal. Most of the guys looked at it as the office playing favorites, but to me, it was an incentive to work harder and get to a better position. Later, when I was in negotiations with New Japan, and even later, when Baba and I made our deal in Dallas (both of which I'll talk about in a later chapter), I knew I had to ask for what I wanted. If we didn't ask, and changed our mind later, it almost was impossible to get them to make a change from what we had agreed to.

For instance, the first time I went to Japan, the office flew us economy class (also known as coach) and we had a stopover in Honolulu, Hawaii. That made for a long trip. However, in 1977, when I made my second tour (that time for New Japan Pro Wrestling), I flew business class on a direct flight. That's what the boys all wanted. I later negotiated a deal with New Japan to fly first class. Eventually, when I was working for All Japan, I asked for first class transportation to and from Japan, as well as a bigger room. It cost a great deal more and was an added expense to the wrestling office, but they must have felt I was worth it because Baba honored that agreement for the entire time he and Mrs. Baba were in charge of the company. When Mrs. Baba sold the company and the new regime took over, I began to fly business class once again. The wrestling business in Japan was facing hard times, and the office didn't want that expense. However, business class is good enough. I enjoyed first class because it made the long trip so much more comfortable, but it was a luxury I could live without.

I got some heat from the other guys when they learned I had a bigger room and was flying first class. I heard several of them grumbling about it not being fair. Business isn't about being fair. It's about business. That was the deal I negotiated with Inoki and Baba for myself. A few of the other guys, like Brody, Terry Gordy, and Steve Williams, made themselves the same deal. When I went to Japan in 1975, I remember Abdullah going first class, but I didn't resent him for it. It just made me think that if I worked hard enough, I might be able to get the same deal someday. Everybody had the opportunity to make their own deal. If they tried, and didn't get it, then the office didn't feel they were worth the price of what they asked. On the other hand, just because somebody gets a better deal doesn't mean they're better than anybody else. It just means there are different positions in life. Work hard and make the best deal for yourself that you can, and don't knock somebody for having a better deal than you were able to get. That's not business. That's jealousy.

I also learned that even though Zbyszko, Jaggers, and I all had about the same experience, our pay was different. Jaggers and I were booked through the Funks, so we received the same amount. Zbyszko was booked through Bruno Sammartino, and Bruno got Larry more money. It wasn't a lot. I think it was in the neighborhood of a couple of hundred a week, but that was big money to me.

It made me realize that I needed to learn the art of negotiating my own deal. Once I learned and began doing that for myself, I kept my business to myself and never talked money to others. Even when I booked new, young talent for Baba years later, I never talked about the money part of it. That just wasn't my deal. I heard that some of the top guys who booked talent would take a percentage of the young guy's money. I didn't think that was the correct thing to do at all. I never forgot how it felt to be paid less than what I had been promised. A hundred dollars is a lot of money to some people, especially the young guys, and the top guys were already getting a good deal from Japan.

On my first tour, Jumbo Tsuruta was getting a big push. I didn't work with him too often because I was way down on the card. Most of the time, he worked with Abdullah or Prince Pullins, or against both when he teamed up with Baba.

At that time, the Japanese and gaijins rode on the same bus. It felt really strange to pull up in front of an arena and all get off of the same bus. In America, babyfaces and heels would *never* (well, almost never) be seen riding together, but that's the way it was back then.

We worked a lot of outdoor shows during that time. The wrestlers were really some of the first gaijins to travel and tour the country. We stayed in some small towns in which very few gaijins had ever stepped foot.

The weather wasn't that bad, but it amazed me to see people sitting on bamboo mats. Even when it rained, they sat on those mats. After the ring was set up, we would make our way to the ring, have our match, and walk back. Everybody was so calm and polite. When we made a good move in the ring, they would clap, even though we were considered to be "bad guys." It was a great experience. The fact that the people were so polite was one of the biggest impressions left on me from that first tour. Unfortunately, those days are gone, and that's sad. Politeness is breaking down in Japan, primarily with the younger generation. It is a different country than it was 36 years ago and Japanese society has changed, but then again, America has also changed during that time period, and in many respects, it has changed for the worst.

There was another big difference in the mindset between the American and Japanese styles of wrestling. Heels were not always heels, and babyfaces were not always babyfaces. An American wrestler who was a really strong babyface in the States might be a heel when he worked in Japan against Japanese opponents. Dory and Terry Funk were good examples of that. However, over time, the people began to cheer them and they switched roles. At his peak, Terry was probably over as a babyface as much as any Japanese.

There also wasn't any set rule about who set the direction of a match in Japan. In the U.S., those calls were normally made by the heel. In Japan, Baba-san was the boss, but as a heel, I still led, although he had the option (as the company owner) to make changes and do things in a match as he saw fit. For the majority of our time, however, Brody and I never gave any thought about who was supposed to make those calls. We simply acted and reacted throughout our matches.

During my career, I worked as both a heel and a babyface, but I preferred being a heel. It was more suited to my personality and style. In my opinion, being a babyface was a lot easier in some ways, but they both had their positives and negatives. As a babyface, you could interact with the people more and you didn't have to worry about the marks. I don't mean to disparage the effort it took to be a babyface, but I think it was harder to be a heel. You had to work harder to get the match over, and you had to work hard to keep the heat. It also was hard at times to deal with some of the babyfaces whose egos would sometimes get out of control. I think it was easy for them to succumb to the cheering and accolades of the crowd. Too often, the babyfaces would let their egos get out of control. They took themselves too seriously. Most of the time, if a match was drawing, it was due to the heat on the heel.

When I was a babyface in Atlanta, I saw some of the babyfaces take advantage of and disrespect the fans. I watched a number of them take the small gifts that some of the blue-collar fans would give to them — small gold chains, T-shirts, things they made — all wrapped up nicely most of the time. They would rip open the package and berate the giver if it was cheap or not of quality. They would come into the dressing room, throw the gifts into the garbage can, and make snide comments about the person who gave it to them. The heels didn't have that problem because we didn't mingle with the fans too much. Whenever we did, we were wary of anything we were given, and we *never* ate food given to us because we were never sure what they might have put into it.

Freddie Blassie did a great job of describing the difference between working as a babyface and as a heel when told me, "*Kid, I worked for thirty years. I was a heel for the first fifteen, and all I did was slowly back away from my opponent with my hands out in front of me, begging him to back off. I spent the next fifteen as a babyface, and all I did was the slow walk forward, no matter what my opponent did to me.*" Wow! I thought that was right on the money. That was the simplest and best description of the psychology of wrestling during his time in the business, all summed up in a nutshell. As a heel, you were sneaky, and sometimes acted like you were scared of your opponent. You backed up and did something cheap to get the heat. As a babyface, you never backed up, regardless of what the heel did to you. Freddie was something.

During my first run in Atlanta, Georgia, which began in October 1977, I wrestled as a heel. At the end of May 1978, I turned babyface against Abdullah the Butcher. I had a good time with Tommy Rich as my partner. We were somewhat of a beauty-and-the-beast type of team. Tommy was a good worker and we had a successful run together. Four months later [September 1978], I turned back heel and tagged with Ole Anderson, only to turn babyface again six months later [March 1979], taking on various partners to wrestle against Ole and Ivan Koloff. It was harder to turn the second time. When you do it too often, you end up toying with the emotions of the people. They weren't dumb, but they were very loyal to us, just as they could get angry with us when we heeled. Each time you turn, it becomes harder for the people to open up and give you their emotions. Ole and Ivan were a great team and both of them were top-notch workers. I really enjoyed that time of my career as the four of us were drawing money together, but I felt more natural as a heel. When I returned to Atlanta in February 1982, I was a heel again, only to turn babyface one more time by the end of the year.

Are you confused? I was.

I once learned a great lesson about signing autographs. For the most part, as a heel, I just didn't do it. I was watching the matches from the stage at the Atlanta Auditorium one night. A boy who was about twelve years old came over and asked me for an autograph. I ignored his first few requests, but he was persistent. He kept asking. I told him "no" a number of times. But in a little while, he would come back. "*I'm your biggest fan. My grandfather loves you. Would you please, please give me you autograph?*" Once again, I turned him down. A few minutes later, he came up and said, "*Mr. Hansen. Please sign this for me. You're my all-time favorite. Please, please.*" He finally got to me. I looked around, but I didn't see Ole (who would have lambasted me for doing it), or anyone else for that matter, so I took the piece of paper and pen. I quickly signed my name and handed it back to him. He held it out in front of himself and looked at it ... and then tore it into little pieces. He almost was yelling as he said, "*I hate you, you sorry #@$%^#$.*"

I almost fell over from laughing so hard. I mean, the energy that kid expended to get me to sign it. Wow! I was impressed. That kid stayed with the program for fifteen to twenty minutes, and when he finally got it, he showed me what he had been planning all along. I thought that was great. That kid is probably the governor of the state now. Of course, I learned not to sign any more autographs.

One of the things which shocked me in Japan was to see men and women in the same restrooms. Jaggers and Zbyszko couldn't believe it, either. It freaked us out. That would never happen in America, but in Japan, it was common.

During the tour, we were able to watch the great boxing match between Muhammad Ali and Joe Frazier, which was broadcast live on Japanese television from the Philippines. We were in a small town in the mountains and we all gathered around noon in a large, tatami-style room to watch the fight. A "tatami" is a straw mat, usually about 2½ ft. by 4 ft. In a "tatami room," the floor is nothing but the straw mats. When you sleep, you sleep flat on the floor. As an example of how apartments and houses are measured, they might be described as a "five tatami room," which means the size of the room is the same as having five mats. It is used in the same way that we use "square feet."

If there is such a thing as a stereotype of what a heel looks like, that person is Ox Baker. Ox was a character, and from what I've seen and heard, he still is. He was what everyone thinks a heel should look like: bald-headed, with thick, bushy eyebrows that turned upwards at the ends, giving him a menacing, almost satanic, look. He was big and hairy, and he talked loud and gruffly. He looked so much the part of the evil heel. His personality and ring presence made him a formidable opponent, but once you got past his look, he was just an average worker. His knees were shot and he couldn't move very well. He also was pretty clumsy, so much so that the Japanese didn't like working with him too often because he couldn't do much inside the ring.

Behind the scenes, he was a nice guy, but for some reason, he didn't get along with most of the boys. I got along with him well. In fact, he taught me a few things about being a heel both inside and outside the ring. While we were there, we had lots of time to talk.

The Bad Man from Borger, Texas

One of the things we talked about was the fact that I was going to wrestle in Dallas when the Japan tour was over. I also was looking for a gimmick which fit me and my style. I had already adopted the "cowboy" gimmick in Louisiana, but I wanted something that stood out. Between the two of us, Ox and I came up with the name "Bad Man." In Amarillo, a man named Richard Oliver, who made custom saddles, made chaps for the Funks and Murdoch. I had Richard make me chaps with skulls on the side, and then added the name "Bad Man" to the back of my vest. Later, I lengthened it to "The Bad Man from Borger, Texas." I chose Borger because it was in Texas and close in proximity to Amarillo. I thought about using Knox City, my real hometown, but Knox City didn't sound bad enough. Borger had that rough edge to it.

Ox used to joke around with the people in the hotels. He looked so wild and different that he always stood out. He would talk loud, until everyone in the lobby would notice him. He played to that all the time. One day, he was talking and kidding around with a group of mama-sans who were cleaning the rooms at the hotel. Ox was talking loudly to them in English, as if they could understand better if he spoke loudly. He smiled at them as he talked, and they smiled back and laughed, not understanding a single word he said.

Ox got our attention and, using pantomime, asked one of the girls how the Japanese bowed. The little old ladies would then bow down as was customary at greetings and departures in Japan. In fact, it is a great custom that is still practiced today. Ox bowed to the other ladies, and they each bowed back. He then told them that he would demonstrate how we bowed in America. He walked over to one of the pretty mama-sans, placed one of his hands on the front of her chest, and the other hand on her back. He pushed on her back and made her bow a number of times. The ladies all watched and laughed as he continued to make her bow. Finally, Ox looked at us, winked, and squeezed the woman's breast, all the time, continuing to make her bow. When the woman finally realized what he was doing, she let out a scream. The women all laughed hysterically. It was all in fun, as Ox meant it to be, and they all accepted it as being funny, including the woman that Ox was helping bow.

We all learned some Japanese, especially for common words like water — mizu. Most of the time, however, we could communicate if we talked slowly and used hand gestures.

On the last day of the tour, Baba came to our hotel and paid us. When he handed me $4,000, I was shocked. In Amarillo, we had been told we would be paid $1,000 a week, so it should have been $5,000 for the tour. I was told that it was $1,000 a week, but the Japanese government had deducted twenty percent for taxes. I was devastated. That was a lot of money. I had budgeted and made plans based on the entire amount, and now I was going to return home with $1,000 less than I had been told. Baba must have read the disappointment in my face because he gave me a ten percent bonus. I shook hands with him and we left on good terms. I still made ten percent less than I had been promised, but it wasn't Baba's fault. Once again, I was reminded that I had to take care of myself and stand up for what was mine. The incident also made me decide to be present on all negotiations which concerned my money. I had been led to believe that I was going to make a certain amount, and the tax situation should have been explained to me. I never left that up to anybody else again. If a third party told me they could get me a certain amount for an independent show, I would confirm it with the promoter to be sure everything was exactly as it had been explained. I didn't blame anyone. It was just a misunderstanding, but the incident taught me to ask a lot of questionis and get all the facts in the future.

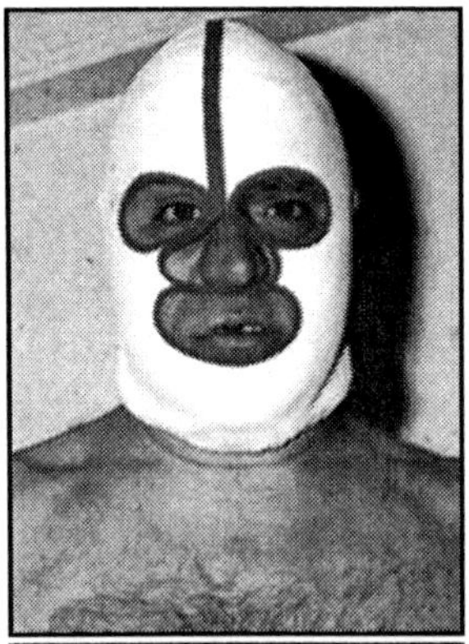
The Destroyer

On the last night of the show, I was supposed to work with the "Intelligent, Sensational" Destroyer [Dick Beyer] in Kuramae Kokugikan, the old sumo building which has since been torn down. Kuramae is an area of Tokyo. Kokugi- means *national sports*, and –kan means *hall.* Destroyer was living in Japan, and for an American, he was over in a big way. In fact, he was so popular in Japan that he had his own TV variety show, which really impressed us. In the ring, he was still wrestling, but he would occasionally do things to make the people laugh. The office didn't like it when he did that, but he was still over and continued to draw money for many years. In addition to being a big star, he was a nice man who worked hard in the ring. In his heyday, he had been a major heel, and his battles with Rikidôzan and Baba are the stuff of legends. We later became good friends and I have a lot of respect for him.

Jaggers and I were really anxious to get home to the States. Before the matches that night, we took our suitcases to the airport and put them into lockers so we could go straight to the airport after our match and take a ten o'clock flight home. We knew we would be on early, as we usually were, but my match was with the Destroyer, and it would be on later than we thought.

When we got back to the arena, Destroyer came up to me and said, "*We're going to have the best match on the card, kid.*" I sure didn't want to disappoint him, so I worked hard, and we had what I thought was a very good match. Destroyer beat me with his figure four leglock, which was his famous finishing hold. My knee had been operated on, so it was weak, and the hold really hurt. My knee was sore all the way home during my flight. I was told that the match I was in was one of the few matches that was televised. They still play that tape now and then.

As soon as the match ended, I left the ring and went to the back. Jaggers and I were worried about missing our flight, so I didn't even bother to shower. We took a taxi from the rear of the Sumo building and barely made it to the airport in time. I had finished my first tour of Japan. I had learned a lot by watching some good workers and top guys, both gaijin and Japanese. I was especially impressed by Abdullah because he was really over with the people in Japan.

I was ready to move on to the next place, which was the Dallas territory.

Chapter 10

White-Meat Babyface

On many flights home from Japan, we made a stopover in Hawaii for a few hours. Many of the guys would spend a few days in Hawaii before continuing the trip home, but once a tour was over, I was always ready to go home to my family. My family could have planned a vacation and met me there, but the timing was just never right. In later years, when we could get a non-stop flight to Los Angeles or San Francisco, it made even less sense to go through Hawaii.

I did work at the Olympic Auditorium in Los Angeles one time when Hulk Hogan and I stopped there to meet a friend of his brother. I don't remember who I worked with, but I remember having a bad case of jetlag during the match. I also worked in Pasadena during that stop.

One of the people I remember from the Olympic was an old, black man who acted as a second and carried the ring jackets back to the dressing room for the wrestlers. When we walked down into the bowels of the Olympic after our matches, he would say, "*That was a masterpiece* (of a match). *You could not duplicate it in a hundred years.*" Of course, he never watched the matches and he said the same thing to everybody. Lord James Blears and John Tolos had imitated him many times, and when the old man said that, I fell out laughing.

I returned to the Dallas territory in November 1975. The main towns in the territory, all of which were potential money towns, were Dallas, Fort Worth, San Antonio, Corpus Christi, and Houston. Fritz von Erich was the owner and top babyface of the territory, but he really only owned the northern side of the territory, which included Dallas and Fort Worth. In reality, the Dallas "territory" was made up of three separate territories. Fritz's power lay in the fact that he supplied the talent to San Antonio and Corpus Christi, which was run by Joe Blanchard, and Houston, which was controlled by Paul Boesch.

San Antonio and Corpus Christi had a large Hispanic population, so in addition to using Fritz' talent, Joe Blanchard used Jose Lothario, a Mexican-American, as his top babyface. If you wanted to make money in Blanchard's end of the territory, Jose was the man to work with. The fans, both Hispanic and American, all loved him. Blanchard himself was in his last years of working, but as the booker, he had solidified his future in the business.

Houston was a major money-making city for wrestling. Boesch ran his show independent of Fritz. He would use Fritz' talent some of the time, but he had no problem flying in top talent from around the country. He flew top guys in every week and worked them in with the talent which Fritz sent. The top guys, in turn, jumped at the opportunity to wrestle in Houston because Boesch paid so well. He was considered the best payoff man in the States. He once made a statement about paying out money: "*You can give it to the wrestlers, or give it to the government in taxes.*" That attitude made him loved by everyone and he never had a problem getting talent. Like Mike London in Albuquerque, Boesch also filmed his own interviews, so his TV show had a different look from the one in Dallas.

The booker at that time was Red Bastien. Red still worked occasionally, but his focus was on booking. The first day he saw me, he pulled me aside and told me I was going to be his number two heel. In that position, I would have an opportunity to work angles in the semi-main events, and occasionally participate in the main event. I really liked the fact that Red Bastien told me up front on how he was going to promote me. It gave me an idea on what I was going to do and the direction in which I was headed. Although I wasn't offered a weekly guarantee (only a handful of people got a guarantee in those days), I knew I was going to have the opportunity to make more money than ever before in the States.

The Mongolian Stomper [Archie Gouldie] was the top heel at the time. Stomper had a great look: bald-headed, muscular build, and tough-looking. More than anything, he knew his character and wasn't afraid to stand up for himself. He had been very successful taking care of his personal business in the various territories, and he wasn't afraid to leave a territory on short notice if the booker and office didn't promote him correctly or treat him fairly on payoffs. He was a good example to me on how to conduct my own personal business affairs. Jim Dillon, who I had met in Amarillo, had changed his name to J.J. Dillon and managing Stomper. They were a good pair.

Fritz, of course, was the top babyface, although Peter Maivia came in and was given a big push, as well. I worked a lot with Peter. He was an extremely strong wrestler from Samoa. In fact, it was somewhat difficult for me to work him because of his size and strength. His body was so thick. As the heel, I wanted to try to lead the match, but Peter wasn't always keen on being led where he didn't want to go. He didn't want to take too many bumps, and as a young heel trying to get over, I wanted to do everything I could. Peter was so strong, however, that if he didn't want to go somewhere, he didn't go. However, I made good money when I worked with him. Of course, Peter was the grandfather of Dwayne Johnson, one of the big box-office attractions in the movies today.

My weekly average hovered around $700 a week. It still wasn't what I considered great money, but it was more than double what I had been making in Louisiana. I was featured in a few double main events in Houston and was paid more than $500 for each show. The Great Mephisto flew in and out as the other top heel on most Friday nights. Frankie told me Paul Boesch had once paid him $2,700 for one match. That was great money, for sure, and it was what I had dreamed about for a long time.

I also worked with Rick Martel, a 19-year-old, white-meat babyface. He was young, good-looking, and could really go in the ring. We developed a good friendship which has endured to this day. Rick was a middle-of-the-card babyface in the Dallas territory, while I was a heel in the same position, but we

Ric Martel

ended up working a lot of the last matches. In the Dallas territory, the main event in Dallas and Fort Worth was not the final match of the night. It was placed in the middle of the card. Fritz said it gave the wrestlers in the main event an opportunity to get out of the building before the crowd, which was a good idea if they had a hot finish and the people were angry. However, Fritz wanted to give the fans a long, exciting match to end the show, and since he only wanted to wrestle for five to ten minutes, he put other wrestlers in that match. It was a great experience for Rick and me, though, and our placement on the card made us feel as if we were actually in the "main event." Our matches often went 30 to 45 minutes, which is tough when you're young and not too experienced, but we learned a lot as we tried to think of things to fill the allotted time. It's only my opinion, but I thought we had some classic matches which stood well against those of the other, more seasoned, veterans of the ring.

"Bulldog" Danny Plechas, another old-time wrestler, now referee in Dallas, was a class act. He had been on top in the '50s and '60s and had made good money. When Martel and I had the 45-minute matches, we would have 30 to 40 false finishes. A false finish is where a wrestler comes close to being pinned, only to kick out at the last second, and the match continues. Each time a pin fall attempt was made, Plechas had to drop to his knees, slap the mat twice with his hand for the two-count, and then get back to his feet. Plechas was an older guy, so it was tough when he had to do that 30 or more times in a match. A few times, when Plechas got tired, he would stomp his foot on the mat to make the count, rather than dropping to his knees and slapping the mat with the palm of his hand. The first time he did that, Rick and I couldn't believe it. When it happened a second time, we just looked at each other in puzzlement.

After the match, when we got to the back, we asked him why he didn't get down on the mat. He calmly said, "*I knew you weren't going to pin him, so why should I get down there?*" Rick and I both laughed, but that wasn't good for business. Rick and I were both trying to have a good match, and it was hard to be serious when Plechas did things like that. We didn't complain, though. We both respected the older guys who were doing their best to stay in the business and make a living for as long as they could.

Another time, Rick and I were working in Fort Worth. I started the match fast and tried to catch him by surprise from behind. Rick moved out of the way and I ran into the turnbuckle. As I staggered backwards, Rick fell in behind me and rolled me up for a three count. The match lasted nine seconds. To her final days, whenever I mentioned Rick Martel's name to my mother, who saw that show on TV, she would say, "*Isn't that the boy who beat you in nine seconds?*"

On January 18, 1980 in Isahaya City, Nagasaki Prefecture, when I was wrestling for New Japan, I got a quick win on live television over Riki Chôshû. I totally ate him up and gave him nothing. I've been told that over the years, he occasionally brought up the story about me beating him in such a short time and in such a significant manner. Up to that time, he had never lost a match that decisively. I don't know if he laughed about it like I did about my match with Martel, but it didn't hurt him. He became one of the biggest stars Japan had ever known.

One of the most life-changing events took place during my first few weeks in Dallas. In late November 1975, my son Logan was born in Amarillo.

While in Dallas, I also met Mike Paidousis, an older, veteran wrestler from the Pittsburgh area. He lived in Dallas, but he was working for the World Wide Wrestling Federation [WWWF] in New York. After seeing me work, he told Bruno Sammartino about me. He told him he had seen a big guy in Texas who could move and take bumps. A month later, he returned to Dallas and gave me Bruno's home telephone number. Of course, I had heard of Bruno. He was the top guy in New York and a legend around the world. It was everybody's dream to work with him.

I was nervous, but I called Bruno. He was nice and told me he was looking for new talent to work with. Mike had assured him that I was a good guy, and on his recommendation, Bruno wanted to help me get booked in New York. I assured him that I wouldn't let him down and that I just wanted an opportunity to do well.

A few weeks later, Red Bastien took me aside and said Vince McMahon Sr. had called and had asked to talk to me. He had told Red they wanted me to work for them. Red was nice to give me the message. He had put time and effort into pushing me in Dallas, but he knew that getting a shot in the WWWF was a great opportunity for me. He didn't stand in the way and must have given his own endorsement of me to Vince. I really appreciated that. I also have Red to thank for giving me the opportunity to establish the Stan "The Bad Man" Hansen character in Dallas. I'll always be in his debt for that.

I talked to Vince and he gave me a starting date for their television. He seemed nice, but he made the comment that it was Bruno who had made the decision to bring me in. I later learned that Vince McMahon Sr. and Bruno didn't always get along. Bruno was a big drawing card in the northeast, so Vince needed him. They had a working relationship, but behind the scenes, they were at odds about many things.

After hanging up the phone, I almost had to pinch myself to be sure I wasn't dreaming. I was so excited. I had been asked to make a run on top in one of the top territories in the U.S. It was going to be my first real shot at the big time.

★ Wrestling Program ★
GULF ATHLETIC CLUB — PAUL BOESCH, PROMOTER
NO. 6055 — FRIDAY, FEBRUARY 13, 1976 — HOUSTON, TEXAS — PHONE: 659-7793 — PRICE 25¢
Texas Title At Stake In Rec Center Friday
Badman Out To Ruin Peter's Title Try!
WORLD CHAMPION TERRY FUNK
ROCKY'S DREAM IS DILLON'S NIGHTMARE!

Houston program, February 13, 1976

Chapter 11

Death Threats

Vince McMahon's territory, which we referred to as the "New York territory," covered most of the northeast. My dad, who came from a large family of 12, had lived in Brooklyn as a child, and he was the only one of his family to leave. My aunts, uncles, and cousins all lived in New York and New Jersey, but I had never been to New York before going to the WWWF. I was raised in Texas, where we brag about everything being big, but in the northeast, the cities were huge and millions of people lived there. There were also many differences between the people in Texas and those on the east coast.

The most striking differences were the accents and mannerisms. In Texas, we talked and moved a lot slower than northerners, and in many respects, even in 1976, the divide between the north and the south was evident. The Yankees seemed to be much more brash and street-smart than southerners, and acted as if the north was where the "in-crowd" lived. We Texans, like most southerners, talked much more slowly, and took a more leisurely approach to life. For the most part, though, I got along with everybody and met a lot of nice people during my stay there.

My wife and I lived in a Ramada Inn for the entire eight months I was in the territory. The hotel management allowed me to use a small refrigerator and a hot plate in the room. We cooked small meals, like breakfast, on the hot plate, and heated things out of a can. Occasionally, we would grill steaks or hamburgers by the pool.

While in the northeast, we went to a few of the major attractions, such as the Statue of Liberty and the Empire State Building. It was 1976 and our country was celebrating the Bicentennial, the 200th anniversary of the adoption of the Declaration of Independence, so we were lucky enough to witness huge fireworks displays on the 4th of July.

The travel in New York was typical of most of the territories. Most of our trips were made by car, except for Pittsburgh, to which we flew. I lived in West Haven, Connecticut, which I believed was more centrally located than New York City. A number of guys lived at the Ramada Inn there, including Bruiser Brody, Skandor Akbar, Pat McGinnis, Doug Gilbert [Doug Lindsay], and me. Jerry Blackwell and Billy White Wolf had apartments nearby. Of course, most of the local guys lived in New York City. Many of them had been working in the territory for years, so they had set down permanent roots in homes with their families. The trips west of New York City were longer, but most of the trips were to the north or east of New York City, in states such as Massachusetts and Maine. The longest trips in the territory were up into Maine, down to Washington, D.C., and to Rochester, New York. Trips to Long Island also took a lot of time because we had to go through New York City, but we understood that traveling was part of the job.

Without a doubt, the New York territory was the top money-making market for individual wrestlers at the time. We could make $3,500 a night on the big shows. Of course, it goes without saying that there was a lot of competition between the wrestlers to work the main event in those cities.

There was somewhat of a long lag, usually a couple of weeks or more, between the shows and our payoffs for those shows. Arnold Skaaland, Gorilla Monsoon, or Angelo Savoldi, who were the main road agents, would usually give us our checks at the shows. When we needed money, we made draws against our future payoffs, although the standard draw was $50. We could request more, but most of the time, that was the maximum advance we were allowed to get. I remember the agents being unhappy about paying Billy Graham his $400 air trans when he flew in from Phoenix. At the time, the office didn't take care of the flight arrangements. We had to purchase our own tickets and not everybody was reimbursed for their airfare. When I realized Graham was being taken care of, I asked the office to do the same for me, and they complied, although I didn't go back and forth to my home much during the time I was there. Pretty soon, others heard about it, and everybody began asking to be reimbursed for their ticket. Of course, the office didn't look at all talent, even main-event talent, in the same way, so only a select few were compensated.

When I first arrived in the territory, there were three managers in New York — Freddie Blassie, Captain Lou Albano, and the Grand Wizard [Ernie Roth]. They were all a part of the on-going wrestling programs, and every heel that came into the territory was assigned to one of them. I was given to Freddie. For all practical purposes, he was a part of the office, and he touted the party line.

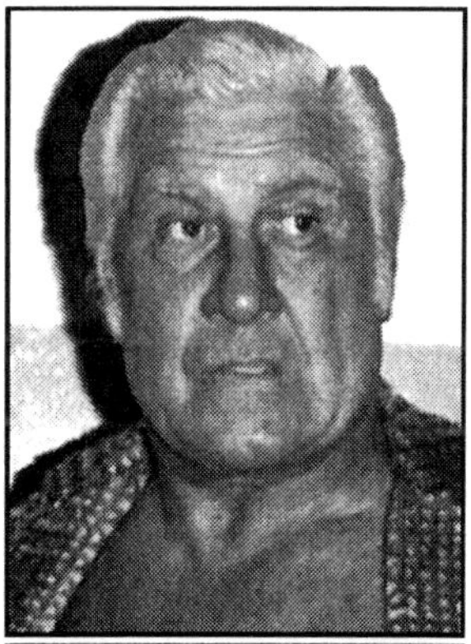
Freddie Blassie

Freddie was a really good guy. He had a long, distinguished background in the business as a top star all over the world. He had also been a booker in the Georgia territory. At first, we didn't really get along. Freddie had his own style and he wanted to do most of the talking on promos. Of course, that caused a conflict right off the bat. In my mind, I was the talent, and I wanted to establish my own personality. In the beginning, however, it was hard to get a word in edgewise. After a few weeks of promos, I called Freddie aside and told him he could start the interview, but after fifteen seconds or so, I wanted take over and make the rest of it. I could tell he didn't like it, but he did what I asked. With our cards all face-up on the table, we got along well.

Freddie shared some of the details of his personal life, including his many marriages and subsequent divorces. When we were together, he told me he had finally found the right girl, and he stayed married to her until he died on June 2, 2003.

From what I understand, Vince had control over all the talent, and made the decisions on the direction of the business. Bruno Sammartino was probably the exception to that rule. I believe Bruno had a lot of say in his programs and matches. At the shows, communication between the office and the talent was handled by one of the road agents, while at other times, the referee would give necessary information to us. The referee was also important to both business and the matches. A couple of referees I remember well are John Stanley and Dick Woehrle. They were both nice guys who did a good job in the ring. Angelo's son, Mario, also was a good referee.

As was the custom for the New York territory, they rotated the heel talent around the champion. The WWWF had been very successful in promoting a top babyface and feeding him an endless string of heels. When I arrived in the territory, Bruno Sammartino was the champion. He was the epitome of everything a champion should be, and he became a true legend in our business. Standing about 5-foot-11 and weighing 275, he was in great shape. He had an extremely thick chest and he was very strong.

My average career weight was 290 to 310 pounds, but at the time, I weighed 315 pounds, which was at the heaviest I had been, or would be, in my entire career. I was too big, though. I felt better when I weighed 290, which was my best weight.

Before I came into New York on a full-time basis, I flew in from Dallas a few times to appear on their wrestling show in order to make myself known and to get some heat which would draw people to the arenas in the hopes of seeing Bruno beat me. I wasn't a big name. In fact, I was pretty well an unknown. I was just one of a long line of heels that Vince had given an opportunity to headline Madison Square Garden.

My first meeting with Bruno in the Garden was scheduled for April 26, 1976. Prior to that, Bruno had headlined shows with title defenses against Ivan Koloff, Superstar Billy Graham, and Ernie Ladd. They were three of the top names in the business at the time, so that was quite an array of talent for a relative unknown like me to follow.

I was really excited the first night I walked into Madison Square Garden. My thoughts immediately went back to the time when my dad and I watched the Friday night boxing matches from the Garden on television. I've always had bad vision, and I remember thinking the building was so big that I couldn't see the fans at the top of the grandstands. The show itself didn't sell out, but it drew 17,493 fans, which was still a respectable number.

Little did I know that my first match with Bruno would end in disaster. Eight minutes into the match with Bruno, I hit him with my Lariat move and put him on the mat, after which I brought him up into position for a body slam.

When I was in the Dallas territory, I had several matches with "High Chief" Peter Maivia. I did a move where I caught Peter coming off the ropes and scoop slammed him. In a variation of that move, I would sometimes reach past the middle of his legs to the outside when I picked him up for the slam. Since my shoulders were stiff and Peter was really stocky, I would do it that way so Peter could slide down my back. He could then avoid being slammed by rolling me up with a pinning move. That habit would result in disaster for Bruno

During my match with Bruno, I scooped him, just like I did Peter. However, Bruno wasn't expecting me to do that. Being uncertain of what I was going to do, he stiffened up. His reaction threw me off balance, and when I tried to go through with the slam, I ended up slamming him on the back of his head and the back of his neck, rather than flat on his back. I went around behind him, pulled him up to a sitting position, and got a head lock on him. Concerned, I held it for a few seconds before whispering, "*Are you all right?*"

He didn't say anything right away. He just sat in place. He finally said, "*Give me a few seconds.*"

Being the man he is, Bruno continued to work and sold for several minutes while he regained his composure. I thought perhaps I didn't hurt him after all. What I didn't know was that when he landed on his head, he cracked three vertebrae in his neck. People would later call it "the break that was heard around the world." I was told later that some of the fans, many of whom had attended every Garden show for years, knew something had gone wrong. Bruno eventually made his customary comeback, only to have the match stopped New York State Athletic Commission doctor, Dr. Edwin Campbell. That decision, of course, automatically set up a rematch between the two of us.

Bruno Sammartino

After the match, I went back to the dressing room and began to get undressed. I was feeling pretty good about the match. As I said earlier, it was my first match on top in Madison Square Garden, and visions of times with my dad again crossed my mind. Before I could get into the shower, Vince McMahon Sr. came into the dressing room. He was seething with anger. "*You hurt Bruno,*" he said. "*You dropped him on his head!*" I wasn't sure if he was serious or not, but he had a sour look on his face and it looked a bit ashen, so I quickly realized that he was.

All I could do was stammer, "*What? I knew he hit his head, but I thought he was okay. I mean, he went on with the match.* " Vince wasn't in a mood to explain. He simply said, "*No, dammit! You hurt him!*" He turned on his heel and left the dressing room, leaving me standing in the middle of the room looking slack-jawed and dumbfounded.

There was a dead silence in the dressing room. I turned to look at some of the other guys, but nobody made eye contact. Most of the guys were looking at the floor, wishing they were anyplace but there. I repeated to no one in particular, "*What happened?*" Nobody spoke up or said anything to comfort me. I was alone in a new territory, and I had seriously injured everybody's meal ticket … Bruno Sammartino.

A few minutes later, a few of the guys came into the dressing room and told us Bruno had a neck injury. A neck injury! Wow! I was in shock. I was scared. But most of all, I felt really bad for Bruno. He was responsible for me being in the WWWF in the first place. He was the one who had given me the

Stan Hansen
vs
Bruno Sammartino

Madison Square Garden
April 26, 1976

opportunity to work on top. And this is how I repaid him. I felt so alone. To make matters worse, Bruno was my only connection to the territory. I didn't know anyone else.

Later that night, and early the next morning, I called around to get details on what happened, but nobody seemed to know anything. I was really anxious, and it crossed my mind to just pack my bags and return to Texas, but I knew I had to face the music. I can't blame McMahon for being upset. The injury put Bruno on the sidelines for the next two months, and McMahon had to rebook every show which featured Bruno and rework the plans he had made. That cost him a great deal of money, time, and effort.

I went back to New Haven, Connecticut, that night without getting any additional information. Early the next morning, and later that night at the show in Portland, Maine, I asked everyone if they had heard anything. Nobody knew a thing, including the office. Eventually, we were told Bruno was in a hospital in Pittsburgh. A conversation with Bruno was going to be the hardest thing I had ever had to do, but I got the phone number of the hospital and began calling. I called and called, but his phone stayed busy and it took me several hours to get through. When I did, he answered the phone. I told him who I was and immediately told him how sorry I was. He said, "*Don't worry about it. Things happen. When I come back, we're going to do some good business.*"

He went on to ask, "*What is it with you Texans?*" When I asked him what he meant, he told me the story about Bobby Duncum breaking his arm the year before. He assured me there was no nerve damage and the years he had spent lifting weights saved his spinal cord from serious injury. As I breathed a sigh of relief, he told me some people had just come into the room, so he had to go. He then said something which made a big impression on me: "*Take care of yourself with the other wrestlers and the office. Don't do anything that will take away from our wrestling together. I want you strong when I get back.*"

As I hung up the phone, all I could think was, "*Wow! What a man.*" There he was, lying in a hospital bed, in traction and with a halo around his neck, and he was thinking about me. Now I know it was about business, but Bruno was a class guy to say something like that without making a single recrimination against me.

One of the things I learned from the situation was that when bad things happen, they can often turn into something good. I didn't see that at the time, but I understood it later. I had injured Bruno, and when he recovered and got back into the ring, the incident would give meaning to our rematch, and the wrestling fans would come out in droves to see him get his revenge. Bruno saw it almost instantly, but it took me awhile before I realized what the event would mean for my career. At the same time, I don't want to sound cavalier, or make light of his injury. At the time of his injury, Bruno was 40 years old. He had been hurt many times before, but this was, by far, the most serious injury he had ever suffered.

I have to credit Bruno for giving green guys like me a chance to work on top. I knew I was green. In fact, that was the reason why Vince hadn't wanted me in the territory in the first place. He gave the same opportunity to Bobby Duncum. Later, when we were both in Japan, Bruno kidded me about the fact that he got broken bones twice in his career, and both times, it was from guys from Texas, and in particular, West Texas State University — Bobby Duncum and me.

When I hung up the phone, a huge wave of relief washed over me. I was so glad Bruno had not taken the injury personally. I was so glad he was the man he was. My future was like clay in his hands, and instead of being vindictive, he molded it to my advantage. I thought about what Bruno had said and determined to take care of myself, which meant not letting others beat me or make me look bad in the ring.

A few of the boys who had been scheduled to work with Bruno around the loop in towns like Boston, Philadelphia, and Pittsburgh, had hard feelings towards me. They never showed it outright, but I could tell there was some resentment. I can't blame them for being upset because it cost them money, but that's one of the risks of the business. Wrestling is a hard and physical sport, and believe me, when you're in the ring with Bruno, you're in for a fight. Bruno believed in giving the fans what they came to see: matches filled with action and intensity. As a rookie, I had a choice to make when I stepped into the ring with him. I could think and act like a rookie, or I could go after Bruno and make a name for myself. In life, you only get the ball (opportunity and responsibility to produce) a few times, and when you're handed the ball in wrestling, you had better carry the ball as far as you can while you have it. When I stood facing Bruno on the opposite side of the ring, I made the decision to do my best and go after him aggressively. By chance, I suppose, that aggressiveness resulted in me breaking Bruno's neck.

In wrestling, there is a fine line between being aggressive and being mean. You should be aggressive and try to dominate your opponent. However, to purposely injure someone is ridiculous. What happened when I injured Bruno was an accident, and I felt badly about it. I felt extra badly because it was Bruno who had encouraged McMahon to bring me into the territory.

I knew that if I was going to make money in the business, I had to be aggressive and make people talk about me. In the early years of my career, it was hard to do that. As a rookie, I was booked in the opening or second match. I was told go out and wrestle with older guys for ten to fifteen minutes. The older guys, however, had been in the business for a long time. They were content to just go through the motions and take whatever money was given to them. Years later, when I was a seasoned veteran, I learned how tough it was to motivate yourself to go out, seven days a week, 52 weeks a year, and work hard for the fans. It was hard to take bumps after traveling 200 to 300 miles in a car, eating in fast-food restaurants, and sleeping in cheap, rundown motels. Those factors all weigh on the body and mind, to a point where you almost become numb. Your only goal was to keep going until you reached the next town, and the next match, and then on to the next city and arena.

When you tried to do something different, or tried to stand out and get noticed by the booker, you often ran into resistance from your opponent. It's almost impossible to get a 300-pound behemoth to do something he doesn't want to do, regardless of how strong you are. As a result, you often had to go out and try to establish your personality without involving your opponent. There were a few wrestlers who blazed their own trails. Their efforts often paid off, as most of them established themselves as top guys in the business. Most of the wrestlers, however, fell into the rut of doing as everyone else did. They looked at their employment as being totally decided by the promoter. I never did. Yes, I had to do business as the promoters wanted, but I was always thinking about how and what I could to do to better myself and my position in the business.

I've always felt that people are given short windows of opportunity in their careers and in their lives. Most of the choices we make don't change our lives at all, but others result in major changes, some good, and some bad. Going to New York and working with Bruno was one of the choices I made, and breaking his neck (accidentally) was a product of that choice. It wasn't something I set out to do, and looking back, perhaps my aggressiveness did cause me to be a little careless in that first match. That incident, however, pushed up my career a notch, and set me on course for a career as a main-event wrestler. My experiences in trying out for pro football showed me how fleeting the opportunity to make big money could be. I looked at every new opportunity as possibly my last opportunity to make it big. I never knew when I might get hurt, and knew that I could easily find myself in the same situation as Bruno, and, so I did my best to make the most out of every situation. My options were to make it in professional wrestling, or go back to teaching and make $477 a month.

When I broke into the business, the promoters were the only people making enough money to be able to save. There were a few wrestlers who saved their money, but the majority of the wrestlers lived day-to-day and saved just enough to pull them through slow times. Even those who had been in the business for a long time were only making a living. They were having a good time, but they constantly moved from territory to territory and had no roots to speak of.

I remember when I reached my first monetary goal in 1978: a house paid off and cash in the bank. When I got into the business, I told myself that if I didn't make it to the top in three years, I would go back to coaching. I wasn't going to be one of the guys who had been in the business for a long time with nothing to show for my efforts.

I had always been told that as a heel, my job was to do my best to cause a riot. In other words, they wanted people to get so mad and upset they would literally come into the ring to do harm to me. In those days, that happened quite often, so being a heel was dangerous. We had to watch in all directions at all times: on our way to the ring before the match, on the way back to the dressing room after the match, and during the match itself. It wasn't uncommon for a fan (often several) to come into the ring to "save" their favorite wrestler. That was dangerous and scary, so we had to be on guard at all times. We worried about getting into the building safely, or getting back to our car after our match. People would wait for us and give us a hard time. Most of the time, we only faced verbal abuse, but knives and guns weren't uncommon. Even when we were away from the matches, such as when we were in a restaurant with our families, people would walk right up to our table and give us a tongue lashing. If we were eating and made eye contact with a fan during a time when we were involved in a hot angle on TV with a popular wrestler, we could tell instantly whether or not they recognized us. When that happened, more often than not, something verbal would be said. The heat we felt around town was as strong as the heat we felt at the matches.

I had studied other heels during my rookie years, and I learned some of the things which had to be done to deal with the "heat" that came with being a "bad guy." The very first thing you have to remember is: never show fear. Whenever you're faced with a possible confrontation, never let people know you might not want a confrontation. If you are approached and yelled at, or taunted, your best bet was to taunt the person back, and show yourself as being ready to do whatever they wanted to do. Most of the time, that attitude prevailed and would scare away a possible threat. However, in most cases, I simply watched the people and tried to look under control while I continued moving towards the dressing room. If we stopped to confront a fan, we would likely become a "sitting duck" for someone else, so the best thing to do was to keep moving slowly and steadily towards the dressing room.

It was several days after my match with Bruno before I realized how much heat I had. McMahon had the details of the incident with Bruno announced on television, and credited Bruno's broken neck to being hit with my Lariat finisher. Being a heel is always a dangerous thing, but with Bruno out of action, and not knowing whether or not he would be coming back, the people really hated me.

One instance I remember vividly took place when I was riding into New York on a commuter train from New Haven. I was on my way to do some interviews and tape a few other things. The train car was full of well-dressed, white-collar workers. I, on the other hand, was dressed in cowboy clothes, a 10-gallon, black cowboy hat, and sported bleached-blond hair and a blond goatee. Needless to say, I stood out like a sore thumb. Sitting across the aisle from me was a well-dressed man who must have been 75 years old. He wore a suit and hat and held a walking cane in his hands. I couldn't help but notice that he was glaring at me, so I tried to avoid making eye contact and minded my own business. I never tried to live my wrestling character when I was out in public. I tended to keep to myself and avoid getting into conversation with anybody.

Most of the seats were taken, but the car wasn't overly crowded. As the train approached a station, the old man stood up and slowly walked toward me. He stopped beside my seat, glared down at me, raised his cane into the air, and brought it down onto my shoulder. It landed hard. In a deep Italian accent, he shouted, "*You cocka-sucker! This is for what you did to Bruno. You cocka-sucker.*" His eyes were blazing. He hit me two or three more times. I put up my arms to ward off the blows, but I kept my seat. What could I do? He was 75 years old. I couldn't punch the old man out. As the train rolled to a stop in the station, he turned and got off the train. I felt so conspicuous. The man was gone and everybody was staring at me. Not one person had moved to stop him. It was embarrassing to say the least, but after a few minutes, I began to smile. I thought about how funny the whole thing must have looked.

One of the things I thought was unfair was that the heels were never paid anything extra for the hassle. We had extra expenses which came directly from our own pockets. Our car windows were broken, our tires were slashed, and sand or sugar was put into the gas tanks of our cars.

The physical dangers were just a part of the job, and many of the guys couldn't stand up to the pressure which came with being an effective heel. They would tell the promoters they wanted to be a babyface. If the promoters didn't do what they wanted, they would either leave the territory, or do a halfway job of making the people mad, in the hopes the promoter would be forced to switch them babyface. When we were young and hungry, however, we would do anything to make an extra dollar, or to get noticed, and possibly get a chance at a higher match on the card.

In the beginning, the people didn't know me, so the heat wasn't too bad, but as people began to recognize me, and the word got out that I had injured Bruno, things got a bit dicey. I have to add, however, that as hot as things were for me during that time, it was nothing like the heat I got later in my career when I was wrestling in Georgia.

Three weeks after my match with Bruno, I returned to the Garden booked against Ivan Putski. I was told to be at the show by two in the afternoon, even though the show wasn't scheduled to begin until seven that night. McMahon preferred for us to get to the show early, in order to avoid the people who congregated outside the building. However, even as early as it was, there were still a couple of hundred people massed around the entrance door where the wrestlers entered the Garden.

The Garden had a well-trained security force which was taught to handle all sorts of rowdy crowds, whether the event was a rock concert, a basketball game, or a wrestling card. Even with the superior security detail, I couldn't help but notice there were a lot of uniformed New York policemen in both the dressing room and the hallways of the building. That was unusual. I was later told that several death threats had been made and that the police took them seriously.

Before the show began, Arnold Skaaland came into the dressing room with contracts for a show to be held the following month at Shea Stadium in Flushing, New York. The show would be broadcast throughout the northeast on closed-circuit TV as the undercard for the famous Muhammad Ali versus Antonio Inoki match. I was told that when the advance gate for the show looked to be a disaster, Vince convinced Bruno to return early to participate in a rematch against me.

Ernie Ladd also was in the dressing room that night. After Arnold handed Ernie his copy of the contract, he walked over and gave me mine. Before I could look at it, Ernie exploded, "*What is this sh—? Two thousand dollars? You gotta be kiddin' me. Arnold, I'm not taking this.*" He wadded up the papers, threw them at Skaaland, and yelled at me, "*Don't sign it, kid. Don't sign it. I don't know what they offered you, but whatever it is, it isn't enough.*"

Arnold picked up Ernie's papers and told me, "*Just sign it, kid. It's a good offer. You ought to be happy with it.*"

Ladd, who was intently watching my expression as Arnold tried to convince me to sign the contract, yelled across the room, "*Listen to me. I'm telling ya. Don't sign that. I don't know how much they're offering you, but you can get more.*"

Noticing me looking at Ernie with a questioning look on my face, Arnold said, "*Don't listen to him. You were a nobody when we brought you in. You owe us this, and you owe Bruno. Just sign it.*"

Ernie wasn't going to give up, and continued to talk to me. "*Listen, you have a once-in-a-lifetime opportunity here. Don't sign it. You have them over a barrel. This is going to be the biggest show ever up here and they have to have you on the card. You can name your price.*"

Arnold turned and said, "*Mind your own business, Ernie!*"

That initiated a shouting match with Ernie. After a minute or so of give and take, Arnold left the room.

Ernie had always been very independent when it came to the wrestling business. He didn't get along well with the office and office personnel. His offer for the Shea Stadium match was $2,000, and he wasn't happy with it. My payoff for the first match with Bruno was $3,500, and my contract for the return match was for $5,000. Given the circumstances, I thought I was really going to make a "score," but $5,000 was much less than I thought I would be paid for such a high-profile match. There was a time when my dad worked for almost a year for that kind of money, and in 1976, that was still considered to be big money, but it was all relative. I was disappointed, to say the least.

Ernie Ladd

I read every word of the contract from the beginning to the end. Ernie finally stood up and left the dressing room. I knew Ernie was right, but it was more money than I had ever made for one match. It was still a big payoff. Not only that, but I wanted to continue making money with New York, and to be able to return again in a few years, as that was the rotation of the territory.

Before the show was over, I had made my decision. I was being given an opportunity to wrestle on the biggest show of my career. I signed the contract. I'd like to add that later, Vince paid me a $1,000 bonus for the match. He said it was separate from the amount we agreed to in the contract and came from the closed-circuit receipts. It was something he didn't have to do and I appreciated it.

The education I received that night was worth far more than the payoff I got, or any payoff I might have been given. I was impressed by the way Ernie stood up for his business. He did what was right for Ernie Ladd. He knew the payoff he had been offered was less than what he deserved, so he stood his ground, regardless of what the consequences might be. In the short term, he lost out on the money and didn't wrestle on that show, but years later, he returned to New York and made more money.

That night, Ernie taught me that there are times when we have to make a stand. I didn't take a stand that night, but in later years, his example played a big part in the way I conducted business with wrestling promoters. He taught me that I have to take care of my own business because nobody else will do as good a job for Stan Hansen as Stan Hansen himself.

The show that evening was sold-out in advance. Putski was being used on top and he was really over, so he wasn't too excited about working with me because he knew I was getting a push, but he reluctantly agreed. As expected, the people rioted when I beat Putski. I realized I couldn't get out of the ring due to the number of people who had pushed their way to the ring apron, and with the people out of control, there was no way for me to leave the ring and get safely back to the dressing room.

Security in the Garden was really good, but when crowds of angry people storm the ring, there is only so much they can do to keep us safe. They came up with a plan, however. Forming a triangle wedge which was three guards deep on all three sides, they forced their way to the ring, pushing and knocking fans out of the way. Backing one flat edge of the wedge to the ring apron, they motioned for me to jump down into the space in the center of the triangle. Grabbing my wrestling tights, they pushed me over at the waist until my upper body was parallel with the floor. Two security guards then jumped up and covered me by draping themselves over the top of the triangle. With my face looking at the arena floor, they proceeded to move quickly towards the dressing room door, which was really a curtain over an opening which went into and under the grandstands. I was completely in the control of the security people.

The curtain was a good 60 feet away and there were a couple of hundred angry people between us and our goal. As we ran, I was surprised to see people looking up at me. In our mad dash, the guards had knocked them down and we were running over the top of their bodies. There was a lot of yelling and noise, and we were drenched with beer and soft drinks that were thrown by the fans, but what hit me the most was the smell of urine and feces. Yes, raw feces. It was an undeniable smell. I soon noticed that some of the people we were stepping over were the security people who had fallen during our mad rush. By the time we got to the curtain, less than half of the security force which came to ringside was still with us.

As we ran through the curtain into the back, the security people said they had never before seen the people in the Garden in such a rage. The New York police then took over and escorted me down the hall, stopping on the way to the rear exit to check every door and room for someone who might be waiting to ambush me. The cops took the possibility of a threat so seriously that a few of them had their guns drawn. It was totally unreal, but it was actually happening to me, and it was a serious situation.

As we reached the back of the building, I saw a taxi waiting inside the huge, overhead doors, which were now closed. The police told me to get into the back of the taxi and lay down on the floorboard. My wife and another girl sat in the back seat with their feet on my body, giving me good cover from anyone who might take a quick glance through the rear windows. When I was settled, the rear door of the Garden was raised and the taxi drove slowly through a couple of hundred fans who were yelling and looking for me. Fortunately, nobody tried to stop the taxi or do anything to cause a problem.

After the show, I was told that the death threats, which I had been told about earlier, had been made against me. I was too inexperienced to realize the danger I was in — until a few days later when a guy pulled a gun on me at a county fair in Rhode Island.

In the WWWF, the wrestling business was usually down in the summer. The best time of year for business was the winter, when it was cold outside and people preferred to watch indoor sports. In the summer, the people wanted to be outside in the fresh air, and they didn't want to go to events in small buildings.

On this particular night, Jerry Blackwell and I were riding together to the fairgrounds. Jerry was one of the best big men in the business. Even at 400 pounds, he could move, drop kick, and take unbelievable bumps. When the matches were over, Jerry and I left the building through the back door and headed to our car. As we walked through a throng of people, a small Puerto Rican guy moved in towards us. He glanced down at the crook of his elbow, which made me look at it, too, and said something to me in Spanish that I couldn't understand. When I realized he held a pistol in his hand, I stopped and stepped back. I didn't know what to do. The guy had an evil grin on his face, so I wasn't sure whether or not I should kick him, charge him, or just turn and run. I chose to freeze and hope he didn't decide to pull the trigger. I didn't want to do anything which might set him off.

Jerry, who was walking a few steps behind me, noticed that we were facing off. Not knowing the guy held a gun, he walked up behind him and grabbed his elbow. As the guy's attention turned toward Jerry, I slipped into a doorway which was right beside me. Spotting a box of empty bottles on the stairwell, I grabbed one of the bottles by the neck and waited for the guy to walk through the doorway after me. I intended to knock him unconscious with the bottle, and do whatever was necessary to guarantee my own survival.

I waited for what seemed like ten minutes, but more than likely, was just a few seconds. I held the bottle high overhead as somebody walked through the door. It was Jerry. He looked as if the blood had drained from his face. He said, "*I didn't see the gun until the guy turned towards me. He looked me dead in the eye, and then just melted back into the crowd.*"

I have no doubt that Jerry Blackwell saved my life that night. Jerry has since passed away and I miss him. He was a nice guy with a good, southern sense of humor, but he also was a tough guy when the circumstances demanded. He handled wrestling heat well. Eight years later, when we met again in Japan, we laughed about the incident. There was nothing funny about it at the time, though.

When word of the incident got back to Vince, he decided to send me home to Texas and keep me out of sight until the big show at Shea Stadium, where Bruno would be making his comeback in a return match against "the man who put him on the sidelines." Vince wanted to be sure I didn't get hurt (or killed) before Bruno's return. No doubt, it wasn't totally an altruistic motive. He was genuinely concerned about my safety, but he also wanted to be sure I was there for the big show.

The Shea Stadium show on June 25, 1976 was eagerly anticipated by the wrestling fans, who wanted to see Bruno come back and "kick my ass." Bruno was "the" living legend, and no wrestler had ever been over with the people of the east coast like he was. The people believed in him. They could relate to him. He was an Italian immigrant, and like millions of other European immigrants, he had made his way to the United States after the war. The majority of them had settled in the northeast, and Bruno represented them. As a member of a poor, blue-collar family, he was one of them. He crossed all ethnic lines. The Europeans loved him. The Puerto Ricans loved him. Everybody loved him.

Bruno represented a special type of man: what we might call a "man's man." He has been described as good, fair, humble, hard-working, and soft-hearted,

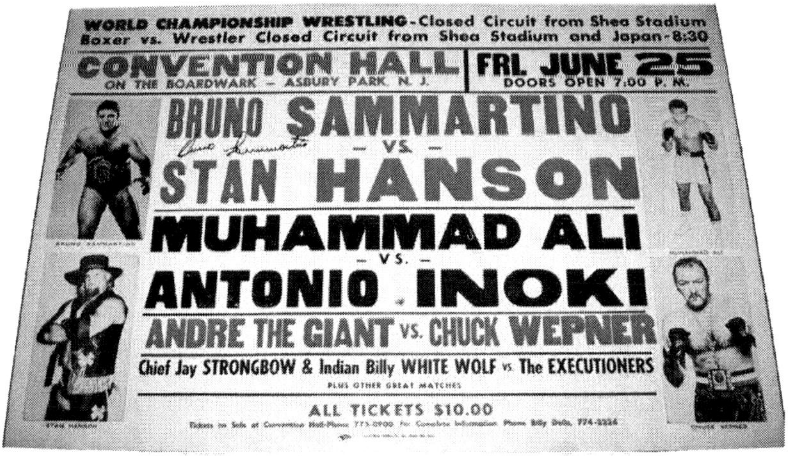

but he could be as tough as nails when it came to a fight. He was a "real man." Bruno wasn't a "superstar" who looked at himself as being more special than the common man. Again, he was one of them. He connected to the average person on the street, and as a result, he had a huge following.

Besides my rematch with Bruno, the live show at Shea Stadium featured a match between Andre the Giant and Chuck Wepner, a former heavyweight boxer who went fifteen rounds with Muhammad Ali in 1975. Other matches at Shea Stadium included Chief Jay Strongbow and Billy White Wolf against the Executioners, Ivan Putski against Baron Mikel Scicluna, and Jose Gonzalez against Kevin Sullivan. The Ali-Inoki and Andre-Wepner matches were aired by closed circuit in 170 locations. Everybody was hoping to make a buck off the Inoki-Ali match. Overall, the closed-circuit show was a huge failure. The show didn't do well in other territories, even in places like Chicago, Houston, and Los Angeles, which held a live wrestling show like the one at Shea Stadium. The WWWF, however, drew more than 32,000 people, who paid more than $400,000, to Shea Stadium to see Bruno make his comeback against the man who had broken his neck. At the time, it was the largest crowd and live gate (more than double) ever to attend a wrestling show in New York. However, the 32,000 people who were at Shea Stadium that night weren't there to see the match between Ali and Inoki. They were there to see Bruno get his revenge against Stan Hansen. Even the newspapers reported it that way. One headline read, *They came to see Bruno.*

Bruno said he really hadn't recovered enough to wrestle, but McMahon convinced him to return early in order to help save the house. It was a dangerous thing to do because if Bruno would have taken a bad fall, he could have been permanently paralyzed. In fact, when he was examined after he broke his neck, his doctor advised him to retire. Bruno accepted the risk, however, and made the decision to return.

There was a fair reaction to the other matches, but when the time came for our match to begin, there was real electricity in the air. The ring was erected on the pitcher's mound. I went to the ring first, making my entrance through the home dugout and accompanied by fifteen uniformed members of New York's finest. They weren't security guards. They were full-fledged policemen.

They told me I could do what I wanted during my match, but they cautioned me that if the heat got too bad, they would take measures to insure there was no riot. When I got into the ring, I warmed up for the biggest match of my career by doing my usual routine of running and moving around the ring.

My wife said she was sitting up in the stands with thousands of well-dressed Italian men and women, some of whom were wearing furs. They hadn't paid much attention to the early matches, but when Bruno stepped out onto the field from the visitors' dugout, there was a huge eruption of emotion. Jumping to their feet, the fans began yelling and screaming wildly. Some, both male and female, cried openly. They believed in and loved Bruno. Their hero was back to take revenge on the big, nasty Texan.

Bruno gave the people the revenge they had been anticipating. He stormed into the ring, hell-bent on paying me back. I tried to charge him, but he was on me quickly and never let up. Bruno seemed to be motivated by adrenalin. After ten minutes, my face was a bloody mask, and after Bruno tossed me out of the ring, I fled towards the dugout. It was good that I didn't get in any offense because a wrong move might have resulted in permanent injury to Bruno. Every move or hold had the potential to cause an injury which might cripple him for life.

As I headed in the direction of the dugout, the cops did their best to keep up with me. As I reached the path between home plate and first base, the people realized that I was abandoning the match. Often, when a wrestler is hurt or in need of time to recoup, they leave the ring, and at times, use it as a tool to avoid getting beat in the middle of the ring. They just head for the dressing room and allow themselves to get counted out. Bruno was still in the ring, so as I passed the base line with the contingent of police, the people realized where I was and what I was going to do.

Being very near-sighted, I could just make out a swell of motion as I looked up into the stands above the dugout. It took a second to realize that a wave of people was charging down towards the dugout. The fans knew I was leaving, and having been worked into frenzy by our actions in the match, they saw and smelled blood. I believe they literally were ready to kill ... me, that is. When one of the cops yelled, "*Sprint,*" we all sprinted to the entrance of the dugout. We could see the wave coming toward us. It was going to be very close. If they reached the field before we could get into the dugout, I honestly believe they would have beaten me to death.

As we reached the edge of the dugout, the wave was right on top of it, and the cops with me dove inside. I landed on one of the benches, which was rough, and felt splinters drive into my arms. There wasn't any time to worry about that as people dove over, or were pushed over, the top edge of the dugout. At the time, there seemed to be hundreds of people, but for certain, several dozen people made their way into the dugout. Three cops and I dove through a doorway which led into a hallway and slammed the door shut behind us. The people immediately began pounding on the door and tried to force it open. We were all wild-eyed and scared, and we were determined to keep them out. We all knew how close we had been to being in what could possibly be a life-threatening situation. Later, I was told that two cops didn't make it through the doorway and had been roughed up by the angry fans, who took out their frustration on them.

One of the cops said, "*Get out of here and go to the dressing room. We'll hold the door.*"

I didn't hesitate. I did exactly what I was told to do. When I walked into the dressing room, the guys were all talking about what they had seen. I have never seen anything like it since, but I know it was my first close call at getting killed by a hostile crowd.

The WWWF main events were always held in the middle of the card so the main event guys could get out of the building before the show ended, thus avoiding the people as they left the arena. That time was especially dangerous for the heels because people often waited around to vent their anger and hatred toward them, and confrontations would often take place between the heels and the fans.

I dressed hurriedly without showering. After leaving the dressing room, I rushed down to meet my wife, who was waiting for me at a pre-arranged exit with two policemen. When I got there, I was met with pandemonium. Three people lying on the floor were being attended to by paramedics. This took place in 1976, before doctors had made the really great medical advances to treat heart attacks and trauma. I could see someone pushing on one man's chest, giving him CPR. Another paramedic was performing mouth to mouth resuscitation, while a third was trying to revive someone else. I then noticed two other people lying on the floor, covered from head to toe with blankets.

My wife later told me that one of the cops said to her, "*I'll bet your husband is really proud to have killed these people.*" That was pretty cold. I felt badly for those people, but they could have dropped dead from a heart attack when they stepped off a train, or while watching a football game. I thought the policeman was wrong to make the assumption that I wanted to see, feel proud, or hope, that somebody died. It was a sad conclusion to one of my most important matches.

Things turned out alright and I had a great run in New York. Bruno and I came back to Madison Square Garden on August 7 and wrestled in a cage. The purpose of the cage was to prevent me from leaving the ring, as I had done at Shea Stadium. This would be my last match with Bruno in the Garden. It would be our third outing and the match in which Bruno would finally get his long-awaited revenge. I had "beaten" him in our first match when the match was stopped after Bruno received a cut above his eye (not to mention the broken neck).

There were a couple of exceptions, but the standard formula was that most wrestlers would get two main event matches in the Garden against Bruno. Due to the circumstances surrounding Bruno's injury, however, I got four main event matches — two against Bruno at the Garden, one at Shea Stadium, and another main event against Putski.

I continued to work in the WWWF through November of that year. I worked with Bruno in the other major cities and we did good business. It was enjoyable to work with Bruno, and it was easy to get heat because he was so over with the people. I also enjoyed working with Pedro Morales, who was very popular with the fans, especially the Puerto Ricans. We worked the secondary shows in the territory. Pedro was tough and really liked to mix it up. He laid in the chops as hard as anyone I had ever wrestled, and in turn, he took the same from me. We had some physically brutal matches which the fans really seemed to enjoy. Pedro and Bruno were legitimately the two toughest guys in the WWWF. Neither one of them ever cried or complained about me being stiff, unlike some of the others.

Out of the hundreds of dressing rooms where I changed clothes over the years, the dressing room in Asbury Park, New Jersey, has to rank as the absolute worst. It was at the old, boardwalk amusement park. There was no toilet in the dressing room and huge rats ran around the room, seemingly without fear of humans. The second worst was probably at a spot show outside of San Antonio, Texas. The weather was blistering hot and there was no shower, so we used a garden hose to wash off behind the building.

After my run with Bruno ended, McMahon teamed me up with my old partner, Frank Goodish, who was now wrestling as Bruiser Brody.

From here on out, I'll refer to Frank Goodish as "Brody," rather than "Frank." I always called him "Brody" when we were in public, but when it was just the two of us, I called him "Frank."

Brody also had worked a series of matches with Bruno, continuing the heel flow of talent with which Bruno would work. Brody and I were big, mobile, and strong, not to mention wild and young. I weighed close to 300 pounds, but I could still move fast, and I had developed a style that was a combination of wild cowboy and tough football player. Steroids had not yet become a major part of the business, so I was considered to be a big man for that time. There were other big men who moved fast for a series of moves, but none of them could move with the quickness and agility that Brody and I did for an extended period of time. We were the first, and our style overwhelmed both the fans and our opponents. The pace we set would literally change the face of wrestling in Japan a few years later.

We worked a lot of matches with Chief Jay Strongbow (the Italian Indian) and Billy White Wolf. Strongbow had been in New York for six years and he had a good name, but as a veteran wrestler, he was suspicious of Brody and me. We were aggressive, wild, and almost uncontrollable. We scared not only the fans, but most of the wrestlers. Strongbow and White Wolf wanted to beat us so badly, and constantly complained about us to the office. Strongbow wanted to keep his name strong, so it was just business to him, but Brody and I felt like they wanted to build their ego and reputation by beating us. I got into a confrontation with Strongbow at a spot show in Connecticut. He and I had a huge difference of opinion on what direction my match should go and it almost came to a physical head. He made the statement that "*it would be good for business.*"

"Yeah," I thought. "*Your business.*"

When I stood my ground, things got a bit heated, but nothing came of it.

Brody and I also got the impression that Strongbow thought he and his partner should come out ahead of us in our matches because we weren't a part of the New York organization, but Brody and I stood our ground. We weren't going to give them what they wanted because we hoped to return to New York someday and work with Bruno again.

One night in the old Boston Garden, I "won" the feature match, which was a battle royal with the stipulation that the winner would receive a $10,000 purse. There was a hotel attached to the Garden where the boys stayed. After the show, while I was checking in, a beautiful girl walked up and began talking to me. She knew my name, which surprised me because it was the first time I had wrestled in Boston. I also was surprised when she came on to me pretty strongly because I looked mean and nasty. I have to admit that I was somewhat flattered by the attention of such a pretty girl. When there was a pause in our conversation, Pete Sanchez, who was checking in at the same time, whispered to me, "*Hey, she's a hooker. She thinks you just won $10,000. She's after your money.*" This "country redneck" learned a valuable lesson that night from "city boy" Pete Sanchez about life in the big city.

I made more money in New York than I had ever made anywhere, although it was nothing compared to what the main event wrestlers make today. Somehow, I got the reputation for not being appreciative of the opportunity to work on top in New York, but that wasn't the case. I had been given an opportunity, and I did everything I was asked to do. I always showed up on time, I never missed a show, I worked hard, and I earned what I was paid. If there ever was a person that could have held them up for more money, it was me. I admit that I did complain to the office about money at times, but that was for the smaller shows.

My experience in dealing with the office over money was a learning experience. I constantly had to fight for my money, and I didn't like having to do that. The wrestlers of today don't have to fight for their money because they have contracts, but in 1976, there was no such thing. The promoters were supposed to pay us a certain amount based on percentages of the gate at the house shows, but they always got "first count" of the box office receipts and it was always in their favor.

In retrospect, one of the big problems I had with the office was the fact that they never looked at me as a true talent, but rather, as a green guy who got a chance break in the business.

Three other top guys I really respected in regards to the way they handled their business were "Superstar" Billy Graham, Ivan Koloff, and Ernie Ladd, each of whom had worked programs with Bruno before me. They all told me what deal they had with Vince — three percent for the big shows, like Boston, Madison Square Garden, and Pittsburgh, and five percent for the smaller shows, like New Haven, White Plains, and Hartford. Vince had agreed to pay them based on those percentages, but he never seemed to want to pay me on the same scale, so I was constantly trying to get the percentage I was supposed to receive. I didn't understand it at the time, but Vince was simply doing what any other businessman would do — get as much out of his talent (employees) while paying them as little as possible. It was simply business and nothing personal.

However, was I a top guy or just a jabroni? Still relatively green or not, I was a top guy, and I never stopped fighting for what was rightfully mine. I even called Vince at home late at night to argue over money. One time, in particular, I was supposed to get $250, and he paid me $200. I wanted the $50 I had coming to me. When he answered the phone, I stated my case. Vince said, "*I can't believe you're calling me at eleven o'clock at night over fifty dollars.*"

I told him, "*Vince, fifty dollars is a lot of money to me. Multiply that times 200 shows a year. That's $10,000.*"

And that was a huge sum of money to me.

I felt that Vince wanted me to thank him for giving me the opportunity to wrestle on top, which I did on a number of occasions, but he also wanted me to be one of his "boys." I wasn't going to be anyone's boy and I didn't have any interest in developing a kinship between myself and the office. I simply did my job as I saw it. That conflict between Vince and other offices carried over throughout my career.

When I first arrived in New York, I went out of my way to separate myself from the WWWF office. Being a Texan and an outsider, I just didn't fit in. I think my attitude of being wary of them was what caused a separation between us. At times, I think back and wish I hadn't gone in with that attitude. I suppose that's one of the things a "green" guy might have done, and regardless of my position on the cards, perhaps I was green after all.

By November, the writing was on the wall. It was time for me to go. If I stayed any longer, I would have to wrestle middle-of-the-card guys, and I wanted to keep my hard-earned position and go out on top. I was ready to move on, and Vince opened the door which led to my next opportunity.

A month before I was supposed to leave the territory, Vince asked me if I wanted to go to Japan. I readily said yes and he booked me into New Japan Pro Wrestling, the promotion which had been founded by Antonio Inoki in 1972. That would turn out to be another one of those pivotal moments in my career.

By the time I left New York, I was having some problems with the office and some of the New York "boys." I just didn't fit in. I was not a "New York" boy. I was independent. I had been booked into New York by Vince McMahon, but I had been my own man for a long time. McMahon, on the other hand, expected his talent to be obligated to the WWWF. I had been broken into the business by the Funks. I respected them and felt a kinship with them, but I thought I was independent of them, too, so I darn sure wasn't going to be controlled by the office. On the other hand, I did appreciate Vince giving me the opportunity, so I thanked him for booking me into Japan and for allowing me to work on top in the WWWF.

In the weeks before I left, the office tried their best to beat me down. The problem with staying in a territory for too long was that you ended up being used and abused. It wasn't something done maliciously by the promoters, although that happened occasionally, but there were only so many things which can be done with a certain talent. A heel could come into a territory, make his money, and then move on to the next territory. That was the formula used in most of the wrestling territories. New York was notorious for running heels through the system. Bruno would eat them up, they would move down to wrestle semi-main event guys, and the company would be through with them within a couple of months.

I was ready to leave, but I wasn't going to let them run over me as I worked my way out. I wanted to come back someday and run with Bruno again. Bruno himself told me to watch myself and not let the promotion abuse me on the way out of the territory. "*You might be able to come back in a few years and work with me again. If you don't allow yourself to be beaten down, it will be easy for us to reheat things when you come back.*" The fact that Bruno told me to take care of myself made it easy to say "no" to the office.

I was surprised to learn that I was booked with Gorilla Monsoon for my last match in the territory. I had my van packed and my wife was ready to drive all the way Texas immediately after the show. It was snowing and it was going to be hard trip.

Monsoon, who had been an amateur wrestler at Ithaca College in Ithaca, New York, took second place in the 1959 NCAA wrestling championships. By 1976, he was at the tail end of his career, but he still had a big name and wrestled occasionally. He had a secure position in the office and worked as an agent for the WWWF.

At 400 pounds, if he had wanted to, Monsoon could easily hurt just about anyone. Before the match that night, it crossed my mind that the office might have told Monsoon to give me a "going-away present." In the dressing room, I focused on our match and thought about what I might have to do to protect myself if he tried to stretch me. I found myself wishing Brody were there to watch my back.

Gorilla Monsoon

Brody and I had a code word we used if somebody seemed to be heading in a direction we didn't want to go. We worked a lot with Danny Hodge, who was one of the top amateurs of all time. He could do whatever he wanted with either one of us and we couldn't have done a thing about it. We decided if somebody tried to stretch us, or do something which might cause us injury, we would yell out, "*Bluejay!*" If Brody heard me say that, or if I heard him say it, we would come into the ring and do whatever was necessary to change the situation. If that meant kicking someone in the face, we were prepared to do just that. We came up with the plan simply for our own protection. Fortunately, we never had to use it.

Unfortunately, on the night I wrestled Monsoon, Brody was booked in another town. Towards the end of my run, they separated us and booked us in different towns. I had no amateur wrestling background, but I was strong and could hold my own. However, I wasn't sure I could prevent Monsoon from doing what he wanted because he was powerful and weighed much more than I did.

Shortly before our match was to start, Monsoon came over to talk to me. He could barely walk. He had hurt his neck and back the night before and was in a lot of pain. He asked me to take it easy on him and avoid touching his neck. He didn't want to take any bumps, either. I was relieved to hear him say that, but the thought lingered in the back of my mind that perhaps he was setting me up. Looking back, it was all just paranoia on my part. We spent the entire match just "walking" and "talking," and before I knew it, it was over and I was on the road headed south.

During the months I was in the northeast, I never had a cross word with Monsoon. I never had a cross word with the other agent, Angelo Savoldi, either. He was a real nice guy who ran a lot of the towns and treated the talent with respect.

In January 1977, I made my first trip for New Japan. Just as I had been booked into All Japan by the Funks, I had been booked into New Japan by Vince McMahon Sr. Unbeknownst to me, Vince had already set up my money deal. Once again, he wanted to be in control of every facet of the wrestlers' lives, which was standard for the Americans who booked talent to Japan. When I asked Vince how much money I was going to make each week, he hesitated. He seemed perturbed that I had the nerve to ask him such a question, but he quickly told me, *"$2,500 a week."*

Having just had a run on top in one of the biggest territories in the world, I wasn't too impressed with the dollar amount. I knew Ox Baker had gotten $2,500 a week during his first tour for All Japan. I thought that after what had happened in New York, I might be in a better position than Ox. I had made a pretty good name for myself, and I felt it had more value than that. Of even more concern was whether or not the $2,500 was the "net" figure, or the "gross," so the first thing I asked McMahon was, *"Is that the net figure?"*

I didn't want another situation like I had with All Japan, where I thought I was getting a gross figure, but got a net figure after taxes. I wanted to know exactly how much money I would be making. McMahon hesitated and said, *"I don't know."*

"I need to know the net figure, or I won't go," I said.

The next day, he called and said it was a net figure. I could tell he had an attitude towards me, although it was probably justified because I had an attitude towards him, as well. Regardless, I thought I had completed a successful first run in New York. I worked there for eight months, and having been in the business for only three years, I thought I had made a name for myself and handled myself well. I had worked with and learned from some of the top talents in the wrestling business in one of the biggest markets in the world. I felt good about what I had achieved.

I was excited to be going to a new place. Before leaving for Japan in January, I moved to Mississippi, where my wife had family. We were expecting the birth of our son, John. It seemed that New Japan wanted me for two tours that year, so Vince McMahon booked me for both, one in January and one in August. In-between tours, I planned to work for Bill Watts in the Louisiana territory. I wanted to be sure that I had work and income, as well as being close to home for the birth of my son.

1976 • Stan with Angelo Savoldi, Harrisburg PA

Chapter 12
Gaijin

When I arrived in Japan in early January 1977, I was picked up and driven to the Keio Plaza Hotel in Shinjuku (Tokyo), which was (and still is) a beautiful, first-class hotel with a large lobby and high ceilings. I was the last foreigner to arrive in Japan, so Antonio Inoki sent a driver to pick me up at the airport and take me to my hotel.

As was the custom for New Japan wrestlers, I arrived two days early. I was the only American on the tour. The other foreign wrestlers, or gaikokujin [foreign-country person], more commonly referred to as "gaijin," were Tiger Jeet Singh, a black guy named Brutus Mulumba from Canada, and Dave Taylor and Pete Roberts, both of whom were from England. I didn't know anybody who worked for the promotion, so I was a little bit apprehensive about going on the tour, but I was anxious for new experiences. After checking into the hotel, I called Dave Taylor to introduce myself to him, but I immediately ran into a problem. I could barely understand a word he spoke. He was from Yorkshire, which is located in the northern part of England, where they have a heavy accent. I thought I'd start somewhere else, so I hung up and called Pete Roberts. I didn't know Pete, either, but he spoke what I considered to be King's English. That phone call marked the beginning of a close friendship which lasts to this day.

During this time, there was a big difference between the two offices: All Japan and New Japan. Under Baba, All Japan was much more American style in their work and in the relations between the Japanese and American wrestlers. On the other hand, New Japan was more Japanese, business style. Everything was run so precisely.

Separation of talent was much stricter at New Japan, too. We were in constant kayfabe mode. One of the first differences I noticed between New Japan and All Japan was that New Japan had a separate bus for the gaijin wrestlers. I was glad of that. The bus driver for the gaijins was Akasaka. He was a nice guy. He was friendly and always greeted us with a smile.

On the bus with us was an older man named Yonetaro Tanaka, or Bon-Chan. We referred to him as Charlie Tanaka. Charlie had worked in the Japan Pro Wrestling Association [JWA] with the legendary Rikidôzan, and was now working as a referee with New Japan. He had scars on his head from when Rikidôzan had beaten him with the bamboo swords which were used for kendo. He was really nice. Most of us gaijin were like babes in the woods in the Japanese culture, so he looked out for us and helped whenever he could. He spoke just enough broken English to communicate, and he walked us through the hierarchy that was the custom in Japan. When we arrived at the arenas, he always insisted on carrying our bags, which was nice, and we appreciated his efforts to please us, but we were somewhat embarrassed by it. I was saddened to hear of his passing in 1996.

Peter Takahashi was the head referee. I didn't know it at the time, but he wasn't well liked by most of the gaijin. Behind his back, the boys called him "Peter the Prick." He wasn't too friendly, and when he was, his friendliness seemed to be contrived. I later heard his father had been killed in World War II, which was the reason why he disliked Americans. World War II had been over for 32 years, but I can see how the loss of his father would cause him to feel bitterness towards Americans. However, he wore his attitude on his sleeve, which made it hard for most of the gaijin to get along with him. I have to say Peter always treated me well and a cross word never came between us.

He was a good referee, though, and he facilitated communications between the Japanese wrestling office and the gaijins. He rode on the bus and could speak pretty good English, but he wanted to sleep whenever he was on the bus. The gaijin were up and moving around, listening to music, or playing cards, and trying to pass the time the best we could. Peter, on the other hand, wanted it quiet. I believe that was the reason for most of the friction between Peter and the gaijin talent. Whenever he could, he tried to separate himself from us. When the bus made a stop, he would disappear and stay out of sight until the bus was ready to leave. Once in awhile, he would point us in the direction of food establishments, but in most instances, Akasaka and Bon-Chan was much more helpful.

I had no interaction with Inoki during those early tours with New Japan. In fact, other than a few times when we ran into one another in the back of the arenas, I hardly even met him, and even then, we only traded polite nods and greetings as we passed. All communication went through Peter, or, on a couple of occasions, Hisashi Shinma, who we knew only as Mr. Shinma. There was never any meeting between talent before the matches, either. I just met my opponents in the ring and we wrestled give-and-take pretty much on the fly.

Tiger Jeet Singh was the star gaijin of New Japan. He was to New Japan what Abdullah the Butcher was to All Japan. Born Jagjit Singh Hans in Punjab, India, he immigrated to Vancouver, British Columbia, in the early sixties and eventually moved to Toronto, Ontario. As the villainous Tiger Jeet Singh, he wore a turban and carried a long, pointed sword when he went to the ring. He was very standoffish and he didn't communicate much at all with Pete, Dave, and I. Brutus Mulumba [Ormond Mulumba], who was from the Caribbean Islands, but was living in Canada, was Tiger's tag-team partner, and they kept to themselves most of the time. We only saw them on the bus and at the shows. When we got back to the hotel, they went their separate ways.

On the first show of the tour, January 7, 1977, I worked against Inoki. Tiger, of course, was in the main event with Brutus against Seiji Sakaguchi and Strong Kobayashi [Shozo Kobayashi].

Before I arrived in Japan, I decided that if I was given an opportunity to work with Inoki, I would be aggressive and unpredictable, and not hold back because of his status as the owner and top guy. That must have been a good decision because through Peter, Inoki let me know that he was happy with our match. Nobody ever told me they had long-term plans for me, so I had no idea of how Inoki was going to use me. He beat me on that first tour, but prior to that, I had been promoted pretty strongly. As time passed, I could tell I was getting some interest from both the fans and the office, but Tiger was far and away the main gaijin.

Tiger Jeet Singh

As Tiger waited to go to the ring for his match, a couple of young, Japanese boys came into the dressing room and took him by the arms. When the ring bell sounded, they opened the door and led him out.

The events which followed changed both me and the direction of my career.

The wrestling fans were packed around the door. Tiger ran out into the crowd, while the young boys tried to hold him back. He proceeded to kick, push, and whack people with the flat of his sword. There was pandemonium as he ran around the building. It was the most impressive thing I had ever seen in wrestling. I turned to Pete and said, "*Wow!*" about 30 times. I couldn't believe it. It was like watching a big fight scene in a movie. People were running and falling, and he was hitting and whipping them. They were scared of him and were really trying to get out of his way. I don't think he really tried to injure anybody with the sword, but he did hurt a number of people during his career. The funny thing is, the wrestling office loved it!

A full five to eight minutes went by before he actually climbed into the ring. I can't remember one single thing about his match in the ring. It didn't matter to me. I was excited and inspired beyond belief by what I had just witnessed. I would later learn that Tiger running through the arenas after crowds of people was a nightly occurrence.

Tiger came back into the dressing room the same way he went out, dragging the two young boys and slamming the door behind him. It was one of the most important moments in my life. Every night for the rest of the tour, I watched and studied him go to and from the ring. I must say that Tiger impressed me with his style.

One week into the five-week tour, Dave Taylor, who was 19 years old and away from home for the first time, began to complain about stomach cramps. He didn't have diarrhea, but it got worse with each day that passed. When the pain got so bad that he couldn't move around at all, somebody from the office took him to the hospital. It was a case of appendicitis. The doctors performed emergency surgery and Bon-Chan stayed at the hospital to take care of him. The Japanese hospitals are much different from the hospitals in the States, where nurses or aides take care of the patients. In Japan, the patient's family has some responsibility in the care of the patient.

The story Dave told was pretty scary. After he was wheeled into the operating room, he was strapped to the operating table. The doctors then used a syringe to give him a local anesthetic (he wasn't put to sleep). While he lay awake on the table, afraid to move a muscle, the doctors cut him open and removed his appendix. That would be terrifying to anyone, much less a 19-year-old who was away from home and in a foreign country for the first time. He really must have been scared.

After being laid up for about two weeks, Dave boarded an airplane and went home to Yorkshire, England. He had only worked one week, and the office used what he had earned to pay a portion of his hospital bills. The office said they were responsible for taking care of the wrestler if he was hurt in the ring, not outside of it. We all felt pretty badly about it.

The fact that he didn't get paid was what stuck out in my mind the most. At the time, perhaps New Japan was justified in doing what they did, but it seemed to me that it was wrong to take the little money Dave had made, which was probably $1,000 for the week. Regardless, the event made me understand that New Japan ran a cold, hard business.

When Dave left, there were just five of us gaijin on the bus, along with Umanosuke Ueda [Yuji Ueda], the blonde-haired tag-team partner of Tiger Jeet Singh. Our next stop was the northern part of Japan where the snow was at least two-feet deep in most places and it was cold. We arrived in a small town early for the show, and checked into a Japanese-style hotel, which had tatami mat floors, a communal bath and toilet, and no heat in the rooms. Since most of the people who stayed at the hotel were business people, and were only there at night, the hotels conserved energy by not running the air conditioning in the summer or the heat in the winter during the daytime hours. Since we checked in much earlier than anybody else, that was really bad for us, especially in the summer when it was really hot and humid. And since the television shows were in Japanese, we were unable to understand them, so all we could do was sleep. And sleep we did. I might add the fact that having to insert a 100-Yen coin into a slot on the side of the TV in order to watch it put a damper on our desire to watch television, as well.

There weren't many rooms in the hotel, so Pete and I were asked to share a room. We didn't mind because we were becoming friends. It was nice to have somebody to pass the time with because boredom makes people depressed, and depression was a serious problem for the gaijins in Japan. Most gaijins had a tough time being away from their homes, loved ones, and things which were familiar. Of course, this was also a time before cell phones and the Internet were available. An overseas telephone call cost five dollars a minute ... when we could get an operator. In addition, since most of the wrestlers trained hard, they needed to eat well in order to perform well in their match. The problem was that the food was different from what we were used to eating. The vegetables we managed to find had a whole different taste from those we grew up eating, and it was tough to eat a diet of rice and fish every day ... fish, by the way, that wasn't cooked.

After the first show in that part of the country, Pete and I went to our room. We were really cold, even with a number of blankets piled on top of us. In a short time, we were looking at our warm breath making fog in the chilly air. We decided we would stay warmer if we pushed our futons together and lay close to each other. It worked, and we didn't freeze. Later, we laughed about how that must have looked — two big wrestlers huddled together under a thick pile of blankets. Actually, we had to laugh at ourselves in order to keep from going insane.

I've already talked about being in a number of riots in America. The natural response of a wrestler to another wrestler in danger was to make an attempt to help save him, even if it put us in jeopardy ourselves.

One night, the bus was parked behind the arena in which we had just wrestled. As Tiger jumped onto the bus, he said, "*Somebody threw something and cut my finger.*" The words were barely out of his mouth when somebody threw a rock and shattered the window beside my seat. I leaped out of my seat, jumped from the bus to the ground, and ran out into the crowd. I didn't know who threw the rock, but it didn't matter. I was angry and beyond rational thought. I picked up parked bicycles and heaved them into the crowd. I was suddenly conscious of rocks hitting the pavement where I was standing, and with it being dark outside, I couldn't tell from where they were coming. As I looked around, I noticed an embankment on which a number of people were standing, yelling, and making gestures at me.

Suddenly, one of the people threw something which hit me in the shoulder. If there was any pain, I didn't feel it because adrenaline was rushing through my veins, masking any feeling I might have had. I charged up the hill, swinging at people and pushing the ones I caught. I felt like I was John Wayne in the movie, *The Alamo*, fighting off a bunch of Mexicans who had rushed the fort.

Placing myself into the midst of an angry crowd was deadly serious stuff, but it also was fun. It was almost like herding cattle as I chased the people around the back of the building toward the bus. As they ran past the bus, I quickly dodged to the side and ran up onto the steps of the bus and stopped. Turning back towards the people, I let out a long yell.

What surprised me the most was they answered my yell with a mimic of my yell. The people loved it!

Tiger, however, wasn't amused. He was concerned about the injury to his finger. It wasn't cut too badly. In fact, it barely bled. My thought was that he could dish it out, but he couldn't take it in return.

Akasaka, Peter, and the rest of the boys sat open-mouthed in their seats. They seemed to be in awe of what had happened. I don't think they had ever seen anybody take it to the people like I did. That event set my attitude and became a precedent for what was in store for my future career. It was as if I knew my destiny. I was determined that when I returned to Japan in the future, I would come back with a much more aggressive style and ring attitude. I would take it to the people and give them whatever it was they gave to me. That night, the foundation for the Stan Hansen character in Japan was set in stone.

When the tour ended on February 10, I returned home to Mississippi and went back to work for Bill Watts in the Louisiana territory. Things were different this time around, though. Watts began pushing me as one of his top heels, booking me into matches with Dick Murdoch, who had been switched to babyface, and Porkchop Cash. I also worked with Bill Watts himself, who was promoting himself in the top babyface spot. Like me, Bill was a big guy and he had played football in college. He liked to have physical matches, but he wasn't what I would consider to be a real good worker. What he lacked in that department, however, he made up for in charisma. He was really over with the wrestling fans, who believed he was one of the toughest guys ever. The chemistry between the two of us resulted in hot and heavy matches as we fought over the North American heavyweight title belt, which I won from Murdoch and defended for a seven-week period.

I'm glad I was able to work for Watts during that time because I got to know him better. I realized then that he had one of the better minds for the wrestling business. Bill had a good mind for the promotion aspect of the business, and he was creative with his TV show. In those days, Louisiana was a hotbed for wrestling and attracted both blacks and whites. New Orleans was the only city of any real size, but each of the small cities which made up the territory was doing very well.

One night in Oklahoma City, Watts and I were fighting outside the ring on the floor. A wrestling fan (we called them "marks" in those days) ran up and hit me in the back as Watts and I were pounding on each other. I turned around, hit the guy with three shots, and he fell to the floor. Forgetting that he was a babyface (or perhaps not), Watts pushed me aside and kicked the guy in the head. When he turned back towards me, we continue fighting where we had left off and made our way back into the ring.

Watts was later sued by the mark. Watts joked that I hit the mark with my first punch, but due to my nearsightedness, I didn't know he was on the floor, so I just kept swinging at the spot where the mark had been standing. That was typical of the way that heels and babyfaces would help each other if there was a threat from the fans.

The heel always had more to do than the babyface. Not only did he have to lead the match, but he had to be aware of what was going on around him at all times, just in case a mark came into the ring to get involved in the match. Of course, without eyes in the backs of our heads, we couldn't see in all directions at the same time, so it was always good to have an opponent who was willing to help out when danger loomed. In fact, many of the babyfaces (like Watts) had been heels at one time or another in their careers, so they knew about keeping an eye on the crowd. Even the wrestlers who were not in the matches, who stood in the back watching, were often expected to help if things got dicey. I ran to the ring from the back of the building to help many times during my career. At times, I simply watched the heel as he walked back to the dressing room, just to be sure nobody tried to attack him from behind. At others times, I had to interject myself into a fight or riot and help the heel get safely back to the dressing room. We didn't get too aggressive with the fans, and we didn't purposely look for a confrontation, but we wanted to make our presence known so fans would think about it before getting involved. Most of the time, our presence alone was enough to keep the fans at bay.

John Tolos also came through the territory while I was there. He was a funny guy … always quick with a joke or rib. He was really old school. Wow! It feels strange to say that now. Now I'm the one who is old school. During his career, John was a huge star all over the world and he drew many sellout crowds in the Los Angeles territory. For his age, he had a great body and a golden tan, hence his name, John "Golden Greek" Tolos.

Pete Roberts tells a funny story about Tolos. While on tour for New Japan (before I went to work for them), they were both on tour with Tony Charles and the McGuire twins, Benny and Billy. I met the twins during my early days in Louisiana. Brody and I worked around the horn with them for a few weeks.

The McGuire twins were huge guys who were advertised at 700 pounds apiece. I had worked with them in Louisiana in 1974 and, at the time, I had never seen anyone that big. At different times in their careers, Benny's top weight was 814, while Billy's was 784. They were huge in size, but they were nice. They talked with a slow, hillbilly twang, and their personality was almost childlike. Several times during the tour, they became frustrated with trying to live in a place built for small Japanese people, and actually broke down crying. They didn't just shed tears. They actually cried for minutes at a time. I witnessed that myself when we were together in Louisiana.

Tony Charles and Tolos were serious "ribbers," which were guys who played pranks on their fellow wrestlers. Wrestlers were famous for ribbing each other. The ribs could be funny, serious, and at times, downright mean. Both Tolos and Charles were good at ribbing. Pete Roberts told me they would spend hours devising elaborate ribs to play on the McGuires.

In the dressing room, it was obvious that the McGuires were pretty simple-minded. I don't mean that in a bad way. They were just two young, naïve, farm boys from Hendersonville, North Carolina who were raised by their grandparents. There was a competition between the two of them as to who was biggest and who was the best wrestler. Now that in itself was pretty funny. At a weight of more than 700 pounds, they couldn't do much more than let their opponents bounce off of them, and then splash (their finish) onto them at the end of the match. Regardless of their limitations, due to their size, they were a huge hit in Japan. There were other big wrestlers, like Man Mountain Mike and Haystack Calhoun, but Benny and Billy were heavier, and they had the additional attraction of being the only twins of that size.

Benny and Billy McGuire in Japan

The Japan tours lasted six weeks, so everybody had a lot of time to get to know each other. Tony Charles struck up a conversation with Billy and they became good friends. Tolos did the same thing with Benny. As they got to know the twins' personalities, Charles and Tolos realized there was some sibling rivalry between the twins. In the dressing room, the McGuires would get into arguments which would get heated to the point where they would get red-faced and "bump" bellies together. Tolos and Charles each built up "his" twin, saying things like, "*You're working harder than your brother,*" "*Your brother isn't really doing his share of the work,*" or "*Why do you have to do all the work while your brother just stands in the corner?*" Over time, the suggestions would cause emotions between the twins to boil over, and the belly-bumping would commence, to the amusement, but straight faces, of the other wrestlers.

They had to make a number of trips by train. The train stations didn't have escalators, so commuters had to climb steps up to, and down from, the platform. When they were making a connection, everybody had to move pretty fast from one platform to the next. "Fast" wasn't a word in the McGuires' vocabulary. Walking up and down steps was pure torture for them. When they arrived at the top (or bottom), they would be sweaty, red-faced, and their breathing sounded like a freight train. Needless to say, wherever they went, large crowds of Japanese would gather around to gawk at them.

One day, Charles ran up to them and said, "*We made a mistake. We have to go to the next platform. Hurry!*" The twins just stood there, speechless, and finally just broke out crying. They realized it was a rib when the boys all began to laugh.

At the time, the McGuires were married to twin sisters from Montreal. They met them through the girls' uncle, who was a referee for the wrestling promotion in Quebec, and were married in the ring at a bullring stadium in El Paso. We had seen pictures of the four of them. The twins were both nice-looking and slim. Billy and Benny, on the other hand, had huge stomachs that literally hung down to their knees. That prompted Tolos to ask one of the McGuires how they managed to make love. One of them told him that he had a harness. When he said that, it set off a whole new line of ribbing from Charles and Tolos. They asked Benny (or Billy) to demonstrate how he would put on the harness. To everyone's delight, he would go into great detail, showing the boys what he would do.

The McGuires were so big that the office used a small delivery truck to transport them from the hotel to the arena. When they could, they would back the truck up to a loading dock and the twins would walk into the back of the truck. One time, they didn't have a loading dock, so the office put bundles of newspapers onto the ground as steps so they could run up the bundles and roll into the back of the truck. Benny was the first to try it. He made without any trouble and was quite happy with his achievement. With excitement in his voice, he yelled for Billy to do it. For them to run, they had to get their stomach to move in the opposite direction of what the front leg would move, so it was very awkward for them. Billy backed up and began to run. As Billy cheered him on, Billy stepped onto the lowest bundle of papers. They promptly slid forward and Billy fell hard under the end of the truck. Everyone was concerned when he began crying like a small child, but in the end, the only thing hurt was his ego. The boys all laughed and walked over to help him up. With everyone's help, the boys were able to push and roll him up and over the tailgate of the truck.

My son John was born in late March, so I wanted to be home in Jackson, Mississippi, every night. Most of the other wrestlers shared rides, and stayed overnight in the towns before driving on to the next booking, which cut down on the number of miles they drove. I wanted to go home every night, so in many cases, I doubled the number of miles I would have normally put on my car.

Bill Watts treated me well by giving me a good push. He promoted me and paid me like a top guy. Business was good and the payoffs were decent. However, Louisiana wasn't a territory where someone would get rich, even on top. I wasn't too concerned because I was just biding my time, preparing myself for my next tour of Japan.

Before I had left the earlier tour of Japan, Mr. Shinma, the business manager for New Japan, came to me and asked if I would return to Japan in August.

He had already talked about it to Vince McMahon. Since I knew I would still be in Louisiana working for Watts until my son was born, I told him, "*Yes.*" It was a good feeling to know I had another job waiting for me, and that I had a safety valve in case something didn't work out with Watts.

Shortly before I left Louisiana for Japan, I got a call from Ole Anderson, who, along with Gene Anderson, was booking the Georgia territory. He said he had heard a lot of good things about me, more than likely from Bill Watts. Ole later told me that he had also talked to Vince McMahon Sr., who gave me a negative rating. Ole told me, "*I'm looking for new talent. I'll give you an opportunity to make a spot for yourself.*" By that, he meant I could come to Atlanta and show him what I could do. If I got over with the fans, he would book me on a regular basis. Before I left for Japan, we set a date for me to start in Atlanta.

"Opportunity" was all I ever asked of promoters. I just wanted a chance to present my character to the fans. It I got over and the people responded, the promoter would see the value of booking me. If not, I would leave without complaint. I liked that type of challenge. The ball was always in my court, and if I didn't get over, I had only myself to blame. I won or lost on my personal ability.

As summer 1977 drew to a close, I became anxious to return to Japan, where I would introduce the wrestling fans to the "new and improved" Stan Hansen.

I returned to Japan for New Japan at the end of August 1977. Blackjack Mulligan and I were scheduled to lead the tour. There were three promotions in Japan at the time: New Japan Pro Wrestling, All Japan Pro Wrestling, and Isao Yoshihara's International Wrestling Enterprise [IWE]. That was Mulligan's fourth tour of Japan, having worked two tours previously for the IWE and one for All Japan.

On this tour of Japan, I decided to take what I had seen Tiger do and integrate his style into my character. Instead of taking a sword to the ring, however, I carried a rope, which fit into my character. Like Singh and his sword, I would swing the rope at the fans, and hit everyone within reach. The more I hit them, the more they liked me. That's really weird, but it's the truth.

I think everyone in the wrestling business, at one time or another has incorporated things into their ring persona that they've seen other wrestlers do. There are a few original moves, but as the old saying goes, "*There's nothing new under the sun.*"

The Lariat was one such original hold. I had learned it when I was a middle linebacker in college. When a tight end would move across the middle of the field, looking for a pass from the quarterback, I would come across from the opposite direction the tight end was running. My job was to intercept him and keep him from getting into a position to receive the pass. One way to do that was to hold out my arm and catch him on the neck with my forearm. I, along with other middle linebackers, inflicted a great deal of pain on tight ends who were preoccupied while looking for the ball. My forearm would lay them out flat on the ground. The next time they came across the field, instead of devoting their full attention to finding the ball thrown by the quarterback, they would be watching me. It worked well for me and many other linebackers, but due to injuries suffered by players who were the recipients, the move is now outlawed in football.

I was the first to use the Lariat as my finish in pro wrestling. Baba did a move which was somewhat like a Lariat. He would catch his opponent's neck with his arm, and then jump up and throw out his feet in the opposite direction. However, I did the move by running at my opponent and hitting him with the full force of my body. It became known as my finish, and I always saved it for the end of the match. I *never* used it as a high spot and I never allowed people to kick out of it, even though there was a lot of pressure from the Japanese wrestlers who wanted to do just that. I did almost everything I was ever asked to do in Japan, but that was the one concession I never made. Since that time, many wrestlers have used the Lariat, or adapted it to fit their own needs. Hulk Hogan's "Axe Bomber," Riki Chôshû's "Riki Lariato," and even Justin Bradshaw's "Clothesline from Hell," were all based on the Lariat.

One time during the New Japan tour, Mulligan and I had taken separate taxis to the arena in Kyoto. We were scheduled to wrestle each other that night. During our match, Mulligan and I took our battle outside the ring. We fought each other all the way back to the dressing room, and then out onto the city street, where we continued to fight in front of both wrestling fans and people who just happened to be on the street. We were still fighting as the New Japan young boys forced me into a taxi cab. Without hesitation, I jumped out the door on the other side of the cab, climbed up onto the trunk of the vehicle, and leaped down onto Mulligan. We continued our battle until the Japanese boys managed to shove us into separate taxis. It was fun and the people really enjoyed the wildness of it all.

I knew from that point on that I was going to do that style. During the days which followed, and throughout the rest of my career, I kept pushing the envelope to see just how far I could go, and how wild I could be. The office didn't object. They let me do what I wanted to do. I believe it was my attitude and style of wrestling that changed the direction of Japanese professional wrestling. Masao "Tiger" Hattori, the primary referee for New Japan, once said to me, "*You really changed the whole style of wrestling in Japan.*" I really appreciated that compliment. I never thought about it until he said that. Riki Chôshû also gave me credit for having done that.

I don't claim to be the first person to do that style. The Butcher and Tiger Jeet Singh had been doing it for years, and from what I understand, King Curtis Iaukea did, too. However, there was a difference between what they did and what I did. None of them moved continuously like I did. When Abdullah and Singh took their battles out into the audience, their match would end shortly afterwards, and the people began to expect that to happen. In contrast, I took the action outside the ring, and then back inside. After I worked in some holds and moves for a few minutes, I would go back outside. I repeated that scenario, over and over, rarely stopping to catch my breath. I just kept going, and the people responded to it. I often chased people for five minutes. The people would run away, tripping over chairs and each other. It was like herding cows. It was exciting for them, and by the same token, it was fun for me. As time went by, and I continued to hit fans with the rope, it became so popular that they would line up in the hopes that I would hit them. To be rope-whipped by Stan "The Lariat" Hansen was a big deal to them. It was almost like a rite of passage.

Stan uses the lariat on an opponent

Working that style, going wild and moving fast, was hard work. It was hard enough to wrestle without blowing up, but taking it outside, and then back into the ring, took a lot of extra gas, so I had to stay in good cardiovascular shape. Of course, football taught me how to train my body for peak cardio performance, and that ability to have the gas needed for that style of work is what separated me from many of the other guys who tried to work that style.

To me, the best part of working that style was that I enjoyed it. I loved to work the brawling style. It wasn't just an act. It actually became a part of me, and I looked forward to doing it every night. It was so much fun. One night, after I had made four or five tours to Japan, I wrapped my rope around a fan's neck and dragged him around the building. Somebody from the office came to me after the match and said that might be a little too much. They weren't mad, but they let me know there was a limit to what I could do. I listened and toned it down a notch.

In the dressing room before each match, I didn't think about what I was going to do, either. Other than knowing where I was going to end up, my matches were spontaneous. I didn't know what I was going to do until I did it. I believe that's the main reason why I got over as well as I did. My matches didn't look planned out ... because they weren't. That is what made my matches so different from just about everything else, and that is what got me over. The New Japan office let me go out and do whatever I wanted to do, and I can't remember them ever telling me what I should or shouldn't do.

One of the things I enjoyed about New Japan was its great organization. Everything was done "Japanese" style. Of course, from the Japanese point of view, that was just standard procedure, but to the gaijin, it was so different from the way things were done in the States. In Japan, everything happens at a specific, precise time. In the States, time is a "rough" figure. I often stated to a new gaijin, "*There are only two things you must always remember: the time the bus leaves to go to the hotel in the next town and the time the bus leaves to go to the matches."*

It was good to see things done on an orderly basis. Our main responsibility was to be on time, and often, Japanese time meant being at least five minutes early. If we were scheduled to leave at nine in the morning, then I would be ready to board the bus at 8:50 in the morning. It became ingrained in me to such a degree that I would arrive early and be in my seat and ready to go at least fifteen minutes before our departure time.

Most of the guys were good about adhering to the time schedules, but as the years passed by, newer and greener guys came to Japan, and many of them were so selfish that they often showed up ten minutes late every day. When they boarded the bus, they would get cold, hard looks from Joe-san, the bus drivers, the Japanese wrestlers, and even from the gaijins who had been on time and were patiently waiting. Everybody wanted to get to the next place as soon as possible. As time passed, the wrestlers who showed up on time would get irritated at the latecomers and tempers would flare up. The office frowned on tardiness, as well. If a wrestler was persistently late, it could cost him his job.

Most of the bus trips were three to four hours at the most, but most were shorter. In the early days, we made many of the longer trips on the Shinkansen, the high-speed railway system known commonly as the "bullet train." In later years, we rode the bus most of the time. Those long trips were brutal, but they were still much better than driving. Whenever I found myself getting negative about the long trips, I would always think back about the road trips we made in the Amarillo territory.

On one bus trip which was going to take close to nine hours, we were all on the bus at seven-thirty in the morning ... except for Harley Race. Joe Higuchi got off the bus and went into the hotel to see if he could find him. Harley was just sitting down to eat breakfast. Joe-san said, "*You need to get on the bus. You're already late.*"

"It's a long bus ride, so I'm going to eat," he replied.

Harley was a big card in Japan and he had a very close relationship with Baba. Harley also was part owner of the Kansas City territory, so he would also book underneath talent for All Japan. As such, Harley had a lot of clout, but by that time, Harley was not the top talent in Japan that he had once been.

When Harley finally got on the bus, everybody was mad. The bus driver had to drive fast because we had a schedule to keep, so he was angry. Joe-san was perturbed by Harley's attitude. The talent was angry because we had already been sitting on the bus for 30 minutes and we still had the full nine hours to go. We weren't necessarily mad at Harley, but we were bothered by the situation. I can't say the incident was the cause, but that was the last tour Harley made for All Japan. Nothing was ever said to us about it, but I never saw him with All Japan again.

Like United Parcel Service [UPS], whose company motto used to be "the tightest ship in the shipping business," New Japan was "the tightest ship in the wrestling business." The company was well-organized and run in a professional manner, and I was always impressed by the way they handled business.

During this tour, Roddy Piper, Blackjack Mulligan, and I had a contest to see who could go the longest without washing or changing our street clothes. After a week or so, we all had a pretty bad odor radiating from us. Mulligan and I finally gave up and Piper was awarded the "unclean" championship. We were all thankful to be able to wash again, but I'm sure everyone else on the bus was more thankful than we were.

That story reminds me of the fact that the Amarillo guys — the Funks, Dusty Rhodes, Bruiser Brody, Bobby Duncum, and Dick Murdoch — all had the reputation of having smelly tights and knee pads. The Japanese wrestlers complained, in a joking manner (I think), about the smell. Joe Higuchi always complained the loudest and was constantly kidding us about it. Part of our reason for not cleaning our ring gear was that in Japan during those times, it could easily cost $30 to have the hotel clean just a few pieces of our clothing. I later discovered small coin laundries in the towns where we stayed. It was ironic that Jumbo Tsuruta was the only Japanese wrestler whose wrestling gear had a bad odor. Everyone said it was because he was trained by the Amarillo guys.

In typical sumo-style heirarchy, the young Japanese boys did the laundry every night for the top Japanese wrestlers, so they always had clean tights. On the other hand (and perhaps as an excuse), we seldom had the opportunity to find a Laundromat, and there were times when we would go almost the whole tour without doing laundry. Later in my career, I was able to wash my tights more often (usually once a week). That was another respect in which I could honestly be called an outlaw.

That third tour of Japan, my second time for New Japan, was a full six weeks long. The office was really giving me a strong push. I wrestled 34 matches against the top talent of the time: Antonio Inoki, Seiji Sakaguchi, Strong Kobayashi, Riki Chôshû, and Kantaro Hoshino. My only pin fall loss in a singles match was to Inoki on September 2, 1977, during a match in which Inoki was making a defense of his NWF [National Wrestling Federation] title belt. I also lost to Inoki by disqualification and went to a "no contest" verdict against Sakaguchi. I won all other singles matches, including a clean pin fall win over Sakaguchi. In tag-team matches, I was either given the win or my tag-team partners were pinned.

I don't quote those statistics in order to brag because a win-loss record wasn't really under my control. I list them because I want people to understand how much faith the office had in me, and how strong a push they were giving me. They definitely had plans for me, and they didn't want anything to hurt my reputation or credibility.

Even with the strong push, when the tour ended, New Japan hadn't given me a return date, so at first, I wasn't sure whether or not they wanted me back. Mr. Shinma did ask me about my plans. When I told him I didn't have anything set in concrete, he asked me if Vince was booking me. When I told him I was booking myself, he seemed very happy to hear that. He said they would be very interested in having me return, and to let him know when I was available. As I boarded the plane to fly back to the United States, I was elated to know I had a job with New Japan. More importantly, it was a good feeling to know they had asked me to return, rather than me asking them.

Chapter 13

Manipulators

In regards to the travel, the Atlanta territory was, by far, the best territory I ever worked. The trips could all be made in less than 1½ hours. They were short enough that we didn't have to leave our homes until five in the afternoon, and we were home by midnight. It was a good time to be home more often because, in January 1979, my daughter Paige was born.

The payoffs were really good, too, so it also was the territory where I saved the most money. At that time, the Charlotte, North Carolina territory was one of the premier territories. The top guys working there could make more than $100,000 a year. However, the downside was they worked seven days a week and traveled six states. In Georgia, we only made $75,000 a year, but the trips were short, which meant road expenses took a smaller chunk out of our payoffs, and we were off on Sundays. That gave us more free time to be with our families, which was important to me.

The territory was on fire at the time. Jim Barnett owned the territory, but Gene and Ole Anderson were the bookers. Gene and Ole worked as a team, both in the ring and in the office, but it was Ole who was the brains and did most of the booking work in the office. Ole put together the matches, mapped out the TV shows, and promoted the talent. He was a smart guy.

I've often been asked to compare Ole Anderson and Bill Watts, the two guys I feel had the best minds in the business. Ole and Watts had both been top wrestlers in their own right. Watts was more of a single guy who had great runs in New York, and he had been influenced by Eddie Graham when he was working in Florida. Ole's early career was primarily spent as the tag-team partner of Gene Anderson. I never had the opportunity to see Ole and Gene wrestle together, but I heard they were one of the best heel teams ever. They had a great run in the Charlotte territory, and Ole was influenced by Jim Crockett Sr. and George Scott. By the time I met them, however, he had developed his own style and he was booking two territories; Charlotte and Georgia. I really liked Ole's psychology in the ring and his constant movement, which is something I advanced in Japan. Next to Brody, my favorite tag-team partner in the States was Ole. Ole was a great wrestling heel and he had a quick mind for the business. He taught me a lot about how to get and keep heat.

When it came to booking, Bill Watts and Ole Anderson were both very smart. They were the two best bookers I ever worked for. Masa Fuchi was a great booking talent for All Japan, but to me, Watts and Ole were the best. Of course, as good as they both were, they were very different in their approach to the business.

First of all, Watts seemed to take care of his friends more so than Ole. Many of the guys thought Ole took care of me, but I believe Ole was more balanced in his payoffs than Bill. I never got the feeling that I was getting a better payoff because Ole and I had a close relationship. As far as I know, the top talents in Atlanta were all getting the same money that I was. I don't knock Watts for taking care of his top guys. That was a part of the business, and those guys were much better talents than I was in 1974 and 1975, so perhaps they deserved it.

The job of the booker was a difficult one. Not too many people were really good at it. Bookers had to be innovative and capable of keeping up with ideas which were to be introduced three to four weeks in the future. Perhaps the toughest job a booker had was the ability to keep and pacify talent. Watts and Ole both surrounded themselves with good talent. No matter how smart a booker is, if they don't get or create talent which can carry their ideas forward, they won't be successful. However, it was hard to handle a roster of wrestlers, each of whom had different egos and personalities. Most of the boys, fueled by a few beers and hours to kill in a car, would be the smartest guys in the business. They (we) would constantly question, advise, complain about what they were involved with in the business. There were a lot of great ideas put on the table during those long trips, but most of them were pretty much self-centered. Bookers, on the other hand, weren't concerned with just one idea or one wrestler. They had to come up with many ideas which involved a large cast of characters, towns, and programs.

Bill Watts

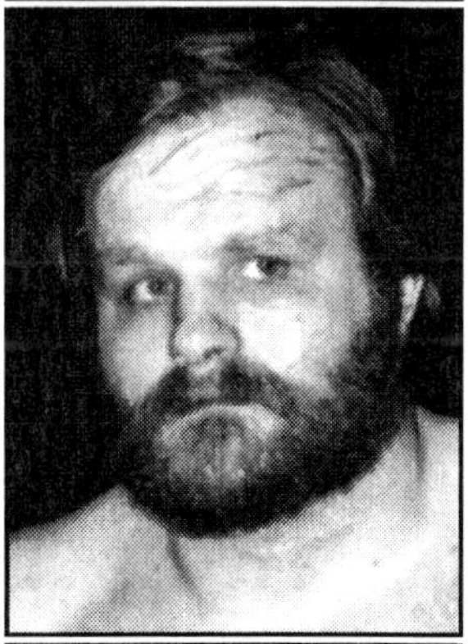

Ole Anderson

One of Watts' traits was that he liked to spell out, move for move, all the details for the end of a match. His ideas would often be long and very complicated. In 1977, when he wasn't able to personally attend a house show, he would send over a tape recorder with his ideas on how he wanted things to go. It was comical in many respects because, as we listened to the tape, there was always background noise, and Watts constantly started and stopped the tape as he added idea after idea. Often, I would picture his face in my mind as he described in detail what and how things could go, more often than not punctuated with curse words. You had to try and filter out the curse words in order to keep up with the flow of his thoughts. As the referee held the tape recorder, we would look at each other and silently laugh as we tried to filter out the extra adjectives and adverbs. That said, I always thought his ideas were good, and in many respects, they were innovative. I was never in a room when Watts made the tapes, but I believe he came up with most of the ideas on his own. When it came to putting those ideas into action, we knew we had better do what he wanted. His word was final.

Ole was a lot like Watts when it came to creating ideas. He knew the direction he wanted to go with his programs, so he had things worked out at least two to three weeks in advance. Like Watts, Ole came up with complex and innovative ideas. Where he differed from Watts was in his style of working with talent pertaining to the end of a match. He would often listen to talent and allow them to have a say in what he wanted them to do. He allowed them to present variations on his ideas, or to suggest their own thoughts on how their matches should go. As his tag-team partner in Georgia for several years, I witnessed many occasions when guys would try to dictate what they wanted, and what they wanted was usually what was best "for them." Ole knew exactly where he wanted to go because he knew what he was coming back with on the next show. He allowed them to talk and say what they wanted, but he would slowly work things around so the final plan was very close to what he had planned all along. In the wrestling business, bookers were also known as "manipulators," and when Ole was booking, he was a master manipulator. He allowed the boys to give their opinions. If their ideas didn't fit into what he had planned for the future, he would take the discussion full circle until he had them back to doing what he wanted to do in the first place. I saw him do that many times with Dick Slater, Mr. Wrestling #2 [Johnny Walker], and many others. Occasionally, he would use their ideas, but most of the time, he would have them agreeing to do what they had earlier said they didn't want to do. And in doing so, he made the talent feel like they had played a part in the decision-making part of the business.

When I went back to work for Watts in 1979, after I had established myself in Japan, I told him I wasn't going to come in and let him take advantage of me. What I did in the States was being seen and reported in Japan, so I had to take care of myself business-wise. We came to an understanding that I would be in control of my matches. He understood my situation and agreed to the condition. We had a good working relationship from then on. Whenever he needed someone fresh or different on his cards, I would come in and work part time between Japan tours.

One time during that same time period, Watts put me with Jake Roberts at the St. Bernard Parish Civic Auditorium in New Orleans. Jake hadn't made it big yet and he was just getting his feet wet in the business, but Watts was giving him a push because he was a good babyface who had a lot of fire. Grizzly Smith (Jake's dad) was running the show that night.

During the match, Jake covered me when we fell to the mat close to the ropes. I saw Jack Howell, the referee, begin to make the count ... one, two ... and as he brought his hand down to count three, I grabbed the bottom rope with my hand. Of course, when a wrestler reaches the ropes, it forces the ref to stop the count and break us apart. Howell was on his knees when he was making the count and my hand was right in front of his face. He looked directly into my eyes and went ahead and made the three-count. The house popped! Needless to say, I exploded and jumped to my feet. I was hot. I knew he saw me grab the rope. I got in his face and yelled, "*Come on, you son-of-a-bitch. I had the rope.*" With his eyes the size of saucers, he backed up and crossed and uncrossed his arms in front of him, meaning, *"No count."* However, I thought he meant "no" to my complaint. I went nuts. I kicked him pretty hard and ran him out of the ring. I then turned on Jake, who was just standing in a corner of the ring, looking like he didn't know what was going on. I picked him up, threw him to the mat, and began kicking him. I finally hit the ropes and was going to drop a stiff knee on his face. As I came down, I looked into his face and saw that he had his eyes squeezed shut. While I was still in mid-air, I moved slightly and gave him a less painful knee to the forehead. It took all my will power to not come down with all my force. I picked him up and threw him out of the ring. When he landed on the concrete floor, he staggered to his feet and ran to the dressing room. I was determined to show the fans that I might have been the one pinned, but I wasn't the one who had lost the match.

I was so hot. I went backstage to find Grizzly, but he had left the building when the match ended (or he was busy doing something outside). Jack Howell tried to tell me that he was trying to say "no pinfall" when he was crossing his arms, but I didn't know whether or not to believe him. I had it in my head that I had been screwed, and it was highly possible that Watts had orchestrated the whole scenario.

I remained angry during the drive home to Jackson. I was supposed to work with Jake later that week in Jackson, but I made up my mind that I wasn't going to go. Not that it made any difference, but Jackson was my home and I wasn't going to play any games there. Later that night, Watts and Grizzly both called me at home to talk about the situation. They told me it had all been a misunderstanding and that I should have been disqualified. They both spent a lot of time convincing me the outcome had been a mistake.

I finally agreed to appear in Jackson, but before I hung up, they told me to show up late and act angry in the dressing room. *"Go to the ring and scare the hell out of Jake,"* Watts said. On the night of the show, I did what they asked and snapped at everyone who came into the dressing room, including the referee. When he tried to give me information about the match, I told him to go to hell. *"I'm gonna do my own match tonight."* The dressing rooms were separate, so I didn't see Jake before the match, but I'm sure he had heard about my actions because everyone else knew I was "upset." I was in the ring long before I was announced, as if I couldn't wait to tear Jake to tiny bits. I hit the ropes several times and glared back towards the door where Jake would be coming out. I paced back and forth in the ring, stopping every so often to kick the ropes. The Jackson Auditorium was a large, round building and the walk from the dressing room was about 25 to 30 yards. Finally, with much delay, Jake began to walk slowly down the aisle. He walked slowly and, as far as I could tell, he really looked scared. He made a couple of attempts to get into the ring, but each time he did, I tried to kick him and he would scoot backwards. When he finally got into the ring, I charged at him. I locked up as stiff as I could and backed him into the ropes. His eyes were the size of silver dollars. I smiled and snickered ... and he realized he had been had. I can't tell you how relieved he looked as we progressed into our match.

Of course, Jake developed into a great talent in his own right, and went on to become one of the top draws in the early days of the WWF.

To be fair to Watts, Ole also used foul language, as most of us did. Over the years, using curse words in the dressing room became a habit. We would never use such language at home, or in mixed company, but there was something about the dressing room which seemed to bring out the worst in most of us.

Watts had a good attitude, but he did separate himself from the average wrestler. He became more like a company executive. I think he did this because he was both the booker and owner of the territory, while Ole was just the former at the time. (Ole eventually bought ownership in the company and later formed his own company, Championship Wrestling from Georgia) The owner has his own money at stake, so he has to make decisions which often upset people. Ole was more down to earth with the guys. He was constantly ribbing and joking, often in ways that offended some, but I thought it was humorous. Nonetheless, both Watts and Ole had an appreciation for their talent. They realized it was the talent that made them money.

In regards to anger, Watts had a bigger temper than Ole. Ole, on the other hand, would cut people to the bone when he criticized them, and that made a lot of people mad. What most people don't understand is that was a part of Ole's sense of humor. He made a lot of cutting remarks to me, as well, but I would just make a smart comment in return. I began to understand that he enjoyed the verbal battles, and he got along the best with people who would give it right back to him.

The wrestlers *never* thought the payoffs were as good as they should be in any territory, but the opinion of most of the guys was that Ole paid out more than Watts, especially since the Georgia territory had much shorter trips than those in Louisiana. I can't complain about the payoffs I received during my second run with Watts in 1977. I just accepted the fact that that was the way the payoffs were. I had a choice — accept them and work, or don't accept them and go somewhere else. I chose to work, so I didn't complain.

When it came to working ability, I think Ole was better. Watts, however, was really over in his Mid-South territory and the people believed in him. To old-time wrestling fans in Oklahoma and Louisiana, Bill Watts is easily one of the most recognizable names, closely followed by Danny Hodge, Dr. X [Jim Osborne], the Spoiler [Don Jardine], Dusty Rhodes, and the Kentuckians [Grizzly Smith and Luke Brown]. Those guys really popped the territory in the early '70s and die-hard fans still remember them. Ole was a fixture in the Georgia and Charlotte territories, being on Ted Turner's old Channel 17 and airing on SuperStation WTBS.

Ole's wrestling brother, Gene, was a good hand in the ring, too, and got along well with most of the guys. Just about everybody liked him. On the other hand, it seemed like Ole wasn't well-liked at all. His personality could best be described as abrasive. Whenever he talked to us, or critiqued our performance in the ring, he came across as talking down to us. As I mentioned earlier, it took me a while to realize that, most of the time, Ole was kidding. He ribbed people constantly. He ribbed the fans. He ribbed Barnett. Most of all, he ribbed the wrestlers. The most amazing thing about Ole was that he could do it without any hint of a smile on his face. Ribbing or not, he *always* came across as being serious. That was the reason why people got so mad at Ole. They didn't know whether he was kidding them or not. Most of the time, though, what he said in his ribbing was exactly what he was thinking, and he didn't mind giving people his opinion.

He started in on me pretty quickly, calling me names like goof, buffoon, and saying I was dumb. I naturally kidded him back. I told him he was short and called him names like runt and midget. Generally, short people don't like to be told they're short. That didn't bother Ole in the least. He fired right back at me: *"If I stand on my wallet, then I'm real tall."* He meant, of course, that he had lots of money. We went back and forth constantly, and I never let him rib me without ribbing him back. I soon realized that Ole enjoyed the give-and-take, and he got along the best with those who gave back a portion of what he dished out. That was the beginning of a great friendship.

Ole also talked to me about saving money. He had a reputation for being close with a dollar, which he was, and being frugal paid off for him. As the booker and a top wrestler in both Atlanta and the Charlotte territories, he made great money. The Atlanta territory thrived under his watch, and Jim Barnett paid him well to keep him there.

Ole was famous for driving a 1970 Ford LTD convertible. When all the top guys got deals on new Cadillacs in the Charlotte territory, Ole passed up an opportunity to buy one. Of the six or seven top guys, he was the only one who didn't. His reasoning was that he didn't have to make payments, his insurance rates were low, and, tax-wise, he had written off the Ford several times over the years. It was a lesson that more of the boys should have heeded. When Ole retired, he had a good nest egg set aside, and he was able to retire in comfort.

We spent a lot of time together on the road, and during the trips, we didn't talk about wrestling as much as we did about investing and saving money. We talked for hours on end about the stock market, and the new and different investments that were available. Ole told me about the timber property and sawmill he owned in Wisconsin. It was a great education. I appreciated that about Ole as much as anything. He taught me a lot. In turn, he found someone in me who was interested in something besides the wrestling business, and our friendship developed around that common interest — saving money.

Ole knew so many wrestlers who were near the end of their career, or already retired, and were dead broke. Many of them left the business without a penny to their name. He told me about guys I didn't know who were living in their cars, or working as security guards at shopping centers. They all spent every dollar they made, never thinking a time would come when they would be too old to wrestle, and without any marketable skills, unable to get a job in the outside world. It was true then, and in many cases, things are no different today. The stories he told put fear in my heart. I was determined more than ever to be in the one percent of the guys who retire from the wrestling business and not have to look for a job and can make a choice as to what I want to do with my life.

Ole had never seen me work, but Bill Watts had told him about me and he knew about my run with Vince McMahon. On October 14, 1977, the first night I worked in the Omni in Atlanta, I was in the second match from the bottom. I worked against a young guy named Preston Nicholas. I was developing my style nightly, and coming from a run in Japan, I had only one thought in mind:

Get over! That first night, I took the match to my opponent. I overwhelmed him and beat him with the Lariat.

When I got back to the dressing room, Ole came running in, looking excited. He said I had really impressed him, and that it was a "pleasant surprise" to see someone who looked like they could get themselves over with the people. Ole later told me that he and Gene watched my match closely, and when it ended, he turned to Gene and said, *"We're going to make money with this guy."* Getting over with the people happens in one of two ways. As a babyface, or good guy, the people get behind you and support you, and as a bad guy, the people hate you and want to see you get beat. I wanted to be the bad guy, and for the next eight months, I was booked as a heel.

When I first arrived in Atlanta, Ole had angles and programs planned out a month in advance. Business was really hot with Dick Slater, the Mongolian Stomper, and Mr. Wrestling #2 on top. Ole and Gene were the top heel team.

Many times, when a new wrestler came into a territory, he was built slowly, and as a result, he got over stronger than if he had been pushed down the throats of the fans. But there also was a place for bringing in someone and doing something really hot right off the bat.

Ideas, on the other hand, were almost always better suited to be developed slowly over time. Taking a long time to get a program into full gear gave promoters an opportunity to determine exactly which direction it should take in order to make the most money and give fans an opportunity to get into it. Most of the time, promoters had a couple of programs going at the same time. One might be long and drawn out over a period of months. Others were fast moving and might be sub-plots of other programs. Still others were teaser programs which were headed in a specific direction to develop future programs.

Programs in Japan were completely different from those in the States. Japan business was based on tours, and not territories, so programs had to be developed and carried out during a very short timeframe. Tours lasted anywhere from two to seven weeks, and most of the business centered around building up to a final match which would take place at the end of the tour.

For the most part, the fans in Japan were interested in the matches from a competitive perspective, rather than personal issues or angles. By the time each tour ended, most of the angles they had developed were finished, and the office would begin preparing for the next tour. Most of the time, successive tours would feature a new roster of gaijin talent, and over time, as guys like Abdullah, Jeet Singh, Brody, and I went over for multiple tours each year, a natural continuation of matches developed between the talent. However, everything was promoted much differently than it was in the States. Everything was done by the actions of the wrestlers in the ring. There were no promo interviews on TV at all. A wrestler got noticed by the fans strictly through his actions in the ring. As a result, it took a long time to get over with the Japanese fans.

For many years in Japan, the fans rarely saw a clean ending in the top matches. The finish would be a count-out, or a disqualification, which became so common that the Japanese fans began to complain. Baba took notice and, to his credit, he listened to the fans and changed the whole direction of his business. He began pushing for straight-forward pinfalls and avoided matches that ended through the use of foreign objects or interference from other wrestlers. I was with the company both before and after the change, and I benefited because I used the Lariat to win my matches decisively. As a result, the people believed in me. Later, when one of the Japanese wrestlers beat me, it meant something. That change was what paved the road to big business for All Japan for a long time.

Ole took his time to get me over with the fans. For the first couple of months, he booked me against young talent like Ted Allen, Jerry Stubbs, Richard Blood (later known as Tito Santana), and Bobcat Rice, as well as veterans like Bill Dromo. He sent me around the territory for a month or so, letting the people see me. During that time, I worked a few matches with a 19-year-old Tommy Rich. Tommy was young, he had heart, and the people would really get behind him. Of course, it didn't hurt that he had lots of young girl fans who loved him.

When I first arrived in Atlanta, the territory was full of talent, and good talent, at that: Dick Slater, Gene and Ole Anderson, Mr. Wrestling #2, Thunderbolt Patterson, Tony Atlas, Pak Song, Dino Bravo, Bob Armstrong, Abdullah the Butcher, and Sgt. Jacques Goulet [aka Rene Goulet], as well as Bill Eadie [Masked Superstar] and Angelo Mosca, who came later. They were all great talent. From October 1977, when I first arrived in Atlanta, through April 1979, we did big business, and had regular sellouts in most of the arenas during that time period.

One month after my Atlanta debut, I was put into a program with Dick Slater. Dick, who I had first met in Florida in 1973, had become a great worker and was really over in Georgia. His one downside was he thought he was a better worker and smarter to the business than others. We got along well, though, but it wasn't until I went to work for All Japan in 1982 that we became good friends. Dick had a good personality and a good sense of humor. Once he knew we were laughing at him, he would go to great extremes to make us laugh. Dickie was very entertaining in the clubs in Japan and many of my best times in Japan were when I was with him.

Stan with Gordon Solie and tag-team partner Tommy Rich

Mr. Wrestling #2, who was best known to the boys as just "Two," had been in Atlanta for five years when I came in. He was over more than just about any other babyface in the territory. He was good at what he did and the people loved him. One night, when we were all in the dressing room in Columbus, Georgia, President Jimmy Carter's mother, Miss Lillian, came in, accompanied by two Secret Service agents. Two other agents took position outside the dressing room. Miss Lillian was a big fan of Two and wanted to meet him. While there, she gave Two a personal invitation to visit them at the White House. Two declined the invitation when he was told he would have to take off his mask. The wrestlers went to great lengths to protect the secrets of the wrestling business, and Two was adamant about keeping his identity a secret from the public, even to the extent of turning down an invitation to the White House by the president's mother.

Thunderbolt Patterson was another top star in Georgia. His wrestling character and style was pretty unorthodox, but he was really over, especially with the black population. He was somewhat hard to work with because he refused to take bumps. However, the people believed in him, and when we worked with him, we got instant heat. Patterson used to drive Ole crazy with his interviews, which were really different from the norm. He had his own style. Most of the time, we couldn't make sense out of what he said. His favorite saying was, "*I'se is full of it.*" During his promos, he would pause for a long amount of time, shake his head, make a face, and say, "*I'se is full of it.*" He would then stop and just stand there, looking bewildered.

Thunderbolt Patterson

Ole would be standing off camera, mouthing, "*What are you full of?*"

Patterson would hesitate, make a face, and start to say something. Ole would be going nuts. "*Say something!*" Patterson would then close his mouth, make another face, say a word or two, and then stop again. At the end of his scheduled minute, he hadn't said anything. He would end the interview by making a face and saying something which sounded like, "*Uh, uh, uh.*" It made absolutely no sense to us, but for whatever reason, it sure did get over with the fans. They loved Bolt's character, which was somehow established through those interviews.

I didn't have what I would consider to be good matches with him, but looking back on it, our styles were completely different. My style of wrestling was hard-hitting and in-your-face. Patterson was more laid back with gimmicky comedy spots thrown in now and then.

One of the things I really respected about Bolt was that he read and studied the Bible in the dressing room, and often had to suffer scorn from the boys. Since he was human like everybody else, and did his own thing, they didn't think he was sincere in his beliefs, and accused him of being a hypocrite. I always took Bolt at face value. If I asked him about Jesus, he would talk to me about Him, but he didn't get into your face and preach *at* me. I don't ever remember Bolt preaching to others without being asked, but if the subject

1977 • Columbus, Georgia
Rock Hunter, Abdul Zataar, Rene Goulet, Miss Lillian Carter, The Invader, and Stan

was brought up, he would gladly share his faith. I thought that was one of the bravest things I have ever seen anyone do in the dressing room. He took lot of ridicule from the guys, but I respected him for taking a stand. In my book, he was really special.

If there is really such a thing as a "man's man," then Wahoo McDaniel was it. His most familiar move was the Indian chop. His chops were as solid as anything in wrestling. He would chop me in the chest and bring blood welling to the surface.

Wahoo also was, quite literally, one of the toughest guys I ever knew. One Saturday morning, he was involved in a bad car accident on Interstate 285, the perimeter loop which encircles Atlanta. Several cars piled up on one another and Wahoo crashed into the rear of the car in front of him. Luckily, he was driving his Cadillac, which protected him from possible fatal injuries, even though the collision totaled the car. He did have broken ribs and facial injuries suffered when he hit the steering wheel.

We were taping television at ten that morning at the old WTBS, Channel 17 TV studio. When I walked into the studio at about 9:15, Wahoo was laying on a table. He was wearing an expensive three-piece suit and it was covered in blood. His face was swollen and dried blood was spattered around his mouth. He was in bad shape.

Ole had a predicament. The entire, one-hour TV show was geared around a match in which Wahoo would be involved in some type of major angle. He also was scheduled to do two interviews during the show, before and after the match, which would set the stage for weeks of main event programs down the line. And here Wahoo was, laying on a table, all beaten up and in bad shape. When Ole asked him if he would make an attempt to do the things they needed him to do, Wahoo agreed to do them. He even wrestled in the match. That was just one example of the toughness of Wahoo McDaniel.

Wahoo McDaniel

I worked with Wahoo many times, but I will never forget one match we had in the Meadowlands Arena in New Jersey. At the time, the American Wrestling Association [AWA] and the National Wrestling Alliance [NWA] were running joint shows in opposition to Vince McMahon and the World Wrestling Federation [WWF]. Prior to that, professional wrestling in New Jersey had always been run under the auspices of the WWWF, which had changed its name to the WWF in 1979. The NWA television show, however, was seen by wrestling fans in the area on Superstation WTBS, the forerunner to today's Turner Broadcasting System. On May 29, 1984, the NWA and AWA promoted "Night of the Champions," drawing 12,000 fans and a $127,900 gate.

Wahoo was with the NWA, while I was the current All Japan PWF champion. The match we had that night is one the guys still talk about. It was brutal. We chopped each other as hard as we could. I couldn't chop as hard as Wahoo could, but I was hitting him pretty hard. After the match, I heard him say, "*Boy, I've been in harder street fights than that match!*" Over the years, whenever we were together, we laughed about how many potatoes [solid blows] landed in that match, and we wondered if the people watching at the time realized how unique that match was.

One time in Charlotte, when Ole was booking the territory, I was at the TV station where the matches were filmed. When they went to the ring, the boys all walked down an aisle from a common dressing room. I was watching the matches from the back of the aisle, along with about 75 other people who were crammed into that small area. Wahoo came out of the dressing room and made his walk down the aisle. He was wearing his trademark, a beautiful, flowing, feather headdress. As he walked by the fans, one of them reached up and grabbed one of the feathers. I don't think he tore the feather from the headdress, but Wahoo turned and threw three hard punches to the guy's face. Without missing a beat, he turned, continued towards the ring, and had his match.

I was watching as the police and paramedics stood over the guy who Wahoo had hit. He was sitting on a chair and the paramedics were checking his eyes. When Wahoo's match ended, Wahoo walked back down the aisle. As he came alongside the guy, he stopped and pushed the paramedics out of the way, and then nailed the guy with a hard right fist to the side of his head. I felt badly for the guy, but I fell out. I couldn't stop laughing. That was typical Wahoo. He never backed down or considered the consequences to his actions. He just did what he felt like doing at the moment, no matter what the repercussions might be. I heard later that the guy sued him for a large amount of money, but I don't know what the end result was.

Another time, Wahoo was leaving Mr. Pips, the bar owned by "Mr. Wrestling" Tim Woods. It was on Steward Avenue out in Hapeville, an Atlanta suburb adjacent to the Atlanta airport. As he walked out, somebody began to give him some flack. One thing led to another and things looked like they were going to get ugly. Wahoo went to his car and opened up his trunk. As the guy came at him, he pulled out his pistol and clubbed the guy over the head with it. Dick Slater, who was coming out of the club, didn't know anything was going on. When Wahoo hit the guy over the head, the gun fired and a bullet ripped into Slater's leg. It went in just above the knee and exited out through his calf muscle. Wahoo didn't get into trouble because Slater didn't say anything. Slater had to endure the pain for a few weeks and was actually back in the ring a week later.

I say with the utmost sincerity: Wahoo McDaniel was "the" real deal. He passed away from complications related to diabetes on April 18, 2002. God rest his soul.

About five months into my run in Atlanta, I suggested to Ole that I wanted to work a program [a series of matches between two or more wrestlers which take place over a period of time] with Tommy Rich. Ole didn't like the idea. He said I wouldn't get over by working against Tommy. He wanted me to work with another top babyface, but I knew Tommy was the type of boy I could get over with. Against his judgment, Ole booked me with Tommy, and, as history shows, we had a great series of matches together, many of them in tag-team situations.

Tommy was the first really young guy to be given a major push on the new nationwide TV show which aired on Ted Turner's Superstation WTBS. He had great talent and became a "heartthrob" with female fans across the country. He had a long run with Ole as booker, but he could have been a major star in any promotion anywhere in the world. For some reason, his career took a downturn. It was a shame to see that happen because he was a great talent and he had great potential.

One of the nicest guys I ever met was the "Russian Bear," Ivan Koloff. I first met Ivan in New York in 1976 a few months after he had his run with Bruno. He was a top guy in New York, and even being as successful as he had been, he was a genuinely nice guy who never acted like he was better than anyone else. Even today, more than 32 years later, I have never heard a single person say anything bad about Ivan. In the ring, he was a machine. He could go and go and go.

When I turned babyface in May 1978, I teamed up with Tommy Rich to wrestle Ivan and Ole in every city in the Atlanta territory. One night after another, we did 60- and 90-minute broadways [draws]. It wasn't easy because we didn't lay in holds for long periods of time. Ivan could really go, and, like me, he wanted to be on the move constantly. To this day, those matches really stand out in my mind due to the fact that all four of us went at breakneck speed for the greater part of those long matches. Before that, when I was still a heel, I made several trips with Ivan. He had a Cadillac and he made me feel at ease with him behind the wheel as he drove me up and down the roads. He was, and is, a classy guy. On one trip, I sat in the back seat, while Ivan and Frank Morrell sat in the front. They were both short in stature and they were both bald-headed, and from my vantage point, that looked pretty funny.

Ivan Koloff

I heard one story about Ivan in Japan when he had been drinking pretty heavily. He was in his room on the 35th floor of the Keio Plaza Hotel. To scare everyone, Ivan went out onto the balcony and climbed up onto the top of the wall, saying, "*I could take a big bump from here.*" Everybody was frozen in place, but after a few moments, he climbed back down and laughed. He was lucky he didn't fall.

I have seen Ivan a few times at wrestling conventions. In the years since I knew him, he has found the Lord and dedicated his life to God's work. He travels around the country, sharing his faith with others. I am happy for him. There is not a nicer guy in the whole wrestling business, past or present.

Much like Ivan, Bobby Duncum was another guy I never heard anyone say anything bad about. When I first heard of Bobby, I was still a student at West Texas State, and he was an alumni. I saw him wrestle on a few wrestling cards at the Amarillo Sports Arena. We teamed up in both the American Wrestling Association [AWA] and New Japan. During the last tour we were together, he broke his ankle when he jumped from the ring apron to the floor. Bobby proved how tough he was after that incident when he continued to work the last week of the tour. I have a photo in my scrapbook of me pushing Bobby in a wheelchair through the Narita Airport.

I always considered Bobby to be a great talent. Eighteen months before I first went to New York, Bobby had been there and had worked on top with Bruno. At the first TV taping I did at the old Philadelphia Arena, I was standing in a room with my back to the Grand Wizard, the legendary WWWF manager. He walked up behind me, turned me around, and said, "*Bobby, how are you …?*"

Bobby Duncum

He thought I was Bobby. I always claimed to have copied the cowboy outfit gimmick from Terry Funk, but until that time, I never thought about the fact that Bobby also might have been an influence on me. That's entirely possible because, as a student at WT, I always enjoyed watching Bobby wrestle.

I really got to know Bobby when Ole booked me out to wrestle for Verne Gagne's AWA in 1979. I only went in for a few days and Verne put me in tag-team matches with Bobby as my partner. Bobby drove me around and took me to his home, where he introduced me to his wife and two sons. Ironically, sixteen years later, one of those two boys — Bobby Duncum Jr. — would become my tag-team partner in Japan.

Jim Brunzell and Greg Gagne were the young, babyface tag-team in the AWA at the time. Of course, Greg, as the son of the promoter, got a big push. I don't say that to take away from his ability, because he was a good talent and he worked well in the ring, but on the other hand, he wasn't big and he really didn't look the part of a wrestler. Together, Jim and Greg were a good team. Nicknamed the "High Flyers," they did numerous spots using aerial moves. Jim was a great athlete who could really move. He was light on his feet, had great jumping ability, and could really get up in the air on dropkicks. Jim was well liked by almost everyone, but Greg had a harder time being accepted by the boys because he was Verne's son. In 1984, they made a tour for All Japan. One night, several of us were talking in one of the hotel rooms, including Brunzell. Someone insinuated something negative about Greg, which, again, was due to his position, more than anything. Evidently, Greg was standing just outside the door and heard what was said. He pounded on the door and was let in. He was hot, and dressed down everyone, but no one in particular. It was almost funny at first, but he had pride, and I guess he had his feelings hurt. He said he was ready to fight anyone, or said something to that effect. Everybody was pretty cool and thought it was funny, but they knew he was mad. The moment passed with nothing happening, which was good, but he was ready to fight. He wasn't that big of a guy, but he wasn't afraid to fight. I respected him for that.

Billy Robinson had a reputation as a really good shooter. Of the wrestlers in the '60s and '70s, if he wasn't the best in the business, he would be second only to Karl Gotch. He worked an unorthodox style with a lot of European moves. In doing so, he took almost everyone out of their own style. I had a hard time working my style with him. He was over in the Minnesota territory, however, and had been a regular in the territory for quite a few years. Verne, being a former amateur wrestler, gave spots to a lot of the guys who had amateur backgrounds, and Billy was one of them.

I met Billy again in Charlotte when Ole was booking there. Billy was going through some personal problems that I could relate to and we became good friends. Years later, after I retired, Billy moved to Tokyo and opened a wrestling gym. I'm happy to know that someone with his amateur background was able to find a niche in the business after retiring from the ring.

The three wrestlers in the AWA who were icons to me were Dick the Bruiser, the Crusher, and Mad Dog Vachon. All three were the kind of classic, unique characters around which the wrestling business was built.

Dick the Bruiser, a longtime mainstay in the AWA, was a real character. Prior to his wrestling days, he played football at both Purdue and Nevada universities and for the Green Bay Packers in the early 1950s. I wasn't familiar with his football career, but he had been an icon in the wrestling business for a lot longer than I had been in the business. I had heard many stories about his matches. He wrestled a strong, brawling style, and was really over in the AWA, as well as his own territory, which was based in Indianapolis. His character was developed over many years of being on top and the people believed in him. Bruiser also was famous among the boys for his ring attire. Each night, he came into the arena carrying a small bag which was about 18 inches square. Inside was an old pair of wrestling boots, a pair of tights, and a jockstrap. That was it. Nothing more, nothing less. He also was famous for never washing his tights. We could smell him before we saw him in the ring. In all fairness, I have to admit that I myself developed a reputation in Japan for having smelly tights.

His partner, the Crusher [Reginald Lisowski], was almost a carbon-copy of Bruiser. Years before he began wrestling as "The Crusher," when he was still wrestling as Reggie Lisowski, Crusher established a reputation as a brawler in the ring. Like Bruiser, he was fairly short, but he was barrel-chested and looked like a tank. As a tag team with Bruiser, even though they disregarded the rules and fought like heels, the fans loved them.

Nick Bockwinkel and I worked as a tag team against Bruiser and Crusher in Chicago's Rosemont Arena. Wow! They were also legends in the business, and I had never worked with either one of them. That night, I actually tried to adapt to their style. They were way past their prime, but still, they were the Bruiser and the Crusher. Period! Even people who weren't wrestling fans knew who they were, and they were respected and liked by everyone. I had never met Bruiser before that night, and I had only met the Crusher once when he came into Atlanta in 1979.

During the match, Bruiser and I wound up in the center of the ring, face to face. I chopped him in the chest. He mumbled something I didn't understand. I remember staring into his bright blue eyes. I couldn't get over how strange it seemed to see blue eyes set on that rugged face. I hit him with another chop, and again, he mumbled something. I said, "*What?*" And once again, he mumbled something. I still didn't understand what he was trying to tell me, but I assumed he wanted me to hit him again, so I chopped him really hard. His eyes got as big as saucers. I picked him up and body slammed him. The Crusher came in and I slammed him. They both rolled out of the ring. Nick was laughing uncontrollably and almost fell off the ring apron. After the match, when we got back to the dressing room, Nick said, "*I would have paid a hundred dollars to see both the Crusher and Bruiser take a slam in the same match. They don't take many bumps these days. In fact, even when they were in their prime, they didn't go off their feet very often.*" Nick loved it.

I also worked with another wrestling legend during my AWA run — Mad Dog Vachon. The Dog was a French Canadian and spoke with a heavy French accent. He had the classic look of an old-time wrestler: short, bald-headed, bearded, and extremely hairy. He was really over, too. Bobby Duncum and I worked with Mad Dog and various partners, which included Billy Robinson, Greg Gagne, and even Verne. In my opinion, our tag-team matches with Verne and Mad Dog were just so-so. From my perspective, Verne and Mad Dog each had huge egos. In the ring, it seemed as if Verne and Mad Dog were competing against each other. They had wrestled in "legends" matches against each other over the years. By 1979, however, Mad Dog was the stereotypical "character babyface," while Verne was the "aging amateur wrestler." Verne always took himself seriously in the ring, which isn't a knock. He was almost bald and looked older as he passed his prime, but he worked well and the people believed in him. On the other hand, Mad Dog didn't do a lot in the ring. He didn't take bumps, he didn't sell, and his main move was gouging the eyes. He was really over with the people, but he was difficult to work with and I had a hard time getting anything out of him in the ring. Bobby seemed to be able to work with him the best. Bobby had been around and lived in the territory.

I flew back and forth from Atlanta to Minnesota for eight months, working a few shots in the territory each month, but that ended when Verne and All Japan had a conflict with dates. Verne wanted to have first pick of my dates, which I can understand, but my allegiance was to Japan. Shohei "Giant" Baba, the owner and promoter of All Japan, never said anything to me. We discussed the conflict of dates which were beginning to happen, but Baba left it up to me. I knew what I was going to do. I was going to give Baba first choice of dates. It was an easy choice to make. In my mind, anything in the States would always be secondary to my Japan business.

I hated to leave Bobby high and dry, but I had to do what was best for my family and career. Bobby had moved to Minnesota and bought a house there. Buying a house and setting down roots was always a problem for wrestlers. It wasn't easy to sell the house and move your family, so the office would take advantage of that and pay them as little as they could. Until Japan became my major source of income, I never bought a house anywhere except Atlanta. I didn't want to lock myself down to any particular territory and I didn't want to be controlled by the promoters.

While I'm on the subject of buying houses, as the saying goes, once I decided to settle down and buy the house, my life took a new path as I began my long career in Japan. When I first began wrestling in Georgia, I moved my family with me. We lived in an apartment complex in Jonesboro, about twenty miles south of Atlanta, where a number of the other wrestlers lived. My daughter was born while we were living there. After a year, I went against the rule of buying a house and bought a house twenty miles east of Atlanta in Lithonia. We lived there less than five months before selling it. With me going overseas so often, my wife didn't want to stay in Atlanta. Luckily, the house sold quickly and we moved back to Mississippi, where I stayed for almost fifteen years.

During that time, I went through a divorce and, four years later, married a woman I met in Japan.

I never moved my family again until my father passed away in 1993. Shortly after that, we decided to make our home in Japan, and we lived there for the next two years. We lived with my wife's family outside of Yokohama. The next time we moved, we came back to the States and built a home in Colorado. By that point in my career, I was only working in Japan, so I could commute from anywhere.

I did the right thing by giving Verne Gagne my notice, but he didn't take it too well and complained to Ole. Ole suggested I call Verne to explain my actions, just to be sure there were no hard feelings. Ole had been broken into the business by Verne, and they were both friends and business associates. I took his advice and called Verne.

Unfortunately, Verne had a long-time friend whose name also was Stan Hansen. It's possible it was only the guy's last name that was Hansen, but I'm pretty sure it was Stan Hansen. When I called Verne, he was listening to the televised presidential debates between Jimmy Carter and Ronald Reagan. For the first few minutes of our conversation, he thought he was talking to his friend. When I told him I was sorry things hadn't worked out, and that we might be able to do business in the future, it dawned on him that I wasn't his old friend, but that "danged wrestler who didn't want to work for him." After I hung up, I wished I hadn't bothered calling because, in my opinion, Verne didn't respond too well, even though I had done the right thing by calling him. The only reason I did it in the first place was because Ole suggested I do it. Later, I made a point to tell Ole that I would not be calling anybody in the future to apologize for my business decisions. Ole said he still thought it was the right thing to do. I ended up going back to work for Verne again in 1985, but the outcome was much different. More on that later ...

Bill Eadie, who wrestled as the Masked Superstar, was another class guy in my book. We found common ground in the fact that we were both school teachers, and for a short time, our back yards bordered one another.

When I sold the house, I recouped most of the money I had put into it, but lost some of the closing costs. Bill Eadie, on the other hand, stayed in Atlanta, and resides in the area to this day. He had a very successful run in both Atlanta and Charlotte, and also found his niche in Japan working for New Japan.

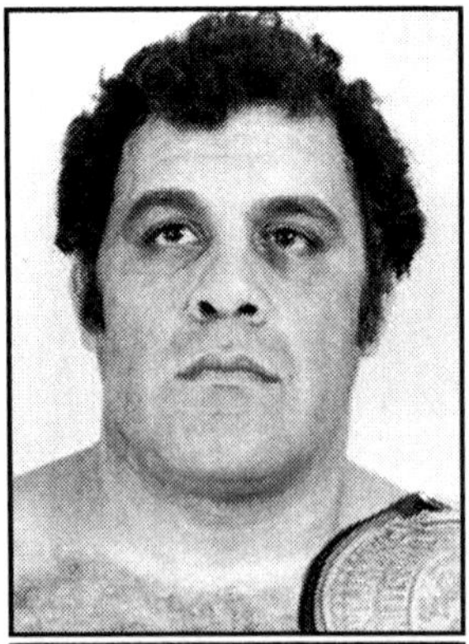

Angelo Mosca

Bill and I, along with Angelo Mosca, traveled together when we were all in Atlanta. We used to rib Angelo at every opportunity. We would meet each day at a designated place. Most of the time, we rode in Bill's van. I would usually arrive first, so I would get into the back seat. When Angelo got in, he was usually in a good mood, but we always found a way to change that. I would say something to Bill like, "*Did you hear about Barnett saying he was going to cut our pay because the Omni was raising the rent on the building?*"

Making comments like that around Angelo was like lighting the fuse of a keg of dynamite. Angelo would explode. He would start cussing Barnett and call him all sorts of names. The trips in Georgia usually took less than 90 minutes, and when we pulled into the parking lot of the arena in Columbus or Macon, Mosca would still be spewing his anger. When we walked into the dressing room, Angelo would throw down his bag and start ranting and raving to anyone within earshot. "*@#$% that Barnett. I ain't gonna take it.*" Bill and I would be biting our lips. We did that at least once a week and Mosca usually took the bait. He would eventually cool down, but it sure made the trips go by faster. Angelo, Bill, and I laugh about that now when we see each other.

I worked and met with a lot of other top talent during the years I wrestled in Georgia. Ray Candy was a giant of a guy who had a high voice which somehow seemed out of place. I first met Ray when I wrestled in Louisiana. He was always quick to smile and he had a great attitude. When I turned babyface, we made several trips together.

Ray and I made one trip to Columbus, Georgia, on the Fourth of July for an afternoon show. We had to leave early because we were also booked on an evening show at the Omni in Atlanta. It was a really hot day, about 100 degrees with 95 percent humidity, and we were going in my old 1974 Ford Ranchero ... and the air conditioner didn't work. We rolled down the windows, so it wasn't too bad while we were moving, but 50 miles outside of Atlanta on I-85, one of the tires blew out. I was never a Boy Scout, so I never learned the number one rule for success in life: *Be prepared.* I had a spare tire, a jack ... but no lug wrench.

Ray Candy

The nearest exit was almost two miles away, so Ray sat in the car while I set out to find help. A little more than a half hour later, a semi-truck driver passed me. He traveled almost two hundred yards before he was able to bring his rig to stop, and then backed up almost a hundred of those yards to meet me. When we got back to the car, I looked in at Ray. He was soaked. Sweat was running off of him like a waterfall. He got out, leaned on the hood, and, in his high-pitched voice, said, "*I think I'm fixin' to pass out.*"

Since we couldn't be at home to enjoy the picnics our families were going on, we both had our wives fix us meals of barbeque to take with us. I ate mine after I changed the tire, but Ray was so hot that he didn't have an appetite. By the time he felt like eating, the food had spoiled.

Ray knew so many people in the Atlanta area. He always brought along a little, black book in which he had the names and phone numbers of his many friends. When we were traveling up north when Georgia Championship Wrestling was going into Ohio, Ray would pull out his book and tell me about his friends who were in the towns we went too.

Sadly, Ray died of a heart attack on May 23, 1994. I miss him because he had a great personality and was a likeable guy.

I first met Hawk and Animal, the Road Warriors, when I was in Canton, Ohio. When I walked into the dressing room, I saw two big guys who were really impressive in size and well-muscled. They hadn't had any matches as of that time and they barely knew enough about wrestling to even lock up, but Ole had plans for them. I noticed some of the other wrestlers eyeing them. In those days, bodybuilding types were looked down upon in wrestling. With the exception of a few, most of the muscle guys who had tried to make it in the business in the past had been dismal failures. Nobody seemed to want to give them the time of day, and I knew they felt out of place, so I took them aside and taught them some basic things they needed to know in the ring. They had been trained by Eddie Sharkey in Minnesota, but they really didn't know much of anything. Hawk passed away in 2003, but whenever our paths crossed, he always took time to thank me for taking the time to help him. Animal did, too, but Hawk did more so. To this day, I do the same thing when I see Terry Funk, who got me into the business and treated me well when I was getting my feet wet.

In 1978, when I switched babyface in Atlanta, I rode to the towns with Tommy Rich and Rick Martel. One Monday night, while we were on our way home from Augusta in Tommy's van, we ran out of gas. Tommy had a habit of letting the gas in his gas tank drop to the extreme empty position before he would stop to refuel. We were on I-285 in Atlanta, close to the end of our trip, and Rick and I were about half asleep. Tommy got out of the van and began walking to find a gas station. We had the album *Some Girls* by the Rolling Stones, and the first cut on the album, *Miss You*, was our favorite. With Tommy gone, I turned the ignition key and cranked up the volume for just a couple of notes. It was amazing how loud it was in the dead quiet of the night. Rick and I talk about that loud two-note when we see each other, and we always break into a line from that song, "With some Puerto Rican girls that are just dyin' to meet you."

I'll talk more about Andre the Giant later, but I had some good times with him in Georgia. He was my tag-team partner one night in Valdosta. At 228 miles from Atlanta, Valdosta was one of the long trips for that territory. It wasn't a regular weekly town, but when Andre came into the territory, the office ran towns that had never seen him before. The arena was packed to capacity and the fans were really looking forward to the wrestling. They were especially excited about seeing "*Andre the Giant, the 8th Wonder of the World.*" The show was held on a Sunday afternoon and, if I remember correctly, we were booked later that night in Macon. Whatever the reason, Andre was really mad at the office, and Ole, in general, who booked him on both shows that day. When he walked into the dressing room, we could tell he was hot about something.

On that particular afternoon, we were booked against Chris Markoff and Rene Goulet. When we got to the ring, I was ready to start the match. It would be natural for me to start, build the match, and make a hot tag with Andre, who would then make an exciting comeback. But Andre said, "*Let me start, Boss.*" Andre called everyone "boss." Based on what happened during the next few minutes, I assumed he had talked previously with Rene about being upset with the office, as both could speak French.

Of course, Andre was huge. He was at least a foot taller than either Rene or Chris, and he was much bigger than me, too. As Andre and Rene went to lock up, Rene kicked Andre in the stomach. Normally, Andre would have shrugged off a move like that, but to our surprise, Andre went down to the mat in a dead heap. Rene proceeded to put the boots to Andre for the next 30 seconds or so, but Andre didn't stir. He just laid there. Rene took his arm and tried to get him to stand up, but Andre refused to budge. Finally, Rene tagged out and Chris came in, kicking Andre for another minute or so. When the people began to yell, I went in and made a little comeback on them, and then the referee forced me out. Chris tagged Rene and they both began kicking Andre. He refused to move, sell, or do anything. He just laid in the middle of the ring. In desperation, Rene got an arm hold and proceeded to work his arm ... but Andre still didn't move. After Rene and Chris tagged in and out a few times, I came in and fought them off, and then tried to drag Andre over toward my corner so I could tag him. He refused to move. He just peeked up at me with a little smile on his face.

Andre the Giant

After six or seven minutes, the people began to boo and make catcalls. Three minutes later, they were yelling really nasty things at Andre and about the match in general. "*Get up, you fat, piece of sh—!*" was one of the milder insults they yelled. Markoff, Goulet and I didn't know what to do. I even went over to Andre and told him, "*Come tag.*" By that time, he was no longer smiling, and he still refused to move.

At the 15-minute mark, I ran into the ring and began to fight with Markoff and Goulet. We went out onto the floor and told the referee to disqualify us, which he did. When the bell rang, Andre was still laying in the center of the ring. After the heels left, Andre slowly rolled to the ropes, got out, and we slowly walked back to the dressing room. The people were livid. They were booing and throwing cups. To this day, I don't really know exactly what happened between Andre and the office, but he sure killed Valdosta.

Andre was a smart guy. He knew what he was doing. His actions that night showed the power he had over his career and position in the business. Nobody, and I mean "nobody," could have done what he did without suffering serious ramifications, but Andre did. Were his actions good for the overall picture of the wrestling business? No, but he sure took a stand and made a statement.

I also learned a valuable lesson while I was in Georgia regarding loaning money. I first met Pez Whatley on a New Japan tour. He and Sonny King were both on the tour. Pez had a funny personality and I thought he was a fair talent. As usual, when you are on a tour of Japan with someone for five to six weeks, you either develop somewhat of a close relationship, or you grow to dislike someone. I developed a good relationship with both Pez and Sonny.

When I met up with Pez again in Atlanta, he asked me if I would be willing to loan him $3,000 for a rock show he had bought and was promoting in Chattanooga, Tennessee. That was a lot of money to loan, and as a rule, thanks to advice I got from Terry Funk in 1973, I never loaned money to anyone. "*Never loan money to anyone because, most of the time, you will not get it back,"* is what he told me. Pez told me he had come up short and really needed the cash to help promote the show. He really sold me on it. According to him, things were going well and they already sold a lot of advance tickets. I would get my money back and would make some from the profits. He told me he had made more than $10,000 on a previous show, and this one was going to be bigger. I made the decision to give him the money ... and I never heard from him again. He ran the show, but never contacted me or made an effort to repay me. I really felt he had taken advantage of our friendship. However, it was a good lesson learned.

Finally, Ric Flair was another guy who came in and out of Atlanta while I was there. I don't care what people say about Ric. They can denigrate his working ability, his lifestyle, or his personal life. When all is said and done, Ric has done it the longest and pretty much the best. He wrestled on top in a money spot for a long time. He is a good athlete and a pretty good worker.

Ric and I had some good times together. He wasn't cheap. At night, he would spend what seemed to me to be a lot of money. He treated the boys and the fans really well. He got to me one night as he was ordering shots of tequila. I don't like hard liquor, so I didn't drink it very often. However, on that particular night, he kept putting them in front of me. For every one I drank, he would drink one, and he was showing none of the effects which I was suffering. After a few shots, it hit me. He had talked to the bartender ... and the bartender was bringing him water. I think he enjoyed playing that game. Regardless, he got me.

One time when we were in Amarillo, he talked to me into letting him drive my rental car to a show. He turned onto an off-ramp of the interstate and began driving north in the southbound lane. He didn't go far, but I was yelling and he was laughing. I swore I would never let him drive my car again.

A few years later, we were both working in Atlanta. After a show, we were at the Ramada Inn in Hapeville and there was a group of the boys over at the TGI Friday's restaurant. He didn't have a ride that night. I had a rental car, but I didn't feel like driving over. He begged me to go. When he said he would drive, I said, "*No way! Not after the last time.*" He took out his wallet, which was flush with cash, and told me, "*Here. You can keep my wallet. If I do anything at all, you can keep it.*"

He all but begged me to let him drive. When he refused to quit, I gave up and climbed into the passenger seat, while Ric got in behind the wheel. Ralph Freed, the promoter from Columbus, got out of the passenger seat and moved to the back seat. Once again, I told Ric, "*Now take it easy.*"

He said, "*Don't worry about it. You have my wallet.*" With that, he started the engine, looked over at me, did his "who-oooo!" thing, and floored the accelerator pedal. He laughed as the car took off like a rocket ... and he never took his eyes off me. It was like John Candy in the movie, *Planes, Trains and Automobiles* when Neal Page (Steve Martin) looked at Candy and he was the devil. All of a sudden, the tires on the passenger side of the car bounced over a couple of cement parking blocks. He never saw them. Both tires blew out and the car skidded to a halt with a terrible screeching sound. I'm sure I had a frightened, dumbfounded look on my face. Ric had a scared look on his face, as well. He had been trying to scare me, but he never intended to hit anything (at least, I don't think he was). He began apologizing and told me he would pay for the damages. All of a sudden, we were both laughing. I returned his wallet and refused to take any money for the repairs. Ric found another ride to the restaurant, while Ralph and I went back to the hotel, knowing "providence" must have saved us from getting out on the highway. I just called the rental company the next day, told them the car had two flat tires, and that they needed to pick it up. Ric felt badly about it, but it's something we can laugh about today.

Bob Armstrong was one of the great talents to emerge from the Atlanta territory, as were all of his sons, although I only knew Brad. All three of us had bad eyesight and wore thick glasses, so we made fun of each other a lot. I later spent time with Brad when he worked for New Japan in July 1986. He was in great shape and he had good timing in the ring. The Japanese wrestlers loved him because he was so funny. He was always practicing his punches on everyone. Rusher Kimura used to laugh out loud at the things Brad would do on the bus.

Stan makes his case on the set of *Georgia Championship Wrestling*

Georgia was a great place to work. I made and saved money during my time there. Towards the end of that 2½ year run, New Japan called and asked me to return. We came to an agreement for me to go back to Japan, and I would be guaranteed a minimum of fifteen weeks per year. I had a family to support and a lot of responsibilities, so the timing of Japan's call was perfect for me. I was excited to go, even though it meant leaving my family. That was the part of the business that wasn't too attractive. On the other hand, it was a method for me to accomplish my monetary goals and provide for my wife and kids. Things are never perfect. We just have to play with the cards that are dealt to us and hope we make the right decisions.

In October 1979, a new face appeared in Atlanta ... a big wrestler named Sterling Golden, who later became famous as Hulk Hogan. Ole wanted to build him, so I wrestled him in the Omni.

I had a great run in Georgia, but I was excited and ready to move on to new horizons. I hated to leave Ole, though. He was one of the few bookers I got along with. He paid well and appreciated the fact that I worked hard. To this day, we stay in touch and our relationship is good. He is one of the few wrestlers I keep in contact with here in the States. When we talk, we no longer talk about how we can invest our money for the future. We talk about the "good old days" of pro wrestling and reminisce about the great times and great characters we met along the way.

Chapter 14
Hansen's Guide to Japan

I'd like to spend a little time in this chapter detailing the Japanese wrestling business, how it was tied in to their culture, how it was different from wrestling in the States, and life in Japan in general. I'll also explain a little about how the tours are set up and what goes on behind the scenes before and after. In order to cover as many bases as possible, I won't be presenting this in a straight timeline. I will be jumping around as I tell stories about the things I learned while in Japan. When the timeframe is relevant to the understanding of a story, or when a subject is specific to a certain timeframe in my career, I will indicate the time element to put things into context.

The tours always begin with a contract. To get booked, we had to sign a contract with the company for whom we were going to work. The contract stated that the office would pay for our travel and hotel, and that they would be responsible for our well being while we were in their country. In later years, the office added a statement that we had to agree with in regard to our obligation to follow the laws. The contract also stated how much we would receive each week, both gross and net, and explained in detail that the Japanese government would take out twenty per cent of the gross for taxes. When we filed our taxes in the States, we received a credit for what we paid in Japan.

If we found ourselves in need of money during the tour, the office allowed us to make draws based on our contract. At the end of the tour, we were paid the balance of our contract. During my first few tours, I was paid in cash, but when I began making good money, it became a hassle to take it back to the States. I found it easier to have the office wire the money to my bank.

After we signed contracts with the Japanese wrestling office, they got in touch with their travel agent in the States, who made travel arrangements for the gaijins. Mr. Ena, who was based in California, was the travel agent for the All Japan office. He had a very big business in downtown LA and a wide base of clientele, but I would imagine that most of them were Japanese.

Mr. Ena would call and ask us to send him our passports, which he took to the Japanese embassy to arrange for a work visa, which normally was for the length of the tour. When I began going to Japan for longer periods of time, I would get visas which were good for three months. That allowed me to travel back and forth without having to send my passport to Mr. Ena every time.

A week or so before the tour, our round-trip air tickets to Los Angeles and Japan would arrive at our hometown in the States, normally via FedEx. When we arrived at Los Angeles International Airport [LAX], we were met by Mr. Ena, who returned our passports and working visas. He stayed around until he was sure we were on the Japan Airlines [JAL] airplane and on our way to Japan. In later years, with the heightened security checks, we needed them in order to check in at the start of the trip, so instead of holding onto our passports and returning them when we arrived at LAX, he would FedEx them to us with our tickets.

The flight to Japan from Los Angeles took 11 to 12 hours. Thanks to the jet stream, the return trip only took eight to 9½ hours. In addition to the flight time, most of us also had a four to five hour flight to Los Angeles from our home states, so it made for a very long day. The travel alone was hard work.

Regardless of whether we flew coach, business class, or first class, the 12-hour trip to Japan is a long time to be cooped up in tight quarters. No matter how big the seat is, the time is the same for everyone. The travel wasn't something I enjoyed, but I was comforted by the fact that the company paid for the ticket and it was a part of the job. I always made the best of it, and I became a million-miler with both Delta Air Lines and Japan Airlines over the years.

Japan Airlines was the best company to travel with. I traveled with them for the majority of the years I went to Japan, and no matter what class of service I flew, JAL was the best at what they did. There was a period of years where I flew on Delta from Colorado to Japan, but there was a constant worry about Delta flights breaking down and not making it on time. Ena preferred JAL, probably due to the fact that they paid more to travel agents, but most of the gaijins had frequent flier miles on domestic carriers like Delta and American. Johnny Ace and a few others often flew on Delta because it was more convenient and it flew out of Portland, Oregon. The office, on the other hand, preferred JAL due to the fact that JAL was almost always on schedule and rarely cancelled flights.

During the early tours, the office wanted us in Japan two days before our first booking. That gave us a full day to rest and recoup from the trip, but I soon realized it was just a wasted day for which we didn't get paid. The office eventually agreed to allow several of us to fly in just one day ahead. They went back to the two-day policy when Delta cancelled a number of flights, which put the first-night show in jeopardy. We never missed a show, but we had some close calls. On one particular trip I made on Delta, the plane had engine trouble and we were diverted to Anchorage, Alaska. When we walked into the hotel where we would be staying, there was a long line of people checking in, so I went straight to the bar and ordered something to eat and drink. Ace got into contact with Mr. Ena, who pulled strings and booked us a flight to Seattle. We landed at five in the morning. Later that morning, we took a JAL flight to Haneda Airport, the old Tokyo airport, instead of Narita International Airport. Haneda handles most domestic flights to and from Tokyo, while Narita handles a majority of the international flights. We arrived in Tokyo just a few hours before the show began. We were lucky, but it was a brutal flight and the office wasn't happy. After that, I flew JAL fairly consistently.

Mr. Ena is really a great guy. He worked hard to get everyone to Japan on time, and was constantly trying to make the trip easy for us. On a few rare occasions, he had to calm the guys who arrived in LAX in a condition in which they really shouldn't have been traveling. They weren't necessarily drunk, but they would be quite tipsy. Thankfully, Mr. Ena and his right-hand girl, Susie, worked closely with Japanese Airlines, and were able to pull strings with JAL to get them onto the plane.

Baba was so forgiving. I only know of one guy who lost his job due to missing his flight from LAX. Joel Deaton missed his flight from Macon, Georgia, and he arrived in Japan a day late. It wasn't his fault, but he got a royal chewing-out from Baba. Joel told me that when Baba talked to him, he was so angry that his eyes were fire-red. He just couldn't get over how red Baba's eyes were. Joel said he was scared he might lose his job. As it turned out, he was correct, at least as far as I know. That was the last tour Joel did. Joel had a good spot, too. He worked hard and the people really got into his character. He was in the "cartoon," or "mikey match," with Haruka Eigen and Rusher Kimura [Masao Kimura]. Mikey is the Japanese pronunciation for microphone. After the match, the fans would ask Kimura to talk to Eigen on the microphone. Joel had a good spot working with Eigen in that match. I really liked Joel. After losing contact with him for years, we recently talked and he is doing well in his hometown, Warner Robins, Georgia. Incidents like that, however, made us realize how important it was to be on time, and to be sure we were there at least one day before the first show.

Joel Deaton

Once we arrived at the airport, we were well taken care of. During my first tour in 1975, we were met at the airport by Joe Higuchi. He could speak English and help us get situated. That was the only time we took a taxi from the airport to the hotel. On future tours, with so many gaijins coming and going, and so much luggage to haul around, the company sent their bus to meet us. Moving through customs was always pretty easy and the lines moved quickly. However, just as things have changed in the States, the Japanese airport security officials are much more thorough since 9/11.

The first thing we would do was check into the hotel. Once again, our hotel accommodations were taken care of by the wrestling office, which was good because the rooms went for $250 to $400 a night in downtown Tokyo. Even the business hotels outside of Tokyo went for at least $100 a night. The only thing we had to pay for was our food and personal charges like telephone calls, but when the gaijin wrestlers first began working in Japan, the office even paid for their meals. When the boys ran up huge bills by purchasing the most expensive meals on the menus, the office decided to end the practice. That wasn't uncommon. It was typical of the wrestlers to take advantage of a good thing and screw up a good deal. On occasion, however, the office would take the whole group of gaijins out for a meal. That happened more often with All Japan than at New Japan, but it was a nice gesture and we appreciated it.

The first few years I was in Japan, we used taxis for personal use to get where we wanted to go. In the '70s, there were thousands of taxis in service, and very, very few personal cars. The taxis only cost about 250 Yen for the first click, which was a couple of dollars, and 50 Yen after that. It wasn't too bad. There also was the option of riding a bus or the subway. The Japanese subway service is second to none in the world. I went to Japan several times over many years before I discovered how convenient it was to use the subway. The subway was easy to access, got us to our destination quickly, and was much cheaper than a taxi. Through the years, as the price of gasoline escalated, so did the taxi fares, and as more and more people drove their personal vehicles, the traffic became congested, resulting in bumper-to-bumper traffic which moved slowly. The subway became the ride of choice because it moved along unimpeded by traffic.

In all my years in Japan, I never felt uncomfortable or scared. Even during my early tours, we could walk around at night and never fear for our safety. That changed a bit during the late '80s and '90s. With a real lack of qualified manual laborers in the country, Japan was forced to open up to all sorts of immigrants, mostly from third world countries. Prior to that, the country was almost pure Japanese. As the different cultures moved in, certain parts of the country began to see the problems we face here in the west and other parts of the world: drugs, theft rings, and culture gangs. Overall, however, the problems were found in a very small part of the whole country. Certain areas were bad, but 99 percent of the country was, and still is, very safe.

I had some good times walking the streets with Brody and some of the Yakuza [Japanese Mafia] bosses. Several of the younger Yakuza guys would walk in front of us, pushing everyone aside as we walked down the crowed street late at night. It was nice to see and experience that. They were showing us off, so I suppose they were getting shown off, as well. It didn't bother us, and other than a few incidents, we never had any trouble being out late at night.

Brody and I figured that as long as the Yakuza kept to the personal business vices which the Japanese culture supported — prostitution, loan-sharking, gambling — then the police would leave them alone. We never saw any drugs around the Yakuza guys. However, by the late '90s, that seemed to change when the Chinese mafia moved in. There was a presence of drugs and drug-related crime which began to grow in Japan's underworld and in the country itself. But again, it was small in comparison to drugs in the States.

When I first went to Japan, honesty was a very important part of their society. It still is, but with the integration of other cultures, that, too, has changed. I first became aware of the honesty of the Japanese culture when my wife left her umbrella on the train. Three hours later, when we realized it was missing, she told me she was going to call the train company. I told her it would be long gone by that time. Nevertheless, she made the call. Sure enough, nobody had picked it up and it had been turned in at the station at the end of the line. Try that in New York.

Another time, one of the boys left their pouch (a small bag that was popular in Japan) in a taxi. The bag contained his passport and more than $500 in cash. We remembered the color of the taxi, so we decided to call the taxi company from the hotel. By the time we found the phone number of the company, the driver had returned to the hotel and brought in the leather pouch, with all of its contents intact. There was *nothing* missing. Even more surprising, another passenger had found the pouch, and told the driver about it. He figured it was one of the gaijin wrestlers and remembered where he had taken us. That was a strong example of how honest the people were in Japan.

As the years went by, I immersed myself in the Japanese culture. I was able to communicate as more and more school children began studying the English language, often beginning in the 7th grade. Before the 1980s, there were few gaijins in the country, but as travel between continents became easier and the cultures began to mix, learning English almost became a requirement. I developed Japanese friends and spent more and more time with them, rather than going out all the time with the guys. That became especially true after Brody left, but I had a lot of good times with Chavo Guerrero [Salvador Guerrero III], Dick Slater, Dan Spivey, Johnny Ace, and Terry Gordy.

As far as the Japanese diet goes, over time, things have changed. In the early years, there was a traditional Japanese diet made up mostly of seafood, noodles, pork, a variety of vegetables, and, of course, steamed white rice, which came with each meal from breakfast to dinner. Rice is a staple, much like bread is here in the States. Sushi or sashimi were low in fat.

Most of the time, we ate at the hotels, especially for breakfast. The hotels offered two standard breakfast menus. One was the "American breakfast," which included two fried eggs, bacon or ham, and toast. The "Japanese breakfast" was miso soup, a boiled egg, dried fish rice, and natto [fermented soy beans]. Most of us chose the American breakfast, especially during the first few years I was in the country. It wasn't until much later that I developed a taste for the Japanese style of cooking, and years later, I ate *only* Japanese style. Very few of the gaijin would eat natto because of the strong smell, but it eventually became one of my favorites. Now that I'm living in the States again, I buy them in the Oriental stores and continue to eat them.

When they make their first tour of Japan, most of the gaijins ask for directions to McDonald's or Kentucky Fried Chicken. McDonald's and KFC were the first American-style fast-food restaurants to come to Japan. There was a statue of Colonel Sanders in front of most KFC stores. Since the Colonel and I both wore glasses and a moustache, Chavo Guerrero used to call me Colonel Sanders. By the '80s, many other fast-food franchises moved in. A few years later, the Japanese were copying them, offering hamburgers and other American foods. The food, however, had a distinct Japanese taste. The proliferation of fast-food restaurants throughout Japan really helped, especially in the smaller towns when we got back late and the hotel restaurants were closed.

In front of many of the restaurants, there were glass display cases which held plastic replicas of all the menu items, with the price written in Japanese Yen underneath each. It was easy for us to get our waitress to step outside so we could point to what we wanted to order.

When fast food became more popular, the standard Japanese diet changed somewhat. They began to eat more meat, which wasn't readily available during the post-World War II years, and the beef which was consumed was imported due to the lack of land on which to raise cattle. As a result, beef was expensive, so there wasn't a big demand for it by the natives. The cheapest beef, most of which came from the U.S.A. and Australia, was found at Korean barbeque restaurants. In later years, as the trade imbalance became a thorn in the relationship between the U.S.A. and Japan, the Japanese began importing more and more American beef into the country, and the average price of beef came down.

The Japanese themselves had a very small market of the Kobe and Matsuzaka beef, which, without a doubt, is the best beef in the world. The cows are raised in a quiet, peaceful setting, fed plenty of fodder (and beer, believe it or not), and are massaged with straw brushes. The meat has a fatty, marbled texture, and is so tender that you can cut a one-inch steak with your fork. It is the most expensive beef in the world, costing upwards of $100 for an 8-ounce steak. Thanks to my sponsors in Japan, who would take me out for dinner, I had the pleasure of eating it often. Thank goodness, I never had to pay for it out of my own pocket.

In the beginning, I searched high and low for western style restaurants, and ate at McDonald's or KFC whenever possible, but when we traveled, we stayed in the small towns and cities, which didn't have them like they do now. In those cases, we would look for a yakiniku restaurant, which was the cheapest place where we could get beef. The Koreans, who were the largest minority in Japan, developed the majority of yakiniku restaurants, and most of them were run by generations of Koreans. Yakiniku, or Korean barbeque, means "grilled meat." We were typical Americans and could never get enough beef. Beef was very expensive during that time. We spent a lot of time and wore holes in a lot of shoes looking for good deals at the yakiniku.

The food sold at the arenas in Japan was somewhat different from what is sold in the States, as well. Most of the time, the concessions were provided by All Japan or private vendors at small tables, especially in the summer when vendors would set up outside the arenas. They offered many different kinds of food. Takoyaki (fried or baked octopus), yakisoba noodles (stir-fried with pork, cabbage, onions, carrots, and a sweet sauce), yaki-tomorokoshi (grilled corn on the cob), grilled octopus on a stick, and yakitori (grilled chicken on a bamboo skewer). Many vendors sold bento boxes. A bento box was a box lunch which consisted of steamed rice, some fried chicken or steamed fish, vegetables, and Japanese-style pickles. Chopsticks and some type of green tea (ocha), oolong (Chinese tea), or soft drink was included in the bento, as well. Many people assume sushi would be sold at the arenas, but for sushi to taste really good, it has to be made fresh and kept cold, which was hard to do at the arenas. And finally, of course, hot dogs. The only concern we had with eating hot dogs in Japan was many of them were fish-based, rather than pork.

After a number of tours, I discovered that every town, no matter how small it was, had what we called a "street of lights." Even though we didn't speak Japanese, that name was something we could say to the taxi driver and make him understand where we wanted to go. On that street, we could find "snack bars," businesses which catered to the late-night crowd, karaoke bars, and shops which sold everything from candy to lingerie.

One of the first things I was taught in Japan was the proper use of chopsticks. It is extremely bad manners to stick your chopsticks into the food, as if you were sticking them in a upright position. I was told it has something to do with offending the dead. Also, the Japanese "sup" their noodles. It is bad manners in America to make that noise when eating, but in Japan, it's acceptable. In no way is it considered bad manners.

Japan was not an easy place for Americans to go and spend a lot of time. There was great frustration which built up as time went by. We were alone, separated from our families, and often, unable to communicate the most simple things. That led to irritability. That is why most of the American wrestlers were hesitant to go to Japan and wrestle on the long tours. Some would come for a six-week tour, but wouldn't return for years, while others would do a couple of tours back-to-back. Most went to Japan just to take a break from their regular territory in the States.

In the early days, it was difficult for me, too. I was lonely and alone. Most of the time, New Japan had a number of Europeans and other nationalities on their tours, but we had little in common. That didn't mean we didn't get along. I ran across a few jerks, but most of the time, we bonded as best we could. The one exception was Pete Roberts, who was from Great Britain. We hit it off and became fast friends. I'll talk more about Pete later, but he helped me understand the Europeans' way of thinking.

The only time we saw the New Japan wrestlers was when we were at the matches. There was very little communication between the Japanese and the gaijins. Once in awhile, we would run into each other in the hallway and we would say hello, but it was difficult because we didn't understand each others' language. Outside the arenas, there was always a sense of kayfabe between the Japanese and gaijins. In those days, breaking kayfabe was a serious offense. We were never in the same place together, but we might be in the same area, or on the street of lights, at the same time. Whenever that happened, we never mingled or talked, and kept the code of kayfabe.

It took time to learn the names of my Japanese associates. Faces are easy for me to remember, but I have a hard time remembering names. They took a little more time. Of course, I knew most of the young boys who had broken into the business over the years, so I had a bit of a head start when I first went to Japan.

As a rule, when the Japanese wrestlers came to the United States, they weren't promoted as well as the Americans were. I don't know if there was a conscious decision to keep the Japanese out of the money, but I believe it was basically because of the limited English most of them spoke. I always had good rapport with the Japanese boys when they were here. In 1973, I went out of my way to befriend Jumbo Tsuruta (who was wrestling as Tommy Tsuruta at the time), who came to the Amarillo territory to be trained by the Funks. The following year, I did my best to help Akio Sato. I also had built good relationships with other Japanese wrestlers, like Rocky Hata [Mitsuo Hata], Umanosuke Ueda, Mr. Sakurada [Kazuo Sakurada], and Genichiro Tenryu. I met Tenryu in Georgia. I thought he was a good talent and could have been used better. He was a good worker and looked good in the ring.

The Japanese talked in their native tongue most of the time, even when they knew and could speak English. That didn't bother me, although I often wondered what they were talking about. I suppose some of the guys wondered if they were talking about us, but I felt secure in my position and didn't think anything about it. At times, when they would laugh about something, I would ask them what they were laughing about. They would tell me the joke, or explain what it was that was so funny.

In the ring, I was in awe of some of the Japanese wrestlers. They could do some really impressive moves. Kenta Kobashi's moonsault was one such move. Mitsuharu Misawa's "frog splash" off the top rope was a legitimate move that really hurt. We had to prepare for his weight to land on us. Jumbo would often direct his running high knee strike to our face, or the side of the head, just to remind us that he was there. I have to confess that I did the same with the lariat. Instead of placing my arm across the neck, I hit several chins fairly hard. It was all a part of getting our "point" across.

My biggest regret in life is that I didn't learn to speak Japanese. If I had learned the language (and I had plenty of time and opportunity to do so), I could be doing all kinds of things in Japan outside of the wrestling business.

One of the questions about Japan I get a lot is whether or not the language barrier caused much of a problem when it came time to communicate information about our matches. Most of the communication between the gaijins and the wrestling office was done with the help of the referees. Peter Takahashi and Charlie Tanaka did the mediating for New Japan. I think they tried their best to keep us happy and in communication with the office. Peter, the top referee, had a good understanding of the English language. There really *was* no language barrier in the ring. We went out and wrestled an old-style, basic match which consisted of holds and counter holds. Most of the wrestlers instinctively knew when to act and react to something an opponent did. When our opponent began working a hold, we intuitively knew what we needed to do and when to do it. That was all a part of the art of the wrestling business, much of which has been lost today as wrestlers choreograph every move from the opening to the closing bell.

Just like in the States, wrestling eventually changed in Japan. The matches became more and more like the American style with lots of sequential moves. More and more spots were laid out before the matches. That really began to happen when the office began to build younger guys like Misawa, Kobashi, and Toshiaki Kawada towards the top. I liked the old style better. The people weren't always able to understand or see the logic behind the new spots. The matches no longer look spontaneous, and the action looks planned. As a result, I believe the fans have lost interest and business is down. I believe that's why my style stayed over for a long time. I did spots that were logical (I'm sure there were some who say illogical) so they could be understood by the wrestling fans. I have to give Masanobu Fuchi credit. He really brought together some great old-school psychology when he began to book for All Japan. In my opinion, Fuchi was the best booker ever in Japan, and a lot of the success All Japan had was the result of Fuchi's booking and laying out the direction of the matches.

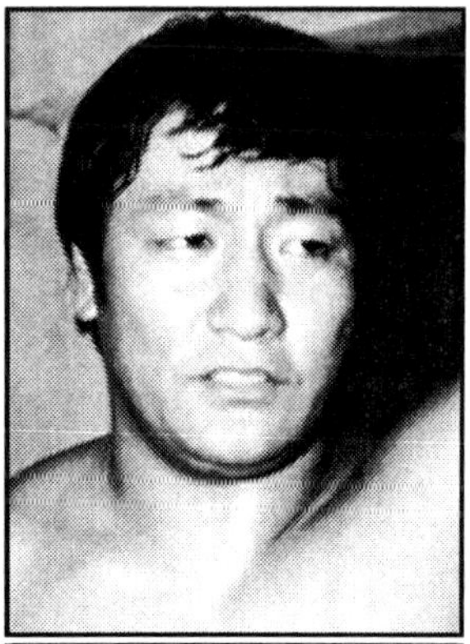
Masanobu Fuchi

The only negative I saw regarding Fuchi's booking (and this is just my opinion) was that the matches became more and more complicated as time went by. As a whole, the matches were good, but they became too lengthy and tended to be repititious. I always wondered why we should do something ten times, when one good time was enough. That was the trend in wrestling, though. The promoters wanted to give the fans more and more, and make every show bigger than the previous show. I don't think that was good for business in the long run. More is not always better. That's one of the reasons why Akira Maeda and the Universal Wrestling Federation [UWF] promotion did so well. They shortened the matches and worked a hard-hitting, shoot style of wrestling. That style got over and was very successful for a long time.

I have to admit, however, that the fans loved those kind of endings because the matches were exciting and very good, and a whole new generation of wrestling fans were developed. My complaint was that it took too much of the individual wrestler out of the match, and the people missed the spontaneous action and reaction in the matches. I also had to wonder whether or not the fan went home questioning the logic of it all. Things no longer seemed to be spontaneous.

I learned early that we mustn't do or say too much, and that we were always under "the eye" in the dressing room and arena. Away from the arena, however, we were on our own. It was there that we really had to adapt to life in Japan. As a gaijin, we stood out because we looked different, and in the early days, there were very few gaijins in Japan. If someone did something wrong or illegal, the news got back to the office pretty quickly. The office, however, was very forgiving, especially All Japan. Most of the talent, including Baba, had spent time in the States and enjoyed the American way of life, which included the nightlife.

I think Baba, like Rikidôzan, realized that the gaijins played an important part in the development of the Japanese wrestlers. There was a period of time when there was great interest in Japanese versus Japanese matches. However, I feel that if the Japanese promoters are honest, they will admit that wrestling and defeating certain gaijins was the defining moment which pushed many Japanese wrestlers to a higher level in the eyes of the fans. Chôshû, Tatsumi Fujinami, Inoki, Masahiro Chono, Misawa, Kawada, Akira Taue, Kobashi, and Jun Akiyama, all fought the top gaijins in their bid to get over, and since then, they have all been successful.

The Japanese wrestling fans were very respectful and seemed to understand how much the Japanese and gaijin wrestlers put into the matches. It wasn't always pretty, and we didn't present the showmanship that wrestling offered in the States, but they respected us for the demanding physical activity involved.

The television shows in Japan changed throughout the years. At first, the TV in Japan was almost a carbon-copy of TV in the States. It was used to promote the matches between the talent, and most of the times, the match-ups were gaijin against Japanese. Later, as I kept coming back, and the same gaijins kept coming back tour after tour, Japanese began wrestling against other Japanese, and gaijins battled fellow gaijins.

The matches themselves were pretty basic. The office might have a few ideas of where they wanted a match to go, but for the most part, the matches were simply between two wrestlers who worked (hopefully) towards an exciting conclusion.

As time went by, that changed, along with everything else, when Nippon Television [NTV] became more involved with the programs. At one time, they told me they wanted me to do specific moves in my matches. I refused to let them dictate to me. When they would come and say something about what they wanted, I would act like I didn't understand what they were saying. I would then go to the ring and do what I felt was right to get my match and opponent over. I'm not sure why I developed that attitude. I realize they got a lot of feedback from viewers on what they liked to see, but I didn't see myself in the TV business. I was in the wrestling business. In addition to that, I respected the wrestling promoters because they knew the wrestling "business," but I had no desire to listen to someone tell me how to do my job when they knew next to *nothing* about our business. I always liked to go out and do what came to me in a split second, and then wait for my opponent to react to what I did. I felt that was much better because it was an authentic reaction to my impromptu action.

Early in my career, one of the moves I really liked was the "flying bulldog," a move many of the Texans and "cowboys" used. When I began to experience back pain, I quit using it. Later, when I was in Japan, the TV executives suggested I begin using it again. Like Dirty Harry said, "*You've got to know your limitations.*" I stuck to my guns because I knew my body's limitations. I felt the same way about taking the back suplex on the back of my head, shoulders, and neck. On June 13, 2009, Mitsuharu Misawa died after taking that move from Akitoshi Saito. The cause of death was later speculated to have been cardiac arrest resulting from a cervical spinal cord injury, but I have no doubt that those kinds of bumps led to the injury. Fortunately, I got out without having neck problems, but the TV execs couldn't have cared less either way.

Even with my refusal to take their orders, they persisted, and I resisted as much as I could. In the later years, even the young Japanese wrestlers wanted things to go in the direction of "entertainment," as the business did in the States. They got their way, but I believe it hurt business in Japan over the long haul. I thought it was great to get a loud reaction from the fans, but in the back of my mind, I wondered about the logic behind what they were doing. Based on box office numbers, the fans began to ask the same questions.

When I was there, wrestling in Japan never reached the stage it did in the States, however, where the matches became entirely choreographed. It took the power and ability out of the talents' hands and put it into the hands of the present-day, so-called booker, who has to hire writers from outside the business to come up with angles and programs.

I'm not sure how much influence the TV stations (TV Asahi, Nippon TV) had on the booking decisions made by the office. I do know that in the beginning, they were pretty much hands-off when it came to the wrestling. However, when I went to All Japan in 1982, the TV executives were part of the meetings regarding my coming to the promotion. And, as the years went by, they had more and more say about what went on in the ring, what direction the programs would go, and which talent should be promoted. They also put TV office staff into the wrestling companies to oversee the books. I wasn't privy to the backstage dealings, but I was once told that the TV paid for the gaijin talent and for the expense to bring them to Japan. Once we arrived in the country, the office took it from there. That was a good deal for the wrestling office because they didn't have to pay us. They just paid the Japanese wrestlers.

The one notable difference between American TV and Japanese TV is that there were no interviews. There might be a message along the bottom of the screen as to when and where the upcoming matches would be, but neither Japanese nor gaijin did promos for the matches. Often, when Baba wasn't involved in a particular match, he would sit at ringside with the color commentator and talk about important angles. That was actually funny at times. As I mentioned earlier, the Japanese fans were quiet, and didn't yell and scream like the American audiences. When something big happened, they might react, but they didn't mindlessly yell throughout a match. Part of the Japanese culture was to be shy and respectful. At times, when everything was quiet, we would hear Baba's deep voice in the background. It was funny to hear him talking in Japanese, of course, and we didn't know what he was saying, but his distinctive voice carried through the arena.

Even though there were no interviews, the promotions had a great deal of coverage in the mainstream news. At the start of each tour, a press conference was usually held at the gaijin hotel. The press conferences were a big deal and gave wrestling an air of importance and mainstream appeal. The office would rent a meeting room at the Ginza Hotel and the press would be there to ask questions about upcoming matches. Most of the time, the final match of the tour was a championship match between two opponents. There would be sometimes 25 to 30 reporters in the meeting room. Of course, they couldn't speak perfect English, so it was hard to get the questions asked. As time went by, however, I realized they always asked the same questions, and they never deviated from them very much.

"What is your condition?"

"What are your goals?"

"What do you think about the final match of the tour?"

We had to be familiar with events that had been taking place in Japan because there were times when we weren't booked on back-to-back tours, and the reporters would ask us about certain things which had happened on the previous tour. That was difficult because the Internet hadn't been invented and news about wrestling in Japan wasn't covered anywhere in the States. As a result, one of the first things we did upon arrival in Japan was to quiz Joe Higuchi, or someone else, about things that had happened.

The reporters would usually direct their questions to an interpreter from the office. In the early years, Joe-san was the main man. He would interpret your answer, but often, if we talked too long, the interpreter would lose his ability to translate our thoughts. I learned pretty quickly to be concise and say just a few words at a time, which made it easier for the interpreter to remember what I said and make the translation. It was a tough job because most of the Japanese didn't have a large vocabulary of English. Of course, we never really knew whether the interpreter was telling the reporters what we actually said.

Wrestling also got a lot of coverage in the wrestling newspapers and magazines. Even the national newspapers followed and covered the matches on a daily basis. Reporters from all major newspapers phoned in an article and the results to their editors each night. The wrestling columns were featured in the sports pages right alongside baseball, sumo, and other sports. That was unheard of in the States

Each tour of Japan lasted anywhere from three to six weeks. Some of the towns were known as the "office towns," or towns run directly by the wrestling office. These were usually the larger, major cities, like Tokyo, Osaka, Nagoya, Sapporo, and Hakata. In many cases, the office usually had a partnership in the larger towns with a "front man," a local guy who would help promote the show. Other towns had a local promoter who actually bought the show from the office for a certain amount of money. I can't recall the name of a single local promoter in Japan, and I only knew a couple by sight. It wasn't unusual for the local promoters to pay $10,000 to $30,000 for the rights to hold a show in their town. That was a good deal for the office because they were guaranteed a specific amount of money that would cover expenses, and they didn't have to do as much legwork to promote the shows. They still had to send front men to help the local promoter, who didn't always have the expertise to do things like set up ticket sales or deal with the building management. The primary job of the office, however, was to supply the talent and arrange for transportation to and from the towns.

After a show, if another wrestling card was scheduled in the Tokyo area, the bus would take us back to our hotel that night. If we were scheduled to move to another town, we would leave the next morning. At times, if we had a real long trip, we would leave after the match, but that wasn't the norm. In the later years, the office tried to book shows in such a way that we could stay in Tokyo most of the time, but I didn't like that as much. I liked the change and I preferred to stay in the smaller towns, not to mention the fact that the bus trips at night killed time. The one downside was those trips were brutal because it was hard to get good sleep on the bus.

Abdullah the Butcher

During the early tours, the buses didn't have videos, so the guys read and played cards. A lot of money changed hands on those bus trips. The generation of wrestlers before me really enjoyed gambling. Moose Morowski, Karl von Steiger, Abdullah the Butcher, and countless others liked to play poker for heavy stakes. Abdullah was a good card player. On the other hand, I had heard stories about Bull Ramos having to borrow money to get back to the States after he gambled away his tour payoff. Cribbage, which would often go on for an entire tour, also was played for a lot of money. When both gaijins and Japanese were on the same bus, there always was a serious card game going on. The really hard-core gaijin gamblers would play a game which had pictures on the cards rather than numbers. That game was very popular with the Japanese.

The first time I went to Japan, I stopped by the Abdullah's room (as it was bigger than ours) and was asked if I wanted to play. "*Yeah, why not?*" Abdullah, Ox Baker, Larry Zbyszko, and Bobby Jaggers were there. I played one hand and lost 4,000 Yen, which was about $25 at that time. That was the first and last time I played cards for money. I learned a lot about the pitfalls of gambling while I was in Japan. I saw a lot of guys lose a lot of money, but what made it bad were the hard feelings that came between the guys over those losses. I tried to take what I learned and convey it to my kids. Just avoid gambling altogether. Money is too hard to come by to just throw it away.

When technology advanced to the point where videos could be shown on the bus, that became the norm. We really enjoyed them for the first few years, but like everything else, they lost their thrill. As soon as the bus began moving, a movie would come on, and we had to endure the same films over and over. It got to a point where within ten minutes of the bus wheels beginning to roll, the guys were all asleep. The constant noise, however, grated on my nerves to a point where I don't enjoy movies even today.

I often told everyone that there were only two things they needed to know: what time the bus leaves for a show, and what time it leaves the next day to move. It was great to not have the hassle or expense of driving ourselves. Japanese traffic was horrendous, and the freeways were often filled with bumper-to-bumper traffic. We could relax, sleep, or talk with each other. The office also had a large, built-in cooler filled with beer in the front of the bus. We could use the cooler to chill our personal drinks, as well. Nobody drank beer, however, until after the show. The one exception to that was Andre the Giant, who began drinking on the way to the show and continued afterwards. He drank a lot, but during all the time I spent with him, I never saw him the least bit drunk.

Umanosuke Ueda stood out from his fellow Japanese wrestlers. He had the classic Japanese face with slanted eyes that were little more than slits, but he bleached his hair blond and slicked it straight back, giving him the look of a true heel. I was told that when Ueda was in his prime, he was one of the best shooters in Japan wrestling history. There was nobody better. One time on the New Japan bus, Ueda was sitting behind Chavo Guerrero. I was sitting across the aisle. Ueda leaned forward and said in broken English in a low voice, "*Excuse me. I don't feel good.*" He leaned a little to the side and let out a long fart. Chavo and I looked at each other and at the same time said, "*Damn.*" Chavo opened his window for a minute or so and then closed it. All was quiet for a few minutes ... until Ueda leaned over to the side again and ripped off another one. Once again, he said, "*Oh, so sorry. Not feel good.*" Chavo again opened his window, this time cussing Ueda directly. Ueda continued to repeat his performance until we were all pretty upset with him.

Umanosuke Ueda

I suddenly noticed Ueda trying to get my attention. He showed me a slingshot-looking metal fork with a rubber band stretched across the tines of the fork. On the rubber band was a five-Yen coin, which has a hole in the center of it. Ueda showed me how he turned the coin to wind the rubber band, and then put it between his legs on a paper book. He leaned to the side and let out what sounded exactly like a long fart, only this time, he stopped for a second, and then continued on with another "burst." Chavo was so mad that he stood up and seemed on the verge of fighting. Of course, the part we had all missed was the fact that there was no odor. Now that I was in on the joke, I began to egg Chavo on, goading him to confront Ueda. At the same time, I was verbally hitting on Ueda in order to make everything seem natural. The whole time, Ueda just kept apologizing. Chavo got madder and madder until he finally moved to another seat.

The next day, Ueda began the whole process again. Chavo got really upset and voiced his displeasure to everyone who would listen. Ueda finally let Chavo "catch him" doing it and the whole bus broke out into wild laughter ... including a chagrined Chavo.

The local promoters paid for the hotel rooms in which the wrestlers would stay before or after the matches. That changed over time. As the local promotions dried up, the office paid for the hotels. Of course, the local promoters all wanted certain matches and the hottest talent in their towns in order to appeal to and draw the largest number of people. Any money that came into the box office, above and beyond the fees levied by the office and the hotel fees, was the profit earned by the local promoters.

In the early years, we stayed in first-class hotels. As time went by, we were booked in business-style hotels. They were smaller and not as fancy, but most were clean and in close proximity to restaurants. Most of the time, we accepted whatever hotel the office gave us. There was only one occasion when I made a local promoter for New Japan change our hotel. The first week we were in his town, we stayed at a lower-class business hotel which wasn't very clean. When we returned to his town on the following tour, he booked us into the hotel across the street, and it was worse than the previous hotel. I made a big deal out of it and he moved us back across the street. Of course, it hadn't improved from the time we first stayed there, but it was much better than the alternative. Andre the Giant was on that tour and was amazed when I made my stand.

Later, in the early to mid '90s, the gaijin wrestlers were staying in first-class hotels. For instance, in Sapporo, the office booked us into the Tokyu Hotel, while the Japanese wrestlers had to stay at the Susukino Green Hotel, a mid-level, business hotel. When the union for the Japanese boys put pressure on the office, they were suddenly moved to the Tokyu Hotel, and the gaijins were shifted to the Green Hotel. That change took place throughout the territory. The gaijins were booked into the business-class hotels, while the Japanese wrestlers stayed in our old, nicer hotels. I noticed the change, but figured that was the way it was and didn't make any bones about it.

Both All Japan and New Japan had a good front office staff who really knew how to promote a show. The office spent weeks, and sometimes months, planning a show. I give the office a lot of credit because they were usually preparing for many shows, all at the same time. The only thing required of us (the wrestlers) was to show up on time on the night of the event, and be ready to wrestle.

Another outlet for ticket sales was the Japanese wrestlers themselves. I wasn't aware of it until the last few years I was in the business, but the office would require them to go out and sell tickets to their acquaintances. Most of them didn't like doing it, but that was a part of the evolution of the business.

I enjoyed wrestling in the small towns. Even late in my career, it seemed as if the country towns were much more traditional Japanese, which was the element of Japan that I fell in love with. There was a kind of innocent mindset and the people lived a simple, traditional Japanese lifestyle. I liked the island of Kyushu because it had a lot of open area on it. Kyushu was the southernmost of the four main islands in Japan. Over time, I visited almost every nook and cranny in Japan. I have made the statement many times that I have probably been to more different places in Japan than any other gaijin ever. I know that's a bold statement, but I believe it's true. I have been to very small islands which had no airport and were only accessible by a weekly ferry. It is in those places that I met some of the most interesting natives of the country. They helped me appreciate the culture of Japan.

As far as the major arenas go, Budokan was the big arena for All Japan for many years. New Japan also ran in Budokan, but it was more of an All Japan building. All Japan booked eight dates a year in the building and really promoted them as big shows. I remember working one Budokan show with New Japan where attendance was so low that they only rented half of the building and a curtain was lowered to divide the building into two sections. When All Japan lost the Sumo Arena, Budokan became our main building in Tokyo. It was a great place to work and I have great memories of wrestling Jumbo Tsuruta, Misawa, Kobashi, Kawada, and others there.

We lost the Sumo Arena when Wajima Hiroshi became a professional wrestler with All Japan. Wajima, who was Sumo Grand Champion from 1974 to 1981, was a Yokozuna, the highest rank in sumo wrestling. He also was one of the stock holders of the Japan Sumo Association. When his restaurant failed in 1985, he used his shares of stock as collateral for a loan to repay his debts. To make matters worse, the loan came from the Yakuza. Outsiders were strictly forbidden to buy stock in the Association, so when Wajima's stock fell into outside hands, he was disgraced. The Sumo Association fired him. The situation caused a deep rift between Baba and the sumo.

To avoid banishment from the Sumo Association, Wajima resigned, and lost all of his benefits and status. Heavily in debt (rumored to be as much as $2 million), he joined All Japan in 1986 and became a professional wrestler.

Nippon Budokan: Tokyo, Japan

When Baba made plans to feature Wajima's Japanese debut in the Ryôgoku Kokugikan, Tokyo's famous sumo arena, the Sumo Association refused to give permission. As a result, Baba refrained from using Ryôgoku Kokugikan from that day forward.

Korakuen Hall was the arena where we held the weekly show. Every promotion promotes there. On each tour, we might have run the Korakuen three times. Often, the TV show was taped there, but not always. Korakuen only held about 2,200 people, but the gate was pretty good at the prices they asked. In September 1982, when I left New Japan and returned to work for All Japan, Terry Funk and I set the record for the biggest crowd there during our hot angle. That was the first year I came back to All Japan, but in my opinion, it was a wasted match that could have drawn many more people in a much larger arena.

We sold out Korakuen Hall and Budokan for at least four years, and I was proud to have been a part of that unprecedented string of sold-out shows. At the 35th straight sellout, the wrestling office gave every wrestler on the shows a metal pin-on button, and continued the practice for every sellout (more than 100) during that run. They also had a Japanese tradition of paying 1,000 Yen ($10) for a sold-out show. It wasn't much, but it was the thought of giving something to us for being a part of the sold-out show. The office even explained beforehand that it would only be a token amount.

Skip Young was wound pretty tight. He did pretty well in the Dallas territory, but he didn't think he was being used as well as he should have been. When he came to Japan, he didn't feel like he was getting a fair shake there, either. Most of the guys all knew how much we would get for the bonus, so at the show in Sapporo on January 30, 1980, they all got together and decided to pull a rib on Skip. Skip was in the ring when the rib was planned. The boys were each going to say they got 10,000 Yen.

Korakuen Hall: Tokyo, Japan

When the office guy came into the dressing room and handed a decorative envelope to each of us, everybody turned their back to everyone else as they opened their envelope. The first guy to speak up said, "*Hey, this 10,000 Yen is going to come in handy tonight.*" A few seconds later, ey""someone else said something along the same lines.

Sold-out buttons

All of a sudden, Skip went ballistic. He was hot. He began yelling and talking about how he got screwed. "*I only got a thousand Yen.*" He looked at Rocky Johnson and asked, "*How much did you get Rocky?*"

"*Ten thousand Yen.*"

Steve Keirn. "*Ten thousand Yen.*"

Even the referee who had brought over the bonuses was in on the rib. Skip was boiling over with anger. He said he was going to go to the office and really complain. Finally, Skip came to me and asked, "*How much did you get?*"

"*I only got 1,000 Yen.*"

Skip yelled, "*You liar! You, of all people! I know you didn't get no 1,000 Yen.*"

Now he was so hot that he wasn't just going to go to the office, but he was going to fight them. Rocky finally told him it was all a rib and that everyone got 1,000 Yen. Skip wouldn't accept it as the truth. He just refused to believe it. I was the only person who told him the truth … and I was the only person he called a liar. Skip finally settled down, but it took some convincing by the guys.

It doesn't have any bearing on the story, but Eddie Graham was a special guest at the show that night in Sapporo. We didn't see Eddie much during his time there, but he and Hiro Matsuda were at the show to watch the match between Steve Keirn and Tatsumi Fujinami.

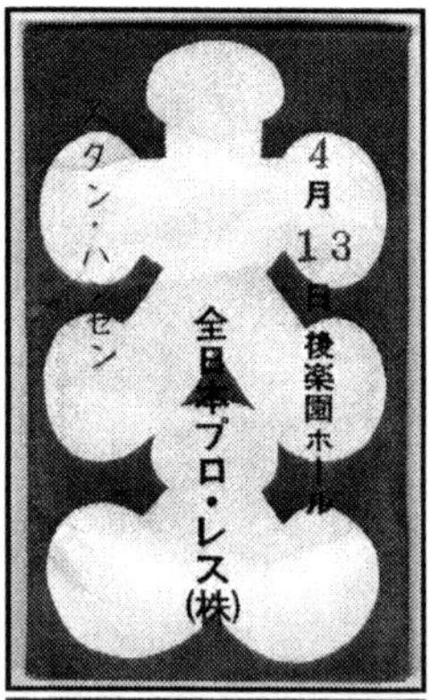

Sold-out button envelope

During the early tours, the wrestling styles of the two offices, All Japan and New Japan, were quite different from each other. Like those in the National Wrestling Alliance, matches in the All Japan promotion were built slowly and featured a lot of holds. I was fortunate to develop my style with New Japan, where the shows were much faster-paced and moved along without a break. Jeet Singh was the first to showcase a wild kind of style, but I took it up a notch by creating a constant-movement, wild style which eventually became known as the "Japanese style." I was credited with establishing the style, which both All Japan and New Japan adapted. I take great pride in knowing that. To me, that is the highest compliment they could have given me.

Through the years, I did get some negative feedback about my style, but the complaints were never from the fans. They were from other wrestlers … primarily my fellow gaijins. If the Japanese complained about me, it was

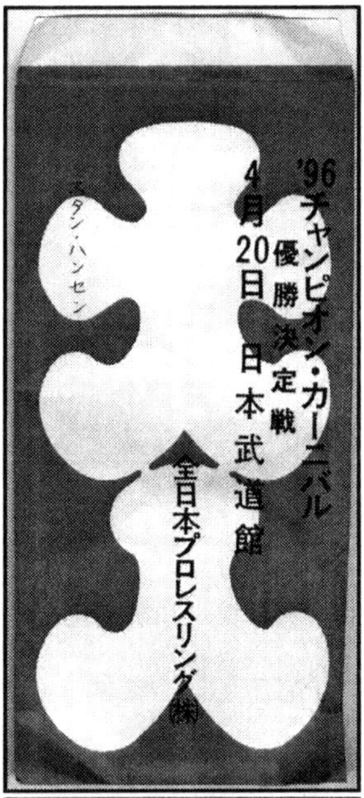

Sold-out payoff envelope
Note: Stan's name is printed on the upper left side of the envelope

behind my back, or in Japanese, because I never heard it. The style was getting over, and business was so good, that they adapted and ran with it. The gaijins, however, felt like I was eating them up and not giving them enough offense.

Del Wilkes, a good talent and upper-mid-level wrestler, wrestled under a mask as the Patriot. I thought he had the potential to be a top guy in his own right. He was big, agile, and had a great look, but other guys began whispering in his ear, so he complained to me: "*They said you're eating me up, and that I shouldn't sell for you because you aren't selling for me.*" When they told him what he should be doing, he listened to them, but in the end, it didn't make any difference. In my opinion, when he said the other guys "told him," it made his complaint irrelevant. Until others told him "what should be," he didn't have a problem because he never recognized the situation. The Japanese office paid me to work that style. It wasn't me wanting to do something on my own. It was what the office (and the people who bought tickets) wanted to see. Hearing him repeat what someone else said only made me see the frustrations of the others, and I ignored their grievances because none of them understood the overall picture of the Japanese wrestling business. After all, I worked the same style against the Japanese wrestlers, and none of them complained. When Del and I wrestled each other after that, he tried to work my style, only against me. Did it make a difference or enhance his career? I don't think so.

The Japanese office paid me to go and work that style. It was not me trying to do it; the office expected and wanted me to work that way.

Other young wrestlers, like Can-Am Express [Dan Kroffat and Doug Furnas], and Johnny Ace, all wanted to make a name for themselves in Japan, and they got tired of waiting for their time to come. I don't blame them. They were all good talent, especially Kroffat, but they didn't understand the Japanese way of doing business. The Japanese knew what was drawing money and what would draw money over time. Their psychology was to put over a few heels as unbeatable monsters, and in a way which would make the people return and buy tickets, in the hopes of seeing the Japanese beat them.

In a nutshell, the real purpose of the wrestling business isn't about making everybody look good. It's about drawing money. That is what made business so good in Japan for so many years. The programs and angles weren't based on ego, on making everyone look equally strong. Everybody can't be the top guy, and it's important for someone to put over the top guy so everyone can make money. The important thing for the guys to remember is that just being on the bus was a great position. Now, they don't even have that.

The prevailing attitude in the States was that everybody was a star. Everybody was a top guy. Basically, ego was controlling their attitudes, rather than the overall business picture. They didn't realize their position (and reason for being in Japan) was to put over the top guys. That position was nothing to be embarrassed about. It was, and is, a part of the business. The young gaijins thought they had all the answers. They crowded into their hotel rooms at night and complained about their lack of movement inside the business (in the States, they would have been complaining in a car as they drove from town to town). They convinced Del and each other that I was the problem. I understand their frustration, but I wasn't the problem. I never suggested one outcome of a match during this time. The office did. I wasn't on top because I was the toughest guy. I was on top because All Japan saw something in me on which they were able to capitalize. They knew who they wanted on top, they knew how to put that top guy over, and their ideas drew millions of dollars of business.

Wrestling had always been successful in Japan because egos were cast aside and someone was put over. For decades, those egos were all held under check by Inoki and Baba. By the mid to late '90s, as the wealth of good, young talent was developed, they lost that hold on the Japanese talent as the wrestlers began to demand an opportunity to "get their spots in." They all wanted more and more of a push. In essence, that "push" pushed them all to the same level, and the focus of the matches was forced to switch from "gaijin against Japanese" to "Japanese against Japanese." The gaijin heel was pushed to the background, and eventually eliminated. That was a new concept which worked quite well for a few years, but the fans ultimately began to lose interest. Who wants to see wrestlers who all look the same, or wrestlers who all do the same moves from the first to the last match? In the end, that's what really hurt the business. Giving into that thinking made business go down in Japan. The fact that overall wrestling business is down and no one is making a living out of Japan speaks for itself.

The States fell into the same trap. The WWE did some of their biggest business ever when Hulk Hogan was the face of their company. Everybody wanted to see somebody topple the great Hulk Hogan from his position as the WWF/WWE champion. Even later, when Hulk became a fan favorite, the fans still wanted to see him beat the heels who challenged him for the title. Today, there is no "one man" who rules the roost in the WWE, or anywhere in the States, for that matter. The wrestlers all look the same, with nothing really striking to differentiate between them. And, like Japan, business is nowhere near the levels of success it was when one or two top guys were the face of the promotions.

However, I do have to give WWE credit. This book is about my recollection of what I believe was the heyday of pro wrestling. In my opinion, it is a bygone time and I am proud to have played a part in that era. However, everything changes over time and the wrestling business is no exception. As my era was different from the late '50s and '60s, today's business is different from that of my era, and it will continue to evolve in the years ahead. The WWE has transformed the way people look at professional wrestling. In fact, they have done such a good job that people automatically think of WWE whenever anyone mentions pro wrestling. They have developed talent, created new methods of promoting in the 21st century, and do everything in a first-class manner. When I attended *WrestleMania* in Phoenix, I really was surprised to see how the business had evolved. I was really impressed by the scale and magnitude in which they conduct their business. I tip my hat to them.

I must say that face to face, the guys all treated me with respect, and I really had no problems with any of them. I certainly have no hard feelings against them.

I don't know if the Japanese wrestling magazines like Shukan "Weekly" Purorseu and Shukan "Weekly" Gong had any influence over what direction the business went, but the editors of those magazines were all close to Baba and Inoki. They covered the matches and wrote articles about all the wrestlers, both gaijin and Japanese. I believe they helped the offices gauge the interest of the fans and gave insight into what interested them.

One of the things which hastened the downfall of our business was the publications which were "exposing" the business and calling the finishes of the matches, primarily in the States. If there is a time in the future when people will look back to determine when the wrestling business began to decline, they will see it was during the time when the so-called "scoop sheets" began to proliferate. There were a number of times when the American dirt sheets [newsletters which reported on pro wrestling news] tried to call the direction of certain matches I was involved in, but they were unable to do so because All Japan protected their business better than any other promotion. Baba knew the trend of the business was moving towards "sports entertainment," but he wanted to keep the wrestling fans guessing and interested by giving them intensely competitive and brutally physical matches. As much as they thought they knew, the dirt sheets were unable to report very little about All Japan's plans. Baba and most of the Japanese hated the sheets, and they expressed those opinions vocally.

I'm sure there were Japanese wrestlers who passed on information, but the gaijins were responsible for most of the information leaked to the sheets. The guys would talk to the dirt sheet writers and tell them what they had heard, who might be getting promoted, and in which direction angles were going. It just baffled me to think anyone would feed information to the very people who were exposing and, in the end, killing the business. The guys didn't realize (or care) that they were hurting the very business which made them a living. Even if they did, their egos got in the way of doing what was right, and they were marks who fed information to the sheets in order to see their name in print. The sheets, in turn, played on the egos of the guys. Like everyone (including me), they wanted to see something nice written about themselves, but to bite the hand that fed them was ridiculous. The business was successful for many decades because the people involved protected it and refused to let outsiders know what was going on behind the scenes. There were guys on the All Japan card who had copies of the sheets as soon as they came out. I read one issue and I never read one again. I was very "old school" and I was proud of it.

Several mainstream magazines also began to push the envelope and expose the business when it came to reporting on matches due to the fact that competition was so tough. There were so many magazines in Japan that they tried to scoop each other by breaking kayfabe and reporting on things which took place behind the scenes. As a result, the wrestling business lost the ability to keep the people interested. I believe the sheets and magazines had the right to publish their opinions, but I don't think the press should dictate business policy, regardless of whether they're a mainstream magazine or a dirt sheet.

In the end, it was the boys themselves who changed the business. They forgot that wrestling was successful because we all worked together and protected the business. Granted, the business was already evolving from an athletic competition into "sports entertainment," but the dirt sheets just hastened the change. Whether or not you question what or how the business operated in the old days is a moot point. I was involved in the business when people believed, and I think that lack of belief is cheating the fans today. The people really want to think, "*Man, those two guys were really pissed off at each other. I don't know about that first match, but in the last match, they were really going at each other!*" The fans miss that excitement.

The women's promotions were really doing well in Japan. I didn't follow them at all, but I was aware that they were doing good business for a time. Rhonda Singh, one of the big-name women wrestlers, who wrestled as Monster Ripper in Japan, was in Mexico when I had my son on tour with me. He was about five years old at the time. Normally, I didn't take my kids to the matches, but as part of my deal with UWA promoter Carlos Maynes, who worked with New Japan, I got to take my family with me for a vacation in Acapulco after a week-long tour in Mexico City. When I left the dressing room for my match, my son got panicky at being left alone. Rhonda, the only other American wrestler who could speak English, was there and assured him that everything would be okay while I was gone. She took good care of him until I returned. I will never forget her kindness.

I went to Mexico just a few times when I was working for New Japan. Carlos Maynes was the booker for Mexico. He would send talent to New Japan, and in return, New Japan sent wrestlers, both Japanese and American, to work in Mexico. Carlos was a nice man and he treated me well. For a country that is so impoverished, they drew huge crowds to the house shows, although the average ticket was less than 25 cents, so the gates weren't very big. Fortunately, the Japanese and American wrestlers were on dollar guarantees, so that helped us. The Mexicans are known for doing a lot of high spots and acrobatic moves. I didn't do their spots.

I worked with two masked wrestlers — Canek, who was a great worker, and Dos Caras, the brother of Mil Mascaras. Masked wrestlers were nothing out of the ordinary in Mexico. On one tour, I was involved in some twenty matches, and I was the only wrestler out of 40 or 50 who did not wear a mask. That is how prevalent the masks were there. During my career, I only worked under a mask one time. I was in the Amarillo territory and it wasn't for an angle. It was just to give me a job for the night. Bobby Hart was wrestling in the territory as the Patriot, so I borrowed one of Bobby's masks. I thought it was a lot of fun. It was like I was hiding behind the mask and it made it easy for me to become a different personality.

Other than matches against those Canek and Dos Caras, who were both big stars in Mexico, I worked mostly tag-team matches. I did my style to the best of my ability. The altitude was 6,500 feet, so the air was pretty thin. In all, I had a good time. It was a completely different style and environment from anything I had been involved with.

One day, I was riding with someone to a town about two hours outside of Mexico City. As we drove up a hill, a huge cloud of thick, black smoke appeared, hiding everything on the highway in front of us. Visibility was down to a few feet. As we slowly pressed onward, the back of a truck loomed in front of us, belching out black smoke from its tailpipe. We swerved just in time to avoid a rear-end collision.

The easiest and most likely way to get work in Japan was to get booked through one of the wrestling offices, as was the case when Vince McMahon Sr. sent me to New Japan in 1977. The Funks were the booking agents for Baba, so the Amarillo talent had a great opportunity to get booked into Japan. Even though the trips were long and the pay wasn't anything to write home about, one of the reasons why talent stayed in Amarillo was in the hopes of getting picked for a tour. Independent wrestlers had to find their own ways to get into Japan.

After I had secured a spot with All Japan, I booked a number of guys for Baba. Baba was always on the lookout for new, underneath talent for tours. He had his top guys, but he liked to keep the gaijin underneath talent fresh. As word got around that I was helping guys get into Japan, I got calls from around the country. I really didn't know much about the money Baba would pay them, so I usually told them it was around $1,000 a week. That's what I got paid when I first went over, so I figured it must be in the ballpark.

Nelson Royal, a former NWA world junior heavyweight champion, was a good friend of Baba. He had a wrestling school in Mooresville, North Carolina, and he broke a number of guys into the business. He booked some of them to Japan for Baba. I also booked young guys for a time when Baba asked me find young talent (we had top talent, but needed new faces) that could work and weren't expensive. Baba told me they had to be ready to do business and, if he didn't see fit to promote them strongly, they would probably be losing most of their matches. This was during a time when everyone wanted to be a star and didn't always want to do what was right for business. However, I never was an "office" type of guy and I wasn't interested in promotion or booking. I just wanted to do my job. I concentrated on my career and the things I was involved with, but I left everything else to the office.

When word got out that I was booking, I began to get tapes and pictures from guys who were trying to get booked. Of course, most of them wanted to go to Japan, primarily for the experience, but to a lesser degree for the recognition. I booked a number of wrestlers out of Royal's camp. For the most part, they were good workers and showed respect to the business.

One of Royal's students was David Isley, a good talent who fit the bill. He later told me how he got booked. I remember him being on tour and have kept up with him since he got out of the business. He was on a wrestling tour of Bermuda with Junkyard Dog. I had a good relationship with the Dog from the days when I was working for Bill Watts in Louisiana. When the Dog suggested he should try to go to Japan, David asked, "*How can I get booked?*" The Dog told him, "*Put together a package of pictures and send them, along with a letter of introduction, to Stan Hansen. Tell him I said you were okay.*" I called David a few months after I received the letter and told him the same thing I told everyone I booked. "*Baba is looking for some fresh talent that is cheap. You'll make $1,000 a week and you will lose every match. If you* *should win a match, you can take that as a gift. If you can work under those terms, then I'll book you."* He agreed and went over on the single tour in 1992, the Grand Carnival tour, which is one of the biggest tours All Japan ran. The gaijin talent on that tour also included Johnny Ace, Big Al Green as Master Blaster (I purposely called him Little Al every time I said his name), Abdullah the Butcher, Danny Spivey, Kimala II [Ben Peacock], Terry Gordy and Steve Williams, and the Can-Am Express. Joel Deaton was on the tour, but he was injured and had to go home early.

Isley turned out to be a pretty good hand to be so green. In Tokyo on March 20, 1992, he was in a six-man tag with Abdullah and Joel Deaton against Baba, Rusher Kimura, and Akira Taue. As Baba threw Isley into the ropes in preparation to give him a big Baba chop, the Butcher yelled to Isley, "*Take a bump! It's the boss."* Of course, Isley knew what his job was and he did it, but I thought it was funny that the Butcher was "looking out" for Baba.

The three-week mark of the tours was the time when most of the gaijins would reach a point where nerves and attitude would be stressed and strained. It affected almost everyone, including the regulars, who often felt the strain no matter how many times they had come over. Almost all the gaijins that came to Japan were somewhat country guys. They loved southern food and, of course, they couldn't get that in Japan. Isley was from North Carolina and after three weeks, he was really hungry for a homestyle, country breakfast. He mentioned that on the bus as the boys talked about the meals they were going to eat when they got back home. One morning in the hotel, Terry Gordy had just finished breakfast when Isley walked in and sat down. Terry told him, "*Man, you won't believe it. I just had a great breakfast. The cook used to work in the States and he just fixed me some biscuits and gravy with ham and grits."* Isley got so excited at the prospect of a good, southern breakfast. Terry called over the waiter and said, "Onige," which mean "the same thing." Terry stood up and left Isley drooling as he anticipated the breakfast that was to come. When the waiter came out, he put down a dish filled with salad and marinated fish, a standard breakfast in Japan, which was what Terry had eaten. Isley was sick when he realized he had been had. When he walked onto the bus later that morning, Terry and the rest of the crew broke out in laughter.

Abdullah was a master of getting goodies from the marks. One night, he took Isley to a small club. As I mentioned earlier, it was always more fun to go out with someone rather than being the only gaijin in the place. After a few drinks, Abdullah asked Isley if he knew it was his birthday. He told Isley to get out a 10,000 Yen note [about $100] and loudly say, "*Happy birthday!"* Isley wasn't sure what he was doing, but Abdullah said, "*Just do it!"* When Isley said it, the other people in the club noticed. Of course, they all knew who the Butcher was, and soon everyone was handing him money for his birthday. Isley told me Abdullah did the same thing a few days later. When he questioned him about it, Abdullah said they celebrated his birthday over a few days. Right! The next time I saw the Butcher, I told him, "*Hey, the least you could have done was share some of it with David for helping you."* Everybody laughed. Nobody "worked" the fans like Abdullah the Butcher.

When I booked young talent, I always told them the same thing I told David Isley: "*You won't win one match. If that bothers you, then don't even think about going."* Everybody I talked to agreed. They just wanted to go for the experience. Unfortunately, Gene Lewis and a small guy from Mississippi let their egos get the best of them and voiced their displeasure to the office about having to do jobs. That was a shame. The office told me about it because I had paved the way to get them into All Japan. I felt so badly about it that I told Baba I didn't want to book talent any longer. To me, it just wasn't worth the aggravation. He understood and turned to others to help secure talent.

Most of the Japanese were good business people and very professional. I never noticed any of them with an attitude about doing what they were asked. They had a lot of pride, but they understood that business was business. In the later years, some of the younger guys who were on their way to the top might have had some negative feelings, but they hid them well and never brought them into the ring. They understood that it never hurt to lose a match in Japan. Wrestling was a contest, and contestants sometimes lose.

I believe one of the reasons All Japan was successful for a longer period of time than New Japan was because they kept the gaijins strong and continually put them over the native wrestlers. New Japan did not. When Jeet Singh and I left New Japan, they never really pushed another gaijin in a position of power. They beat everyone pretty quickly, and as a result, their business suffered. Sure, they brought in Hulk Hogan and Van Vader [Leon White], but they never really put the ball into their hands. It's possible that might have happened at New Japan because of the problems that developed after Brody jumped to New Japan. As time passed, both companies gave a stronger push to the Japanese teams, and that is the way it should have been. When that time came for me to step back, I never argued. The Japanese wrestlers had helped promote me without complaint for years, and I was more than happy to return the favor. As a result, we had a great run of business.

I also believe the primary reason why All Japan kept people like Brody and me on top was to force the younger, up-and-coming wrestlers to really work for the opportunity to knock us out of our position. Very few of them reached the top spot, and it took years for many of those who did. Not only was that good for the company, but it built the character of the young wrestlers who strived to reach the top.

Japan was, and is, an affluent society. Most of the people live in small houses that have unbelievable value, and they're less than 1,000 square feet. The apartments they rent are even smaller. I've been in some apartments that were less than 300 square feet and their rent was $400 to $700 a month. And yet, even though the cost of living in Japan is high, the people still manage to save.

By our standards, ticket prices in Japan were high. At $10, children's tickets were the cheapest. General admission was $25, while ringside went anywhere from $50 to $60. We (the wrestlers) used to dream of promoting a town in the States and getting those prices.

During my first few tours of Japan, the fans were primarily male "salary men," a term used for men who worked white collar jobs, although women also were sometimes a part of it. They came to the matches wearing a suit and tie. They often would be in groups who enjoyed business and private time together after work. A lot of bonding took place after office hours, which routinely were long ten to eleven hours days. By eight or nine o'clock at night, the restaurants would begin to fill up. With so many salary men anxious to unwind and get together with friends and co-workers, there was plenty of business to go around. Business catering to this part of Japanese social interaction was a huge part of the overall Japanese economy. At night, in certain areas of the city (the areas which I always referred to as "the street of lights"), activity was alive and bustling. Anything pertaining to any kind of business had their doors open: flower shops, women's' dress shops, department stores, night clubs, convenience stores, small bars (by the hundreds), and any kind of restaurant you can imagine. There were also many establishments open for those with a taste for illegal or immoral vices, all of which were run openly by the underworld. We speculated the police allowed many of those things to happen as long as people were respected. That changed later when the Chinese gangs and other outsiders made their way into Japan.

By the late '80s and early '90s, the demographic began to change and the crowds were mainly made up of young girls and boys. I'm not sure why we lost the older salary men, but we did.

When I became a main event talent, there was never any pressure placed on me. Everybody — the TV producers, the local promoters, the Japanese talent, the gaijin talent — had their job.

In my opinion, the strength of the Japanese wrestling business, and Japanese business in general, is that they think long term. They don't let short-term things influence their long-term plans. They had their top guys in place for a long-term business opportunity. There was a saying I heard a lot during my time in Japan: "*It takes a long time to get over in Japan, but once you do, you can stay over for a long time.*" That's a true statement.

I wasn't involved in the long term planning of the direction the business would go. There were a few times when Baba would come to me and discuss things on a personal level, and there were a few occasions when I would go to Baba and make a suggestion or two. He usually said, "*Take it easy. Relax. Don't worry.*" I took that to mean he knew exactly where he was going with his business, and that I was just a passenger on his "train." That was fine with me. Under that circumstance, I had the best job in wrestling. All I was expected to do was do my job in the ring, get to the bus in time to leave for the next town, and wire money home to my family. There was nothing else expected of me, so I concentrated on learning about Japan between towns and enjoying my family between tours.

When I worked for New Japan, they were run like a true Japanese corporation. Everything was done in the traditional Japanese fashion. I'm jumping ahead in time here, but one of the things I noticed when I went to All Japan in 1982 was how lacking in organization they were compared to New Japan. That was (in my opinion) partly due to the fact that All Japan used a lot of Japanese wrestlers who had learned their craft in the States, which had a much different business plan than that used in Japan. Everything was so laid back in America. The Japanese wrestlers enjoyed both the undemanding lifestyle and loose structure of the wrestling business in the U.S. The wrestlers could go and do what they wanted to do, and show up in the town on their own. There was no strict hierarchy of wrestlers in the States, either.

The problem began when they returned to Japan and had to readjust to that strict hierarchy. Most fit right back into the Japanese wrestling culture, but others had a hard time, and even brought back some of the different ways of thinking and liberal actions that they had been exposed to in the States. Many of them had a different attitude than what was expected by the Japanese wrestling company.

Those attitudes caused a big shift in the way business was done in Japan. Their exposure to the American way of doing business made them reluctant to blindly follow the directives issued by the Japanese office. The guys who came back began to demand an opportunity to rise in the ranks quicker than they would have under the traditional path, which promoted slow advancement. Genichiro Tenryu, Riki Chôshû, Misawa, Kawada, Akihisa Mera, Kazuharu Sonoda, and Keiji Mutoh all wanted their chance in the top spots during their physical prime, and didn't want to wait for the traditional hierarchy promotions. In the end, both New Japan and All Japan were forced to give in to those demands, and their decision to concede changed the face of the wrestling business in Japan forever. Whether those changes were a benefit or a detriment to the business is a subject of never-ending debate.

Was allowing young talent to dictate and losing control of the talent good for overall business? I think we can look at the business they're doing now and see the answer. I have always felt that, in any territory, whether it's in the United States, Japan, Europe, or wherever, the entire card cannot be promoted as a main event. There cannot be twelve main event matches on a card. There have to be some underneath matches. Wrestling has been successful using that formula for decades.

People like to see a young guy, or what we call "white meat," who is the underdog against somebody they perceive to be superior in ability, experience, talent, and size. When they give their all to the match, and fail in the end, the wrestling fans feel sympathy for them. They relate to them. They know what it's like to compete against somebody who is superior because they do that every day in the real world, so they want to watch an underdog, in the hopes he just might catch a break and prevail against insurmountable odds. That's part of the psychology of wrestling that has been lost in today's product. Everybody today is a top guy, so they don't get sympathy, and that's sad because the people really want to feel for a wrestler. I believe the fans get the most excited when they see their favorite wrestler getting beaten up, and not necessarily when they win their match. It is the fact that they are getting "beaten up" that gets the most reaction. The biggest emotions are fear and anger — fear of the possibility that their favorite wrestler *might* get beat up, and anger when he is being beaten up. They like to see them make a comeback, but there is less intense emotion than when he is on the receiving end of the punishment.

Chapter 15

Elevator Stampede

My fourth trip to Japan (my third time for New Japan) was my first in which I got booked without going through an agent, such as Vince McMahon Sr. or Dory Funk. I negotiated my own deal and I was quite happy with the results. For the next 2½ decades, I booked myself into Japan, and I *never* had to fight for my money. I worked for both Giant Baba [All Japan Pro Wrestling] and Antonio Inoki [New Japan Pro Wrestling], and they always treated me fairly. I always knew how much I was going to make each week. I liked that because a weekly guarantee allowed me to set a budget for myself. I didn't get a raise in pay when I returned, but I was getting the same money I got on the previous tour, and that was more than I could have expected to make in the States. One of the things I hated about wrestling in the States was always having to fight for my money, and that assurance of my money was the basis for my decision to dedicate myself to a career in Japan. And, since the money was guaranteed, which it wouldn't have been in the States, I was able to plan my living expenses based on that amount. Knowing exactly how much I was going to make allowed me to plan for a specific amount for both savings and spending. That was, of course, during the time before the wrestling offices were handing huge contracts to the talent.

When I returned to New Japan, I had my rope and I was ready to use it. I could not use it in the States like I was planning to use it in Japan, but I was bent on establishing myself as a top wrestler in Japan. I knew it was going to require hard work to reach that level, so I was going to do my best to establish my character. If that meant putting in lots of time, then I was willing to do fifteen weeks or more to get over.

I grew to respect New Japan so much. It was a very organized company, run in the traditional style of the Japanese corporation. In America, we had to make our own travel arrangements, so the time of departure was very general. In Japan, the schedules were specific and everything was very punctual. From leaving the hotel, getting to the arenas, and leaving the following morning, they had all the bases covered. That was difficult for most of the gaijins to accept. I overslept very few times, and when I got onto the bus, there was a silence which was an obvious statement of dissatisfaction. That was more notable later in All Japan when I had to ride the bus with the Japanese for a while.

Antonio Inoki

Seiji Sakaguchi

Strong Kobayashi

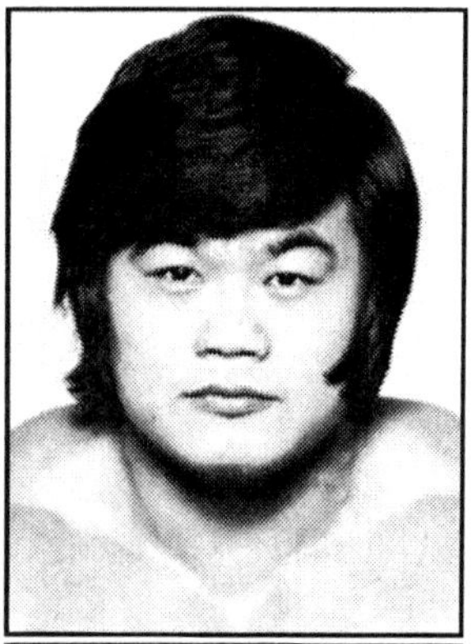
Kuniaki Kobayashi

Kenta Kobashi

New Japan had a good roster of wrestlers during the time I was with them. Inoki, Seiji Sakaguchi, and Strong Kobayashi were the top three guys. Of course, Inoki was the top man, but both Sakaguchi and Kobayashi were really over with the fans. Also about this time, a young Tatsumi Fujinami was beginning his career. He was young, good-looking, and a fresh face, and, as with Tommy Rich in Atlanta, that was to his advantage. He drew a lot of young ladies to the arenas. We helped Fujinami get over quicker by beating him up and making him "fight out from underneath," as I call it. That was what made the fans believe in him. He took a licking, but he refused to give up. Over time, that became part of his character.

I need to clarify a few names to keep people from getting them confused. There were four Japanese wrestlers with similar names: Strong Kobayashi, Kuniaki Kobayashi, Kenta Kobayashi, and Kenta Kobashi.

The original "Strong Kobayashi" was born on December 15, 1940. Working for New Japan, he was second only to Inoki, and the two wrestled each other in a high-profile match on March 19, 1974. After making the jump to New Japan in January 1975, Kobayashi and his tag-team partner, Seiji Sakaguchi, held the Japanese version of the NWA North American tag-team title.

Kuniaki Kobayashi was born on January 11, 1956 and began wrestling in February 1973. He was a good junior heavyweight who had several acclaimed matches against the two Tiger Masks, Satoru Sayama and Misawa. He wrestled in Los Angeles in 1982 as Kid Koby [short for Kobayashi] and held the NWA Americas heavyweight title. He is currently the caretaker of the New Japan dojo. Referring back to the original Strong Kobayashi, I used to call Kuniaki "not-so-strong Kobayashi."

"Kenta Kobashi" began his career in Ryuo, Shiga, on February 26, 1988. Kenta was one of All Japan's top stars until he left in May 2000, when Misawa formed Pro Wrestling NOAH and took all but two of All Japan's native wrestlers, Kawada and Masanobu Fuchi.

"Kenta Kobayashi" didn't make his wrestling debut until May 2000. He was one of the last two trainees of the All Japan dojo [physical training facility] and made his pro wrestling debut with them, but shortly after that, he followed Misawa to Pro Wrestling NOAH. For the first year of his career, he used his real name, but due to confusion in the marketplace with his mentor, Kenta Kobashi, he began billing himself as KENTA, with his given name in all caps.

Inoki always made sure he pushed himself as the number one talent for New Japan. He promoted himself constantly. He was the top guy and everybody knew it. Obviously, he had an ego, but that served to his advantage most of the time. The Japanese wrestling fans believed in him so much that even when he promoting himself in situations which embarrassed him, he was almost beyond being able to hurt himself. Take, for instance, his "classic" battle with Muhammad Ali. The end result was embarrassing for him, but nothing he did seemed to be able to bring him down. No matter what anyone thinks about his style or ego, that is the true definition of "being over."

When it came to promoting, Inoki wasn't afraid to stray from wrestling and promote different types of shows. He promoted kick boxing contests and shoot fights. He also promoted shows in other countries. In the end, however, Inoki lost control of his business when he gave in to the demands of the younger wrestlers.

Inoki wasn't a particularly big man, but somehow, he projected size. I never knew exactly how he did it, but he did. He would come to the ring wearing a bulky robe, and when he took it off, he would look bigger than he really was.

I enjoyed working against Inoki for many reasons. First of all, he was as quick as a cat. He could really move. I think that was his strongest point. He could get behind his opponent with lightning-like speed, or get in and out of the ring rapidly. For a big man, I was pretty fast, and both of us moving quickly was one of the things the fans enjoyed about our matches.

Inoki also had a good knowledge of basic wrestling. Not only did he have a big repertoire of moves, but he was very innovative. He was always experimenting with new moves and holds. When we tested each other, he often kept me off balance.

He didn't complain if he got hurt, either, as many of the wrestlers did. Of course, to be honest, most of the complainers were the Americans. The Japanese wrestlers were pretty tough. They didn't whine when I hit them hard with my fists, or when I whacked them across their backs with a chair. Their only response was to come right back at me.

I remember one match with Inoki when he jumped up and kicked the back of my head. He did it so quickly that it knocked me out for a fraction of a second. When I came to, I was falling to the mat. I have been knocked out a few times, but that was the first time it happened in Japan. Later in the match, I picked him up for a side suplex and dropped him over the ropes onto the ring apron [the part of the ring floor which extends beyond the ropes]. He landed hard and fell to the floor.

That was the way it was. As the expression goes, it was "tit for tat." I give one to my opponent, and he gives one back to me, "one" being a hold, a bump, a blow, or a kick. In wrestling, the "one" given back is called "a receipt." In part, that was the way my style developed. I tried to give out more "ones" than I took.

Inoki was known for his big jaw, which jutted out. I was in awe of that characteristic. Sometimes, when I would have him down on the mat, lying flat on his back, his jaw seemed to stick up far above the rest of his body. It was a funny and awesome sight.

Seiji Sakaguchi, the number two guy behind Inoki, had a totally different style of wrestling than that of Inoki. They fit well together as a team because of that variation in their styles. For one thing, he wasn't very quick and he didn't move around as well as Inoki. However, he was a judoka with a fifth degree black belt, which he won in the 1965 All Japan Judo championship. That was an extremely prestigious award to hold in Japan. With his judo background, he was able to throw us from almost any position. His legs were his real power. By any standard, Sakaguchi was big, tall, and strong. I had some good matches with him.

One quirk about Sakaguchi was that he didn't like to take a body slam, or, perhaps, he didn't know the proper way to be slammed. He was known as one of the toughest guys to slam in the wrestling business. No matter how hard we tried, it was almost impossible for us to slam him. His height and judo training made it almost impossible to pick him up for a slam. He had that power base in his waist and legs, and we just couldn't get his weight transferred to a position where we could pick him up and rotate his body. Whenever he sensed we were going to try it, he would roll away, shifting his weight away from us. It became such a challenge to us gaijins that we would make bets on who was going to be the first to slam him. There were occasions when a few of us caught him off guard and got him up, but I can't remember anybody ever turning him over to slam him onto his back. At that point, it was almost like we were in a cartoon. We just dumped him to the mat. There was only so much we could do with 265 pounds of dead weight. I only did that a couple of times because I hurt my back when I attempted to lift him. There also was the fact that dropping him made us look weak. In retrospect, I don't remember anyone ever slamming him cleanly.

Sakaguchi also was the president of New Japan during a time when they did great business.

I often wondered whether or not Baba and Inoki were on friendly terms. Inoki did his best to put Baba out of business. However, I don't know if Baba looked at it as being "just business" or on a more personal level. One thing I do know is that Baba and Seiji Sakaguchi, the number two man at New Japan, got along.

Strong Kobayashi was the third top man in New Japan in those days. He had a good following and he had certain moves which always got a response from the people. One of those moves was to hit us across the chest with a forearm, after which he would back up and spread his arms, as if stretching. The people would respond in a positive way.

Unlike his partner, Kobayashi didn't have a problem with being body slammed, but one of the things he did when someone picked him up was to grab their crotch. I don't know why he did that, but I assume it was to make us aware that if we slammed him too hard, he could hurt us by pulling on our balls. Naturally, most of the guys didn't like it one bit, but he often got away with it. When he was in that position, he would look up and give us a little smile, knowing that even though we were slamming him, he had control of the situation.

Outside the ring, both Kobayashi and Sakaguchi were nice guys. I ran into them several times over the years and they were always friendly. Even though he worked exclusively for New Japan for the better part of his career, I believe Sakaguchi had a good relationship with Baba-san. Baba occasionally mentioned having spoken to him about something or another, and he always had something nice to say about him. Then again, I never heard Baba say anything bad about anyone.

Hisashi Shinma was a whole different story. He and Inoki had a relationship which dated all the way back to 1966, when they, along with Michiharu Toyonobori, formed the original Tokyo Pro Wrestling company, in opposition to the Japan Pro Wrestling Association [JWA]. A year later, the company was dissolved and Inoki went back to work for the JWA. In 1971, after Inoki and Baba tried to take over the company from President Junzo Hasegawa, Inoki took the heat and was fired in December of that year. Inoki and Shinma immediately formed their own company, New Japan Pro Wrestling, and held their first show on March 6, 1972. Since then, Mr. Shinma has been both the manager of Inoki and the general manager of New Japan's sales division.

For the most part, we gaijins never knew what the various company employees did. For that matter, most of the time, we didn't even know *who* they were. Not being able to understand the Japanese language made it almost impossible to understand the real structure of the wrestling business in Japan, and that was often a problem. Whenever we tried to voice a complaint to someone, we would always be told that the person we were talking to didn't have any authority.

By the mid-1970s, we began to realize that Mr. Shinma was the man to whom we should talk about business, particularly when we needed to get information about our money and contracts, and whether or not we would be returning for future tours. Shinma always listened carefully to what we had to say and treated us with respect, and he did his best to make our stay in Japan as uncomplicated as possible. When I moved into a good position was when he really began talking to me. Until then, he spent a lot of time talking to Tiger Jeet Singh, but he rarely spoke to me.

In late 1980, I was teamed up with Hulk Hogan. One of the big tours for New Japan was the Madison Square Garden [MSG] Tag League Tournament. The first MSG tournament took place from November 21, 1980 until December 10. It became the big tournament of the year for New Japan and Vince McMahon sent talent from the WWF. I hadn't talked to Vince since I left the WWWF in 1977. Vince had heard that I had told New Japan I was booking myself. I'm sure he didn't like that, and from that moment on, he didn't seem to have much time for me.

The MSG tournament, which lasted for three weeks, was loaded with talent — Antonio Inoki and Bob Backlund, Andre the Giant and The Hangman, Tiger Jeet Singh and Umanosuke Ueda, Seiji Sakaguchi and Strong Kobayashi,

Tatsumi Fujinami and Kengo Kimura, Willem Ruska and Bad News Allen [Allen Coage], Kantaro Hoshino and Riki Chôshû, Ox Baker and Johnny Powers, and Hulk Hogan and myself.

Hogan began wrestling when he was 24 years old, which is considered old to be breaking into the business. Prior to that, he worked in construction and played bass guitar with a Florida-based rock band for ten years. He stood 6-foot-7, but was tall and skinny, weighing less than 200 pounds, and had long, blond hair which hung down to his waist. After working out at the gym with Eddie Graham's son, Mike, Hogan caught the attention of Jack and Jerry Brisco, who convinced him to give wrestling a look. Mike sent him to Hiro Matsuda. Matsuda, who had a reputation as a real good wrestler and shooter (meaning submission type of wrestling), owned a percentage of the Florida territory and trained many big names in the ring at the Tampa Sportatorium. Matsuda wasn't impressed with Hogan, and promptly took him down and broke his ankle ... on purpose. Nobody thought Hogan would come back, but he did. In a few months, after his ankle healed, Hogan showed up and asked for another shot at the business. Matsuda was impressed with his perseverance. After training Hogan for almost a year, he broke him into the business in fall 1977 as the Super Destroyer, a masked wrestler.

Hulk Hogan

The Florida office booked him for two months, but his bookings pretty well dried up after that. A short time later, he went to the Pensacola territory and worked there as Terry Boulder until July 1979. From there, he went to Memphis, and then Atlanta, which is when we first met. Once again, he changed his name and was billed as Sterling Golden. We hit it off and began to hang out together. In November 1979, Vince McMahon brought him into New York, where he was given the name Hulk Hogan.

When Hogan left the WWF in May 1981, he immediately went to Japan, which is where we met again. He later worked in the AWA for Verne Gagne, or as we called it, the Minneapolis territory. In those days, the AWA was a great territory. A wrestler only worked about 17 days a month, but made as much money as they did in other territories working seven days a week. The downside was that it was bitterly cold in the winter and the travel was hard. The territory was spread out across the map, from the west coast to Colorado, Nebraska, Iowa, Minnesota, Wisconsin, and Illinois. Most of the top boys flew in a chartered turboprop airplane. It was the best way to go, but the stress of flying in bad weather was real tough on the wrestlers.

Hogan got over big in Minneapolis. He became a huge star there and really enjoyed working for Verne. If Verne had played his cards right, he could have had a big run with Hogan in his territory, rather than losing him to Vince McMahon, who changed the face of pro wrestling and made millions of dollars with Hogan on top. Hogan told me he had a falling out over money from T-shirt sales. It was only a few thousand dollars, but in hindsight, it probably cost Verne many times that amount when Hogan left for the WWF.

Before leaving, Verne, a two-time NCAA champion in the late 1940s at the University of Minnesota, and an alternate at the 1948 Olympic Games, had a physical altercation with Hogan. The story is that during a heated exchange between the two at a TV taping, Verne shot in to scoop up Hogan's legs and take him down. Hogan threw his legs back and sprawled on Gagne's back, hooking him with a guillotine and taking him to the ground. It was a foolish move by Gagne. At the time, Hogan was 27 years old. Gagne was 57. Hogan also had 100 pounds on Gagne. The incident did show the character of Verne. He had been a great amateur wrestler in college, but he was 30 years older. And yet, he still believed he had the ability to do what he thought needed to be done.

Verne just could not accept the fact that wrestlers of the modern era were not the same as the guys of the past. The wrestlers were more educated and expected to make a decent living. Verne and so many other promoters never understood that in order to have loyalty from the wrestlers who worked for them, they had to treat them fairly and with respect. Instead, they continued to operate like the old-time promoters, holding on to the old ways of having complete control over the wrestlers.

I'm glad Hogan had the success he did. He had a lot of adversity thrown at him when he tried to get into the business, and he wasn't booked too well during the first few months, but he ignored the difficulties and persevered.

When Hogan and I were in Japan, we were together quite a bit. I enjoyed getting out in public with him and that was where we got our first taste of Japanese life outside of wrestling. Hogan had a friend in Japan who really helped us adapt to life there, taking us to restaurants and showing us things we never saw from the lobby of the Keio Plaza Hotel.

I also spent a lot of time with Andre the Giant. I first met him in the Amarillo territory. I didn't work with him there, but I watched him work with Don Leo Jonathan. They were both big men, and they had a match which was really impressive.

We ended up on the same tours when New Japan began giving me a good push. One night, I was actually booked against Andre. There's quite a difference between seeing Andre in a personal setting and in the ring. Words are almost inadequate to describe how big and powerful he looked when we stood facing him from a corner of the ring. His fist was the size of both of mine combined. His head was the size of a large watermelon. That's a Texas watermelon, not the Japanese version. His shoe size was a 24, compared to my size 14.

Most of the time, Andre dominated his opponents so much that the battle looked uneven. He threw his opponents around the ring so effortlessly that they looked like rag dolls. But with my style of wrestling being what it was, I took the battle to him.

I believe the first time I wrestled Andre was on May 18, 1979, in Niigata, Japan, which was during my fourth tour of Japan. I was really trying to establish myself and the office was giving me the opportunity to get over. Andre, who was in a class by himself, came in for almost a month. For some reason, I was concerned about losing whatever momentum I had built towards becoming a top gaijin for New Japan, so I went out and fought in my usual style. I think I surprised him that night with the intensity I put into our match. He liked

(top) Stan and Hogan vs Bob Backlund

(above) Weekly Gong Magazine volume 14, number12

(top right) Killer Kahn, Hogan and Stan
"This photo in the dresssing room shows the pressure of long tourrs. Almost everyone was wishing they were home."

(bottom right) Stan and Hogan at the Shinkansen (bullet train)
"We must have had a hard night. The t-shirt Hogan is wearing is mine!"

having someone push him back, as opposed to the guys who usually let him control them. I wouldn't sell him as much as the other wrestlers, either. Most of them seemed to do that automatically because ... well, after all ... he was the Giant. I was probably the first person to really give Andre any real offense, and the people seemed to buy it, especially in Japan. Andre was smart enough to listen to the people and sell me. The more he sold, the more it made for a better match. Andre also was happy to have a big gaijin to work with because he could only wrestle the smaller Japanese wrestlers a limited number of times. In the eyes of the people, I became a formidable opponent. When a wrestler is a "special attraction" type of character like Andre, there are a limited number of things the promotion could do with him. Once they've seen him do his thing a few times (bulldozing over his opponents), his style becomes less "special." I believe working with me taught Andre that he could go out and have a program which people would buy, and in return, he took his new "style" to other territories and found himself in much more demand than before. He was no longer billed as a "one-night special attraction" in every major city in a territory. He was able to go back for several weeks in a row and work angles and programs. He really took advantage of that experience when he went to the WWF and had his long run with Hulk Hogan.

Contrary to what some people say, Andre was very unselfish in the ring. He would occasionally give me some ideas on the match we were doing, but for the most part, he adapted to "my" style. The result was that he was one of those who were very instrumental in getting me over in Japan.

My matches with Andre became quite a draw for New Japan. Business was good everywhere we went, and even though we weren't always featured in the main event, a lot of the people came to see the two of us butt heads. I was always excited to work with him, because it gave me another direction to go in order to keep my matches with Inoki from getting stale.

Our series of matches came to a head on September 23, 1981 at Den-En Coliseum, the big tennis stadium in Tokyo. It was a match which had been built up over a long time. From what I was told, when the last ticket had been sold, more than 3,000 people were standing in line outside the arena to see the match. I'm not sure I recall any match in which the fans were as excited as that one. There seemed to be electricity in the air that night. It also was the first and only time I body slammed Andre. I can still remember him coming to the ring. I was waiting for him. As he raised his leg to step over the top rope, as only he could really do, I charged him. He kicked me in the face as he stepped over. What perfect timing from his point of view! In the end, I ducked a lariat from Andre and he hit the referee, Peter Takahashi. Andre was disqualified and the match was over. It was one of the most memorable matches of my career.

Koji Miyamoto, a friend in Japan who I always called "Lou Thesz' manager," says the show that night was one of the best in the history of New Japan. "*Inoki vs Kim Duk was the main event after Hansen vs. Andre,*" said Koji, "*but all the audience was so excited by Hansen vs. Andre. Inoki vs Duk was very calm, non-exciting circumstances. The match itself was just so-so.*"

One of my fond memories of Andre was of the times we went to the movie theater. When we were working for New Japan, we would always leave around nine in the morning for the town we were going to wrestle in that night. New

1981 • Stan vs Andre the Giant

Japan wanted us to get there early so we had time to eat and relax. Since we all rode the bus, we would always be there on time, which was usually around noon. Not having anything else to do in the towns, Andre and I would go see movies. As soon as we arrived in a town, we would ask around to find out the location of the theater and the name of the movie that was playing. We must have seen more than 200 movies over the years.

It was almost impossible for Andre to fit into a movie seat, so he usually picked up a bench in the lobby and carried it into the theater, placing it in the aisle. The two of us would sit on the bench together, eating peanuts and drinking cokes while we watched the movie. We always timed it so we had just enough time to get back to the hotel and get dressed for the matches. When the movie was over, we would go outside and flag down a taxi. The sight of Andre getting into the back of a Japanese taxi was a funny thing to watch. He would completely fill up the back seat. It was impossible for him to sit in a normal Toyota-sized taxi. He would get in head first and crawl to the other side and remain on all fours, and, depending on the size of the taxi, he occasionally had to hang his head out the window.

Andre was famous among the wrestlers for his ability to drink. In fact, he loved to drink. His beer drinking is legendary. He drank it by the case. He once drank 253 beers at one sitting in the United States. When he went to a club, he would order 50 beers at a time so he didn't have to wait. In his huge hand, a normal-sized beer can looked like one found in a child's toy box. When he wrapped his hand around a can, you could barely see it. He would upend the can, take two swigs, and it would be gone. He would drink two to three bottles of wine in one evening. Occasionally, he drank Crown Royal whiskey.

New Japan built a special, larger-than-normal seat on the bus for Andre. Next to the seat was a large, blue, Japanese-style trashcan. It was always filled with large bottles of Kirin, Asahi, or Sapporo beer that were covered in ice. The first thing Andre did when he got on the bus was open a beer, and no matter how long of a trip it was, he drank almost constantly. When he got back onto the bus after the matches, he would continue where he left off. I have never seen anyone who could drink like Andre, and yet, due to his size, his body was always able to accommodate the alcohol. When he was in Japan, we went out together many nights, and in all those times, I never saw him drunk or even a little bit high from the alcohol.

One time at the Keio Plaza Hotel, I was on the way to catch the bus to the show. I was waiting for the elevator to stop at my floor. It was a huge elevator and held at least 25 people. When it stopped on my floor, the door opened and it was crammed full with Japanese people. Standing in the very back of the elevator was Andre. He towered over everyone in the elevator. We make eye contact, but we didn't say anything to each other. I was just able to squeeze into the very front of the elevator as everyone pushed back into the elevator to make room for me. The doors closed right in front of my face and the elevator began the long descent to the lobby. My room was near the top of the hotel and the elevator moved slowly down the thirty-odd floors to the lobby.

As was usual for elevator rides, the ride down was quiet. Everybody stood still, looked straight ahead, and avoided making eye contact with anybody else. A few seconds after we began to move, a really loud and exceptionally long fart broke the silence. It just went on and on for what seemed like a couple of minutes. If anyone in the elevator was deaf, they probably would have felt the vibrations. It was so loud that nobody could begin to imitate the sound with their lungs. It was obvious to everyone that it was coming from the rear of the elevator, so everybody began shuffling forward, pushing me face-first into the doors. It also was apparent to everyone that only one person could possibly be responsible for such a "giant" fart. I tried so hard to keep my composure, but I began to laugh and turned around to look at Andre. He was just standing there, staring directly at me, with a huge smile on his face. He looked so proud. When the doors finally opened, the crowd stampeded off the elevator and pushed me out with them. When I was able to stop, I turned around to see Andre walking off the elevator, giggling like a schoolboy. We laughed all the way to the bus. Of course, the first thing I did was tell the other boys about it.

Most of Japan was a really great place to be in the 1970s and 1980s. Before Japan opened its doors to the world and a lot of the world's problems, one could go out and never worry about getting into trouble. The society itself was pure Japanese in its culture and personality. Everyone was extremely polite and very nonviolent. One really had to be doing something wrong or acting like a jerk to get into trouble. The Japanese went out of their way to accept us gaijins and our different tastes.

One of the places we enjoyed going to was Roppongi, located in Minato, Tokyo. The Roppongi district had a huge selection of nightclubs, bars, and restaurants, many of which were open all night long. We could easily arrive in the district at night and walk out as the early sunlight was breaking. The restaurants included everything from traditional Japanese dining to McDonald's and Hard Rock Café. One of the few country music places in Japan at the time, a club called Mr. James, also was found there. During that time, the average Japanese citizen didn't own their own personal car. The primary mode of transportation was train or taxi. Late at night, we would find a forest of neon lights advertising everything from electronics to food, and entertainment could be found far off the beaten path in the most out-of-the-way places. In those areas, taxis would be lined up for blocks. The taxi drivers knew when the nightlife would begin to wind down and waited patiently for customers to leave the business establishments. The line of taxis moved slowly as they picked up passengers, one by one. It was all done in an orderly fashion on very narrow streets which were barely wide enough to accommodate two small, Toyota-style vehicles.

Sometime in 1979, when I was working for New Japan, Andre and I met a number of All Japan's gaijins in Roppongi at the Lexington Queen, an underground nightclub which catered to models and celebrities. New Japan wrestlers often would meet talent from All Japan during our off days. Almost every night, it was packed with an equal mix of Japanese and gaijins. Most of the gaijins were either models, both male and female, or from some part of the entertainment industry. We met so many "beautiful" people there. Of course, we stood out like sore thumbs because there are few "beautiful" wrestlers.

After spending time with the All Japan gaijins, one of which included Terry Funk, Andre and I decided to leave. Terry was staying in the Ginza district, which was closer to Roppongi than Shinjuku, where Andre and I were staying. Andre and I walked to the line of taxes and took our place at the rear of the line. When we reached the front of the line, we got into the taxi which pulled up beside us. A long line of people had formed behind us and the line of taxis couldn't move until our taxi got under way. I told the driver, "*Keio Plaza Hotel,*" which made him happy because it was an expensive trip. I believe the fare was $40 or so. As the driver pulled away from the curb, Terry Funk appeared out of nowhere and dove onto the hood of the cab. He laid motionless for a minute or so, which seemed a much longer time than it actually was. The driver wouldn't move because he was afraid he would hurt him. I got out of the cab and pulled Terry off the hood. As soon as I got back into the cab and shut the door, the driver began to drive off. Once again, Terry came running up and jumped back onto the hood. The taxi driver slammed on the brakes and stopped the vehicle. Once again, I had to get out of the cab and physically pull Terry out of the way. I got back in and told the driver to hurry up. "*Haiaku! Haiaku!*" For the third time, just as the wheels began to roll, Terry appeared. This time, he laid down on the hood, and then rolled onto the street in front of the taxi. While this was taking place, there was a long line of taxi cabs waiting to pick up customers, but they couldn't because our taxi was blocking the street. By that time, Andre and I were mad. It was no longer funny because we had a long way to go and it was late. No matter what we said, Terry wouldn't stop. He repeated his actions over and over. After the fifth or sixth time, I just stayed in the taxi and watched Terry "act" as only he can act. Andre and I finally began to laugh because it was really funny to see the extreme lengths that Terry went in order to "get" us. The horns were honking like crazy and the people in line could do little but stand and watch the "crazy gaijin." Andre and I were laughing so hard that tears were running down our cheeks. After a good ten minutes from the time he first appeared on the hood of our cab, Terry simply stood up and walked down the street, as if it was just another night in Roppongi. That incident was classic Terry Funk. He could, and *would,* go to the extreme to "get" the people. That creativity is why Terry is one of the best talents in the wrestling business.

Years later, when I was with All Japan, Dick Slater, a Japanese friend named Koichi Yoshizawa, and I were out with some other people in Matsuyama. Koichi, who was a young magazine writer when Brody and I were first together in Japan, lived close to that area. We were on our way back to the hotel late at night on the deserted streets of the town. The owner of the yakitori restaurant, a lady in her mid 60s, was playing like she was getting a headlock on Slater and me. Somehow, Slater and I ended up lying down on the street. Mama-san then covered us like someone would do in the ring. Koichi got down on his knees and counted us both out ... to the roar of the ten to fifteen patrons who had followed us outside.

Only in Japan!

Considering the fact that everything in Japan cost much more than it did in the States, the decoration of the Lexington Queen must have cost millions of dollars. The club catered to the high-end gaijin talent and they allowed us in without a cover charge. One night, the club was filled almost wall to wall with the "beautiful" people all dressed to the nines. All, that is, except for two ... Jim Duggan and myself. We were "belly up to the bar" in t-shirts and Levi's jeans.

Jim and I got along great. We were both big guys and we both wore thick glasses. Jim's glasses really exaggerated the size of his eyes. To say we were wild looking would be an understatement. We were well aware that we weren't part of the "beautiful" crowd and we were proud of it. As we stood drinking and talking at the bar, a male model walked up to us. He was just being friendly and said, "*You guys sure stand out!*" Neither one of us had any idea of what the other was going to say, but at the same exact moment, we each said loudly, "*So what?*" The guy spun around and made tracks. Jim and I looked at each other and burst out laughing. Later that night, we met Joe Cocker and some of his band members. Years later, when I was living in Mesa County, Colorado, I learned that Joe also lived in that area. Knowing some mutual friends, I mentioned to them that "*I met Joe in Roppongi in 1979.*" I barely remember it and I'm sure he doesn't.

After moving to All Japan and meeting Yumi, my future wife, I quit going to Roppongi and did not go for a number of years. During that time, the other boys kept going and I kept up with what was going on by listening to them. It seemed as if things were slowly changing and the guys talked about it becoming laced with a lot more gaijins from Southern Asia, China, and Africa. I later went back occasionally to meet with some friends and I could not help but notice how much the area had declined. There were more open "soaplands" [brothels doing business as bathhouses] and lower-end, shady-looking businesses built around the sex trade. It was still a very famous area and there were a lot of businesses, but the average Japanese working man was absent and the gaijins seemed to be the primary clientele. Also during that time, some of the boys got into trouble for engaging in fights with military personnel and other gaijins. From what I saw, I was glad that I no longer frequented the district. I felt like Japan lost control of one of the great entertainment places in the country, which is too bad because at one time, it was a high-class area.

I have said this many times over the years: Andre got Stan Hansen over with the people in Japan. I worked hard, and New Japan promoted me well, but it was my matches with Andre which got me over. Whenever I met up with Andre in later years, I always took time to thank him for getting me over, and how I never forgot how he had helped me become a top wrestler in Japan. Even later, when he came to All Japan, when his health was spiraling downwards and he couldn't move around too well, I would sneak over to his dressing room and thank him personally. He always appreciated it. I think of him often and was saddened by his untimely death. I will always think of him as a special man. To me, he was a giant ... not just in size, but in heart and character. I miss him and hope God shines on him.

There weren't too many new boys brought on board while I was there, but I was honored to have worked with several of the younger Japanese wrestlers when they were in the beginning stages of their careers. I'm not quite sure what steps the young Japanese boys take to get into the business. I do know someone has to recommend them, and only a very select group of guys were offered the opportunity. It was important that they have some special athletic ability or background in another sport, like judo, amateur wrestling, or sumo. I understand that when the office took the young boys in as potential candidates for the business, they also took over all responsibilities for their welfare. It was set up like the old days, when a youngster would become an apprentice to a skilled worker and be trained in his business for a number of years.

It was a very humbling experience by American standards, for sure. Each boy was usually assigned to a veteran wrestler. They would be considered one of the veteran's boys and they were expected to do whatever they were told to do. They learned the discipline of the professional wrestling system. They were subservient to all the older wrestlers. They washed the veterans' clothes. They packed their bags and took care of them. They never walked. They ran everywhere. They would unload the bus, and help set up anything that might be needed at the show. They were expected to undergo tough workouts in the ring, and do brutal, physical training [PT]. It wasn't uncommon to walk into a dojo and hear the boys crying, or screaming out in pain, as the veteran wrestlers put them through their physical training. The young boys would often undergo this training process for two to three years before they were allowed to have their "debut" match.

Eventually, the young boys are placed under the care of an older wrestler. He looks out for them and helps them, but in no way do they take it easy on their charges. Most of the time, they are the most demanding and brutal towards them. Each one of the boys is broken down, both mentally and physically. It is the same in sumo, judo, baseball, and most other sports. Where Americans would rebel against such treatment, it is the standard in Japanese society, even to a point in the business world.

Today, the training they underwent would be considered abuse in any court of law, but that was the way it was in those days. The daily training schedule included 1,600 sit-ups, 500 back extensions, 1,200 push-ups, 500 squats, hours of sparring, and 300 to 500 "bumps" (body slams, backdrops, etc).

One of the things they all did was work on flexibility. The trainers would make the young guys sit on the floor with their legs straight out in front of them. They then would lean with all of their weight on the young boys' backs and shoulders, forcing their faces down toward their knees, while screaming at them to keep their legs straight. I have seen two or three guys pushing down, with all their weight, on the backs of some of the young guys. The young guys would scream in pain. As brutal as that sounds, it was not done with malice. Everyone who got into pro wrestling in Japan had to undergo the same routine. The very top Japanese wrestlers all had to endure the same treatment the new, young boys did. It was the culture of Japanese pro wrestling.

Every day before the show, the young boys trained and did hours of PT. There were no exceptions. Everybody worked out ... even the top guys. They didn't always work out in the ring, but they always did something like weights or stretching. The veterans were teaching the importance of PT, but the real lesson being taught was that they do it, therefore "you" are going to do it, and it will teach you to respect the business. As the young boys slowly made a name for themselves with a promotion, they wanted everyone else to go through what they went through. It was hard and humbling, but with everyone going through the same thing, they all developed a common bond. That mindset was practiced and taught at both All Japan and New Japan.

I saw so many young boys start their career in Japan. It was very tough for a Japanese boy to break in and many didn't make it. Not too many gaijins were willing to go through the training I saw the younger Japanese wrestlers doing, although a few tried. Allen Coage, better known as "Bad News Allen," trained at the New Japan dojo, while Doug Furnas' brother Mike, Richard Slinger, Maunakea Mossman, and Kurt Beyer (son of Dick "The Destroyer" Beyer), all went through the process with All Japan.

Bad News became a really good worker and made many tours for New Japan. Doug's brother hurt his kidneys during training and had to quit, while Slinger, who was Terry Gordy's nephew, made it through the program and had a good run with All Japan. Mossman spent most of his career with All Japan and was given a push almost from the start. When Misawa left the promotion in 2000 to form Pro Wrestling NOAH, Mossman was one of the very few who stayed loyal to Mrs. Baba and All Japan.

Kurt Beyer tried to get into the business at the late age of thirty. He went through the hardest part of the training and seemed to have done well. However, he wanted to graduate into the gaijin status too quickly, and quit after he was told he still had to put in his time as a "young boy." A few others, like John Tenta, went through training, but soon left for reasons unknown to me. That was too bad because he had the potential to be a top guy in Japan. Tenta was a former sumo wrestler, so he knew some of what was expected and adapted to All Japan really well, but after a year or so, he went to the States. I believe he left because he just couldn't adapt to the Japanese hierarchy and style of business. It is hard to come from a complete different society and adapt to a style of living where one becomes subservient to others.

That hardly ever happens in America. That was Japan, however, and if a gaijin wanted to break into the business in Japan, they had to learn the old adage, "when in Rome, do as the Romans do." That applies to Japan, as well.

The veteran gaijin didn't receive any special treatment, either. They either put up with the hard, physical style of wrestling or they didn't return for another tour.

Mitsuharu Misawa, Toshiaki Kawada, and Kenta Kobashi were three of the young Japanese boys I watched being broken into the business and I was there as they slowly moved up in the ranks. There were other youngsters who tried to break in, but they left quickly. It wasn't easy to get into the business in Japan. As I mentioned earlier, the young boys had to go through thousands of hours of brutal training and abuse, both mental and physical. The Japanese wrestling business was built on that system, and even sumo and amateur wrestlers had to go through it. As they became established wrestlers, they wanted everyone else to go through what they went through. It was hard and humbling, but it made them close to their peers, as they had something in common.

Often, competition developed between students and that led to hard feelings, as it did between Kawada and Misawa. They had a few serious fights in public, which led to their eventual separation as they established their independent personalities and groups. As in everything, some are meant to lead and others are meant to follow.

One of the big differences between Brody and I was our attitude towards the young talent. Brody looked at most young talent as future competitors. He felt like he had worked hard to get his position, and he wasn't going to give it up to anyone younger or newer in the business. I can remember him saying, "*I'm not going to help anyone. You never know if they're going to take your job.*" I never looked at it that way. When I broke into the business in 1973, the wrestlers in Amarillo all took me under their wing and taught me the ropes (pun intended). They didn't look at me as someone who was there to take their jobs. Granted, over time, I did pass many of them by, but that was the natural process. In order to "pay it forward," as they say now, I decided to do the same for the younger boys who crossed my path. If I had no other reason for doing it, I thought it was important to teach them the correct way to do things in a way which would protect the business. In the past 30 years, I have had the opportunity to see and help so many young wrestlers who just needed a little guidance. Most of them appreciated the fact that I (and others, as well) took the time to watch their match and give them constructive criticism. And, just as I ended up passing many of the veterans who helped me, many of the young wrestlers have passed me by, and for that, I am delighted to know that I may have played a part in their good fortune.

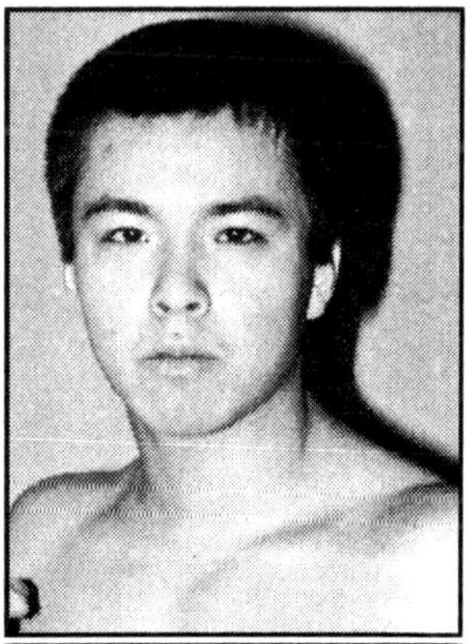

Yoshinari Ogawa

Three of the young boys who stick in my mind are Yoshinari Ogawa, Kenta Kobashi, and Tsuyoshi Kikuchi. Of the three, Ogawa would have been the one I wouldn't have thought would make it. He was small, even by Japanese standards, but to everyone's surprise, he made it through the training. He took a lot of punishment and was given no mercy, and yet, he endured and went on to become a top boy. He worked hard and overcame his size limitations through sheer determination. He became Misawa's tag-team partner and earned a spot in the upper echelon of All Japans talent.

Tsuyoshi Kikuchi

Kikuchi, who had been a good amateur, was a junior heavyweight. He settled into a good mid-level spot, but unlike Ogawa, who advanced through politics and friendship, Kikuchi advanced as far as he could given his size and talent.

Kobashi and Kikuchi began their careers at the same time. In my eyes, Kobashi really stood out. From the first day, he was the best young boy I had ever seen. He was determined, hard working, and almost a natural in the business, but the first thing I noticed about him was his size. He was physically bigger than the average Japanese, and he was strong, too. In my opinion, only Steve Williams was stronger. I always thought Kobashi had the most potential of the three. He had heart and he trained harder than any of the young boys who broke in while I was working for All Japan. What was even more impressive about Kobashi was the fact that he lost his first 63 matches. He made his debut on February 26, 1988 and didn't win his first match until May of the following year. Through it all, he never complained. He simply went about developing his character and abilities. Like I said, he caught my attention from the first time I saw him and it was no surprise when he developed into one of the top five wrestlers in Japan.

Stan Hansen vs Kenta Kobashi
Nippon Budokan: July 29, 1993

Kobashi was one of my favorite opponents. Whenever we wrestled, I knew he was going to be stiff from start to finish, and he never complained when I potatoed him. As the saying goes, he was as tough as a boot. One night, when I was wrestling him in a tag match, I picked up a chair and hit him with it. What I didn't realize was that the chair was damaged and had a piece which protruded outwards. When the chair hit him, the piece slashed his forearm almost to the bone. It was really bad and he bled a lot, but he never said anything to me about it and he never complained. We both loved to work stiff, but that went over the line. I felt really badly about it. I still used chairs on occasion, but from that night on, every time I picked up a chair, I remembered the night I cut open Kobashi's arm. As a result, I became more cautious of the damage I could unintentionally do with a chair, and to be honest, the Japanese became more fearful.

Away from the arenas, I had a few good times with Kobashi and Kikuchi. I ran into them on the street one night when they were on their way back to their hotel. I knew most of the young boys loved to eat, so I invited them to go out with me for dinner and a drink. We walked around town until we found a small club.

Most gaijins did not understand Japanese, and by that I mean both the language and the culture. I didn't speak the language very well, but I did understand the "Japanese style" of going out to the clubs. There was no cover charge, but if we weren't careful, we could wind up with a bill for a lot of things we didn't order. I was aware there were table charges, snack charges, and even hostess charges. The table charge was one of the things which almost always got to most of us gaijins. The amount of the table charge was left up to the owner of the bar. Once we were seated, the hostess would bring a basket of peanuts or pretzels to our table. We would eat them without thinking, only to be told later that there was a charge for them.

To our delight, one of the unique things we discovered were the geisha girls, or hostesses, who would sit at our table, pour us a beer, and make conversation with us — until we were told there was a table charge — not just for the beer, but for the amount of time the girl sat at our table. There seemed to be no end to the hidden charges. That was tough, especially when the beer itself was anywhere from seven to ten dollars apiece.

I learned this firsthand because, in the very early days, I ventured out a few times with a few of the wrestlers. Before we knew what was happening, the bill would be more than one-hundred dollars, so we learned early on to not go to those kinds of places on "our" dollar. At one time or another, every gaijin got "taken" by being handed a huge bar tab for what wasn't very much beer. It was, however, a part of their culture, and in the '70s, '80s, and early '90s, Japan was probably the richest country in the world.

Harley Race

Harley Race once told me a story about meeting and going out with a big sponsor. They went from one club to another, taking two or three cabs in the process. As the night wore on, the sponsor picked up the tab in every venue they visited. The total bill must have been in the thousands of dollars. Harley, of course, was the NWA world champion at the time, so it was well worth it to the sponsor to be seen in the company of such an important man. As they prepared to leave one club, the sponsor called for the bill. Nice guy that he is, Harley told the sponsor, *"I'm going to pay for this one."* The sponsor tried to refuse, but Harley said, *"Don't worry."* When Harley looked down at the bill, he saw it was for 200,000 Yen, which was something along the lines of $2,000. Harley had left the hotel with only a few hundred dollars in his wallet, so as everyone made small talk, he reached under the table, tapped the sponsor on the leg, and passed him the bill. Harley was relieved when the sponsor took it without question and didn't say anything to anyone in their party. Harley learned a great lesson that night.

The charges for "extras" could add up quickly, and over the years, there had been numerous confrontations between the gaijin wrestlers and club owners over those circumstances. That was why, very often, when we opened the door to a club, the host would step in front of us and cross their arms, wordlessly telling us, "*No gaijins!*" I had been involved in some of the conflicts with club owners, so whenever I went into a small club, I quickly learned to find out how much things cost. My experience taught to always ask how much it cost for "one beer." I learned to always ask, "Beer-o equra?" That meant "*How much is a beer?*" in Japanese. By asking that, we could get an idea of how much a few beers were going to cost.

During the time I was in Japan, most Japanese seemed to be doing well economically, and there seemed to be no end to going out and having a good time. I don't know how many thousands of "snack clubs" [small businesses that sold drinks and snack food] there were, but they all seemed to be doing business. We (gaijins) used to marvel at how often the Japanese went out at night, and we were excited to be able to go out and do the same after work.

On the night I took the young and green Kobashi and Kikuchi in tow to a small club, I asked how much a beer was and it was within reason. We only had one beer and stayed just a little while. It was already late and they needed to get back to the hotel since they had countless jobs to do taking care of the older Japanese wrestlers. When we got up to leave, I asked for the bill. It was 20, 000 Yen, which translated to about 215 dollars.

I went nuts. I said "*No way!*" I got into an argument with the establishment and refused to pay the bill. I had been in that type of a situation before, but no club owner had ever tried to screw me over in such a short time for so much. I made too big a deal out of it, of course, probably due to two reasons: I had been drinking and I didn't want to lose face in front of the two young boys I had with me. I kept refusing to pay. Kobashi and Kikuchi were embarrassed, I'm sure. They didn't know what to do or make of me. I finally ended up paying and we left. However, I know they had taken advantage of me and ran up the bill in a big way. That isn't right whether you're Japanese or gaijin. I'm sure that since the economy is suffering, some of those hundreds snack clubs that have gone out of business wish they had treated some of their customers a little better during the good times. Perhaps they might have stayed in business during the hard times.

Those were the negatives but we had a lot of good times at the clubs. One of the things we really enjoyed doing was finding a four- or five-story building in one of the night districts. The buildings were full of the snack clubs. By looking at the street signs, we could see which clubs were on each floor. We had a lot of fun getting on an elevator and riding up to one of the upper level floors. On each floor, there would be four or five snack clubs. Most of them were less than 500 square feet, often with just enough room for a bar and a few tables. We would walk to the first door and open it, never knowing quite what to expect because each one was different from the other. It was an adventure to walk into the clubs because they were all decorated differently. One might be decorated like a jungle, or a Roman setting. The host might tell us not to come in by crossing his arms over his chest, or we might not get any reaction at all. One club might be completely empty. Others would be crowded with people who would wave us in when they saw us. Often, the patrons would invite us in and ask us to sit at their table. They would treat us to drinks and a good time. It was a pleasant experience for every one of us.

When visiting the clubs got old hat to some of us, we enjoyed taking out new gaijins who had never experienced it. I had a lot of fun showing the Japanese style of night life to the new guys. I had the pleasure to show so many guys during the two decades I was there, and in all that time, I never got into trouble because we used common sense. Of course, there were a few times when some Japanese got out of control, but it was hardly ever a problem. Most of the guys at All Japan were taught how to act by someone like me, who was taught by Brody, who was taught by King Curtis Iaukea. You had to be a real jerk to get into trouble. Japan was very pro-American and, since wrestling was very big, the Japanese people recognized and liked us.

Another aspect of Japanese culture was common baths, or public bathing. In the past, many homes in Japan were not equipped with bathtubs, so the public bath was a place where people could go to wash, relax, and/or socialize with friends and neighbors. The custom in Japan is to wash someone else's back. It would be odd to see that in America, but in Japan, it's a common act. The young wrestlers were expected to wash the backs of the veteran wrestlers, and to be sure they had everything they needed, like soap and a towel. I can't see Americans being subservient to other guys. Washing their clothes, cooking for them, and washing their backs in the baths would seem degrading, but in Japan, it was a part of their culture.

While he wasn't what I would consider a "young boy," Akira Taue also became a top wrestler. He came to All Japan in January 1988, just one month before Kenta Kobashi made his debut. Taue got a big push due to being a well-known sumo wrestler. The thing which impressed me the most about Taue was his height. Of course, Baba was taller than anyone, but in height, Taue is second only to Jumbo Tsuruta. Coming into the business at age 26, Taue had to learn at an older age than most sumo wrestlers who came into pro wrestling. It took him a while to become a top talent in the eyes of the fans, but he slowly worked his way to that position. He did not have the luxury to go work in the States, as did Tenryu. It is harder to learn the wrestling business and develop ones style inside the hierarchy than it is to go out and develop it by working with wrestlers of varying styles. What did help Taue considerably was having the opportunity to team with Jumbo.

Akira Taue

Taue developed the jumping high-kick, a move I feel was second to none. The move is a lot like Baba's trademark "big boot." However, Taue put a twist to the move that added something special. Instead of waiting for his opponent to "run into" his outstretched foot, Taue would jump up and kick them, adding power to the move. It became one of his most successful spots.

When Kawada was injured, Baba put Taue and me together as a tag team. We teamed together for the first time in Kashima on October 24, 1999. We teamed together a total of 27 times, with our last match together taking place on May 30, 2000.

During our time together, Taue proved to me that he has more talent than most people give him credit. I developed a lot of respect for him because he worked hard and often carried our matches. Our styles were nothing alike, but he was always in the right place at the right time and never complained when mistakes in communication happened, as it does in most tag-team matches. When Mitsuharu Misawa died on June 13, 2009, Taue was named as Misawa's successor and became the president of Pro Wrestling NOAH.

I first met Akira Maeda in 1977 when he was a young boy. I remember him well because he was tall and lanky. He stood 6-foot-3, which was unusually tall for a Japanese. What also sticks out about our first meeting was his strength. Blackjack Mulligan also was on that tour. Mulligan was about three inches taller than Maeda, and second only to Andre the Giant in overall size. His hands were big and he was strong. He liked to joke around with the young Japanese boys. He would shake hands and have a test of strength with anyone who would accept his challenge.

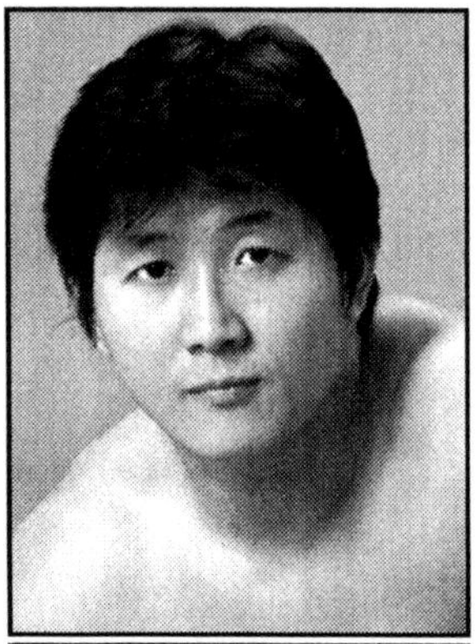
Akira Maeda

At the time, Maeda was working as a second. One of his jobs was to bring the ring jackets back to the dressing room. One night, when he came back after a match began, Mulligan challenged him to a test of strength. He wanted to do the thing where the two men face each other, put up their hands, and interlock fingers. The object was to force the other man's hand backwards. It is a good test of your hand strength and grip. I was sitting on the other side of the room and wasn't paying attention to what was going on. But all of a sudden, Mulligan called over to me and said, "*Hey, this guy is really strong.*" Throughout the tour, Mulligan kept messing with him. Each time, Maeda stood his ground and pushed back. Jack must have mentioned to me a number of times how strong Maeda was. He was really impressed with him.

At one time, Maeda was being groomed by Shinma to be Inoki's successor as the top star of New Japan. Shinma, the figurehead president of the WWF at the time, sent Maeda to work for Vince McMahon Jr. On March 25, 1984, he beat Pierre Lefebvre for a new version of the International heavyweight title, which was the major title recognized by New Japan.

Meanwhile, in the wake of scandals involving himself, New Japan, and Inoki, Shinma was kicked out of the company. Shinma promptly formed his own promotion — the Universal Wrestling Federation — in the hopes of re-creating the success he had with New Japan, and convinced Maeda to go with him. However, things didn't work out. From what I understand, the business relationship between Shinma and McMahon soon went south when McMahon was forced to choose between Shinma and New Japan, with whom he already had a business relationship. McMahon chose New Japan, but continued to use Maeda, who was promptly relegated to wrestling older talent like George Steele and Rene Goulet.

When Maeda left the WWF, he was disenchanted with the heirarchy aspect of pro wrestling. He resented having to do business with what he considered to be "past-their-prime wrestlers" like Steele and Goulet. When Shinma began using him as the top guy in the UWF, he used his influence to change the direction of the promotion from a traditional, pro-wrestling style to a more martial arts-oriented style. Several others in the promotion, most notably Yoshiaki Fujiwara, Nobuhiko Takada, Kazuo Yamazaki, and Satoru Sayama, all had martial arts backgrounds, and they were enthusiastic about Maeda's ideas. Fujiwara had the reputation of being one of the top shooters when he was with New Japan. Trained by Karl Gotch, he was Inoki's enforcer. He had the reputation of being tough. One night, when I was going to the ring, I accidentally hit him with my rope and he gave me a look. The upshot was that the UWF promotion incorporated realistic moves, submission holds, and kickboxing-style kicks to create what has come to be known as "shoot-style wrestling."

Shinma, however, didn't approve of the new style, and after a power-play between himself and Sayama, Shinma found himself on the street and out of the wrestling business.

Maeda eventually returned to New Japan, where he was accepted by the fans as one of the hottest talents in the business. I was told he had problems with Inoki and, due to the fact that neither man could come to an agreement over the direction his push would go, it was only a matter of time before they went their separate ways. Sadly, they never worked in a singles match against each other in what could have been a huge, money-making program. Maeda also supposedly got into a fight in a bar with Keiji Mutoh, another one of New Japan's rising stars. In April 1986, Maeda took advantage of Andre's bad legs and took him down (which was unheard of) and not letting him touch him. When the match ended, Andre was blown up and unable to get to his feet. The final straw was broken when, on November 19, 1987, during a 6-man tag-team match, Maeda kicked Riki Chôshû in the eye, breaking Chôshû's orbital bone and putting him on the sidelines for more than a month.

Maeda was suspended, but given an opportunity to return under specific stipulations. He refused and, along with Takada, formed the second version of the Universal Wrestling Federation [UWF]. The UWF not only became the hottest wrestling promotion in the world, but it was the first pro wrestling event to ever sell out the Tokyo Dome, drawing a gate of $2.9 million. One year later, the UWF was dissolved due to mismanagement of finances.

Despite his differences with promoters and proclivity to do what he wanted, regardless of what was expected of him by his bosses, Maeda brought a lot of positive influences to our business. In particular, he popularized a stiffer style of working, and his emphasis on giving the fans clean finishes influenced other promotions, including New Japan and All Japan.

Nobuhiko Takada was another young boy for New Japan who went on to become a top talent. I also remember him when he was a young boy. He was a good-looking boy who trained hard. I remember one instance when I realized he was tougher than the average wrestler. He was still in training at the time and hadn't had his first match. While returning to our hotel after going to eat, four of us gaijins passed by the Japanese boys' hotel. I don't remember who the other guys were, but I think Steve Keirn was one of them. Takada was just walking into the hotel and we called him over. He was wearing short pants and a nice t-shirt which was very different. One of the wrestlers jokingly said he wanted his tee shirt and pretended like he was going to take it off. Takada took him seriously and tensed up, refusing to let him have it. He began to fight him off. Of course, that only encouraged the rest of us to step in and take his t-shirt. He kept fighting, but we finally pulled the shirt off over his head. When someone said, *"Let's get his shorts,"* he really began to fight. It took all four of us to overpower him and take them off. When we let him go, he ran naked into the hotel.

The next day, we were told he had broken a rib while fighting us. We were shocked and felt badly that he got hurt. Wrestlers were always ribbing each other, but at times (like this one), it turned out to have serious consequences. He missed a week or so of training. To his credit, he never said anything or complained to us about it. Then again, that rib was *nothing* compared to the hazing the young Japanese boys took from the older Japanese wrestlers.

I tell this story because it demonstrated Takada's character. His refusal to give up, even when faced with overwhelming odds, showed us just how tough he was. It might have embarrassed him at the time, but we all developed a respect for him. Of course, he later became a wrestling superstar with both New Japan and Universal Wrestling Federation, and in the year 1996, moved from professional wrestling to mixed martial arts.

Kantaro Hoshino is another New Japan wrestler about whom I have good memories. He was short, but he was very thick and stout. He also had short legs, but they were well-muscled and strong. In the ring, he could move quickly. He took a pounding from the larger wrestlers, but he never complained. The other Japanese wrestlers kidded him about being a Korean, and when the gaijins heard that, they started in on him, too. I don't know if he liked it, but whenever wrestlers learned something which bothered someone, they would keep doing it just to irritate them. He passed away as I was making my final read-through of this manuscript.

Kantaro Hoshino

Riki Chôshû also was getting his start when I was with New Japan. Chôshû had been a good amateur in college and participated in the 1972 Olympic Games for South Korea. He wasn't too tall, but he had great balance and good legs. The office eventually gave him a good push. In 1983, he was featured in an inter-promotional program which did perhaps the greatest run of box office business in the history of New Japan Pro Wrestling. New Japan sold out many of their house shows during the following 12 months, and the TV show was among the top five television shows in the country.

Chôshû used my Lariat as his own finishing hold. Many wrestlers used in over the years, but Chôshû adopted it as one of his main moves. He wasn't the only one to do that, but rather than be irritated or resentful that other people were using my finishing move, I took it as a compliment that they would want to use it. I can't say I was happy about it, but there just was no stopping the boys from doing what they wanted to do.

I don't think anybody used the Lariat at New Japan until after I jumped to All Japan. Hulk Hogan was one of those who did, calling it the "Axe Bomber." In time, almost everybody was using it, but to the fans, the move was always synonymous with Stan Hansen. My version is the one they remember the most, primarily because I fought to keep it strong. I never cheapened it by using it early in a match. When I used the Lariat, the match was over. Today, we see wrestlers using it ten times in one match. Obviously, if it isn't used to end a match, it couldn't hurt their opponents too much. No matter what someone else called it, the fans knew there was only one Lariat. They knew the difference. It was a devastating-looking move.

Riki Chôshû

Chôshû later came over to All Japan and we had some good matches. He was at the height of his popularity and he had some classic battles with Jumbo Tsuruta and Genichiro Tenryu, and held the NWA International tag-team belts with Yoshiaki Yatsu for an entire year. During that time, he mentioned that he remembered the time I beat him in less than a minute. The match took place on live television on January 19, 1980 in the Isahaya-City, Nagasaki prefecture [governmental bodies that are comparable to states in America.] when we were both working for New Japan. He was just a green boy at the time. Time is usually a factor on TV shows, so when I asked how long a match they might need, they said, "*Short. Doesn't matter.*" Since it didn't matter, I went out and beat him in less than a minute. He badly wanted to even up the score by beating me in a singles match, but I held out. He was never given the opportunity. Over the years, he told the press many times that I had beaten him in less than a minute.

I have heard different things about Chôshû as a booker and owner — some good and some bad. I do know we have a mutual respect for each other.

During the time when Chôshû was being given such a big push, I just sat back and took part in matches which weren't promoted too heavily. I worked hard and was kept in view, but I was never really promoted during that time. It was very frustrating for me because I was in my prime. I felt strong and I was ready to forge ahead with my career, but I could only stand by and watch as Chôshû came and took all the main interest for a while. The matches between Jumbo, Tenryu and Chôshû did good business for two years. By February 1987, when he had taken as much as he thought he could get, he jumped to New Japan and took several wrestlers with him. To those of us in the business, we called that "raping and running." He did give All Japan the bounce it needed at the time, but I don't remember business falling off too much. I never took much interest in those events, but I do know Baba kept going and started over with the talent which had remained loyal to him. He offered exactly what the Japanese fans wanted to see.

At the same time, there was a movement in the States with the TV companies buying control of the wrestling companies. Huge sums of money were being made and offered to wrestlers. Hulk Hogan called me a few times and said he could get me on with the WWF. He was in a good position with the company, and he knew we could do good business together. I have to admit that I was tempted by the possibilities, but I decided to stay in Japan. Baba had asked me to be patient. Baba called me over to talk during Chôshû's run and said, "*I'm going to put you on the back burner and let the Japanese go against each other. I have plans for you. Let it play out. You are important to the company, and this thing with* Chôshû could be short-lived. W*hen the time is right, I will just heat you back up.*" I trusted him. I just went out and did my matches, and even though I wasn't figured into things too strongly, my pay remained consistent.

That is just one example of how much of a broad understanding Baba had of the business. He was doing good business with Chôshû and his group. The TV was giving them top billing and the ratings were doing well. At the same time, he also was smart enough to keep me and a few other gaijins in a position to help if things changed.

I also was approached during that time by Paul Orndorff at the Atlanta airport. I was amazed when he told me he would make upwards of $700,000 that year. All I could say was, "*Wow!*" That was huge money in wrestling. I could hardly believe it, but I knew Paul and didn't doubt what he said. He said he had just turned from heel to babyface, so there was a great opportunity for a good heel. And since I had been out of the States for such a long time, I would be a relatively new face to the fans. He urged me to think about it, which I did. I had a tough time making a decision, but there were several factors which led to my decision to stay in Japan. One was that my kids lived with me between tours of Japan. I couldn't take care of that responsibility if I worked in the States, and I wasn't going to sacrifice my home life for money. Secondly, and I'm repeating myself, I had promised Baba that I would be there for him when he called, even if it meant sitting on the back burner until such a time arrived.

The money I was making with All Japan was nothing like I could have made in the States, but I was comfortable with my life and the money I was making. It was a missed opportunity in many ways, but I have never regretted my decision. I could have made more money, but I would have had to work something like 320 days a year to get it and I would miss valuable time spent with my children.

It also was during that time that I had met and began a relationship with a wonderful and beautiful Japanese woman. That alone could have been the main reason why I decided against pursuing a deal in the States. We underwent a long courtship which proceeded slowly, but it turned out to be the best thing that has ever happened to me. Over a period of time, we fell in love and got married. We now have two sons and we are really happy.

I always operated under the idea that my wrestling career was public, but my private life was just that — private. During the time of our growing relationship, I was pretty much at the peak of my popularity in Japan. I was very aware of and valued my privacy. I kept my relationship quiet and a secret from the All Japan office. I didn't want any publicity or attention drawn to it. Even when we got married, I kept it to myself. Other than Pete Roberts and Brody, I didn't tell the office or anyone else in Japan because I didn't want a "big deal" being made out of it. Eventually, the office learned about it, but by then, I had been married for more than three years.

In a sense, being put on the "back burner" allowed me to spend time preparing to get married and starting a new chapter in my life. Today, more than twenty years later, I am happy and very much in love with my wife. We have a great relationship and enjoy living our life together in the mountains of Colorado.

As I look back on my fellow gaijins who left Japan to pursue their dream in the WCW and the WWF, I find that many of them made good money, but their careers ended far sooner than they expected, and things didn't always pan out like they had hoped. Many times, I warned my close friends that "the grass is not always greener on the other side of the fence," but my warning fell on deaf ears. Unfortunately, things didn't work out for many of my friends. By contrast, my career in the ring lasted until November 2000, several years longer than most of theirs.

It's also interesting to note that I signed a contract with Baba at our first meeting in Dallas, but the duration of the contract was for just three years. I worked for Baba for two decades and never signed another contract. We trusted each other and sealed every agreement between us with a simple handshake. That was the type of man he was, and I suppose he saw something of the same in me. I never knew another promoter like him. He was one of a kind.

Many of the wrestlers told me they were hoping for a good money deal when they went to WCW and the WWF, but no matter how closely their lawyers studied the contracts, there was always something hidden which affected them negatively down the road. Both WCW and the WWF had the last laugh. The contracts were never as they seemed and things did not work out for them. Several of them came back to Japan to work, but they were often put into a lesser position than they had been in when they left. On the other hand, there were guys who left Japan to work in the States, and they made great deals for themselves, but they were the exception to the rule. Steve William was the perfect example. He left Japan two times, once to WCW, who he said messed him around and didn't honor their contract, and then to the WWF. Dan Spivey did the same thing, but his career, for whatever reason, never took off in the States. Regardless, they were both great talents.

I decided that no matter what, I was going to stay in Japan. I loved the country and the people, and it became my home away from home. I have never looked back and I have no regrets about staying in Japan.

Tatsumi Fujinami was (and is) someone I respect, although he had been in the business for more than a decade by the time I knew him. When I was wrestling for New Japan in 1979, he was Inoki's number one partner. He had great athletic ability and could move well in the ring.

I still see him occasionally and he seems to stay in good shape. I heard he had a bad back for a while and it held him back in his wrestling. It's hard to me to believe he's now in his mid 50s. To me, Fujinami, Chôshû, Takada, and Maeda will always be the young wrestlers they were when I was with New Japan, but it's a sobering thought to think the boys of New Japan who were young in 1979 are now almost retired. That is a long time to be wrestling.

On April 27, 1979, Jack Brisco came to New Japan for a two-week tour and negotiated a good payoff for a high-profile match between himself and Inoki. That was big news to us because, in years past, as the NWA champion, Brisco had worked for All Japan. He made a challenge to Inoki and offered to place $10,000 on the line, with a winner-take-all stipulation. The match, held on May 10, 1979 in Fukuoka, the biggest city of Kyûshû Island, was billed as a "Prize Match." Chavo Guerrero and I were watching from the back of the arena. Inoki and Brisco had a good match, with Inoki winning. After the match, Brisco presented the $10,000 dollars in 1,000 Yen notes to Inoki. Inoki took the money and threw it out into the crowd. The people were in frenzy as they attempted to grab the money. Chavo and I went nuts. It was all we could do to keep ourselves from running out into the arena and grabbing the bills which were floating around the arena.

Jack Brisco

Chavo and I just shook our heads and returned to the dressing room. We were thinking about how nice it would have been if Inoki had just split the money among the young boys, and paid the remainder to the veteran talent as a bonus. Somebody could have bought a pair of shoes, or something extra for their family. Instead, he threw it out to the fans. It was a popular move for Inoki, but his "troops" went without.

Things like that happened a lot in New Japan. Inoki also seemed to put himself ahead of everyone else. Now, there's nothing wrong with promoting yourself, especially if you are the boss, but the bosses, whoever they are, are only as good as their employees. I feel that most of the underneath wrestlers were kept on the short end of the money too often. It is good to be young and hungry, but in my book, to throw money away, rather than give it to those who are dependent on you, isn't right. But then again, I have no first-hand knowledge of how the Japanese office made those decisions.

During the tour, Jack Brisco told me he didn't know how much I was making, but wondered if I was taking care of myself on the money side of the business. He told me he was paid a lot of money to come over and work for the two weeks he was there. When I told him I was making $2,500 a week, he said a lot of guys were making $5,000 a week, and pointed out that the arenas were selling out. "*Stan, you're a major reason why they're drawing those big houses. You really should be sure you're getting paid your fair share. Nothing lasts forever. You'd better ask for a raise while you're still hot, because things can change fast.*" He gave me good advice.

I didn't want to make too many waves because I was enjoying myself, but I still was in the business to make money. Two weeks before the end of the tour, I went to see Mr. Shinma about getting a raise. He went back to the office, I'm sure to discuss things with Inoki, and came back with an offer for $3,500 for that tour and the tours later that year. He told me I would get a raise the next year if things kept going well. It wasn't $5,000, but I took it and was happy knowing it was the first step in the process.

I believe the gaijins were paid more in the early days, especially the top talent. The Japanese wrestlers were paid on a different pay scale and they were given expense money for their meals. However, after the Japanese boys formed and joined a union, they negotiated for better money deals. By the late 1990s, the top guys were making very good money.

In 1981, Dusty Rhodes came to work for New Japan. One of the connections between Dusty and me is that he also played football at West Texas State. I didn't know Dusty when he was at West Texas, but he was there when Brody was playing. Dusty quit school and went into wrestling long before either of us.

Dusty was a big star in the States during that time. His "American Dream" character was really over with wrestling fans. With the advent of wrestling on Ted Turner's cable channel, SuperStation WTBS, Dusty became one of the first true superstars in the U.S. who traveled from territory to territory on a show-by-show basis. Andre was actually the first, but Dusty was really over in the NWA territories. House show attendance would jump when Dusty was billed on a show, regardless of who he was wrestling. And, in turn, he was paid very well.

Dusty Rhodes

The benefit of having Dusty come in for New Japan was that he was a wrestling character that wrestling fans in Japan recognized, and bringing him in for New Japan would definitely add something positive to a card. Billed as the Texas Outlaws, he and Dick Murdoch had been to Japan twice before. The first time, in June and July 1973, they worked for the old International Pro Wrestling company, which was being booked at the time by the AWA. Two years later, Dusty worked for All Japan, and now (1981), he was coming to New Japan through Eddie Graham's relationship with the promotion. Dusty talked to Mr. Shinma a lot. Shinma did everything he could to make Dusty happy, and Dusty took advantage of the situation by constantly asking for gifts. Shinma would almost always accommodate him. The result was that the gaijins, including me, all began asking for gifts, too. To his credit, Shinma tried to make everyone happy, but it caused a lot of friction between the boys.

The one problem Dusty had was that he worked a really different style which did not fit into the direction in which Japanese business was headed. His style was slow, methodical, and very showy. On the other hand, I worked hard and fast. I didn't slow down from the time I left the dressing room until the time my match was over. I kept moving and demanded that my opponents keep up with me. I didn't stop and sell, or lay in a hold, for too long. And in those days, I had a lot of gas [endurance] and could really go for a long time. Remember, wrestling in Japan wasn't that fast-paced until I helped establish the style. That might sound like bragging, but I really did speed it up.

Having worked with Dusty in the States, I knew he had things his way most of the time. When I worked with Dusty in the Georgia territory, I accommodated him and worked as much of his style as I could. When he came to Japan, however, I expected him to follow my lead. I wasn't going to sit back and let him slow my momentum, or do funny things to make the people laugh. I liked

Dusty, but I had seen how he always took care of himself in the U.S., regardless of the cost to his opponent (or territory, for that matter). I was determined he wasn't going to use or abuse me in Japan, especially since I had been given the opportunity to get over. By that time, I was beginning to feel that Japan was "my" territory. The other gaijins were just coming in and working on a part-time basis. That gave me the determination to not let Dusty or anyone else turn down the steam I was building.

We had a number of matches while he was there. Several times, he was Inoki's partner. One night, he ran from the dressing room to the ring to "save" my opponent in my match. He charged across the ring hard and hit me on my temple with his elbow. It connected solidly and I almost blacked out. I actually stood motionless for a few seconds while I regained my senses. I thought it was an honest mistake, but then again, it was a mistake in his favor. It made me wonder if he was really trying to move into my space.

The next time we met in the ring, I was ready for him, and we went at it. It wasn't too long before he couldn't keep up physically. He began to tire, but I kept going after him. When he tried to buy time to recover by getting out of the ring, I went right out after him. His face eventually turned a deep blue color from the lack of oxygen. He finally fell to the mat and lay on his back, trying to suck in enough air to keep from passing out. I just kept going after him, and began stomping him. When his partner came in, I gave him the same treatment. By the time the match was over, the fans had no doubt as to who had been in control of the ring.

I give him credit for not complaining. He knew it wasn't anything personal. It was just business. We got along real well outside the ring.

Most of the time, however, when one of the gaijins blew up, I would give them time to get their breath. I would do something like throw them out of the ring so they could rest, or I would go out and herd the people around the building for a few seconds. I could get after some of the young boys who were stationed around the ring. I always found something to do which would give my opponent an opportunity to regain his composure. I wasn't trying to embarrass anybody. I had been on that end of things myself, so I knew that a few seconds respite would allow the guys to catch their breath. And to be perfectly honest, there were times when I would leave the ring and chase the fans around the arena for several minutes. When I got back to the ring, my opponent would have to let me catch *my* breath for a few seconds.

I mainly wrestled the Japanese during that time. They never complained about anything. Never! I whipped them with my rope. I smacked them over the head with steel chairs, sometimes splitting them open (by accident). Again, no complaints!

I also teamed with Jim Duggan when he came to New Japan in 1981. He had played football at Southern Methodist University [SMU] and had been signed by the Atlanta Falcons of the NFL, but was released from the team due to knee injuries. Jim wore glasses like I did, and he had an eye which looked off at a different angle.

On one particular night, we were enjoying the late nightlife in the city of Aomori. It was one of the few times that Andre decided to return early to the hotel. Duggan and I decided to go to one more place. We found a small club and met a wrestling fan who was really nice and could speak good English.

He showed us some good times and took us to a number of clubs. As we were leaving one place, he said he could take us across town to another place. We walked up to a Lincoln Mark V, a very nice, and expensive, American car. It was really expensive to get a car like that in Japan, where there were few American cars on the streets.

Jim Duggan

It was a two-door car. I went around to the passenger's side of the car and got in. The man opened his door, pulled up the seat back, and with his hand, gestured for Duggan to get into the back seat. When he stuck his arm through the doorway, I grabbed his arm and pulled him into the back seat. Duggan pushed the seat to an upright position and sat down behind the steering wheel. We were all feeling good from the beer we had been drinking.

As soon as Jim sat down, the fan became stone-cold sober. We had no intention to take the car for a ride. We thought about what perfect timing it had been to pull him into the seat and laughed at his reaction. Duggan, however, noticed the keys in the ignition, and a light seemed to turn on in his head. He reached out, turned the key, and started the car. The guy began talking very fast in Japanese. To make him even more nervous, Duggan pressed the accelerator pedal and made the engine roar. After a few seconds, he put the car into gear. The wheels had been turned sharply towards the curb, so when Jim put the car into gear, it jumped the curb. Jim slammed on the breaks and the car stopped a few inches short of a brick wall. By that time, the guy in the back seat was almost crying. Jim backed up and drove us around the block to the front of our hotel, where we got out. The guy was so happy that the ordeal was over. We thanked him and all was well.

Thank goodness nothing happened. It was one of those spontaneous moments, all done in fun.

Around two in the morning, we went to a soba shop, which was located around the corner from the hotel, and ate udon noodles. Everybody goes to soba shops to close out a night of entertainment. We were laughing about the look on the man's face when the two big gaijins took control of his expensive car. There was a group of about six guys sitting nearby on a tatami mat, eating and drinking.

One of the men stood up and went to the toilet. On the way there, he stopped and said something to us in Japanese. We didn't know what he said, but his attitude and tone were clear. He was being hateful. Duggan and I just looked at each other with raised eyebrows as he walked off. We immediately put it out of our minds. We had been out on the town many times and it was very unusual to get into, or to find, trouble in Japan. That was one of the nicest things about the country, especially in the early '80s.

When the guy came out of the restroom, he stopped in front of our table again. He bent down between us, almost touching our faces, and motioned for me to take off my glasses. Now, Jim and I both wore glasses, and we both knew that when someone in school asked us to take off our glasses, we were fixing to fight. Allowing someone to take off their glasses was common courtesy, even to schoolyard bullies.

It was a direct challenge, but I ignored him. I just kept looking across the table at Jim, hoping the guy would just leave. He moved his face closer to mine, to where he almost was touching the side of my face with his. I still refused to acknowledge him. Duggan was watching me closely, trying to read the situation in case he had to act. I stared right at Duggan. I finally gave the guy a hard shove to get him away from me, after which I turned to look again at Duggan. I suddenly sensed the guy taking a swing at me from behind. I ducked just in time, stood up, and hit him with a short punch to the face.

Immediately, all hell broke loose. His buddies jumped up and charged at us. With my left arm, I grabbed the guy in a headlock, and began jabbing at his friends with my right fist. Meanwhile, Duggan was backing up towards the exit door. Still holding the guy in a headlock, I slowly followed Duggan in the direction of the front door. There was a lot of yelling and pushing as we moved towards the door, but I kept my new friend in a headlock between me and his pals, and punched and kicked at anyone who came close to me.

I was wearing flip-flops, which were shower shoes that we wore a lot during the summer. There was a small step-down just before the door opening. When I stepped down, the shower shoe tore off, causing me to fall hard against the wall which separated the dining area from the kitchen. In the wall was an opening through which the cooks passed the food to the waiters. I hit the wall with such force that the wall collapsed into the kitchen. Pots were hung on the kitchen side of the wall, and dishes were stacked on shelves. There was a tremendously loud crash as they all left their assigned spots on the wall and fell to the floor. The cook and his help all began to yell in Japanese. Meanwhile, other things in the kitchen began to collapse, and it looked like the roof was going to cave in. Evidently, the building was not built too well, and the wall I fell into was probably a load-bearing wall.

I stood up, still holding the guy in a headlock, and stepped out the front doorway. "*Now give me some fightin' room!*" I yelled, quoting a line I remember from an old movie called *The Great Race.*

Duggan was already outside and had taken off his glasses. He was ready to fight. As I released the guy I was holding, I told Duggan to wait. The owner of the soba shop and the customers all ran outside, closely followed by steam and smoke, which billowed out the door of the soba shop. We all came to our senses, suddenly aware of how much damage we had done, and I knew there was going to be legal trouble in store for me.

There were about 50 taxis lined up in the street, all ready to take people home. Several of the drivers left their vehicles and came running over, all acting like policemen. There was a lot of loud chatter in Japanese. Of course, I didn't understand any of it, but I knew the fighting was over. I told Duggan, "*Go to the hotel and get Peter Takahashi. I'll probably be going to jail.*"

Duggan didn't want to leave me. He was afraid more fighting might break out, but I told him that with all the people there, it was probably over. Shortly after he left, the police showed up. They talked to everyone, including the owner. Now, the owner saw everything that happened, and he knew how it all began, but I was afraid he was going to take care of his regular customers and put the blame on us. We were just gaijins who happened into his place of business. For all he knew, we would never be back there again.

I was watching the guy who started the incident. He was rubbing an oshibori [a wet hand towel offered to customers at most Japanese restaurants] under his eye, trying to irritate the skin so his face would look worse from my half-punch than it really was.

When Peter arrived, the police told him we all had to go down to the police station to figure things out. I pointed to the guy who started the fight and told the police in English, "*He started it.*" When they looked over at him, he pointed to the red bruise on his face. At the police station, the owner admitted that Duggan and I were simply minding our own business when the other guy accosted us. That was a nice thing to do since it would have been easy to say we were at fault. All the while, the guy continued to rub his face with the towel, which was now almost raw and looked pretty bad. I knew what he was doing. When we made eye contact, he gave me a small smirk.

We were leaving town the next day. If we didn't settle things before we left, we would have to come back to court a day later. We had bookings to fulfill, and we couldn't change our schedule, so the wrestling office paid for the damage and gave some money to the guy who started the fight. The office never said anything to us about the incident, and I don't know if it was ever reported to the press.

The incident made me realize how well the office took care of a wrestler depended on who they were. I thought back to the incident where Dave Taylor had the appendix operation and they made him pay the medical fees. Now, the same office had paid several thousand dollars to put an end to the trouble, and they never asked me for one cent. That was the nature of the business.

I ran into trouble one other time while on tour, but this time, it was at the arena in Sapporo. This incident took place on the same night we played the rib on Skip Young, which I related earlier.

I was wrestling Inoki at the show that night. I had Inoki bent over the metal railing which surrounded the ring and was choking him. Facing the crowd, I noticed a fan standing about five feet away. Suddenly, he ran forward and punched me in the face. Without breaking my hold on Inoki, I bent my head down and he hit me on the top of my head. I released Inoki, jumped the rail, and ran after the guy, who had turned around and was off to the races. I am really near-sighted, so I can't see too much in the distance, but my radar was locked in on that guy. The people in the audience were running and stumbling over each other as they tried to get out of my way. I knew if I chased him far enough, he would trip over something. Sure enough, when he glanced back to see how close I was, he tripped and fell to the floor. I was on him in a second. I smacked him across the face with a couple of open-handed slaps, and then grabbed him by the hair and slung him to the floor. I then turned around, and with a maniacal look in my eyes, I began to herd the crowd back toward the ring. I loved going wild and being out of control with the fans. It was so much fun. Everybody ran as I made my way back to the ring. Inoki and I finished the match and I went back to the dressing room.

Early the next morning, Peter came to my hotel room and told me I had to report to the police station. They wanted to talk to me about hitting someone in the audience in Sapporo. He would go with me to translate and (hopefully) help smooth things over.

We had a show in Sapporo again that night. I was at the police department from nine in the morning until mid-afternoon. They had me sit at a small table in a room which was barely big enough to hold a small desk, one chair for me, and two chairs for the police interrogators. Peter was asked to remain outside in the reception area. As I walked into the room, I noticed that behind my chair, the plaster wall was cracked, and it was stained with something which looked like blood stains. I wasn't sure if someone's head had been bounced off of it or not, but I was definitely guarded.

One of the policemen could speak a smattering of English. I told them the story of the fan hitting me, and how I chased him down and hit him back. I explained that I wasn't trying to hurt him. I just wanted him to understand that he couldn't get away with attacking other people. They asked me to repeat the story many, many times, and asked the same questions over and over.

By mid-afternoon, they put some papers on the desk and asked me to sign them. They were written in Japanese, so I didn't know what they said. The policeman told me I wasn't going to get into trouble, but I had to sign the papers. I refused and asked them to let Peter read it, which he did. There was an admission of guilt buried in the papers, so I asked them to remove it. After we went back and forth for another hour or so, they simply decided to release me, and I never had to sign the papers.

When we got back to the hotel, I only had fifteen minutes to get ready before we had to leave for the show. Peter later told me the guy I had hit had apologized for causing me so much trouble. At that point, all I wanted to do was to forget the whole incident, so I just shook my head in agreement, and then began to turn around and walk away. What they said caused me to stop dead in my tracks. "*He wants to make it up to you by taking you out to dinner after the show tonight.*"

I was stunned. My jaw dropped to the floor. I was at a total loss for words. The guy who hit me, and who I hit back, wanted to take me out to eat? When I talked to Steve Keirn about it, he said, "*It sounds like a setup to me.*" That did it. I wasn't going out with the guy. When I gave my decision to Peter, he said the guy was a huge fan of Inoki, and that he was really sorry. Peter was so convincing that I finally decided to take the guy up on his offer, but only if Peter would come with me.

As I walked to the designated restaurant after the show, a man with a large bandage on his nose walked up to me. He bowed deeply in the traditional Japanese manner and began apologizing, and through Peter, he told me he did not go to the police. When he went to the hospital to get his nose taken care of, they filed a report with the police. Regardless, he was very apologetic. We were both somewhat guarded at the beginning of our meeting, but as time went on, we became very relaxed and we have a good time together.

The man's name was Mr. Takamori. Having Peter to translate made our conversation easy. It was obvious that he wasn't in the Japanese mafia, but he did have connections with them due to him owning late night entertainment businesses, which included several bath houses. He was always surrounded by associates, and throughout the night, he was constantly talking what seemed to be business with many people.

I learned something important from that experience. During the years which followed, I was invited out often by fans, or again, as we called them, sponsors. Going out alone with the "sponsors" was not as much fun as having one or two other wrestlers along. It was always fun when one or more of the boys were with us. So, from that time on, I always invited one of the boys to go with me.

Fate can sure take some strange twists in our lives. After that night, Mr. Takamori became a good friend and sponsor. He was the owner of several nightlife businesses in Sapporo. When I moved to All Japan in 1981, he followed me as a sponsor, taking care of me and a number of my friends during the two decades which followed. Whoever would have thought that someone who attacked you would become one of your best friends? Looking back on the incident, I'm so glad it took place. Mr. Takamori was one of the great acquaintances I met over the years in Japan. He showed me some great times and took care of me.

December 13, 1980 • Mr. Takamori, Stan, and Charlie Tanaka

I have been out in Japan late at night hundreds, if not thousands, of times, both before the incident and afterwards. I never ran into trouble like that. There were a few times when people got a bit unruly, but those incidents were not the norm. One of the great things about Japan was the fact that we could go out and have a nice time, without worrying about getting into trouble or into a fight. People would drink too much at times, so we had to use common sense and restraint, but seldom did we run across people who were mean or looking for trouble.

On May 8, 1981, while we were taping TV in Kawasaki, I was standing with Hulk Hogan and several others when we heard a commotion. Abdullah the Butcher sauntered into the building, closely followed by reporters, who were taking pictures and trying to get an interview. At the same moment, Hogan and I turned to look at each other in shock and disbelief. New Japan had made a huge score. Somehow, they had enticed the Butcher to jump from All Japan.

Abdullah was Baba's top heel, and had been with him since December 1972, so we knew it would hurt All Japan very badly. In fact, Abdullah had been on my first tour of Japan when I worked for Baba. I had seen how well he had been treated, and how they had catered to him, so his arrival in New Japan came as quite a shock to me. I even remember thinking his arrival was going to change a lot of things. In retrospect, it ended up being the beginning of the best thing that could have happened to me.

Abdullah walked over to us and said a few words. We were all gracious and welcoming, but Hogan and I were somewhat reserved. We were naturally thinking things like, *"Where does this leave us?"* Abdullah was a major coup for New Japan, but in our eyes, it meant they were looking for more talent ... and if they were looking for talent, perhaps they didn't think we were able to do the job. The office was giving Hogan and me a push, but where did we stand now that Abdullah was in the picture? What did the future hold for us at New Japan? Did we even *have* a future at New Japan? It made us stop and reevaluate our position. I believe that was when Hogan decided to move back to the States and branch out in a new direction of business, although he kept a great relationship with Inoki and was used well there for years. On the other hand, I decided I was going to stand and fight. I would wait to see how things played out. Besides, I didn't have the options in the States like Hogan did.

Within a week or so after Abdullah's first appearance, Shinma asked to meet me in private after one of the shows near the end of the tour. He tried to reassure me that my position with the company was secure. He also said I was the focus of their future business plans. But then he said something which shocked me. "*Don't worry about Abdullah. He is a fat piece of sh—. He will be dead in a few years, so don't worry."*

I was really taken aback by his statement. If he said that about Abdullah, who was a major player in the wrestling business, especially in Japan, then I wondered what he was saying to others about *me*. That was when I lost respect for Shinma. It also was when I came to the realization that professional wrestling in Japan was a cold, hard business. I wasn't friends with Abdullah. He was my competition, but I respected his ability and the position he had worked so hard to get. A few days after bringing him over from All Japan, Shinma was already saying negative things about him to me. It sure it was done to put me at ease, but he shouldn't have put him down as a person. He was a major talent who would help their business for many years. That one statement told me a lot about how New Japan looked at their talent. Perhaps they only viewed the gaijin talent that way, but they made me realize that we were just pieces of meat. It also made me remember what Jack Brisco had said to me about getting what was due me, and that things didn't last forever.

After that, Shinma went to great lengths to make me happy. He gave me a $500 per week raise, which brought me up to $4,000 a week, and when I was told I would be working in Japan for almost 17 weeks in 1981, I was in high spirits. I still wasn't entirely satisfied, though, because I didn't think I was being paid on an equal level with the other top talent. I was doing good business for them. It wasn't like Abdullah had come to New Japan at a time when business was bad.

I felt like Vince McMahon and I had not gotten along very well since 1976 when I broke Bruno Sammartino's neck. I'm sure that was just one of the reasons, though. He seemed upset with me for negotiating my own bookings, especially with New Japan. I also thought he wanted his wrestlers to be indebted to him, although he wasn't alone in that mindset. Most other promoters had the same attitude towards the wrestlers who worked for them. However, that was in direct contradiction to the way wrestling promoters had always operated their business. They always insisted that wrestlers were independent contractors, and not employees, which meant we had to provide our own health benefits, life insurance, retirement plan, and so on. From Vince's point of view, his hard feelings towards me might be justified, but I was in business to support my family and make the most money I could make. To do that, I chose to be independent and make my own choices.

Vince McMahon Sr.

Vince also had to contend with my independence when New Japan booked me to work in New York in early 1981. My bookings in New York were set up by the New Japan office with Shinma making the contact. Shinma seemed to like the idea of me working Madison Square Garden. There was a certain prestige to having one of the top guys in New Japan working in the Garden. Shinma said he was going to talk to Vince and tell him that he insisted on certain conditions. The most important condition was that I would not lose a match by pin fall. I would get myself disqualified or counted out. The only other request I can recall making was transportation expenses back to Mississippi. I told Shinma that the McMahons would never accept his terms. Shinma told me, "*Don't worry about it. Just leave it up to me.*"

On August 9, 1980, Shinma, his female Japanese interpreter, and I met with Vince McMahon Sr. and Jr. at a hotel in downtown New York. Shinma gave them the terms he wanted for allowing me to work for the WWWF. I was shocked when the McMahons both agreed, albeit somewhat reluctantly, to abide by the conditions set forth by Shinma.

After leaving the hotel, the first thing I did was go to Shea Stadium to find Bruno, who was wrestling in the main event there that night against Larry Zbyszko. I told him New Japan and Vince had agreed to have me come into the territory to work with him and Bob Backlund. I also mentioned the terms which had been agreed upon: no pin falls. Bruno looked surprised. When I asked him how he felt about that, he said he didn't have a problem with it. I took that to be a positive sign and looked forward to having a good run.

On October 21, 1980, I flew to New York and wrestled on a TV taping in Allentown, Pennsylvania, and in early December, I returned for a TV taping in Hamburg. In early January 1981, I began what would turn out to be a five-month run in the northeast.

I wrestled some good talent during my run there. One of the guys I'd like to mention is SD Jones. He always had a good attitude and was a good worker. Even though he had a long career in the WWWF, he didn't get the top spots, but he was one of the guys who really did a great job getting the top heels over when they came in. I accidentally hurt him one night when I hit him in the stomach as he came off the ropes. I was told he spit up blood from his stomach for a number of weeks. I felt badly about it, but he didn't complain. An individual with a lot of class, he passed away on October 26, 2008.

Other talent included Dominic DeNucci, a class act from the old school, and Baron Scicluna, both of whom were close friends of Bruno. They were both near the end of their careers, but they were solid workers in the ring and had good attitudes. Baron had a deep voice and wore thick glasses which exaggerated the size of his eyes. What I remember about him the most was that he was always telling funny stories or mimicking someone.

Pedro Morales, a former holder of the WWWF heavyweight title, was a great worker. He really laid in the chops. He liked to work stiff, which suited me perfectly, so we got along well in the ring. I remember one particular match around Newark, New Jersey. We had a brutal match that had the boys talking and the office personnel thinking we were out to kill each other. The fans in New York didn't see too many matches like that. I really enjoyed working with Pedro. He was over and he fought. What else could I ask for in a match?

During this time, I lived with Hulk Hogan in his apartment in West Haven, Connecticut, a suburb of New Haven. We were eating lunch at a family steak house when Hogan said the office had told him that Sylvester Stallone wanted to talk to him. He thought someone at the office was playing a rib on him. We talked about it and he tried to decide whether or not to call the phone number. He finally stood up and walked over to a pay phone (remember those things?) and dialed the number. About five minutes later, he came back with a huge smile on his face. *"I talked to Stallone."* Of course, I had to ask if he was sure it really was Stallone. He said, *"I'm sure it was. It sounded just like him. He wants me to be in a scene in* Rocky III.*"*

Wow! We were both excited. Hogan told me Stallone wanted someone with a certain look and that Hogan fit the character to a T. He also said nobody else was auditioning for the part. Hogan and Stallone agreed on a time and date to meet in Los Angeles. When I asked Hogan if he mentioned any money figures, he said he was going to take whatever they offered. I thought that was a smart answer, although it's an answer that most of us wrestlers wouldn't have given. Most of the boys would have tried to make a big score. I heard later that Hogan got something like $10,000 for the part. Of course, the money wasn't the big score. He parlayed the notoriety he received from the film into millions of dollars. That was a smart business move for Hogan.

Towards the end of my time there, Arnold Skaaland, an agent for the WWWF, told me Backlund was going to pin me. I stood my ground and refused to let them force me into doing something to which we had not agreed. *"A deal is a deal,"* I said. The second time they asked me to put over Backlund was just before our last match together. Again, I refused. I told Bob that I hoped he understood. He didn't say anything, but I got the impression that he was a little annoyed when he heard me say I wasn't going to put him over. My matches in Japan with Bob were just average. We each had our own style of working. He was very systematic and methodical in what he did, while I was wild and unpredictable, so our styles just didn't seem to mesh. When he wanted to, though, Bob could get out of his style. In some of our later matches, towards the end of my time there, he began to adapt to my style and we brawled in and out of the ring.

I heard a number of the boys voicing opinions that Bob did not do a good job as the WWWF champion. I always thought Bob was, without any doubt, the right guy for the position. He was the best-conditioned athlete in professional wrestling. However, like Pedro Morales, he had to compete in the shadow of Bruno Sammartino. A good comparison would be Brian Griese following John Elway as quarterback of the Denver Broncos. It just was a hard act to follow.

They also wanted Bruno Sammartino pin me. Again, I refused. They were persistent. Several times during my run there, I had to say, "*A deal is a deal.*" I believe Bruno, like Backlund, wanted me to do the job, but he never asked. He never had an attitude with me over the fact that I refused, either. Bruno and I have crossed paths many times since then and we get along well. I respect him for the unique position he attained. In my opinion, nobody has *ever* gotten over as big as he did when he was at the peak of his popularity in the '70s and '80s. He was truly over as much as a wrestler could ever be. I do think it would have been good for the WWWF business if I had put him over, but we had made an agreement. It wasn't something I personally had demanded, but it *was* agreed upon by all parties involved. Not only that, but I planned to make my living in Japan, and not New York, so it wouldn't have been in my best interest to do a clean job. The fact that I refused to deviate from our original agreement put me in a bad position, but my relationship with New Japan was more important. From that point on, word got around to other promoters that I put my "Japan business" ahead of everything else, and many of the offices in the States would not work with me. Several of my friends told me that promoters had heard I wouldn't do business in New York, so they worried that I might not do business with them, either.

And ... they were right.

That was the one-and-only, time a Japanese promoter, in this case Shinma, gave me instructions on how I should handle business in the States. Later, when I went to work for Baba at All Japan, he never told me what I could or couldn't do between tours. He assumed I knew enough to put "my/our" business first, and that business did not include me losing matches in other territories.

The New Japan 4th Annual MSG League tournament, which was held on May 8 through June 4, 1981, was very memorable, especially the opening ceremony. Prior to the opening ceremony, we were in the dressing room. We had all been given little rubber balls to autograph and we were going to throw them out to the fans. Vince McMahon Sr. was there with us. He was going to open the ceremony with a few statements. I jokingly told him, "*Vince, when we get into the ring, I'm going to throw this ball and hit you square between the eyes.*" He didn't smile or show any expression whatsoever. He simply stared at me.

I made that statement in front of all the other wrestlers in the dressing room. I was joking, of course, but as time passed, almost every one of the wrestlers told me that I did not have the "balls" to do it. Most of them knew there was tension between Vince and me, so they egged me on by saying I wouldn't dare hit him.

When the opening ceremonies began, we all got into the ring and the wrestlers all threw their rubber balls out into the crowd, but nobody took their eyes off me. They were watching to see what I was going to do. I threw about twenty balls out to the audience. When I was left with one ball, I looked over to see Vince standing across from me on the opposite side of the ring. He was standing tall and straight, and he looked very distinguished. He looked every bit the refined dignitary he was. With the palm of my right hand facing upwards, I tossed the ball straight up into the air and caught it when it came down. After doing that a few times, I had everybody's attention. I looked straight at Vince and took a big windup, like I was pitching to Randy Bass, the starting first baseman of Japan's Hanshin Tigers. I threw the ball straight and hard, aiming at a spot about one inch over the top of his head. Everybody was relieved when the ball took the path I intended ... including myself. I was thankful I didn't miscalculate and hit him. It came very close to his hair, but Vince never flinched. He just stood there looking distinguished. It was all in fun, but he certainly didn't take it that way.

From that day on, as far as I know, Vince McMahon Sr. never said one good thing about me. Ole Anderson told me that on several occasions when they talked on a promoter-to-promoter basis, Vince really expressed his dislike of me.

Granted, I might have been a bit out of line when I threw the ball at him, but the other things he held against me were all just business. In 1976, I was in a unique position to "hold him up" for more money on the Shea Stadium show, and almost anyone else in those circumstances would have done the same. The money was not out of proportion to the house he drew based on my feud with Bruno. As far as booking myself goes, I didn't see why I should have let someone else make a deal for me when I was perfectly capable of doing it on my own. And, finally, when the office wanted to change our agreement in 1981, they should have acknowledged the deal we made and not act like I was asking for something I didn't deserve. In the end, they did honor the original deal because I was never pinned during the four months I worked there. In all respects, when it came to business, I treated Vince McMahon fairly, and he did the same for me. Regardless of the bad feelings he seemed to have for me, I sincerely hope he rests in peace.

In 1980, during my sixth tour with New Japan, the gaijins were all coming back from a show outside Hakata-ku, Fukuoka. Andre the Giant, Hulk Hogan, Bob Backlund, Dusty Rhodes, Tiger Jeet Singh, Wilhelm Ruska, and several others were on the bus. We were drinking beer, singing to country music, and just having a good time. When the driver pulled the bus into the hotel parking lot, we didn't get off. We were having too much fun. Peter Takahashi and Akasaka [the gaijins' bus driver] finally got off the bus and left, but we stayed on the bus for at least another hour. When we finally got off, we went out onto the streets of Hakata-ku. We were a bunch of wild cowboys in the old west who were just riding back into town after a long cattle drive. We weren't looking for trouble. We were just being loud. Most of the people who met us were entertained by seeing us in that mood. I believe some of the Japanese people wished they could "let their hair down" like we did, but their culture didn't allow them to carry on like we were.

While walking across a bridge, we saw a Japanese man performing some kind of a ceremony with a samurai sword. When one of the guys walked up to him, the man turned and swung the sword at him, which gave all of us quite a scare. We quickly began walking again, laughing about what had just happened. We knew when to move on.

There was a lot of talent on the bus that night. Since then, I have often thought about how we all were 10,000 miles away from our homes in the States, trying to make a living in a foreign country, and how there probably will never again be a group with as much talent all in one place. It was a very memorable moment for me.

Now that Abdullah was with New Japan, rumors began to circulate that All Japan was going to go out of business. Shinma even told me that it was just a matter of time until Baba's company folded. We didn't know for sure that All Japan was in trouble. We only knew what we were told by people like Shinma.

In reality, New Japan's business increased about twenty percent after Abdullah came over, although some credit for the upswing in business should probably be given to Satoru Sayama, who wrestled as Tiger Mask, the popular Japanese manga [comic book] hero. Sayama became a big star for New Japan and put their junior heavyweight wrestling division on the map. The thrust of the promotion, however, was always Inoki and his opponents. When he came to the ring, the people always stood and chanted over and over, "*Inoki! Inoki! Inoki!*" On the flip side, All Japan's business didn't suffer too badly. For the most part, their business remained relatively stable, and when it did decrease, it was by no more than five percent. Due to Abdullah's jump, however, they were looked at as the "number two league" by the newspapers, magazines, and fans.

That caused me some concern. From my first day in the business, I had been aware of how important competition was between wrestling companies. We all knew that if there was only one promotion, then the wrestlers would have no power at all. In Japan, that was more obvious than anywhere else. Isao Yoshihara's International Wrestling Enterprise had gone out of business around this time, so I was very concerned about the future of All Japan. That fact, however, was one of the catalysts for convincing me to jump to All Japan.

I was teaming up with Hogan most of the time, so we renewed our friendship during that time. We talked openly to each other about our business, and we often voiced our concerns about where we stood in the future plans of the company.

A few weeks before Abdullah showed up, I had talked to Wally Yamaguchi, a reporter for the wrestling magazines. The boys referred to him as "The Weasel." I don't know what his business dealings were, but he had deep relationships with both Inoki and Baba. He also was very close to Abdullah, so he might have acted as the go-between for Abdullah and New Japan. He had a good command of the English language, so he could "stooge" information from the gaijins to the Japanese, and vice versa. For all I know, he might have played a big part behind the scenes, but at the time, all I knew for sure was that he was a reporter for the wrestling magazines. During our meeting, he told me there was a rumor that Butcher would be coming to New Japan. I don't know how Wally knew anything about New Japan business, but we wrestlers were always the last to know things like that. I believe he told me in order to gauge my reaction and see how I felt about it. I tried to hide my feelings, but I'm sure he was able to tell that I was surprised and disappointed.

In late April 1981, after returning to my home in Mississippi following my 9th tour of Japan, my telephone rang. To my surprise, when I picked it up, I heard the voice of Terry Funk on the other end of the line.

Chapter 16

Clandestine Meeting

I wasn't surprised to hear from someone from All Japan. In fact, I half expected someone to contact me sooner or later, but I never thought it would be Terry Funk who would make the call. After we caught up on what we had each been doing, I said, "*I've been expecting to hear from you.*"

I think it took him by surprise. He said, "*What do you mean you were expecting to hear from me?*"

"*Well, it's been years since we had last spoke. You must want to talk to me about something important.*"

It was important. When he asked me about my feelings towards Abdullah coming to New Japan, I told him I wasn't shocked (which, I was), and that I was confident it would help our business. He then asked me if I was happy at New Japan. I told him I was, and that was the truth. New Japan had given me a good spot and they had treated me well.

However, what I didn't tell Terry was that I had just begun negotiating a new contract with New Japan. Terry launched into his purpose for calling. "*How would you feel about talking to Baba?*"

After thinking about it for a few seconds, I told him, "*I'd be willing to talk, but I won't guarantee I'll move from New Japan, and it will take a lot of money for me to even consider it.*" I also emphasized that there must be complete secrecy about the meeting. "*I don't want to talk to anybody but you and Baba, and I insist on absolute secrecy. I want it kept between the three of us and nobody else.*" Terry assured me he would and that he would be back in touch.

I didn't hear from Terry for awhile. When he did call, he said Baba would like to meet with me at a hotel on the grounds of the Dallas/Ft. Worth International Airport. I suggested a date in June 1981 because I planned to attend a big family reunion at Possum Kingdom Lake, which was about 100 miles west of Dallas in Graham, Texas. I had to drive from Mississippi through Dallas, anyway, so Dallas was a convenient place to meet. Baba also had other business to take care of in the States. I later learned that he also had a meeting with Tiger Jeet Singh, with whom he also was negotiating.

After hanging up the phone, I was faced with mixed emotions. I enjoyed working for New Japan. I didn't know for sure what the future held, but they had always treated me well. They gave me a good push and an opportunity to get over. On the other hand, they kept putting me off whenever I asked for details of my new contract, and I was relegated to lower spots on the cards. They were putting their efforts behind Abdullah and Jeet Singh as a tag team, and Rusher Kimura as a single. I was getting the uncomfortable feeling that they didn't have me figured for a top spot in the future. I talked to Shinma several times and we negotiated, but I could tell he was in no hurry to put anything in writing. Of course, I was anxious to hear what All Japan had to offer and I looked forward to my meeting with Baba, so there wasn't any urgency on my part, either.

One of the things which bothered me was that every time I met with Shinma, he had something negative to say about All Japan's business, or Baba's financial stability. He would say things like, "*They're on their last legs,*" or, "*The TV is going to cancel their contract. It's just a matter of time.*" I did have reason to wonder whether or not All Japan was having trouble. Nippon TV aired their TV show on Saturday afternoons at 5:30, which was *not* a good time slot. That was prime time for weekend television in America, but in Japan, 90 percent of the young wrestling fans were outside during that time, and the VCR was not yet a standard item in Japanese homes. Hearing Shinma say those things made me feel a sense of doom. In the back of my mind, I kept thinking, "*If there isn't any competition, where will that leave all of us wrestlers?*" Without competition, our value to the company would diminish because the market would be flooded with talent looking for work.

Shinma did make an attempt to put me at ease. He would frequently take the time to talk to me, but the subject matter was of no real importance. I usually kept quiet and let him do most of the talking. I expected the office to do what was going to benefit them the most, so the early details of the negotiation didn't concern me, but I was having a hard time getting Shinma's comments about Abdullah out of my mind. They had spent a lot of money to get him to jump to New Japan, and yet, they talked about him in such a negative way. I thought, "*Why would they think any differently about me?*"

I also was beginning to feel that New Japan wasn't counting on me as much as they had been, especially since they had convinced Abdullah to jump. They had also picked up some Japanese wrestlers from Isao Yoshiwara's promotion, International Wrestling Enterprise [IWE], which had gone out of business after losing their television. Rusher Kimura, Animal Hamaguchi [Heigo Hamaguchi], and Isamu Teranishi all came to work for New Japan when the company closed its doors. Yoshiwara was later hired by New Japan as a booker, but passed away in 1985 at the early age of 55.

I was a businessman, so during the negotiating process, I continued to do my job. I did it to the best of my ability and I worked hard. At the time, I was teaming with Dick Murdoch, who had also left All Japan and made the jump to New Japan. Hogan had gone back to the States and was spending most of his time working for Verne Gagne's AWA promotion. It was good to have Murdoch as my partner. He was a good fit for me. I thought he was one of the best big men in wrestling. He could move, he was quick, and he was one of the masters of crowd psychology. I also enjoyed working with him because he was from Amarillo, Texas. There is a bond between Texans which can only be understood by other Texans.

When Shinma continued to stall negotiations, I began to feel that New Japan wasn't taking me seriously as a businessman. In some ways, perhaps it was my fault. I was young, and I joked and messed around a lot. I would do my job in the ring, but as soon as the match was over, I wanted to get out of the arena and have a good time. I was having a great time in Japan, which is the reason why I stayed in Japan for as long as I did. I loved the country and its people, the Japanese culture, and my private time away from the business. It was like America in the 1950s ... or, at least, as I imagined it had been. I admit that I was a heavy drinker at night, but I quickly learned that my system could not handle hard alcohol, so I only drank beer. It was the lesser of two evils, but I was always ready for the next day's matches, and it never affected my job performance. I didn't take myself too seriously, either. I could have acted more like a "top guy" by being more mature in my interaction with the fans, but that wouldn't have been "me."

At the time, there were large numbers of young fans who followed the gaijins. At times, there would be 50 to 75 fans at the hotel when we would leave for a show. Most of them were high school or college girls, but there were also many male fans in that number. When the bus pulled up in front of the hotel after the show, the fans would be waiting. Did they go to the shows? I'm not sure, but it was pretty neat to see so many there to greet us. I had a great time joking and kidding around with them.

I suppose, for those reasons, they thought I was happy-go-lucky or immature (I probably was), even though I told Shinma several times that I was a businessman whose goal was to take care of his family. I knew that being in a good spot was often a short-lived thing, and if I didn't get a good deal for myself while I was still an asset to the company, everything I had worked for could disappear. I kept thinking about IWE going out of business, and Shinma talking about the financial trouble All Japan was facing. If All Japan went down, it would leave only one company — New Japan — and if one company held all the marbles, how long would it take before the company would cut my money? Even worse, how long would it be before they hired someone to replace me? At that point, I set my sights on getting a good, long-term deal for myself, and I was willing to sign a deal with whichever company wanted me the most.

On the way to the family reunion, my parents were involved in a major automobile accident. My mom's knee was crushed and my dad got a cut and a knot on his forehead when it hit the windshield. My family and I were in their own car, so we had just arrived at the reunion when we got word of the car wreck, which had taken place a short distance behind us. I immediately drove to the hospital in Graham where I found my mother in terrible pain. She screamed when they moved her leg. It was a terrifying moment.

After my mother got settled into a room, I went in and spoke to her. One of the first things she said was, "*Be sure you go ahead and have your meeting with Baba.*" Throughout all the pain and misery she was undergoing, she was thinking of me. I felt badly and wept. Yes, even big, tough, mean wrestlers cry.

I later chartered a private air ambulance at a small airport in Graham, Texas, to fly Mom and Dad back to Jackson, Mississippi. After seeing them off, I drove to DFW Airport to meet with Baba and Terry at the Hyatt Regency DFW Hotel. To my surprise, Terry wasn't there. Baba told me he had been delayed due to the June 14 funeral of Rip Blackburn, son of acting AWA president

Stanley Blackburn. Rip had been a local promoter for spot shows in the Amarillo territory, and his family was close to the Funks.

Present at the meeting were Baba, Mrs. (Motoko) Baba, and a TV executive from Nippon Television [NTV] who I did not know at the time, but who later became an important figure in both my business and All Japan's. Baba spoke and understood English well, so there was no interpreter. In Japan, he normally used Joe Higuchi as an interpreter and buffer between himself and whomever he might be speaking, including me. In time, however, as Baba felt more comfortable dealing with me on a one-on-one basis, we had many short, personal conversations without the use of an intermediary. On the day of this meeting, however, Baba spoke English. Baba said we could wait for Terry to arrive, but we ended up talking business.

Giant Baba

Mrs. Baba always treated me with great respect. She was the "strong woman behind the man" we always hear about. She ran the everyday nuts and bolts of the company so Baba could concentrate on the business of matches and talent. One of her primary jobs was to run Giant Service, the merchandise end of the company. Whenever I negotiated with the company, though, I always dealt with Baba, although I'm sure she was privy to what Baba was doing. At this meeting, however, she was not involved in our discussions.

The only request I had was that I be allowed to continue using my own style of wrestling. At the time, All Japan was known for matches which moved at a leisurely pace and featured lots of holds, as opposed to my "perpetual motion" style of wrestling. I would not compromise my style. Baba answered me simply: "*We want your style most of all.*"

We talked about a number of other things pertaining to the business. Having been told that All Japan was in danger of losing their television, I wanted confirmation that NTV was dedicated to continuing to do business with them. The NTV executive gave me verbal assurance that the TV station was resolutely behind All Japan and was committed to the future growth of their business. That promise was the key behind me making a decision.

I asked for a few other minor considerations and we came to an agreement on all of them. It was not one-sided. I conceded some points and Baba gave in on others. One of the things I was concerned about was a clause in my New Japan contract, which stated that if either of us failed to honor the terms of the contract, the person at fault would have to pay a $10,000 fine. I can't remember what those terms entailed, but I wanted to be sure it was paid and that I did everything correctly. I didn't want New Japan to have any grounds to come after me legally, and I wanted everything to be done in a business-like manner. I didn't want anything to jeopardize my future in Japan. I was putting all my eggs into the All Japan basket and I didn't want problems to crop up after I went over. I knew I was going to burn a bridge, but I didn't want to blow it up, as well. Baba told me that I shouldn't worry about the fine and that it would not stand up in court, but I was adamant about paying it. I wanted to leave without any outstanding obligations.

I also let Baba know that I was obligated to do the three remaining tours for New Japan in 1981. During early contract negotiations with New Japan in the spring 1981, they weren't offering me much of a raise. Since we couldn't agree on terms by the time my current contract would come to an end, New Japan had offered me a $500 a week raise and asked me to sign three individual tour contracts for the remainder of 1981. It was a good deal for both of us because that would allow them to lock me in for the rest of the year, and give us more time to negotiate. I signed because I didn't know what the outcome of my meeting with Baba would bring.

Working on three more tours was going to be tough. I wanted everything to be kept quiet. If word leaked out, things could get really nasty. As it turned out, it became one of the best-kept secrets in Japan, especially given the time between my meeting with Baba and the date of my first appearance. To my knowledge, the only people who knew anything at all about the negotiations were Baba, Mrs. Baba, Terry Funk, and the TV executive. During the meeting, Baba told me he also was negotiating with Tiger Jeet Singh.

About two hours after the meeting began, Terry Funk joined us. Baba-san and I had already reached an agreement. I'm glad it worked out that way. I liked Terry, but I always preferred to do business one on one. I didn't like going through others. The deal was made between Baba and me. In the years ahead, as Baba got to know me, we developed trust and a personal relationship. I believe he was glad he had been able to negotiate with me man-to-man, rather than through the Funks or anyone else. It wasn't that he didn't trust them, because he did, but it was just good business for Baba to have a one-on-one relationship with his top talent. By dealing with talent on a personal level, there was less chance that communications could get mixed up or misunderstood.

When I originally told Terry it would take a lot of money to make me jump over, I didn't expect the money Baba and NTV put on the table. Let's just say I was extremely happy with the offer. We all shook hands and signed the contracts. I don't know if they would have held up in court because we wrote in the price we agreed on, but the thing I felt good about was the fact that I had Baba-san's handshake. From what I knew about him, that was worth more than reams of paper. Bruno Sammartino and others had talked about Baba with high regard. When I was leaving New York in 1976, Bruno said that even though Vince Sr. had a working relationship with New Japan, he (Bruno) had a personal relationship with Baba, and that Baba was a man of his word. Wrestlers were always voicing their opinions on different people, both good and bad. Not one time during my career did I hear anyone say anything bad about Baba ... not even when I was wrestling for "the other side." The one thing I consistently heard about him was that "his word is gold." In other words, we could always count on Baba to keep his promises. Knowing that, I never doubted that I had made the right decision.

I worked for Baba for the next 17 years, and in all those years, long after that original contract expired, we never had another written contract between us. Our future agreements were all done on a handshake.

I could have asked for more concessions, or made a better deal for myself, but in the end, I was happy. After dealing with New Japan and other promotions, I wanted to develop a good lasting relationship with Baba. I wanted them to leave the table thinking of me not as a "commodity," but as a partner. I wanted them to be at ease and know that I would work hard. I wanted to be someone they could trust. To reach those ends, I was willing to make less money, rather than ask for the very last dollar in negotiations. That said, I made a great deal for myself during the years which followed. In fact, I made much more than I ever would have imagined in my early years.

I also felt that perhaps I could help their business. There was a lot of talk about the possibility of them going out of business. I had no idea whatsoever how much trouble All Japan was in financially, but I knew that if they went out of business, it would spell disaster for the wrestlers, both American and Japanese. Like I mentioned earlier, competition is what makes things happen, and I wanted to be able to have a choice. If there was no choice for the wrestlers, then the remaining offices would control everything, including our lives.

At this time, New Japan seemed to be more attractive to the Japanese male. New Japan seemed to be drawing 80 percent men and young boys, while 50 percent of the All Japan audience was men, and the remainder was teenage girls and children. There was a big difference in the types of crowds. New Japan also was doing better business. That could not have gone overlooked by Baba and NTV for too long. It was a combination of those statistics, and the fact that Inoki had taken the Abdullah, which caused Baba to make a change in direction.

I took a big risk because I really did not know how business was conducted at All Japan. On the other hand, I knew how they worked at New Japan, and some things they did bothered me. I made my final decision based on the fact that I wanted to base my career in Japan. I was willing to forget wrestling in America. That was a huge decision because there were many places to go and make money in America. To this day, I look at it as the best business decision I ever made.

Tiger Jeet Singh also came to an agreement with Baba. However, he made his All Japan debut just weeks after his meeting. Singh wrestled in New Japan's MSG League tournament between May 8 and June 4, 1981, and made his last appearance for New Japan on June 5 at the old Kuramae sumo stadium. On July 3, Tiger made his first showing with All Japan.

My family was waiting for me downstairs during the meeting. We left immediately after the meeting and drove back to Jackson to see my mother. She was in bad shape. She was a large woman, so there was a very real possibility that she might not walk again. The surgery to repair her crushed knee had taken more than five hours. The doctors took part of her hipbone and attached it to the end of her tibia. My mother was facing a long recovery, but she never complained or gave up. Through it all, she never thought of herself, but worried about how it was affecting us. She was and has been an inspiration to me many times in my life. She was a very religious Christian and her faith was unwavering, and she passed those qualities on to me, although I sure didn't act like it at times. I knew she was one tough lady because I had seen her endure physical pain so many times. As time passed, she slowly recovered, but she never did walk completely right. She had to use a cane to get around. Three years later, when she was 60 years old, she had a stroke, but she lived to be 78. I am so proud of her. She had an unbendable spirit. The poem *Invictus*, by William Ernest Henley, which she loved, sums up my mom's character to a T. I only hope I can be half as tough and strong in life as she was.

Closing the deal with Baba was bittersweet because it was during this time that my marriage began to fall apart. I found myself in the beginnings of a long and prolonged divorce which had a lasting effect on my life. I have talked about how money-driven I was in the business. That was my reason for getting into wrestling. I didn't get in to hear the fans cheer, or for an ego rush. I was in it for the money. However, after the divorce, I made a promise to not let the business rule my life. In the end, I decided to spend fifty percent of the time at home with the kids. At the time, they were seven and four, respectively. They were young, but since I was doing tours in Japan, I could spend most of my time with them. By working half of the year in Japan, I could be with them for the other six months, which was a luxury that wrestlers in the States didn't have. I tried to be a good father and I put my kids first on my list of priorities. In hindsight, God works in mysterious ways. The divorce was something I ended up having to endure. However, even though it marked the end of one chapter in my life, it opened up the best and most blessed chapter as I met my current wife.

I don't know if wrestlers have more marriage problems than other occupations, but I do think the travel and separation are hard on a relationship. Travel is the one thing wrestlers do a lot of, and sometimes, separation from our families was the hardest part of the job. I did my best to get home as often as I could. When I worked in New York, I would take a late-night flight to get home, even if it only meant spending one day with my family. That's just not enough, however, and often, when we do get home, we just want to relax. We don't want to think about anything. We don't want to do anything. On the flip side, the wives have been "stuck" at home with the kids and taking care of the home front. I didn't understand that for a long time, but I eventually came to an understanding of what wrestlers' wives had to go through. While we were out playing cowboys and Indians (some of us literally) and having what seemed to be an exciting life, the wives were tired and bored. In the end, I realize nobody is without fault. We all made mistakes and definitely weren't perfect.

I went to see the movie *Kramer vs. Kramer* a number of times in Japan. I remember it being a depressing movie, but in the end, the main character was a lot like me. After my divorce, when I was at home in the States, I was Mr. Mom. When I went out on the road, they stayed with their mother. Considering the circumstances, it worked out as well as I could have hoped. For children, though, there is nothing really "good" about a divorce.

I really got to know the kids well between tours. Between trips to and from school, I was cooking, washing, ironing, and shopping. It was a lonely time for me, but it was a good time that I will never forget. My parents also were able to spend a lot of time with the kids because they had moved into an apartment I had built onto my house. I had opportunities to work a full-time schedule, and I made occasional shots in Georgia for Ole, but my focus was on bonding with my children. I was resolute in my decision to stay at home. I really enjoyed it. I was making more than a living in Japan, and between tours, I could be at home and have somewhat of a normal life.

When I re-married and was spending long periods of time in Japan, I made the decision to call home every day. International long-distance calls were very expensive back then, but it was an expense that was well worth every penny spent. I told everyone I knew in Japan to take care of their home situation. If spending money on long-distance calls meant doing without beer, or anything else, for that matter, then make the sacrifice and call your wife. And when you call, don't spend time complaining about how hard things are on the road. Listen to her talk. Listen to her tell you how she had a hard time dealing with the kids when they went to the grocery store, or how she had trouble finding a part she needed to fix the sink. If you do that, you will have a much better chance to survive the long time apart. For that matter, what else did we have to do with our free time in Japan? Why not apply it to good use … the building-up of our homes? In my experience, time spent "listening" on the telephone came back tenfold. I remember Johnny Ace saying he took my advice and it seemed to work for him. A number of the others did, too. When you and your wife are on the same game plan, you can get along in this business, but it takes a lot of work.

Most of all, I realized that I had to change the one constant in my life — me! I didn't want to keep making the same mistakes I had made in life. I wanted to learn from them. I didn't enjoy living with the repercussions of bad decisions I had made. I became determined to change myself on a personal level, and hopefully, that change would be for the better.

While I was working for All Japan Pro Wrestling, I met my wife in Japan and we began dating. That was the beginning of the best part of my life. After we got married, I took my children to Japan on several occasions, but not when I was on tour. Years later, when my son John was a teenager, he accompanied me on some tours. On D-Day, June 6, 1993, my father passed away and we had to put Mom into a nursing home. By that time, my wife and I had two boys ourselves, Sam and Shaver, and we all moved to Japan. I wanted them to know their heritage, so we moved in with my mother-in-law. My wife's dad had passed away when she was just 14 years old.

Sam was three years old when we enrolled him in a Japanese kindergarten. He was the only gaijin kid in the school, which made it tough at first, but he adjusted and it turned out to be a great experience. The school authorities were very strict compared to American schools, but Sam did well. Everyone wore uniforms and they had to change together into clothes suitable for physical-education classes. It was a very structured environment for a three-year-old, and one that is unheard of in America. He had a strong will and often was the dominate kid in his class. Shaver was six years old and going into the first grade when we moved. He attended a Japanese school which offered assistance for international children. He was the only American in the school, but there were six other children from South America and Europe. He learned to read, write and speak Japanese. It was a great experience and one he fondly remembers.

When we lived in Japan, I would commute to work by train, and then travel on the company bus to the towns. Shaver and Sam never traveled with me when I was working, but they did attend two or three shows during the two years we were there. John came over and traveled with me on the bus during two or three tours. We went out many times and I showed him the nightlife. There were a number of times when he was asked for his autograph. He thought it was funny and he got a big kick out of it. Paige came one time and stayed at my wife's house while I was on the road. One time, between tours, we all went to Tokyo Disneyland.

After two years, my wife and I felt like it was time to move back to the States, primarily because the boys were losing their ability to speak fluent English. We also wanted to get our boys back into American schools to learn this country's culture and sports.

During one tour of Japan when my son John was with me, we were in Kumamoto on Kyushu island, the farthest southern island which makes up Japan's mainland. I was with an old, retired Japanese wrestler, Atsushi Hongo, who had worked for Isao Yoshihara's IWE International promotion when it was in business in the late '60s. In 1973, he went to work for Baba, wrestling as Munenori Higo. He retired in 1978 and became one of the All Japan promoters on Kyushu Island.

Like many of the retired wrestlers who opened snack shops and night clubs, he opened a club in Kumamoto. When the boys came to town, he took care of them and let us eat and drink at his club. Of course, he advertised around town that we were going to be there, so our presence brought him extra traffic.

On this particular night when John was with me, I had not seen Hongo for a while since we didn't go to Kumamoto on every tour. He took John and I out to a late night yakitori [grilled chicken] house to eat. It was pretty late since we had matches that night. John was about 14 at the time and was really enjoying seeing this part of the Japanese culture. As were sat and ate, I noticed some Japanese Mafia-types at a table across the room. It was late and they were getting pretty loud. It also looked like they weren't feeling any pain. When they noticed Hongo, they motioned for him to come over to their table. I noticed right away that Hongo was deep bowing to them. They poured a beer and they all began drinking together. As the Mafia boss talked to Hongo, his voice got louder and louder. I got John's attention and told him I wanted him to pay close attention to what I was going to tell him. *"If I tell you to go, that means you are to run to the front door and go out into the street, and I want you to get out as fast as you can. I will be right behind you."*

He stiffened, looked around, and said, *"What's wrong?"*

"Never mind. Just do what I say if I tell you to go."

Not more than a minute or two later, the Mafia boss stood up and threw a heavy beer mug at the head of Hongo, who ducked down to avoid being hit. I yelled "Go!" and John took off for the door without looking back. As an all-out brawl erupted, I stood up, walked out of the building, and walked back to our hotel with John. John was worried about Hongo, but I was angry with Hongo for putting my son in that situation. It might have been different if it had just been me, but I didn't want John to get involved in a situation like that.

A month or so later, Hongo invited me to go out with him again, but I wouldn't do it. I told him, *"You put my son in danger, and I don't appreciate that."*

I knew that anyone who owns a bar, or a late night snack club, has to deal with and are close to the Yakuza. I have had a number of nice guys from the Yakuza who treated me well, and in return, I treated them with the same respect. The problem with Hongo, which really wasn't his fault, was that he wasn't an actual member of the Yakuza organization, but one of the myriad of people with whom the Yakuza did business.

Getting back to the story of my going to work for All Japan, in the weeks that followed my meeting with Baba, when All Japan and I were in Nagoya at the same time, I decided to visit with Brody. I wanted him to know what was going to happen. We had history together and the wrestling press was always talking about the possibilities of seeing us together, so I knew we would be a natural team when I went to work for All Japan. I followed what he had been doing with All Japan and he did the same with me, but we never really thought of ever getting back together as a tag team. I wanted him to know that there was the possibility of us becoming a team again.

I knew Brody's attitude was going to be very important if we were going to score and make a big impact on All Japan Pro Wrestling. He was very conscious of his career. He was very independent, too, and he didn't like surprises. He was being pushed at All Japan at the time, and like Abdullah had at New Japan, I would be coming in and getting a big push, as well. I never thought about who would get "over" more. I was content simply to do my thing and see how things progressed. I did know that if we became a tag team and combined our styles, we could be very successful. I was excited about the possibilities which lay ahead.

I took a taxi to the Lions Plaza Hotel where Brody was staying. We had gotten together a few times before when we were both in Tokyo. Brody and I walked to a small park and sat on a bench. It was sunny, but cold. I told him I would be showing up in All Japan soon and that I thought he should know. I told him I had asked the All Japan office to keep it quiet and not mention it to anyone. When I asked him for his opinion, he said he appreciated me telling him and that he wouldn't have been happy to have been surprised. I knew what he meant. I didn't like Abdullah showing up out of the blue when he walked into the building in Kawasaki. I didn't want Brody to feel the same way. Brody didn't reveal much about how he felt about the situation, but he was excited about the possibilities with us both on the same side. We liked each other and we were both getting over with the Japanese fans. I believe he thought my arrival would enhance his position, as well.

Looking back on my meeting with Brody, to me, that was the most important meeting I had in Japan, second only to my meeting with Baba in Dallas.

I was looking forward to working for All Japan, but I was going to do my very best for New Japan. I felt like I owed them something for giving me an opportunity and never doing me wrong. I knew that no matter what I did, Inoki and Shinma would feel like I double-crossed them, but I didn't want them to look back after I left and say I laid down on them. I still wanted them to do good business, even though it was their own fault for paying too much attention to Abdullah and not getting me signed earlier. They obviously thought I would wait around until they were ready to make a deal. They also could have made me content by treating me as an equal in all respects to the Butcher. They decided, for whatever their reasons, to not take me serious and not treat me like a businessman.

Knowing I was going to All Japan at the end of the year placed a lot of stress on me, especially psychologically. There was nobody I could talk to about the situation. During the first tour back, Shinma began to apply pressure for me to sign a long-term contract. They began offering me more and more money. Each time they came to me with a new offer, I put them off by saying I had to talk things over with my wife. Of course, my wife and I were separated and almost divorced by that time, but that excuse took care of the first tour. On the second tour, I evaded them as much as possible and never gave Shinma any promises. I have to admit that he worked hard to convince me to sign, and he was sincere in his negotiation. He offered me a lot of blue-sky (imaginary) incentives. He once told me that Inoki owned an island in the Pacific, and showed me a picture of a small island among several others, all overgrown with trees. Hanging from one of the trees was a banner which said "Inoki Island." I don't know if that was the truth or something they made up, but I accepted it as the truth. I was shocked, however, when he offered me an island. He said it would be named "Hansen Island." Now that was a nice gesture, but how many times would I ever visit an island in the south Pacific? Not too many times, I would imagine.

Shinma also said I could have a few percentage points in the company. That was a tempting offer. I spent a few days imagining myself as part owner of New Japan Pro Wrestling. I never really thought it was a serious offer, but I enjoyed going over the possibilities in my mind. I'm sure no other gaijin had ever been offered points in the company. It was a nice gesture, but after thinking about it, I just didn't believe it would really be done. In my mind, however, it raised all sorts of questions as to how I would be able to know the truth about the promises they made.

I think it's worth mentioning that on June 24, 1981, shortly after my meeting with Baba, Abdullah the Butcher made his first live appearance for New Japan. We teamed up against Inoki and Yoshiaki Yatsu. Abdullah and I pretty much ate up Yatsu, primarily because I wasn't going to allow myself to look like the weaker member of our team.

The last New Japan Pro Wrestling tour of the year, and my final tour for the company, took place from November 19 through December 10. By that time, I needed to confide in somebody, if for no other reason than to find a release for the stress which New Japan was putting on me. Dick Murdoch was my tag partner, but other than Brody, the only people I told were Pete Roberts, who I trusted implicitly, Hulk Hogan, and Andre the Giant. I confided in Pete during the August tour, and broke the news to Hogan in October. They both kept the information to themselves, which confirmed my belief that they were true friends.

Hogan, who was on the final tour with me, also was in a position to possibly move to All Japan. I even mentioned that he should think about coming over to Baba with me, but he knew that when I left New Japan, he would have an opportunity to advance his position as a single. And that's exactly what happened. Shortly before I left, they split us up and began giving him more of a push. They obviously looked at him and his connection to Vince McMahon when they decided to push him as a single. He stayed with New Japan and he did very well in Japan in the years which followed.

The only other person I told about my move ahead of time was Andre, and I didn't tell him until the day of the last show before I went over. I hated to leave him. Andre had played a big part in my getting over in Japan, so I felt like I owed it to him. When I went to his hotel room before the December 10, 1981 show in Osaka, I said, "*Boss, I won't be seeing you anymore.*"

"*What do you mean?*"

I told him I had made a deal with Baba and that I was going to work for him after that night. I also told him that nobody knew. He grinned and said "*Go for it, boss! I might see you down the road sometime.*"

Andre called everyone "boss," and in turn, it became a habit for me to call him "boss," as well. It was just a funny little play we had when we talked to each other. I never called anyone else "boss," but I felt comfortable using it with Andre, as did many other wrestlers. I sure did respect Andre, and I appreciate so much all he did for me in Japan. In my opinion, our matches were what really got me over in Japan, not just the ones with Inoki. They were good and helped, but I believe Andre and I working together was the main reason.

I left the matches that night with a clear conscience. I had let my closest associates in on my secret.

Nobody knew what my money deal was with Baba, but the dirt sheets reported he doubled my salary from $4,000 to $8,000. That was typical of them. They printed rumor and innuendo without verifying their facts. Let's just say I received an increase in pay that was beyond my wildest dreams. As I said earlier, I could have asked for even more, and I might have gotten it, but I decided to establish a relationship with Baba by not asking for an outrageous guarantee. Both over time and in the end, Baba and I were both very happy with the deal between the two of us.

I refused to discuss or reveal money deals with anyone else. As I said earlier, I was happy that Terry Funk did not make the original meeting with Baba because it left him out of the loop. I trusted Terry, but when it came to business, I always tried to keep details between myself and the other party involved. The Funks were very tight with Baba and could be trusted with anything relating to All Japan business, but I wasn't sure they *were* privy to all of Baba's business dealings. To my way of thinking, they weren't Japanese, so they weren't, and neither was I. The money Baba was paying me was my own business. I didn't share that information with the boys or anyone else. For that reason, the dirt sheets never did get the figures correct, even though they pretended to know by printing bogus information. I didn't want to know what anyone else was making, either. That way, greed and envy didn't enter into the equation. Not knowing made it easier for me to control my own ego. If I was happy with the deal I made, it didn't matter what anyone else made. As the saying goes, ignorance is bliss.

I became more and more excited as the time drew nearer for my move to All Japan. Shinma was stopping by frequently, asking for a decision on what I wanted and what terms I wanted in the contract. With each day that passed, he began to pressure me more and more. In the final days before I left, they offered me as much money as All Japan had. I was absolutely shocked one afternoon when Shinma said, "*Name your price.*"

Their offers had no interest for me. I was going to All Japan regardless of what they promised. I had made a deal and shook hands with Baba, and that was that. I would never break a deal on a handshake. I lived by the very thing I told Arnold Skaaland in New York … "A deal is a deal." I was not going to bend to pressure or greed. For Stan Hansen, a deal was a deal.

I have to admit there was a time during the last tour when I had some misgivings. I overheard Shinma once again mention that All Japan was going out of business. He said Nippon TV (channel 4) had canceled their TV show and things were so bad that Baba was selling his Honolulu condominium just to get enough money to make his payroll. I should have known better, but that got to me.

In November and December 1981, both All Japan and New Japan had big tag tours running at the same time. Feeling overwhelmed over all the rumors and stress from my previous tour, I found out where the All Japan wrestlers were staying and called Terry Funk, who was on tour with them. I would not leave my name. When I finally got in touch with him, I told him I needed to talk to Baba personally, and soon. He called back just a few minutes later and we set up a meeting at the Hyatt Regency Tokyo in Shinjuku, across the street from the Keio Plaza Hotel, where the New Japan gaijins stayed. I met Baba in a room where we had total privacy. Joe Higuchi was there, as well, but he never entered into the conversation. It was strictly between Baba and myself. I told Baba what I had heard about his financial troubles and that he was selling his condo. He just smiled and confirmed that he was selling it, but that he was buying a much bigger one on the seafront in the same building. The statements made about Nippon TV canceling the All Japan show were nothing more than rumor, too. History would prove that to be correct as Nippon TV supported Baba from the day he opened All Japan [October 22, 1972] until his death [January 31, 1999]. Baba smiled and said, "*Everything is alright.*" The whole meeting took less than 30 minutes. I breathed a sigh of relief and never looked back from that point forward. I was going to All Japan.

Back at New Japan, Shinma was polite and never lost his cool, but I could tell he was beginning to feel the heat of not signing me. At times, he seemed to be frustrated. I actually felt somewhat sorry of him, but he had ignored me too often in the past, and now, in the final hours before my last contract was about to end, he was trying to hardball me into signing. In addition to that — and I know I must sound like a broken record by now — but I just couldn't get past the comments he made to me about Butcher and others.

Shinma and Inoki might have had an idea of what was going on, but I never got word of it. Japan is a small place. Rumors are rampant and the press was always snooping around. And yet, there was no talk about the possibility that I might go to All Japan. Looking back on it now, I believe New Japan thought I was more preoccupied with playing around and having fun with Jim Duggan and my other friends than I was about business. We had good times together. We would do immature things like shoot water pistols at the fans. However, I believe that was one of the things which endeared me to the fans. We were different and down to earth. New Japan didn't look at it that way. They saw it as immaturity.

When Dick Murdoch came over to New Japan from All Japan in August 1981, the office put us together. Shinma held a press conference, saying something like, "*As revenge for All Japan picking up Tiger Jeet Singh, we picked up Tiger Toguchi [Kim Duk] and Dick Murdoch.*" Dickie was a good match for me and he was a great worker in his own right. However, he was not in my confidence, like Pete Roberts, and later, Hogan and Andre. Dusty Rhodes also was coming in at the time and getting his fingers into the office. He milked his worth real well. I had some good old "Texas" times with Dusty and Dickie on that last tour. However, Dusty was always blowing smoke about what a great relationship he had with Shinma. It might have been true, but Dusty was another person that Shinma spoke about in a negative way during our discussions about my future with New Japan.

I don't know who made the hard decisions for the company. As the point man, Shinma took all the heat, but it's hard to say that he wasn't following Inoki's advice.

In fall 1981, shortly after Murdoch came to New Japan, we visited a small fishing village on the coast during one of our rare days off. Looking to have some fun, Duggan, Murdoch, and I borrowed three small motor scooters from some of the local people. We rode them hard for several hours. We went up hills so steep that the scooters eventually came to a stop, unable to drive us any further. To the villagers, it must have been a funny sight to see three 300-pound men riding small scooters around their community. Later, in the hotel, which was shut down during the day, the three of us stalked each other with water pistols on both floors of the hotel for at least a couple of hours.

I tell this to demonstrate the things grown men will do to entertain themselves when they have time to kill in a place where there is no communication, no TV, and no entertainment. I also mention it because that was probably one of the instances where the New Japan office got the idea that I was immature and not serious about business. Granted, I did act immature at times, but I was deadly serious when it came to business.

On December 10, I sat in the dressing room in Osaka, knowing it was going to be my last match with the company. I was fairly certain that we had kept the entire matter quiet. As far as I knew, other than Baba and the people I had told, nobody in either company knew about it. However, people in the wrestling business are almost always talking and spreading rumors, and there is a saying about Japan: "It is the smallest country in the world when it comes to keeping a secret." I believe that's true. And if word had leaked out, I didn't rule out some kind of a double-cross taking place in my match that night. It didn't happen, but I was on my toes. I wasn't going to fall prey to a quick count, that was for sure.

Outside the business, especially after I jumped, I often looked over my shoulder, wondering if somebody might be coming after me. I was wary. Japan was a small country with certain elements which were dangerous, like the Japanese Mafia, of which I had heard many stories. They had their hands in most businesses, or at least had a relationship with most organizations. For that reason, I wondered whether or not they had a relationship with New Japan, and if they did, would they come after me? Perhaps I was being paranoid, but that suspicion lingered in the back of my mind during the first few tours after I jumped to All Japan.

One of the strange things about the whole scenario was that I never felt like New Japan had scaled back on my push. Normally, when a wrestler's contract is ready to expire, or he is going to leave, the company either quits pushing them or tries to beat them. That never happened to me. In fact, my last appearance for New Japan was in the main event in Osaka on December 10, 1981. Dick Murdoch and I wrestled and lost to Inoki and Fujinami. Murdoch lost the fall when Fujinami reversed Murdoch's signature brainbuster move and pinned him cleanly. When I think about it, though, it would have been hard for the office to beat me because of the matches I had with Andre, not to mention the fact that I had beaten Inoki once. I also believe they kept pushing me because they were confident they would sign me.

I tried to avoid Shinma on my final night. He didn't go to all the towns, but I knew he was there that night. As I expected, Shinma came into the dressing room and asked one more time about trying to get a long-term contract signed. He seemed to be very concerned about the fact that I hadn't signed, and asked if there was anything he could do for me. When I said no, Shinma must have known something was up. If I didn't have other plans, I would have signed by now. I didn't get any feeling, however, that he suspected I might be going to All Japan.

After my match, we all took the Shinkansen [Japanese bullet train] back to the Keio Plaza Hotel. I wished everyone good night and went to my room. Murdoch still didn't know what I was going to do. The next morning, I took a taxi to the Ginza Tokyu Hotel, where the All Japan office had me registered under an assumed name. I spent the night there alone. That same day, the New Japan gaijins took a bus to Narita International Airport for the flight back to the States. I would have enjoyed being a fly on the wall of that bus. My conspicuous absence must have lent itself to a great deal of interesting conversation.

I later returned my unused ticket to New Japan. Baba had agreed to pay for my flight back to the States. Up to that point, it was New Japan's responsibility to see that I "come into and leave the country," so I wanted that taken care of so there wouldn't be any problem later when I applied for a new working visa.

When I first began going to Japan, before any of the gaijins got into serious trouble, the wrestling office accepted "full" responsibility for our "welfare" while we were in their country. They provided transportation to and from the countries of origin, and while we were in Japan, to and from the arenas. There also was something in our contracts regarding their duty to provide medical care when we got injured. Later, after a number of the boys got into legal trouble with the police, the office added a stipulation in which we agreed to abide by the laws of Japan. If we broke the law, they would disavow any responsibility for our welfare. The office also began making background checks in both Japan and the States before issuing a visa. A number of the wrestlers who had gotten into trouble in the States had a hard time getting a working visa for Japan.

At two o'clock the next day, December 12, I was picked up by Yoshihiro ("Yoshi") Momota and driven to Yokosuka, which is two hours south of Tokyo in the Kanagawa Prefecture. The show in Yokosuka that night, which was the next to the last show of the year for All Japan, featured the semi-finals of the Real World Tag League tournament. The gaijin wrestlers on that tour included Terry Funk, Dory Funk, Bruiser Brody, Jimmy Snuka, Tiger Jeet Singh, Harley Race, Larry Hennig, the Sheik [Ed Farhat], Mark Lewin, Baron von Raschke, and Killer Karl Krupp. It was a great lineup of top talent.

I arrived at the show early and went to the dressing room. Not too many people saw me when I walked in. There were a number of smaller dressing rooms in the building, so Brody and Snuka were dressing alone. Brody was in a bad mood. When I asked him why, he said the office kept him completely in the dark about me coming to All Japan. Of course, he knew about it because we had discussed it in Nagoya, but he felt like the office should have included him in such an important piece of business. As their up-and-coming young talent, his pride was hurt. Of course, Baba and Terry Funk had promised *me* to keep it a secret, and perhaps they weren't sure just how Brody would respond to me coming over. Brody might not have trusted the Funks as much as I did, for whatever reason. He also had his tag-team partner and good friend, Jimmy Snuka, to think about. My entry into the mix gave Brody some things to discuss with the office about his own position with the company.

I felt Brody's participation was important. Even then, I didn't think of myself as being separate from Brody in stature with the company. I wanted us both to have a successful run, so I determined to smooth things out. I sent word to the office that I wanted a meeting with Baba, Brody, Snuka, and the Funks. We agreed to meet at the Takanawa Tobu Hotel, which was located two blocks from the Shinagawa train station, and where the All Japan gaijins were staying.

After the matches, Yoshi drove Brody, Snuka, and me to the hotel. Present at the meeting were Mr. Baba, Mrs. Baba, both of the Funks, Brody, Snuka, Joe-san Higuchi, and myself. We sat down and discussed the plans for the company. An hour or so later, everybody was appeased, including Brody. We were told that if everything worked out, we would all be pushed on an equal level. I would not be coming in to be pushed ahead of Brody or anything like that. And that was exactly the way I wanted it. I can understand Brody's feelings. He felt left out, much like I had when Abdullah came over to New Japan. I think it helped that we were friends and that he trusted me because he could have looked at my arrival as a threat to his stature with the company. I did everything I could to relieve him of that notion, which was my reason for calling the meeting. I wanted everyone to be happy.

I wondered what the Terry and Dory thought of the hastily-called meeting and its conclusion. It was obvious from what was said that Baba wanted things to go smoothly for Brody and me. There was some underlying strain between Brody and the Funks which I wasn't aware of until I arrived at All Japan. They had been doing business together for a number of years. Quite often, he was their opponent in the ring, and since they were the bookers for All Japan, there had been some small conflicts and misunderstandings come up between them.

That was where Brody and I differed in personality. We were close friends and were 100 percent dedicated to each other as a team. However, Brody was always suspicious of everything that came his way. He looked at every situation from a hundred different angles to determine if things were as they seemed. He also spent most of his free time thinking about his personal wrestling business — of what was good both for himself as an individual and for us as a team. I, on the other hand, tried to take things at face value, and believe with faith that things were as they seemed. I felt that was the major difference in our personalities. Brody was non-believing, while I took a "wait and see" attitude. However, our differing approach to the business served us well as a team for many years. Brody looked much further down the road than I did in terms of our business. I was content to adjust as we went along. Often, I would be a calming effect on Brody when he got upset, or when things did not go as he wanted them to go. On the other hand, he was able to head things off by recognizing the different directions our business might take in the future. During our time together, however, in public, we always were a united front. We never let anyone get between us, and we never let anyone else see that we were even discussing different opinions. I feel that was a real strong point in our relationship and one of our unique strengths.

We were all excited as we left the meeting. We were ready to move forward and turn All Japan's business around. That meeting was the foundation for a long and prosperous time for All Japan and all parties involved.

The following night, December 13, was the final show of the tour for All Japan. It was held in Ryôgoku Kokugikan, the old sumo arena also known as Sumo Hall. I showed up early again in order to stay out of sight as much as possible. The show was sold out for the finals of the 1981 Real World Tag League tournament, in which Brody and Snuka faced the Funks in the final.

I never showed my face until I walked to the ring with Brody and Snuka. I was wearing my street clothes and a cowboy hat. I can still remember the electricity of the crowd as we walked down the aisle to the ring. The closer we got to the ring, the more people began to notice me. The fact I was there was quite a shock and put the fans in a mood of excitement. Brody had a great partner in Jimmy Snuka. Snuka was a top talent in his own right, but the Japanese fans knew about my past connections with Brody. Stories about our time together in the States had been written about a number of times. In fact, fans had voted us as the "dream team" they would most like to see together.

When we got to the ring, the people responded wildly. I was there merely to be a "second" to Brody and Snuka, so I kept a low profile during the early part of the match. During the closing moments of the match, Terry Funk bumped into me on the floor and we began to fight. As could be expected, before too long, all five of us were into it. When we began to get the best of the Funks, Baba and Jumbo came to the ring, and chaos broke loose in the building. People were throwing futons [small seating cushions used at Sumo Hall] as we fought toe-to-toe. When Baba hit me in the forehead with a big chop, the blood began to flow, and the excitement of the people reached a new high. I mixed it up with Baba as much as I could. He was the top guy, and I wanted to be sure we were going to be "connected at the hip" from that night on. Finally, after a wild end to the match, we stormed through the crowd and went back to the dressing room.

After we had been sitting in the dressing room for a few minutes, an idea crossed my mind. I stood up and charged down the hallway toward Baba's dressing room. Brody didn't know what I was going to do, but he followed hot on my heels. I didn't know what was going on in Baba's room, and I didn't even have a set plan in mind, but I was going to run in on him and attack him. It was a totally-unplanned scenario.

I managed to stay in character, but I was unprepared for what I saw when I stormed into the room. I couldn't have timed my impromptu actions any better. The dressing room was full of people — pressmen, fans, TV reporters, photographers, and all the young Japanese boys. I can still picture the shock on their faces when I kicked open the door and ran inside. With blood pouring down my face and my shirt covered with blood, I must have been a sight. As I'm very near-sighted, I really had to work to spot Baba in the crowd of people, but when I did, I attacked him. He fought back, but was hampered by the people who surrounded him. When Brody joined me, we stood side by side and carried the battle to anyone and everyone. Baba was my main focus, however. After a minute or so of turmoil, Brody and I backed out the doorway and returned to our own room.

Baba never told me in so many words, but I know he was extremely excited that I took the initiative to do what I did. That spontaneous action was exactly what he had hoped I would bring to the business.

The scene was caught on camera and still photos went over big in Japan. The best thing about it was that the whole thing was unplanned. It was as real as it could be. That event set the whole tone of what the Hansen/Brody combination was going to be about in All Japan. We were wild, unpredictable, and spontaneous.

My spontaneous reaction to go into action was something which just couldn't be written into a script. I felt that if I didn't know what I was going to do next, then the office didn't know, either, and as a result, the fans wouldn't have a hope of guessing what was going to happen next. I feel that was a very real part of what All Japan evolved into and why we did such good business in the days and years which followed. I must say that it took "gas" to do it. It was hard work, especially at the end of matches when everyone was tired, but I feel the extra effort and unpredictably we generated made Bruiser Brody and Stan Hansen a valuable asset to All Japan Pro Wrestling.

I still have a photo that was taken that night of me coming out of the dressing room with Brody right behind me. The photographer captured the moment which set the tone of things to come in All Japan. The intensity with which Brody and I worked during those times was unique. Just like the unplanned moment when I ran into Baba's dressing room, Brody and I consistently acted on impulse, doing things which were unexpected. We simply reacted to whatever situation in which we found ourselves. That was the foundation of our success as a team. "Don't plan, just react." Nobody knew what we might do or where we were willing to take a match. That mindset, coupled with our size and strength, were the two main things that made us the dominant tag team in Japanese wrestling.

On December 13, 1981, my direction was set. The change was complete. I looked out to see a whole new frontier for me to challenge and take on. I was excited to the highest degree. I felt the goals I had set for myself in the business were finally within my reach. I had worked long and hard to get to a position where I could make an impact and be well paid for it. I had been through so many trials and tribulations. I had bruised and lacerated my knees. I had suffered a cut Achilles tendon. I had slept three-to-a-bed to save money. I had struggled for months not having enough money to eat properly or pay my rent. I had spent countless, lonely hours on the road, and paid the additional price of going through a divorce which, in large part, was caused by my absence from home. It had been a long struggle.

Now that I had arrived at All Japan, my future was in my hands. My story was mine to write. I had no illusions that there would be many challenges ahead. In fact, if Brody and I were going to get the push I expected, I would be facing more pressure than ever. We were going to make a concerted effort to work hand-in-hand with Baba to increase his business. That provided me with an opportunity which only comes once in a lifetime to a very few people. I was going to be an integral part of a company, and I wanted to do my best for them. It was Baba's company, but I was determined to be somewhat instrumental in deciding the direction his future business would take. I was looking forward to the challenge.

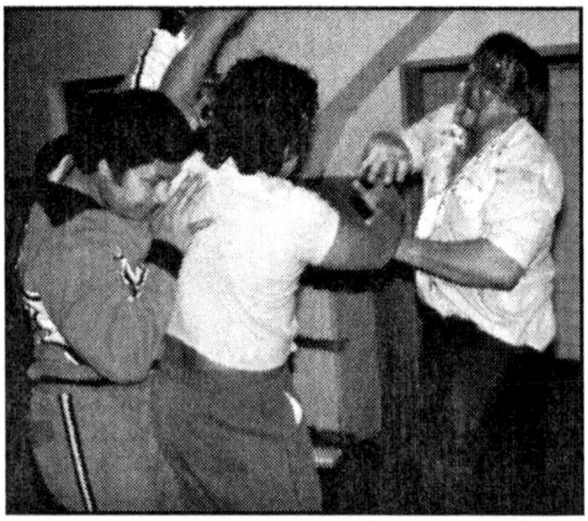

Tokyo, Japan
Ryogoku Kokugikan
December 13, 1981

Chapter 17

When in Japan ...

I didn't say anything negative about Inoki or New Japan Pro Wrestling after I left. In fact, I didn't mention them much at all during the years that followed. I maintained a friendly relationship with Seiji Sakaguchi, Akasaka [the gaijins' bus driver], and Ms. Kurakatsu, one of the office ladies I met at a number of functions. I bumped into Inoki a couple of times — once on a flight to Los Angeles after Jumbo passed away, and another when we were both on the same flight to Japan. We had a nice conversation both times. He even said I was welcome to come back to New Japan. In his eyes, what I had done was all about business, and nothing personal. I respect him for that. I also saw Shinma during a flight from Tokyo to Fukuoka, but we only talked for a few seconds, not saying much more than hello. We were polite, but we really had nothing to say to each other.

I would not say I had friends in the New Japan office. For the most part, it was business. The years to come at All Japan wouldn't be much different. I had many Japanese acquaintances, but friendships were rare for me. Even among the gaijins, friends were few and far between. I got along with just about everybody, but the only people in Japan who I considered to be more than acquaintances were Pete Roberts and Brody (which goes without saying). I was also close with Terry Gordy, Steve Williams, Danny Spivey, Ted DiBiase, and Johnny Ace.

In wrestling, you make very few friends. At least, few who can be considered "real friends." We are friendly with just about everybody, but true friends in the wrestling business are few and far between. On the other hand, there seemed to be more camaraderie in those days than there is today, a time when everybody is out for themselves. The huge egos of the guys today run hand-in-hand with the huge salaries they're paid. I'm glad they're being paid the huge salaries, but the egos have made everybody separate and individual, rather than encouraging them to work as a team. Before wrestling became a business controlled by TV ratings, the boys (wrestlers) were dependent on house shows to make a living. Our pay was determined by the number of people who bought tickets (the gate) to attend the matches. So from the top of the card to the bottom, everyone went out and tried to do their very best. And even though there was quite a difference between the payoffs of the opening guys and those of the top guys, everybody got their own little piece of the pie. The more successful the house shows were, the more money there was for everyone. The difference might be as little as five or 25 dollars a night, but that small amount meant a lot. That extra percentage might allow us to sleep in a motel, rather than our car. We might be able to eat a good meal in a restaurant, rather than a bologna-and-cheese sandwich. More importantly, those few extra dollars meant there was more money to send or take home to our families. To achieve those goals, everybody (for the most part) worked together. The boys respected each other as professionals as we worked towards our goal, which was to earn an opportunity to appear in the main event. We knew that to get noticed by the people who made the decisions, even if we were only in the opening match, we had to go out and work with the right mental and physical attitude.

As I said in an earlier chapter, during the time I worked for New Japan, I had little personal communication with Inoki. He was always in another dressing room or on a different bus. Mr. Shinma delivered most of the business which went on between us. At All Japan, however, I dealt strictly with Baba-san, and our meetings almost always took place at the arenas. Only in my later years did I go to the All Japan offices, and even then, in more than twenty years with the company, I only did that a few times. By contrast, I never went to the New Japan office once during the entire five years I worked for them.

There were a few times when I asked Joe Higuchi to deliver my questions or comments, but if they were too complicated, a meeting with Baba was scheduled. Surprisingly enough, we only had ten to fifteen meetings about business over the next seventeen years. Of course, I saw him at the matches and we would greet each other, but most of the time, even when I was his partner, there was quite a separation between the gaijins and the Japanese talent. I believe the reason for that is due to the fact that the Japanese are more reserved than us gaijins. I did what I was asked to do and Baba left me alone. That is one of the reasons why we had a long and successful business relationship. My situation was pretty much problem free. That was the main reason why I passed up on the bigger money in the States. All I had to do was get on the bus at the scheduled departure time, do my job in the ring, and wire the money home.

I also got to know the ring crew and office personnel at All Japan. Baba-san had some family members who helped out in the office. One of the first things I noticed about All Japan was that they were very laid back, especially in contrast to New Japan's pure Japanese style of management. Of course, All Japan was so laid back that it wasn't always well organized, and things didn't always run as smoothly as they could have. Things at the company improved when Mrs. Baba took over as office manager. Her organizational skills were part of the reason for All Japan making a turnaround, and over time, she became a powerful figure in the office. She was strong and she ran a very tight ship, directing the Japanese wrestlers and office staff more like a Japanese corporation. She also ran the marketing of products for the business. It really took a lot of stress and strain off Baba. Personally, she treated us all cordially and with respect. I heard some talk about her alienating the Japanese wrestlers, but I don't know what the conflict was about. It might have been due to the reality of Japan's male-dominated society.

There was a big difference between New Japan and All Japan in those days. All Japan was considered a pro-American promotion. They spent a lot of time and effort into pushing the gaijins. New Japan, on the other hand, didn't.

Tiger Jeet Singh was over, for sure, and they used a lot of European wrestlers, but other than that, they just rotated through the gaijin talent they had available without giving them a lot of buildup. From the perspective of the gaijin wrestlers, that wasn't good, so for a gaijin, All Japan had the reputation of being the company for which to work.

In 1982 and 1983, I made a total of nine tours of Japan. In between, I spent the majority of my time in 1982 working as Ole Anderson's tag-team partner in the Atlanta territory, and in 1983, I turned babyface and teamed with Tommy Rich. Ole, who was running Georgia Championship Wrestling at the time, was really good to me. We traveled together whenever I was in the territory. Not only was he a fair person to work for, but with me going through my divorce, he was a true friend who helped me out during that difficult time in my life. He didn't treat me like he was the booker, but as a friend.

Emotionally, I hit the bottom during that time, and I was really depressed. We were at the Richmond Coliseum on one of the nights when I was feeling especially disheartened. At that time, almost everybody knew I was having personal problems. While I was talking to someone, I said, "*You know, sometimes I just feel like ...,*" and I put my forefinger to the side of my head, like I was holding a gun. Sgt. Slaughter [Bob Remus] saw me and walked over. He said, "*What the hell are you doing? Don't be stupid!*"

It took me a second to figure out what he was talking about. I never gave any real thought to doing something like committing suicide, but I was wallowing in self-pity and made the gesture as a joke. Bob Slaughter's reprimand made me stop and take a hard look at myself. That night, the wounds of my personal problems began to heal, and I began concentrating on the All Japan tours which were lined up ahead of me. I don't think Bob has any idea of the impact he made on my life that night, but if I ever see him again, I intend to thank him for making me see the light. In 2010, when I was invited to introduce Antonio Inoki during his induction into the WWE Hall of Fame, I had an opportunity to see Bob once again. Unfortunately, he was too busy to talk, but I will never forget what he said some 25 years before.

Ole also was very understanding when it came to working around my Japan dates. Most of the other promoters wanted their talent to work for them first, and put Japan second. Ole knew I had to protect my reputation because Japan was my primary focus, so he used me well. In return, I gave him as many dates as I could so he could run some programs with me, and we made money together. As time went by and my divorce was finalized, I cut back on my work in the States.

On January 14, 1982, I arrived at Los Angeles International Airport. It would be the first tour of the year for All Japan and I was anxious to start work. I felt the pressure of wanting to be there on time and establish myself as one of the key players in the promotion. Unfortunately, my flight to Los Angeles had been behind schedule. I couldn't believe it. I was on my way to make my first tour for All Japan and I had missed my Japan Airlines connection to Narita. I immediately called Mr. Ena, who was still the go-to person for travel with the All Japan promotion. Strangely enough, the company he owned was called "New Japan" Travel. I was quite relieved when he booked me on a China Airlines flight which would get me into Haneda Airport around eleven in the morning on the following day.

When I arrived at Haneda, there were a number of people from the office and a TV crew waiting there to meet me. They had rented a large van which would seat at least twenty people. As we made the trip to Shinagawa, Tokyo, the TV crew filmed me doing nothing but sitting in the seat and watching the scenery go by. The TV crew produced the footage they shot as a short video, as if I was reflecting on my first tour with All Japan in 1975. To be honest, they were right on the money. I couldn't help but think back to that tour, which had also been my very first trip to Japan. I remembered being impressed with the buildings, and how they had reminded me of the Godzilla movies I had seen as a kid. In future years, each time I flew into Haneda and took a taxi to the Ginza, I would always think of the scenes from those movies.

When we parked in front of the Takanawa Tobu Hotel, my first reaction was one of disappointment. I couldn't help but feel let down as I stepped down out of the van. When I worked for New Japan, the gaijins stayed at the Keio Plaza Hotel, a first-class hotel that was very spacious and beautiful. In contrast, the Tobu Hotel in Shinagawa was older and a business-class hotel, at best. The rooms were all painted a drab, white color with midsize beds. The gaijins who worked for All Japan used to stay at the Ginza Tokyu Hotel, a first-class hotel in the Ginza area of Tokyo, but they had all been forced to move to the Tobu. The Tobu Hotel cost something like $80 a night, where lodging at the Ginza Tokyu went for almost $300 a night. It was cheaper and much more liberal towards the antics of the boys. Part of the reason All Japan made the change may have been due to the expense, but to be honest, the gaijins brought the situation on themselves. Due to their misbehavior and abuse of the rooms over the years, they had been told they were no longer welcome at the Ginza. As time went by, we were moved from one hotel to another: Ginza Tokyu (first class), Takanawa Tobu (second class), Hotel Pacific (first class), and finally, back to Ginza Tokyu for the remainder of my time with All Japan.

For those who might not know, the Takanawa Tobu was the hotel in which David von Erich died in 1984. Brody told me that David didn't make it to the bus on time. After waiting an extra five to ten minutes past their scheduled departure time, Joe Higuchi went to his hotel room to get him. Ten minutes later, Brody went to find out what had delayed Joe. When Brody walked into David's room, he saw Joe-san frozen in place, staring downwards, with his hands pressed flat against the wall. When Brody shifted his gaze down at the bed, he saw David's lifeless body. Brody said David's eyes were open, but when he went over and put an ear to his chest, there was no heartbeat and he was as cold as ice. Brody had a long and personal relationship with David's father, Fritz von Erich (who broke Brody into the business), and all of his sons. He knew David very well, and the coldness of David's body left a long and nightmarish effect on Brody for a long time.

Getting back to 1982 and my first day with All Japan, the other gaijins were wrestling in Yuasa that night, a town located in the Wakayama Prefecture, so I checked into the hotel and went up to my room. To say the least, it was depressing. I just laid down on the bed and thought about what lay ahead of me. I had a lot on my mind. I had just gone through a divorce and I was facing a lot of hard work in the weeks to come. As I stared out at the four, dingy, white walls, I could feel myself sink into a depression. No doubt, it was a combination of the divorce and the jet lag. As I lay there thinking about all that had transpired, I reflected on my life. What mistakes had I made in the past, what mistakes were I likely to make in the future, and where was my life headed? I suddenly came to the realization that there was only one constant in my life ... me! I came to the conclusion I didn't need to be in that state of mind. If I was going to be an asset to Baba's company, I needed to be strong and confident.

I also thought about the balance I had to establish between work and home. For months, a question had been popping up in the back of my mind: What could I have done to have made things work in my three roles as husband, father, and provider? At the time, I didn't have a good answer, but I did come to a couple of conclusions. No matter what else happened, if I was given another opportunity to find a wife and mate, it was going to be for life. To reach that end, I would always strive to put work *second* to my home. I was going to find the balance in my life which would make that happen. I didn't want to be successful, and not have someone else with whom to share it.

Also, the one constant in my life was "me." I knew if I did not make a personal decision to change for the better, then my life would keep repeating itself. I had to change Stan Hansen, and I was determined to do exactly that.

I also decided it wouldn't hurt to talk to Baba and negotiate better accommodations. The truth was, Baba didn't have to negotiate anything. Everything was spelled out in the agreement we had reached in Dallas several months before. However, Baba did me a big favor and moved me back to the Ginza Tokyu Hotel when I returned to Japan in April for the next tour. Needless to say, it made for a little heat with the other gaijins, but I didn't let it bother me. I planned to spend a lot of time in Japan, and while I was there, I wanted to live comfortably and in a nice location. The Ginza also gave me some privacy when I wasn't wrestling since the other guys were at the Tobu. My divorce had been finalized and I was moving on with my life. Months later, I met a Japanese lady, and being separated from the office and the other guys allowed us to have somewhat of a normal relationship. It also kept us out of the constant scrutiny of the wrestling fans, not to mention the press, which seemed to loiter around the Tobu. Baba really helped me out by allowing me to have that privilege.

Yoshihiro Momota

To explain more about the housing situation with All Japan in the days which followed, after a year or so, Baba made a deal with the Hotel Pacific Tokyo, a first-class hotel in Shinagawa, and moved all the boys there. It was just one block from the Tobu, but in respect to class, there was a world of difference between the two hotels. His primary reason for asking me to move to the Hotel Pacific was to make things easier for Yoshi, who usually was responsible for picking me up at the Ginza and driving me to the shows held in the Tokyo area. Yoshi took care of me for more than a year. I heard he took a lot of ribbing from the Japanese wrestlers about being "Stan Hansen's chauffeur," but if it bothered him, he never mentioned it to me. I went out of my way to avoid taking advantage of the situation. I always treated him with respect and as a friend, especially when I was around the Japanese boys. Sadly, he contracted liver cancer and passed away on November 22, 2000.

We stayed at the Hotel Pacific for a number of years, until ... once again, the boys messed it up. During that time, the guys, mainly the muscle-heads, all wanted to wear muscle shirts and spandex tights. They really stood out in a crowd of Japanese. In that setting, they looked like trash in a high-priced hotel. I was never a formal dresser, for sure, but when the other hotel guests began to complain to the office about the boys wearing gym attire in the lobby, the office told them to wear nicer clothes. As always, the boys, being the boys, thought they looked cool, so they ignored the office's request. The expression "When in Rome, do as the Romans do," never entered their minds. Eventually, their method of dress, and some sickening ribs pulled on some of the guys by the British Bulldogs (Davey Boy Smith and Dynamite Kid), got us kicked out of the hotel. It was unfortunate. The hotel had a wonderful swimming pool, was located directly across the street from the train station, and had a McDonald's and other fast-food restaurants right next door.

It really got me hot. It could have been prevented with just a modicum of compliance, but they were just too dumb and immature to listen. The office was hot, too. They really laid down the law. We moved back to the Ginza Tokyu Hotel and stayed there until Baba passed away in 1999. Baba treated us like royalty. Most of the boys respected Baba, but wrestlers will be wrestlers. Some of the guys took advantage of his kindness and abused the privileges he passed our way. I'm not trying to paint myself as an angel. I was *far* from it. I did my share of crazy and wild things, but I knew who was paying the bills and I appreciated the opportunity I had been given to work. I knew when to back off. Some of the guys just didn't care and never seemed to get it.

Normally, I didn't mind staying in business-class hotels. When we stayed overnight after wrestling outside Tokyo, the local promoters paid for our lodging, so they put us in economically-priced hotels. I always looked at the situation as "a room is a room."

As I said earlier, one of the few times I protested my housing situation was shortly before I left New Japan, after I had already made the decision to leave the company. They moved us from a medium-standard business hotel to a very cheap, lower-standard hotel. Several of us had stayed there on earlier tours, so we knew how bad the living conditions were at that hotel. The entire gaijin crew was upset, but everybody, including Andre and Hogan, reluctantly accepted the change. I decided we deserved better treatment, and knowing I wasn't going to be with the company much longer, I chose to take a stand.

The hotel we were moved to was directly across the street from the one in which we usually stayed. I called Peter Takahashi and told him we would not stay the other hotel. "*Make some calls, or do what you need to do, but we aren't going to stay in this rundown, piece of crap hotel.*" At first, he thought I was kidding, but when he realized that I was serious, he wasn't too happy. That wasn't anything new. Peter was fairly hard to get along with. He was a company referee and had nothing to do with making any decisions, other than to stooge to the office about what the gaijins did on the bus. I refused to budge on my demands and stood in the lobby with my bags at my feet until he got the local promoter on the phone. A short time later, Peter returned and we walked across the street to check into the other hotel. I remember Andre looking at me with a questioning look in his eyes. He was surprised that I was making a big deal out of it. In the end, however, he was happy that we moved back to the other hotel. Hogan knew I was leaving, so he just followed along.

Needless to say, the rest of the crew was glad we changed, as well. That night at the show, the local promoter came to me and apologized. I treated him courteously and thanked him for moving us. The promoters also talked to me after the show and asked if the "new" hotel was more to my liking. Of course, I graciously told them it was and thanked them for their consideration to all of us.

During my first tour with All Japan in 1975, the Japanese boys stayed at smaller, Japanese-style hotels which were built for the Japanese people. Most of them live in small apartments, and even million dollar houses are not much bigger than 1,200 square feet, so they didn't complain. They weren't acceptable by our American standards, though. Years later, in the early '90s, the Japanese boys got a Union and negotiated for lodging at the hotels where the gaijins stayed. They also got daily meal expenses, which is something we never got.

The wrestling office paid for our hotel rooms in Tokyo, but when we were on the road, our rooms could have been paid for by either the wrestling company or the local promoters. New Japan allowed us to stay in luxury hotels in Tokyo and Osaka, but on occasion, we often found ourselves in substandard hotels, such as the Tobu. In the early days, the hotels used by All Japan in Tokyo were pretty much equal to those in which we stayed with New Japan. In the later years, all the wrestling companies began using business-class hotels, which weren't nearly as nice. When wrestling out in the country, we stayed in nicer hotels than those provided to the guys by New Japan. As the company ran more and more shows, they tried to cut back on expenses as much as they could. Even if the difference between a luxury hotel and a substandard hotel was only $10 a night, they would put us in the cheaper hotel. It really didn't bother me too much because the office paid for the rooms, and that was an expense which didn't come out of my pay. And not only did the Japanese companies pay for our hotel rooms, but we each got our own, separate room. The only exception to that was when we were on a boat overnight, or in a small town which had only a small, Japanese-style hotel. No matter how small the hotel was, however, it was a much better situation than I experienced in the States when three or more of us had to "heel a room."

During the years I worked in Japan, I always stayed in a hotel. I never had an apartment, which cost $2,000 to $3,000 a month, although I did live with my mother-in-law for a couple of years. When I was booked on almost every tour of the year, I kept my Japan clothes at the hotel between tours, and traveled light going to and from the States. When we moved back to the Ginza after getting kicked out of the Shinagawa Hotel Pacific, the management of the hotel was kind enough to store the bags for the boys who were making back-to-back tours.

The Ginza Tokyu was one of the first and most famous hotels in the Ginza district of Tokyo. All Japan used it for its business for more than 30 years. After some 40 years of existence, it was sold for some 900 million dollars. It was torn down and an office building was built in its place. In Japan, buildings are considered to have no value. It is the land that is important.

Getting back to the time of my first tour for All Japan, the gaijins arrived later that evening. I was happy to see some familiar faces, especially the "Intelligent, Sensational" Destroyer. He had been on the first tour I made to Japan in

1975. Now, seven years later, he was setting off on a new profession as an Elementary Physical Education teacher at Akron Central School in Akron, New York. He had worked out some kind of a deal with Baba to appear in Japan once or twice a year, usually in the summer when school was out in the States. I always thought the Destroyer did a better job of handling his business than anyone else. He was able to make the transition to another career and still maintain his long-time relationship with Baba which he had developed over the years. I also thought he had the best run in Japan of any gaijin wrestler. His career there spanned more than four decades and he was a legitimate superstar who had been instrumental in helping Baba build his business.

I was glad to have someone like him on the tour, and I talked to him extensively about his career. I never reflected on my own situation, or what I was going through, but he made me feel like I had made the right decision when he told me he never regretted putting his trust in Baba.

Mark Lewin also was on the tour. He was a big influence on Brody, for sure, although I'm not sure in what direction. Brody talked of Lewin often, especially about his dealings with him when Lewin was a promoter. Mark, who promoted wrestling in Australia, New Zealand, and Singapore during the late '70s and early '80s, had the reputation of being somewhat "out of bounds." I believe his strongest influence on Brody was in teaching him to "screw the promoters before they screw you." That was his attitude and I believe it rubbed off on Brody. Lewin was a good talent in his own right, and because of our mutual friendship with Brody, we got along well on the tour. He was real smooth and reserved, though, and I never could read him well. Then again, who could really read anyone. I later heard that Baba had a conflict with Lewin and I believe that tour was his last. From what I understand, Mark was smart about business, saved his money, and is now retired.

Most of all, I was looking forward to working against Baba. I had worked against Inoki a number of times, but this would be my first opportunity to work with Baba. He was really over with the Japanese people. He was a huge man. Most people only remember him in his later days, but when he was young, as well as in middle age, he was a very impressive man. He stood nearly 7-foot tall and was exceptionally strong. He had a natural strength in his tendons that was very deceptive. However, over the years, what I learned about him that impressed me the most was his toughness. When he was in his late 40s and early 50s, we could see the pain he was suffering from arthritis. He did more than just endure it, though. He fought through it and never let it affect him. He didn't complain, either. To the very end, he gave 100 percent whenever he wrestled. It must have been hell on earth for him to do that. I know, as most of the other wrestlers do, how hard it is to perform while suffering through the aches and pains caused by years of abuse to our bodies. When arthritis is added into the mix, it makes it doubly hard to perform. Baba, however, was a master at hiding the pain he was undergoing each time he stepped into the ring. In my eyes, he was in a class all his own.

My first show with All Japan was January 15, 1982. I hadn't been booked on the first two weeks of the tour since the publicity was already out when I made my jump on the last night of New Japan's December tour. The first match was one I remember so well. I wrestled Ashura Hara [Susumu Hara], a former member of the World Rugby Team, in Kuragata Sports Hall in Kisarazu-City,

Chiba. He was built like an American football fullback ... solid and hard as a rock. He didn't give me anything during the match and made me work for everything I got. At one point, he hit me in the chest with a big chop that left a hand print for several days. The match ended when I dropped him with a big lariat.

The fans, the press, and most importantly, the office, all enjoyed the match. I think even Hara was happy with the match. In fact, I could not have done what I did without a talented opponent like Hara. He handled himself well. I worked hard to establish the fact in everyone's minds that my style was not going to change. It was important to establish myself as the same Stan Hansen that I had been in New Japan. That was the main thing I worried about when I initially met with Baba in Dallas. After my match with Hara, though, there was never any thought given to changing my style. Like Baba had said during our initial meeting in Dallas, "*I want your style.*"

However, I was not prepared for the next thing that happened. When we walked outside, the gaijin bus was nowhere in sight. When I was with New Japan, the bus was always waiting in a pre-designated location. If the bus wasn't directly outside the arena, I would be escorted by some of the young Japanese boys who had not yet had a match. On that night, I followed Ricky (Mitsuo) Momota as he began his search for the bus. As we walked, I looked behind me to see hundreds of fans following us. We walked a long way to the corner of the building ... no bus. Turning around, we retraced our steps and headed back the way we came. All the time, the fans dogged our every step.

It had always been my custom to go to and from the building much like I did going to and from the ring. I was used to running, or moving hard in my style, from the bus to the building, and back again. I would swing my bullrope around and around, spreading out the fans, and occasionally hitting them. They really liked that. It was a part of my personality. Now I was wandering around like a lost soul, trying to find the bus. I wasn't too happy.

We walked all the way to the opposite end of the building and turned the corner. This time, we found the bus waiting. We got on and found most of the other wrestlers already seated. I noticed Jumbo, Genichiro Tenryu, and Baba were conspicuously absent, only to learn later that the company had a Dodge van which transported the top Japanese talent to and from the matches.

I would discover that organization was the big difference between New Japan and All Japan in those early years. New Japan was run as a very strict, Japanese-style business. Everything was organized efficiently, run on schedule, and nothing was left to chance. After five years with New Japan, I had become accustomed to (and preferred) the strict and defined style of organization.

I was really disappointed. I felt good about my debut match because the people saw what they came to see and were excited about it. My objective, however, was to not only present my style and attitude of my character in the ring, but also on the way to and from the bus. Events like the one which had just taken place exposed my character. Granted, I tried to stay in character while we were looking for the bus, but wandering around aimlessly did *not* allow me to look confident and act like I knew what I was doing.

The other situation I wasn't happy about was being on the bus with the other Japanese wrestlers. I wanted to maintain strict kayfabe at all times. I was going to battling those guys in the ring, and it didn't look good for us all to be on the same bus. It wasn't good for business. After all, we weren't a troupe of actors traveling from one playhouse to another. We were athletes who would be locked in competition against each other on a nightly basis.

While in Japan, I tried to stay in character as much as possible. I thought of myself as an "old-school" heel and didn't cater to the fans like Terry Funk, and later Hulk Hogan, did. Normally, when we walked into the lobby of our hotels, there would be 25 to 30 people waiting to see us, most of them fans. When our bus pulled up to the hotels or arenas, people would surround us. By moving quickly, I could avoid shaking hands or having my picture taken without appearing to be rude. I didn't charge the crowds or run through them like I did in the arenas, but there was a time or two when I left the bus and swung my rope towards them to let them know I would hit them if they didn't move. That might seem callous on my part, but it was actually what the people came to expect. Most of the time, they moved. I didn't see well because I didn't wear my glasses all of the time, so I'm sure I might have scared some younger children, but if I saw kids or older people, I would change directions to avoid them. I always thought it was funny that, in the later years when the wrestling fans began to like me, they actually lined up to be "whipped" by Hansen.

Pete Roberts enjoys telling the story about the time I left the All Japan bus to go into a building. We often arrived at our destination around five in the afternoon when it was still light outside. Most of the shows began at six-thirty. There weren't a huge number of fans at the back of the building that day, but as I stepped off the bus, a big, burly, young man walked up to me. In broken English, he said, *"Hansen sign!"* and held an autograph board (the square piece of cardboard sold for autographs) in my face. I had the rope on a short grip. Without saying anything, I hit him on the head. I didn't hit him too hard, but I did hit him. He didn't react at all. He simply looked at me and said, *"Hansen sign!"* Since he was standing in my path to the door, I hit him again, this time somewhat harder. Once again … no reaction. *"Hansen sign!"* He said it more forcefully and really pushed the cardboard into my face. This time, I really hit him. He backed up, but stopped and repeated what he had said before. *"Hansen sign."* Pete was behind me when it all happened. I turned and looked at him and we broke out into wild laughter. I turned back around, took the sign, and signed it. We laughed all the way into the building, and today, we still laugh about it when we get together.

As a celebrity, it was hard to maintain any semblance of anonymity or privacy. We were constantly approached by fans in public venues. There were very few people in the metropolitan areas of Japan who weren't familiar with professional wrestling and the wrestlers. When we went to a restaurant, we would try to get a table away from the windows where people couldn't just walk in and bother us. People who didn't intend to buy anything weren't welcome by most business owners, so that kept many of the younger fans away. I don't mean to sound ungrateful for the attention we got because it was nice to be recognized and we truly appreciated the fans, but there were times when we just wanted to sit and relax. I learned to say, *"Private time,"* and put my arms into an 'X' to express what I was trying to say. In almost every situation, the Japanese fans respected my request.

Early in my career, I didn't sign any autographs at all. Later, I relented and began to sign some, and the fans were appreciative when I did. The problem we had was that once the people saw you sign something, everyone came over to get one, and it was hard to walk away when there were people who had been patiently waiting their turn.

In the 1980s and 1990s, it was hard to get away from people who wanted to talk with us and it became fun to try to outsmart the fans who were lined up waiting for us to come in. I have to admit that, at first, it was funny to have 20 to 30 fans walking behind Brody and me. We tried to keep them behind us so we could at least walk without having camera flashes go off in our faces, but after a number of years, it became a hassle just to get a cab or go someplace without people walking right beside us. After several years, we began going out late at night after most of the fans had gone home. I learned there was good food to be found in the basement of department stores. I would go there to eat Japanese food and would then return to my room. There were other nights when I would not go out at all.

I know a person's "one moment of fame" is fleeting, but to be honest, I'm glad that part of my life is over. I don't mean to sound big-headed when I say that and I don't take myself or my "fame" too seriously. As a rule, the people were nice and polite, and very few people came across as being obnoxious. With smart phones and the ability to send photos sent over the Internet instantly, I can't imagine life as a celebrity today. There would be no privacy at all.

Brody and I held the same view in regards to our interactions with the fans. We wanted to "do the right thing for business" because we were both old school. We didn't mistreat the fans, but we didn't go out of our way to win them over. In Japan, we felt that the less approachable we were, the better it

"This is an example of some of the artwork drawn for me by fans. It's a shame this image doesn't show the color in the drawing.

was for our characters and, ultimately, business.

I believe that after Baba and I made our deal, Nippon TV [NTV] and Baba both resolved to become a more Japanese-oriented company. One of the NTV executives began traveling with Baba and became involved in some of the office work. I don't know to what extent his involvement was, but more than likely, he was there to help with the organization and maintain their accountability to NTV. I have no knowledge of that to be a fact because I never asked or discussed it with anyone in power, but it was just something I observed.

The next time I had an opportunity to talk to Baba, I told him I thought he should make some changes. Since they would be my opponents, I wanted separation from the Japanese wrestlers. Shortly after our discussion, he put the top four or five gaijins in the van, while he and Jumbo began making trips on the big bus. That arrangement changed about a year later when they hired a new driver and bought a medium-size bus. That bus would carry twenty passengers, while the big bus could transport 60 or more.

Business at the time was only fair. Even with all the hype about me jumping from New Japan, and the talk about my debut match, the house show in Kisarazu-City was not sold out, although it was a good house. I was told the house was up from what it had been in weeks past, and I remember it being pretty crowded, but I knew we had a lot of hard work ahead of us. I knew I couldn't do it by myself. Kisarazu-City was the perfect example of that. Just putting Stan Hansen on the card was not enough to make the people want to buy tickets. It was going to take a combined effort by Baba, Jumbo, Dory and Terry Funk, Brody, myself, and every one of the All Japan wrestlers, to turn around the business. Everybody would have to do their part. Kisarazu-City, though, was a start, and we were all excited and ready for the challenge.

I made several new acquaintances during the tour and re-established friendships with those I had worked with in the past. Nikolai Volkoff was a gentle giant of a man. He was big and strong, but he was a real nice guy. I had heard stories about Nikolai wrestling Bruno Sammartino at a fast pace for one solid hour. I also got to know Nick Bockwinkel on that tour. Nick was a classy guy who had been through it all both professionally and personally. He listened to me and gave me moral support as I went through the final stages of my divorce. I really appreciated his "ear" during a time in my life which was exciting on a professional basis, but tough on a personal level.

Kelly Kiniski was a good guy who had huge shoes to fill. His father, Gene Kiniski, was highly respected as a former NWA world heavyweight champion. Kelly played football at West Texas State, where he received varsity football letters in 1978 and 1979, but that was after I was there, so I didn't know him. Kelly was the first person to take me to a public bath, and on the recommendation of his dad, Kelly got a massage from an old Mama-san. Pat O'Connor, another former NWA champion who I had met when I was first introduced to the wrestling fans in Amarillo, was 58 years old and stayed pretty much to himself.

Gypsy Joe [Gilberto Melendez] also was a great person to be around. He was double tough and so funny. He loved to take chair shots to his back and would allow the guys to hit him as hard as they could. In fact, that was his "gimmick" in the ring. Somebody broke a chair over his back almost every night — not just the wooden chairs, but also those made of metal. He would sell the shot for a few seconds, and then stand up and look composed. I really liked Joe. I had met him years before in Louisiana. He was a good heel who took a lot of bumps and got solid heat. I find it amazing that he's still wrestling today because he's in his seventies. Wow! I'm glad he's able to continue doing what he loves (but I'm glad I'm retired).

Gypsy Joe

One time, we were in Kagoshima, the capital city of Kagoshima Prefecture at the southwestern tip of the Kyûshû island of Japan. Sakurajima, an active volcano which covered the city in ashes in 1914, is situated directly across the bay from Kagoshima. We were staying at a really nice western-style hotel which had large glass windows facing out to the bay with Sakurajima framed in the background. At the time, Sakurajima was billowing smoke and ash. As active volcanoes do, they often release built-up pressure with a loud explosion. We were all relaxing in our rooms when a huge blast let go, sounding as if it was directly outside the large, plate-glass window. It was so loud that I thought the glass was going to break. When we looked out the window, we saw a huge cloud of ash mushrooming into the air. We all decided to go outside, and as we opened the door to the hallway, there was Gypsy Joe crawling on the floor with a frightened look on his face. We kidded him about that for a long time.

Tor Kamata, another good hand who was really over in Japan, also was a good bump taker. He was easy to get along with. Not too long ago, shortly after Tor's death, I was in Hawaii. When I stopped at a small souvenir shop on the north shore, I saw a large picture of Tor on the wall. It turned out that his family owned the store.

I finished the tour with a good feeling because things went really well. I was even more excited about future tours because Brody wasn't on the first one. We had not yet had an opportunity to tag up, and that was something I had been looking forward to for a long time. The wrestling fans also looked forward to the team of Stan Hansen and Bruiser Brody, and the anticipation was mounting. We were looked at as a fantasy team. They knew of my history with New Japan, and they knew Brody's background with All Japan. They also knew about our history as a team in the States.

Business did begin to pick up shortly after I arrived. Baba-san was smart enough to know that he shouldn't rush us into a match too soon. Brody was already involved in a program with Jumbo and the Funks, Dory Jr. and Terry, so Baba waited a full three months from my arrival in All Japan before putting us together. Our first match as a team in Japan took place in Nagoya on April 20, 1982, when we wrestled Baba and Jumbo. From that date until our last match together on December 12, 1984, we teamed together 56 times. That doesn't seem like a lot considering all the talk about the Brody-Hansen team in Japan, but it was a time I hold dear and will never forget.

When we began wrestling as a tag team, Brody and I decided to continue the character style we had developed when I was with New Japan and when he was with All Japan. Some of his style was patterned after what he had seen King Curtis Iaukea do, but he added the extra style of going out into the audience, much like the Butcher had been doing at All Japan. We both knew we were going to continue to do our styles, and, if anything, we were going to make it wilder and more out of control.

The two of us would out into the audience and send the fans scattering in fear. It was like herding sheep. As they ran, we would turn them and move them around the building. It was fun for us and we really enjoyed it. To anyone watching, it looked like we were beating them unmercifully with my bullrope and his chain, but we did our best to avoid injuring anyone. I have to admit there were times when I really tried to hurt someone, but it was only in retaliation against someone who threw a chair at me. I would go after them and "teach them" a lesson, but even then, I never tried to injure them. Most of the time, the fans panicked and ran away. There were some who acted as if they were going to stand their ground, but 99 percent of the time, they broke and ran. If they didn't, we laid it on them pretty stiff, but again, we never did anything to really hurt them.

It took a lot of gas to go out into the audience and run the people, and that's probably why nobody else did it. We could keep the people moving for four to five minutes at a time. That was hard work. Jeet Singh couldn't do it for that long, and he was in good shape. Abdullah couldn't, either. A few of the gaijins tried it a few times, but it never lasted too long. We were proud of the fact that we were the only ones who could do that for an extended period time. Not only that, but the office didn't want everyone doing the same thing. One of the things which hurt wrestling in the past decade is that everyone tries to be like everyone else. There are no styles which stand out as being different or unusual from others.

One time with New Japan, we were somewhere in Kyushu, the southernmost of the four main islands of Japan. Bad News Allen was my partner that night. I was "working the floor" and herding people around the building. Bad News didn't often go out on the floor, but he was my partner, so he followed my lead. We were standing shoulder to shoulder and pushing our way through the maze of chairs, many of which were scattered and turned over. As we changed directions, we found ourselves moving towards a small man who was dressed like a monk. He had a little, white, pointed beard and he was holding a walking cane. The people around him all scattered, but he just sat in his seat and didn't move a muscle. As we ran up to him, he still didn't budge. Bad News and I broke off on either side of him as he sat silently in his chair. We continued running the crowd and then headed back to the dressing room. When we were safely inside, we both broke into laughter at our reaction to the "monk" not moving. We joked about how embarrassing it would have been if he had stood up like Mr. Miyagi of the movie *Karate Kid* and beat up the two big gaijin wrestlers.

Brody and I didn't always work the same tours, and contrary to what people assume, as a tag team, we were only booked four or five times on each tour. I think it was important that we kept our separate identities most of the time.

I never held back when I worked with Baba. Again, I worked pretty stiff. If I have any reputation at all, that's the one I hear most often. When I worked against Baba, or Terry Funk, or anybody else, for that matter, I hit them almost as hard as I could. I didn't do it with intent to injure them, but I wanted my work to be as solid as it could be. Baba never once asked me to loosen up. In fact, he gave back as much as I gave him, and he never failed to get my attention with his stiff chops. Occasionally, after his knees got bad, I would give him time as he got to his feet, but overall, he never asked us to take it easy. If it's even possible, I would say the Japanese wrestlers gave it to him even harder, as I witnessed much later when I was his tag-team partner in the December Real World Tag Team Tournament. That's one of the reasons why he was over as strong as he was. Everybody knew he was in pain from arthritis. Towards the end of his career, he worked mostly in tag-team matches with Haruka Eigen and Rusher Kimura.

Baba really knew the psychology of wrestling, especially the Japanese psychology, and he never ceased to amaze me with his wrestling moves, to which the people always responded, and every once in awhile, he would pull out a move which nobody had seen in years. I can't imagine how good he must have been in his prime, although I have seen some old black-and-white footage in which he moves and does some amazing things. It took a lot of skill just to move all of that height and size around the ring. Most people don't realize how big a man he was. Only a few wrestlers were close in height, and that is what set him off from all other Japanese. Andre the Giant, Pak Song, Big John Studd, and Blackjack Mulligan were a few of the wrestlers who could stand in the ring and not be dwarfed by Baba.

Baba and I had so many matches over the years that it is hard to keep them all from running together. In singles, tag team, and six-man tag-team matches, I was in the ring against Baba 163 times. We were good opponents for each other. I believe my style often forced him out of his own character, which was good, because most of the time, he dominated his matches. As the general, or leader, of his matches, he was always able to direct things in a direction he wanted to go, and he usually had a game plan. I think I was able to take him

July 7, 1984 • Tokyo: Giant Baba & Tenryu vs Stan Hansen & Alexis Smirnoff

in directions he might not have gone with another opponent by forcing him to react to things he didn't expect. That, in turn, made for interesting matches which were truly competitive, and the fans were often caught by surprise when we didn't do the moves they expected. They really got into the matches because they didn't look laid out.

I have always thought a real reaction was so much better than one that was thought out beforehand. Before wrestlers began choreographing their moves from start to finish, wrestlers might discuss a few things and be told where they were going to end up, but it was up to them to determine how they got the finish. We didn't sit in the dressing room and map out our moves. We reacted to one another and made spontaneous decisions in the ring. Things changed somewhat later in my career, but at the beginning of my All Japan run, that was how we did things.

I think one of my strongest points was that ability to force wrestlers to react. Due to the fact that I didn't know what I was going to do until I did it, my opponents never knew what was going to happen, and couldn't plan ahead when it came to moves. They were always off balance because I didn't do the conventional. In my mind, I always tried to do the opposite of what my opponents might anticipate. For all practical purposes, their reaction to my unexpected moves was "real," and the people could tell it. That was one of the reasons why I got over, and why the promotion kept me over for as long a time as they did. On the other hand, I have to admit there were matches where I could have done a better job of planning out what I was going to do.

My style was to dominate my opponent and not show any weakness until it was time for their comeback. Even then, I wouldn't sell too much. Later, when I worked with the younger generation of wrestlers, and after many matches with Mitsuharu Misawa, Toshiaki Kawada, and Kenta Kobashi, I did tend to sell more.

I remember one night in Tokyo, shortly after I made the jump to All Japan, when I was the PWF heavyweight champion. I was facing Baba in Tokyo in one of the big arenas which had been built for the Olympics. As a rule, I always tried to vary the start of my matches. I did that by constantly changing the things I did, either before or after the opening bell sounded. Those variations at the beginning of my matches became my signature.

On that particular night, I was moving around the ring, working myself into the proper frame of mind. I never can remember the details because my mind was always so focused, but I'm pretty sure the announcers and flower girls were still in the ring. Baba was standing in his corner, watching me warily. He had held the PWF championship three times for a period of more than ten years. He took a lot of pride in the belt and had defended it many, many times. On this night, however, I was the champion. The belt had heavy, gold-colored metal attached to the leather. It also had chains and hooks attached which were used to fasten it around someone's waist. On impulse, I took off the belt and slung it across the ring as hard as I could, directly at him. The belt soared through the air, traveling across the ring in a straight line … and hit Baba right in the face. He went down hard and blood poured from his face.

I didn't give Baba much warning, but I thought he had seen me preparing to throw the belt. If don't know whether he looked away at the last moment, or if

1983 • Stan Hansen vs Giant Baba

he wasn't paying attention, but I do know he could have suffered serious injuries. Luckily, the belt didn't cut him so badly that he needed stitches, but he was bleeding pretty heavily. By the time I realized he was bleeding, though, I had already rushed across the ring. I had no choice but to put the boots to him, which had been my plan when I ran towards him. I tried to give him a second or two to recover, but I continued with my onslaught and drove him into the corner of the ring. To Baba's credit, he never complained or asked me to ease up.

I never gave any thought to the fact that throwing belt at Baba might have caused him serious injury, such as putting out one of his eyes. However, looking back on my career, I realize I could have (and probably did) hurt my opponents, not to mention the fans. At one time, I had been critical of Tiger Jeet Singh for accidentally stabbing a number of wrestlers and fans with his sword. Having caused injury to Baba due to my over eagerness, I found myself in a comparable situation.

Once in Sapporo, Brody and I gave Baba a double football tackle. We hit him with such force that he flew backwards, with his head up and his legs extended out in front of him at a 90-degree angle to his body. His back hit the ropes and his body slid downwards to the mat, with his head bouncing off the top and middle ropes on the way down. Brody and I looked at each other, knowing we had overdone it, but Baba never said a word. Then again, some of the guys told us he couldn't have said anything at that time if he had wanted to.

There was a fine line in my actions that is hard to explain. I often ran blindly and wildly through the crowd as I made my way to the ring. I stepped on a lot of people, or caused them to fall over as I ran forward. I didn't set out to hurt anyone, but it was a natural consequence of the wildness that was a part of my character. The more I did it, the more the people wanted to see me do it.

I can't explain what it was about my style that excited the crowd, but I suppose it was something akin to the "running of the bulls" event which takes place each year in Spain and Mexico. It was the pro wrestling style that Baba-san had come to Dallas to get, and when I made it clear that I did not want to change my style, he agreed. He explained that he wanted me to help All Japan move away from the conventional NWA style of wrestling, and the predictable matches they had been featuring for years.

On the night I threw the belt, Baba got a first-hand look at what was to become the new style of All Japan Pro Wrestling — the Stan Hansen style of wrestling. As we continued with our match, I couldn't help but wonder if he had second thoughts about signing me to a contract. Regardless, after he recovered his wits, we had a good match. One of Baba's great talents was his ability to sell, and after a few minutes of taking my abuse, he made a big comeback.

Brody once told me that Jumbo Tsuruta was the hardest person he ever worked with. Like me, Brody had his own style. It was somewhat like mine, but he would wrestle more. Jumbo was strong-willed and unmovable in the ring, and to get him into a position to do something was like "pulling teeth." In the hierarchy of Japanese business, Jumbo had a lot of power, and he wasn't going to be anyone's stepping stone. That made him even more difficult to wrestle.

During my time in Japan, I began to understand more about the Japanese culture. There is a hierarchy in most of Japan's businesses, and the wrestling companies were no different. Since Baba was the top man in All Japan, Jumbo was relegated to the number two position for the majority of his career. He was, of course, a top man and a very important part of the business. As an amateur, Jumbo won the 1971 and 1972 All Japan amateur wrestling championships in both Freestyle and Greco-Roman as a super-heavyweight. He also competed in the 1972 Summer Olympics in Munich, West Germany. His credentials brought a lot of respect to All Japan, and his contribution to the company business was invaluable.

However, being unable to pass Baba in the hierarchy must have been frustrating. As was the custom with most Japanese, they hide their emotions, so Brody and I often speculated on how Jumbo must have felt.

When people ask me about my favorite or most memorable matches, the matches I won aren't the ones I remember first. The one which sticks out in my mind first and foremost is my April 18, 1989 match with Jumbo in Tokyo's Ryôgoku Kokugikan. I believe that match comes to mind first because it was the first time Jumbo went over me in a singles match.

At the time, Jumbo was the NWA International heavyweight champion, while I held the United National and Pacific Wrestling Federation titles. The match was billed as a unification of the three titles, with the winner to be declared as the first AJPW Triple Crown heavyweight champion.

The match was a physically tough match with both of us moving at an exhausting pace. After being handed the title belt, Jumbo climbed up onto the ring post and held the belt up high for all the fans to see. As I watched, I remember thinking of how he had finally been given his due. He had played second fiddle to Baba for many years, and the match established him as a top star in his own right. The fans began to look at him on the same level as

Baba. In large part, Jumbo being elevated in the eyes of the fans was due to Baba, who moved himself down a notch. That's one of the reasons why I had so much respect for Baba. He had his ego under control. Inoki, on the other hand, always promoted himself first, but he was successful in doing that. Sadly, when it was Jumbo's time to really take over as the top Japanese wrestler, he contracted Hepatitis C, which eventually cost him his life.

Jumbo also had some long and impressive matches with Brody during the early years I was with All Japan. He also had some classic battles with Genichiro Tenryu, who also was trying to establish himself as a top wrestler with the company.

On February 20, 1982, Brody and I worked with Jumbo and Tenryu at the Bayfront Center in St. Petersburg, Florida. It was a big show for the Florida territory and featured mostly American wrestlers. In addition to our match, Ric Flair defended his NWA world heavyweight title against Mike Graham, NWA International champion Dory Funk Jr. put his belt on the line against Hacksaw Reed [aka Butch Reed], and the finale of the night was the U.S. Open Double Battle Royal. Nippon TV was going to videotape our match, as well as Dory's, for later airing in Japan.

Brody and I really dominated Jumbo and Tenryu. We were on our home turf, so we didn't give them very much offense. When they did make a comeback, we didn't do much selling. After the match, when we went back to the dressing room, the American wrestlers just stared at us and shook their heads. They couldn't believe we had been so aggressive with our Japanese opponents, especially since the reason for bringing us to the States was to get a good match for Nippon TV. That was our style, though, and our decision to overpower our opponents proved to be a good one because Baba never came to us and complained. If he had disagreed with what we had done, he would have told us. He knew that what we did was the best for business. The American wrestlers, of course, knew that Brody and I had chosen Japan as our primary careers. However, most of them had no idea of the style we worked in Japan, and they were somewhat awed by the energy with which we wrestled. I got the distinct feeling they were happy they didn't have to work with us.

Brody and I didn't go to the ring that night with the mindset of working stiff. We just decided we weren't going to look bad in the States. We knew Jumbo and Tenryu were top boys and the top team for All Japan, but Brody and I knew we had to work hard to uphold our reputations.

That match did so much to enhance our reputation in the States, not to mention establishing the overall style of Japan wrestling in the minds of the fans in the States. Having heard about the good living Brody, Abdullah, the Funks and I were making in Japan, most American wrestlers wished they had the opportunity. It sounded like a good deal. They could wrestle and make good money for a few weeks, and then return home. It looked easy, and quite a few of them thought about doing it. However, I was told that after word spread through the territories about Brody and me kicking the hell out of Jumbo and Tenryu, the gaijins seemed less inclined to make the trip. The wrestlers in America fought hard to keep their spots, but what they saw us do in St. Petersburg was almost scary to them. In that respect, the match served a dual purpose. Not only did it enhance our reputations in both America and

1984 • Bruiser Brody and Stan Hansen

Japan, but it kept many of the gaijins out of "our" back yard. In many ways, Brody and I looked at Japan as "our" country.

Brody and I both developed a reputation for being "outlaws," but there was a big difference between the two of us. My reputation came from standing up to promoters and expecting them to pay me what I was due. Brody, on the other hand, expected his money, but he also fought with the promoters over other things, like the direction of his matches and bookings. He looked at misunderstandings and differences as being personal, rather than business. His attitude wasn't necessarily bad, but it wasn't what promoter were used to dealing with.

I also was placed into the "outlaw" group of wrestlers due to my relationship with Brody. I believe we were labeled "outlaws" way back in the early days, when we were both in Louisiana, and there was no questioning the fact that promoters looked at us as outlaws when we wrestled in Japan and Puerto Rico. When we were the U.S. tag-team champions in Louisiana, we didn't show much respect for the belts. When we walked into the TV studio, we would drag the belts on the ground behind us, or toss them around. To us, we were just showing our displeasure on being booked in the second-tier towns. It also enhanced our rebel characters. I don't know if Watts minded our disrespect of the belts, but other wrestlers told us we should show more respect for them. Of course, most of them wanted the belts themselves. We held the belts for almost nine months, but in hindsight, Watts did the right thing when he took them from us.

I never tried to do anything to dispel my outlaw reputation, and at the time, I thought of myself in those terms. Later, I thought of myself as an "independent," rather than an outlaw, and working for All Japan gave me that independence. Of course, to most wrestling promoters, being independent was what made us outlaws.

One thing for which I have to give Watts a lot of credit was splitting up Brody and me. Watts was smart enough to realize that Brody and I needed time apart in order to develop our own styles and talent. I didn't like it at the time, but when I look back on it, he did us both a big favor.

The Funks had been with Baba since he formed the All Japan Pro Wrestling company in 1972. Siding with Baba, they became his closest allies in the States. They booked gaijin talent for the company, were trusted in the most important decisions, and gave Baba good advice about his business for a long time. They were as much a part of Baba's inner circle as anyone else, including the Japanese office personnel. The fact that Terry was invited to the initial negotiation meeting between Baba and me gives credence to that. My speculation, based on the hours of discussion I had with Brody, was that the Funks had the unique position of being the only gaijins to ever have influence over the direction of company business.

Inside the ring, the Funks had engaged in feuds with most of the Japanese wrestlers over the years, in both New Japan and All Japan, before becoming fan favorites. At that point, they began wrestling their fellow Americans, and developed a spot in Baba's business which was almost as important, if not as important, as that of Baba and Jumbo. Personally, I think the Funks were over *more* than the Japanese during that time. I also believe that in the back of Baba's mind, he felt like he had lost control of his business. Not to someone he didn't like or trust, but to someone who was not Japanese.

When I came to All Japan in 1982, it was a fact that Baba's business was not doing as well as Inoki's. Inoki had kept himself as the focal point of New Japan's business. Inoki was not necessarily a better wrestler than Baba, but he did a better job of promoting himself at that time. The Japanese fans were really interested in Inoki, and believed in him, mainly because he constantly pushed himself as the top man in the company. He became obsessed with doing things he thought were innovative, but in the end, those ideas became self-serving, and the company lost ground as a whole.

That was one of the major differences between Inoki and Baba. Inoki pushed himself relentlessly, and was successful in doing so. Baba promoted himself, as well, but he knew that for the long term, he had to take a step back and pass the baton. He did not let his ego dictate (at least not out in the open) his business decisions. If I had been in either of their shoes, it would have been tough to not promote myself. More than likely, my ego would have driven me to that end. I'm sure there are a number of gaijins who waited for their opportunity to advance in Japan, but I never got out of the way, so to them, I would probably be considered an egomaniac. The decision to keep me on top, though, was Baba's, and not mine. I didn't have anything to do with the results of my matches or the direction of the business. I just showed up for each tour and did what the office dictated.

One of the most important things I learned was knowing when to look strong and when to sell. In wrestling, it's important to give and take, but you have to learn to give and take at the right time. I didn't give to just anyone, either. I gave mainly to the Japanese. I worked a little differently with the Japanese than I did with the Americans. I found that most Americans were too impatient. The wrestling business is just that ... a business. Everybody wanted to be the top guy, and I understood there were many gaijins who had to wait (and wait and wait) for the opportunity to become the top gaijin. But it wasn't my fault that I maintained that position for as long as I did. The office promoted me, and one of the reasons for that was that I had the ability to "make" the young guys. The young Japanese wrestlers went out and beat other Americans, and yet, they still didn't get over to a point where they would be considered top guys. The office kept me strong so I would be the guy the young talent had to beat in order to get over. To that end, I did my best in every way to make the younger Japanese boys fight for every inch they were going to gain on me and my position. The harder I made it, the more the fans bought it, and also the harder the young Japanese had to go to get over me. And when they did finally get over me, it made them. That might sound like I have a huge ego, but it's the truth. I made it hard by making *them* work hard. When they finally went over, the people believed they were a top guy.

Another difference between Inoki and Baba was that Baba had let the emphasis of his company switch to the Americans. Baba was much more accommodating to the gaijins than Inoki. He had seen the success Rikidôzan had working with foreign talent, and Baba also had been involved with the Destroyer and the Butcher. The Japanese vs. gaijins format was very successful. However, in the early 1980s, gaijin talent like Harley Race, Mil Mascaras, and Dick Slater were really over with the Japanese fans. Ricky Steamboat also was a draw in Japan, but he wasn't in the same class as the others. During that time, Baba and Jumbo seemed to have been pushed back a notch. That attention given to the Americans caused a lot of jealousy on the part of the Japanese wrestlers. They didn't show it outright, but there were definitely some serious concerns going on in the minds of the Japanese wrestlers. Years later, when the Japanese boys formed a union, one of the primary demands was to be taken care of like the gaijins. However, to my knowledge, and to their credit, they never showed any bitterness or animosity to the gaijins.

The Japanese vs. gaijin formula was usually developed over a long period of time. The first thing that had to be done was to put over a heel and build him over time. Along those same lines, the Japanese did things correctly by slowly grooming their young talent towards the top spots, and often took ten years or more to move them to that level. Most of the time, other than Jeet Singh, Abdullah, or myself, a heel from the States would start off strong. After having a blow-off match at the end of a three to six-week tour, they would return to the States. If the office thought they were good enough to return for another tour, they wouldn't be brought back for six months or more. In later years, All Japan used the same crew of wrestlers on every tour. It was easy and successful for awhile, but there is only so much they could do with limited talent, as it is in any territory.

I think Baba realized that in order for All Japan to survive, he needed to promote himself and Jumbo into the top position. He respected and appreciated the Funks for what they had done for the company, but he also knew that, in the end, the Japanese fans want to cheer for a Japanese wrestler. The fans are Japanese. The Japanese might like a gaijin, but they naturally would like to see a Japanese wrestle and beat a gaijin. There is nothing wrong with that. It's human nature to want to see one of your own countrymen defeat someone from outside the country. That is what the Olympics and other international sports are all about.

I also believe that at that time, no matter how badly Baba wanted himself or Jumbo to be the center of their business, the Funks held that position, and, in particular, Terry Funk.

There was a lot of history between me and the Funks, and Japanese fans were anxious to see us wrestle. Terry, of course, had broken me into the business. To this day, I am grateful for him for that. By doing so, he changed my life. Thanks to him, I was able to make good a good living and travel the world. I really do appreciate him for giving me that opportunity.

My breaking away from the Funks at such an early time in my career might have developed some hard feelings between us, but there is no heat between us that I am aware of. When I left their Amarillo territory, they could have looked at me as not appreciating the fact that they broke me into the business. They needed talent when I left, and I never really went back to work in the territory on a regular basis. They might have thought I should show my loyalty by staying and working for them. I looked at the situation in a different light. When I asked Dory Jr. to book me out to a good territory, he sent me to Louisiana, which was one of the lowest-paying, hardest-traveling territories in the country. As I mentioned earlier, it might have been that no other promoter would take me, but I don't really believe that to be the case, for the following reason.

Dory Funk Jr. had just finished up as one of the most successful NWA world heavyweight champions. He drew great business for all of the NWA territories, so the promoters were somewhat indebted to him. I believe he could have made a few telephone calls and gotten me booked in Portland, Oregon, where I told him I wanted to go. I mentioned several others, as well. Specifically, however, I told him I wanted to go *anywhere* but Louisiana. When they chose to book me there, I made my decision to book myself. In my opinion, the Funks treated their talent much better than other promoters. Their decisions were always based on what was in the best interest of their territory, and not out of disrespect or contempt for the talent.

In a way, it all worked out for the best, for several reasons. Grizzly Smith gave me my first opportunity to really get into character. He shot an angle with me and gave me a chance to work with him in main events around the territory. Brody and I also hit it off there and we became good friends. We spent time with Grizzly's partner, Luke Brown, who nurtured us and gave us tips on tag-team psychology.

Bill Watts, the promoter, had been double-crossed by quite a few wrestlers over the years, and he probably had good reason to feel like he was on the opposite side of a fence from the talent. On the other hand, Brody felt like we had been mistreated by Watts during his early years in the business. I was there. I saw it happen. Brody never forgave him, and his experience in Louisiana was the catalyst for Brody's distrust of promoters for the rest of his life. From that time on, Brody looked at the business as a struggle between wrestlers and promoters. When I worked for Watts, he laughed and made fun of me to other wrestlers. I never forgot that, but I didn't take it personally. At the time I probably did, but when I went back to work for Bill in 1977, I let all those old feelings go. Brody had a much harder time forgiving. He kept those feelings bottled up inside him for the rest of his life.

Baba was one of the only promoters Brody really liked and respected. Baba had promoted him heavily during the time Inoki was promoting me at New Japan. I don't think Brody ever quite got the push that I did at New Japan, but I do know Baba pushed him pretty hard. However, since the Funks were the bookers of gaijin talent, they worked hard to keep themselves in the top positions. Fortunately, unlike most promotions, which only promoted one team on the very top, Baba looked at us as two distinct "camps" for his company, and pushed us both heavily.

A match between Terry Funk and me seemed to be a natural. I had already worked with Baba a number of times, so it was good to have someone else to work with. Although we both had a wild fighting style, our styles were unique to each of us. Terry was a super babyface in Japan, and at the peak of his popularity in the early 1980s, he was over more than just about anyone, including the Japanese. He developed his character during his time there. He fought hard, bled a lot, and even though he sold strongly for his opponents, he never died. Win or lose, the people always believed in him. I was bigger than Terry, so I didn't sell as much, and I handed out more punishment ... most of the time, literally.

When Terry and I wrestled each other, we worked as stiff as we could, which was the Japanese style. We really laid in the chops, chopping each other so hard that our hands would be bruised and our chests would be bleeding. To tell the truth, I never hit anyone as hard as I hit Terry, but he never complained. Nine times out of ten, he would issue what we called a "receipt," or a return blow. I was working hard because I was trying to establish my position with the company. On the other hand, Terry wanted to hold onto the position he already had with All Japan, so he wasn't going to show any weakness, in or out of the ring. That is where real competition comes into play in professional wrestling matches. The fact that we were competing for the top spot in the company, as well as status in the eyes of the wrestling fans, was the main reason for our competitive matches. In our eyes, the stakes were huge.

It would be hard for fans today to visualize the type of matches that Terry and I had. From the second we came out of the dressing room, until the time when we went back, our matches were all "act and react." One of us would "act" (not "act" as in pretending, but in the sense of doing something), and the other would "react." It was like the football drills we did at West Texas State.

We reacted to what our opponents did. Most of our matches were almost entirely in that "act-react" style. We also adjusted our actions and reactions to the crowd response. Not knowing what was going to happen next, and both of us reacting to each other, made for some really exciting matches.

So ... is there real competition in professional wrestling? I think this is one example of that being the case. I came to Japan to establish myself as a top talent. I wasn't going to give an inch to the Japanese, so I had no intention to give anything to the gaijins. I really didn't have a game plan. I just knew Baba had made it plain that he wanted my style, and that meant not giving anyone a break. Again, that was where the real competition came in, and the Funks fought just as hard to maintain their position.

June 23, 1990 • Stan Hansen vs Terry Funk

I respect Terry Funk a whole lot. He is one of the toughest wrestlers I have ever faced. There might be better wrestlers, but none were as tough as Terry. I think our battles in my early years with All Japan should stand out as some of the best examples of true competition in Japanese wrestling history. It was a real fight ... a fight between two Texans which started out as just a match, but ended up being an honest-to-goodness, brutal battle. Brody and I versus the Funks would be in the limelight of Japanese wrestling for many years, but the real link was the matches between Terry and me.

On June 23, 1990, Terry and I worked on an outdoor show in Pennsauken, New Jersey for ECW. I flew in from Japan, stopping in Hawaii for a few days, and then flew on to the east coast. My plane was late, so I went directly from the airport to the show. To say the least, I had intense jet lag. Terry and I had one of our classic matches, battling all over the grounds. We fought in the lake and in the dressing room trailer. The people had never seen anything like that. It just kept going and going. When the match was over, one of the fans said, "*I've never seen a more controlled act of violence.*" I didn't know exactly what that meant at the time, but that became ECW's standard. I think the violence is okay if kept within reason, but I feel like ECW took it too far. Since then, there has been a big following of what fans call "hard core wrestling." I suppose there are fans for that kind of thing, so the promoters just give them what they want to see.

Terry Funk has become an icon to wrestling fans, both in the States and Japan. Throughout his career, he never changed his style. That style is what made Terry Funk one of the best talents the wrestling business has ever known. To me, personally, he is a legend.

Chapter 18

The Gravy Train

To make a change in the direction of All Japan's business, Baba had to change the emphasis of the promotion from the American babyface wrestlers (the Funks) to matches between himself and Jumbo, a babyface Japanese team, and an American heel team ... Brody and me. Like my matches with Terry Funk, a feud between the Funks and Brody-Hansen was a natural draw. The Funks were both legends in Japan and the established gaijins, while Brody and I were the (relatively) new kids on the block. I played to the fact that they were "older" than we were. They weren't really that much older, but they had been in Japan much longer than we had been.

Our first match together was held at the Kuramae-Kokugikan [Sumo Arena] in Tokyo on December 13, 1982, with Lou Thesz as the substitute referee. When we knocked out Joe Higuchi, the main referee, Lou got into the ring. Brody and I double-teamed him and threw him out of the ring. Lou called for the bell and disqualified us. I thought there might be some heat in the dressing room afterwards due to the way we manhandled Lou, but he wasn't mad at all. I did hear later that he was upset about us tearing his new referee shirt, which his wife, Charlie, had made by hand. Lou was 66 years old at the time, but when I grabbed him in the ring, I couldn't help but notice that his muscles were as hard as a rock. One thing I remember about Lou was that he always ate the watercress greens when we ate at the Pacific Hotel in Shinigawa. Watercress is really expensive, but since then, I eat a lot of it when given the opportunity.

I got to know Lou pretty well when we were both in Kuwait in April 1985. As the booker of foreign talent for the promoters, he contacted me and brought me over for the tour, which lasted a little more than a week. I was quite impressed by him. Lou was 69 years old at the time and he refereed every match on the tour, from the opener to the main event, in cold weather. I was worried about him when he caught a bad chest cold, but he was so strong. He never took a day off.

We stayed at the Marriott Hotel, which was a converted ocean liner which had been dry-docked on land. It was a first-class ship, but it was still a ship. We had a real variety of food to choose from, but other than breakfast, we had to pay for our meals. In addition to wrestlers from the Charlotte territory, Abdullah the Butcher and Afa and Sika Anoa'i, along with their sons Little Sam and Big Sam, were also on the tour.

Before we left for Kuwait, we were warned that customs officials were very strict and that alcohol, drugs, and sex magazines were forbidden. I didn't have to worry about any of those things, but I dreaded not having a beer to drink under the circumstances. Another tour of foreign wrestlers had gone to Kuwait the week before and one of the guys had gotten into trouble for bringing something in that he wasn't supposed to.

When I reached the front of the customs line, a customs agent began looking through my wrestling bag. As I watched, I noticed the corner of a small magazine protruding from my gear. He seemed to see it at the same time and pulled it out. It was a paperback novel that I had bought at the airport in the States. I breathed a sigh of relief when I saw what it was, but when the customs agent opened the book, danged if it didn't have two or three pages of pictures, and one of them was of a topless girl. He looked up at me and then called over someone dressed in the typical headdress of the Kuwaitis. The man opened the book and looked at the picture. He then looked at me and shook his head from side to side. In perfect English, he told me to go on. To say the least, I felt a little weak-kneed.

The promoters were from Kuwait, but we never knew who the main guy was. When we arrived, they insisted on taking our passports. Abdullah and I refused to give up ours, even when Lou asked. Abdullah and I did that "iggy" look we did when we were getting paid by promoters, as if to assure the other we weren't going to give them up. Somehow, Lou covered for us and we were allowed to keep them.

During the tour, the promoters took some of the guys to the markets where gold was sold cheaply and bought gifts for some of them. I patiently waited my turn, but it never came. You win some and you lose some.

The shows were held outdoors in a soccer stadium in Kuwait City. Halfway through the tour, the promoters brought in three Pakistani wrestlers who were supposed to be shooters. On their first night in, we all sat around the dressing room and watched them suspiciously. They were pretty much in awe of the Butcher. They just kept staring at him. Deciding he would give them a little something to think about in the event they had plans to shoot on us, Abdullah opened his bag and took out one of the forks he used as his gimmick. He then took his time wrapping adhesive tape around the tines of the fork, leaving the ends uncovered and jutting out. Acting nonchalant, as if he was the only person in the room, he slowly stabbed himself in the forehead, over and over again. He didn't push too hard, but he used enough force to show them what he could do in the right situation. The Pakistanis couldn't speak English, so they just watched with fascination, and perhaps a little fear. One of them finally got our attention and, with his hand, pointed to himself, and then to his scarred forehead, and pantomimed the action, as if to say, "*Don't do that.*" Abdullah and I looked at each other and broke out laughing. The ice was broken. Neither Abdullah nor I worked with them, but the guys who did didn't encounter any trouble from them.

When the time came to pay us, the promoters gathered us together and told us we were going to have to stay an extra day. They were very emotional, claiming the shows had not drawn well and they had lost money. One of the promoters said he would be going to jail because he lost so much money. I don't know if that was true or just something to get us to do what they wanted, but we stayed the extra day. A big argument occurred when the promoter told us we would have to work the extra day for nothing. It was hot and heated, and for the first time since I arrived, I actually thought the promoter might do something to us. Lou stepped in and promised us he would see to it that we would get paid for the extra day. When I asked him if it was coming out of his money, he gave me a vague answer, but I got the feeling that at least some of it did.

I don't know about anyone else, but the Butcher and I were paid what we had been promised, as well as the money for the extra day. I had received 50 percent of the guarantee up front and the rest was paid from Lou's bank, where the money had been held in escrow. By the time the final show was over, we were all relieved to get on the British Airways flight and leave Kuwait behind.

After our time there, and dealing with problems that arose with the promoters and the conservative laws of Kuwait regarding alcohol, it was nice to be on a British Airways flight back to London. As soon as I settled into my seat, I ordered a couple of beers. Shortly after takeoff, I fell asleep. An hour or two later, a loud noise woke me. The cabin was pretty dark, but it was light enough to see figures. The first thing I saw was either Afa or Sika Anoa'I literally running up the aisle with someone draped across his shoulder. I could hear laughter and talking going on behind him. I did a double-take to be sure I had seen what I thought I saw. I closed my eyes and went back to sleep.

As we were preparing to land at London Heathrow Airport, the captain's voice came over the loudspeaker: "*We would like to thank the Samoans for entertaining us during our flight back.*" The whole cabin of passengers broke out into a loud cheer. I laughed out loud because I could just imagine what they must have been doing during the four- to five-hour flight.

While we waited to board to the plane which would take us to John F. Kennedy International Airport in New York, Little Sam and I went to a restaurant to get a quick bite to eat. In the distance, we saw one of the Samoans talking to Charley Pride, the country-music singer. They were laughing and cutting up when, all of a sudden, the Samoan grabbed Pride in a headlock and began leading him around the concourse. Little Sam said, "*Well, I'd better go and get this calmed down.*" There wasn't any real problem, but Little Sam wanted to be sure Pride was okay. Pride thought it was funny and everyone laughed when it was over.

I know Baba was excited about the possibilities that Brody and I brought to the table. It was up to him to direct us along what looked to be a long and turbulent road. He had just shocked the wrestling world by raiding New Japan's talent roster and bringing me and Tiger Jeet Singh over to All Japan. I don't think he wanted a "war" on talent, but Inoki initiated it when he wooed Abdullah to New Japan.

Not too many people really know the true story of what really went on behind the scenes between Baba and Inoki. I often wondered whether or not Baba and Inoki were on speaking terms. Inoki did his best to put Baba out of business. However, I don't know if Baba looked at it as being "just business" or on a more personal level. One thing I do know is that Baba and Seiji Sakaguchi, the number two man at New Japan, got along.

Baba was too smart and deep-thinking to let any of us in on any more than what was absolutely necessary. A few of us gaijins were privileged with certain information, but only a handful of people really knew everything that went on behind closed doors. Then again, perhaps only two people were totally on the inside ... Baba and Inoki. Brody used to love to speculate about that. We spent countless hours discussing this over beer at our favorite Japanese restaurants. There was one thing we knew with absolute certainty. Brody and I probably knew very little about what really went on in the office.

One of the reasons why people knew little about what went on with the company was because Baba didn't talk a lot. He was confident enough in his abilities that he didn't feel the need to prove himself to the people outside the circle of his business. He moved with precision and often had numerous things going on at one time. Today, we call it multi-tasking, and he was the master of it. It takes great intellect to keep a major wrestling company moving forward in a positive direction. I have known a lot of promoters and bookers who were able to do that efficiently, but I would have to class Baba-san as a genius when it came to running a wrestling company. He had a lot of people under contract, each with their own individual deals and problems.

When Brody and I began going on tours together, we got over in a big way. Nobody laid down for us, for sure. On a nightly basis, we fought our way to the ring, fought hard in the ring, and then fought our way back to the dressing room after the match. I don't think we were that much better than the other wrestlers. It was our "wildness" that got us over most of all. We both weighed around 300 pounds, and yet, unlike other big men, we could move fast and keep moving. Nobody had been able to combine speed, quickness, and size into one package. There are many huge men in the wrestling business today, both in height and weight, but I don't think any of them could have kept up with Brody and me.

Brody and I ate and trained hard to gain body weight. We realized size would be a key to our success. However, we had a base on which to build, and we both thought that base was football. I believe football is the toughest sport in the world. Not only do the players have to develop great cardiovascular systems, but they have to have strength, knowledge of their game, quickness, and mental toughness. It is the only true contact sport where they are literally trying to knock their opponents out of the game. There is something about practicing for three to four hours, and then running ten 100-meter sprints at the end of that practice, that stays with a person for a lifetime. We all wanted to quit, but we just kept plugging along. At the end of the day, we went back to the locker room and looked around at each other, knowing with pride that we had done things which most people wouldn't do. I'm sure other athletes feel the same about their chosen sport, but I lived American football. Brody and I talked about that often. We both agreed that we owed our success in wrestling to the tough training we received in football at West Texas State. Those base years in football kept us in a top position in wrestling, even when we should have been past our prime.

Brody and I were having the time of our lives. We were doing something we loved — wrestling — and we had one of the best spots in the business. Not only that, but we were in Japan, a country which we both loved. As Brody and I became more and more familiar with the culture of Japan, going out to enjoy the nightlife became an adventure to us. That was one of the main reasons why we loved doing business there.

Brody taught me about life in Japan, just as he had been taught by King Curtis Iaukea during his early years in the country. I didn't really have anyone to show me the country when I was working for New Japan. I enjoyed the time I spent with guys like Pete Roberts, Hulk Hogan, and Dick Murdoch, but we didn't venture out much at night. Most of the time we just went to the nearest western-type restaurant, and after we had a meal, we would go right back to the hotel.

Together, Brody and I went out and learned a lot about the customs of the average Japanese "salary man" and the after hour social "work" which was required of them.. We preferred going out on our own because most of the other gaijins were into western food. We never went to Denny's or Royal Host unless it was really necessary. We wanted and looked forward to experiencing authentic Japanese food and culture. We would eat and drink while we mixed business with pleasure, discussing business and enjoying the nightlife. On most nights after the matches, we would shower and then go out to eat. Occasionally, if it was late, we would just wash our face and hands without bothering to shower, spray on some cologne, and hit the streets. We justified it by saying it added to our character. We both developed a love for a large variety of Japanese food. Brody already knew about a lot of the food and was anxious to teach me what he knew. We discovered Iobatayaki, yakitori, and even sushi and sashimi. Long before sushi became popular in the States, we were sitting down nightly to plates of fresh sashimi ... with their gills still moving. The chefs would flay the outsides of a live fish, without gutting them, and lay them on a bed of ice. The fish still moving when it arrives at your table is pretty common in Japan.

We also developed a taste for Japanese beer, which we decided was the best beer in the world. We decided early on that we would only drink beer. I had drunk whiskey a few times when I was in college, but I quickly learned that I couldn't handle it. It usually ended up handling me. On the other hand, I liked the taste of beer and it wasn't too potent, so I set a rule that I wasn't going to drink anything but beer. Brody did pretty much the same thing. We would always say, "*Beer only.*" It never seemed to get a look of astonishment from whoever was asking us because most Japanese begin with beer, but move to whiskey pretty quickly. Of course, I have to admit that we drank a *lot* of beer. We discovered that when we ate, we could drink a lot and not get drunk. We never set out with the intention of getting drunk, although there were times when we drank much more than we should have, but that was the exception. Most of the time, we just went out and drank beer slowly and steadily as we ate at different restaurants.

At times, we would go to the small cabarets which were scattered all over the "street of lights." I also learned that no matter how small a town is, it has some kind of a "street of lights" where we could find a good, late-night restaurant. We also frequented karaoke bars. Most Japanese could at least carry a tune, but neither Brody nor I could even come close to being considered good singers. I can't recall Brody ever singing. I did a few times, but I was pretty bad.

Quite often, when we were at a restaurant, we would be invited by other patrons to join them at a small club for drinks. Most of the gaijins never

Stan Hansen and Bruiser Brody on the streets of Japan

experienced that kind of nightlife. Everything was so traditional Japanese and different from anything found in the States. We loved it. Sometimes, Brody and I went on our own to the little clubs. When we opened the front door and looked in, they might invite us to come in. At other times, when they realized we were gaijin, they would cross their arms and shake their head from side to side. Gaijins weren't welcome in those clubs. That didn't happen very often, but it did happen occasionally. Most of the time, however, they were receptive to us and invited us to join them. It was fun to just walk down the sidewalks and open doors, not knowing what lay behind a door. Every establishment was different from the one that preceded it. Some were full of people. Others were empty with just one woman standing behind the bar. Most of the clubs were only wide enough to accommodate a bar and a row of stools. Often, if we had a group of three or more, someone would go into a club while the others continued walking down the street. If nobody saw them leave the group, we would have to double back and look for them. Or when they came back out onto the street, we might be in another club, so they would have to open doors to find us.

In the beginning, Brody and I were able to enjoy our time out without being noticed too much. Later, when we became more popular, we attracted a pretty big following, to a point where we couldn't walk into a restaurant without being noticed. We didn't mind that because it was nice to mingle with the fans and the public. Most of the time, we weren't approached by fans who had been at the matches, but by businessmen who were out of the town after a hard day at work. People would want to pour us a glass of beer, and often sent bottles to our table. The Japanese tradition is that you pour the beer into the glass of your company. If someone is doing that for you, you always hold up the glass for them to pour it into. It's considered impolite to let the glass sit on the counter as it's being filled. We learned that when a stranger came to our table and poured us a glass, they would usually leave a bottle or two at our table. It was a nice tradition and we usually were unable to finish all the beer that came our way.

It wasn't long before we learned other customs and fit right into the late-night eating places. As time passed, we became recognized more frequently. It was nice for the most part, but sometimes, the attention led to trouble.

I don't think the attention Brody and I received was any more than that given to Terry and Dory Funk. Wrestling in Japan was very popular at the time. I can imagine just how much attention the Japanese wrestlers received from the wrestling fans. I don't know how Tenryu or Jumbo were able to go out and eat without drawing huge crowds of adoring fans. It was impossible for them to go out in public and not be recognized. It wasn't uncommon to see 15 to 25 fans hanging out in the hotel lobbies. When we would leave the hotel, big groups of fans would follow behind us, or run ahead of us and take our picture.

At first, it was nice to be recognized, but after a while, it became uncomfortable to always have someone watching us. That gets old really quickly. I know most people don't understand nor have sympathy for people in that position. However, until you experience it, you just can't understand how annoying it is. We cherished every minute of "private" time we experienced. We knew we were having our "fifteen minutes of fame," which means everyone is supposed to be famous for a short time and then it is over, but we wanted to enjoy ourselves without the constant scrutiny of the public. We began to do things which would allow us to elude the fans and the people. We would sneak out the back door. We would run outside and jump into a taxi, leaving the people behind. Of course, that didn't always work as well as it sounds. Eventually, losing our followers became a game for us. We would go to real extremes to elude the fans.

We looked at the situation as "us" against "them," and we would go to real extremes to evade pursuit. We weren't too serious about it, but it was our way of not conforming to what the fans wanted from us. I can remember getting off an elevator on the second floor, walking down a flight of stairs, and then leaving through an exit which led into an alley on the back side of the hotel. It wasn't that I was unsociable, but it got to be a hassle walking the streets with 25 to 30 people walking beside and behind me. We would get into cabs and hand the drivers written notes with instructions on where take us. If someone from the hotel came out and told the driver where we wanted to go, the people would hear it and follow us in other taxis. Once we were way from the hotel, however, we didn't get an undue amount of attention from the fans. I can imagine the loss of privacy today with the easy access of digital cameras and live feeds to the Internet. I'm glad I was there before those things were available.

It was a costly mistake to lose a hotel room key. The hotel would drill the lock, make a new key, and charge us at least $100. The rule was to drop off the key at the front desk, rather than take it out of the hotel. I did that for years, but as time went by, I would take my key with me and I never lost one. Another problem was that we would be in different hotels every night, so we would often have trouble remembering the name of the hotel in which we were staying, or we couldn't pronounce it well enough for the taxi driver to know where to take us. I learned to stop at the front desk of the hotel and get a card which had the name and phone number of the hotel. All I had to do was show it to the driver and he would know where to take me.

Most of the other gaijin wrestlers liked to hear the people call out to them, or to be noticed in public. In the ring, Brody and I were heels. We loved being the "bad guys," but that wasn't our attitude in real life. We didn't go out looking for trouble, or act like we were tough guys. We didn't treat people badly when they interrupted our private time. It's hard to explain. We wanted to experience the Japanese life, and that meant eating, drinking, and talking with the average person who might be at a restaurant or club. However, we tried to maintain a distance. Even though we were hospitable to people, we never really wanted to get too close to them, and if somebody happened to step over a certain line, we would rebuke them. I believe that was a part of our popularity. We could be friendly, but nobody knew for sure how we would react, and that unpredictability was what was unique about Brody and me. We didn't set out to promote any kind of an attitude. It was just a natural and spontaneous response.

In the years after Brody and I went our separate ways, I continued to go out and experience the great life of Japan. The knowledge about Japanese culture had been passed from King Curtis to Brody, and from Brody to me, was passed through me to others. I took out Terry Gordy, Danny Spivey, Johnny Ace, Steve Williams, Ted DiBiase, and many others, to experience the great food, nightlife, and culture of Japan. They all made a career in Japan and grew to love it as much as I did. One of the great joys I had was to take out young, first-time gaijins. It was always fun to watch the new talent try sushi, or other traditional Japanese food, for the first time. Or to see them react to someone pouring a beer for them, and learning the custom of pouring it back. Not too many gaijins could adapt and give up western food, especially fast food like McDonald's, but those who did found a whole new world waiting for them.

Of course, as I grew older, I didn't frequent the clubs as often. As western culture began to worm its way into the country, western problems followed. As I mentioned earlier, I even lost my desire to go to Roppongi because it became so westernized that it was like going out in the States or another westernized country. Roppongi changed so much that there were more gaijins on the streets from Europe, Africa, and the Middle East than there were Japanese. It lost the lure of being "Japanese." I wanted to go out to see Japan, not "Tokyo New York."

Today, Japan is still the best foreign country to visit. If you stay away from gaijin clubs and go to the places where the Japanese go to eat and relax, you can have a great time.

Pete Roberts was, and still is, my best friend in the business. Our friendship began during my first tour with New Japan. Brody and I were close for a long time, but my friendship with Pete has lasted for more than 30 years. When I negotiated my first contract with Baba and All Japan, one of the things I asked Baba was that he bring over my friend Pete Roberts sometime in the future. I didn't expect Baba to bring in Pete as a top man, but Pete was a good talent who wrestled the European style, a style which is much different than the *catch-as-catch-can* style of wrestling. It moves at a slower pace and uses more holds and reversal of holds. European wrestlers like Billy Robinson and others used it to great effect because it looked so different from anything else in the ring. Jumbo Tsuruta and Dory Funk liked that style and always mixed some of it into their match when they worked together.

Pete lives in southeast England in a county called Kent. Kent borders East Sussex, Surrey and Greater London. He is a carpenter by trade and, after working thirty-odd years in Europe and Japan, he opened his own two-man remodeling company.

He is now retired and comes to visit me and my family once a year in the States. I have visited him in England, as well. Pete loves the American west, so we always take a trip out west when he comes over. He loves the old western movies and we watched *Lonesome Dove* together for the first time on the bus in Japan. It is our favorite movie. I live in western Colorado, so we travel out to Monument Valley, and places like Lincoln County, New Mexico, where Billy the Kid broke out of jail and killed a deputy. We always travel to some historical place from the Wild West. We drink a few beers and reminisce about our time in Japan and the wrestlers who were there at the time.

Pete enjoyed the nightlife in Japan as much as I did. One day, while we were walking down a street in a small Japanese town, we saw the light of a sign about ten blocks down the street. It was in a residential area of the town. As we walked, a man came up to us and began talking. He could speak a smattering of English. He didn't recognize us, but he had heard that wrestling was going to be held in the town later that night. He ended up inviting us to his home for dinner. We were astonished. I mean, what a nice, trusting person he was. He and his wife cooked tempura and we had a great time visiting with them.

It's amazing how things happen when you're in need. Pete and I were both somewhat depressed. We were far from home, in a town where there was little to do, and there wasn't a restaurant anywhere close to the hotel. Call it fate or God's providence ... either one will fit the bill. What a truly unique experience it was to just happen to run into such a special person. That story always comes up whenever Pete and I get together. I don't know of any place other than Japan where someone would invite a total strange to their home for dinner. Is it any wonder why I love that country so much?

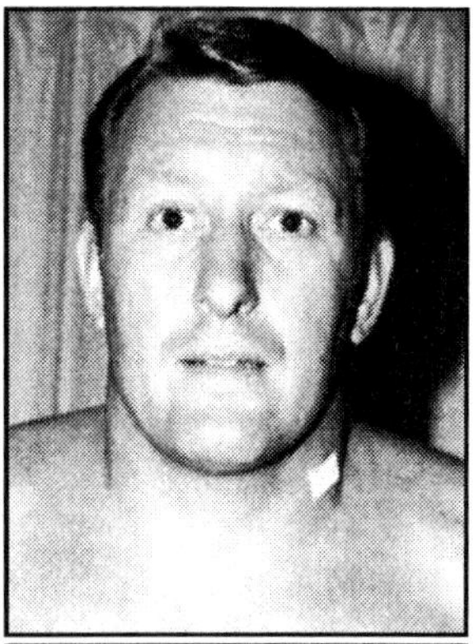

Pete Roberts

That enjoyment of life in Japan stayed with me for my entire career. It is one of the reasons why I was able to stay and work there for so many years. If life here in Japan has been unattractive, or unpleasant, then I wouldn't have stayed, no matter how much money I would have made. There were so many people who offered me their hospitality and friendship that I couldn't begin to mention them all. To every one of the Japanese people who made my life so enjoyable, I thank you from the bottom of my heart.

One of the other great characters I met in Japan was Lord James "Tally-Ho" Blears. Blears had a remarkable story, which is documented in the history of World War II. On March 26, 1944, during World War II, he was one of five survivors of a Merchant Marine ship which was torpedoed in the Indian Ocean. The crew was captured and tied together in pairs. As the line slowly marched by the conning tower of the submarine "I-8," the Japanese methodically hacked off the heads of the sailors. As Blears got close to the front of the line, he and another man dove over the edge of the ship. The Japanese shot and killed his mate, but Blears freed himself from the corpse and escaped. He swam for more than eight hours to reach the floating wreckage of his ship, where he found four other crewmen hanging onto floating debris. Days later, they were picked up by an American ship and dropped off in Ceylon, which is now called Sri Lanka, and they worked their way back to England. There were only five survivors out of 103. After the war, the captain of the Japanese submarine was executed for war crimes.

Lord Blears

In 1945, after the rescue, he wrestled for three weeks for the New York office run by Toots Mondt, Al Mayer, and Rudy Miller, when his ship, the Nieuw Amsterdam Dutch Liner, was docked in New York harbor. When he left the service, he made six tours of France and England, and then moved to New York. He had quite a career in California and won the world light heavyweight title from Wild Red Berry in Phoenix, Arizona, which was then part of the California territory run by Hugh Nichols. Blears and his tag-team partner,

Gene Kiniski, moved to Hawaii in the summer of 1955, where he stayed for several years. In his later years, as the commissioner for the Pacific Wrestling Federation, Blears made appearances with All Japan two or three times a year. He would read the announcement at the opening ceremonies for the big tournaments and scout gaijin talent for Baba.

Blears would sing jingles and recite poems, one after the other. He knew hundreds of them. He just loved to talk and be around the boys. I have to admit that we would often get annoyed when he went on and on, but he was a man who was always upbeat and loved life.

I used to kid him about his job as the commissioner of the PWF. "*Blears, I wish I had a job like yours. You're on the gravy train.*" When he was giving his speech during the opening of a tournament, I would try to disrupt him by moving around, or charging the other wrestlers. It became a rib for me to go after him and make him lose focus on his speech. One time, I tripped (or was pushed) and fell on Blears, trapping him between me and the ropes. When I got back to the dressing room, he was really hot at me. He pulled up his pants leg to reveal a black-and-purple bruise on his thigh. It really looked bad, and he let me know how upset he was. "*What were you thinking? I'm your dad's age! You could have seriously hurt me!*"

His statement really hit me hard. I really felt badly. I apologized and never did anything to him again. We became fast friends after that, and we often had breakfast together at the hotel when he was in Japan.

The old saying "what goes around, come around" really came true for me. In 2001, Blears developed some physical problems and was unable to make the long trip back and forth to Japan. I retired from the ring around that same time. That was when Mrs. Baba appointed me the new "commissioner" of the PWF. Blears never let me live that down. From that day on, he ribbed me about being on the gravy train.

Today, he is frail and bed-ridden, and he lives in a nursing home in Hawaii. I called him recently, and although he doesn't sound as chipper as he once was, he quoted me an Irish rhyme just before he hung up the phone. Lord James Blears is a class guy.

Chapter 19

Killer Khan and the Gorilla

The All Japan tag tour always takes place from the middle of November through the first week of December, and Thanksgiving always falls during that time. Thanksgiving is an American holiday to celebrate giving thanks for food and a harvest in the fall. It goes back to the earliest settler from England and the sharing of the harvest with the Native American Indians. It is a tradition for the American family to get together and enjoy a large meal of turkey, cornbread dressing, and many other dishes. I was fortunate to be home to celebrate the Thanksgiving holiday for more than twenty years, but we had to observe the holiday early. I would have dinner at home with my family before leaving for Japan and the tour.

Brody and I spent a number of Thanksgivings together in Japan. For some reason, the office always booked a show in Obihiro on Hokkaidô Island on the last Thursday in November. For three or four years in a row, we sat in the Gaslight Restaurant on the top floor of the Washington Hotel and enjoyed our Thanksgiving dinner together. We didn't have turkey, but we treated ourselves to a nice meal at a fancy restaurant. On those nights, we always seemed to reflect upon our careers and life. We would stop and give thanks for our blessings. We talked about how lucky we were: how we were two relatively-poor boys who were a long way from West Texas State; how we had made a spot for ourselves in the world of professional wrestling; how we had fallen into a good position in the wrestling world of Japan, and into one of the top positions in the whole business; how we were dining in a first-class restaurant halfway around the world, eating fancy dishes and not worrying about what they cost. We talked about being "on top of the world" as we looked out over the night lights of the city from high on top of the Washington Hotel, a very high-class hotel chain in Japan. We marveled at it all. We never took our good fortune for granted, but for a short period of time, we allowed ourselves a moment to relax and enjoy the moment. There was no worrying about tomorrow, no worrying about money, or discussion of anything negative. I just gave thanks to God that we were there to enjoy the moment. We did talk about how we would have rather been at home with our families on that day. However, since we couldn't be, we voiced our appreciation of the situation we found ourselves in and gave thanks for it.

In the later years, Mrs. Baba would go out of her way to prepare a Thanksgiving dinner for the American wrestlers, and often had turkey flown in from Tokyo to serve to us. I know it was her idea and it was much appreciated. She did it out of the goodness of her heart. We all thanked her for helping us feel a little less sad over not being at home in America with our loved ones. That was just one example of how Mr. and Mrs. Baba went out of their way to make us feel at home and at ease. They didn't have to do that. We were grown men, but she treated us with such kindness, just like we were her own family. That is just one of the things which separated the Babas from all the other promoters.

I've had several regular tag-team partners through the years, but the best partner I ever had, hands down, was Bruiser Brody. We were together at the right time in Japan. Brody was a big man, but he could move like a lightweight. Together, we ran over the competition, and whatever we did, we did "together" for our interests as a team. That's why it came as quite a surprise to me in 1985 when Brody told me he was in talks with Inoki and New Japan. He was excited and said he was seriously thinking of going over if the deal was right. I was at a loss for words. The only thing I could say was, "*Why?*" I just couldn't understand why he wanted to break us up, or why he would want to move in that direction when things were going so well for us in All Japan.

He asked my opinion of the situation. I gave him advance notice of my coming to All Japan in 1981, so I guess he felt he owed me the same respect. He didn't mention anything about the money deal he might be offered, but I was sure he wouldn't go for less or the same money. I told him to "*be careful because things might not be as they seem there,*" which was my honest opinion at the time. He knew what I had been through in New Japan because we had talked about it over the years. I simply reinforced the details of my experience with New Japan and I said it was up to him to decide whether or not he could trust them. He responded that he felt he could handle himself with them and that he was going to take Jimmy Snuka with him. I thought that was a good idea because Jimmy was a good partner for him.

He never mentioned the name of his go-between contact so I don't know who he was working through, but I told him there was one thing to keep in mind. "*All of the gaijins who have come over to Baba have been treated well. Not one of them has been screwed over. You can't say that for New Japan. Most of the guys who worked for New Japan have had some major complaints and felt they got shafted.*" I went on to name a couple of them, like Abdullah and Dick Murdoch. Even Masao "Rusher" Kimura, who was a big star in Japan since 1970, seemed to have been mistreated by New Japan. He later came over and found a unique place in All Japan's business.

Brody said he had a solid deal and the company had big plans for him. I was saddened at the thought of Brody leaving, but I wished him well and kept quiet about his plans.

In April 1985, Brody and I were both booked together into Australia by a wrestler named Larry O'Day. It was the first time we had been together since he had left. Years earlier, Jim Barnett, the promoter in Australia, and Larry, who was the booker, used American and Japanese wrestlers for outside talent. I had never met O'Day before that time, but I had heard about him from a number of wrestlers. He had the reputation of making promises, and then trying to renege on them. Brody had worked for him in 1977 when he was hanging around with King Curtis and Mark Lewin. Larry made a deal for

Brody and me to come to Australia for ten days. We were scheduled to work in Sydney and Melbourne. The money wasn't very good, but I had decided to take the trip because Brody had said it should be good. I also wanted to see Australia. There wasn't much business going on there and it might be a once-in-a-lifetime opportunity for me to see the country. As a tag team, we worked against Jay Youngblood and Ron Miller, and as a single, I worked several matches against Miller and Mario Milano.

During that time, Brody and I had some real heart-to-heart talks about what had transpired in our careers, our feelings about our relationship, and the business as a whole. It was a good time and we enjoyed seeing and doing things together like we had done years earlier in Japan. As things turned out, it would be one of the last times we would spend real time together. After that, he left for New Japan. Ten months later, he had a falling out with Inoki and he was out of Japan for the next 22 months.

During our free time in Australia, some people took us around Sydney and we went to the Sydney Zoo. Jimmy Suzuki, a Japanese reporter, was there to follow us and report on our matches. Also on the tour was Masashi Ozawa, who wrestled in the States as Killer Khan. I knew Ozawa from the time when we both wrestled for New Japan. He was one of the bigger Japanese wrestlers, but he was used in the middle of the card most of the time. When he was given an opportunity to wrestle in the States, he really got over and drew big money in the WWF, Florida, Louisiana, and other territories. In my opinion, Khan and the Great Kabuki [Akihisa Mera] were the two Japanese who did the best in the States. Khan had the perfect look for a heel. He had a huge head, and with it shaved, he looked downright scary. More than anything else, he got over due to his look.

Killer Khan

While Khan and Suzuki wandered around the zoo, Brody and I stopped at the gorilla exhibit. Gorillas were, and are, an endangered species, so we were really anxious to see it. The compound in which the gorillas lived was really nice. It was a large semi-circle with a larger area of grass and fallen trees on which the gorillas could climb. When we walked up to the railing, we saw one of the gorillas laying on its back in the grass, relaxing in the sunshine. He was a huge, magnificent animal. There must have been 50 people standing around the semi-circle, all watching the gorilla. At the same time, the gorilla seemed to be watching the people that lined the low wall.

Suddenly, the big gorilla jumped up and stormed toward a portion of the wall to the right of where we stood. His eyes were red and his teeth were exposed, and he unleashed a deep, guttural yell. As he passed a huge tree that was lying down, he picked it up off the ground with one hand, and then dropped it and headed up to the edge of the grass. He ripped a large chunk of grass from the ground, threw it towards the wall, and let out a huge scream. Everyone noticed the unusual behavior of the gorilla. At the same time, everyone looked down the wall to see what had made the gorilla so angry. When I turned my head to the right, I saw Khan bending slightly with his hands on the wall. As I looked at his profile, I remember thinking that his facial features resembled those of a gorilla. All of a sudden, Khan realized that everyone was looking at him. Brody and I fell bent over with laughter. We knew what the gorilla was doing and we just couldn't keep from laughing. Khan was embarrassed and casually stepped back from the wall. Brody and I wouldn't let him leave without pointing to him. We were laughing so hard. It was just a natural reaction. When a zoo official heard the commotion, he came over and told Khan that he shouldn't tease the gorilla. Of course, Khan had just been standing there and didn't do anything to provoke it. When Brody and I talked to the official, he said that when a male gorilla feels challenged by another male gorilla, he makes those charges and throws things at his competition. That was what the gorilla thought of Khan. It was so funny.

For years after that, whenever I saw Khan, I would yell, "*Kong! King Kong!*" Khan didn't like it, but it was just in fun. I have never seen a more impressive reaction than the one from that gorilla in Australia. It was a real reaction.

Khan now operates a snack bar in Shinjuku, a major commercial and administrative center in Tokyo.

During our time "down under," Brody and I talked about his move to New Japan. He opened up more than he ever had before and told me the main reason he had moved was because he "wanted to be number one." He wanted to be the quarterback and have the opportunity to run with the ball. I could understand that. However, "we" had the ball with Baba. I had always thought of "us" as "one." I had never given thought to which one of us was over more, or who was paid more, or who was being given the biggest push. In fact, I never knew what he was paid. He didn't know my business, either. But his decision to jump boiled down to him wanting to do things "on his own" as a single, as opposed to a tag team.

I, too, had done things on my own when I went to All Japan. When I made my deal in Dallas, I had been hoping for a job which would give me security, but also one in which I could balance my personal life. Baba's deal gave me the best of both worlds, and I never tired of working for All Japan. I also had my single run with Baba and Terry Funk, but I thought Brody and I together were a unique team that was perfectly situated for business. We were one of the strongest teams of all time. I never gave a moment's thought to who was number one. I knew who I was and that was enough for me. However, I couldn't blame Brody for wanting whatever the move might have done for him. I understood his reasoning, but I never thought too much about heirarchy. I'm sure that when a person looks at someone else who might be in front of them, or is positioned where they want to be, it gives them focus. I know in my early years, I looked at the Funks, Bruno Sammartino, and even Abdullah and Jeet Singh, as people I wanted to surpass. I am also sure that over the years, Terry Gordy, Steve Williams, Danny Spivey, and other gaijins looked at me the same way. That attitude just adds to competition. That drive to succeed and surpass others was what drove Tenryu. It also drove Kawada, who wanted to establish and separate himself from Misawa. It also was the factor which drove Brody to go out on his own and try to establish himself in the position he set for himself.

Brody's run in New Japan didn't work out as well as he had expected. He didn't come right out and tell me that, but everybody knew it had been a mistake. He told me about some of the things that had happened, most of which I wasn't surprised to hear. He told me there had been a big problem in the very first match he had with Inoki, and that had set off the whole relationship on a bad foot. They worked out their differences and did some business for awhile, but in the end, they parted company. Brody quit New Japan and was out of business in Japan.

I have heard that Inoki talked badly about Brody. A lot of what I heard came through interpreters, but I did hear his comments from a number of people, both gaijin and Japanese. Inoki made it clear that the Japan wrestling business should never allow another gaijin to get into the position which Brody held. He lumped all gaijins into the same pot and he said we were all the same, which meant me, Vader, the Funks, and every other gaijin who ever drew money in Japan. Inoki has the right to his opinion, but it was building and fighting gaijins which helped make Inoki one of the most popular wrestlers in Japan. I believe that by going along that route, he created a big hole in the gaijin talent, which to this day has not been replaced. New Japan wanted to control the wrestling business, which they did for a time, but in the end, they lost control of their own (Japanese) talent and their business never recovered.

"Hansen and Brody"

I don't know all of the details behind the situation. I'm sure New Japan has their side of the story to tell, as well, and they acted as they saw fit to protect their own interests. I also know Brody wasn't an easy businessman to get along with. He told me he had lost a lot of money over the years by sticking to his principles. He reacted to his treatment by New Japan and the rest is history. Ultimately, Brody lost out on a great place to work, and by leaving the way he did, he also burnt his bridge to Japan behind him. He was forced to go out and work the independent market, which doesn't lend itself to steady income. He went from being paid a good income to earning money when and where he could find it. He had to haggle and deal with promoters every day, which was a constant hassle. There's no question that Brody worked the indy circuit better than anyone else ever did, but by no means was it easy. He told me he would often double book himself in advance because some of the independent promoters would cancel at the last minute, and he would lose the guarantee he had been promised. He did a great job at booking himself, though, and became successful as one of the best independent talents in the country.

In October 1987, Baba-san gave him another opportunity and brought him back to All Japan. I don't believe anybody other than Baba would have done that. It was his character, and showed his uniqueness in dealing with people. That is why I chose to stay loyal to Baba during all those years.

Chapter 20

Showdown in the Shower

In September 1985, I went to Minneapolis to work for Verne Gagne and the American Wrestling Association [AWA]. As I related earlier, I had worked for Gagne for a short time in 1979 when I was working out of Atlanta. For some reason, we just never seemed to get along. I was still working for All Japan, so I had a choice as to when and where I worked in the States.

Verne had a dominating personality. He ran the AWA promotion with an iron grip. He got what he wanted and his word was final. Hulk Hogan, who had drawn a lot of money for Verne in the early 1980s, told me the story about what happened between him and Verne. Hogan was making great money and he liked the territory, so he didn't want to leave. However, Verne had agreed to pay him a percentage of the revenue from t-shirt and picture sales. When he reneged on giving Hogan his cut of the money, Hogan questioned him about it. It was all over $25,000 or so. That wasn't a great deal of money to Verne. It was just a tiny fraction of the revenue Hogan was bringing in for Verne in cities throughout the territory. However, it was quite a bit of money to Hogan.

Verne Gagne

They had a confrontation and Verne tried to take Hogan down to the ground. Hogan front face-locked Verne and sat down on him. Verne had to give up under the pressure of the hold. Verne then tried to do it again, and Hogan repeated his earlier performance. Verne had to concede again.

Hogan left the territory in 1983 and made a deal with Vince McMahon to work for the WWF. The rest is history. Hogan went on to become a huge star and drew Vince a lot of money. On the other hand, Verne let someone go who was a good talent and had been drawing the AWA large amounts of money ... all over a relatively small amount of money (to Verne) and the control he wanted to hold over the wrestler.

When Hogan left, Verne seemed determined to find someone to replace him. Scott Hall was just breaking into the business. He was a tall, impressive-looking guy and they tried to promote him as the "next Hulk Hogan." There was one difference between Hogan and Hall. Hogan was a veteran who had years of experience, while Hall was still very green. He wasn't a bad talent, but he was inexperienced. The office felt like they could make "anyone" a champion, but I could see they were pushing him too quickly. Scott Hall later had great success in both the NWA and WWE, and a lot of that success came from the exposure he received during his time with the AWA.

Verne had a lot of great talent in the territory while I was there. Nick Bockwinkel, or Nicky-Poo, is one of the true legends of professional wrestling. During the period of 1975 until 1986, Nick held the AWA heavyweight title a total of four times. There was no gray area with Nick. The guys either liked him or they didn't. Verne promoted him on top for so long that a lot of the guys were jealous of him. No matter what anybody thinks about him, there's no denying the fact that he's a class act. We became friends during my first tour after I made the jump to All Japan in 1982. I was going through my divorce and he helped me get through it. He was there for me and gave me some good advice. I appreciated him helping me through those hard times. I didn't spend a lot of time with Nick during my time in the AWA because we were on opposite sides of the dressing room. We got along both in and out of the ring, but we didn't socialize often. Nick also was a part of the office, which a lot of guys held against him, although their bitterness towards him was nothing more than jealousy.

Nick Bockwinkel

Buck "Rock 'n' Roll" Zumhofe was a great guy. He was funny and a good, gimmick heel who would carry a huge boombox to the ring. Kevin Kelly and Rick Steiner were both green guys and were getting broke into the business at the time. Kevin was tall and lanky with long, stringy, light-blond hair. I worked with him a few times on TV and he put me over. He was pretty stiff, but I didn't mind. I heard later that he got out of the business after a physical confrontation with Vince McMahon over a dispute about money. He was quite a tough guy.

Verne loved guys like Rick Steiner, who had placed second in the Big Ten amateur wrestling championships in 1983 while wrestling for the University of Michigan. I worked with him a couple of times. He was short, strong, and green. I later worked with Rick and his brother, Scott, when they were being pushed as a tag team in World Championship Wrestling [WCW]. They were doing some really dangerous moves as a team ... "dangerous" to their opponents. One of the moves, known as the Steiner Device, involved one of the Steiners hosting an opponent onto their shoulders, while the other would climb onto the top turnbuckle and drop onto them with a clothesline. It was a devastating move, one which should have been a finisher, but they used it as a high spot. They tried to get me up onto their shoulders a few times when I was working for Ole Anderson in WCW. In my opinion, it was the type of move that looked spectacular, but illogical. How can anyone keep someone perfectly balanced on their shoulders until someone else hits them with a clothesline? To me, it was an expose of the business as the person on the shoulders would have to cooperate with them. It looked planned, and I didn't like it. When the Steiners tried to get me up onto their shoulders, I just kept "losing" my balance in one direction or the other. I didn't want to take a bump onto the back of my neck or head from that height. I had seen many others take it and they never landed the same way twice. I refused to jeopardize my health for a move that someone else considered to be a "high spot."

Without a doubt, one of the greatest guys in the territory was Baron von Raschke. Raschke was one of the few guys in the business about whom nobody ever had a bad thing to say. In his role as a German heel, he had a fantastic look for the business. His bald head and oversized ears gave him a menacing look, but he was (as were most heels) the nicest guy anyone could ever meet. He was a good talent who did great interviews and could really get the old-style heat, and he had a great run with Verne for more than eighteen years. In my book, he was a class act.

The Freebirds — Michael Hayes, Terry Gordy, and Buddy Roberts — were also in the territory. Of the three, I knew Hayes the least, but Terry, who had been with Hayes almost from the day he got in the business, had talked about Michael a lot. Of the three, I thought Hayes was the least proficient worker, but he knew his gimmick. His strength was in his interviews, and his persona was wild and cocky. In my opinion, his persona carried over outside of the ring. I suppose he might have been the "brains" behind the Freebirds, which is what some people tell me.

Buddy Roberts and Terry Gordy were both good in the ring. Buddy wasn't as big as Terry, but he fit well in the team. I saw him take a stand for the Freebirds in Winnipeg, a stand which I believe cost him his job. Jack Lanza was the agent for the office and was running the show for Verne. When Lanza asked Buddy to go in a direction that would make him look weak, Buddy refused. The Freebirds didn't mind doing "business" in the ring if there was a purpose behind what the office wanted them to do, but they weren't going to look bad just for the sake of a match that meant nothing. When Lanza left the room, Buddy explained their policy and asked me what I thought. Lanza returned to the dressing room several times and tried to convince Buddy to do what they asked, but Buddy stuck to his principles. He got dressed and refused to wrestle. I'm not sure whether or not he got fired because it was my last shot in Winnipeg, but I don't remember seeing Buddy again. I admire him for standing up for himself and the Freebirds.

Steve Regal was Wilbur Snyder's son-in-law. The first time we met, he came to Atlanta as a babyface. He was another good worker, although he was a bit on the thin side to be a top babyface, and he was always in a good mood. He ran with Tommy Rich occasionally when Tommy was my tag-team partner. We were in Japan together in 1985 and he was a pleasure to be around. When we were in Atlanta, we were always messing with each other in the dressing room. I walked up to him one night and was going to knee him in the thigh. I misjudged the distance and hit him really hard. He got really hot at me, and rightly so. The experience taught me that it was best to not mess around because if someone got hurt, even by accident, it could cost them money.

One night, when Jerry Blackwell and I were making a trip in Wisconsin, we pulled into the drive-thru of a Dairy Queen. Speaking in his Georgia drawl, Jerry spoke into the speaker and told the cashier what we wanted. At the end of the order, he said, *"Ad I want your largest strawberry milk shake."* As we waited in line, we talked about the town in which we found ourselves. When we drove up to the cashier's window, a girl leaned out and held out a huge cup. It looked like the medium-size popcorn bucket you'd buy at the movie theater. She asked him, "Is this the size you want?" Jerry shook his head up and down as if to say yes. She began to turn around, but stopped and asked him again. *"Are you sure you want this size milk shake?"* Jerry glanced at me and then shook his head up and down again. The girl left the window, only to turn around and walk back, asking again, *"Now, you're sure you want this size?"* As Jerry began to shake his head again, I leaned over towards the car window so she could see my face. In a somewhat raised voice, I said, *"Look at him! He wants the largest strawberry shake you make. Just look at him. Why do you keep asking him? HE WANTS THE LARGEST SHAKE YOU CAN MAKE!"* She quickly turned and left the window. Jerry had that possum grin on his face. In a few moments, she came back and handed him the large cup full of strawberry shake. I told her rather sarcastically, *"Now, thank you for getting him the LARGEST strawberry shake."* Jerry put the car in gear and we drove off laughing. I'll bet she remembers that today, more than 30 years after the fact.

There is another great story about Jerry Blackwell that happened when we were wrestling in Georgia. Jerry owned some acreage in the country. Also working for in Atlanta at the time was a underneath carpenter (wrestling term for good wrestlers who work the underneath matches to get the top talent ready for the main event) named Snake Brown. He was tall, thin, and had wiry hair. I remember he almost always wore a welding, baseball-type hat. It seems that Snake did some odd work around Jerry's place and was often there taking care of his place when Jerry was on the road. It seems that on one particular occasion when Jerry was gone, Snake did something to really tick him off, and when Jerry got home, he physically went after Snake. Snake ran out into the woods to get away. Jerry got a shotgun, got into his car, and drove up and down the road calling out (in his slow, southern drawl), *"Snake! Snake! Come out Snake!"* He tried and tried to get Snake to come out, but he never did. Just a great story on how southerners often settle things. I guess they settled their differences after a while, but I can picture Jerry driving up and down the road yelling out, *"Snake! Come out, Snake."* And I can see Snake running low through the woods in his welding hat.

Jerry Blackwell

I also met Leon White while I was in the AWA. He was being broken into the business by Verne. Leon was an ex-football player who, by any standard, was big and strong. We had a lot in common and we got along well. We worked together a few times during my run in the AWA and he made me look strong.

In 1985, while I was working for the AWA, I worked with him one time in the Meadowlands Arena in East Rutherford, New Jersey. I was doing my style and he was going along with me. There was a commissioner sitting at the timekeeper's table on the floor at ringside. Leon and I were having a serious match, but when I looked down at timekeeper and commissioner, they were laughing about something. More than likely, it was something which didn't even pertain to our match, but I took offense to them joking around and distracting the people at ringside while Leon and I were trying to do business in the ring. I whispered to Leon, "*Those guys at the timekeeper's table are clowning around. Go over the turnbuckle and land on the table.*" I whipped Leon into the corner of the ring and he hit the turnbuckle with every bit of his 360 pounds. It seemed as if he was moving in slow motion as he flipped over the top turnbuckle. As he went over, he might have made an attempt to grab the top rope and break his fall, but he was either too green or he just missed it. He landed on the table with a big "splat" and everything came to a stop for a second. Suddenly, a huge cracking noise was heard the table split and everything except Leon seemed to fly up into the air. The guys at the table scrambled to get out of the way. I can still picture the look of horror on their faces as that huge wrestler came over the ropes and onto the table in front of them. It was a real look of fear. I loved it. I rolled out of the ring and grabbed Leon before anybody could move. I ran him over to the other ring post and whispered in his ear, "*Beautiful, baby,*" which was the comment made to me years earlier by Johnny Valentine.

In 1987, he began wrestling for New Japan as Vader. I really got to know him when he came to WCW with his Vader gimmick in 1990. We traveled together a lot during that time. He also had a guy travel with him who helped him with his outfit.

Leon learned his lessons well and later developed into the top gaijin for New Japan. He was working pretty steadily for them when New Japan got together with All Japan on February 10, 1990 to promote a joint show in the Tokyo Dome. I never liked those shows very much. Granted, the shows were a money maker, but the money didn't seem to trickle down to the boys. A few of

Stan Hansen vs Leon "Vader" White

them got the lion's share, but most of the money went to the offices. I also felt like All Japan was doing good business without the help of New Japan and the other offices. I know the Japanese wrestlers liked working the Dome shows because they were prestigious, but we were regularly selling out the Budokan every month.

The promoters put Leon and me together on the show because it was a match that everyone wanted to see. Leon was a horse in the biggest sense, and I mean that in a good way. He was strong, and for a big man, he was quick.

Leon had never forgotten about how someone had written some negative remarks about our match in the Meadowlands. He brought it up a number of times, talking about how they had said they "had never seen a more one-sided match than Leon White vs. Stan Hansen." I thought it had been a good match. He was pretty green at the time and it was good for business. Well, then again, maybe it was good for Stan Hansen's business, and not so much for Leon White's, but it was still good for business. As far as I know, he didn't hold a grudge or anything, but I'm sure the memory lingered in the back of his mind.

Now, several years later, we were working for two competing promotions and were going to be looking at each other from opposite sides of the ring. I can imagine what was going through his mind. I'm sure neither he nor New Japan wanted him to look like he did at the Meadowlands. Of course, to a certain extent, I was thinking the same thing, only from my viewpoint. After all, we were in Japan, and I was representing All Japan.

When the bell rang, I realized the match was going to be a stiff one. He began hammering me and I hammered him right back. To be honest, much of the time, I was just hanging on. He was so massive and unworldly strong. He backed me into a corner and began wailing on me. He wore black gloves and threw some wicked boxing combinations that were pretty hard and stiff. He was excited and I'm sure he was trying to make a good showing for the people, but he was letting me know that he wasn't going to be the patsy he had been during our match at the Meadowlands. I knew exactly what was going on, so I just laid them back into him. We went tit for tat and I hit him in one of his eyes a couple of times. All of a sudden, the crowd let out a huge roar as he backed up and pulled off his mask. I'm pretty blind without my glasses and I can't see too far, so I wasn't sure what he was doing. I could see enough, though, to think, "*It looks like his eyeball is hanging down on his cheek.*" Vader grabbed his eye and yelled at both me and the crowd. Again, the people went wild. He charged me and we went at it again. In-between the punches we were both throwing, I yelled, "*Take it easy, Leon.*" He hit me with a stiff punch, and I gave him a receipt. For the second time, I yelled, "*Take it easy, Leon!*" We went at it for a little while and then went into the finish, which was a double countout.

I wasn't sure what to expect from Leon when I got back to the dressing room. As I waited for him to come back, it crossed my mind that he might try and go at it in the dressing room because of what I had done to his eye. He came into my dressing room and said, "*Great match, man.*" I was relieved that he wasn't pissed off. I'm sorry it happened like it did, but I didn't intend to injure his eye. Things like that occasionally happen in the ring. I was bruised pretty badly, too. Years later, he told me he has permanent damage to his eye, with the eye being moved off center. I don't think the term "fake" pertains to our wrestling.

The next day, Mike Tyson was scheduled to defend his heavyweight boxing title against Buster Douglas in Tokyo. Several of the wrestlers were staying and going to the match. Leon mentioned that he was going and had ringside tickets. I told him neither Tyson nor Douglas would be landing any harder punches than what we had just given to each other. I could have cared less about the boxing match, so I took the next flight home. As it turned out, the match was the biggest upset in boxing history when Douglas beat Tyson by knockout in the tenth round.

Eight years later, Vader came to All Japan after New Japan quit using him. I talked to Baba for him and Baba brought him over on my recommendation. Soon after Baba passed away and Mrs. Baba took over, Leon and others seemed to move towards Mitsuharu Misawa's power-play and away from Mrs. Baba. I chose to stick with Mrs. Baba. It was not a hard choice. Mrs. Baba was Baba-san's wife, and Baba-san was my friend, first and foremost. I don't knock anyone for doing what they thought best for their career, but old saying "where money lays, honor dies" seemed to ring true during that time.

When I arrived in the Minneapolis territory, it was not in good shape. Verne was behind the curve on almost everything that was going on in the wrestling business at the time. The territory itself, however, was a dream come true for wrestlers who were used to being on the road for seven days a week. In Minneapolis, we worked three to four days, and then we went home. In the summer, it was even better because the AWA ran even less shows. In fact, the territory almost shut down in the summer. That was a real draw for talent because it gave us time to do something other than work, and allowed us to spend time with our families. The colder territories were known as "winter territories," meaning the best time of the year for the wrestling business was during the winter months. When the weather warmed up, the people were eager to get outside and go to the lake, or do outside activities. They were tired of being cooped up due to the cold weather. When the temperature dropped in the fall, they were ready to go to arenas to watch sports and other forms of entertainment. The big cities ran year-round because the promoters had to keep their hold on the buildings, but the smaller venues closed down when winter took hold.

Our longest trip was to Winnipeg, Manitoba, to which almost everyone flew. There also was a loop called the "North Dakota loop," but I never made that trip. I did make a few shots into Fargo and a few other North Dakota towns, but I always flew. In those days, most of the guys drove, and the North Dakota loop was a brutal trip, especially in the winter when they had to deal with "killer" ice and snow.

I went into the Minneapolis territory with no expectations of getting a big push. I thought that as a top talent, I would have a good run and be promoted as any top heel would be when coming into a territory, but I wasn't close to the office and Verne knew my allegiance was to Japan. I went into the AWA with no other aspirations other than to make money, and hopefully, make some for the AWA and help turn their business around as a strong heel. Verne and Baba, who had been trading talent for many years, came to an agreement which would allow me to keep my Japanese dates as a priority. My dates in the AWA would always come second to Japan.

From my first day in the territory, I assumed I would be making a normal heel run, with the promotion building my reputation towards a run against Rick Martel, who was the AWA heavyweight champion. I had met and wrestled Rick previously in both the Dallas and Atlanta territories. He was a great-looking babyface who worked hard in the ring.

One of my most memorable matches took place on September 28, 1985, in Chicago at Comiskey Park [now known as U.S. Cellular Field]. It was during a time when the AWA was trying to compete with the WWE and the NWA. The promoters were all promoting extravaganzas which were expensive and hard to promote. Verne put together a show called *Superclash '85* with Rick making his first defense of the AWA heavyweight title against me. Verne also brought in top talent from around the world, including Mil Mascaras, Giant Baba, Jumbo Tsuruta, Genichiro Tenryu, Harley Race, Kerry von Erich, Ivan Koloff, Nikita Koloff, Magnum TA, and even the NWA world champion, Ric Flair.

The ring was set up on the pitching mound and ringside seats were set up all over the infield of the stadium. As in Shea Stadium in New York, and Hiram Bithorn Stadium in Puerto Rico, the wrestlers came through the dugout on their way to the ring. Having worked my wild style in Japan and the other baseball stadium shows over the years, I had a idea of what I was going to do when I stepped out of the dugout. With the ring set out in the middle of the field, and 21,000 people in the bleachers, it is hard for the fans to see and get into the match from such a distance. Since the promotion wants to be sure the show is a success, they favored a lot of organization, particularly in the way the matches are introduced. They played music and told the wrestlers to take their time going to the ring.

I went to the ring first. When Martel came out, he had barely reached the ringside seats when I bolted out of the ring and sprinted towards him. I grabbed him and whipped him into the fans who were seated at ringside. Rick was a talented worker, so he instinctively reacted and came right back at me. We fought each other through the fans, around the ring, into the ring, and back out again. At one point, I grabbed a handful of Martel's hair and ran him towards a fan who was seated in the front row. I can still picture the fan's face as we approached. He was smiling and enjoying the action. As I got closer, he just sat there, refusing to move. I could tell he was thinking I wouldn't dare throw Martel into his lap. That, of course, was all the incentive I needed. I brought Martel to a few feet of his seat, pulled him backwards by the hair, and threw him as hard as I could into the guy's lap. The fan lost his courage at the last moment and dove to the side, as Martel landed on the chair. I guarantee you it was the most exciting action the fan had seen that night. He might not have looked at it that way, but it was.

I was in America, a country where most of the boys did things differently than they did in Japan, but that was my style. I couldn't get away with doing that today due to the threat of a lawsuit, but Japan wasn't lawsuit-crazy. I understand it had been my responsibility to avoid hurting the fan, but in the dying art of professional wrestling, where everything isn't choreographed, I wanted to work a style where the fans couldn't expect or anticipate what I was going to do. By working my style, I could still get the fans to "believe." The fan in Chicago that night believed, if only for a short time, but he believed enough to know that he had better get out of the way or Martel would be sitting in his lap. I believe, too. I believe that excitement of the moment is what the fans want to experience.

That match only lasted, officially, 2½ minutes, but during that time, the people saw a "real" match. Real in the sense that Martel's reaction to my initial attack was real. He wanted to have a good match, and he wasn't going to let Stan Hansen run over him, so his subsequent action was real. And my reaction to his action was real. We didn't have any idea of what we were going to do next. And the fans loved it. They loved it because they knew the match wasn't choreographed tumbling. It was a down-and-dirty fight. Some fans are only interested in getting their face on television, but most of them come to see the matches. They don't want to think about it as a show. They want to get lost in the action and go home saying, "*That was a heck of a fight.*"

Believe me, it is much easier to go out and follow a plan. *Let everyone go out and get their little high spots in and everyone will be happy.* But in doing so, we have lost a big part of what has made wrestling great for decades.

Yes, you can label me "old school," but I'm proud to be an "old-school guy."

One night, Rick came to me and said, "*Verne told me I'm going to drop the belt to you.*" Given my status with the company, that was the last thing I expected to hear. I never thought I would be given an opportunity to get the belt. Rick went on to tell me to keep it to myself because the office wanted to keep it a secret. I thought that was good business. The fewer people who knew something, the more important it would seem when it took place. At the time, the promoters and (most) wrestlers tried to keep their business hidden from the fans. Unfortunately, the dirt sheets were just beginning to get a foothold in the business and we wanted to keep them from publishing information about matches before they took place. It was hard to keep things secret because even some of the wrestlers had begun feeding information to the sheets. Rick said he told Verne he would be happy to do it, but he wanted to ask for something in return. He was promoting in Canada and wanted me to return the favor there. Without hesitation, I told him I would be happy to do the favor. All he had to do was call and we'd book the date. That was a big favor because of my business in Japan. I was All Japan's top guy, and what I did elsewhere reflected directly on Baba's business. But I liked Rick, so I made a promise to him. Five months later, on May 12, 1986, we worked together in Quebec City and he beat me cleanly in the middle of the ring.

On December 29, 1985, we were booked in East Rutherford, New Jersey. Verne took me aside and told me Rick could not speak English well and that he wasn't drawing as a champion. Verne wanted me to take the belt that night. When I told him I already knew, he seemed to be surprised. I told him I would be happy to represent the company as champion, but also reminded him of the fact that my Japan dates would take precedence over anything else. He agreed with my request. I won the title that night at the Meadowlands Arena. I was happy to know that Verne trusted me enough to have me as his champion, and excited to have an opportunity to make serious money, as most of the champions were able to do. Unfortunately, the good feelings didn't last too long. I quickly realized how disorganized the promotion was.

They seemed to be hung up on inventing a new "Hulk Hogan."

The TV tapings in those days were supposed to be used as a vehicle to promote upcoming matches and programs. The matchups and angles would give the fans something to stimulate them into attending the house show matches, which is where the promoters made the majority of their revenue. To get over with the people, the wrestlers had to do something to stand out, and we had just a few minutes during the 60-minute TV show to make an impact on the viewing audience. How we did it was normally up to the booker, who controlled the direction of the business in a territory. I did my best to get over in the AWA by working the wild and unorthodox Japanese style. However, the TV matches I had were just simple matches against an opponent whose only purpose for being there was to get me over. The "job guys," as we called them, were an important part of our business, and they had a lot of my respect for the job they were asked to do.

One day, I questioned Verne's son, Greg Gagne, about the direction they were going and the fact that the TV shows weren't promoting any specific angles. He looked me in the eye and said, "*Our forte is the TV show. We are just really good at it.*"

I almost laughed out loud. I thought he was kidding, but he wasn't. I just went back to the dressing room and shook my head. That was when I began to realize that things might not work out for me as I had hoped. Each week, when I showed up for the tapings, I would look at the booking sheet and see something which looked like this:

Greg Gagne vs ________________
Stan Hansen vs ________________
Sgt. Slaughter vs ________________
Rick Martel vs ________________
Nick Bockwinkel vs ______________

On a separate sheet of paper, they had a list of part-time guys who would be coming to the TV to work. Their reason for being there was simply to put over the top talent. When they showed up, either Verne or Greg would put their names in the blanks. There was no rhyme or reason for any of the matches. They were simply matches which meant nothing to anyone. When I realized they weren't shooting angles and planning for the future, I knew all was lost.

At one particular taping, I was doing my style on the way back to the dressing room. I picked up a chair and waved it around my head as I came up to the desk where Greg Gagne was talking as the color man for the commentator. Greg also wrestled. He was a babyface in the territory. As I walked towards him with the chair, I gave him plenty of time to see me so he could get out of the way, but he just stared at me and kept talking on the microphone, as if nothing out of the ordinary was happening. Thinking he would move, I swung the chair down hard. He didn't move. I nailed him with the chair and then went back to the dressing room.

A few minutes later, Greg came into the dressing room. He was really pissed off and seemed to be ready to fight me. One thing for which I have to give Greg credit is that he wasn't scared to fight anyone. I never saw him in a fight, but I knew he wasn't scared to engage in one if the opportunity presented itself. He was really hot that day. He yelled at me and complained about me hitting him with the chair. I told him, "*You saw me coming! You should have moved! Why would you sit there like I didn't exist?"* I didn't understand it. Who in their right mind wouldn't move out of the way when confronted by 6-foot-3, 300-pound wrestler who was waving a steel chair over his head? By sitting there, looking calm and composed, he forced me to hit him. The fans liked my style because it was natural. It didn't look planned or put on. I wanted them to believe my character was wild and fanatical. With that being the case, when I approached Greg with the chair over my head, what sense would it have made for me to just stop what I was doing and return to the dressing room?

I wasn't trying to stir up anything or cause problems, either. I just wanted to make an impact. I was wrestling on TV in a no-interest match for the umpteenth time. I didn't want to waste time doing squash jobs that didn't mean anything. I wanted to start an angle with someone that would be of interest.

I felt Verne lost a lot of potential business by holding fast to his TV format. He wanted to continue doing business in the same manner he had for the previous 25 years. By that time, the wrestling business had changed with the times. The WWF had gone nationwide with their product, and there was a lot of competition for the limited number of fans in each town who would buy a ticket to see a show. To keep a market share of that business, the promoters had to be innovative. I thought Verne was behind the curve in that respect.

Stan with the AWA title belt

I also realized Verne's criticism of Martel was unwarranted. Rick was a good-looking guy who was in great shape and he had a lot of talent. It wasn't Martel's fault they didn't do business. Verne just didn't promote him correctly. I soon came to realize that I had been put into the same position. I didn't get promoted, so the AWA belt didn't mean a whole lot. The belt had to mean something in order for it to draw.

I tried to give the office some ideas to promote the belt, but eventually, Verne and I had a big falling out over my suggestions, all of which were turned down. One of my suggestions to Verne was to do something which would involve Curt Hennig, the son of the legendary Larry Hennig. I thought Curt was a great talent. Better still, in my opinion, he *was* the talent. He was over pretty good. He was a young, good-looking babyface and a good worker who would fight from underneath. He had a huge shadow to get out from under in his father. Most second-generation wrestlers had a hard time getting past their dad's reputations, but I feel like Curt had the talent to do so, and to this day, I think Curt was the guy who could have taken the AWA back to the top. He was literally bursting with charisma and talent. He could have had a good run either as the champion, or in chasing the belt.

Verne, however, wanted to do things his way because he felt like he owned the belt. I suppose he did, but I was the champion, and I wasn't willing to just sit and do nothing. I wanted an opportunity to make some money with the belt. To do that, they needed to do some hot angles, but their idea of promoting belt was to just have me defend the belt at house shows.

I suddenly came to the realization that they really didn't want me to get over. They hadn't figured me into their plans. Verne was simply using me as a transitional champion, like McMahon did when he used Iron Sheik [Hossein Khosrow Vaziri] to switch the WWF belt from Bob Backlund to Hulk Hogan. I didn't know whether Verne planned to put the belt on Scott Hall, Curt Hennig, or Nick Bockwinkel. What I did know was that he wasn't interested in promoting me as the champion, and in my opinion, just having the belt wasn't enough to draw money. As a heel, I felt I could get over as someone the people wanted to see beaten.

Stan Hansen wrestling figure (Remco, 1985)

I was only the first of a long line of disgruntled wrestlers. I personally saw Sgt. Slaughter walk out on Verne at an ESPN taping at the Showboat Casino in Vegas. I admired Bob for standing up for himself and watched as Verne tried to talk him back, but to no avail. More than likely, Bob already had another place to go. Having another territory lined up was a trump card for wrestlers. My trump was Japan. Without those alternate territories in which to work, the office had complete control over the talent. I always thought that was a no-win situation for the talent. If there is only one major company, and no competition, the talent will wind up on the short end of the stick. If there are only one or two companies for which a wrestler can work, or if they lose their spot with one of them, they don't have much of an opportunity to find work elsewhere ... and that puts them at the complete whim of the existing companies.

I left the territory after Verne and I had a confrontation at a show on July 29, 1986 at McNichols Sports Arena in Denver, Colorado. I didn't leave because of the confrontation, though. I was booked on a tour of Japan. On the night of the match, most of the boys were in one big dressing room. I hadn't been there too long before Verne and Nick came over to me and asked me to join them in the showers to talk. The shower room, or the toilet area, was the place where private talks were held. "Going to the shower" to talk amongst the boys was an ongoing joke, but it also was where some very horrible confrontations took place, the most well-known being the incident in Puerto Rico where Brody was stabbed. I'll weigh in on that later, but having said that, I wasn't the least bit worried about something like that happening with Verne and Nick. I simply thought we were meeting about the match. On that particular night, the shower room was big, roomy, and well lighted. Verne and I faced each other, while Nick stood somewhat off to my left and a little behind me. Without any fanfare, Verne said, "*We're going to put the belt on Nick,*" and without pause, continued with, "*Do you have any ideas?*"

I wasn't really expecting it, but I wasn't shocked. It was just typical of how haphazardly I thought their business was run. There were all kinds of things for me to consider. As the champion, it would have been logical for me to be in the "loop" of what was going on, particularly when it had to do with the belt. Earlier that day, when we were leaving the hotel, Greg, Verne and I all got onto the elevator together. We exchanged some small talk, but nothing of any importance was discussed. That would have been the perfect opportunity for Verne to tell me his plans, but obviously, either he didn't think I was important enough to let me know anything, or he wanted to keep it a secret from me. More likely, he didn't care about me or about what I might think. I really believe that was the case.

When Verne told me he wanted to put the belt on Nick, I looked him right in the eye and said, "*I don't think so.*"

His mouth dropped open and he said, "*What?*"

"I'm not doing it."

Verne's face turned beet red. He stepped up and got right in my face. I didn't back down. I just stared at him, face to face, and with my peripheral vision, I kept an eye on Nick. I wasn't really worried about Nick. He had too much class to do something like attack me, but situations like that were uncharted territories. I liked Nick, but I also knew he had worked almost exclusively for Verne for 16 years. Needless to say, his loyalty was with Verne, period, which was as it should be. Verne glared at me and said something like, "*It's my belt and you'll do what I tell you ...*"

I interrupted him and said, "*I didn't ask for the belt, but I haven't made any money and it's too soon to switch it!*"

Verne edged closer and growled, "*You're dropping it!*"

Placing the flat of my hand against his chest, I extended my arm and pushed him back away from me. I said, "*Don't get in my face.*" All the while, I was still watching Nick out of the corner of my eye, but most of my attention was on Verne. I didn't think Verne respected me because I didn't have an amateur wrestling background, so he probably questioned my ability to handle myself in a shoot. In a flash, I remembered the story Hogan had told me about his confrontation with Verne. In a louder tone of voice, I said, "*I ain't doin' it, and that's that!*"

I turned and walked out of the shower room, almost stumbling over Jim Nelson as I passed through the doorway. It was obvious I must have been one of the few who didn't know about the title change. Jim, who had a real talent for imitating people perfectly, immediately began to tell everyone he saw what I had said to Verne ... "*I ain't doin' it, and that's that!*"

I've heard so many variations from the boys on the story of that confrontation, the most exciting being the one where I yelled out the "Rebel yell" and threw chairs. However, there wasn't much more to it other than what I just described.

I've talked to Nick Bockwinkel a number of times since that night. He told me he had warned Verne. "*You had better not surprise Hansen. He won't like it.*" If, in fact, he did that, he sure had me pegged.

I really didn't like to leave a territory without giving notice, but I knew Verne had made up his mind and was not going to give up any ground, so I decided it was in the best interests of all if I just left. I remember Verne following Sgt. Slaughter out of the arena and trying to talk him out of leaving. I didn't think Verne had no intentions of doing that with me, and even if he did, I had no interest in getting into an altercation. I walked right over to my bag, picked it up, and walked out of the dressing room ... and I took the belt with me. I took a taxi to Stapleton International Airport, which was Denver's primary airport before it was replaced by the new Denver International Airport. I flew to Long Beach, California, where my wife was staying with the family of one of my best friends, and we were both headed to Japan the next day as planned. I had no plans to return, but I did plan to return the belt. I had no interest in promoting myself as the AWA champion without a relationship with Verne and his promotion. The news of what had happened reached Japan, however, and Baba had already booked a number of AWA title defenses for that tour, so I just took the belt and worked the matches as the champion. I didn't have any contact with Verne during that time. As far as I was concerned, I was still the champion.

Stan in Japan with the AWA belt

Not too many weeks after my confrontation with Verne in Denver, while I was driving with my family on I-285 in Atlanta, Jerry Blackwell pulled up beside me and waved me down. Neither of us had known the other was there, so we pulled over onto the shoulder of the road to talk. I respected Jerry Blackwell so much. After catching up on what each of us had been doing, he asked me what my plans were for the AWA belt. He was working for the AWA during that time. I told him I was hot that I had not been promoted and given the opportunity to make some money. I felt the office should have put me in an angle with a hot babyface. I remembered how we popped Atlanta when I worked against "white meat" babyface Tommy Rich.

Jerry told me Verne was really upset and that he had gone ahead and awarded the belt to Nick, which I already knew. When he told me Verne wanted the belt back, I told him I was keeping it. I understood that Verne didn't want me using the AWA belt in my wrestling, but I was mad about how things had been handled. I'm sure Jerry must have called Verne as soon as he left me. I really liked and respected Jerry. As far as I was concerned, he had saved my life in 1976 when I was working in New York. But Jerry had been working for Verne for a long time and I knew he was really close to the office. There's nothing wrong with that, but I knew he would feel obligated to tell Verne about our conversation.

A week or so later, I received a registered letter from a law firm in Minneapolis. It stated that the American Wrestling Association was a copyrighted name and the title belt was the property of the company. They demanded that I quit using the belt, that I stop promoting myself as the champion, and to immediately return the belt to the office. I had no reason to keep it. I know it was just a matter of time before I would have to return it, but I was hot! I was being painted as the bad guy. I didn't stay awake at night thinking about it, but again, I didn't feel like I had been given a fair opportunity to make money. I never dreamed about having title belts, like a lot of the guys did. I knew I wasn't in the fold. I knew I was looked at as an outlaw. I was just happy to be a heel and to work to the best of my ability. However, when I was given an opportunity to be a top guy, I wanted to "score" and score big. I wasn't interested in playing games or in being a "token" champion whose sole purpose was to hand off a title from one babyface to another. I don't mean any disrespect to Nick, but I wanted to work with someone new, someone with whom I could have rematches in order to grab the interest of the people. AWA wrestling fans had seen Nick "win and chase" the title many, many times. In the end, I realized that Verne wanted to do with my career what he wished. What he didn't realize was that I have always had first call on my career, and I wasn't going to change for him or anybody else.

Having said that, I wasn't like a lot of guys, who always thought the promoters were out to screw them. I respected the fact that they invested money to promote talent and they had a right to a good return on their investment. I had to find a balance between my welfare and the promoters making a fair return.

I always knew I was going to return the belt, so when I returned to Mississippi from Japan in August, I called FedEx and arranged for a pickup. There are many rumors about what I did to the old belt before I returned it. I pounded it down into a small heap of metal. I shot it full of holes with a shotgun. The truth is, I didn't intentionally do anything to it. I had an old 1950-era tractor sitting on my property. It had two big wheels on the back and two small wheels in the front. It just so happened that while I was waiting for the FedEx truck to come to my house, I was driving around on the tractor, "enjoying" the belt for the last time. Somehow, the belt slipped from my waist and fell down under the tires of the tractor. Before I could apply the brakes, the tractor ran over the belt … not just once, but four times! Weird things happen sometimes.

That old AWA belt had been around for a long time. As championship belts go, it was quite large. It also was dinged up quite a bit. I later learned something else about the title belt. The office had a newer belt in the office which they had planned to present to Nick when he beat me ... which is exactly what they did.

Once again, I had been involved in a confrontation with a promoter, which added greatly to my reputation of being an outlaw and non-conformist. I was happy to be labeled an "outlaw." I was glad the promoters thought of me that way. In my opinion, being an outlaw was standing up for what I felt was right. I wanted to change the scenario that Martel faced when he was handed the impossible task of trying to make money with the belt.

I'm sure there were a number of reasons why Verne wanted to switch the belt. For one, I had been in Japan a couple of times when Verne had a big show at the Metrodome in Minneapolis. I flew in to make the title defenses, but flew right back out to finish my tour of Japan. One such instance took place on April 20, 1986, when I accepted a booking from Verne for a show called *Wrestlerock*. Unfortunately, the Dome show fell during a scheduled trip to Japan. When I called Baba and told him about it, he said if I could make the travel arrangements, I could leave Japan for a few days to make the show.

I took Mitsuharu Misawa along with me. He was booked on the show to give him some international recognition. He wrestled on the show as Tiger Mask against Buck Zumhofe. We left in the middle of the tour. The flight from Japan to Chicago took more than twelve hours, and from there, we caught another flight to Minneapolis. On landing, we immediately went to the Metrodome where the show was already in progress. The show featured a great lineup of matches with 50 wrestlers competing. I was booked to defend the AWA belt against Nick Bockwinkel. To say the least, it was tough. I had been up for more than 24 hours. Nick's style was quite the opposite of mine. He was more of a wrestler. I tried to do my style with Nick, but after a few minutes, the jet lag hit me hard. I ran out of energy. We had a match that I would rate as being just so-so and I regret that. On my way back to the dressing room, I had such little energy that I almost collapsed. The show was still going on when I left.

I went back to the hotel near the airport and was fast asleep by ten o'clock. At midnight, the phone rang, waking me out of a dead sleep. It was Jerry Blackwell, who wanted to know if I wanted to go out to eat with him. I looked at the clock. It was midnight! *"No thanks, Jerry. I'm dead tired."* Unfortunately, I couldn't get back to sleep. There was a sixteen-hour difference between the time zone I was used to in Japan and the one in Minneapolis. It was midnight in Minneapolis, but three in the afternoon in Tokyo. I eventually got up and Misawa and I caught an early flight back to Japan. We arrived in Japan at four in the afternoon and a company car drove us to an outdoor show in Chichibu where All Japan had booked an outdoor show. I went into the bus, changed into my wrestling gear, and went right out to the ring. I teamed with Ole Anderson and Ron Bass against Isamu Teranishi, Yoshiaki Yatsu, and Riki Chôshû. That was a brutal series of trips, which took place over a four-day period, two of which were spent traveling.

Later, when I received my payoff, I was very happy with it. Verne had promised me a guarantee and he honored it. Many of the other wrestlers, including Brody, complained to me about their payoff. They were really upset and wanted to know how I felt about what I had been paid. I told them Verne had honored our deal, but I didn't tell them how much I made. It wasn't their business. I didn't like to discuss money with anyone. Even Brody, my best friend, and I didn't discuss money matters. If we made a deal together, we were up front with each other, but when we made separate deals, we kept it to ourselves. Neither one of us wanted money issues to come between us. I didn't want to know what anyone else was making, either. I realized that if I knew someone was making more than I was, especially if we were at the same level, I couldn't help but feel jealous and envious.

It's ironic that Verne and I fell out over money. When it came to money, I never asked Verne for a written agreement, even though I had heard many people say they had money disputes with him. I do have to say that the one time I had a handshake agreement with Verne regarding money, he upheld his end of the bargain. The problem wasn't getting what he had guaranteed me, but he wouldn't do anything which would allow me to make more than he had guaranteed, which, ultimately, would have put more money in his pocket, as well. I wanted to get promoted as the champion and be paid, and I felt like he wasn't promoting me properly. However, in the one deal where there was an opportunity for him to stiff me on the payoff, Verne kept his word, and I respect him for that.

Verne thought the AWA champion's loyalty should be the AWA first and foremost. He thought he should have first booking of "his" champion. I don't deny that he had a valid argument, but in my mind, my primary allegiance was to Japan. Verne never promoted me to my fullest potential as champion, so I wasn't making the money the champion should have made. Japan, on the other hand, was my bread and butter. They did everything for me that Verne didn't, which included promoting me to the best of my abilities.

Ten years went by before I ran into Verne again. Through the efforts of the "Intelligent, Sensational" Destroyer, I was honored at the 1996 meeting of the Cauliflower Alley Club in Studio City, California. It was the first time I had been to the annual meeting and it was nice to be recognized by my peers. I'm not sure if the sponsors knew of our past differences, but if they did, they pulled a big rib when they seated Verne and me at the same table ... directly across from one another. It was our first encounter since Denver years earlier. When we locked eyes, I wasn't quite sure what to expect. After we stared at each other for a few seconds, he slowly shook his head, smiled, and (to my relief) said, "*You son-of-a-bitch.*" I smiled and reached over to shake his hand. I said, "*It's too bad things happened like they did, but it was just business.*" The tension eased and we had a good time. We didn't talk much, but as the old saying goes, "*Time heals all wounds.* I'm happy we parted that way. From what I hear, he has been through some very tough times in recent years. My prayers are with him and his family.

Stan gives Vader a boot to the chest

Chapter 21
Opportunity

In the early days of Japanese wrestling, it was very hard for the Japanese wrestlers to develop unique and separate personalities. When they begin training for the business, the office decides the position they are going to hold and the pace at which they are going to be brought along. The structure of their training is very strict, and innovative thinking is frowned upon, which makes it hard for them to break out of the hold placed upon them by the office.

Their training consists of a planned regimen which allows no change. That is good in respect to teaching the mechanics of wrestling, and the Japanese are some of the best mechanics in the ring, but their ability to innovate, or adapt to changing circumstances, is much weaker than wrestlers from other countries. We often remarked on the fact that they all learned to do the same moves in the exact same way, and we saw no deviation of common moves.

All wrestlers have to learn basic methods and moves in wrestling. However, the method by which we learned them was very important. My generation learned the basics during training sessions, but most of what we learned took place in the ring before a live crowd. Every night, we learned that nothing was ever the same. We had to change our moves and holds on a daily basis. We might do something in a match one night which might not come up on the next. We had to constantly think, change, and try new things. Everything was done spontaneously. By doing things that way, each of us developed our own personal style.

In the 1970s and 1980s, a few of the Japanese had an opportunity to go to the States, so they were able to develop their own personality and style. Examples of wrestlers who fall into that category include Jumbo Tsuruta, Hideo Koma, the Great Kojika, and Great Kabuki [Akihisa Mera]. They all returned to Japan with a style much different from that of their fellow wrestlers. The Japanese also picked up on different moves since the Americans have been able to wrestle in Japan and show their styles. To their credit, the Japanese picked up on different moves and perfected or took them to new heights. That is the strength of the Japanese. They are able to change when they see something new or different. In the end, however, they still continue to teach everyone the exact same moves.

Today, wrestlers everywhere, not just in Japan, are carbon copies of the people who taught them the moves. You can hardly tell one wrestler from another. It's hard to stand out when everyone looks the same and does the same things. That isn't really their fault. The fault lies in the fact that with the territories out of business, there are no places to go where they can learn different techniques and styles. There are only two major wrestling organizations, and both of them have their own schools which teach new talent the business as they want them to learn it. Having been under the influence of the same trainers, when students leave the schools, they come out looking almost the same as everyone else.

From what I hear, there is a lot of steroid use in the business, and what I see tells me the stories are true. Yes, the drugs do make the guys get bigger, but I believe there's going to be a price to pay in the future. I'm proud to say I never used them. Brody told me he never used them, either, and I believe him. He just never had the look of a user. On many occasions, I did see him eating three or four cans of tuna fish and downing desiccated liver pills by the handful, but he didn't do steroids. Our size was natural. To me, it's easy to the difference between natural muscularity and muscles developed through the use of steroids. Bodies created with the use of enhancement drugs are almost too muscular and look artificial. However, as I write this, that look has become accepted and is the look desired by wrestlers in the States. I don't believe widespread use of steroids has crossed over to the Japanese boys yet, but I'm sure it will eventually. There might be exceptions, but I think most of the Japanese have trained hard with weights to gain size and muscularity. I'm not knocking the guys who use steroids. It's their personal choice. I can just imagine the pressure they're under to look muscular and ripped.

More than fifteen years ago, several of us were talking in the dressing room about the use of steroids. There was twelve gaijins on the tour and I was the only guy who had not used them during training. I couldn't believe it. Most of the guys I know who used them in their early years have quit using them, but most of the young, green wrestlers are under pressure to get bigger. Huge, muscular bodies might be the choice of the promoters, but when it comes right down to it, the use of steroids is a choice which young wrestlers make on their own.

One of the Japanese wrestlers once told me that I was one of the few gaijins who did not have the 'artificial" look which most of the gaijins developed in the weightlifting gyms. I was glad that no one ever accused me of taking steroids and that I looked "natural." I often joked about it and told people, *"Nobody has ever accused me of taking steroids. Just look at me."* Of course, what I meant was that my body wasn't lean and muscular. I was not sitting idly by, however. I trained hard. I did lift weights when I was in the States, but throughout my career, my main training was my cardiovascular system.

When in Japan, I would train at the hotel every day. I would get up early in the morning, long before the others, and go to the stairwell of the hotel. I would then do step-ups on the steps. I would do hundreds of step-ups and squats. I also would do stretching and calisthenics during my workouts, but the emphasis was on the legs and stamina. There were very few wrestlers who could keep up with me in the cardiovascular arena. I took great pride in being able to really go in the ring. Most of the gaijins looked like bodybuilders, so they looked like they were in better shape, but I knew that very few of the guys I worked with could keep up with my movement in the ring. I might not have been as fast as some, but like the Energizer bunny, I could just keep going and going. Keep in mind that I was able to do that even when I was in my mid 40s. I took real pride in the fact that I was able to leave almost all the gaijin behind in that department, and even the Japanese had to really work hard to keep up with me.

The legs are the most important things a wrestler has going for him. In most professional sports, especially football, basketball, and wrestling, it is the legs that are the foundation to the success of the athlete. Most people think the overall "look" is important, but it is the "wheels" that are the most important. During my career, I spent more time keeping my legs in shape than any other body part. However, towards the end of my career when my knees were in constant pain, I slowly lost the ability to work them as I should. That became the driving factor for my decision to retire when I did.

I came into the business during a time when the proving ground for professional wrestling was football. Many of the top stars of the '70s and '80s came from the gridiron: Dory Funk Jr., Terry Funk, Bruiser Brody, Dusty Rhodes, Ernie Ladd, Bill Watts, Angelo Mosca, Paul Orndorff, Dick Slater, Wahoo McDaniel, Bob Bruggers, Tito Santana, Charlie Cook, Barry Windham, Greg Gagne, Curt Hennig, and countless others. They all developed their base in strength, toughness, and agility through football. That doesn't hold true today. Wrestlers today come from the ranks of bodybuilders and weightlifters. I have to admit that they're in great shape. Their bodies are well-muscled and cut up, but their bodies are developed more for show, which is the direction in which the business has gone. Wrestling is now "sports entertainment," and the wrestlers all talk openly about it being a "show," as opposed to competition.

1985 • Stan vs Baba

To a certain point, professional wrestling has always been a show. However, in Japan, it has always been athletics and competition first, and a "show" second. It was that way in the States, too, until the promoters decided to move to an entertainment format. The new form of pro wrestling has proven to be very popular in the States, and a whole new generation of wrestling fans have latched on to the showmanship format, so I really can't knock it. I don't "like" it, but I can't knock it. It remains to be seen how long the "show" form of wrestling will keep its popularity. I have been told that it might have peaked and is now moving in a downward direction as people have grown accustomed to it as a show. Many people, however, don't like the showmanship style of wrestling, which is why I think "ultimate fighting" and "mixed martial arts" have become so popular. Professional wrestling endured in the States for almost a century because of its competitive nature. Japan tried to keep itself separate from the "show" style of wrestling long after the States made the move in that direction, which is why I believe it continued to do well for a longer period of time. However, Japan has slowly moved in the same direction as the States.

I will credit today's wrestlers as being better athletes than many of the wrestlers who were in the business when I broke in. However, the innovation and development of styles was much more diverse, which added to the excitement and spontaneous reaction of the crowds. It's my opinion that if promoters today did away with the fireworks, smoke, props, and lighting, the shows would seem flat and boring. Granted, we are living in the age of technology, and it takes more to keep the interest of people, but in the old days, it was up to the wrestler alone to go out and "get" the people. We had nothing to rely on other than our ability.

One of the Japanese wrestlers who developed his own unique style of wrestling and personality was Genichiro Tenryu. He had great talent. To me, he was the best Japanese worker of them all in almost every aspect of wrestling. He was in the brawling style of Terry Funk, but he could adapt to any style.

Tenryu came into professional wrestling from sumo wrestling, a sport in which he was highly respected. As a sumo, he was ranked as a sekitori in the makuuchi division, the top division in professional sumo. His highest rank was Maegashire, the fifth-highest rank in sumo wrestling, and the lowest of five ranks in the makuuchi division. In September 1976, at the young age of 26, he retired from sumo after a dispute with the Japan Sumo Association. He was signed by Baba-san and sent to the Amarillo territory, where he was trained by Dory and Terry Funk, and made his professional debut in 1976 against Ted DiBiase.

I first met Tenryu in 1978 in the Atlanta, Georgia territory. I had already made two tours for New Japan, and expected to make more, so I went out of my way to befriend Japanese wrestlers whenever I could.

Genichiro Tenryu

I was living in Mississippi at the time and was going in and out of the territory. I rented an apartment in a suburb of Atlanta and discovered that he lived there, as well. The apartment complex, which was called Falcons Rest, was famous (or perhaps infamous) in the wrestling world. The owner was an older lady named T-Bell who was a wrestling fan. She had known and rented to wrestlers for more than twenty years, and she treated the boys very well. We really liked her and made sure we treated her and her apartments with respect. It wasn't a modern place, but it was inexpensive and gave the wrestlers a base from which to work.

I knew that many of the Japanese could cook, and I had heard that sumo was a good training ground for cooking since they all cooked for each other in their stables. Tenryu was a good cook. He invited me to his apartment many times and he would prepare dinner. I would bring food for him to cook and we would share the cost of the meals. My favorite meal was probably hot dogs and pork and beans. I could eat them every day. Almost every time I went over, I took a package of hot dogs and a couple of cans of beans. He got sick of them after a while, but I loved them and never changed my routine of bringing them.

Years later, when I went to All Japan and he was back in Japan, we would talk about our experiences together in Atlanta. He never failed to bring up "hot dog and pork and beans" and he would tease me unmercifully.

Tenryu didn't speak English very well at the time. The apartment was very drab and colorless. He bought a bunch of high-wattage light bulbs and put them in every lamp and light socket. The room was really bright, almost white with light. Every time I went to visit, I commented on the bright light, and he would say to me, "*Dark light!*" Now "dark light" did not make sense, but that is what he would say. I thought it was amusing.

During his stay there, his apartment became infested with fleas. The person who rented the apartment before him must have owned a dog, and the fleas must have laid eggs which hatched in the carpet after he moved in. He came to me one day making gestures with his hands, trying to make me understand that something was biting him. I finally had to go down and check it out. Not too long after sitting down on his couch, I was bitten. We left and bought several cans of flea spray. That put an end to them.

By 1979, Tenryu had become a good worker and was working regularly throughout the Atlanta territory. There was a tendency, however, among most of the promoters to pay the Japanese less than their abilities warranted. Kojika did well working as Kung Fu Lee in the Amarillo, Dallas, and Kansas City territories. Killer Khan [Masashi Ozawa] was a big star in Florida and Georgia. However, while it was the norm for most Japanese to come to the States and get experience, most did not make much more than a living. The Great Kabuki did well in Dallas and other territories, but later told me he thought he got the short end of the payoffs. He felt he didn't get paid as much as the American wrestlers who were being pushed on the same level. He also said Gary Hart, his manager, always involved himself in the matches and took advantage of the situation. Wrestlers who weren't able to talk and do promos had to rely on a manager to do their talking for them. I always thought a manager could be an asset to a match, but I never thought they should get pay equal to the wrestlers they managed. Kabuki told me Gary negotiated a better deal for himself than he did for Kabuki. That bothered Kabuki because was one of the hottest Japanese talents ever to work the States, and he harbored ill feelings toward Gary for a long time.

At one time, I tried to get Ole to push Tenryu, but much of the business in America was based on interview ability, and Tenryu's limited English skills made it hard for Ole to give him much of a push. The fact that most of the Japanese boys were unable to communicate in English limited their opportunity to work the top programs.

Regardless of his ability to talk, what I remember the most about Tenryu was the he was talented and could work a real good match. I had the privilege of working with him many times when we were both wrestling for All Japan. He was a good opponent for me. He was big and he was as quick as a cat. Sometimes, the fans can see something happening when two wrestlers work against each other. It's just a natural thing and the people can just feel the competition between them. That was the way it was with Tenryu and I. We really worked stiff and enjoyed seeing who could hit the other with the hardest chop. He and I had good rapport in the ring, whether we were working "against" each other or in a tag-team match as partners.

Stan vs Genichiro Tenryu

The thing I liked the most about Tenryu was his ability to "fight from underneath." Whenever his opponent seemed to have him close to defeat, he would make a comeback and have the wrestling fans on the edge of their seats. "Comebacks" were a part of every match, but Tenryu had a way of doing it which captivated the fans. Tommy Rich and Terry Funk both had that same unique quality, and that was an ability which can't be taught. The key to fighting from underneath is all based on "selling," which is reacting to your opponent's moves. If you can't sell, then you can't get the fans to feel sympathy for you. It seems like everybody think the key to getting over is "being strong," but I believe it comes from selling. The more you sell, the more you draw the fans into your plight, and when you finally make your much-anticipated comeback, the fans make a comeback right along with you.

We had some classic matches. I worked stiff, but he would give it right back to me. He could chop hard and kick like a mule. One night, he kicked me in the back of the head and almost knocked me out. I believe he also was the first to use the move he called the "Powerbomb." The first time he used it on me, my weight sent me hard to the mat, and the force of impact knocked me out for a second or two. I came to as the referee counted "Two" and I almost didn't kick out. Later, when we were involved in a series of matches, he knocked me out completely for a few moments. When I regained consciousness, I attacked him, and then ran around the building and chased people. I hadn't regained total control of my senses, so I really wasn't quite aware of everything I was doing. I can still see the look of surprise on Kabuki's face as he tried to calm me down.

We also had a hard match up in Hokkaido one time. I kicked him in the forehead with the instep of my boot and split him open over one of his eyes. A few minutes later, I bent him over and kicked him again, cutting his forehead over the other eye. After the match, he had to go to the hospital to get stitches. When I saw him the following night, the first thing I said was, "*Sorry.*"

"Good for business," he replied, which was the standard answer for the Japanese boys. They never complained about getting hurt.

There was no BS in Tenryu's matches. The people believed everything he did. For that matter, I personally believed in a lot of what he did. We kicked and chopped each other brutally for years. As a result, the people always believed what we were doing. And why wouldn't they? Most of our matches were as stiff as they come.

One time, I was working against Tenryu and Ashura Hara in a tag. Hara had come in and kicked me off of Tenryu while I was covering him. When Hara turned and headed back to his corner, I stood up and charged him. I hit him from behind just as he was stepping through the ropes onto the apron of the ring, sending him face first into the ring post. He wound up having 30 stitches to close a big horseshoe-shaped wound that encircled his eye. I didn't mean to injure him. Perhaps I should have known better than to hit him from behind when he was off balance. I felt badly about it, but that was my style. I saw him the next night and apologized. He didn't say too much. He just looked at me and smiled. I will never forget that. Hara was one tough man. My respect for him grew that day, for sure.

I remember when Chôshû, Yoshiaki Yatsu, and their "invading promotion" group came over to All Japan in 1985. The first tag match between the teams of Chôshû-Yatsu and Jumbo-Tenryu was a memorable one. Brody and I were still together at the time and we watched the match from the back. It was not pretty from Jumbo and Tenryu's point of view. In my opinion, they were pretty much dominated by Chôshû and Yatsu. Being the first match in their program, it was all very interesting to Brody and me. We were anxious to see how things were going to go.

Brody and I had been in that same situation when we first tagged up. Jumbo and Tenryu were not going to allow us to take advantage of them, and now, they were being taken advantage of by the new guys. Chôshû and Yatsu really took the match to Jumbo and Tenryu. Brody and I were hot. We had worked hard with Jumbo and Tenryu, and when it looked like Chôshû and Yatsu were going to beat the hell out of them, we felt like it made us look bad. Brody and I decided we were going to protect ourselves, and in doing so, we also would be protecting the reputation of All Japan. However, it was not long before Jumbo and Tenryu were able to adjust to Chôshû and Yatsu, and ended up doing good business with them. I think the first match just caught them by surprise. In future matches, Jumbo and Tenryu took the match right back to Chôshû and Yatsu, and didn't allow them to dominate them. Brody and I were glad to see that. We were just employees of All Japan Pro Wrestling, but we had pride, both personally and in the company.

In 1987, Tenryu separated from the main group at All Japan and formed a stable of wrestlers known as "Revolution." Two years later, we became tag-team partners and we stayed together for more than a year. I had a number of partners over the years, and I think we were one of the better combinations.

Being teamed up with Tenryu during that time, I came to the realization that there was some serious discord between him and Baba. I don't know how long their differences had been building, but from Tenryu's perspective, it was obvious that their business relationship was not good. He constantly complained about the direction, or lack of direction, of the business, and he wanted to have more input. I just kept my mouth shut. I didn't know what to make of it all. All I knew was that I was a gaijin, and it would do no good to get involved in problems between two Japanese. So, I just kept quiet. There were times when I wondered if Tenryu was telling me things just to test me and see if I would go talk. I never did. I simply minded my own business.

I stayed away from the politics of the Japanese. I dealt strictly with Baba. I was friendly with Tenryu and most of the Japanese, but I was not in the circle. Part of the reason for that was because I was gaijin, an outsider. I believe the Funks might have been close at one time, and Abdullah to an extent, but for the most part, it was strictly Japanese. The bottom line, though, was that I preferred it that way. One of the reasons I chose Japan was because I did not have to be involved in all the rumors, the stooging, or the behind-the-scenes antics which went with booking and trying to keep one's position. I liked Japan because it was stress free. I just got on the bus, went to the building, and gave my 100 percent in the ring. I did what Baba and the office needed and wired the money home, and between tours, I went home and spent time with my family. That was the beauty of the job. As far as I was concerned, I had the best job in professional wrestling. It just kept going on and I was never involved in the nitty-gritty of the business.

In 1990, when Tenryu left All Japan to form his own wrestling company, Super World of Sports [SWS], I once again found myself in a unique position. Several times over the years, I have been at the summit in my career, and in a position where I could have begun to slide down the back side. However, events always seemed to happen to keep me in a strong position with Baba. Tenryu leaving the company was one of those events.

Nobody contacted me to ask if I wanted to go with them. I suppose they thought I was totally loyal to Baba ... and they were correct if that was what they assumed. I can't say I wouldn't have been tempted if they had offered me a huge amount of money, but I wasn't approached. Tenryu did call me when it happened. I think he might have been feeling me out, but he didn't bring up the subject.

The wrestling business in Japan went through different cycles. Things would change around me, but I always stayed true to my style and did what Baba asked of me, even when I wasn't promoted in the top position. I know "life is change," but I just kept doing things my way the best I could. I never asked for special favors and I always tried my hardest, no matter how small the show was, or who was on the wrestling card. I always worked hard and never laid back and took the money. I often did what I felt was best for myself, but that also was almost always what was best for Baba's long-term business.

One of Baba's strong points was his ability to keep things going and make subtle changes in his business over time. He had number of really good young boys coming up under Jumbo and Tenryu. When Tenryu left, he took a large number of the upper hierarchy: Yoshiaki Yatsu, Ashura Hara, Shunji Takano, The Great Kabuki, Hiromichi Fuyuki, Tatsumi (Koki) Kitahara, Masao Orihara, Isao Takagi, and referee Hiroyuki Unno.

Baba must have been worried because the exodus left a huge void of talent to fill. However, the mass exodus gave an opportunity to a number of young

Japanese wrestlers who were not yet established main-event wrestlers. Mitsuharu Misawa, Toshiaki Kawada, and Kenta Kobashi were three wrestlers who were ready for the opportunity. Until then, they had been stuck behind Tenryu and others in the hierarchy of All Japan.

During the time when Jumbo, Tenryu, and Baba were the focus of All Japan, Mitsuharu Misawa was getting a push as the second-generation Tiger Mask, a character inspired by the comic book character created by Ikki Kajiwara. The original Tiger Mask was New Japan wrestler Satoru Sayama. Pete Roberts had worked with Sayama on a number of tournaments in Germany and Europe and knew Sayama really well. He even took me to Sayama's home for dinner one night.

When Sayama retired from wrestling in August 1983, Baba bought the rights to the Tiger Mask character from Kajiwara and put the mask on Misawa. Misawa was young, tough, and he could move, and he wrestled as Tiger Mask for six years. The mask gave Misawa time to develop and establish himself with the fans, even though everyone knew he was one of Baba's young boys. I think that was good booking on Baba's part.

Mitsuharu Misawa

When Tenryu left All Japan, Misawa was in the right place to move up to that well-deserved top spot. It seems there is a style that goes with wearing a mask. Most masked men seem to do a lot of high-flying, acrobatic moves. Misawa mastered many of those moves. Of course, most of the masked high-flyers are smaller in stature than the average professional wrestler. Misawa was not a small man, which makes it all the more astonishing that he could do those moves. However, the force placed on a big man's body is almost more than one can handle. I believe that was the case with Misawa. The bumps he took had to be punishing. Misawa was one tough man. Anyone who has worked with me will attest to the fact that I hit hard, whether I'm using my fists or a chair, and yet, I never heard him complain. He took everything I threw at him. On the other hand, Misawa had many signature moves of his own, including the flying elbow and the splash off the top rope. His forearm was second to none. He took every opportunity to lay his forearm onto the bone behind my ear. The force of it would stagger me. It was the real deal.

On August 22, 1992, Misawa won the Triple Crown title from me in Tokyo. For the next eight years, he was a dominant force in the All Japan rings. When Baba-san died on January 31, 1999, Mrs. Baba began running the All Japan company and Misawa was appointed company president. On June 16 of the following year, Misawa and all but two of the All Japan wrestlers [Kawada and Fuchi] held a press conference and announced they would be forming a new promotion called Pro Wrestling NOAH. Two months later, NOAH made their debut at the Differ Ariake Arena in the Ariake neighborhood of Tokyo.

I don't know what went on behind-the-scenes events between Misawa and Mrs. Baba, but I know she had the power and ran a tight ship, so she probably had a lot of heat with the boys. Add to that the fact that there is a cultural bias against women in Japan, she had the deck stacked against her. From what I understand, her main concern was simply to hold the company together until the 30th anniversary of the company in September 2002. At that time, I was told she sold the company to Keiji Motoh and he became the new president of All Japan. All Japan Wrestling was no longer associated with the Giant Baba name.

I didn't blame Misawa for what he did. I understand business. Inoki and Baba did pretty much the same thing in 1972 when they both broke away from the Japan Pro Wrestling Association for form their own promotions. My loyalty, however, remained with Baba-san.

Sad to say, Misawa died on June 13, 2009, during a match in Hiroshima in which he broke his neck taking a belly-to-back suplex, a move which was dangerous, to say the least, but one which he had taken many times before.

Tenryu's departure also elevated Toshiaki Kawada. Even though Kawada's tag-team partner, Hiromichi Fuyuki, jumped to SWS with Tenryu, Kawada made the decision to stay with All Japan. That was a wise decision on his part. Kawada had worked hard as a young boy and impressed me from the beginning. Now, with a number of the older and more highly seeded wrestlers out of the way, he was given an opportunity to step up and become a top boy much quicker than he would have if things had remained the same.

Kawada was a member of Tenryu's "Revolution" group, so it came as quite a surprise to me when he and Yoshinari Ogawa decided to stay loyal to Baba, rather than follow Tenryu. It showed me just how little we gaijins really knew about the inner workings of the Japanese business and mental state of the Japanese wrestlers. I had long since given up trying to figure out where Baba's mind was on certain issues. He was almost impossible to read. The gaijins, on the other hand, readily show their attitude and mood. The gaijins are more likely to show their attitude and mood, while the Japanese keep their feelings to themselves. We tend to fly into a rage when something upsets us and we don't care who knows that we are upset. I suppose showing our feelings is part of the gaijin culture, just as hiding their feelings is a part of the Japanese culture.

It was a great benefit to Kawada to stay loyal to Baba. I later heard he and Misawa had been good friends in high school, so I understood more of why he didn't follow Tenryu. I didn't know it at the time the exodus took place because we knew very little about most of the Japanese wrestlers. I spent more than two decades in Japan and, in all that time, I knew them only in a very shallow way. On the other hand, the gaijins traveled together for several weeks at a time, so we got to know one another fairly well. Even when we weren't on the road, there wasn't much of anything to do, so we just hung around together. We learned about one another's family, work, lifestyle, and attitude.

Kawada, like Misawa, had a great deal of pressure placed on him when his push began in 1990. The pressure wasn't as great in the beginning as it would be later, but it was pressure. In my opinion, Kawada benefited more from Tenryu's departure than Misawa. When Tenryu left All Japan, Misawa was quickly thrust into a position where he had to carry the company. Kawada, on the other hand, also was given an opportunity to better himself, but the office didn't expect as much out of him.

Kawada began to develop his character when he was working as part of Tenryu's "Revolution" group. In my opinion, he was the better wrestler of the two. Terry Gordy and I worked with Kawada and Tenryu in the Budokan, and I worked with them several times around the country with other gaijins as my partners. During those matches, Kawada "worked up" [worked above his ability] most of the time, and in so doing, he established himself as a top talent. I believe that success if often the ability to take an opportunity and capitalize on it, and Kawada did that as well as anyone else.

Kawada had a distinctive style. He was shorter than many of his peers, so the fans looked at him as having a disadvantage. More importantly, since the fans themselves were smaller than most wrestlers, and especially the gaijins, they felt like they could relate to him. To compensate for his lack of height, he began lifting weights to build his body. I believe the Americans brought weight training to wrestling in Japan. It took a while for the Japanese to catch on to the advantages of weight training, but once they did, they adopted weights into their daily training regimen. Tenryu, Kawada, and later Kobashi, were the first to really start training with weights at All Japan. Since then, Kawada and Kobashi have become almost legendary on how hard they train with weights. Kawada used the strength he developed from weight training and his ability to karate kick to establish his style. They have served him well.

Stan vs Toshiaki Kawada

The first time we wrestled in Tokyo was June 5, 1992. My All Japan Triple Crown title was on the line and the match was voted Match of the Year by *Tokyo Sports* newspaper. Kawada and I faced each other many times, and for a long time, I always came out on top. I believe the fact that he couldn't beat me is what endeared him to the fans. He had the ability to open his heart to the fans and let them see his character. They knew he had set a goal of defeating me, and they returned regularly in the hopes he would one day win over me ... which he eventually did. On April 7, 1998, during the annual Champion's Carnival tournament, he pinned me cleanly in the middle of the ring in Kumamoto City.

Most of the gaijins wrestlers, however, did not particularly like Kawada. They thought he was cold and aloof. However, I always felt that was just a part of the personality and character he developed. I also think a lot of it had to do with Kawada being Japanese. Most of the gaijins don't understand the Japanese very well, and when they don't understand something, they take offense. I spent so much time in Japan that I began to understand the Japanese mindset, but no gaijin will ever really understand because we are not Japanese. I learned a long time ago not to get upset about things I didn't understand. I accepted Kawada as he was. We were never friends, but we had respect for each other.

One other wrestler who benefited from Tenryu's departure was Kenta Kobashi. When Kobashi was moved up the ranks, he gained the respect of the fans, as well as his peers. He learned many "high-flying" moves and perfected the back somersault, the move known as a moonsault, off the top rope. The moonsault became one of his signature moves and nobody that big did that move any better. Vader used it occasionally, but not as often as Kobashi. It takes great balance and strength to stand on the top rope, do a backwards flip, and land flat across the chest of your opponent. There are so many things that could go wrong. You could slip as you pushed off the ropes. You can misjudge where you were going to land, and in so doing, injure your opponent or yourself. It was a dangerous move and one which takes a toll on the body. Many of the young guys use it to impress others (and themselves), but often, it is just a matter of time before they make a mistake and injure themselves.

I learned early in my career that the human body can only take a certain amount of punishment before it begins breaking down, and the bigger you are, the harder falls from the top rope are on your joints and body. Misawa and others have done unbelievable things off the top rope. They are impressive moves, but you have to be in good shape and very agile to do them. I couldn't do them even in my youngest years. One time, I blew out my knee just jumping off the top rope onto one of my opponents.

The price many of the guys pay for doing that is that they eventually hurt themselves. Of the boys who got their start while I was with All Japan, Misawa was one of the first to suffer serious problems. In 1985, he was out of work for quite some time when he blew out his knee and had to undergo surgery. When he came back after his recovery, he still did moves off the top rope, but he didn't use them as often. Kobashi has had serious problems with his knees and elbow, as well. The lesson many of the veterans have learned is that "Old Man Gravity" is a hard man to beat. He will hurt you and you can never beat him.

Baba had so much young, Japanese talent in a position to take over the reins of those who had left. He also had some of the top gaijin talent, like Terry Gordy, Steve Williams, and Dan Spivey. All of a sudden, All Japan was featuring new match-ups between wrestlers who had never faced each other before, giving the fans many interesting matches to watch. When the young Japanese wrestlers were thrust into top matches against the gaijins, they were given the opportunity to show and develop their characters. More importantly, they were given a chance to "establish" their characters. Looking back, I can see how hungry the Japanese boys were. Misawa was under a lot of pressure to step up and produce, and it was that pressure which drove him. He worked hard to move up to that top position. It didn't come fast or easy. It was a hard-fought battle.

Nobody could have predicted it, but the exodus of Tenryu and his crew to SWS was the key to the rejuvenation of Baba's business. All Japan's business not only didn't go down, as most had expected, but it went up. I believe that to some degree, Baba himself was surprised with the outcome.

Tenryu, on the other hand, wanted to be the boss. He wanted to make the score and see what he could do as a promoter. It turned out to be a tougher task than he thought. He told me it was much easier just working for someone else and getting paid, and the thing which weighed on his the most as "the boss" was his responsibility to his talent. But even though his promotion collapsed after two years, he did well financially and invested his earnings in a sushi restaurant.

Today, Tenryu and I remain good friends. Whenever I make a trip to Japan, he is one of the few friends I always seek out and attempt to visit. Tenryu is a true icon in Japan. At 60 years old, he is less than one year younger than me, he still wrestles for promotions in Japan. The things I remember the most about him are: he was not an underneath guy, he had a lot of pride, and his primary goal, as he put it one time, was "*taking care of my family.*"

Stan vs Kenta Kobashi

Chapter 22

The Show Must Go On

I wrestled in some strange places during my time with All Japan. On April 5, 1990, we wrestled on a cruise ship that was moored at the dock in Beppu Bay. I also wrestled on shows on top of department stores, in the vegetable sheds for truck companies, in the large lobbies of public bath houses, and countless outdoor shows.

All Japan ran a lot of outdoor shows in the spring, summer, and fall. They would go to faraway places and set up in empty fields, or on parking lots. They invested a lot of money in trucks that would transport hundreds of wooden and metal chairs, and trucks that would haul large tarps, most of which were royal blue in color. They had thousands of feet of metal cable to string between portable posts, and at times, they would drive in stakes to hold down the cables which supported the tarps which functioned as the wall of the show. Most of the time, they were set up in squares or rectangles with the ring set up in the center of the area. Portable posts supported cables which stretched out hundreds of feet to hold the ring light over the ring. Often, if we were in an area where there was no available electricity, the company would bring a huge generator so they could operate the ring lights and sound system.

The bus was our dressing room, so we didn't always have access to a toilet, but most of the time, we would use one of the portable units brought in for the fans. The first time I went to Japan, we went to an outdoor show and it was drizzling rain. The office provided bamboo mats for the fans to sit on. The price of the most inexpensive ticket was $15 and ringside went for $60. Sometimes, they were sold shows, which were shows sold to local promoters for a certain amount, who would then sell the tickets to the public and, hopefully, would make more than the show cost them. I heard they sold shows to local promoters for anywhere from $15,000 to $30,000. If they were able to draw a couple of thousand people at an average price of $20, it was a good deal for all concerned. Most of the time, the attendance was in the range of 500 to 1,500 people.

There would be one opening in the canvas walls surrounding the show. The tarps were a good ten feet tall so no one could see over them and were tied down with stakes into the ground and lashed together. Only in Japan could you have a show like that. In the States, someone would slice open the tarp and sneak in, but in the Japanese society, it was a very feasible way to promote. Inside the front opening, the office would have tables set up from which they sold t-shirts, hats, towel, books, and other trinkets about All Japan Pro wrestling and its talents. Giant Service was the merchandising arm of All Japan and Mrs. Baba ran that end of the business. On occasion, I was paid extra for merchandise sold which featured my likeness or name. I took what came my way and didn't question whether I should have been paid more. To me, it was just gravy on top of the good money I was already making. I was there to wrestle, so I concentrated on that.

A crew of about ten to twelve people was involved in the actual running of the show. The crew drove the trucks, set up the chairs and ring, indoors and out, and stringing the ring lights. Even at indoor shows, they had to crisscross the ring lights from the top rafters, over the ring, and to the rafters on the other side of the building. I never saw that done because everything was always set up by the time we got to the building. The crew worked real hard and put in long hours. During the show, they filled whatever positions were needed. The referees all had dual jobs helping out with the promotion side of the business, from ticket-taking to hawking concessions for Giant Service. After the show, they had to tear everything down, fold and load the chairs, repack the merchandise, and travel to the next location.

The office was always setting up new ways to engage and promote the fans. The talent would sit out front behind the merchandise tables to greet the fans and sign autographs. The office also developed the idea of taking pictures of the fans with the talent. It was a long process of engaging the fans and making the most out of the promotion.

Behind the tables and out of reach of the people was Baba's chair. He would be visible for all the fans to see as he sat there to oversee everything. Once in awhile, he would talk to friends, or address issues which needed to be taken care of, but most of the time, he just made his presence there for all to see. He felt (and I agree) that his presence put his mark and reputation on the show. The people knew that if they saw Baba, they were going to get their money's worth. I didn't understand at first, but over time, I realized that his presence gave stability to All Japan, and it indicated a high standard that the people appreciated.

At almost every event, the company had a custom of providing a bento box for everyone involved in any part of the venture. The crew would take a short break before the show began to have this meal, and often, if the travel was long, they would also have one after the show. There must have been a whole business which catered to this type of need as I have seen it at the Nippon Budokan and other Japanese arenas.

I was in awe at how well-run and smoothly the whole operation ran. It was really something to see. I don't know what kind of money the ring crew made, but they sure worked hard. And, like most Japanese companies, they were very efficient at whatever job they did.

One night, I was working with Jody and Dean Malenko on the roof of a department store during a thunderstorm. The rain let up just enough to get in some of the matches. Often, when a show was in jeopardy of being canceled, they would "turn the show upside down," meaning the main event would take place first, followed by the semi-final, and so on down the card. That allowed the people to see the top matches, even if the weather turned for the worst, and kept the promoters from having to refund the show. On that particular night, we were in the third match from the top.

By the time we got into the ring, there were puddles of water on the mat. I immediately charged the Malenkos, picked up Jody, and body slammed him. Jody hit the mat and skidded out under the ropes to the floor. I then slammed the other one and he slid out, too. The slick mat was dangerous, but we still went at it. Later in the match, I picked up Jody outside the ring with the intention of slamming him on the floor in a puddle of water. He turned in midair and landed on his hands and feet. I laughed under my breath. That took a lot of coordination.

Like their dad, who wrestled as the Great Malenko, Dean and Jody were good people. I gave them a hard time when they came to All Japan, although it was all in good fun. They wore matching warm-up clothes. Since they were short (compared to most wrestlers) and well built, I would kid them about looking like a trapeze team from the circus. When they went to the ring, I would sing the tune for circus attractions.

Jody was the real deal. He was a former amateur wrestler who learned to shoot under the tutelage of Karl Gotch. We talked at length about how hard and dedicated he had to be when he trained under Gotch. His training took so much of his time that he missed out on a lot of high school functions. Even so, he is well-educated and eventually moved on from wrestling into private business as a pharmacist who works for drug research companies and other businesses. He was and is one of the smartest guys I ever knew in the business.

Most of the time, when I worked with them, due to the hierarchy of Japanese wrestling, I went out and ate them up. Of course, they went along with it, but it bothered Jody. There is no doubt in my mind whatsoever that I couldn't have laid a finger on Jody if he hadn't allowed it. He was that good. We got along great, though. We keep in touch and we laugh about those matches and days.

Tenryu once told me that on some of the shows when it was cold or rainy, the Japanese wrestlers would just groan when they realized they were working with me or my team. They wanted to take it easy, but they knew I wouldn't allow it. I took pride on giving it my all, regardless of how small the crowd or bad the venue. I was told the wrestling press often wrote about that fact. No matter how begrudging the Japanese wrestlers were when we met in the ring, I usually got them fired up. More often than not, it made them mad, but that in itself made for a good match.

"This bus was used as a dressing room at an outdoor show. Blue tarp walls, all set up by the ring crew, enclosed the show. It was hard work."

Stan Hansen merchandise

Chapter 23

Silent Heat

In the early morning of December 17, 1987, around one-thirty in the morning, I heard what sounded like a loud crash of dishes breaking, and then I heard my dad call my name. I had returned from a tour just a few days before. My mom and dad lived in an apartment I had built onto my house. It had one bedroom, a kitchen, living room, and bath. When I looked through the window of their front door, I saw a wall of fire. I had seen public service commercials about not opening doors or touching the door knobs of a house that was on fire. Even so, I slowly reached for the knob, but decided against touching it. I got in through a common door which connected our house to their apartment. My mom had suffered a stroke several years earlier, so I hurried into the bedroom to help my dad get her into her wheelchair. As we did, the ceiling began to fall in. Luckily, there was a back door leading from their bedroom, so we pushed her through it. I then ran back to our part of the house and woke up my wife, who was nine months pregnant at the time. I woke her up, and then proceeded to get John and Paige out of their beds. By the time I herded them out the back door and into the yard, the smoke hung down about five feet from the ceiling throughout the house, and flames were reaching up through the roof.

It probably wasn't the wisest decision I ever made, but I went back into the house and crawled to my office to call 911. I was surprised when the operator didn't answer. I was later told that one of our neighbors had woken up and was talking to them. As we walked around the house to the front yard where I had an old Ford Ranchero parked, we could see that the apartment, along with two cars which were in the carport, was engulfed in flames. We got out wearing our underwear and carrying a few blankets, and at twenty degrees Fahrenheit, it was the coldest night of the year in Jackson, Mississippi. However, we were thankful that we all survived with no injuries. Later that evening, while we were at a hotel, my wife went into premature labor. Twenty four hours later, on December 19, she gave birth to my son Shaver.

A television crew later came out and interviewed me about the fire. Not because I was Stan Hansen, but because we had survived a fire. Apparently, there were two other fires in the area that night and somebody had died in both of them. At first, I thought the fire might have been set by a renter I had evicted some days previously. However, after an investigation by the fire department, it was determined that the fire was started by an automobile drop light we had put into a dog house to keep our dog warm. The cord had shorted out.

The house was pretty much a total loss. However, I had a great insurance policy, which paid to rebuild the house and replace almost everything. I lost some personal possessions, but I was able to recover many of them, thanks to the brick wall which separated the apartment from the main house. My parents' apartment burned to the ground, so they lost everything.

Seven months later, I was in the Pacific Hotel in Shinigawa when my telephone rang. It was the middle of the night and Terry Gordy was at the other end of the line. He said his wife had just called and told him that Brody was dead. "*I just heard Frank was stabbed in Puerto Rico. He's dead, Stan.*" I was stunned, but in some strange way, I wasn't too surprised.

This is going to be the hardest chapter for me to write. For a long time, I didn't talk about Brody's death at all because of the sadness it brings to me. However, it is a big part of my past and it will do me good to get it out.

Brody and I had been going to Puerto Rico for a number of years. We worked in Japan almost full time and neither the WWF nor WCW would use us on our off dates due to our commitment to Japan. Puerto Rico gave us a place to go and team up together outside Japan. We liked that because it was a place where our style was not only accepted, but it was a necessity for survival. It was a good place for wrestlers to go and make money. The weather was nice, the beaches were great, and the trips were short. But the most attractive thing about Puerto Rico was a new group of opponents with whom we could work our style. In Puerto Rico, the wrestling was as violent as it was anywhere in the world. Long before Atsushi Onita and ECW developed the so-called "hard-core" style of wrestling, it was thriving on the islands of the Caribbean. Brody and I had a hard time working in the States, where the offices (and most of the talent) wanted control over us and our matches. We didn't like to work under anybody else's rules. Japan and Puerto Rico both gave us the independence to go out and take "our" match to our opponents for our fans. We worked the stiff style for which we were known.

The promoter was Carlos Colón, a native Puerto Rican. He was really over with the people on the island. He also was a great opponent for us. He was solid and laid everything in, and he never complained when we gave him the same.

If you were a heel in Puerto Rico, you literally took your life in your hands whenever you went to the ring. I've handled heat in the States, so I was used to it, but Puerto Rico is a step above when it comes to fan violence. We never knew when we were going to get hit with a rock, or stabbed on the way to the ring. We had to be conscious of everything going on around us at all times. We worked in a lot of baseball stadiums, but we couldn't sit in the dugout to watch the matches because young kids would use slingshots to fire rocks at us. When we left the buildings, there was usually a crowd of ill-tempered fans that would pelt us with rocks and anything they could get their hands on. Believe it or not, there were even vendors who sold rocks to the fans as they made their way into the venues.

Puerto Rico was *not* an enjoyable place to work, but there was a lot of potential for doing good business and making big money.

Abdullah the Butcher, who had been working in and out of Puerto Rico for a long time, ended up being a tag-team partner with Carlos after spending many years as his opponent. In 1984, they teamed together against Brody and me and we drew more than 25,000 fans to each of two stadium shows. I was told they were the biggest gates in the history of Puerto Rico to that time. We sold out many other arenas around the island, including some large baseball stadiums. The Butcher and Carlos were a hot team, and the people believed they were the only team capable of standing against us. We had violent and bloody matches that the fans really loved.

The fact that we didn't act afraid of the fans and their acts of violence was what separated Brody and me from most other wrestlers. If we saw a fan throw something, or if a fan came at us in a threatening way, we would go after them. Neither Brody nor I really wanted to do that, but we knew if we showed fear, or even hesitated, they would take it as weakness and attack us.

Puerto Rico:
Stan vs Abdullah the Butcher

I never tried to play to the fans too much. I always thought it was more logical to be focused on my opponent, and I believe the fans felt that way, too. I did do a few things that played to the fans, like hold up my arm and adjusting my lariat before using it. However, that was a habit from Japan where it got a big reaction. I just never focused on specific fans. My emphasis was always on the match and my opponent.

There was a fine line when it came to retaliating against fans who hit us. Most of the time, if someone took a soft shot at me, I tried to ignore it. However, in some cases, that could be interpreted as backing down, or being afraid to fight back, which emboldened them even more. If a fan hit me hard, I would hit them back, or give them a good, hard shove in the chest. Most of the time, it wasn't anything I had to think about doing. It just came as a reflex action.

Brody and I would watch each other's back for people who might attack us, or even for somebody who might throw something. We had to dodge bottles, spark plugs, chairs, needle-pointed darts, and even knives that were thrown into the ring.

When our match was over and it was time to return to the dressing room, I would jump out of the ring and onto the floor where a mass of people stood, threatening us. Brody and I learned that if we stayed in the ring too long, the people would think we were scared of them, and that would make them more likely to come after us. If the people seemed to be too out of control, we would wait to see if the security guards were going to do their jobs and help us get out. There were many times when the guards were too scared to come out to help us. In those cases, we just had to go out and take a chance on making it back to the dressing room on our own. That usually meant fighting, kicking, and attacking the fans who seemed to be determined to hurt us. It's no exaggeration when I say it was wild and dangerous, but it was the only option we had.

There was more than one occasion when a guard walked up to me and said, "*You've got "balls."* One time, when I asked the guard why he said that, he said, "*Didn't you see that guy with the knife? You walked right by him.*"

I'd like to say I was just brave, but, of course, I wasn't. Again, my eyesight is so bad that I couldn't see the knife. There were times when I did see them, but I'm sure there were many more that I didn't see. Regardless, no matter what the situation, we had to rely on our own nerves and courage to get us back to the dressing room. Of course, having Brody as a partner was as good as it got. He was like me. Unlike our ring characters, we weren't the bravest guys, but we knew we had to take care of ourselves physically, and we did.

We often had to go after the fans, and at times, we went into the crowd after them, hoping they would break and run as we chased them. The fans believed we were crazy, and it was important to keep them believing that, so we were forced to stand tall without wavering when we were confronted with danger. I have to admit, however, that we were often scared. At times, though, being scared sometimes made us do what we had to do. It worked for us.

I wrestled Carlos at a baseball stadium show. While the ring announcer was introducing us, a knife with about a 10-inch blade flew from the grandstands and the point buried itself in the center of the ring. If it had hit either one of us, it would have buried itself to the hilt. Carlos and I turned our heads to look at each other. Simultaneously, we grabbed hold of each other, fell down to the mat in a heap, and began rolling around the ring. The fans thought each of us was trying to wrestle and get the advantage, but in reality, each of us was trying to pull the other one on top of himself to protect himself from another knife or thrown object.

Puerto Rico:
Stan vs Carlos Colon

Another time, in a small, sold-out house show, I was standing in the back watching Brody fight Abdullah. The office had put a "manager" with Brody. He was supposed to help Brody if he got into trouble. The manager was supposed to stay at ringside, but on this night, the fans seemed to be so worked up and violent that he stayed back at the dressing room door.

When the Butcher pushed Brody's back onto the ropes, a fan ran out of the stands and grabbed Brody's hair from behind. With Abdullah's weight mashing Brody against the ropes, and a fan holding his hair so his head could not move, Brody was in a dangerous position. His "manager" froze. I could see it. In old wrestling terms, that's called "chilling." He was just too scared to go out and help Brody. When I read that in his face, I sprinted out of the dressing room. By that time, the aisle was completely full of fans and they stood twenty deep on all four sides of the ring.

On this show, the only seats available were in the bleachers. There were no ringside seats because the security guards couldn't control the crowd if they were that close to the ring. The fans, however, left the bleacher seats and came down to ringside, where they overwhelmed the security guards who were there to protect the heels and keep order. As I sprinted to the ring, the fans had their backs to me, so they didn't know I was coming. I either bowled them down or parted them like a boat going through water. By the time I clawed my way to the ring, Brody had broken loose from the guy who held his hair. We turned together, threw up our arms, and side by side, we ran back through the crowd. We had the surprise element on them. When they saw us coming, they broke, ran, and scrambled to get out of our way. They were in "herd" mentality, which means everyone was looking out for themselves. It was the surprise, and resulting fear, that got us out safely that night.

In another town, I was wrestling Carlos Colón in a singles match. After the match, I slowly moved back towards the dressing room. A number of fans threw spark plugs at me. They were firing their "missiles" from about 30 feet away. I picked up a metal folding chair and held it in front of my face and body, deflecting the spark plugs. They were being thrown so hard that I could see dents appear on "my side" of the chair. I knew then that they were really trying to kill me. I picked my spot and threw the chair sideways at the feet of the fans. They all went down into a pile of bodies as the chair knocked their legs out from under them. I didn't care if they were injured or not. It was survival. They had been trying to seriously hurt or kill me.

One of the buildings in which we wrestled had a shower with the walls open at the top. Since it was in the tropics, the weather is warm all the time, so the buildings were open-aired but always enclosed by chain link fences. The fans would climb up onto the fence which surrounded the building and stand high over the shower. After our match, when we went in to take a shower, they would look down at us, and often, if we weren't paying attention, they would urinate down on us.

There were a couple of times when Brody and I were coming back to a town where we had wrestled before. The police would come in and say some nut had threatened to kill us at the matches that night. I can remember telling Brody that if anything happened to me, I wanted him to tell my family that I loved them, and to explain the details of what happened. It sounds a little corny to write this, but that's exactly the way it was. There were times when we were scared like that, but we knew we had to go out and do our job. That was real heat. People really wanted to do harm to us ... and all over a wrestling match.

One time, Roddy Piper was wrestling a local favorite in Trinidad. He had the wrestler on the ropes and was kicking and beating him. The security guards surrounded the ring to hold back any fans who might try to get into the ring. All of a sudden, the captain of the guards jumped into the ring and pulled out his gun. He put it to Piper's chest and said he would shoot if Piper didn't stop. Of course, Piper stopped.

I wrestled Tony Atlas in a small-town, high school gym in Georgia. Tony's fans, about 95 percent of them black, were packed to the rafters. Tony and I had been working around the territory and they came to see him get his revenge. There were no ringside seats and the ring was set up in the middle of the basketball court. As I stood in the ring, waiting for Tony to come out of the dressing room, a fan ran out onto the court and began running around the ring, yelling and swearing at me. All of a sudden, he jumped up on the ring apron.

In the world of professional wrestling, the ring is the private territory of the wrestlers. The fans should not touch or try to get into the ring. If we let one person get in, then everyone else would want to try to get in, too. When I saw the guy jump up onto the apron, which meant he was just one step away from getting into the ring, I charged him and gave him a hard shove. He fell off the apron and onto his butt, sliding backwards a few feet on the shiny gym floor. Until the guy appeared, the fans were all yelling and getting worked up about the upcoming match, and this guy just excited them more. When he hit the floor, the whole gym got deadly quiet. There wasn't a sound to be heard! It went from a loud roar to silence in one second, as if someone had flipped a switch. Not a sound!

Tony Atlas

The guy jumped up and cussed me even more, and all the time, he was running faster and faster around the ring. He finally threatened me, yelling, "*I'm going to kill you, you son-of-a-bitch!*" He was yelling other thing, too. As he raced around the outside of the ring on the floor, I kept my eye on him and followed him around the ropes inside the ring. I could read the rage, so I took him seriously as he continued to threaten me verbally and make gestures at me. The whole time, the people remained absolutely quiet.

I was wondering where Tony was and when he was going to come to the ring. When he finally came out of the dressing room, he got no reaction whatsoever. The people sat stock still and didn't utter a sound as he walked to the ring with the referee. The guy on the floor continued to run around the ring as I shifted my eyes back and forth from him to Tony. When Tony stepped through the ropes and into the ring, the silence continued. I charged at him and said, "*Kick my ass!*"

He began kicking and hitting me, while I made motions as if I was trying to defend myself, but I just let him go after me. Tony Atlas was the audience's favorite wrestler, and he was kicking me around the ring ... and there was absolutely no reaction whatsoever. That went on for three to four minutes, which is a long time to just take a beating. It especially seemed like a long time because there was absolutely no noise in the building except for Tony's and my breathing.

What we were experiencing was what we called "silent heat," which is the most serious heat a wrestler can get. I had heard about it, but I had never experienced it before that night. Silent heat doesn't happen very often, but when a heel does something that really angers the crowd, like I did when I attacked the fan, the people get serious and divorce themselves from the atmosphere of the wrestling matches. It was eerie and was something I will never forget.

Eventually, the people began to get into the match and they reacted to what Tony was doing. However, the reaction was slow to build and it took quite a while before the majority of the fans got into the match. When the match ended in my disqualification, I scooted out of the ring and went to the dressing room.

In less than a minute after I got to the back, a couple of plainclothes policemen told me I should dress fast and they would escort me out of town. They told me the guy I had pushed off the ring apron had just been released from the state prison the week before. He had served five years for murder and they took his threat seriously. Needless to say, I did, too.

Brody and I had never experienced silent heat, but we were no strangers to serious heat and death threats. We knew it wasn't unusual for that type of violence to happen in the Caribbean, so we were always cautious. We kept our eyes on everyone that was yelling or making gestures, and we specifically watched their hands. We *always* watched the hands because that is where people will have something which could hurt us.

The last time I worked in Puerto Rico was in 1987. Carlos brought me down for a big show and put me in the final match of the evening. It wasn't the main event, but it was the match which would keep the people there to the end. As I left the ring and turned towards the dugout, I saw a fan standing about 35 feet away. I realized he was going to throw something at me, but I had no time to react and move. What he threw was a rock which had been wrapped up in a Coke cup. It hit me in the fat part of my cheek, stunning me and dropping me to my knees. I stood up and tried to go after the guy, but the security guards had already grabbed him and were taking him out of the stadium. I walked back to the dugout and dressing room on wobbly legs. The rock had hit me in the perfect spot of my cheek. If it had landed just a little bit higher, it would have broken my upper teeth. If it had landed a little lower, my bottom teeth would have been smashed. To the left, my cheekbone would have been crushed. I got to the dressing room with nothing more than a big horseshoe-shaped bruise on my cheek. The bruise was visible for three weeks. That was when I decided I would not return to Puerto Rico. I wasn't going to risk my life for a few extra dollars. By that time, I was working every tour in Japan and it was just not worth it.

When Brody went to work for New Japan in March 1985, he also began to work more often in Puerto Rico. When he had his falling out with Inoki in December of that year and left the promotion without giving notice, he wrestled in Puerto Rico a lot. He eventually became a babyface and his character became very popular.

Brody couldn't find work in Japan again until October 1987, when Baba needed a strong draw to replace Ric Flair, who was pulled from the tour at the last minute. One month later, Baba brought in Abdullah, who had jumped to New Japan in July 1981. I was glad to see them return. They had both sent word to the All Japan office many times, requesting a meeting with Baba to discuss the possibilities of being brought back. I remember thinking that bringing Brody back would make for all sorts of potential programs between us. It was exciting to think of the business that could be done. That wasn't going to happen, however, until Baba was ready for it to happen. He was not in a big hurry. When Brody did return, he was very thankful to Baba for giving him his spot. He was looking forward to working with me in whatever programs the office had planned. I really think the time Brody spent on the independent market, and being unsure of when he was going to have work from one week to the next, humbled him somewhat. At least, it seemed to be that way in Japan.

As for the Butcher, he was and is a unique character. He was an icon and definitely had some value. He tried to come back in a top position, but I think Baba's plan was to keep him in a supporting role. Abdullah worked hard, but he had passed the point of being a regular main eventer in the business. As time went by, he got over as a babyface due to his history and character. He wasn't over as a babyface in the sense of Jumbo, Tenryu, or Misawa, but as a character, like Rusher Kimura. The style of wrestling in Japan had also changed to more of my style, and physically, he just couldn't do it. I really respected Abdullah. He handled his business and marketed himself as well as anyone could. He kept himself strong in the independent market in the States and continued to go to Puerto Rico. However, like me, his love was for Japan. He had many sponsors who catered to him and he knew how to milk Yen out of a tour. I enjoyed being around him.

On November 22, 1987, Brody and I worked *against* each other for the first time ... in a tag match. Terry Gordy was my partner and Brody teamed up with Jimmy Snuka. In time, I believe Brody and I could have had a very interesting rivalry, although I have trouble thinking about working against him. In my mind, Bruiser Brody will always be my partner.

While I was in Atlanta making a movie called *No Holds Barred* with Hulk Hogan, Brody called me at the hotel where I was staying. He told me he had been talking to a promoter about working in Germany and wondered if I knew anything about them. He also asked my opinion on some other things. He told me he was still going back and forth to Puerto Rico and that he had a good position there. He also told me he was so happy to be back with Baba and that he was looking forward to reestablishing himself in Japan. We had a nice talk and I was glad he had taken the time to track me down to ask my advice. We talked for quite some time and closed by saying we would see each other in Japan later in the year.

That was the last time we talked.

I really don't have anything to add in regards to what took place on the night Brody was stabbed, and I don't think anybody will ever know exactly what happened in Puerto Rico on the night of July 16, 1988. All I know for sure is that he was stabbed a number of times and left to bleed in the dressing room for more than an hour before an ambulance arrived. Only a few people will admit to having seen the incident, and many of those who did seem to be scared for their lives. That's a shame, but that's the way it is in some parts of the Caribbean.

When Gordy called with the news about Brody's death, I called his house to talk with his wife Barbara, but whoever it was who answered the phone didn't seem to know anything about what was going on. Barbara had already flown down to Puerto Rico. Alone in a hostile country, she went to the authorities and tried to get some details on what happened, but there were no witnesses still on the island who were willing to talk. She also had to undergo the pain of identifying the body and making all the arrangements for Frank's cremation.

Everybody in Japan was stunned by the news of his passing. Regardless of the differences he had with Baba, he was over in a big way with the office, and even more so with the fans. And, sad to say, he was elevated even more in death than he was in life.

On August 29, 1988, as a tribute to Frank, All Japan held a "Bruiser Brody Memorial Night" at the Budokan. During the program, Barbara presented me with Brody's chain. The Butcher wanted to use the chain in an angle, but I didn't like the idea. I returned the chain to Barbara and told her to keep it. I didn't have any use for it and I wanted to keep it out of all the bullshit that some people wanted to make of it. I do think Brody would have laughed at the ideas some people were making of his chain pertaining to business. Professional wrestling can be a cold world.

I have witnessed the untimely passing of many other close friends during the past twenty years.

Terry Gordy. What a great guy … just a great guy. I felt so much for his wife and family. He was really a nice guy and he had a great heart.

Gary Albright. He could be a little moody when his sugar diabetes hit him, but at heart, he was a good guy. He knew I loved blues music, so he gave me a number of his albums and got me hooked on Stevie Ray Vaughn.

Bobby Duncum Jr. was almost like a son to me. I knew his father very well and I was close to him over the years. I remember Bobby Jr. when he was a high school kid living in Minneapolis. I wish Bobby had never left Japan, but he returned to the States to chase his "Big-Time Wrestling" dream. Once there, there seemed to be nobody who could hold him back in his life style. I sometimes wonder if there was anything I could have done to help him stay in Japan, but like so many others, he wanted to try to make it big in the States. I can understand that, but it's a shame things turned out as they did.

Jumbo Tsuruta. I was at the Budokan when All Japan held a memorial for him. I met with his wife and three sons in private. It was a moving moment for all of us.

None of those deaths, however, affected me as deeply as Brody's.

Almost twenty-three years have gone by since Frank passed away, but I think of him almost every day. He was a true friend in a business in which real friends are hard to come by. We didn't always see eye to eye on things, but we were connected in spirit and friendship. I sure do miss him.

Bruiser Brody

wRESTle In Peace
Frank "Bruiser Brody" Goodish
June 18, 1946 — July 17, 1988

Photos at right: Nagano, Japan: July 27, 1988
Stan beat Genichiro Tenryu to win the PWF world and NWA United National titles.
Bruiser Brody died July 17, 1988, so photos were displayed at all shows during the tour.

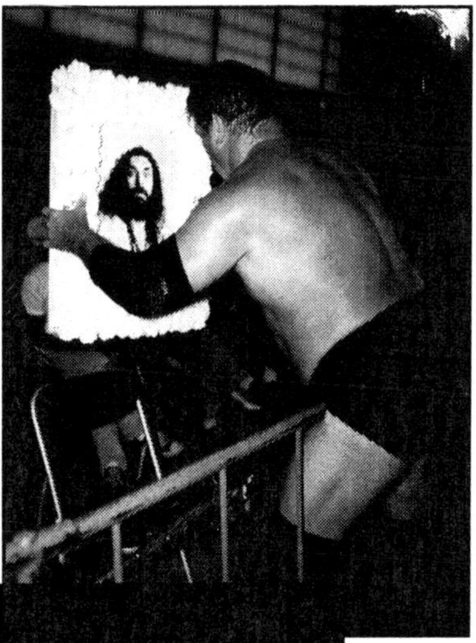

Chapter 24
Veteran Gunslingers

As far as tag-team partners go, Brody stands alone, but I participated in tag-team matches with a variety of partners after he left for New Japan. The ones I consider to be regular partners include Ted DiBiase, Terry Gordy, Danny Spivey, Genichiro Tenryu, Johnny Ace, and Gary Albright. Ole Anderson would be included as a regular partner, but that was only in the States. I had other partners, but I didn't consider them partners in a tag-team sense. They were just wrestlers who teamed with me for matches which really didn't have any real meaning.

My tag-team partners learned to just not ask me what I was going to do at the beginning of a match. For the most part, I didn't know what I would do until I was in the ring. I always played things by ear and tried to keep the fans guessing. I wouldn't discuss who was going to start the match, either. There were nights when we would agree that my partner would start the match, but when we got into the ring, I might decide to start it myself. I suppose some might say I was selfish, but I think it was more important to keep the wrestling fans off balance and unsure of what I would do. In the same respect, my opponent had the option to "act and react" to what I did.

I can remember one time when the office asked me to hold off my attack until the ring announcer finished introducing the participants of the match. I wasn't too happy about that. Of course, there were times when I would let the announcer do what he was paid to do, but at other times, I wanted to get right to business. The office wanted to have more order to the matches, but I had never been one to follow order. That was part of what made me different from other wrestlers. I know I was wrong, but my character was so deeply ingrained within me that I did what I felt I had to do. I respected the fact that Baba and the office ran the business, but I felt that when it came to what went on inside the ring, nobody had the right to tell me what to do or how to do it. I felt at home in the ring. It was one place where I felt somewhat in control of myself.

It's a fact of life that we all get into the same rut or routine. We become familiar with a certain way of doing our jobs and we continue to do them that way. In some ways, that holds true for wrestling, but while a routine might work for a profession like teaching or carpentry, doing the same thing in the ring, night after night, isn't good for the business.

My partner in 1986 and the first half of 1987 was Ted DiBiase. I first met Teddy when he came to visit West Texas State as a high school senior. I was finishing my degree in teaching at the time and working as an assistant coach of the freshman team. He later attended West Texas State on a football scholarship. We didn't cross paths again until he was in the wrestling business, a product of the Funks' promotion. He had done well for himself in different parts of the country and several promoters considered him as a candidate for the NWA world heavyweight title.

I was still wrestling for New Japan when I noticed DiBiase again. When I could, I would watch All Japan's TV and he was on it a number of times, usually in the Funk's corner. I noticed that he was a very good worker. Of course, he had been trained by the Funks, and they were among the best in the wrestling business. Teddy was big and he moved well in the ring.

After I made the jump to All Japan in 1982, Teddy appeared on ten of the tours I was on. When Brody made his move to New Japan in 1985, Baba asked me to team with Teddy. The one hesitation I had with Teddy at first was that he was a babyface at heart. He was well-liked by the fans and it was going to be hard to change his image. He had been the young "Funk boy" for a long time. However, he was tired of the image, as well, and he wanted to establish his own identity. Brody's move had given him the opportunity to change the direction of his career, one which would set him out on his own personal road. However, being a fan favorite was somewhat hard to change.

Ted DiBiase

I told him that Baba had asked me to take him as a partner, but I was only willing to do that if he agreed to listen to me and do what I wanted him to do in the ring. He listened to everything I said and we got over as a team. It was a good fit. He was a good partner to me in so many ways. He was a good scientific wrestler in the Jumbo Tsuruta-Dory Funk Jr. style. Of course, my style was wild and uncontrolled, so our styles complimented one another. Many times, the most successful tag teams consist of two wrestlers who have different styles. Teddy would get into the ring and wrestle our opponents, and when the timing was right, I would tag in and take it to them physically.

I believe I helped establish Teddy's style and personality, at least in the beginning, but it wasn't long before I ran out of things to teach him. As time passed, he developed his own personality and adopted the attitude of an arrogant, egotistical heel.

Teddy and I got along really well. We both grew up in Texas, so we had a common background. He had also moved to Mississippi, where his wife grew up. I wanted to get out of the limelight, which was one of my reasons for moving to Mississippi. Teddy, on the other hand, liked to keep himself visible, so he became well known there. I had been there for several years, but not too many people knew I was living there because I kept a low profile. The good thing about working in Japan was the fact that when I came home to the States, there was absolutely no publicity surrounding me. I was able to keep my life quiet and private.

1985 • Ted DiBiase and Stan

Teddy and I had a lot of fun together doing the nightlife in Japan. One night, after we ate dinner, we began walking back to our hotel. Someone recognized us and invited us to a small club. There were just a few people there when we entered, but within an hour or so, the place was packed with customers. The music and talk was loud and everyone was in a good mood. Teddy and I enjoyed that scene because it was so typically Japanese. At one point, most of the people in the club began to dance. Teddy and I were reluctant to join in, but we finally agreed and stepped out onto the dance floor. We were dancing with 30 or more people. After a few minutes, we came to the realization that the only people dancing were men. Teddy and I looked at each other, and at the same time, reached over the bar and grabbed hold of the girl who was mixing drinks. We literally hauled her up and over the bar and onto the floor. We put her between us and began dancing with her. We weren't quite sure what was going on, but we didn't like the idea of people seeing us dancing with a bunch of guys. We felt much better to have a woman dancing with us.

That was Japan. It's hard to describe life in Japan to people who have never been there. Most of the time, we got along with everyone, and the people treated us like we were special. Being a wrestler had its special treats for us for a long time. I appreciate the Japanese people who treated me so well. They made my life in Japan so much better than it might have been.

1986 • Ted DiBiase and Stan

I think Teddy and I were successful as a team and we had many important matches during the eighteen months we were together. More importantly, Teddy established himself as a top competitor and one of the best gaijin talents ever to wrestle in Japan.

In 1987, Teddy got a call from Vince McMahon and was offered an opportunity to wrestle for the WWF. He was given the character of the Million Dollar Man. It was perfect for Teddy and he became very successful through his own efforts. I hated to see him go, but I'm glad he moved on and created his own destiny. I enjoyed tagging up with him and I hope I helped him on his way to becoming the wrestler he became. I know he helped fill the void when Brody left.

When Teddy left for New York, we were the PWF tag-team champions. I'm not sure why Baba didn't ask us to drop the title, but I chose Austin Idol to be my partner.

In October 1983, when I was working in Memphis between Japan tours, I worked with Austin in my last match in the territory. On that same night, Roughhouse [Sonny] Fargo came to the ring in the match before ours. Fargo made a cartoon out of his match and completely exposed the business. I was so angry. When Austin got into the ring, I was determined to prove to the fans that I wasn't a cartoon character, and that wrestling business was a serious undertaking, and not a vaudeville show. I chopped and beat Austin so badly that, after the match, he complained and got me fired. I suppose I should have been fired, but I was so upset because I had never seen anyone like Fargo expose the business like he did. I was too much into the Japanese mindset and style to accept it. Looking back on my actions, I was wrong to react as I did, but that was me.

I made it up to Idol by helping him get booked with All Japan in September 1987. Austin, however, was not a Japanese-style wrestler. He wrestled strictly the American style and wasn't into the hard-and-stiff physical style. That worked well for him in the States, but not in Japan. One month after we began teaming together, in our first and only title defense, we dropped the title to Genichiro Tenryu and Ashura Hara in Nagoya. During the tour, Austin "hurt" his ribs and wasn't able to work much. Somebody in the office told me they were "suspect" of his injured ribs because of his reluctance to do a job. That was a ploy that even some of the Japanese wrestlers used.

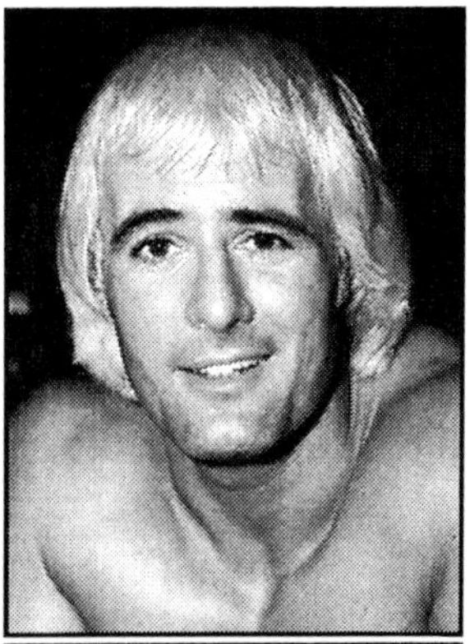
Austin Idol

While he was on the tour, Austin wore a new pair of tennis shoes called *Air Jordans* which had just come onto the market. As far as I was concerned, they were just another brand of tennis shoe named (I thought) after Jordan Airlines. That shows how much attention I paid to advertising. Austin told me they cost $100, which I thought was outrageous. When Austin got hurt, he was complaining about the pain and talking about how he might not live through it. The first thing I said to him was, "*Can I have you shoes if you die?*" That was the amount of sympathy a wrestler typically got. None.

At one time, Austin and I were pretty close. Our families got together quite often and we enjoyed each others' company. When the doctors found a tumor in my arm, I wasn't sure how things were going to turn out. He was a good friend to me during that time.

Austin Idol and I had previously worked together on a small independent show promoted by Johnny Hunter in Mocksville, North Carolina on November 8, 1986. There were no more than 25 to 30 people in the audience. With such a small crowd in attendance, I made sure I got paid before I went to the ring. As I sat in the dressing room and got dressed, the young wrestlers all circled around me and asked for my autograph. It was so funny. They were fans more than they were wrestlers.

When Idol and I wrestled, there wasn't a sound in the building other than the noise of our breathing. Not one sound. I did make a little noise when I chopped him, but other than that, the crowd was dead silent.

We made a double shot that weekend. More people were in attendance at the second show than there were at the first, but neither one had a very good turnout.

I heard the most successful show Johnny Hunter ever promoted was in his hometown. From what I understand, he died on February 4, 1989 ... at one of his shows. That's sad, but he loved the business so much, I believe that's the way he would have wanted it. He was a nice guy.

Another nice man who worked on the show in Mocksville was Rick Link. I booked him to Japan when Baba was looking for new (and cheap) talent. Rick's gimmick was eating raw chickens. That was what I call a real gimmick. Rick and I kept in touch for several years. I heard he became a preacher.

During the months of August through November 1987, I participated in several tag-team matches with partners like Dick Slater, El Medico [Carlos Jose Estrada], and Joel Deaton. For some reason, I don't have any memory of teaming with El Medico at all, and nothing of note sticks out in my mind about teaming with Slater and Deaton, other than the fact that I considered them to be really good talents.

On November 21, 1987, I began teaming with Terry Gordy on a regular basis. Aside from a brief period from August 25 until October 28, 1988, Gordy and I teamed up through July 1989.

Terry was a natural in this business. He could do it all and he was so believable. Pete Roberts and I both thought highly of Gordy's talent. Pete once said that Gordy was the guy who had the talent to take over when I was finished. Like Dick Slater, he was a natural talent with superstardom written all over him. He had size, the ability to move, youth, and most importantly, he understood the psychology of wrestling.

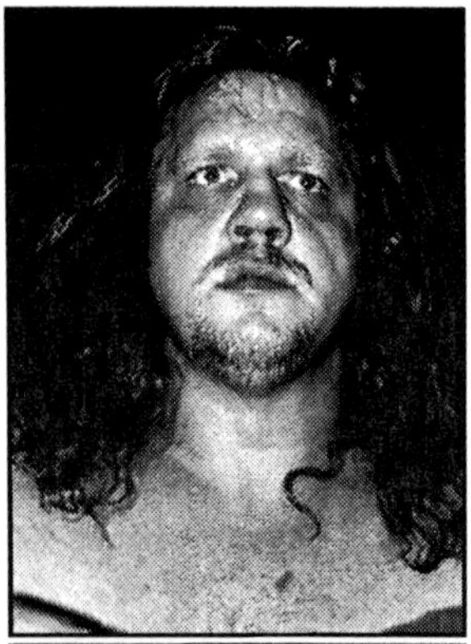
Terry Gordy

Gordy and I worked well as a team and the people believed in us. The one problem Gordy had was that he liked to drink too much. In the States, with Michael Hayes and Buddy Roberts, he had been a member of the tag team known as the Freebirds. The Birds had a reputation for living in the fast lane, and they promoted it. Their drinking and partying was legendary in the Dallas territory.

In Japan, Gordy and I enjoyed the nightlife together. I liked to go out and have a good time experiencing the nightlife. However, as I got older and matured, I knew when it was time for me to stop drinking. Gordy had a much harder time knowing when he had reached his limit. He could drink heavily without noticing any debilitating effects, but it was inevitable that he would eventually get drunk. I wouldn't say he was as wild with me as he was when he was with the Freebirds, but many times, he drank far beyond his capacity. The truth is, we all drank beyond our capacity, but I learned when I needed to stop. Many others did not.

I don't want anyone to think I'm judging him, because I'm not. When most of us were younger, we all tended to overdo it. I'll be the first to admit that I did. I drank more than my share of beer. However, I believe that as we grow older and mature, we learn to have a good time without overindulging. For some people, that's a harder lesson to learn than with other. It took me a long time, but I finally learned to stop short of getting plastered. It also was much more fun to enjoy the nightlife when I didn't overdo it, not to mention feeling better when I woke up the next morning, or when I was involved in a brutally hard match with Misawa, Kawada, or Kobashi.

Terry Gordy and Stan Hansen

I really believe part of the reason I changed was because I witnessed so many of the guys go too far in their indulgence. As Japan changed, they became stricter on gaijins. I watched several guys drink to the point of no return, and that made me think more about what I was doing. I realized how close I myself had been to stepping over the line and getting out of control. Often, it got to a point where I had to make a choice of whether or not to stay with my friends, or leave and return to my hotel room. I made it clear that if someone passed a certain point, I wouldn't stay around to get them out of trouble. Most didn't get that far every night, but when they did, I often left and got myself away from the situation. I figured I couldn't stop anyone from doing what they were hell-bent on doing. They were grown man who had to take responsibility for their own actions.

That was a pivotal point in my career. That was when I decided to not follow or get caught up in the crowd. I wasn't going to jeopardize my job for anyone.

Unfortunately, over the years, I watched several of the guys fall into the bottomless pit of self-indulgence, and most of them were good friends. It was a shame and a huge waste of talent. They just could not control their drinking, and that, mixed with prescription medication, led many to an untimely death. I really felt badly for them. Baba personally gave many of them numerous "second" chances. I think Baba had more tolerance of the gaijins than anyone else.

One time, Joe-san received a late-night phone call from employees of a family-type restaurant in Kanazawa, which was located about a block or two from the hotel. They said Gordy had gone to sleep in one of their booths and they couldn't wake him up. Joe-san had to go out around two in the morning. He walked into the restaurant, hoisted Gordy over his shoulders, and carried him back to his hotel room. That was quite a feat, especially considering the fact that Gordy weighed more than 300 pounds and Joe-san was more than 60 years old at the time. Joe-san complained about it the next morning while we were eating breakfast.

Most of the time, the guys who drank in moderation looked out after those who drank too much, but it's like the old saying, "You can lead a horse to water, but you can't make him drink." That is the way it was with some of the guys. We all tried to keep them on the right track, but ultimately, they just refused, or were unable, to change. That is one of the saddest stories in wrestling to me because many of the gaijins had immense talent that was curtailed when they were unable to change their lifestyles.

In 1990, All Japan began grooming Gordy to replace me in the top spot. That was a very good business decision on their part since Gordy was really over with the fans. When Steve Williams began touring Japan, he and Gordy were pushed as a second gaijin tag team. At the time, Dan Spivey and I were regularly teaming together. It was only natural that the office would program Spivey and me against Williams and Gordy. I was excited to have that competition between us because I knew it would be good for All Japan's business. However, since we were competitors in the ring, the four of us had to quit hanging out together. We still rode the same bus, but we quit doing anything together in public after work.

The first time I remember Gordy being involved in controversy involving All Japan business was in April 1990. All Japan Pro Wrestling, New Japan Pro Wrestling, and the WWF combined talent for a show at the Tokyo Egg Dome called "U.S. and Japan Wrestling Summit." The main event was supposed to feature Terry Gordy against Hulk Hogan. I wasn't even on the card.

The day before the show, Gordy decided he wasn't going to "do business" with Hogan. He knew he was in line for a top spot with the company, and he didn't think it would be a good career move. Finding himself in a tough spot without a top talent for Hogan, Baba called my home in Mississippi and asked my Dad if he knew how to get in touch with me. I was enjoying time off at my wife's house in Japan. Baba got the necessary information from my Dad and called me. He seemed to be more in shock over the fact that I had been married for more than three years without his knowledge than he was over the predicament with the big show. He explained that Terry had backed out and asked if I would take the spot. Baba said he was in a bad position since Gordy was one of his boys, and it made him look bad to both New Japan and the WWF. I was happy to take the match. We made a deal and I was happy to make the extra good payday.

The next day, which was the day before the show, we held a press conference at the Capitol Tokyu Hotel ballroom. I stood up and challenged Hogan. During our give and take, Gordy stood up and came up on stage. When I handed him the microphone, he just stood there looking at Hogan and me. I didn't say a word. I respected Terry and wanted to let him say what he wanted about the situation. Everybody was on edge, unsure of what he might do or say, but he didn't say anything. He simply stepped down and left the building, probably feeling a little embarrassed. When he was gone, Hogan and I got back to promoting the match. I was told that until that time, there were only a few thousand tickets sold, but they sold more than 30,000 the following day.

Hogan and I had a lot of history together, but we hadn't stayed in touch. He had gone on to become quite famous with the WWF. I'm happy things worked out for him. He worked for everything he got and wasn't given a free ride to the top. We talked a little that night, but we didn't discuss much other than our match. We had each moved on in our careers. I had won a match with Hogan many years earlier when I was with New Japan, so I had a feeling that this night was going to be my night to even the score. Baba thought we should have a clean match with no controversy. When Hogan took the fall on me, the fans thought they had seen a good, physical match with a definitive ending.

One of the reasons why Baba liked to deal with me was because I always had my ego in check. Baba had an ego, as well, but he always put his ego aside if it was good for business. The way I looked at it that night, I had won hundreds of times more than I lost. As far as I'm concerned, the people in Japan respected me because I worked hard, not because I was never (or seldom) beaten. Baba said the match needed to be clean and with no controversy. He wanted the fans to go home with a smile on their faces. That was the difference between Baba and the other promoters. For the sake of their egos, the others would rather present a match that stunk, or make the people mad. Baba just wanted people to get value and entertainment for the money they paid. He had the fans' interests at heart. That's why he was "Baba."

I never refused to do anything I was asked to do by Baba. If it was done the right way, and it was going to be good for business, then I wasn't going to argue. Regardless, it was Baba's company and Baba's decision, so I did what was asked of me. Baba, in turn, was smart enough to keep me over. The wrestling fans believed in me because the office put me over and kept me strong. The key to doing business was to have someone, preferably a heel, who was so strong that the people would die to see him get beat. I believe that's one of the reasons why All Japan did consistently good business over more than twenty years. When I lost to Jumbo and Tenryu, and later for Misawa, I did it the right way. Sometimes, you can tell when wrestlers aren't happy about doing something they are asked to do. I learned to control that attitude, rather than let it control me.

I do have to say that even with the three promotions all trying to get their talent over at the Summit, I didn't detect any tension behind the scenes. Everybody went about their business in a professional manner. When the matches were over, both Vince McMahon Jr. and Hogan came up and thanked me. Vince even sent me a little bonus later on, which I thought was a nice gesture on his part. He even said that if I ever wanted to leave Japan, to give him a call.

In the summer of 1990, the office called and requested a meeting with me in Nagoya. It was unusual for them to invite me out for dinner by myself. At the dinner, they asked me what I thought about Gordy. They wanted to know my honest opinion as they were grooming him to replace me as the top gaijin for the company. I was glad the office thought enough of me to ask my opinion, and to let me know that things were going to change. At the same time, Misawa was replacing Jumbo as the top Japanese wrestler. Jumbo had developed Hepatitis C and was unable to work a hard schedule or long matches. He basically just stepped back and turned over the reins to Misawa. It was sad because it happened at the time when Jumbo had just attained the top spot from Baba.

I assumed the plan was to work towards a program between Misawa and Gordy, a series of matches which would undeniably draw big business for the company, while Jumbo and I would be given the position of the "veteran gunslingers." I felt confident that Gordy was the one who could have taken the ball and run with it, so I answered them honestly. "In my opinion, Gordy is 'the' guy. He has great talent, and if anybody can get over, he can." A short time later, on July 17, 1990 in Kanazawa, I lost the AJPW Triple Crown heavyweight championship to Gordy. I had been wrestling in Japan for 13 years at that point, and that was my first clean loss in Japan to another gaijin.

Fate once again took an unexpected turn as, shortly after I dropped the title, Gordy's heart stopped beating at a night club in Roppongi. Fortunately, he was revived and didn't suffer any noticeable health problems. The plans for his career, however, were curtailed. Ten days later, on July 27, I took Gordy's place in a match with Misawa, with the winner of the match being crowned the new Triple Crown champion. I regained the title and was given another opportunity to keep my career going.

That type of situation happened several times over the years. Someone else's misfortune became my fortune. Each time someone found themselves in a position to take over my spot, they did something to postpone it. The same thing happened to Steve Williams. He got into some trouble and had to stay out of Japan for a year, right at a time when Baba was planning to give him a major push. Others in line for a push were lured away to WCW and the WWF with promises of big, guaranteed contracts. Unfortunately, for most of those who chose that route, things didn't work out as they hoped. The sad thing is that most of the guys who messed up never fully recovered their potential position. Fortunately for me, however, Baba always had the foresight to keep me strong and in a position where I could step up and take the ball when given the opportunity. When it was necessary, I was able to have programs with the younger Japanese guys. I had seen so many gaijins, who had an opportunity to stay and do business for many years, lose the opportunity because they could not control their lifestyles. I don't mean to sound opportunistic, but I watched some of them, and the results of their actions helped keep me focused on the fact that I was doing the right thing. I always kept in mind the reason why I was there: To make a living!

It seemed that Gordy lost his chance at the top spot, but Baba continued to push him, albeit in a lesser capacity. Steve Williams, who was a very good talent, had just come over and they were put together as a tag team. Gordy and Williams together made a great pair. I believe if they had been around when Brody and I were together, we could have had some great matches. Steve told me part of his job was to take care of Gordy when he went too far. Steve did that for a long time and extricated Terry from many dicey situations, but in the end, Steve couldn't stop Terry from doing what he wanted to do. Again, in the end, we are all responsible for our own actions.

Three years later, in 1993, Gordy passed out during a flight to Japan when they were about an hour from landing. When the plane landed, he was rushed to the hospital, where he lay in a coma for five days. Baba brought him back for 12 days in July 1994, but he was not the same Gordy who had been there before. Whatever caused Terry's problems had taken its toll because Gordy seemed to be a shell of what he had once been. Baba had no other choice other than to let him go. Gordy was only 32 years old at the time. I find that so sad because I believe Gordy would be the top gaijin in Japan today. There is a great lesson for everyone in Gordy's story.

Just eight years later, on July 16, 2001, Terry Gordy died of a heart attack caused by a blood clot. He was only 40 years old. He was a great talent, but most of all, to me, personally, he was a great friend. He was a nice guy and he loved his family so much. We were always talking about our kids and how lucky we both were to have a supportive wife at home.

Danny Spivey was a good friend and one of my favorite tag-team partners. He was big, strong, and he could move. We had a good run and we were together from March 1990 through the end of 1991. Baba put Spivey and I together during the time when I was teaming with Genichiro Tenryu. In regards to my matches in Japan against other gaijins, I think the matches Spivey and I had against Steve Williams and Terry Gordy were second only to the matches that Brody and I had against the Funks. The match I remember the most was the one we had in the Budokan during the finals of the Real World Tag League tournament on December 7, 1990. The action never let up and neither side gained the advantage for too long. Steve pinned me with just one second left to go in the thirty-minute match. It was one of those matches where we felt proud of ourselves for having given the fans our best.

Danny Spivey

In my opinion, Steve Williams was the strongest gaijin wrestler to wrestle in Japan. There were very few wrestlers who were stronger than Steve. He had both size and extreme power. He impressed me more than just about anybody else. I had some great matches with him over the years in both singles and tags. There are a few things Steve did that left me in awe. He could pick up his opponent and effortlessly carry or throw them across the ring. One night, when I rebounded off the ropes, went behind me, picked me up, and threw me into a spin. He controlled me as if I was a light pillow, turning me in midair and slamming me down onto my back. At the same time, he landed on his butt, adding his weight to the force which sent me to the mat. The thing that was so amazing about it was that he did it so effortlessly. Another time, he jumped off the top rope and hit me with a tackle in the center of the ring. That in itself wasn't so different, but he landed on his feet all the way out in the center of the ring. That takes great leg strength and agility.

Steve Williams

In his day, Williams was one the toughest guys in the business. We used to kid each other about our faces, which are covered with numerous scars and blemishes. We know what we look like and we never thought of ourselves as "pretty boys," unlike a lot of the wrestlers. We were and are proud of the fact that we are as we are. We never put on airs about our appearance. We knew that we were on the ugly side of the scale, but we didn't care. We accepted that and liked ourselves as we were.

A number of times, we would be wrestling around with each other, rolling around face to face, each trying to get the advantage. Our faces would be just inches away from each other. Our eyes would be slits due to the sweat running into them, and our hot breath was blowing into each others' face. One of us would say, "*Damn, you're pretty!*" Of course, we both knew we were pretty ... pretty ugly!

Steve never complained, either. I potatoed him with a chair a number of times, but he never took it personally. To him, it was just a part of the job. I also cut him open with my fist a few times. He had those heavy eyebrows which seem to split open easily. He used to say his wife and kids didn't like me because he would be all taped up over the eyes when he came home from a tour. They looked at me as someone who was beating up their husband or father. I knew how they felt. My family saw me come home all beaten up and sore from the punishment I took in the ring. That was a part of the business, though. When a wrestler is finished with a match in Sapporo or Tokyo, the fans go home and forget about most of it, remembering just a few of the things that stood out in their minds. We had to go home and allow our bodies to heal in the short amount of time we had before we had to hit the road again. The schedule in Japan was much harder than it was in the States. The wrestlers might work more dates in the States, but the matches in Japan are much more punishing and exhausting. I hope the wrestling fans in Japan appreciate how hard the wrestlers work there.

Between tours of Japan in 1991, Spivey and I came to the States and went to work for WCW. Due to backstage politics, he lost his job, and I have to claim partial responsibility for it happening. On June 22, 1991, we were scheduled to wrestle Tom Zenk and Rick Steiner in Chicago. The people in charge wanted Spivey to do the honors in the middle of the ring for Zenk. At the time, we were the world tag-team champions in Japan, so that wouldn't have been good business. I didn't think it was the right thing to do because there was no reasoning behind it. If they had an angle and long-term program in mind, then perhaps we might have done business, but that wasn't the case. It was my belief that they were testing him, to see how far they could push him. I suggested he not do the job. He didn't cave in to the pressure and told them he wouldn't do it. I admired and respected him for taking a stand. However, over the long run, taking that stand cost Danny some money. It kept us going to Japan for a while, but six months later [January 1992], we went our separate ways. I never was quite sure why that happened, but at the time, I thought he got a contract in the States and decided to go in that direction. I had seen so many guys lured away from Japan by lucrative contracts being handed out by both WWF and WCW. I don't know many guys who were happy for having made that choice in the long run.

I have a lot of respect for Spivey, both for his hard work and for being a good partner. However, I believe injuries held him back from his full potential. I would put him behind Brody and Gordy as my best partner in Japan and I really missed him when he left. He moved to Odessa, Florida, where he now lives and works for his family-run construction business.

When Spivey left, my next partner was Johnny Ace. I enjoyed teaming with Ace, and he was a good talent, but our styles just didn't mesh. Regardless of how hard he tried to be a heel, for all intents and purposes, he was a babyface. The first night we tagged together, he wore a black cape with a huge pink heart embroidered on the back. Before we left the dressing room, I looked at him and said, "*Wow! We really look like a team.*"

Johnny became a student of the Japanese wrestling business. He could do a lot of the Japanese high spots and had a great memory for remembering long, drawn-out finishes. That served him well because, by the time we were teaming, Japan was moving towards presenting long, planned-out, choreographed matches. I was against it, but that was the direction in which Misawa and the other young bucks wanted to go. That style worked for a while, but in the long run, it took the unpredictability out of the business and smartened up the fans. I believe that shift in attitude influenced Ace in a big way and became his modus operandi when he went to work for the WWE in 2001. Going to work for the WWE was good for Ace. He was a smart guy. Even when we were teaming, he frequently told me he was more geared to being an office guy, rather than an in-ring performer. I'm not saying he wasn't a talented wrestler, but rather, he was intelligent and used his talents in a creative capacity. I'm sure he put a lot of what he learned in Japan to use for the WWE. From what I understand, he was recently promoted to the position of executive vice president for the company.

Johnny Ace

When Ted DiBiase came back to Japan after his big run in New York, Baba wanted to put us back together. Ace was upset because he was having a good run and was getting a big push as my partner. He went to Baba, who told him not to worry, and then began pushing Ace as a single.

I spent most of 1993 and 1994 working as a single. In 1995, I teamed with a variety of partners, which included Johnny Smith, Dan Kroffat, Tommy Dreamer, Rob van Dam, Doug Furnas, Mitsuharu Misawa, and Bobby Duncum Jr. I had some important matches with both Bobby and Gary as my partners, but the matches with the others were pretty much throw-together matches.

Not to be confused with the original Dan Kroffat, who wrestled primarily in Calgary and Vancouver from 1969 through 1985, the "Dan Kroffat" I tagged with was Phil Lafond. Lafond was a big fan of the original Dan Kroffat and adopted his name when the original retired. Dan [Lafond] was underrated. I considered him to be a great worker, one of the best I've been around. He learned a great deal about wrestling from Bobby Jaggers, who I always considered to be a good ring general. Kroffat moved on to team in Japan with Doug Furnas. Calling themselves the Can-Am Connection, they had a good run in Japan.

I teamed with Baba quite a few times beginning in 1993. We worked hard together and the people really got with us. When we teamed up in the Real World Tag League tournament in 1994, I thought the people would love to see us win the tournament, but Baba was smart and Misawa and Kobashi won the tournament. That was another prime example of Baba having his ego under control. Before the match, Mrs. Baba told me he was really "*inspired and excited*" by the reaction we received from the fans about us being together.

It revitalized him one last time to have a series of matches that the people could really get into. The Japanese didn't take it easy on him, either. He bumped hard and took a beating, which must have been a physical nightmare to him, but he never complained. I never stopped doing my style, and that was a part of what made our combination so good. The noise when the people would chant "*Baba! Baba! Baba!*" was almost deafening. During thirty-minute broadways, he really sold for our opponents, and that provided the fans with some really exciting matches.

Rob Van Dam was a good talent and could do the great moves that the junior heavyweights like to do. However, I often thought that over time, he began to rely too heavily on premeditated moves and routines. His matches looked too much like two wrestlers "working together" to be considered logical. That's just my opinion because the fans, as well as the Japanese wrestlers, enjoyed his style. When I saw him in Japan a few years ago, I told him I had heard that he had done well in Extreme Championship Wrestling [ECW] and congratulated him. He let me know that he "sure was making a lot more money now" than he did for All Japan. I thought that was an odd thing to say, but good for him. If he had bad feelings for the time he spent in Japan, he must have forgotten that was where he learned his style and developed into the "star" that he is now. I do hope he appreciates all the top talent who worked with him when he was green.

In May 1995, I hooked up with Bobby Duncum Jr. In many ways, Bobby was like a son to me. I had never seen anyone in the business — anyone — who was so quick-footed and willing to learn. Bobby was one of those no-fear type of guys. He just didn't show fear at all. He told me about a number of fights he had at school in Austin, Texas, and how much he enjoyed it. But while he might have lacked guidance in his personal life, in the ring, he would (and could) do anything and everything that anyone asked of him. As I said, he was like a son to me and I took him under my wing in Japan. We tagged up together when I was on the back side of my physical ability, so he was a perfect fit for me at the time. For such a young man, Bobby had a lot of injuries, many of which he got when he played football for the University of Texas. He never complained, but it was obvious he was in pain all the time. He had to take pain pills just to be able to get into the ring to wrestle. He was surrounded by people in Japan who looked out for him, but I don't know about his situation in the States. In the end, it is the responsibility of the individual to take care of himself.

The last time I talked to Bobby was early January 2000. He was very depressed over the many personal and physical problems he was facing. He also mentioned that Gary Albright's passing had really upset him. As I listened, I became worried. When we ended our conversation, I told him to be careful, and that in time, things would get better. A couple of weeks later, as I was boarding a plane to fly to Japan, I heard he had passed away. Bobby was recovering from reconstructive rotator cuff surgery when he died on January 24, 2000 from an accidental overdose of a prescription pain killer. He was only 34 years old at the time of his death. If he had been given time, he could have been a top talent.

Finally, one of the most powerful and strongest wrestlers I had the pleasure to team with was Gary Albright. Gary was a legitimate wrestler who used his amateur background in the ring. As an amateur wrestler, when he was the

Montana state heavyweight champion, he compiled a record of 55 wins and two losses. He went on to wrestle for the University of Nebraska. During the 1985-1986 season, he scored the Nebraska state record for scoring the most falls in one season: thirty six. He was a three-time All American and a two-time Big Eight champion. He wrestled in the U.S. freestyle nationals (which he won in 1982), the U.S. Greco-Roman nationals, the AAU freestyle nationals, and the NCAA championships. As a professional, the wrestling fans bought and believed everything he did.

Gary Albright

I witnessed a close encounter between Gary and Bobby Duncum in Japan one time. We had arrived at a hotel after a long six-hour bus trip. Everybody was tired and in an irritable mood. As we got off the bus and piled into the lobby of the hotel to check in, there was a commotion outside by the bus. It seems someone had taken one of Gary's shoes. Gary was a diabetic, and when his blood sugar got low, he became very moody. Bobby and Gary had been hanging out together at night, so I guess Bobby had taken his shoe as a joke. Gary was really hot and limped into the lobby wearing just one shoe, pulling his luggage behind him. He was in the worst of moods. Most of us were at the check-in desk and we didn't know what was happening. Gary was complaining loudly. About that time, the sliding door of the hotel opened and a shoe flew in across the lobby. It was Gary's. A few seconds later, Bobby walked in with his bags. When Gary saw him, he assumed Bobby had taken his shoe and unloaded on him verbally. Bobby stood nose to nose with Gary. He didn't yell back, but he stood his ground and refused to back down.

Not only did Gary know how to handle himself, he also was one big man. He weighed every bit of 315 pounds. Everyone but Bobby knew that when Gary got into one of his diabetic mood swings, they needed to steer clear and give him his space. They finally gave it up and went on to their rooms, with Gary and a couple of other guys getting to the elevator first. I followed with Bobby later. As we walked onto the elevator, Bobby said in a low voice, "*If he wants to fight, I'll fight. I ain't scared of him one bit.*" I told him to not take it personally and to just forget about it, but as we stepped off the elevator, Gary was walking the hall to his room. The two of them stared at each other and Bobby began muttering to me again. Nothing came of it and we all went to our rooms.

Later, I went downstairs and overheard Bobby telling someone else that he wasn't afraid to fight Gary and he was going to tell him that to his face. I just couldn't believe that after more than an hour, he was still thinking about it. That was Bobby, though, and that was Gary.

I liked to think of Gary as a gentle giant. He was big, strong, and he looked tough, but he was a nice man. When Gary learned I liked blues music, he gave me a number of Eric Clapton and Stevie Ray Vaughan albums. Sadly, as was too often the case, Gary died much too soon. On January 7, 2000, he collapsed in the ring during a match in Hazleton, Pennsylvania and died of a heart attack. He was 36 years old and passed away just seventeen days before Bobby Duncum Jr. God bless his soul.

Chapter 25

"Get 'em, daddy!"

In August 1990, Ole Anderson brought me to Atlanta to work for World Championship Wrestling [WCW]. Before I agreed to go in, I told Ole that Japan would always have precedence over WCW. He said we could work around my schedule, but that I might have to commit quite a bit of my off-time in the States. My wife was expecting our second son and I knew that if I was to have one last run in the States, this would probably be my last opportunity. Ole got me $500 a shot, transportation expenses, and a rental car. I knew that several of the boys had huge guaranteed contracts, but in my mind, $500 was a good payday, especially if it would allow me to continue to work Japan.

The company treated me pretty well. I worked a limited schedule and they worked around my Japan tours. They paid me a guarantee, took care of the expense of my rental car, and flew me in and out of Jackson, Mississippi, where I was living at the time.

Most of the talent with WCW wanted to look the same: sleek, muscular, and pretty. In some respect, even the heels wanted to be looked upon as being good-looking or cool. I wanted to be different. I wanted to be the most ugly, nasty-looking heel the fans had ever seen, or what I viewed as a "real heel." I didn't want the "heel fans" to cheer for me. Many of the other heels wanted that kind of attention, and the office seemed to be okay with that, which told me they didn't understand the psychology of wrestling. As far as I was concerned, everybody else could be a "pretty boy." I wanted to stand out by being as nasty as possible.

I decided to push my Texas character by chewing tobacco and letting it drip down my chin. I had chewed tobacco for a number of years during my lifetime, but I had quit during the ten years preceding my arrival in WCW. I would run to the ring, wrestle for five to ten minutes, and then run back to the dressing room. The entire time, I had tobacco juice running out of my mouth and down my throat. It takes a cast-iron stomach and strong lungs to handle that. When I would get back to the dressing room, I would bend over and cough in an attempt to get the tobacco and juice out of my lungs and esophagus. I really worried about doing long-term damage to my lungs. But the more I did it, the more the people seemed to get into my wild style. When the heel fans tried to befriend me as I made my way to and from the ring, I would spit juice on them. Without a doubt, I was the most nasty wrestler who ever went to the ring. I heard someone else in the business did the gimmick later on, but I was told he chewed liquorice. If it really *was* tobacco, then I have to tip my hat to him.

After a couple of weeks, Ole began getting flack from the TV executives who felt I was too disgusting for television. When Ole told me they said I was "a bad example for the youth," I said, "*Tell them that Stan Hansen is a good example of why kids shouldn't chew tobacco.*" Looking at how far they've pushed the envelope on television since then, with the unrestrained sex and cursing, it's hard to believe they were concerned about a cowboy who chewed chewing tobacco.

I also lost every TV match by disqualification, rather than win an endless series of squash matches, which had been the standard for as long as I could remember. And yet, even though I lost the matches, there was never any doubt in the viewers' minds as to who the real winner of each match was. Ole really bought into that idea, but sadly, the wrestling executives didn't like the idea of me losing matches. "*Here we are, pushing this guy, and he can't even win a match on TV.*" They began to pressure Ole to make me change. That just shows the short-sightedness of their understanding of the business, especially since I was getting over. Bob Armstrong, who was wrestling in Alabama at the time, told me that "*everyone in the buildings is talking about you.*" And it was because I was different. It was a real shame they didn't get behind the idea and run with it because ninety-nine percent of the people wanted to see me get beat. And that's what it's all about, isn't it? I'm not sure the people in charge at WCW knew that. Ole fought for me, but I eventually had to win on television in order to pacify the office.

I didn't change my style, either. I wasn't going to go out and lay in a hold just because I was in the States. I hit the ring on the run just like in Japan and kept going the entire time, and all the time, I was chewing tobacco. Sting and Lex Luger were leery of me because of that. They were the two top babyfaces and they were making big money. (Good for them, and I mean that) I worked against Luger a few times. I had heard a lot about him from the boys and most of what they had to say was negative. They considered him to be cocky. All I can say is that I never had a problem with him. He did complain about me one time when I hit him with the U.S. title belt, but other than that, he was great to work with.

I only wrestled Sting a few times, but the first time I wrestled him, we had a good match. When we got to the back, he said something like, "*Hey, you aren't stiff at all. That was good.*" I told him, "*Yeah, I just look stiff. It's too bad we didn't' have the opportunity to wrestle more often before now.*"

During my run with WCW, I had a confrontation with Jim Herd. Herd was the executive vice-president of the company at the time, but I reported directly to Ole, who was the booker. Herd was Ole's boss, but Ole was my boss, so I don't remember having very many conversations with Herd. He seemed to take a liking to the other top guys, but he didn't come around and talk with me. Of course, that was fine with me. My attitude during my entire career was, the less interaction I had with the office, the better.

I was chewing tobacco and trying to look as nasty as possible during my interviews. When we were in Chicago, Ole pulled me aside and told me Herd wanted him to fire me. I had been expecting it, but when Ole told me, it naturally made me mad. I said, "*Hey, you don't have to fire me. In two seconds, I'm out of here and on my way to the airport.*"

Ole said, "*No, wait a minute. I want you to go to Herd and tell him you want a raise for one-thousand dollars a night.*"

"What? He wants you to fire me, but you're saying to ask for a raise? Are you ribbing me?"

There was definitely something strange going on, although I knew Ole and Herd were butting heads about the direction the business was going. Ole knew a lot about the wrestling business, and I suppose Herd knew something about the restaurant business (which is what he did before he got into wrestling), so there was a huge gap between the two in regards to knowledge of the business. I also knew the upper brass didn't like me or my style because it was wild and out of control. The TBS "suits" hated my obnoxiousness and tobacco-chewing, although I have to admit that most of the top babyface wrestlers hated it, too. I can't blame them because I was pretty disgusting, but I wanted to be different. I wanted to be a "true" heel.

So when Ole told me to ask for a raise, I didn't understand his thinking, but I found an opportunity to pull Herd aside and ask for a raise. In the back of my mind, though, I still wondered if Ole had an ulterior motive for asking me to do this. I got in Herd's face and said simply, "*I want one-thousand dollars a shot. Most of the top babyfaces are talking about getting huge contracts and guarantees, and I'm a unique talent, so if you want to keep me, I want a raise.*"

Herd looked at me for just a few seconds, just long enough for the silence to sink in, and then said, "*Okay.*"

I almost reeled backwards with astonishment, but I recovered, said "*Thanks,*" and walked out. To this day, I don't know why Herd gave me the raise, but I was really appreciative.

I walked back to where I had left Ole and told him Herd had agreed to my demand. As was his custom, he reached over, grabbed my forearm, and gave it a squeeze. We both burst out laughing. In the end, Ole could not save his job (which was WCW's loss), but he did help me get a better deal.

In the latter part of 1990, Ole told me he had been fired and was going to Wisconsin to oversee his sawmill business. I knew my time was marked. My relationship was with Ole, the booker, and not WCW. My youngest son was due to be born, so I looked in my date book and began calculating my exit date.

The company continued to treat me well after Ole left and Dusty Rhodes took over as the booker, but from what I saw, he wanted to take the company to a cartoon level, and I wasn't interested in being a part of that.

One of the shows I was booked on was Wrestle War '91, which was held in Phoenix, Arizona on February 24, 1991. It was there that they asked me to do an angle with Missy Hyatt. She came into the dressing room looking for Brian Pillman, who she was attracted to. Instead, she found me sitting in a chair, wearing nothing but a pair of boxer shorts. As usual, I was chewing tobacco. The guys had been egging me on for weeks to spit tobacco on Missy. She told me she knew everyone wanted me to do it and she asked me not to. I didn't.

On Wrestle War, I was scheduled to wrestle Leon "Vader" White. The company had seen tapes of the match at the Tokyo Dome between Leon and me, so they thought that was reason enough to put us together in a match. Before the show, the company told me they had big plans for an extensive program between us, but nothing ever came of it. There wasn't much they could do with us because we were both very conscious of our positions in Japan. Before our match, they set off fireworks and explosions when we went to the ring. Leon and I had learned our lesson in the match in Tokyo, so our match at Wrestle War was much more controlled. Our match ended with both of us being counted and we fought our way down the ramp as we made our way back to the dressing room. We were still fighting when they set off the fireworks for the match which followed ours. When we got to the back, Vader told me he could barely hear because the fireworks had exploded right next to his head.

As the company continued to move in the direction of cartoon-land, I became more disgusted. Dusty wanted me to manage Dutch Mantell and Black Bart, who would be called the Desperados. They would go on TV and make funny interviews about me, saying things like, "*Have you seen Stan Hansen? We're looking for him, but we can't find him.*" Everything had to have a humorous twist. I liked both Dutch and Bart, and perhaps their little skits might have gotten over in time, but the idea was against everything I had worked hard to develop in Japan. I remember Dusty telling me that wrestling was going to move away from competition and towards entertainment. I was dead set against the idea, but in the end, that's the direction our business went. I wasn't ready to go that route, so I began looking for a time to bow out gracefully.

I do wonder if the change in direction was good for WCW, but other than that, I really have nothing bad to say about the company or the time I spent with them. They stood by their word as far as money was concerned.

One story which stands out in my mind was tagging with Sid Vicious in Memphis on November 8, 1990 against Sting and Lex Luger. Sid was from West Memphis, Arkansas, and he loved to play softball. From what I understand, he made a big name for himself in the semi-pro slow-pitch softball leagues. A large number of Sid's friends and family were in at ringside. Sid was talking to everyone about his sister being there. From what he said, she was somewhat like my sister, a good athlete who pushed Sid in every way until he just outgrew her. He made the comment that at previous shows, she had gotten into confrontations with both fans and his opponents. Without a doubt, Sid is one of the most impressive guys who ever came into the wrestling business. However, at that time, he was still pretty green. When Sid won the first fall of the two-out-of-three-fall match, the crowd reacted wildly, especially his family and friends. WCW allowed a period of rest between falls, so I eased back to the dressing room. Since Sid won the fall, he would be starting the second. I figured I would wait until I heard the bell sound, at which time I would make my way back to the ring. All of a sudden, Sid came barging into the dressing room with a wild look on his face. "*The match is fixin' to start! We're gonna get counted out!*" He was frantic. I stood up and said, "*Well, what are you waitin' for? Let's go?*"

He turned and sprinted all the way back to the ring, which was a good ways from the dressing room. I was jogging at a good clip, but he was flying. I can still see him jumping up on the ring apron and soaring over the top rope ... all to the cheers of his friends and family.

I didn't think about it until I wrote this, but it was a lot like the rib Karl von Steiger pulled on me during my third match in Abilene, Texas. I guess it didn't hurt me, so I'm sure it didn't hurt Sid. We all got a kick out of it, though.

Sid got me back later when he, Mike Rotundo, and I went to see the movie *Arachnophobia* in Jacksonville, Florida. We were killing time before the wrestling show, so we went to the afternoon matinee. The theater was just about empty. The plot of the movie revolves around a large South American spider getting loose and killing people. During one intense scene, Sid snuck up behind me and lightly brushed one of my earlobes. Jumping to my feet, I slapped at my ear and hair, and yelled out loud. Before I realized what had happened, Sid had sprinted up the aisle and out of the theater. You know what they say about paybacks ...

My run with WCW would be the last time I would work a "territory" on a regular basis. From that day forward, other than making a few shots here and there for independent promotions in the States, my entire focus was on Japan.

One of the independents I worked for was Eastern Championship Wrestling, the company which later became known as Extreme Championship Wrestling. Eddie Gilbert was booking the promotion at the time. He brought me to Philadelphia for television on August 7 and 8, and then booked me to wrestle there on September 18, 1993 at an event called *UltraClash*. Unfortunately, shortly before the show, Gilbert had a falling out with the company owner, Tod Gordon. On the day of the show, we were told that Gilbert had been fired and Paul Heyman was the new booker.

A few years earlier, I had a run-in with Heyman at an independent show in Alabama. At the time, he was a photographer and writer for the *Pro Wrestling Illustrated* magazine. He strolled into the dressing room like he owned the place and without any introduction, asked me what had happened between Verne Gagne and me. I didn't know who he was. As far as I was concerned, he was a mark ... and he was in *my* dressing room. I tried to be polite and told him to "*get out of here,*" but he just stood there and repeated his question. At that point, I pointed at the door and yelled, "*Get the hell out of here!*" When he didn't move fast enough for my liking, I stood up and chased him out. He stumbled as he ran, giving me enough time to stop and pick up a folding chair, which I proceeded to throw at him. When he saw the chair flying in his direction, he took off running down the hall. I yelled after him, "*If you come down to the ring during my match, you'll regret it!*" I probably peppered the threat with a few choice curse words, but that was the gist of what I said.

Later that night, I went to the ring. Heyman didn't come down.

A few years later, he's the booker of a wrestling promotion. Wow! How things can change. I'm sure Heyman is a good booker. He obviously put a lot of time into learning the business, but at that time, I didn't know him.

When Heyman walked into the dressing room, I was sitting with Abdullah the Butcher, Kevin Sullivan, and Terry Funk. Heyman walked up and said something like, "*The boss wants a clean finish. It doesn't matter who does the job, but someone has to do it.*" We didn't say a word. We just stared at him until he turned around and left. He came back in and repeated it two or three more times. Each time, he was met with stony silence, and as soon as he left the room, we all looked at each other and laughed. It was so comical. I knew good and well that Abdullah and Terry weren't going to do a job, and I would imagine Kevin Sullivan was going to take care of himself. And what I knew for sure was that Stan Hansen wasn't going to do the job.

I guess it goes without saying that there was no job in that match. Terry and I wrestled Sullivan and Abdullah and we all got disqualified.

From what I can remember, Tod Gordon was a nice guy. When we met that night, I told him I wanted to be paid up front. Abdullah saw me do that, so he did, too. "*No checks for us,*" he said. "*I've been down that road too many times.*"

During my first trip to Philadelphia for ECW, I wrestled Shane Douglas on television. Shane was Johnny Ace's first partner when they wrestled for WCW in 1989. Ace told me a great story about a time when he and Shane were wrestling as the Dynamic Dudes. They had bleached-blond hair, wore teeny-bopper clothes, and carried skateboards to the ring. They wrestled in Baltimore one night, a town which had a lot of hard-core wrestling fans. Hard-core fans didn't automatically cheer the babyfaces. In fact, they were more likely to cheer for the heels. As Ace and Shane made their way to the ring, the fans went wild. Unfortunately, considering the fact that Ace and Shane were the babyface team in their match, the fans weren't yelling what you might think they were. In unison, they chanted over and over, "*Shane sucks Johnny's co—! Shane sucks Johnny's co—!*" Ace and Shane could hardly keep a straight face. When the match was over, the fans repeated the performance as the two walked back to the dressing room. Of course, Ace and Shane ignored the chants and stayed in character, waving and acting like the fans loved them. When they walked into the dressing room, Jim Barnett, the Georgia Championship Wrestling promoter, came up to them and said (in Jim's famous lisp voice), "*My goodness. I have never heard such heat for a babyface team!*" Of course, coming from Barnett, that was really funny.

Nothing else stands out other than the fact that I took my family with me. While we were in the area, we went to visit my aunt, uncle, and cousins from my dad's side of the family. My daughter Paige, who was in junior high school, had never seen me wrestle live. During my match, everyone was booing and hollering at me. I remember bending my opponent backwards over the ropes and seeing Paige standing on the last empty row of chairs, whistling and yelling, "*Get 'em, daddy!*" What a great memory. Once, while watching the premiere of the movie *No Holds Barred*, Paige walked up to me at the end of the scene where the character Zeus beat me up and pulled out my hair. She climbed up into my lap, patted me on the neck, and said, "*That's okay, Daddy. That's okay.*" I thought that was sweet.

I never smartened up my kids, but I did tell them not to worry about me and that I would be alright. The only thing I told my parents was that it was hard work. They never questioned me because they saw how physically beaten I was whenever I came home between tours. My sons saw how tough it was when they came to Japan. I took Sam and Shaver to three shows, including one at the Budokan and my retirement show. I think it was at the retirement show when they first had an understanding of the position I had achieved in Japan. I had another opportunity to take them to Japan in the summer of

2006, but it had nothing to do with wrestling. They went to play baseball in the Goodwill Series, an annual event where "Team America" plays Japanese all-star baseball teams from five or six prefectures. When word got out about who their dad was, the press came and gave them a lot of time. I did my best to keep it about my boys and their baseball, but the press always tried to steer the conversations back to wrestling.

Japanese wrestling magazines

Chapter 26

Terry Gordy and the Birthday Girl

During my time in Japan, I met a number of interesting people. I first watched sumo while I was with New Japan, as did many of the other gaijin wrestlers. Since most TV shows were produced with Japanese dialogue, sumo was something we could watch and understand. At first, I was attracted to it because it was a sport, but I was drawn to it because the action resembled American football's big offensive linemen going one-on-one.

As time went by, we developed our favorites. The first sumo wrestler I met was Takamiyama Daigoro [Jesse Kuhaulua], the first foreign-born sumo wrestler to win the Emperor's Cup [1972]. We just happened to be in the lobby of the Keio Plaza at the same time. I can still remember his deep, gravelly voice, and the strength in his hand as I shook it. However, for a number of reasons, I developed a liking for Wajima, primarily because he was left-handed. In sumo, you hook your opponent with your dominant arm and try to throw him, and being left-handed, Wajima often caught his opponent by surprise. Being left-handed is something that made an athlete stand out. I did my lariat with my left arm, which was something on which the announcers frequently commented. Wajima had good size, but by sumo standards, he wasn't a really big guy. That made him an underdog when he competed against Kitanoumi Toshimitsu, the dominant wrestler at the time.

When Hiroshi Wajima left sumo, Baba broke him into the wrestling business. That was big news in Japan because he was the first grand champion to become a pro wrestler. Baba sent him to Hawaii for training. It's only my opinion, but I thought he was rushed into the business before he was properly trained. It was a real thrill for me, however, to meet and work against someone of whom I had been a fan when I was young. That was the second time that happened to me. I told the story in an earlier chapter of playing football in 1971 with my idol, Johnny Unitas, when I was at the Baltimore Colts training camp. That had been a dream come true. I didn't have that same feeling about Wajima, but it was nice to meet and work with somebody I had looked up to. The thing that impressed me

Hiroshi Wajima

the most about Wajima was his strength. The years of sumo training had given him a really strong trunk, which is the area from the shoulders down through the hips. I don't think anybody impressed me in trunk strength like Wajima. It was almost impossible to bend or twist his back.

Wajima could have been a big card in wrestling, and he did boost Baba's business for a short time, but I believe he got in too late in life. He treated me with respect and I enjoyed meeting him. I still see him occasionally on television shows, but I have no idea what he did when he left wrestling.

One of the first young sumo wrestlers I noticed was Chiynofuji [Mitsugu]. He was small, but the thing that made him stand out was that he looked like he trained with weights. He seemed to have a lot of confidence as he would come up for the face-off and stare at the opponent for a long time. We discovered his nickname was "The Wolf." He developed a real following, especially among the gaijins, due to his being somewhat of an underdog. We watched as he slowly moved up the rankings ladder. Over time, he became a Yokozuna. Chiynofuji's popularity was a real shot in the arm for sumo, and I believe he did a lot to bring the sport into a new age.

Later, when I was with All Japan, someone set up a meeting between us. He had been told that I liked to watch him wrestle, so someone took me to his stable where I could watch them work out. During our time together, we visited and ate chanko-nabe (which we called chunko), the sumo soup that is so delicious. *Nabe* means "pot" (or a meal simmered in a pot), while *chanko* is the meal eaten by sumo wrestlers. There is no hard-and-fast rule about what goes into the pot, but common ingredients are chicken, tofu, vegetables like Welch onions and Chinese cabbage, all cooked in a seasoned soup stock.

Chiynofuji told me he was raised in Hokkaidô. When he was a young boy, he had gone to a wrestling match and I was on the card. I left the ring that night (as I did almost every night) and went out into the crowd, swinging my rope wildly. He told me that as I came close to him, he had been somewhat

Sharing a meal with Chiynufuji Mitsugu

scared of me. Who would have guessed that years later, we would be sitting together and talking about it?

One of the great pleasures of my time in Japan was meeting Randy Bass. Everyone in Japan knows the name Randy Bass. Randy was the starting first baseman of Japan's Hanshin Tigers and an MVP with the Nippon Professional Baseball League. During his career, he became the greatest foreign hitter (of over 400) to ever play baseball in Japan. He set an all-time season batting average mark of .389 in 1986, is the only player to win back -to-back Triple Crowns, and hit 200 home runs faster than any man in baseball history. From 1998 to 2003, he worked as a scout for the Tokyo Giants.

I knew who Randy was before I met him. Of course, I don't think there was anybody in Japan who didn't know the name Randy Bass. I watched the baseball highlights every night on TV. The very first thing I noticed about him was his size. Randy was, and is, a much larger man than most baseball players, especially in Japan. His exploits on the baseball field were featured almost daily on television news programs.

Randy Bass

Evidently, several of the Japanese baseball players often told Randy that he looked somewhat like me. Somehow, that reached the ears of the sportswriters and they began trying to get us together. Randy invited me to come to the stadium in Kobe on one of my days off. I had been in Osaka the night before, so I made the twenty-mile trip the next day. Randy showed me around I watched the pre-game practice. They offered to let me take batting practice against the batting practice pitchers, but I declined. I don't remember why I made that decision, but that is one of my big regrets. I wish I had at least taken a few swings. Many times, when I found myself in venues other than wrestling, I tried to stay out of the limelight. That caused me to miss a great opportunity to try to hit against a major league pitcher. I wish I could be given that opportunity again.

As time went by, Randy and I developed a good relationship. He was from Lawton, Oklahoma, and knew a football player with whom I went to college. Of course, Oklahoma is an arch-rival to Texas, and there has always been competition between the two states in sports, so there was a lot of good-natured kidding going on between the two of us.

Randy invited me to his home in Kobe a number of times. He had a nice family who were very friendly and hospitable. I particularly enjoyed the opportunity to get away from the hotel scene and being served a home-cooked American meal.

One night in Nagoya, when Terry Gordy and I were together, Randy was staying at a nearby hotel. Having been invited to a friend's birthday party, he called and asked us if we would like to go with him. It was after midnight, but that was prime time for us back then. We called a taxi and set out for the party, which was being held on the top floor of a high-rise building located on the outskirts of Nagoya.

Randy was a celebrity, so he was often invited to parties by friends and acquaintances, but he didn't always know the host or honoree. That was the case on this occasion. When the elevator doors opened, we saw around 50 people enjoying themselves. There was food spread out on a large table and everyone seemed to be having a good time. When we walked in, somebody handed us a beer and introduced us to a small group of people. Gordy, who already had a few beers earlier that evening, asked, "*Who's the birthday girl?*"

One of the girls in the group said, "*I am.*"

Gordy said, "*Well, happy birthday!*" And before any of us knew what was happening, he opened his can of beer and poured it over her head. The girl was furious. She began yelling and cursing at Gordy. Everybody was upset, including Gordy, although I never did figure out why he got mad. He ended up kicking a wall before getting another beer and sitting down quietly on the floor.

Randy and I had already made a plate of food and were beginning to eat when Terry poured the beer over the girl's head. As if on cue, Randy and I began to wolf down our food, knowing the mood towards us by the people there had changed and our time was short. We left a few minutes later. As we were getting into a taxi, several unopened beer cans sailed out the window of the room where the party was taking place and exploded on the street near the taxi. The three of us looked at each other with wide eyes. We talked about going back up, but better judgment prevailed and we left. Randy and I talk and laugh about that incident every time we get together.

Years later, when Randy was at the height of his popularity in professional baseball, his son got sick. He had to choose between his family and business. He made the right decision and returned to the States. He had to end his career prematurely, but the family was much more important. I really respect him for making that decision and know he has no regrets about his choice. Of course, he left in the middle of the baseball season and the team didn't understand why he would put family before company. The Japanese culture is so different from that in America. In Japan, especially in those days, a person's first loyalty was to the company. The family came in second. It's hard for Americans to understand that mentality. I believe we can each learn from the other. Over time, I came to understand the Japanese mindset when it came to business. Much of what the Japanese do is so good, and we should take lessons from them. However, when family is sick or in need, the Japanese need to learn from us.

I really respected Randy for his strength to make the right decision, even though it caused problems between Randy and the front office of the baseball team. When all was said and done, he was no longer welcome to return to play baseball in Japan. Randy put his family before money and business, and that just reinforced my decision to do the same thing. Randy Bass was a good example for Stan Hansen.

In spring 2009, I met with Randy while I was traveling through Lawton. He is now a state senator, but still conducts business in Japan. He also goes back to Japan for an occasional "old-timer" baseball game.

In Osaka, I met Muddy Waters, my all-time favorite blues singer. I couldn't believe he was staying at the Plaza Hotel where I was staying. I had a few drinks with him and several members of his band. He was living in Mississippi at the time, so we had that in common. A few weeks later, I arrived home from a Japan tour to find an album one of his business associates sent to me.

One day, Jesse Jackson and I were on the same flight to Jackson, Mississippi. We were all sitting in the first-class section and I heard them talking about getting off in Jackson, which I knew would result in huge TV news coverage. I had been on a long tour of Japan and my dad was bringing my son and daughter to the airport to meet me. I knew the TV cameras would be there, so since I was sitting in the front seat, I made sure I was the first person to walk off the plane ... just a few feet ahead of Jesse Jackson and his entourage. As I walked through the doorway into the gate area (this was before airport security tightened the rules), the camera lights hit me, expecting Jackson. When my kids saw me, they bolted to me. I picked them both up and gave them big hugs. I continued to block the doorway as I stood upright with my kids in my arms, and my big ten-gallon, cowboy hat further obstructed the view of the cameras. As I talked to my kids, Jesse and his group had to sidle around me.

Later that night, I watched the news coverage of Jackson's arrival, but they didn't get a single shot of him walking through the gate. I thought it was really funny.

I met Jackson years later in Japan at a lounge. We talked for a few minutes, and when I told him I was from Mississippi, he said, "*Oh, a home boy.*" I thought that was a nice thing for him to say, although I wouldn't have dared use those same words to him.

On another flight, I was flying from LA to Tokyo with Steve Williams and Terry Gordy. We were flying first class on a Boeing 747, so there was a lot of space between the seats. I was sitting across the aisle from Terry and Steve, and in front of me was George Kennedy, on his way to Japan to make a movie. Several hours into the flight, I woke up as I felt something bump my seat. When I opened my eyes, I was Steve laying on the floor, pulling himself up beside Kennedy's chair. Kennedy was wearing one of those eye covers which keeps the light out. When Steve looked up, he saw Kennedy peeking out at him. Steve just stood up and went back to his seat. I don't know why he was on the floor, what he had planned to do, or how long he had been there, but it struck me as funny. Kennedy later signed an autograph for Steve to put on the wall of his gym.

Eating with chopsticks

Chapter 27

Return to West Texas

There was a time in my career when I began to realize that I was no longer able to do some of the physical things I had done for most of my career. I became aware of the fact that youth was no longer on my side. I used to take pride in my movement and speed, but in the latter part of my career, I knew I was slowing down. As with most wrestlers, my knees were the first to go, and that is the most difficult injury to overcome. My knees hurt so badly during my last five years in Japan that I had a hard time walking up and down stairs. I could still do certain moves in the ring, but I could tell my mobility was going. The long, physical matches I had with Baba, Jumbo, Tenryu, Misawa, and the other younger wrestlers, took their toll. I had been fortunate to not need any surgeries since my early days in wrestling, but my knees just slowly wore out. The years of wear and tear, of having them kicked and yanked on, finally caused them to weaken.

On October 21, 2000, I worked in Nagoya with Tenryu in the semi-finals of the All Japan Triple Crown Tournament. In a match a few days before, my legs went numb after I took a body slam. That had never happened before and it really caught my attention. I took a couple of days off and, even though my legs were still weak, I went through with a scheduled match with Tenryu. During the match, when Tenryu power bombed me, the back of my head hit the mat and I was knocked unconscious. I don't remember getting pinned or how I got back to the dressing room, but when I came to, Steve Williams was picking me up off the dressing room floor. As he sat me down into a chair, I was told that I kicked out after being pinned and went wild through the audience. When I walked into the dressing room, I collapsed. That was when Steve picked me up. When my head cleared, I decided right then and there that God was telling me it was time to stop.

I thought about how we used to notice Baba as he tried to get up from a chair. He was a big man and his knees had been under pressure for a long time. Finding myself in the same situation, struggling at times to get up from a seated or crouched position, I can imagine how bad it must have been for Baba. He was older and taller, and when I looked at him, I could see that he was in a lot of pain. I will always have the utmost respect and admiration for him. He persevered through it all. He stepped back and slowed down in his later years, but even then, at times, he would amaze us all by going all-out during a six-man tag against Misawa, Kobashi, and Kawada. He could have taken the easy way out and stood on the ring apron, coming in only to make a big comeback, but instead, he would allow himself to be bumped around the ring. Having been in that situation, I don't know how he did it, but he did.

Many years before, I had seen veteran wrestlers hang on long after they had any business being in the ring. Many of them embarrassed themselves by trying to do things in the ring they were no longer capable of doing. It was sad to see so many of the legends go down that road. After seeing that scenario repeat itself over and over, I made a promise to myself that I would not hang on when I found myself in that position. When the time came to retire, I would accept the fact that it was time and I wouldn't look back. During the previous two to three years, I had been in a lot of pain and I knew God was speaking to me, so I listened.

After my match in Nagoya with Tenryu, I showered and changed clothes, and then I went directly to Mrs. Baba and told her I was retiring. Baba had already passed away and she was running the business until Baba's thirtieth anniversary. She was really disappointed. When the chips were down, she knew she could always trust me. Most of the wrestlers with All Japan were against her, and when Misawa formed Pro Wrestling NOAH, he took 24 of the 26 All Japan wrestlers with him. Toshiaki Kawada and Masanobu Fuchi were the only two native wrestlers who stayed with All Japan, along with referee Kyohei Wada. They had promised Baba that they would help carry out one of his last wishes, which was to "keep All Japan Pro Wrestling alive." I, myself, was totally loyal to Mrs. Baba because she was Baba-san's wife, and alive or not, I was still loyal to him.

I was scheduled to wrestle a few times after the tournament, but Mrs. Baba gave me time off to recuperate. I had already missed a few matches since my legs went numb earlier in the tour. It made the news that I had missed a show for the first time. That's pretty incredible considering the fact that I made 131 tours of Japan.

I missed six shows on the tour, but I put in an appearance at the first three before missing the fourth and fifth shows. On October 20, I wrestled Tenryu in Nagoya, and then missed the four shows which followed. On the final night of the tour, October 28, 2000, I participated in a six-man tag-team match in the Budokan. I teamed with Steve Williams and Wolf Hawkfield against Masa Fuchi, Yoshiaki Fujiwara, and Johnny Smith. I tried to do some things in the ring, but for the most part, I stood on the apron of the ring in the corner. My legs were much too weak to carry me for long in the ring. That was the very last match of my career.

When I got back to the States, the doctors did an MRI and found a cyst pressing on my spinal cord. It was close to the area of the spinal cord which controls the bladder. A week later, they operated and were successful in removing it. I recovered quickly and was on my way home within three days. To this day, three of my toes are numb from the damage the cyst did to my spine. Two weeks after the back operation, I had both knee joints replaced at the same time. That night, I was up and walking with the assistance of a walker. Finally, in late 2006, I had both shoulder joints replaced. My doctor tells me that only one-tenth of one percent of the people in the world have four artificial joints … my new claim to fame. I also weigh almost 50 pounds less than what I did when I was wrestling. The only complications I had was an infection in my left shoulder, on which I had four operations to cure.

I was supposed to appear on the next tour, which was a tag-team tour, but due to my surgery, that obviously wasn't going to happen. On November 19, 2000, Mrs. Baba announced that I would be retiring. I had never seen Mrs. Baba in the ring, but I was told she got into the ring that night and made the announcement.

On January 28, 2001, I returned to Japan for a show which featured my retirement ceremony. It coincided with the first anniversary of Baba's death. I have to say that Mrs. Baba and All Japan really went out of their way to honor me and treated me warmly. They flew over my whole family. Also in attendance was Pete Roberts from England, and Mike and Judy Levy (good friends from Atlanta). My mother-in-law came from her home in Japan. They put us all up at the Tokyo Dome Hotel, which served as the site of numerous get-togethers and interviews during the three-day event. They gave us a private box inside the Dome from which we could view the wrestling matches and ceremony.

I can't recall all the names of the Japanese and American wrestlers who attended, but I have a photo of them lined up outside the Tokyo Dome Hotel. I believe it was published in the newspaper. Some of the legends brought back included Abdullah, Terry Funk, Toshiaki Kawada, the "Intelligent, Sensational" Destroyer, and Atsushi Onita. New Japan boss Seiji Sakaguchi came and presented me with a nice gift during the ceremony. I thought that was a great gesture since they have always been the rival company to All Japan. Lord James Blears also was there in his last official act as president of the PWF.

The Tokyo Dome banquet hall was filled with more than 50 huge poster-sized pictures of various matches, all mounted in frames, along with numerous trophies and gifts from the sports newspapers and other institutions.

In November 2000, I had a spine operation, and in December, I had both knees replaced. Now, just one month later, it was a long walk from the dugout to the pitcher's mound where the ring was set up, but I did it and climbed up into the ring. I dressed up in a coat and hat, something I hadn't done in Japan for more than 25 years.

During the two days leading up to the show, I did interviews with several newspapers, sports magazines, and television shows. On the day after the show, I was invited to the prestigious annual Japanese Professional Sports Association ceremony which included the retiring Sumo grand champion, Akebono Tarô, and star baseball player Hideki Matsui of the Tokyo Giants (later with the New York Yankees and now playing as a free agent for the Los Angeles Angels). Matsui made it a point to get over to have a picture made with me. I was excited to meet Matsui because I had watched him play baseball since he was in high school. I was a huge baseball fan and knew many of the players.

Going to and from the ring with thousands of people chanting my name, *Hansen! Hansen! Hansen!*, was something I can't even describe. I've heard that before over the years, but I must say, that time, it really hit an emotional chord with me. Pete Roberts used to tell me that I never understood how over I was, but I never thought about it. I just went out and did my job. On that night, however, as the fans poured out their feelings, it humbled me. I can never give back what they have given to me, not only that night, but through all the years I wrestled in Japan.

I didn't realize it until my retirement ceremony, but one of the things I'm going to miss the most is the wrestling fans. I was a heel, so I never set out to win fans, but inevitably, over time, some began to like me. I still can't figure out what it was about me they liked. Perhaps it was the wildness, or the style which didn't change over time, that attracted those fans. However, even when I realized that I had a following, I stayed in character and never tried to work to them. Today I consider myself blessed to have had the support of those fans, and I'm thankful for everyone who has supported me over these years. There are a few fans who have stuck with me for more than twenty years, and I have special relationships with individuals in Osaka, Tokyo, and Nagaoka. They were just kids when I first met them. Now they're grown up, married, work a variety of jobs, and have children of their own. I wish them luck.

It goes without saying that I could not have been successful if I had not had great opponents to wrestle. Japan provided me with the best talent with which to learn my profession.

My family and friends really enjoyed themselves during the retirement events. We ate some great food and just had a great time together witnessing that great outpouring of feeling from the wrestling fans. I will never forget them. I think my kids, both the grown ones and the younger ones, had a different impression of what their dad had been doing in Japan all those years. On the other hand, to them, I was still just DAD.

After that, I became the president of the Pacific Wrestling Federation. I was just a figurehead with no power, but it was an easy job and I enjoyed keeping my hand in the business. I didn't do much more than read the ceremony scroll before the matches and tell the fans that I had given official sanction to a specific match between two wrestlers. I often told the guys that I had the position that couldn't help or hurt anyone. I had seen Lord Blears fill that role in the past and knew it was a position of respect for past allegiance. I remember thinking back to the time when I gave Lord Blears such a hard time when he was in that position. Whenever he tried to read the ceremony scroll, I would charge him and try to get him flustered. One time, I accidentally hurt him and that put an end to my antics. Now that I was in that position, I fully expected somebody to pay me back for all the havoc I had dished out, but nobody ever did. I never looked at the position as anything but a gift and I was happy to make the "easy money."

I enjoyed working with the company while Mrs. Baba still had control, but when Keiji Mutoh took over as the new president of the company, things changed. The office treated me with respect, but they began to cut back on some of my perks. When they asked me to fly coach instead of business class, as most of the talent did, I refused. That, of course, resulted in them cutting back on the number of times they brought me over. When we couldn't get together on money and travel expense, Tiger Kihara, the long-time All Japan ring announcer, called to ask me to resign and make an official statement to that end. When I refused, the company made the statement themselves and appointed Hiroshi Hase in my place in June 2007. It was all just business and it was cheaper to put somebody in the position who lived in Japan so they didn't have to pay the transportation. Hase was, and is, a good guy and I liked him. I sincerely wish them the best.

Wresting in Japan today is in a flux. I don't know where it is going, but it is changing, and it will continue to change with or without Stan Hansen. I have seen change in the Japanese society over the years. The changes are sometimes slow and hard to see, while others are easier to notice.

I've written quite a bit about hierarchy. Hierarchy is a part of every society, but it has played a huge part in Japanese society. It has been the foundation of everything from sumo wrestlers to workers at a factory. I believe hierarchy is something that has given stability and order to Japan. Other countries, like the United States, envy Japan for the order they've maintained in their society. This system has worked well in Japan for a long time. It is inevitable, however, that it will change. I already see the younger people beginning to change and move away from that order. Some of the change is for the better. It will allow more innovation and opportunity. However, as the country continues to travel down the road of opening their doors to societal change, there will be no "putting the Genie back in the bottle." Over time, the change will continue to evolve in all sectors of their society, no matter what. The same is true for professional wrestling.

However, there will never be another Giant Baba or Antonio Inoki. They established themselves as godlike icons in Japanese society. I don't think we'll see their likes again. They are also the last of a special breed of wrestler, and I was fortunate to have worked for both of them.

I've written a lot about Baba-san in this book, but I just can't say enough about the man. It was a pleasure to work for both Inoki and Baba, but to me, Baba was everything the head of a company should be: honest, humble, and fair. In addition, he always placed business and the company before his ego. I think it would be almost impossible to find anyone in today's world who has those character traits.

As I write this, I think of our meetings over the years. I'm surprised when I realize there really were not that many, and the few times in which we did meet were for important business. We didn't have to meet to work on our relationship. It was based on an honest understanding of each other and trust that we were each going to do what was right for each other. I feel that was what made our relationship so unique. No, it wasn't a personal relationship. It was a working relationship, but I felt that it went beyond just that. It was a special bond between an "owner" and a "worker" which developed into a truly unique relationship between two men set on a parallel journey through their lives. We happened to meet along the way, and with time, formed a connection which could not be shaken or doubted.

Based on past experience, I had negative feelings about promoters, so my relationship with Baba was truly a godsend. My life would have been completely different if I had not joined him in Japan. He was the reason why I stayed there for most of my life. He gave me the opportunity to make a great living while doing what I enjoyed. Through my association with his company, I met my wife and fell deeply in love. It's strange. My wife is Japanese, but I've been a part of Japanese society for so long that I no longer realize she *is* Japanese. I just don't see it now. We also had two sons, both of whom are so important to me, as are all my children. I was honored to be the only person to hold the AJPW Triple Crown both as a unified championship and as separate components [NWA International heavyweight title, NWA United

Giant Baba and Stan vs The Patriot, referee Joe Higuchi

National title, and the PWF world heavyweight title]. When they decided to combine the three titles, they booked me against Jumbo Tsuruta at the New Sumo Hall in Tokyo on April 18, 1989.

Finally, Baba-san's generosity allowed me to prepare for retirement. To give credit where it's due, God led me in the direction he wanted me to go, but Baba was so instrumental in paving the way.

I know that in the complex world of running a business in Japanese culture, and specifically the business of professional wrestling, one has to deal with the TV network, promoters, talent, staff, the venues, the economy, and other relationships. Baba was truly the master of bringing these all together. Some people have asked how he managed to do that. In my opinion, he mastered them by standing first and foremost on his word. I don't think he could have stayed in business all those years and been successful without establishing his character first and foremost ... that character being "straight and honest."

To sum things up, there was only one thing in Japan that never changed ... and that one thing was Baba-san.

It has been ten years since Baba passed away. Since then, All Japan has evolved, and will continue to evolve for many years. I don't know much about what goes on behind the scenes now, but I do know that a power vacuum is present. There is nobody who has shown the capability of replacing Baba and all that he stood for. However, I believe there is a future All Japan Pro Wrestling, but there will be a long and difficult transition period before the company ever reaches the heights of popularity it once held.

Pride is something good. I know the Japanese wrestlers are proud. They take pride in their ability and fighting spirit. I know they all want to stand tall and be looked at with pride by the fans. Ego, on the other hand, is something different. Ego is negative, especially if there isn't somebody in control to put a check on that ego. If there is one thing which will destroy a person or an organization, it is ego. It can easily misguide someone if they let their ego overrule their common sense.

I'm sure Baba-san faced situations when it was hard to keep his ego under control, but he persevered. He also worked hard to keep the egos of his wrestlers under control. He did that through both hierarchy and example. His guidance will be sorely missed as the young promoters and wrestlers navigate through these uncertain times.

I, too, have made such a trip in my life. From school and sports in the States, into pro wrestling in Texas, and finally, to Japan, my journey was somewhat like that traveled by my grandfather and father. My life has been beset with everything from physical hardships to personal problems, but I left them behind me as I kept my sights set towards the future. I tried to stay steady and straight, just as my grandfather did on the oceans of the world back in the late 1800s, and as my father did when he landed on the beaches of North Africa, Italy, Sicily, and the south of France during World War II.

It has been a long trip; but a joyous one. The past 60 years have slipped by so quickly that it's hard for me to believe that many have gone by.

On October 10, 2009, I attended a reunion of West Texas football alumnae during homecoming weekend at West Texas A&M (formerly West Texas State University). About 35 to 40 guys from the Kerbel era showed up, including his youngest son, Sammy, and his daughter, Sherri. We had a great time as it brought together players (who are around 70 years old) from Kerbel's first class in 1960 and the last group of players (my class, who are around 60). Terry Funk and I were the only two professional wrestlers there. Most of the guys came to see each other because they knew it might be for the last time. We told stories and relived the great experience we all had under the watchful eye (and sharp tongue) of Coach Kerbel.

Everybody at the reunion had a "Fat Man" story or two ... or three. I was reminded of a few:

On October 30, 1970, when I was a senior, we played the Eastern Carolina University Pirates at the Buffalo Bowl field at West Texas. Not only did they lose the first three games of the season, they didn't score a single point in those games. I was playing middle linebacker. The Pirates came onto the field and scored three touchdowns in the first half. The "Fat Man" went ballistic. He gave the players and coaches hell in the worst way.

When the gun signaled the end of the first half, we gravitated towards the locker room, which was located behind the dirt hill which wrapped around both ends of the field and, along with the grandstands on the sides, made the Buffalo Bowl a "bowl." As the visiting Pirates went up and over the hill, I noticed Harold Stewart, a senior linebacker from Odessa (who was the spitting image of Jim Brown, the great pro running back), hurrying at almost a sprint up the ramp towards our locker room. I thought to myself, "*That Harold is hurrying to the locker room to get some orange juice before Coach Kerbel can get there and kick over the table.*" A number of times over the years, when things didn't go well for the team at the half, Coach Kerbel would kick over the table and nobody would get any juice at the half. When I saw Harold sprinting, I figured I'd better do the same so I could get mine, as well. As I topped the hill, I saw Harold in the middle of the East Carolina team, fighting for his life. I ran down the hill and into the midst of the players, swinging and kicking at whoever got in my way. Harold and I stood back to back and fought like men possessed. We were getting pounded, but we kept fighting, hoping to hold out until the rest of the Buffaloes arrived to give us some help. When they reached the top of the hill, they charged down and the battle was on. Charlie Reade, Ed Howig, Windy Williams, and Ray Brown were the first four to make it into the melee.

The fight went on for four or five minutes, which is a long time to fight, and quite a few people got knocked out. The coaches from both teams finally separated us and we all went to our separate locker rooms, while Coach Kerbel and the other coach had a meeting. There wasn't a sound to be heard in the room as we waited for Coach Kerbel to come in and unload on us. When he walked in, he paused in the doorway, stared at us, and said, "*That's the way to kick those son-of-a-bitches.*" We all began yelling and screaming. The people in the stands never knew the riot had taken place because the stadium was blocked by the hill. We were fired up when we went back out on the field for the second half. We beat them by two touchdowns, 42-30.

Two weeks earlier, we played Lamar Tech in Beaumont, Texas. It was the first game of the season and we were expected to beat them. We played a really bad game. The temperature was close to 95 degrees and the humidity was about 98 percent. We rallied back and scored a few times, but lost the game 33-28.

The plane ride back to Amarillo was one we all would love to forget ... except for one thing. Everybody was quiet and deep in their own thoughts during the trip. We all wondered if we would have to run sprints when we arrived at the field house at WT, just as we had done after other games when we didn't play well. It didn't matter that it was three in the morning and everybody on campus would be sleeping comfortably in their beds. Many times, he made us run 100-yard sprints back and forth between two parked cars which were facing each other with their headlights glaring. We ran out of the dark into the glare of lights, and then we would turn around and run back into the dark. He would make us repeat that over and over.

Halfway through the flight, Coach Kerbel suddenly jumped up and yelled out loud, grabbing his stomach. Everybody stopped and stood quietly as he yelled out a second time. Windy Williams, Harold Stewart, and I were sitting in a three-seat row, while Coach Ostrander, the defensive back coach, was sitting across the aisle. We all thought Coach Kerbel was having a heart attack. In all sincerity, Windy prayed quietly, "*Lord, don't let him die.*" I immediately prayed, "*God, don't let him die,*" and without thinking, added, "*until my senior year is over.*" Harold then prayed, "*Lord, let him die.*" We all looked at each other and began to snigger. Of course, we didn't mean it ... or perhaps we did. All we were thinking about were the laps he would make us run when we got home. We leaned over towards coach Ostrander and asked, "*Is the coach going to be all right?*"

"*I don't know,*" he said. "*I hope the son-of a-bitch drops dead.*"

Wow! Later, we all laughed about it, especially when we were told that Coach Kerbel was only suffering from a bad attack of gas pains.

The reunion was a lot of fun. Thirty-five players from that era were in attendance. Two of Kerbel's coaches I played for were there: Clarance Dirking and Joe Granado. Granado was one of the assistants who was pushed out the door with Kerbel when he was forced to resign. I also saw two student coaches who had been at WT during my freshman year: Jim Young, of Muleshoe, Texas, and Ronnie Mankin, of Amarillo. I also saw my cousin, Tom Lair, who lives in Canyon. He played one spring for Coach Kerbel and attended two days of the homecoming activities, which included riding on a float in the homecoming parade.

I've always heard that over a lifetime, your true friends can be counted on one hand. I find that to be true. I met two of those people during my college football days. Both were linebackers and both were coached under Coach Dirking and, later, Coach Burl Woods, who also played for Coach Kerbel before I came to West Texas.

The first was Windy Williams. Windy was one year behind me in school, but we ended up being roommates for a few years. He was from the small town of Panhandle, which is located about 30 miles east of Amarillo. He was a good football player who fought for a position at outside linebacker. He only weighed 195 pounds, but he was quick and he knew football. However, what I remember the most about Windy was the fact that he was a Christian. Throughout his twenty-five years of coaching after college, he let his Christian values dictate his coaching style and philosophy. Where other coaches would have bowed to the pressure to win and done things which were dishonest, Windy stayed on the Christian course, even when it cost him on the field. He had a great coaching career and ended up coaching a state champion team from White Deer, Texas. He also is still married to his high-school sweetheart. We have remained close through the years and we communicate regularly.

Charlie Reade was the other. Charlie was a linebacker who transferred from a junior college in Redondo Beach California. He was about the same size as Windy and was a good football player, too. After moving back to California, Charlie became a paramedic/firefighter and retired after thirty years of service in Los Angeles County. He played tackle football annually for almost twenty years in the huge rival game between LA County firefighters and the police association. He also is still married to his high school sweetheart.

These two men, who I consider my brothers, have been a great influence on me. I make specific mention of them because we have had an enduring friendship for more than forty years. They followed me throughout my career ... not as fans, but as friends ... and no matter where I was or what was going on in my life, they were there for me when I needed them.

Terry Funk told several stories about me breaking into the wrestling business. I thought it was interesting that the wrestlers who played for Coach Kerbel — Terry, Dory Funk, Bobby Duncum Sr., George Allen (wrestled for Joe Blanchard), Dusty Rhodes, Bruiser Brody, and myself — all ended being top "heels" in the wrestling business. I think that has something to do with the fact that we were all influenced by the Fat Man.

We all had several things in common when it came to Coach Kerbel: we feared him, we hated him, and we avoided him, but most importantly, everybody there respected him. We took pride in the fact that we were able to endure the tough physical and verbal abuse he heaped on us. We were proud to have had the opportunity to play for him and never have a losing season. More than 30 of Kerbel's players either played pro football or were invited to tryouts. A few players were All-Pro and others played on Super Bowl teams. Two players, Jesse Powell and Mercury Morris, played on the 1972 Miami Dolphins team, which still holds the record for going 16-0 and winning the Super Bowl.

The guys there had gone on to be top insurance executives, police officers, and coaches. Most of us succeeded in life in one way or another. I think Coach Kerbel had something to do with that. He helped develop our character and work ethic. We are indebted to him for that.

When we were playing for him, we had a love/hate relationship, but after so many years, we remember the good things, and the bad ones just fade away. One thing is for sure: Joe Kerbel was the most dynamic individual I have ever met. He was a larger-than-life personality who, in retrospect, we all loved.

It's now the year 2011 and I go to the gym at least five times a week, which is more than I did when I was in the wrestling business. I have four artificial joints, so I know my limitations. I can't lift heavy weights, so for my heart, I push myself hard for 45 minutes on a stationary bike. To me, that is the most important exercise I do. I also do a range of motion lifting with minimal weight just to rehab the joints. I have lost 50 pounds from my wrestling weight and have kept it off. I feel good, but I am limited as to the activities in which I can participate. I feel many of the aches and pains that come from a lifetime of wrestling, but overall, I am in good health.

On January 8, 2010, I attended Steve Williams' memorial service in Denver, Colorado. There must have been 300 people at the service, most of them from the Lakewood Colorado area where Steve was raised and attended high school. The people there came to show respect and reflect on the life of a man who was a son, brother, father, football player, amateur wrestler, professional wrestler ... but most of all, we remembered him as a devout Christian. He wasn't only strong physically. He was strong mentally and his faith was unshakeable. I just can't say how awed I was at the outpouring of love and respect for Steve by people from all walks of life. The service lasted for more than three hours as multimedia of his life was shown and friends share testimonials of what Steve meant to them.

Former University of Oklahoma football coach Barry Switzer, and Stan Abel, Steve's wrestling coach at Oklahoma University, shared humorous and moving memories of Steve. His college teammates told stories about his unbelievable physical strength and mental toughness.

Steve's toughest and most impressive fight, however, was his battle against cancer. Stories were told about how he fought throat cancer and had his larynx removed during surgery, and close friends talked about how he continued to make a living in order to support his son and step-daughter, even during the dark times when the cancer threatened to return.

The most significant testimonies were of his loyalty to and faith in Jesus Christ. One of the central themes that everyone talked about was of Steve's loyalty to his friends. Having worked with him for close to a decade, I can attest to that fact. When it came to his friends, there was no middle ground with Steve. Either he was with you or he wasn't. Everybody at the service who knew him closely bore witness to that. Steve had that same attitude when it came to his faith. He relied on his faith in Christ to see him through years of pain and disappointments.

Steve and I became brothers in Christ in Japan during the time when he teamed with Terry Gordy. We were all on the 1990 Real World Tag League tour which ran from November 15 through December 7. Danny Spivey was my partner during the tournament. One night, we were all on the ferry after a show in Akita, which is located in the norther part of Honshû. We were going to the next show, which was south on Shikoku Island, the smallest and least populous of the four main islands of Japan. Mrs. Baba had the Tokyu Hotel kitchen staff prepare turkey, dressing, pumpkin pie, and many other Thanksgiving dishes, and fly everything to the ferry. I can't begin to calculate how much that must have cost, but it must have been in the thousands of dollars.

To say the least, as we all gathered around a table in the first-class lounge of the three-story, 200-foot ferry boat, we were excited. As we moved towards the food, Steve suddenly said, "*We should say a prayer ... a prayer of Thanksgiving.*" Most of us weren't paying attention and we continued moving towards the food. Steve spoke louder and said, "*We should pray a prayer.*" My first thought was that we had all been drinking beer, and not knowing Steve that well, I thought he was trying to be funny. When everybody realized he was serious, we got quiet and bowed our heads. Steve then said a nice prayer, thanking God for the many things with which we had been blessed. That was a brave thing to do. We were in a non-Christian country, surrounded by Japanese, and he was just getting to know some of the wrestlers.

It was always difficult for me to express my faith in public, mainly because I didn't always act like a Christian. I'm sure many of my colleagues would be surprised to learn that I was a Christian. I had to constantly focus on doing the right thing and I occasionally failed, but I never gave up my Christian foundation. If I offended some people during my life (and I'm sure there were many), I hope they will forgive me. Being a Christian is not an easy road to travel.

That was the beginning of what became a very personal relationship between the two of us. Our relationship centered around our faith in Christ and it endured through both good and bad times. I have no doubt whatsoever that he is no longer in pain and is enjoying his reward in Heaven.

Steve's faith served to influence others. He led by example, even in his final days. He not only "talked" his faith, but he "walked" it. I really respected him for that. He would text me often, usually saying something like, "*God is good all the time.*" On Christmas day, he sent me a text which said, "*God is so good! I am leaving the hospital today and all is well. I am going to be home with my boy today.*"

Steve passed away five days later ... December 29, 2009. He was only 49 years old. He was a real man. He was the "horse of all horses." He was my friend.

I had an opportunity to talk with Terry Taylor at Steve Williams' memorial service. I hadn't seen him for fifteen years or so, but I knew he had great success in the WWE and now in TNA. Terry told me the thing he remembers the most about me was that I just kept moving and never stopped. I took that as a compliment, but he continued on to say I was very intimidating to other wrestlers, which wasn't a compliment. When I asked him why that was, he couldn't give a reason, but said I was intimidating to the guys in the dressing room. I guess over time I used sarcastic humor when I kidded the guys, but I never thought they took me seriously. Of course, it's too late to make amends to anyone I might have unintentionally offended, but looking back from their perspective, I can understand how they may have thought I was serious. I do remember kidding Barry Horowitz to a point where he showed his dislike for me. In that case, I definitely overdid it, and I'm sure there must have been other who felt the same. I feel badly about it now, but at the time, I was simply teasing.

I do know I was intimidating in the ring. There were times when I even went after my own partner when they tried to work in the American style. My contention was that we were in Japan and Japan was a different style. When I first began working for Baba, he told me he hired me for my style and the direction I could take All Japan. My objective was to always do what was good for All Japan, and in that spirit, I tried to develop that style.

Shortly after returning home from Steve's memorial, I talked to Danny Spivey. I told him about Terry's comment and how I was taken aback by it. Danny proceeded to tell me about a time when Terry was in a six-man tag-team match in Shirakawa [July 10, 1990] with Spivey and me against Jumbo Tsuruta, Masa Fuchi, and the Great Kabuki. Terry did an American move which was more show than it as the Japanese style. I got into the ring, chopped Terry, and threw him out of the ring. When he came back in, I told him, "*We don't do that stuff here.*" I don't remember that, but Spivey had no reason to make up such a story. It sure was possible. If anything, it was a part of my character and made me look even wilder than I was ... at the expense of Terry, I guess, and for that I apologize.

Not everyone could or should work like I did, but I was expected to lead the change of style in Japan, and I believe that change was for the better. Many of the wrestlers didn't see it that way, some of whom included those I considered to be my friends. Even Spivey said he thought I didn't like many of the guys. It hurt to hear that, but if Danny said it, then perhaps I did come across that way. There is nothing I can do to make things right with the guys I might have offended, but I hope there are a few who understand why I did what I did, especially in the ring.

My mom passed away in 2002. She never fully recovered from the 1981 car accident, although she had been able to go back to work for a number of years. She later suffered a stroke and was paralyzed on her left side. She never cried or felt sorry for herself, and she never wavered from her faith.

When I visit Japan, people still walk up and introduce themselves. Most of the people who were my fans are now the 35 to 50-year-old "salary-men" and are integrated into the Japanese business society. They all are respectful and seem to have fond memories of the "golden age of wrestling," which is what they call that time and era in Japan. I'm very proud to say I was a part of it. Thanks to the Internet and shows on networks like ESPN, there are people who still watch some of my matches.

My heart goes out to all of Japan as they deal with the effects of the earthquake and tsunami. I have fond memories of both Sendai and Fukushima, where I stayed and wrestled many times. They are going through a horrible time, but the Japanese culture is strong, so the people will endure and get through it. The world is seeing the true character of the Japanese people and I am proud to know many of them personally.

I recently was in a mattress store in Arlington, Texas, buying my son Sam a mattress for college. A guy looked at me and said, "*Say, you aren't that wrestler, are you?*" I don't ever offer that information unless someone else brings it up, but if someone recognizes me, I usually acknowledge who I am. That's what I did this time. "*Yeah, that's me.*"

"*No, you're not,*" he said. "*You're pulling my leg.*"

I didn't say anything, but continued to go through the process of buying the bed. A few minutes later, he said, "*Yeah, you sure do look like him, but I know you aren't.*"

I told him again that I *was* Stan Hansen the wrestler. "*Oh, come on,*" he said. "*I know it isn't you. You're not as big as he is. You're not him.*"

Sam noticed I was getting hot, so he told him, "*Hey, it is him. You'd better take his word for it.*"

The guy continued to insist that I wasn't him. Sam and I laughed as we walked out. "*I can't convince anyone that I'm me,*" I said.

I remember talking to Ray Stevens in September 1979 when I was living and working in Atlanta. He told me he had been in the business for 29 years. I thought to myself, "*Twenty-nine years!*" I couldn't believe he was still wrestling. Most of the guys who got into the business before me got in at a much earlier age than I did. Ray Stevens and Terry Gordy were teenagers when they got into the business. I was 23 years old when I broke in. And yet, at the time, I was dumbfounded to think someone could have been wrestling for 29 years.

At the time of my retirement, I was in my 27th year in the business. Twenty seven! And 25 of those years were in Japan. When I look back, I wonder how that could possibly be. Those years seemed to be long at the time, but now they seem to have blown by so quickly. It seems like just yesterday that I was knocking on the front door of Terry Funk's house with the hope of getting a job. Or getting off the airplane at Haneda Airport in 1975 and staring in awe at the buildings that looked like the ones I had seen being destroyed in the movie *Godzilla* when I was a child.

On the personal side of my life, I have few real regrets. Some early decisions I made have haunted and followed me through time, but they were my decisions and nobody else's. As much as I'd like, I can't go back and change them.

In regards to business, I think about my first goal … to have a house paid off and a few thousand dollars in the bank. At the start of my career, I gave myself three years to make it to the main event level, or I would get out and go back into coaching and teaching. Three years later, I was going to work for the WWWF in New York. I was going to be in the main event in the most famous arena in the United States — Madison Square Garden.

I went through some hard times during those first three years, but those years led to the development of Stan "The Lariat" Hansen.

My face is now weathered and scarred, and as Steve Williams and I used to say, "*It sure ain't pretty.*" I had always wanted to develop character in my face. Well, twenty-seven years of ring battles sure did put some "character" on it. There are scars and wrinkles all over it, but they are mine and I accept that.

I have turned down many offers to get back into the ring. I did make a trip for Inoki a few years ago as an observer for a few matches, but other than that, I have never given a moment's thought to returning. I have retired and I am not coming back like so many of the guys did. Tenryu tried to talk me into coming back after Misawa left, but I told him I wasn't interested. All Japan and Mrs. Baba had honored me with a huge, and very humbling, retirement ceremony in the Tokyo Dome. I just couldn't bring myself to come back as other wrestlers did. My time has passed. It has been a great ride!

I have retired.

YEE-EEEEEEEE HAA-AAAAAAA!

Stan's Japan Tours

Compiled by Koji Miyamoto

1. 1975 (All Japan) Sept. 26 to Oct. 30
2. 1977 (New Japan) Jan. 7 to Feb. 10
3. 1977 (New Japan) Aug. 26 to Oct. 6
4. 1979 (New Japan) Apr. 27 to June 7
5. 1980 (New Japan) Jan. 4 to Feb. 8
6. 1980 (New Japan) Mar. 28 to Apr. 4
7. 1980 (New Japan) Apr. 25 to June 5
8. 1980 (New Japan) Aug. 22 to Sept. 30
9. 1980 (New Japan) Nov. 21 to Dec. 13
10. 1981 (New Japan) Apr. 16 to Apr. 23
11. 1981 (New Japan) May 8 to June 4
12. 1981 (New Japan) June 24 (one-day show at Kuramae Sumo Hall)
13. 1981 (New Japan) Aug. 21 to Sept. 23
14. 1981 (New Japan) Oct. 8 (one-day show at Kuramae Sumo Hall)
15. 1981 (New Japan) Nov. 19 to Dec. 10

Stan Hansen moves to All Japan. 16th tour to 131st tour, All Japan only

16. 1982 Jan. 15 to Feb. 4
17. 1982 Apr. 16 to Apr. 22
18. 1982 May 14 to June 10
19. 1982 Aug. 26 to Sept. 15
20. 1982 Nov. 26 to Dec. 13
21. 1983 Mar. 25 to Apr. 28
22. 1983 Aug. 19 to Sept. 8
23. 1983 Oct. 14 to Nov. 3
24. 1983 Nov. 25 to Dec. 12
25. 1984 Mar. 23 to Apr. 26
26. 1984 Jul. 6 to Aug. 2
27. 1984 Aug. 23 to Aug. 28
28. 1984 Nov. 22 to Dec. 12
29. 1985 Mar. 29 to Apr. 25
30. 1985 May. 10 to June 13
31. 1985 June 28 to Jul. 31
32. 1985 Aug. 23 to Aug. 31
33. 1985 Nov. 23 to Dec. 12
34. 1986 Mar. 29 to Apr. 26
35. 1986 Jul. 4 to Jul. 31
36. 1986 Aug. 30 to Sept. 11
37. 1986 Oct. 16 to Oct. 23
38. 1986 Nov. 22 to Dec. 12
39. 1987 Mar. 28 to Apr. 24
40. 1987 Jul. 3 to Jul. 30
41. 1987 Aug. 21 to Sept. 17
42. 1987 Nov. 21 to Dec. 11
43. 1988 Feb. 20 to Mar. 11
44. 1988 Mar. 26 to Apr. 1
45. 1988 Jul. 2 to Jul. 31
46. 1988 Aug. 20 to Sep. 9
47. 1988 Oct. 15 to Oct. 28
48. 1988 Nov. 19 to Dec. 16
49. 1989 Mar. 25 to Apr. 20

50. 1989 May 26 to June 8
51. 1989 Jul. 1 to Jul. 28
52. 1989 Sept. 30 to Oct. 28
53. 1989 Nov. 17 to Dec. 6
54. 1990 Feb. 10
The above show was a New Japan Tokyo Dome show. Baba sent some top names from All Japan to show his courtesy to Seiji Sakaguchi, new president of New Japan.
55. 1990 Feb. 21 to Mar. 6
56. 1990 Mar. 24 to Apr. 19
57. 1990 June 1 to June 8
Followed by one more week New Japan tour
58. 1990 Jul. 7 to Jul. 27
59. 1990 Aug. 29 to Sept. 3
60. 1990 Sept. 29 to Oct. 12
61. 1990 Nov. 15 to Dec. 7
62. 1991 Jan. 2 to Jan. 27
63. 1991 Mar. 23 to Apr. 18
64. 1991 June 1 to June 7
65. 1991 Jul. 6 to Jul. 26
66. 1991 Aug. 17 to Sept. 7
67. 1991 Sept. 27 to Oct. 24
68. 1991 Nov. 16 to Dec. 6
69. 1992 Jan. 2 to Jan. 28
70. 1992 Feb. 22 to Mar. 6
71. 1992 Mar. 20 to Apr. 17
72. 1992 May30 to June 5
73. 1992 Jul. 4 to Jul. 31
74. 1992 Aug. 20 to Sept. 9
75. 1992 Oct. 2 to Oct. 21
76. 1992 Nov. 14 to Dec. 4
77. 1993 Jan. 2 to Jan. 31
78. 1993 Feb. 19 to Mar. 4
79. 1993 Mar. 25 to Apr. 21
80. 1993 May13 to June 3
81. 1993 Jul. 2 to Jul. 29
82. 1993 Sept. 3 to Sept. 9
83. 1993 Sept. 29 to Oct. 23
84. 1993 Nov. 13 to Dec. 3
85. 1994 Jan. 2 to Jan. 29
86. 1994 Feb. 19 to Mar. 5
87. 1994 Mar. 19 to Apr. 16
88. 1994 May 13 to June 3
89. 1994 June 30 to Jul. 28
90. 1994 Aug. 20 to Sept. 3
91. 1994 Sept. 30 to Oct. 22
92. 1994 Nov. 19 to Dec. 10
93. 1995 Jan. 2 to Jan. 29
94. 1995 Feb. 7 to Mar. 4
95. 1995 Mar. 21 to Apr. 15
96. 1995 May20 to June 9
97. 1995 June 30 to Jul. 24
98. 1995 Aug. 19 to Sept. 10
99. 1995 Sept. 30 to Oct. 25
100. 1995 Nov. 18 to Dec. 9
101. 1996 Jan. 2 to Jan. 28
102. 1996 Feb. 17 to Mar. 2
103. 1996 Mar. 22 to Apr. 20
104. 1996 June 29 to Jul. 24
105. 1996 Aug. 17 to Sept. 5
106. 1996 Sept. 28 to Oct. 18
107. 1996 Nov. 16 to Dec. 6
108. 1997 Jan. 2 to Jan. 26
109. 1997 Feb. 16 to Mar. 1
110. 1997 Mar. 22 to Apr. 19
111. 1997 June 28 to Jul. 25
112. 1997 Aug. 17 to Sept. 6
113. 1997 Sept. 27 to Oct. 21
114. 1997 Nov. 25 to Dec. 5
115. 1998 Feb. 14 to Feb. 28
116. 1998 Mar. 21 to Apr. 18
117. 1998 May 1
All Japan first Tokyo Dome show
118. 1998 Aug. 22 to Sept. 11
119. 1998 Oct. 3 to Oct. 31
120. 1998 Nov. 14 to Dec. 5
121. 1999 Feb. 20 to Mar. 6
122. 1999 May 2
Giant Baba Memorial Tokyo Dome show
123. 1999 Oct. 9 to Oct. 30
124. 1999 Nov. 13 to Dec. 3
125. 2000 Jan 31
Giant Baba 1st Anniversary Memorial Tokyo Dome show
126. 2000 Feb. 12 to Feb. 27
127. 2000 May 20 to June 9
128. 2000 July 23 (Budokan show only)
129. 2000 Aug. 20 to Sept. 2
130. 2000 Oct. 14 to Oct. 28
Last tour as active wrestler
131. 2001 Jan. 28
Tokyo Dome show, Stan Hansen retirement ceremony

PHOTO GALLERY

Before New Japan singles tournament
Keio Plaza Hotel
"This was very formal dress for me. Bobby Duncum is behind me. Andre and I had words during the event."

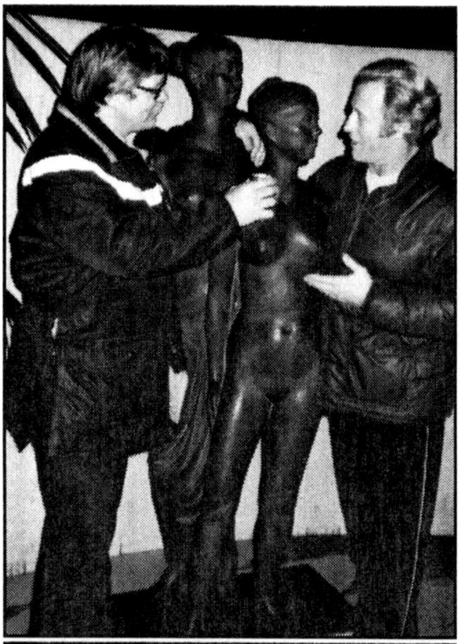

"Nick Bockwinkel really knew how to charm the women, but even he couldn't get over with these women. Nick was a class act."

(above and below) The Destroyer's birthday party

Stan and Dick Murdoch
New Japan

1976 • Stan in Amarillo with his sister, Jan
"My sister, Jan, a true hippy, and me just trying to look as foul as I could."

Yokohama, Japan: April 21, 1993
Stan Hansen vs Mitsuharu Misawa, referee Joe Higuchi

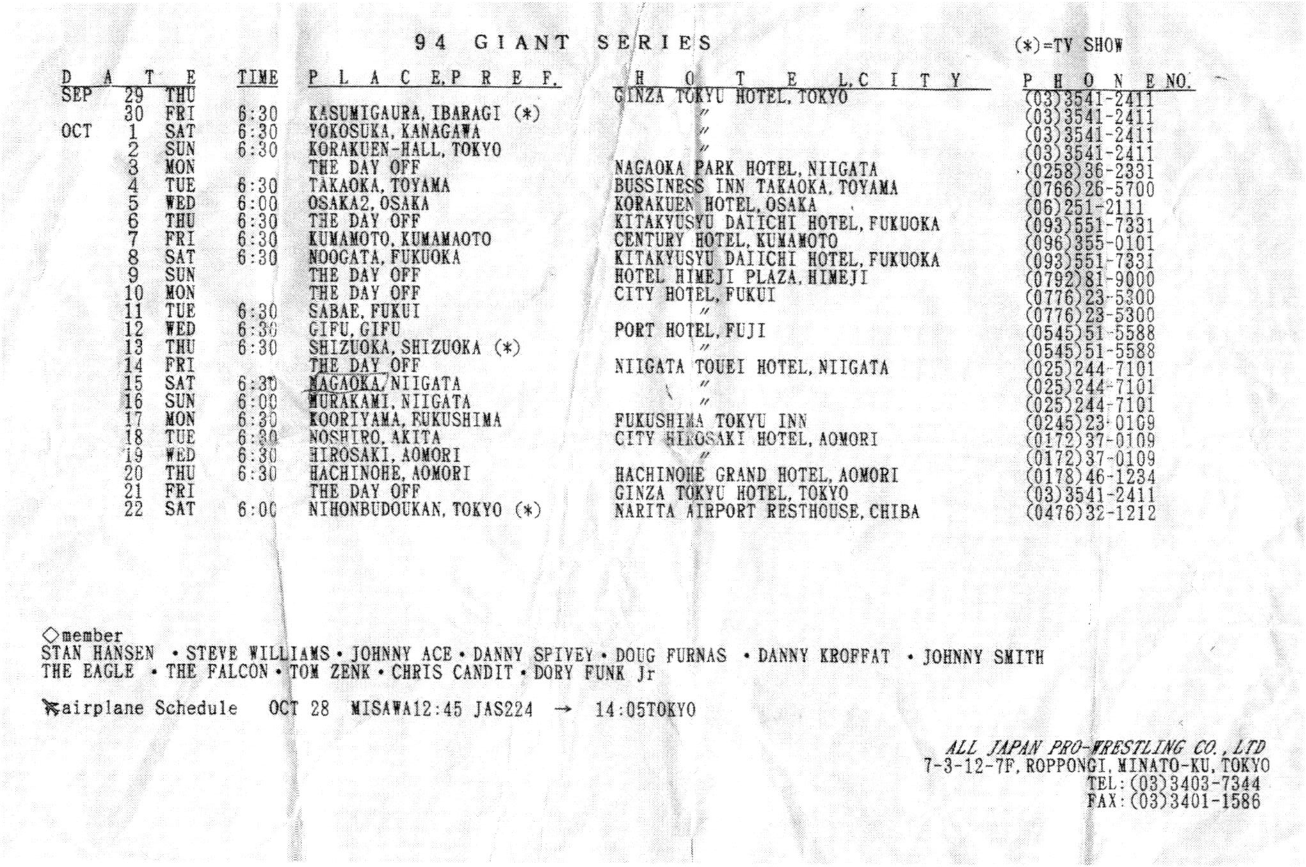

94 GIANT SERIES (*)=TV SHOW

DATE			TIME	PLACE,PREF.	HOTEL,CITY	PHONE NO.
SEP	29	THU			GINZA TOKYU HOTEL, TOKYO	(03)3541-2411
	30	FRI	6:30	KASUMIGAURA, IBARAGI (*)	〃	(03)3541-2411
OCT	1	SAT	6:30	YOKOSUKA, KANAGAWA	〃	(03)3541-2411
	2	SUN	6:30	KORAKUEN-HALL, TOKYO	〃	(03)3541-2411
	3	MON		THE DAY OFF	NAGAOKA PARK HOTEL, NIIGATA	(0258)36-2331
	4	TUE	6:30	TAKAOKA, TOYAMA	BUSSINESS INN TAKAOKA, TOYAMA	(0766)26-5700
	5	WED	6:00	OSAKA2, OSAKA	KORAKUEN HOTEL, OSAKA	(06)251-2111
	6	THU	6:30	THE DAY OFF	KITAKYUSYU DAIICHI HOTEL, FUKUOKA	(093)551-7331
	7	FRI	6:30	KUMAMOTO, KUMAMAOTO	CENTURY HOTEL, KUMAMOTO	(096)355-0101
	8	SAT	6:30	NOOGATA, FUKUOKA	KITAKYUSYU DAIICHI HOTEL, FUKUOKA	(093)551-7331
	9	SUN		THE DAY OFF	HOTEL HIMEJI PLAZA, HIMEJI	(0792)81-9000
	10	MON		THE DAY OFF	CITY HOTEL, FUKUI	(0776)23-5300
	11	TUE	6:30	SABAE, FUKUI	〃	(0776)23-5300
	12	WED	6:30	GIFU, GIFU	PORT HOTEL, FUJI	(0545)51-5588
	13	THU	6:30	SHIZUOKA, SHIZUOKA (*)	〃	(0545)51-5588
	14	FRI		THE DAY OFF	NIIGATA TOUEI HOTEL, NIIGATA	(025)244-7101
	15	SAT	6:30	NAGAOKA, NIIGATA	〃	(025)244-7101
	16	SUN	6:00	MURAKAMI, NIIGATA	〃	(025)244-7101
	17	MON	6:30	KOORIYAMA, FUKUSHIMA	FUKUSHIMA TOKYU INN	(0245)23-0109
	18	TUE	6:30	NOSHIRO, AKITA	CITY HIROSAKI HOTEL, AOMORI	(0172)37-0109
	19	WED	6:30	HIROSAKI, AOMORI	〃	(0172)37-0109
	20	THU	6:30	HACHINOHE, AOMORI	HACHINOHE GRAND HOTEL, AOMORI	(0178)46-1234
	21	FRI		THE DAY OFF	GINZA TOKYU HOTEL, TOKYO	(03)3541-2411
	22	SAT	6:00	NIHONBUDOUKAN, TOKYO (*)	NARITA AIRPORT RESTHOUSE, CHIBA	(0476)32-1212

◇member
STAN HANSEN • STEVE WILLIAMS • JOHNNY ACE • DANNY SPIVEY • DOUG FURNAS • DANNY KROFFAT • JOHNNY SMITH
THE EAGLE • THE FALCON • TOM ZENK • CHRIS CANDIT • DORY FUNK Jr

airplane Schedule OCT 28 MISAWA12:45 JAS224 → 14:05TOKYO

ALL JAPAN PRO-WRESTLING CO., LTD
7-3-12-7F, ROPPONGI, MINATO-KU, TOKYO
TEL:(03)3403-7344
FAX:(03)3401-1586

All Japan gaijin booking sheet

Early 1980s
Giant Baba vs Stan Hansen

Korakuen Hall: March 1989
Stan Hansen vs Genichiro Tenryu

Stan with Johnny Ace and Pete Roberts (photo Koichi Yoshizawa)

Louisiana 1974

April 1989
Stan Hansen vs Jumbo Tsuruta

Matsuyama, Japan: April 12, 1983
Stan Hansen and Ron Bass after winning the International tag team title

INDEX

BRUISER BRODY

The Last Laugh
by Bill DeMott
with Scott Teal

WRESTLING
IN THE CANADIAN WEST
VANCE NEVADA

ASSASSIN
THE MAN BEHIND THE MASK
by Joe Hamilton
with Scott Teal

"Wrestlers Are Like Seagulls"
From McMahon to McMahon
by James J. Dillon
with Scott Teal & Philip Varriale

DRAWING HEAT
BY JIM FREEDMAN

"Is That Wrestling Fake?"
The Bear Facts
by Ivan Koloff
with Scott Teal

Wrestling With
The Truth
Bruno Lauer

ATLAS
Too Much ... Too Soon
by Tony Atlas

THE SOLIE CHRONICLES
The Life and Times of Gordon Solie
Robert Allyn
with Pamela S Allyn and Scott Teal